Human Behavior
and the
Social Environment

MACRO LEVEL

Human Behavior and the Social Environment

MACRO LEVEL

Groups, Communities, and Organizations

Second Edition

Katherine van Wormer

Fred H. Besthorn

UNIVERSITY PRESS

2011

OXFORD
UNIVERSITY PRESS

Oxford University Press, Inc., publishes works that further
Oxford University's objective of excellence
in research, scholarship, and education.

Oxford   New York
Auckland   Cape Town   Dar es Salaam   Hong Kong   Karachi
Kuala Lumpur   Madrid   Melbourne   Mexico City   Nairobi
New Delhi   Shanghai   Taipei   Toronto

With offices in
Argentina   Austria   Brazil   Chile   Czech Republic   France   Greece
Guatemala   Hungary   Italy   Japan   Poland   Portugal   Singapore
South Korea   Switzerland   Thailand   Turkey   Ukraine   Vietnam

Copyright © 2007, 2011 by Oxford University Press, Inc.

Published by Oxford University Press, Inc.
198 Madison Avenue, New York, New York 10016

www.oup.com

Oxford is a registered trademark of Oxford University Press

Library of Congress Cataloging-in-Publication Data
Van Wormer, Katherine S.
Human behavior and the social environment, macro level:
groups, communities, and organizations/Katherine van Wormer, Fred H. Besthorn.—2nd ed.
p. cm.
Includes bibliographical references and index.
ISBN 978-0-19-974057-4
1. Social ecology.   2. Social psychology.   I. Besthorn, Fred H. II. Title.
HM861.V36 2011
307—dc22   2010010363

9 8 7 6 5 4 3 2 1

Printed in the United States of America
on acid-free paper

*To our students of human behavior and the social environment
and to students of human behavior everywhere who seek
to understand why people do the things they do.*
—Katherine van Wormer

*To my children,
Marc Jared Besthorn
and
Abby Louise Besthorn,
who are constant sources of joy and wonder!*

*And thanks to three special women in my life:
My late mother, Mollie Besthorn
My loving and patient older sister, Kathleen S. Besthorn
My best friend and partner, Nancy E. Browne*
—Fred H. Besthorn

Acknowledgments

I would like to express gratitude to Oxford University Press, specifically to Maura Roessner, editor for social work, and Nicholas Liu, assistant editor, for their guidance and expertise in shaping this book. From this end, I'd like to thank my student assistants Lynn Rutz, and William Lounsbery, whose skills in proofreading, knowledge of computer technology, and construction of charts and diagrams were invaluable in the completion of this project. Finally, appreciation is extended to my son, Rupert van Wormer, a social worker himself, and to my husband, Robert van Wormer, for their fine photographic contributions.

—Katherine van Wormer

Thanks to my colleague and friend Katherine van Wormer, without whose vision, dedication, and persistence this book would not have been begun nor completed. Thank you, Katherine.

Thanks also to my sister Kathleen S. Besthorn, photographer and designer, and to Margie Hays, photographer, aLightGoesOn Inc. (www.alightgoeson.com), for their excellent contributions to this effort.

—Fred H. Besthorn

Contents

Preface

Since the publication of the first edition of the *Human Behavior and the Social Environment, Macro Level*, events that have taken place in the economic realm have ricocheted across the entire social structure. Scarcely a community, organization, or family has been spared from the impact. Bankruptcies, foreclosures, and job layoffs have become daily occurrences. We are talking of what is now called the recession of 2008/2009 and could be called the Great Reckoning. For there is every possibility that the enduring economic crisis will lead to a profound rethinking of free-market economics and wasteful consumerism. Already, during the space of two short years, America's boundless optimism, the acceptance of mass indebtedness, and the "eat, drink, and be merry" lifestyles are giving way to more sober reflection in many quarters. The realization seems to have struck that unchecked economic growth is not sustainable any more than is a devouring of the earth's resources.

Dramatic changes in the ecological landscape combined with a new global awareness of the interconnectedness of nature and human life have alerted the world community to the need for planned and drastic action. Consider, for example, the impact of the giant oil spill on human and nonhuman life in the Gulf of Mexico. This disaster gives a special urgency to the agreements reached in the 2009 Copenhagen climate accord for the promotion of the economic development of nations within the context of environmental sustainability.

Sustainability: An Organizing Theme

Sustainability is the notion that humans must live in harmony with each other and with other species while preserving our natural resources for future generations. Long known in agriculture where the benefits of conservation of the natural resources are most obvious, the concept of sustainability is applied today to economic and social as well as to ecological components of the society. A sustainability ethos alerts us to the future impact of present wasteful practices. Consistent with the pervasive and dominant ideologies of laissez-faire politics, such practices include the continuing deforestation, mass production of farm animals, chemical pollution of the water, soil, and air, and the economic mortgaging of our children's future.

Across the span of human history the impetus for sustainability has never been more front and center than it is today (Brown, 2006). This ethos is shaping everything from the buildings we live and work in to the crops we grow and eat to the way we dispose of industrial and other wastes. The sustainable thrust is endorsed in government funding incentives for the development of solar energy, the harnessing of wind power, electric cars, other green technologies, and the popularity of organic farming.

Conservation, recycling, and preserving biodiversity are common themes that span the core academic disciplines. The discipline of psychology has its ecotheory; religion, its deep ecology; agriculture, its conservation; women's studies, its ecofeminism. And what about social work? Social work has its emphasis on healing and resilience. Nancy Mary's groundbreaking (2008) *Social Work in a Sustainable World* anticipated the present academic focus on the importance of preserving a safe, nurturing, and sustainable environment. A proliferation of college courses are offered with sustainability as a major theme. The advantage of such a theme at the university level is that it lends itself to community service and student-led clean-up and recycling campaigns.

Some universities are even framing their entire liberal arts core curriculum within a sustainable rubric (for example, Warren Wilson College near Ashville, North Carolina, and Central College in Pella, Iowa). Nationwide between 2005 and 2009, the numbers of majors, minors, or certificates in energy and sustainability-focused programs at colleges expanded from three to over 100 programs (Association for the Advancement of Sustainability in Higher Education, 2009). This surge is driven by student interest in the courses in addition to employment interest in hiring graduates with training in the concepts of sustainability. In response to such efforts by individual colleges, the National Wildlife Federation publishes a national report card to chart the sustainable movement in higher educational institutions that make exemplary efforts.

Social work programs increasingly are offering courses in sustainable development. For the 2010 CSWE annual conference in Portland, Oregon, in fact, sustainability in social work was chosen as the basic theme. The emphasis will be on promotion of sustainability. The selection of this theme is consistent with Mary's (2008) proposal for the development of a new paradigm of sustainable practice for social work. The focus of this model is on prevention, community development, and a recognition "that the natural environment is an integral part and the foundation of our world and must be sustained as a living and sacred part of our global social welfare" (p. 25).

Inspired by the sustainability movement and informed by the knowledge that human development is intertwined with the state of the ecosystem, *Human Behavior and the Social Environment (HBSE), Macro Level* in its second edition infuses sustainability content throughout the chapters of this book. Thus, attention will be devoted to the sustainable community, the impact of economic globalization on populations and families, the qualities of sustainable organizations and policies, environmental justice, and, as in the first edition, to ecosystems analysis.

Readers of the earlier edition of *HBSE* will find the chapter organization and the topic headings familiar. New to this edition are the following:

- The infusion of a sustainability focus throughout all the chapters
- Many new boxed readings and photographs
- Updated academic references and government statistics
- The replacement of theoretical designs with new models and designs
- A heightened emphasis on ecosystems as opposed to general systems models
- Increased Latino/Latina content
- Rewriting of large sections of the theory, group dynamics, family, community, and environment chapters

Knowledge at the Macro Level

Historically, the study of social work has been characterized by as sharp a divide between micro and macro as between theory and practice. On the micro side of the equation, theorists who were inspired by psychology have focused their attention on the human mind, often to the neglect of the normative and institutional constraints on human behavior. At the macro level, the influence of sociology has directed attention to social structure and to socialization within that structure, but often to the neglect of the human being and, accordingly, of life itself.

The person-in-environment framework that guides *Human Behavior and the Social Environment, Macro Level* considers the impact of the individual acting in concert with others on the social environment and the impact of the environment on the person. Because this book is geared toward the macro side of the micro-macro continuum, readers will find concepts and applications here that demonstrate how social and environmental issues are intrinsically linked.

Thinking about human behavior as interchanging configurations of person and environment requires a holistic, multidimensional approach. The beauty of social work is its ability to draw on a wealth of knowledge across academic domains so that we can suit the intervention to the situation, to the cultural context, and to the individuals involved. This is where our social work imaginations come into play—in fitting the intervention to the need and, even more than that, in determining the need in the first place.

Like the skilled anthropologist studying culture, the social worker must seek to know the pattern in the chaos, the "method in the madness." The need is to address poverty, oppression, and injustice at every level of society, from the local to the global. Encouraging a critical consciousness of this context of social work practice is an essential obligation of the human behavior and the social environment (HBSE) curriculum. At the heart of much of the pain and suffering that the social worker's clients face are macro-level forces—the global economy, political ideology, the corporate media, and commercial culture.

And yet most social work textbooks and course curricula on HBSE concentrate on the smaller dimensions of human life. The bio-psycho portion of the bio-psycho-social-spiritual equation typically focuses on body and mind. The term *social* usually refers to family and small groups, and the spiritual realm, if included at all, may only be mentioned in terms of an external support system such as the church. Social work departments offer the required course work on macro practice—community organization and policy courses, for example. But missing is the scientific study of human behavior at the wider level—specifically, the study of the social psychology of groups, of social movements, of the dimensions of globalization, and of the natural, as well as social, environment.

The ecosystems model is sufficiently broad to do justice to these phenomena. The ecosystems model is not a body of knowledge. Rather, it offers a framework for organizing the facts and theories of knowledge relevant to human behavior at the macro level. Although ecosystems proponents traditionally have emphasized homeostasis in contrast to conflict and adaptation to stress, we go where our vision leads us. We adapt the theory to the facts and not the facts to the theory. And the facts in today's world cry out for radical social change. In any case, it is our belief that systems concepts relate to social change as readily as they do to social stability. As a nonlinear, nondichotomous approach to human behavior, ecosystems theory is concerned with the dimensions of interconnectedness. The *eco-*, or ecological, portion of the term brings our attention to the environmental domain, a term that in our usage includes the natural, as well as the social, environment.

This model, in our view, has the best potential for serving as an organizing framework to encompass the broad-based material that is the subject matter of this book. This macro human behavior perspective complies with the Council on Social Work Education's (CSWE's) (2008) accreditation standards that require competencies for practice with individuals, families, groups, organizations, and communities. Students who obtain professional degrees in social work are expected to have an understanding of the person and the environment and to "recognize the global interconnections of oppression" (p. 5). Graduates are also expected to be "knowledgeable about theories of justice and strategies to promote human and civil rights" (p. 5). Much of this material is incorporated in courses on human behavior, typically in a second or more advanced course.

What does the study of human behavior at the macro level entail? Macro-level behavior concerns the functioning of people within communities and organizations and the groups that compose them. The *macro* social environment is the configuration of these communities, organizations, and groups in which individuals live and work and within which social workers conduct their practice. These larger units are the products of social, economic, and political forces, both within the society and globally.

Purpose of the Book

And what is the purpose of studying macro factors in human behavior? Why do social workers who work mostly with individuals need to concern themselves with larger systems at all? Group membership—status, class, race—affects our behavior, directly or indirectly. Our organizational and community ties define who we are and affect our everyday life. The impact of economics—local and global—is substantial. The first major purpose of this book is to enhance the reader's understanding of the inner workings of the broader social systems—groups, families, organizations, and communities—and to help social work students realize how these social institutions influence the behavior of their clients, so many of whom are caught in the throes of structural oppression. To this end, theory and empirical findings related to gender, culture, race, and social conflict are drawn from social work and sociological literature.

A second, but not secondary, purpose is to prepare would-be change agents for roles in addressing systemic issues that are in need of

change—to better enable them to work within (or outside) the system to change the system. Because social workers generally carry out their functions in organizations and work through organizations in their broker-advocacy roles, organizational workings and theory are addressed.

The vision of social work is expanding. In recent years, the profession of social work has broadened its horizons commensurate with the increasing globalization of society. The National Association of Social Workers (NASW; 1996) includes in its sixth standard a digest of the social worker's ethical responsibilities. Those that have a special bearing on macro concerns follow.

Standard 6. Social Workers' Ethical Responsibilities to the Broader Society
6.01 Social Welfare
Social workers should promote the general welfare of society, from local to global levels, and the development of people, their communities, and their environments. Social workers should advocate for living conditions conducive to the fulfillment of basic human needs and should promote social, economic, political, and cultural values and institutions that are compatible with the realization of social justice.
6.02 Public Participation
Social workers should facilitate informed participation by the public in shaping social policies and institutions.
6.03 Public Emergencies
Social workers should provide appropriate professional services in public emergencies to the greatest extent possible.
6.04 Social and Political Action
(a) Social workers should engage in social and political action that seeks to ensure that all people have equal access to the resources, employment, services, and opportunities they require to meet their basic human needs and to develop fully. Social workers should be aware of the impact of the political arena on practice and should advocate for changes in policy and legislation to improve social

conditions in order to meet basic human needs and promote social justice.

(b) Social workers should act to expand choice and opportunity for all people, with special regard for vulnerable, disadvantaged, oppressed, and exploited people and groups.

(c) Social workers should promote conditions that encourage respect for cultural and social diversity within the United States and globally. Social workers should promote policies and practices that demonstrate respect for difference, support the expansion of cultural knowledge and resources, advocate for programs and institutions that demonstrate cultural competence, and promote policies that safeguard the rights of and confirm equity and social justice for all people.

(d) Social workers should act to prevent and eliminate domination of, exploitation of, and discrimination against any person, group, or class on the basis of race, ethnicity, national origin, color, sex, sexual orientation, age, marital status, political belief, religion, or mental or physical disability. (NASW, pp. 26–27)

A third goal of this text is to provide dynamic case studies and narrative descriptions that emphasize cultural strengths and individual and group resilience within a context of situational and social oppression. This goal is consistent with the NASW Code of Ethics (1996) statement on cultural competence. Section 1.05 ("Cultural Competence and Social Diversity") states that social workers should understand culture and its function in human behavior and society, recognizing the strengths that exist in all cultures.

HBSE, Macro Level is conceived as a companion volume to *HBSE, Micro Level*. These textbooks can be used in one course or in two separate courses, as is customary in the HBSE foundation sequence. Each volume offers an analysis of human behavior with attention to the bio-psycho-social-spiritual elements, but the first volume focuses much more on the psychological aspects. Micro-level concerns, as one would guess, are more with the internal

processes—dreams, feelings, thoughts, and so forth. A macro lens expands this vision into the wider, more external realm, while still maintaining a focus on the person-environment configuration. At the macro level, the *biological* part of the equation—rather than focusing on physiology of the body and the neurological dimension of human behavior—is concerned with elements in our habitat, such as the air we breathe and the water we drink. Nowhere is the concept of a global village as relevant as in our management of physical resources. Contamination of the soil in one country may produce water contamination somewhere else, for example, and war destroys the earth for those who dwell there and beyond. The *psychological* ramifications of social and systemic phenomena, including despoliation of the earth, are considerable. Additionally, the study of social psychology bridges the gap between psychological principles of human behavior and the *social* side of group membership—class, race, and gender.

Finally, we come to the *spiritual* dimension. Here, too, there is an expanded vision, a shared morality that takes people beyond their more mundane, everyday concerns into the realm of the unknowable and nonmaterial. Spirituality is often experienced as a sense of connectedness to the universe, to one's ancestors, and to "all creatures great and small." Religious worship or ritualism may or may not come into play. Many people who do not believe in divinity and who do not regard themselves as religious nevertheless may experience a sense of oneness with humanity or a Presence, perhaps, in nature. Spirituality thus figures in the macro, as well as in the micro, or personal, level of human experience. (For an exploration of spiritual growth and development across the life cycle, see *HBSE, Micro Level* [van Wormer, 2011].)

A word about micro-macro considerations: The distinction made between these two entities is only that—a distinction based on size of social system. The common division of HBSE courses into these divisions should simply be regarded as one of convenience, not one of philosophy. In reality, there is no dichotomy here any more than there is a dichotomy between theory and practice or between international social welfare and domestic welfare. Individuals are profoundly affected by their social environments, even as the social environments are affected by the individuals who constitute them. Micro and macro should be regarded as opposite ends of the systems continuum on the basis of size, with families and small groups somewhere in the middle. We explore systems in some depth in the introductory chapter.

Unique to this text, compared with others in the HBSE field, are the following:

❥ Study of group dynamics drawing on research from social psychology
❥ Use of an ecological, interactionist framework for the study of macro-level human behavior
❥ Emphasis on matters pertaining to globalization
❥ Infusion of the empowerment perspective within an ecosystems framework
❥ Attention to the physical environment and to the interrelationship between nature (and the despoliation of nature) and society
❥ Emphasis on the need for a sustainable world
❥ Linking of spiritual concepts and the natural realm
❥ Inclusion of restorative justice and human rights content

Plan of the Book

The organizing theoretical framework for this book is the ecosystems perspective built on concepts of empowerment and the sustainability of resources. Chapter 1 introduces the concepts that underlie this model, as well as alternative conceptual frameworks for understanding human behavior within larger social systems. The *ecosystems framework* helps us see the interdependence and connection of all living and nonliving systems (Lee, 2001). *Interactionism*, or reciprocity, a guiding motif of social work theory, is integral to ecosystems theory because it directs our attention to the person-in-environment and environment-in-person

configurations. The sociological formulations—structural functionalism and social conflict theory—are also examined in the opening chapter, and their relevance to the study of human behavior is explored. Many of the principles and concepts from all these key theoretical perspectives are visited again and again in the following pages. The person and his or her social environment are viewed in constant and dynamic interaction throughout this text.

Empowerment is a second major theme (in conjunction with the ecosystems framework) of this text. Whereas the ecosystems framework is the equivalent of a three-dimensional map for envisioning relationships in society and showing how parts interact in tandem with each other and fit into larger wholes, empowerment perspectives are infinitely more personal and more political. Whereas the former is about physical vision, a way of seeing interconnections, and is borrowed from science, the latter is more didactic and provides a vision of a different sort that relates to working with people and communities. At the macro or societal level, an empowerment perspective turns our attention to power dimensions in the social environment, as well as to the empowerment practice with communities, organization members, and marginalized populations within the environment. The emphasis is on finding strengths in individuals and their communities and in helping people tap into their inner resources.

Chapter 2 starts at the micro-macro level, with the person as member of the group. Here the emphasis is on social conformity to groups and collective norms. Susceptibility to manipulation—whether by politics or the mass media—obedience to authority, prejudice, and the influence of authoritarian versus democratic leadership on the human behavior of group participants are basic themes. This chapter seeks to answer the question *why*: Why do we do the things we do? This discussion provides the theoretical foundation for Chapters 3 and 4, which are devoted to social work group practice and family dynamics, respectively. After describing the functions and structure of the small group, Chapter 3 relates the theory to specific strategies for social work group practice.

The small group with which we in our society are the most familiar is the group we are born into or adopted into. This is, of course, the family, which is discussed in Chapter 4. This chapter is an extension of the concluding chapter from *HBSE, Micro Level*. Whereas the focus of the companion chapter was on human behavior and relationships within the family circle—brother with sister, father with son, and so on—the focus here is on macro-level concerns. Pressures from the workplace on individual families are considered; attention is paid to ethnicity and same-sex partnerships within society as well. Family violence against girls and women is viewed locally and globally. The chapter ends with a section on progressive family innovations from across the globe.

The topic of culture comprises the following two chapters, the first on culture and society and the second on community and community development. Close attention is paid to the study of cultural value orientations, especially the dominant beliefs and ideologies of North American society. In the community chapter, contemporary issues are addressed in terms of opposing viewpoints. Whether community life has disintegrated in today's fast-paced world or whether the community is alive and well—this is the key question. Case examples of thriving communities and community-based initiatives relevant to social work are provided.

Complex organizations are discussed in Chapter 7. Because it is the foundation of the economic structure of postindustrial society, the modern corporation is a central concern. This is not the usual dry, organizational theory chapter. We do consider the leading historical and contemporary theories on leadership and bureaucracy. But here we also consider what the new technologies and globalization bring to modern bureaucracy and how such developments may lead to a sense of alienation in the worker. Heightened productivity, outsourcing, replacement of people with machines, and the impact of the market economy on social work are among the issues discussed.

Expanding our vision even further, we devote Chapter 8 entirely to the physical environment, to the natural world that surrounds us. Generativity at the micro level—a major theme of the life span

chapters of volume 1 of this series—is matched by sustainability at the macro level, and violence against people is paralleled in the second volume by violence against Mother Earth.

Ecological disaster is described in terms of natural disasters such as the great Indian Ocean tsunami and Hurricane Katrina. The interaction between people and their environments is shown in regard to the impact of people and their industries on the atmosphere and water resources, as well as the impact of nature on the human population. A unique history of social work efforts to bridge the gap between the person and the environment is provided.

There is yet one higher level of understanding. Chapter 9 takes us on a journey into the metaphysical or spiritual realm. This concluding discussion explores the nature of spiritual development and aspects of religious expression, some harmful and some helpful, in seeking the meaning of life. Contemporary controversies of special relevance to social workers are addressed. Readers will find much material for critical reflection in the pages of this final chapter, and hopefully of this book.

References

Association for the Advancement of Sustainability in Higher Education. (2009). Bachelor's degree programs in sustainability. Retrieved March 19, 2010, from http://www.aashe.org/resources/bachelor.php

Brown, C. (2006). *Plan B 2.0: Rescuing a planet under stress and a civilization in trouble*. New York: W. W. Norton.

Council on Social Work Education. (2008). *Handbook of accreditation standards and procedures* (6th ed.). Alexandria, VA: Author.

Lee, J. (2001). *The empowerment approach in social work practice: Building the beloved community* (2nd ed.). New York: Columbia University Press.

Mary, N. (2008). *Social work in a sustainable world*. Chicago: Lyceum.

National Association of Social Workers. (1996). *Code of ethics*. Washington, DC: Author.

van Wormer, K. (2011). *Human behavior and the social environment, micro level: Individuals and families* (2nd ed.). New York: Oxford University Press.

Human Behavior
and the
Social Environment

MACRO LEVEL

Theoretical Perspectives

There is nothing as practical as good theory.
—KURT LEWIN

Field Theory in Social Science, 1951

Individually, as well as collectively, social workers intervene at the intersection of the personal and the political. Consider the following scenarios in which the social worker:

- Is awarded a grant to study the results of family group conferencing in ensuring child safety as compared with the traditional agency-centered approach; this innovative approach was modeled from the child welfare program in New Zealand
- Travels to the Gulf Coast following Hurricane Katrina to help displaced persons with resettlement issues
- In the face of the national economic crisis, works with a family threatened with the foreclosure of their home
- In her role as a school social worker helps refugee and Mexican children adjust to life in a U.S. school
- Is employed as a mental health professional at a state prison and is concerned about the large numbers of persons with schizophrenia sentenced to the facility. He contacts a legislator to provide funding for community mental health treatment.
- Testifies at a legislative session on behalf of single working mothers in need of affordable, high-standard child care
- Specializes in helping prospective parents adopt children from countries in Eastern Europe
- In her capacity as the administrator of a substance abuse treatment center, is interviewed on TV to speak in favor of increasing the cigarette tax
- As a member of the city council, delivers a speech in support of a nondiscrimination ordinance to protect the rights of gays and lesbians

In the preceding vignettes, the social worker is involved through his or her agency in community work or is otherwise working in the context of the larger social environment. Some of these activities relate to political advocacy on behalf of clients, whereas others relate to community involvement that is performed on a volunteer basis. In all these scenarios, professionals would rely on the interviewing skills they have obtained in practice courses, as well as on an accumulated wisdom about human behavior—what might be termed their *social work imagination*. Such imagination encompasses knowledge bolstered by resourcefulness. Given the social worker's responsibility to engage in client advocacy for the improvement of social services and to work for social change in social systems, large and small, an eclectic knowledge base is crucial. Underpinning such change efforts is knowledge concerning the functioning of social systems, the power of political persuasion, the dynamics of social and economic oppression, and environmental policies for sustainable development.

The study of human behavior at the macro level comprises the study of individuals and macro systems and the reciprocity between them. Comprehending the dynamics of human behavior requires a holistic approach that encompasses everything from the biological to the spiritual. Knowledge about groups, families, communities, organizations, and the natural environment is important in understanding human behavior because of the key role these entities play in shaping our very humanness. The family and social group make life possible, while the community and natural surroundings sustain life and provide purpose.

In his or her daily work, the social worker is drawn to explore nuances of culture and relationships and to seek the pattern, the rhythm in things. The ecosystems perspective is especially relevant to social work practice because social workers intervene at the interface between the individual and society. Knowledge of the wider pattern is key to unlocking the secret of human resilience and survival. The miracle of resilience (even in the face of the most horrendous of human tragedies) is not foreign to the social worker. Resilience in itself is a pattern, the kind of pattern with which the study of human behavior is vitally concerned— how people, groups, and whole cultures will, as William Faulkner (1951) once famously said, not only endure but prevail. To help make that happen—that is empowerment.

From an empowerment perspective, this book explores the ecosystems of life, ecosystems that are intricately interconnected. Compared

with its counterpart, *Human Behavior and the Social Environment, Micro Level* (van Wormer, 2010), this volume represents a shift from the person-in-the-environment to the environment-in-the person, a progression from small things to larger and more complex entities. This shift in focus is graphically represented in the book cover designs of the two companion texts. In Volume 1, the individual grains of sand correspond to the poetic theme—"to see the world in a grain of sand". For this volume, in contrast, the publishers have chosen an entire ecosystem of beach plus ocean. And lest we forget the human dimension, there are footprints in the sand.

The concern of this, the macro volume, is the study of the often bewildering behavior of humans within the context of the social institutions which shape and are shaped by human behavior. The study of personality and individual behavior across the life span (the subject of Volume 1) is fascinating, as the wealth of the literature on these themes, both fiction and nonfiction, will attest. But human behavior of groups, of the masses, is every bit as fascinating and the subject, too, of great literature. To make the subject especially compelling, the emphasis here, as in the first volume, is on the unconventional, as well as the conventional, in human organization.

The scope of *Human Behavior and the Social Environment* extends from macro-micro (the impact of the social environment on the person) to macro-macro phenomena. (the impact of one layer of the social environment on another layer, for example, of the global market on the average worker or family or on the social service agency) and their attendant values of commercialism and structural "reform." The reader will note that as the investigation into human affairs broadens, so too does the opportunity for controversy. Macro-level theory is ideological and political in ways that theories about individual growth and development are not because it relates to macro-level concerns such as globalization and social justice.

The shaping of this book is consistent with the notion that social work, first and foremost, is social. Social workers operate in and have to be sensitive to a multiplicity of contexts, from the local political to the global realms (Dominelli, 2004). Students of social work are trained as *generalists* to intervene in systems of all sizes— families, groups, agencies, communities—and, unlike those in other segments of the helping professions, to encompass efforts toward systemic change in their work. Even when engaged in therapy with individuals, social workers generally deal with issues of relationship; draw on support systems, including the family, as a major resource; and strive to achieve *cultural competence*. Cultural competence is a term that, as seen in Chapter 5, has relevance not only at the personal level but also for human service organizations in terms of policies and practices—at the systems level, in other words (see Raheim, 2006).

In the role of educator, the social worker may strive to help the client think critically about the harmful impact of group pressures, the corporate media and company sales appeals, and other manipulative activity. Intervention, moreover, includes linking the individual to community services and, at times, working in the wider political sphere to influence state and local policy. Social work, defined by Popple and Leighninger (2010) as "the policy-based profession," is unique among the helping professions. In their role as social service administrators, social workers might shape policy directly and advocate for staff and clients with agency boards. In all these ways to improve social functioning and well-being of people, knowledge of the intricacies of decision making and behavioral change is vital.

To get a clear idea of the extent to which members of the profession are called on to work at the macro level, read these sample headlines from recent issues of *NASW News:*

"NASW calls for action on CEDAW
   (Convention on the Elimination of All
   Forms of Discrimination Against
   Women)" (Malamud, 2009)
"NASW, New York chapters file brief in
   same-sex parenting case" (Sfiligoj, 2009a)
"NASW weighs in on student strip search
   case" (Sfiligoj, 2009b)
"Social work day at the U.N. celebrated:
   Global poverty—challenges for social

work practice was this year's theme"
(Sfiligoj, 2009c)

This chapter presents an introduction to the study of human behavior with a special emphasis on concepts and theoretical perspectives that pertain to social life within the wider social and cultural orbit. An ecosystems model is introduced as the theoretical framework for the book, a model that encompasses an empowerment perspective.

This model can be envisioned as a *holon*. In a holon, each part is a whole in itself as well as a part of a larger whole (see Figure 1.1).

Figure 1.1. The holon. Each part is a whole in itself and a part of a wider whole. This sculpture was constructed on the Portland State University Campus in honor of systems theorist Gordon Hearn. Photo by Rupert van Wormer.

This discussion can be conceived of as groundwork for the chapters on group dynamics, family forms, communities, and organizations that follow. More specifically, this chapter includes a discussion of the nature of theory, critical thinking about dominant and alternative theoretical approaches, a description of the major macro theoretical approaches, and the values that shape theory. Because of their relevance to macro-level social work and their explanatory power with reference to the mechanisms of social change, we have selected the following for emphasis: ecosystems theory, structural functionalism, and conflict theory from the discipline of sociology; anti-oppressive social work theory and the empowerment/strengths perspective from the field of social work; and the feminist approach from social activism.

Think of this as the theory chapter. Be prepared to reflect on the significance to the profession of the study of macro aspects of human behavior, a study that extends to the physical and global environments. Be ready also to review or learn about the major relevant theories, several of which are from sociology, and portions of which appear again and again throughout the pages of this book. Think of the purpose of this chapter as foundational: to provide an expanded ecological framework informed by principles of empowerment and anti-oppression analysis. Critical thinking is a major theme, as are the reciprocity of person and environment and the analysis of cultural ideology and value systems that permeate the society as a whole. The chapter is highlighted with two case studies: one a personal narrative of a woman's awakening to feminism and the other an article about a small agency's struggle to help the homeless.

Paradigms, or dominant perspectives, simultaneously shape and reflect the institutions and processes shared by people in a society (Schriver, 2010). In many ways, since that period of great awakening of youth and of a host of minority groups that occurred in the 1960s and 1970s, the predominant paradigm of social work has grown ever more refined and inclusive. Whereas the profession has continued the fight against injustice and oppression, mainstream politics from the 1980s through the

early 2000s took a 180-degree turn to the right. With the return of the Democrats to power in 2009 came a new impetus to address the plight of the poor, the unemployed, and the uninsured. Attention to the need for sustainable social welfare (health care) policies was matched by a heightened awareness of the consequences of unsustainable environmental and economic practices. Global warming has been a major concern of the twenty-first century (see Gore, 2006, *An Inconvenient Truth* and Gore, 2009, *Our Choice: A Plan to Solve the Climate Crisis*).

The age-old dilemma between the macro realities and the individual, problem-solving focus of much of social work, like the conflict between youthful idealism and the bureaucratic imperative, are not easily resolved. If the challenges facing social workers are severe, those facing our clients are even more so. To meet their needs and help them cope, professionals rely on theories often without any awareness that they are doing so, theories that involve assumptions about human nature and that guide the treatment process. Among the questions with which macro social work theory and this book grapple are these:

➤ How do decisions made at the macro level affect the lives and well-being of people of color, women, immigrants, and other vulnerable groups?
➤ What accounts for shifts in the public sentiment regarding explanations of poverty from one historical period to another?
➤ How can sociological theory inform social work theory and practice?
➤ What is the role of the media in public persuasion?
➤ How does the deep ecology movement link environmental concerns with spirituality?

A society fortified for war through massive spending with tight control of the media is generally a society of declining social benefits for the people. Within such a political climate, when the social work knowledge is out of sync with mainstream politics, the necessity for critical thinking about mass psychology and political persuasion is paramount. Given the contradictions between social work values (to promote the well-being of people and confront oppression) and the current work environment at many social service agencies, an environment shaped by external bureaucratic controls, Mullaly asks, "What should social work do?" (2007, p. 24). He finds the answer not in revolution but, more practically, in theory construction. The kind of theory Mullaly has in mind is built on expert knowledge about power dynamics and a comprehensive understanding of the nature of oppression.

Theory Construction

Theories are ideas abstracted from experiences and observation. In everyday usage, theories explain why something happens or, in the case of human behavior, why people behave the way they do. Popular thinking about society is informed by theory—people have theories about human nature, about justice, about causes of crime, about ethics, about sex-role behavior, and about child-rearing practices. In social science, the word *theory* is used in a more formal sense. Theory offers to behavioral scientists a general conceptual framework for understanding behavior in a wide variety of situations and a foundation for conducting research.

Social scientists talk of *small-range theory*, or principles that are useful in practice, such as the notion that a client's motivation is enhanced by taking even small steps. *Middle-range theory* is more comprehensive but specific enough to be grounded in data, whereas *grand theory*, which is highly abstract, offers explanations of social life as a whole (Buchinger, 2004). Robert K. Merton (1957) was the chief proponent of the former theory, and Talcott Parsons (1967) of the latter. The key variable here has to do with the scope or sweep of the referents.

Macro theory, as the term is used in this book, encompasses all three levels of sociological as opposed to psychological theory. Macro theory, in other words, relates to persons in the plural in interaction with each other and with forces in the environment. The environment may range from the family system to the global community in the social realm and

from housing to the wider natural environment—air, soil, and water—in the physical realm. To think in macro terms, think in the collective—of housing instead of house, of the behavior of the group—in short, of the group—rather than the individual mind. But don't stop there; think also of political-economic forces that influence social institutions and ideology through global institutions such as the world banks and the information technologies that support them. Macro-level forces emanating from the global market imperatives have reoriented the social work practice agenda to comply with government dictates (Dominelli, 2004).

Theories can be classified in terms of scope, in other words. Within macro theory itself, there is a further breakdown in the literature between theorists who conceive of society in terms of consensus or *order* and those who stress *conflict* and disorder. Mullaly (2002, 2007) and Payne (2005) take this approach. Mullaly (2002) categorizes theory dichotomously in terms of the order perspective, including the neoconservative and liberal paradigms, and the conflict perspective, including social democratic, Marxist, and structural paradigms. Mullaly views these two perspectives as mutually exclusive. Payne (2005), similarly, organizes theoretical perspectives on the basis of order, or individual-reformist, and of conflict, or socialist-collectivist, dualism. Under the category *individualist-reformist*, Payne includes social development, systems, and cognitive-behavioral approaches, and under *social-collectivist*, he includes anti-oppression, feminist, and empowerment approaches. Most conceptions of social work, as Payne acknowledges, include elements that cross the boundaries between these perspectives.

Lundy's (2004) use of a continuum to show the degree to which a theory adheres to assumptions of order or conflict is more useful, because it is more reflective of reality. This conceptualization allows for the ordering of consensus-based and conflict-based perspectives according to their unique and differentiating characteristics.

As we read through the social work journals and examine the various theoretical frameworks that are used, it soon becomes apparent that social work theory's greatest strength—

flexibility—is likewise its greatest weakness. Some theoretical frameworks with different names are relatively similar—for example, the empowerment and anti-oppression perspectives, conflict and structural theory, and systems and ecosystems frameworks. And others by the same name are different—for example, functionalism (as used in social work and sociology) and the ecological perspectives (which can have conservative connotations or be of a more liberal bent). Mullaly (2007) refers to the "confused theory base" (p. 33) and hodgepodge of beliefs that characterize the state of theory development in social work today and calls for a unifying framework, a complete reformulation of social work theory (p. 18). Such a reformulation is required to address the contemporary issues, chief among them of which is economic globalization. The field of social work, however, notes Mullaly, "has been unprepared to confront social and economic change, and has lacked the analytical or theoretical framework to understand global capitalism and to deal with its negative consequences" (p. 42).

Reformulation appears unlikely, however, because social work is a profession so closely linked to the social system. Various theoretical schemes have been proposed as alternatives to existing models, and, as Payne (2005) notes, their authors tend to exclude one another, almost as if in competition over territory. The alternative theories, in reality, are not so much alternatives as theories with a particular emphasis; some focus more on the individual in the environment and others on the environment itself, some on race and gender, and still others on empowerment or strengths. Generally, though, as Payne further indicates, most conceptions of social work include elements of each of these views.

Contemporary social work theories share a common ground in regard to the dominant social work values; these values are summarized by Mullaly (2007) as humanitarianism and egalitarianism. The well-being of the general public is primary. Social work ideology, as Mullaly (2007) suggests, has more in common with socialist than with capitalist paradigms. Agency practices are another matter, however.

Within a social structure in which market forces have gained priority over people and in which many agencies and health care facilities have now become private, for-profit organizations, a conflict between social work helping norms and corporate interests may be apparent. In their field placements, social work students often for the first time become aware of the constraints of managed care and fiscal crises as they affect the helping mission. The discrepancy between theory and practice then comes to a head. The next section explores such structural concerns from the standpoint of critical analysis.

Critical Thinking at the Macro Level

Think for a moment about a social problem, such as suicide, as if you were a social scientist. What kind of information would you want to have? You might be concerned with suicide rates across gender, race, class, age, and so forth. Your focus would be on patterns related to differences in the rates. Cross-cultural data that could show to what extent the problem is specific to any one social group (for example, the suicide rate among elderly men) or whether the incidence of suicide is spread evenly across the population. You might also want to look at data from the World Health Organization to compare rates in various countries.

When a social phenomenon is endemic to one social group—say, white elderly widowers—or high in one nation, such as Japan or Denmark, the researcher might develop hypotheses or hunches as to why. This is the fun part, because here, as art joins science, we can give our imaginations full rein. This quality of imagination enables us to grasp biology and psychology and the relationship of the two within the social system. In examining data concerning infant mortality, childhood deaths, and life expectancy, for example, the need to think sociologically is apparent. Consider the research that reveals that health and longevity are correlated with social class and that, in the United States, social class determines such life-shortening phenomena as inadequate or poor medical care, poor nutrition, high work stress, and other stress related to poverty. Behavioral factors, including unhealthful habits such as smoking, of course, also come into play. Next, consider behavioral statistics such as crime and incarceration rates. A critical analysis of such data reveals a confluence of biological, psychological, and social factors that affect everything from the nature of the crime committed to the quality of legal representation to the severity of the sentence meted out.

Two key aspects of critical thinking delineated by Keefe (1980) are empathy and critical consciousness. Each of these twin social work skills complements the other; each relates as much to individual as to social change. We discuss these attributes of critical thinking, along with a third and closely related concept—cultural competence.

Empathy, the ability to put oneself in the place of another, is a quality usually associated at the individual level with getting in tune with the other's emotional state and circumstances through imagining ourselves in his or her place. This is the art of social work. Empathy can be extended to whole peoples and cultures and populations, as well, such as survivors of the Holocaust or Stalin's Gulag. Keefe's (2003) use of the concept *profound empathy* uniquely captures the essence of this quality at a level that is higher still:

> The first step away from the subjective realization of a continuity with nature can be a step toward a profound empathy. One realizes one's nature is the same as other sentient beings, other manifestations of awareness. Consequently, this empathy is the first post-experience value; other values may follow from it. So one's cultural values are now conditioned by empathy with other living things and may be reexamined in this light. Our unconditioned awareness is precious and, by extension, that same awareness is valued in other sentient beings. (Keefe, 2003, p. 10)

Critical consciousness involves an understanding of the encompassing social-structural context of human problems. A keen awareness

of the fact that there are serious problems with the economic structure of this society and that the status quo is not static is an essential part of the professional's collective wisdom.

This kind of resourcefulness, which exemplifies the use of both a critical consciousness and social work imagination, is seen in the form of collective field activities that developed in Latin America under the charismatic leadership of Paulo Freire, an exiled Brazilian educator who lived in Chile. These grassroots activities functioned outside of the mainstream and involved organizational work among the poorest and most needy groups of society. Chilean social work education was revolutionized as a result of the pedagogical instruction of Freire. From 1965 to 1973, when a military dictatorship intervened to suppress the program and persecute the social workers who were organizing the countryside, a real participatory democracy characterized social work education. Today, while human rights are being restored in Chile and throughout Latin America, schools of social work continue to train their students in this collectivist form of organization. Freire (1973) eloquently described his emancipatory pedagogy as follows:

> The critically transitive consciousness is characterized by depth in the interpretation of problems; by the substitution of causal principles for magical explanations; by the testing of one's findings and by openness to revision; by the attempt to avoid distortion when perceiving problems and to avoid preconceived notions when analyzing them; by refusing to transfer responsibility; by rejecting passive positions; by soundness of argumentation; by the practice of dialogue rather than polemics; by receptivity to the new for reasons beyond mere novelty and by the good sense not to reject the old just because it is old—by accepting what is valid in both the old and new. (p. 17)

The influence of Freire is widely echoed among social activists today, such as feminist educator bell hooks (1995, who articulates Freierian premises in terms of "teaching/learning to transgress" and critical thinking as "the primary element allowing the possibility of change" (p. 202). A related aspect is, of course, cultural competence. *Cultural competence*, as discussed in Chapter 5, entails a recognition of society's prejudices—ethnocentrism, sexism, classism, heterosexism, and racism—and of our own possession of many of these traits and our need to strive to overcome them (see NASW, 2001). An important part of cultural competence is understanding one's role as an oppressor as well as of being oppressed (which is usually obvious to the victims). In *Becoming an Ally*, Anne Bishop (2002) explains that it is difficult for us to see ourselves in the role of oppressor, both because this is uncomfortable to us and also that it is equated with normality, universal standards and values, and political and cultural neutrality. Becoming aware of such less obvious roles that we play and positions that we occupy in society is one of the challenges of critical thinking.

To enhance the "possibility of change" of which bell hooks speaks, a vision across time and *space* is essential. The concept of space as used here refers to region or places and takes into account neighborhoods, social institutions such as the church or social service agencies, communities, and physical environs. These are all topics addressed in later pages of this book. *Time* relates to a sense of history. Take the passage of a piece of legislation as an example. Considerations of time would address the question: What is the history of this legislation? Has it been introduced before, and with what results? In other words, are conditions ripe for change? Kuhn's (1962) concept of paradigm shift, discussed in the next section, is relevant to this discussion.

The way social ideas are constructed changes over time: Whether an idea receives any consideration or is rudely discarded depends on the public sentiment and the taken-for-granted notions of the age. The influence of media images can be a decisive factor in captivating the attention of the masses. Ten years ago, who would have thought, for example, that marriage could take place between persons of the same sex? Who would have thought that single women might choose to have a baby through artificial insemination, or that people from all parts of the world could simultaneously be exposed to the same news sources and the same mass culture? The rapid communication of ideas and innovation helps pave the way for shifts in ideology, shifts that can reach far and wide.

Paradigm Shift

The welfare state is in crisis, as it has been at least since the Reagan era. Government retrenchment in social welfare services has led to the formation of Depression-type food banks, widespread homelessness, and futile attempts by churches and other voluntary organizations to meet the demands for food and shelter for the poorest of the poor. And yet no economic depression exists, but, rather, a strong economy internationally, characterized by increasingly massive sums of wealth concentrated in the hands of a few. The crisis in social welfare and, therefore, in the profession most closely associated with it, social work, can be viewed in terms of a shift in the predominant worldview or paradigm. Kuhn (1962), in *The Structure of Scientific Revolutions*, popularized use of the term *paradigm* to refer to a particular cognitive framework of a discipline and to the social context in which it functions. The ideological values, beliefs, and goals of a particular paradigm determine the interpretation and explanation given to social problems (Mullaly, 2007).

Kuhn viewed the Great Enlightenment of the eighteenth century as ushering in a shift in thinking in Europe away from an emphasis on the authority of the church and monarchs to an emphasis on rationality and the scientific method. Professionally, remnants of this advance are present today in the impetus in social work practice to use only practice methods that are "evidence based." An alternative view, *postmodernism*, is a reaction to the previous modernist thought that relegated science to a status superior to art and to the tendency to see reality in terms of mutually exclusive either/or categories. Schriver (2010) differentiates traditional or dominant paradigms from alternative ones that may exist at the same time. The latter paradigms, he suggests, are inclusive on the grounds of race, class, and gender and more consistent than the former with the core concerns and historical values of social work. Schriver urges that we, as social workers, draw on multiple worlds of understanding, that we find a proper balance between art and science. There are many ways of knowing.

The social construction of ideas changes with the times. A paradigm shift occurs through what Kuhn termed a "scientific revolution," at which time a completely new worldview comes about, one that represents a revolutionary break with past ways of viewing reality. The shift is precipitated through actions taken by a dissatisfied segment of the community. Through such activity, all or parts of the older paradigm are replaced with a newer one, as Schriver (2010) indicates. Or a crisis such as a war, economic depression, even a great plague can cause people to lose faith in the "old ways." Craig Mosher (2009) speaks of certain watershed events such as Hurricane Katrina that may help to shift many peoples' thinking. Then there are "the slower, catastrophic, events … also coming into greater focus: melting glaciers, deforestation, HIV-AIDS, dead zones in the oceans, polluted breast milk, and so on" (p. 14). We can use the metaphor of a pendulum to describe swings in the political thinking of an era, whether the thrust was to eradicate poverty and rehabilitate criminals or to leave the poor to fend for themselves and mandate harsh punishment for crime. Such causal attribution has important treatment and public policy implications.

We can characterize the growth and decline of the American welfare state in terms of paradigm shifts or pendulum swings between two opposite poles, with the focus of individual attribution at one end and the focus of social reform at the other. When the focus was on social reform, the field of social work expanded in accordance with the ideology. The Progressive Era that preceded World War I, the period of the Great Depression, and the 1960s and 1970s were the healthiest times for social workers and social activists. The times in between were characterized by conservatism, individualism,

and a throwback to a strong social control emphasis. As of this writing, a certain disillusionment with free market capitalism has set in. Today, according to Mary (2008), there is the realization in some quarters that the goal of unlimited progress and reliance on paradigms that have outlived their usefulness is no longer functional. Mosher (2009) perceives the opportunity for a paradigm shift related to our awareness of an impending environmental crisis. He calls for a new paradigm to be based on work toward a more just and sustainable society. This new worldview would be based on interdependence rather than individualism and a long-term rather than limited perspective.

Macro-Level Research

Research knowledge is valuable to social workers in helping them to provide high-quality services, to initiate change, to improve practice, and to evaluate programming. The NASW (1996) Code of Ethics stipulates that "social workers should promote and facilitate evaluation and research to contribute to the development of knowledge" (Section 5.02b). Because research tends to be funded by the government or by private foundations, each having restricted interests, research that compares multiple theoretical approaches tends to be limited (Payne, 2005). Macro-level research is rarely funded by the government, especially during times of fiscal (and political) conservatism. Such grant money that is available is marked for the area of health care and/or to support research concerning specific practice interventions with persons who are battling conditions such as depression, addictions, or eating disorders. Research concerning evidence-based practice is in demand (Surface, 2009). Because insurance companies reimburse for treatment interventions of proven effectiveness, medically and psychologically based research with individuals is the favored empirical research design. Yet, as Witkin (2001) suggests, too heavy a reliance on evidence-based procedures aligns social work practice too closely with dominant as opposed to alternative paradigms. And as

Mosher (2009) indicates, with regard to academic journal publications, one problem with overreliance on evidence-based methodologies is that it casts the social worker in the role of expert and narrows the focus of research questions and methods to the neglect of the physical and social environment.

Macro social workers conduct research to obtain information they need to carry out their work of bringing about a better society (Brueggemann, 2005). For example, if you are engaged in community work, you will want to find out as much as you can about community needs and resources. Conducting focus or structured discussion groups with community members on topics of concern is an excellent way to gather qualitative data in a systematic fashion (see Chapter 3). If you are studying an organization's effectiveness, as Brueggemann further suggests, you might conduct a survey to locate areas in which breakdowns occur and to gauge problems in need of correction.

The study of structural events such as the impact of social welfare policies on family life or of the global market on the regional workplace or of environmental pollution on human health and life span is every bit as scientific as the study of mental and emotional process or treatment interventions. Social structures may not be tangible entities that can be seen on a computed tomography (CT) scan, yet their effects are tangible and can be measured accordingly. In the aggregate, besides, it is much easier to predict human behavior or the consequences of a given policy than it is to predict what a given individual will do. And yet collective behavior often does surprise us. Consider, for example, voting patterns by many poor whites that go against their personal and class interests. Such surprises or paradoxes can lead to a reappraisal of the social theory underlying an earlier faulty prediction. Often a structural analysis of the hidden uses of power is enlightening.

As with all investigations, the researcher's bias enters in at every stage of the research, starting with the questions asked. Hutchison (2008) lists the following areas as those most likely to involve bias: funding sources that have their own agendas; selection of the variables studied; choice of sample to be studied; and manner in which data are collected. Industry-funded research has been shown to be far more apt to be positive toward the product studied (for example, a new medication compared to an older one) than negative (Tavris & Aronson, 2007). Studies by nonprofit organizations yield far different results. The scientific community that once valued objectivity in research and a separation of science and commerce has now given way and is less concerned with conflicts of interest as universities urgently seek new sources of revenue. The general public pays the price for the unreliable and tainted findings. Social workers need to be wary of research findings financed by private interest groups.

In addition to drawing on research about treatment effectiveness, social work, because of its concern with matters social, tends to draw on the social sciences and especially sociology for its knowledge base. But drawing on the social sciences for our knowledge base raises some important concerns. The first concern is the sheer magnitude and diversity of social science theory and research. With so much knowledge constantly expanding, how do we discover and incorporate what is most useful and salient? The second concern is related to the first. Just as there is a vast sea of knowledge to confront, there is also the great depth of knowledge with which to contend. So, for example, if we are observing aggressive behavior on the part of an adolescent boy we are working with, is the behavior a function of the dynamics of the activity group of which he is a member? Is it the product of the violence he experienced earlier in his development? Or is it a function of his drug use?

Yet research at the group and macro levels is vital for social change efforts. First, there is the data collection, and then, the analysis. Data may be gathered by using a small group based on a sample of the population under study. Data collected from mass populations are often available from government sources in the form of crime reports, victimization surveys, sentencing data, and census data. Data analysis is vital to understanding the true nature of social problems and also in countering media hype and irresponsible political claims with the facts.

That the use of hard statistical data is subject to abuse and misuse is shown in the following situations:

➤ The government's pie chart on U.S. tax dollar spending, which seriously underestimates the level of military spending by consolidating categories (see http://www.warresisters.org)

➤ Data from Uniform Crime Reports showing steady decline in crime rates while politicians continue to "crack down on crime" (see http://www.ojp.usdoj.gov/bjs)

➤ Political arguments purporting to show that the death penalty is a deterrent to crime (see http://www.amnestyusa.org/abolish)

➤ The case against global warming, despite evidence to the contrary (see www.sierraclub.org).

➤ Media accounts announcing that women are as violent as men in relationships (for the real facts, see the Justice Department statistics at http://www.ojp.usdoj.gov/bjs)

➤ Arguments by the National Rifle Association that gun ownership saves lives (see http://www.jointogether.org and www.vpc.org, the Violence Policy Center, for figures on gun-related deaths)

➤ The widespread but erroneous belief that drug use is primarily a problem among racial and ethnic minorities (see http://www.drugpolicy.org)

➤ The belief that Social Security is in a state of crisis (see http://www.aarp.org/bulletin/socialsec/changing-ss.html)

Students of social work take courses in research and statistics so that they can critically analyze claims such as the preceding ones. Such knowledge of research techniques and interpretations enhances critical thinking. Access to a wide range of sources on the Internet enables the skeptical citizen to check on political claims that seem to represent an agenda to pursue a given cause. To advocate for a cause, such as prison reform, for example, one needs to have accurate and reliable data at hand and to be able to refute false claims. Social activist organizations might furthermore conduct a needs assessment in order to advocate on behalf of marginalized populations in need of services and to demonstrate the cost effectiveness of greater investment in home health care, affordable day care, public health care clinics, and housing for persons with mental disabilities, for example.

The need to include the populations being studied—the persons with the disabilities, the homeless, and so forth—in the design of the research is crucial; moreover, it is politically empowering. Social work researchers such as Brueggeman (2005) and Surface (2009) stress the ways in which such inclusion can contribute to the research effort, even, in some cases, radically changing the purpose, process, and assumptions that underlie a particular project. Brueggemann (2005) terms such community- and consumer-centered research *action research*. The tendency in existing models of research is to treat the people being investigated as "other," to make an artificial distinction between researchers and the researched. Even in outcome evaluations, staff members rather than service users are generally the persons who provide the data. Shalowitz, Isacco, et al. (2009), in their review of the literature on community-based participatory research discuss the advances that have been made in research that is conducted as an equal partnership between traditionally trained experts and members of a community. Participatory research to be truly participatory must involve community members at every stage of research: in formulating the research question, in conducting interviews, and in analyzing the findings. These are among the ways that empowerment-oriented researchers can return as much control as possible to users, whatever their abilities or circumstances.

Paige (2009) examines the use of language in empowering therapy with women in recovery from sexual assault. From this perspective, therapists create language and meaning that fit with the relational experience of women and celebrate their strength and resilience. Healing possibilities are seen as emerging through achievement of mutual understandings and reframing of experience. The choice of words is important as well in doing research. Words, according to Rapp, Shera, and Kirsthardt (1993), should come from the vernacular of the people in the study rather than from research jargon. Consumers talk about jobs, for example, and researchers about "instrumental role functioning" (Rapp et al., 1993, p. 732), and friends and families become "social support systems" in research-speak. When a report is written in laypersons' language, the results can be widely disseminated and used by the people in question. Such client-centered and collaborative research, like client-centered therapy, can help break barriers between professional and client and be a consciousness-raising experience for all concerned.

Introduction to Macro Theory

We move now from research to the theoretical perspectives on which much of social work research and practice are based. Many of these perspectives (loosely referred to as theories) are derived from the social science that is concerned with social phenomena in the broader context—sociology. The systems framework (borrowed originally from the biological sciences), structural functionalism, and conflict theory are major sociological perspectives. Ecosystems theory (a hybrid that combines systems and ecological concepts originally from biology), anti-oppressive theory, and the empowerment perspective are social work contributions. Keep in mind, as you explore these theoretical concepts, that they are not static but subject to change over time and to varied interpretations as each theorist adds on ideas and adaptations of his or her own. Despite the differences among theorists and critics, generally speaking, the progressive theoretical concept of the preceding period is apt to be viewed as conservative and limited in scope by the next generation. Theoretical concepts are thus continually expanded and reconceptualized; the intellectual development of theory tends to parallel paradigm shifts in the wider society. In accordance with the new thinking, new perspectives are born and many of the older ones abandoned or modified. The civil rights movement, women's liberation, feminist research, and activism by gays and lesbians,

disabled persons, and the like, for example, have been instrumental in transforming knowledge and advancing theory in the social sciences (Lundy, 2004). Today the emphasis on spirituality, the natural environment, and the impact of globalization are expanding theory into areas that were previously overlooked.

Theories, then, are ideologically based and reflect cultural and personal biases of the theorist and the period. For this reason, it is often educational to read the classic theories and judge them within the context of the day while appreciating many of the insights that were presented. Often we tend to overlook many of the great theoretical insights from the past.

Each of the macro perspectives that we examine in the pages that follow has strengths and weaknesses. As an aid in critical thinking and in the interests of fair play, we ask the same questions of each theoretical perspective:

1. What are the basic assumptions and concepts?
2. Is the theory verifiable?
3. Does the theory incorporate issues of diversity and oppression?
4. What is the contribution to social work?
5. What are the major criticisms of this theory?
6. What does the theory teach about human behavior?

Because of their contribution to the study of groups, families, organizations, and communities, we have chosen the following perspectives for consideration: general systems; ecosystems; structural-functionalism; conflict and structural; and the feminist, empowerment, and anti-oppression frameworks. As we examine each theoretical perspective for its relevance to macro social work, let us keep in mind the definition of social work provided by the International Federation of Social Workers (IFSW, 2005):

> The social work profession promotes social change, problem solving in human relationships, and the empowerment and liberation of people to enhance well-being. Utilizing theories of human behavior and social systems, social work

intervenes at the points where people intersect with their environments. Principles of human rights and social justice are fundamental to social work. (IFSW, 2005)

Ecosystems Theory

In this section we describe the ecosystems framework. This framework is basically a combination of systems theory and an ecological, interactive perspective. The formulation of this theory was developed in conjunction with feedback from critics, a fact that was highly appropriate to a mode that is itself centered on the concept of feedback. We start with the early formulation of systems theory, then provide a brief description of concepts from the school of ecology; finally we trace the development of ecosystems theory as a combination of the two.

Concepts from General Systems Theory

Following World War II, systems concepts gained currency through observations of the new science of information technology (Walsh, 2009). Notions of feedback, feedback loops, and inputs and outputs were later borrowed from the machine imagery of information technology and used in the social sciences. The general systems framework first came to the full attention of the scientific community in the 1960s through the efforts of Ludwig von Bertalanffy, a biologist (Greene, 2009b). Systems theory is not really a theory at all because it does not explain anything, so the term is used here in a general sense only. What it does do is show how parts fit into the whole. Greene describes this perspective as a model or framework for describing and analyzing any living system, such as an organism, or any nonliving system, such as a group or organization.

Systems conceptualizations are in sharp contrast with Freudian perspectives that were prevalent in the nineteenth century. Sigmund Freud (1924/1975) saw the human organism as driven by instincts that needed to be satisfied.

Psychodynamic theory, based on the teachings of Freud and his followers, heavily influenced the development of psychological and social theories throughout the twentieth century. Until the end of the 1960s, it was the dominant organizing framework in social work (Haight & Taylor, 2007). After that time, the social and behavioral sciences broadened their knowledge base considerably by viewing the human organism interactively. Maslow's (1970) famous hierarchy of human needs can be considered as portraying a kind of *open system* designed to discuss individual needs but with equal applicability to the duty of society to see that the people's needs are met to help them collectively achieve a state of higher actualization.

Systems concepts were brought into social work in the 1970s as a reaction against psychodynamic theory, which focused on the human mind (Payne, 2005). The basic premise of systems liberates us from earlier linear, atomistic, and mechanical views of human behavior to include truths from sociology as well as psychology. This more holistic framework broadened the scope of social work considerably. From this perspective, social workers could view their workplace, the agency, within a wider context.

Recognizing that social workers work with complex systems, Gordon Hearn (1969), with several contributors, realized the utility of general systems theory for the social work profession and introduced some of its concepts. (Think back to the odd-shaped sculpture of the holon pictured at the start of the chapter [Figure 1.1].) This sculpture was constructed in honor of systems theorist Gordon Hearn. As Hearn asserted:

> Individuals, small groups—including families and organizations—and other complex human organizations such as neighborhoods and communities—in short, the entities with which social work is usually involved—can all be regarded as systems with certain common properties. If nothing else, this should provide social work education with a means of organizing the human behavior and social environments aspect of the curriculum. (p. 2).

The translation of general systems concepts into family therapy revolutionized the way families were viewed. Virginia Satir (1972) adapted systems concepts of roles, boundaries, feedback, and triangles in her practice with families. Satir's teachings in her writings and workshops were highly influential in social work and substance abuse treatment circles. She taught family therapists to look for family communication patterns, especially dysfunctional ones, and to help family members analyze the messages they were sending.

Thomas Keefe (in private correspondence with van Wormer of May, 2006) tells that when, in his clinical practice, he was participating in a mental health team meeting, a case was presented in which a client's problematic behavior was explained with equal plausibility by a psychiatrist with a psychoanalytic explanation, including unresolved conflicts, and by a psychologist with a behavioral explanation, including ways the client's behaviors were being rewarded by significant others in the client's life. The social worker, meanwhile, tried to turn the group's attention to pressures on the family and within the family. Because each explanation led to a different approach to intervention, the team was in a dilemma concerning which position was the true one. From a systems perspective, the explanations, like the influences on the patient's behavior, could interact—for example, the mental conflict might initiate the behaviors that are then sustained by the interpersonal responses. A holistic approach such as that based on systems understandings gives us a way of thinking that dissolves artificial categories and better reflects the complexity of human behavior.

Although systems theory broadened the social work perspective from the individual to the family, we often frame practice with families as family treatment and target the family as the system for change with very little attention to the need for change in the social systems that create poverty, unemployment, and family difficulties (Mary, 2008). General systems perspective is an organizing framework that is sufficiently broad and inclusive to cover all the social sciences in their interrelationships, as well as one particular social science, such as

social work. Our concerns about the integration of social science knowledge spring from the nature of social sciences: The social sciences are vast; they are expanding; and they address different levels of analysis for what outwardly might be seen as a single phenomenon. Clearly, if social work is to usefully draw on the social sciences and on some portions of the biological sciences to serve as its knowledge base, the profession must employ an organizing framework that makes some sense out of the ocean of information, and it must identify the level or levels of analysis it is employing in given assessments and interventions. Related to the concerns of the profession previously identified, von Bertalanffy (1968) was concerned with the degree to which specialization in the sciences leads to difficulty in communication. In von Bertalanffy's words:

> Modern science is characterized by its ever-increasing specialization, necessitated by the enormous amount of data, the complexity of techniques and of theoretical structures within every field. Thus science is split into innumerable disciplines continually generating new subdisciplines. In consequence, the physicist, the biologist, the psychologist and the social scientist are, so to speak, encapsulated in their private universes, and it is difficult to get word from one cocoon to the other. (p. 30)

Yet communication among specialists is necessary to fully and adequately address the kinds of problems that confront humankind in our historical era. Von Bertalanffy believed that there were parallelisms of principles that could serve as a kind of bridge between persons from different fields.

Whereas von Bertalanffy sought to help sort out general principles of organization across the sciences, social workers, having a pragmatic bent, are interested in the application of such principles in situations and problems that affect people. So, for example, if the problem were a polluted river, people from a variety of fields would need to communicate to adequately address the problem—biologists, chemists, engineers, waste disposal experts, economists, lawyers, politicians, law enforcement personnel, and others. These specialists would have to address components or processes of multiple systems—physical, ecological, economic, social, and even interpersonal.

Formal and informal organizations range from nation states to communities of interest or locale; they manifest the ways humans organize. These organizations comprise *small groups*, which, in turn, comprise individual or *micro behaviors* within the realm of *interpersonal relations*. The academic disciplines that correspond to the study of the exchange of commodities, organizations, and group behavior are economics, sociology, and social psychology. When applied to micro systems, concepts from these disciplines have enhanced thinking about the ways parts of a system—individuals in groups or families—affect each other, seeming to interlock and mutually influence each other in indirect ways.

Whole-Part

Biologists have come to understand that the mitochondria in animal cells are derivative of thousands of bacteria that have contributed part of their genes and functions to the cell (Dawkins, 2004). This whole-part idea relates well to social work's traditional person-in-situation (Germain, 1979; Hollis, 1965) construct and its variations.

Von Bertalanffy (1968) used the metaphor of the Roman god Janus to illustrate how we perceive reality. Janus was often represented as a two-faced god, the statue of whom was carved into the archways of building entrances. One face looked within and the other outward. This symbolized the idea that the universe is made up of systems that are all wholes in and of themselves with their own subsystems and also, simultaneously, parts of larger systems. This principle also illustrates the significance of studying phenomena from more than one angle. See Figure 1.2 of the gorilla looking out of the glass cage at the photographer looking in.

Moving from macro to micro systems, the universe is made up of the ecological system, nations, communities, the workplace, and the family. The family is a whole of which each individual is a part. Considering human systems, each person is a system, and each person

Figure 1.2 "Looking from the outside in or the inside out." Photo by Kathleen Besthorn and Margie Hayes.

is made up of a variety of systems—circulatory, respiratory, digestive, nervous, reproductive, and so forth. The whole-part concept helps us to think of both context and underlying structure when we consider aspects of human behavior—not only is everything connected but everything is also both a whole and a part of larger systems.

Open and Closed Systems

Von Bertalanffy distinguished between open and closed systems. A *closed system* is shut off from its environment, and it will eventually become *entropic*, that is, internally deteriorate. By contrast, an open system continuously exchanges mass, energy, and information with its environment. This *steady state* of exchange with its environment makes it possible for the open system to grow, specialize, differentiate, and become more complex. Generally, living things or systems made up of living things that conduct this *steady state* of exchange with the environment are open systems. Closed systems are nonliving and, lacking the steady state of exchange, move naturally toward randomness or entropy.

On a larger scale and in the nonliving realm, the notion of systems in interaction with other systems enriches our analysis of organizations. Even as bureaucracies, most organizations have the qualities of open systems. Importing and exporting energy, some of it in the form of revenue and information, the bureaucracy will grow new and ever more specialized divisions, departments, and offices. Cutting or expanding the steady state of exchange of revenue and information is often the subject of political debate.

Boundaries

Of all the concepts that constitute general systems theory, the concept of boundaries is perhaps the most useful for social work practitioners. *Boundaries* are the defining limits of systems. And, therefore, the concept of boundaries can often serve at different levels of analysis. Boundaries signify what is inside and what is outside a given system. The shell of an egg is

a well-defined, material boundary. Family therapy is the area of social work most closely associated with the concepts borrowed from systems analysis. The roles that individuals play in a family are viewed as complementary and interactive, and much attention is paid to the boundaries between individuals as they play their complementary roles. This concept of boundary has an expanded usage as well: Privileges, access, the surface of a person's body, family secrets, a person's social roles, the streets that define a geographic community, or the borders of a country can all be considered boundaries that define particular physical, psychological, social, or political systems. Human beings continually draw boundaries through use of language, culture, educational achievement, and so forth that serve our individual and social functioning, sometimes to the exclusion of outside groups.

The concept of boundaries can provide us with a useful perspective on systems relationships: A healthy or functional boundary is firm enough to allow adjoining systems to grow and develop normally and is flexible enough to allow communication between the systems. Thus, the health or functioning of a relationship is not judged by particular values or a list of characteristics so much as by the degree to which boundaries are firm and flexible, allowing optimal development. In other words, in employing the concept of system boundaries, we can analyze a system's boundaries—whether the system is an individual, a family, a group, or a community—as to its health and functioning.

In social work, we deal with systems in which a simple cause-and-effect explanation does not suffice. A behavior may be rewarded by several contingencies. One family member's responses may affect another's responses, which then affect the first. This is interactionism. These systems concepts delineated here can be viewed as building blocks for the later theoretical approach known as the ecological school of social work.

Teachings From the Science of Ecology

Germain and Gitterman's (1996) *life model* of social work practice is the major formulation of the ecological systems perspective (Payne, 2005). Based on the metaphor of ecology in which organisms are interdependent with each other and the environment, the life model dominated the field in the 1980s. Commentators such as Hartman and Laird (1983) applauded the dawning of a new era in social work—the shift toward rigorous but holistic theories that broaden the parameters of social work practice:

> A revolution has been brewing for some time now, in the social sciences, in the helping professions, and in social work. Since the late 1950s and 1960s, social workers have been exploring the potential of general systems, cybernetics and ecological theories.... A scientific revolution has been in the making, one which in Kuhn's sense is ushering in a new paradigm. (p. 3)

Ecological thinking singularly brought the attention of social workers not only to the person *in* the environment but to the person and environment in interaction. Such interaction was viewed as constant and dynamic; attention was thus brought to patterns of behavior and to the networking of subsystems within the unitary system as a whole. This framework has also enhanced our understanding of stress and coping in meeting the demands of the environment and one's ability to function in a hostile neighborhood or community setting (Greene, 2009a). Conceived as ever-widening concentric circles, this model has inspired the risk and resilience approach in social work with families.

Key concepts from an ecological approach are as follows:

- *Niche:* a particular place that is suitable for the growth and development of the organism
- *Transactions:* interactions between people and others in their environment
- *Energy:* borrowed from systems theory, refers to the power that springs forth and takes the form of input or output depending on the direction of the energy
- *Targets of change:* the source of the social work intervention can be individuals, groups, or whole communities

No other conceptual frame of reference since the introduction of Freudian psychology has had as significant an impact on mainstream social work thinking as have the ecological and systems formulations. Taken together, these frameworks build on each other and are enlightened by their shared conceptualizations.

Combining Ecological and Systems Models

Systems and ecological perspectives have a lot in common; both operate at a high level of abstraction and are concerned with patterns of behavior. Both theoretical perspectives look at the interactions and interdependence between the person and his/her environment (Rogers, 2006). In addiction, both approaches lend themselves to analysis of minority as well as mainstream cultural values and expectations, and to an understanding of cultural clash between divergent systems (Greene, 2009b). Solomon's (1976) concept of the ethnosystem emphasized the interdependent interrelatedness of ethnic collectivities in society and brings our attention to variations in cultural and language patterns that may have a bearing on communication as well as access to resources.

Rogers (2006) helps us differentiate these twin approaches. Although both perspectives focus on systems, each offers a slightly different way to think about how systems impact one another and how people adapt to their changing circumstances and surroundings. Systems theorists, for example, focus on the roles that individuals play to help maintain order within their systems. Ecological theorists take a broader view by looking at the settings in which people play out those roles and at the impact of those settings on people's functioning. In social work and other literature, concepts from these two approaches has been combined for an ecosystems approach. Then ecosystems theorists have delved into areas such as the impact of the natural environment on human and nonhuman life that were never tackled before. Such is the beauty of good theory; it lends itself to innovation, reformulation, and expansion.

Mullaly (2002) sees the limitation of the general systems perspective, or "order theory," as being that it does not adequately deal with structural variables such as class, race, and gender, nor does it adequately deal with power relations or conflict. A neglect of history in favor of a focus solely on the "here and now" is another serious flaw. Hutchison and Charlesworth (2008) point to the heavy emphasis on equilibrium and on traditional family roles that gives traditional systems theories a conservative slant. Contemporary formulations have begun to recognize power and oppression, although fleetingly.

The replacement of the concept equilibrium from general systems with that of balance by ecosystems theorists is a major improvement in the framework, in our opinion. The concept of nature in balance (as articulated for example in Al Gore's [1988] *The Earth in Balance*) refers to replenishment of natural resources, fertility, and growth in the life cycle. Equilibrium, in contrast, is a more static concept, one with political connotations related more to social stability than to social change.

Ecosystems, which interact with the geophysical phenomena, are historically recognized as conditioning aspects of human activities. In recent years, the interactions of humans with the natural environment that affect social welfare have been increasingly recognized, such as with issues of distributive justice and the effects of alienation of people from the natural environment (Besthorn, 2003).

The best illustration, perhaps, of the ecosystems conceptualization is provided in a beautifully photographed film about the prairie. Called *America's Lost Landscape*, the film was produced by biology professor Daryl Smith (2005) of the University of Northern Iowa. Although the prairie has all but disappeared from the landscape of the American Midwest, we learn from the film of efforts made in Iowa and Kansas to return the earth to its natural state, to the ecosystem in balance. The prairie is not linear, as the film narrator informs us. In its native state, grasslands reached a height of 5 to 10 feet, and plant and animal life was abundant. The Plains Indians experienced life as a circle of growth and death and new growth. Life is circular, as are the seasons; anything that was at one time will be again. The Indians relied on the wild bison and planted crops for

sustenance while ensuring that these resources endured for the use of future generations. The principle they followed was that of sustainability. As preparation for our discussion of the concept of sustainability, we look at how ecosystems writers modify the person-in-environment configuration.

Focus on Person *and* the Environment

Germain and Gitterman (1996), as stated earlier, modified their theory in response to theoretical criticism to include notions of coercive and exploitative power, such as when dominant groups withhold power from workers or endanger community health through environmental pollution. The aim of social work practice from the life model perspective is to improve the fit between people and their environment by alleviating life stressors, thus increasing people's personal and social resources to boost their coping mechanisms and influence environmental factors for the good of people (Payne, 2005).

From the ecosystems perspective, the term *environment* refers to the habitat in which a person lives. This might be a house, a neighborhood, the workplace, or school (Hutchison, 2008). Sociologists Massey and Denton (1993), authors of *American Apartheid*, for example, argued through the use of demographic data that segregation in the urban areas studied is the root of many problems that African Americans face today. Similarly, Massey and Fischer (2006), in their analysis of data from their longitudinal survey of first-year college students, were able to document the effects of segregation and housing on later academic performance. Black and Latino college students were found to be severely disadvantaged by external factors in the environments compared with other students. Such research findings can serve to bolster ecological theory regarding the person-in-environment and the environment-in-person configurations.

Social work theorists today are infusing such demographic research related to segregation and poverty into their writings on the macro social environment. Tester (1994) earlier envisioned an ecosystems model for social work practice in an ecological age. To Tester, history, the economy, and culture are strong determinants in shaping the physical environment, which, in turn, shapes the economy and culture. Kirst-Ashman (2007); Morales, Sheafor, and Scott (2010); and Zastrow and Kirst-Ashman (2010) use ecosystems perspectives throughout their texts, which examine the human behavior in communities, organizations, and groups; a focus on poverty and minority status is evident throughout their writings. Although these writers such as others of the basic social work texts do not employ the term *sustainability*, we can infer from their criticisms of the U.S. social welfare system and the unbalanced distribution of income and the impact of unmet needs on people from all walks of life that current government spending practices are viewed as unsustainable. In their entry on human needs in the *Encyclopedia of Social Work*, Dover and Joseph (2008) urge ecosystems proponents to further develop need-based theory and research to reflect the reality in which social workers work, a reality that is centered on human need. Our discussion of sustainability that follows is consistent with Dover's urging.

Sustainability

Sustainability is about meeting current needs of the population without threatening the lives of future generations. Throughout the sustainability literature, this concept is often used in close association with its opposite—unsustainability. Thus, we often hear today such statements as "Our overuse of the soil and pollution of the waterways are unsustainable" or "Our mass consumption of our natural resources is unsustainable"; of course, the same is said about present government economic practices. Today our increased ecological and economic spending consciousness is rooted in crisis. Relevant to the environment, most often we hear about global warming, and we are treated to photographs revealing the steady melting of the glaciers at the North and South Poles. Relevant to the U.S. economy, figures concerning the national debt and rising unemployment rates commonly appear on the TV screen.

Sustainability is a concept that is integral to ecosystems theory. Among the basic assumptions we can glean from the science of ecology with special relevance to sustainability are the following:

- The biological organism exists in dynamic interaction with its environment.
- Force exerted by the organism affects the environment, which in turn affects the organism. This concept is called *interactionism*.
- The organism *adapts*, partially adapts, or fails to adapt to stress induced by changes in the environment.
- Organisms work together to form a *system*: the whole is greater than the sum of the parts.

From the 1970s, organizations such as Greenpeace and Earth First! tried to raised the public consciousness about environmental destruction through radical direct action. After 1980, a growing body of literature published by scientists and academics suggested that we are on a collision course between human exploitation of natural resources and nature. More mainstream organizations such as the United Nations Environment Programme and the World Wildlife Fund contributed to the proliferation of documents, conferences, and the establishment of environmental protection agencies throughout the world (Berry, 1988, 2009).

Generally speaking, however, the emphasis in the 1980s and 1990s was on short-term consequences. The publication of Al Gore's (1988) *The Earth in Balance* and Brundtland's (1987) *Our Common Future* did receive considerable notice within many intellectual circles.

Sustainability as a guiding concept is often traced back to the writings of Aldo Leopold (1949), author of the *Sand County Almanac*. To Leopold, land was not merely soil but included a fountain of energy flowing through a circuit of soils, plants, insects, birds, and other animals. Uniquely, Leopold advocated a conservation system based on rights rather than wholly on economic considerations. Today his thinking lives on in the conservation movement, and his book is considered a cornerstone of the movement.

The Dream of the Earth is another classic on the subject of sustainability by Thomas Berry (1988). Like Leopold, Berry writes eloquently of the wonders of nature and the need to preserve our streams, oceans, plants, soil, and water. Berry calls for a new ecological age, an age in which there is an economics of the human as a species as well as an economics of the earth. "Only within the ever-renewing processes of nature," he writes, "is there any future for the human community" (p. 74). To damage the earth community or ecosystem is to diminish our own existence. Influenced by the feminist movement, Berry sees the biggest threat to human life and the planet as emanating from four patriarchal establishments: the classical empire, the ecclesiastical establishment, the nation-state, and the modern corporation. He contrasts devotion to the fatherland with reverence for the Earth Mother. For guidance, instructs Berry, we need to listen to the earth. Berry's concept of the human of the species is "less a being on earth or in the universe than a dimension of the earth and indeed of the universe itself" (p. 195). Now let us look at the specifics of practices that can be considered sustainable or not.

Sustainable Land Use

At the local and regional level, there is the crisis in agriculture in the rural areas and the crisis of urban sprawl and industrial wastes that extends across the continent. Consider modern farming and the impact of the disastrous consequences of the heavy use of chemical fertilizers, pesticides, and herbicides on the land. The popular 2008 film *Food, Inc.* (directed by Robert Kenner and featuring interviews by experts on agriculture) provides a grim look inside America's corporate-controlled food industry and shows how Monsanto breaks the backs of farmers who wish to save their seeds for replanting.

As a result of monocultural crop farming, mainly of corn and soybeans, the precious topsoil for which the Midwest is famous—a layer of soil that was produced and protected for the last thousand years in the unique interworkings of climate, plants, animals, and fire—is now being reduced to a fraction of its original depth.

And gradually, through the planting of row crops, heavy use of pesticides and herbicides, and the replacement of native plants and animals with domesticated species, modern farming has threatened the balance of nature. As early as the 1960s voices have cried out in the ever-diminishing wilderness to stop—stop the abuse against the soil, the bulldozing of the forests, and the pollution of the fresh water. Today organic farming, which uses natural processes to cultivate the land, is increasing in popularity and profits as more and more people willingly pay more to avoid buying food produced with chemicals.

At the Land Institute in Kansas, an experimental station for organic farming, the planting of crops is based on the way the native prairie works. Emphasizing sustainable farming methods such as polyculture and biodiversity of plant life, the Land Institute has as its goal a structural restoration of the tall prairie grassland ecosystem. In Baraboo, Wisconsin, the Aldo Leopold Foundation utilizes restoration ecology in the tradition of Aldo Leopold's land ethic.

Increasingly, it is realized today that social development and even economic development depend on the sustainable and productive use of the earth's natural resources. Clean water, tillable soil, and fresh air are essential to life on the planet. Missing from traditional systems theory is an emphasis on the interconnectedness between human welfare and the natural environment; it is occasionally mentioned but not emphasized. Ecosystems-based social work, in contrast, views all life forms, human and nonhuman, as interconnected and interdependent, and the earth's resources as finite, so we need to preserve them.

Sustainability and Social Work

"What is the responsibility of social work in ensuring that we have a future?" asks Nancy Mary (2008, p. ix), in her book on sustainability. "What is our role in influencing decisions that will help in influencing decisions that will help sustain families, communities, ratios, and even the planet?" In light of the new literature on systems, globalization, and the world community, Mary calls for a new sustainability model of social work, one that involves an expanded ideology and mission.

Mary's work is reminiscent of that of Coates (2003), who drew on notions of ecology to introduce a new paradigm for social work practice at the macro level. His focus is on sustainable development in all societies, rich and poor alike, and on the global interconnectedness of communities in today's world. Because the earth as a whole is a closed system in terms of available natural resources, preservation of the limited resources is a major emphasis. According to Coates, we must promote environmental as well as social justice.

Sustainable development is defined in *The Dictionary of Social Work* (Barker, 2003) as an "international goal of achieving more economic well-being within the existing physical environment" (p. 426). An economy, from this perspective, is sustainable if it uses but does not deplete its resources. Sager (2008), writing in the *Encyclopedia of Social* Work on the topic of social and urban planning, views sustainable development as a necessary advance to address the problems related to urban sprawl and environmental degradation. Sager views sustainable development as a sound economic principle through responsible land use. This brings us to a closer look at issues related to the economy.

Economic Sustainability

But sustainability is not just about being green. Economic solvency and the preservation of our natural resources go hand in hand. There is a need at the macro level for society to be economically sustainable. Macro economics, including a materialist perspective, addresses economic activity in terms of the balance of trade, worker productivity, and the strength of the banking system. Today, as we emerge from the worst economic crisis since the Great Depression, there is a burgeoning interest in global economics and government spending priorities. A listing of some recent headlines from the mainstream media brings the extent of this crisis into focus:

"U.S. Downturn Dragging World into Recession" (Faiola, *The Washington Post*, 2009)

"Economic Casualties Pile into Tent Cities" (Bazar, *USA Today*, 2009)

"Thriving Norway Provides an Economics Lesson" (Thomas, *The New York Times*, 2009)

"Socialism Is the Best Medicine" (Connolly, *Newsweek*, 2009).

"Why Capitalism Fails" (Mihm, *The Boston Globe*, 2009)

"Ohio Shooting Puts Face on Foreclosure Crisis" (Associated Press, 2008)

Taken together, a clear picture of economic disaster emerges. Several of the headlines are self-evident. The article on Norway explained how the government kept large reserves in the event of economic collapse and how their welfare system insulates the people from economic declines. The *Newsweek* article cited a study that showed Americans wait longer to see primary-care physicians than do patients in countries with strong public health systems. The headline on the Ohio shooting referred to the case of a 90-year-old woman who attempted suicide in the face of foreclosure.

The economic crisis came about through what we might consider a tragic flaw in capitalism: the fact that modern finance is a system built on risk and collective investment and indebtedness. Collapse was inevitable at some point because the homes people purchased were often beyond their means, and individuals were borrowing on their credit cards to a degree that guaranteed future indebtedness. In a society with a weak social welfare system, a bout with major health problems might be enough to throw the family breadwinners into bankruptcy. The barrage of news stories concerning the rise in homelessness among families, the rise of whole-family murder-suicides by fathers in crisis, and the timely release of Michael Moore's (2009) satirical film, *Capitalism: A Love Story*, all reflect the foundational flaws of our economic system that bring us to a new level of public awareness.

Economist David Korten (2009) brings much insight to the issue and shows how reliance on global markets and the outsourcing of employment overseas is counterproductive. Korten emphasizes the importance of buying and banking in the local community. For solutions to problems, he urges us to look upstream to the source, which is a system of continuous economic growth that only serves to make a few people very wealthy at enormous social and environmental cost to the rest. In Korten's words:

> It is now acknowledged that we humans are on a course of self-destruction. Climate chaos, the end of cheap oil, collapsing fisheries, dead rivers, falling water tables, terrorism, genocidal wars, financial collapse, species extinction, thirty thousand child deaths daily from poverty—in the richest country in the world, millions squeezed out of the middle class—are all evidence of the monumental failure of our existing cultural stories and the institutions to which they give rise. (pp. 9–10)

In his *Agenda for a New Economy*, Korten proposes that we measure progress not in terms of the gross domestic product, which basically measures spending, but that we construct a happy planet index to measure life satisfaction and life expectancy in terms of the ecological cost. Economically, we must "turn from Empire to Earth Community," argues Korten (p. 100). This book would be an excellent resource for teaching economic literacy to social workers and social work students.

The burgeoning field of behavioral economics has been catapulted to prominence by such books as the bestselling *Animal Spirits: How Human Psychology Drives the Economy, and Why It Matters for Global Capitalism* (Akerlof & Shiller, 2009). *Animal Spirits*, in fact, reportedly is being studied closely by the Obama administration to learn the facts about financial decision making and how to help people change their wasteful ways (Grunwald, 2009). As Akerlof and Shiller indicate, free market capitalism when left to its own devices will exhaust the earth's resources, create wealth for the few and poverty for the many, and lead to all kinds of excess. Under unregulated capitalist economics, people will consume too much and save too little. These economic truths have been overlooked by traditional macroeconomic theory;

free market economists failed to predict the recent economic collapse because of a neglect of the human element in the system—this is what Akerlof and Shiller call the "animal spirits" of economics. As we learn from this work on behavioral economics, not only does economics drive psychology, but psychology also drives economic behavior.

Given the impact of the Great Recession on social work agencies and on social workers' clients, major efforts in social work education are underway to teach the fundamentals of economics. A collaborative educational project, the Economic Literacy Project has recently taken shape among five New York City schools of social work: Hunter College, Fordham University, Yeshiva University, Lehman College, Touro College, and Long Island University. As described by Jessica Rosenberg (2009 in listserv correspondence to the Baccalaureate Program Directors [BPD] of November 23):

> Specifically, this project seeks to develop social work curricula (assignments, readings, trainings) that are designed to train social work students to better meet the needs of clients and client groups who have been adversely affected by the recession. The severity of this economic downturn has resurfaced a traditional client need, and concomitantly, a social work responsibility. More people than ever need social services targeted toward addressing financial-based needs, such as entitlements counseling, as well as skills in the assessment of psychosocial problems that might be exacerbated by economic insecurity. As a result, skills in Information, Referral, and Advocacy services that lift people out of poverty, and guarantee that the Safety Net is in place, are of paramount importance in today's world.

What we need to teach is a sustainability-first ethos. Nancy Mary (2008) contrasts the pervasive markets-first scenario, which places trust in the globalization and corporate wealth as a remedy for environmental problems, with the sustainability-first ethos. This ethos, according to Mary, is ripe with new paradigm thinking that would involve international collaboration as well as regional efforts to displace values of consumerism, competition, and individualism with those of simplicity, cooperation, and community. The connection between consumption patterns and the waning of energy resources is becoming clear.

An emphasis on sustainable development rather than on economic growth would help us move in the right direction. This concept—*sustainable development*—which according to Brundtland (2002) was beginning to enter the general vocabulary during the time of the groundbreaking world environmental conference in 1992 at Rio de Janeiro, is one that we would do well to heed today.

We have discussed sustainability as a concept widely applied to the environmental and economic realms of human behavior; now we continue with a brief discussion of the spiritual dimension as a relatively new addition to ecosystems theory.

Deep Ecology

Besthorn and McMillan (2002) have added to ecosystems theory an articulation of the interconnectedness of human beings and nature.

This conceptualization is in sharp contrast to the previous portrayals of individuals as living essentially independent of nature and as subduing the natural elements. Today many people as formerly are finding a spiritual essence in nature.

Throughout history, men and women have experienced a dimension of the spirit that seems to transcend the mundane world (Armstrong, 1993). A small but growing movement within social work, Deep Ecology, echoes this theme. As described by Besthorn (2002):

> Deep-Ecological spirituality recognizes that humans share a common destiny with the earth. It celebrates an ongoing cultivation of a deeper identification of self with the whole of the cosmic order. From this vantage point, self-interest becomes identical with the interest of the whole. Humanity and nature cannot be separated—the sacred is in and of both. (p. 4)

This ethic of interconnectedness takes us into the spiritual realm as we envision ourselves as one small part of a greater organic whole. (See Figure 1.3 for a typical Kentucky

Figure 1.3. Consider this Kentucky farm pond as an active ecosystem. It is teeming with frogs, fish, and plant life. Photo by Rupert van Wormer.

rural landscape.) The concept of Deep Ecology is developed further in Chapter 8 on spirituality. For now let us put the ecosystems framework to the test and examine this formulation in terms of the criteria we are using for theory evaluation.

Is Ecosystems Theory Verifiable?

The major criticism that is directed toward general systems theory applies here as well. Because ecosystems is actually just a useful framework for illustrating how parts relate to the whole, there are no variables to operationalize. Because it is not explanatory, it is hard to test empirically. Still, we can draw on our powers of observation of human behavior to examine relationships and role playing in families and work groups. And we can look to numerous field studies from anthropology and biology that support ecological principles. As Hutchison and Charlesworth (2008) indicate, a long tradition of research supporting a systems perspective can be found in anthropology and sociology, but empirically based studies of their perspective in social work are lacking.

Does the Theory Incorporate Issues of Diversity and Oppression?

The bulk of the literature of the ecological school of social work does not address diversity or oppression (Mullaly, 2002). The life model pays little heed to issues of oppression apart from the addition of power concepts in response to criticism. The ecological framework, due to its comprehensiveness and focus on interaction, however, lends itself to the incorporation of ideas from other approaches such as public health. Studies of housing policy and low-income, segregated neighborhoods show that these ecological niches deprive residents of the resources they need (Massey & Denton, 1993).

Greene (2009b) points to several basic assumptions of this perspective that are consistent with a focus on cultural competence. Among these is the idea that humans must be viewed as a culture-producing and culture-produced species. An examination of cultural environments and of organizational responsiveness to cultural diversity is thus essential to the model. Another critical issue is the goodness-of-fit between the organization, such as the work organization, and the wider social environment. Hostile environments lack resources and take a physical and psychological toll on the people within them. In sustainable environments, on the other hand, the inhabitants tend to flourish. Discrimination determines which people live in the hostile environments and which do not. Greene suggests that within the ecological perspective oppression can be addressed from an empowerment perspective through a study of power relations. This is our choice, as well, as an organizing framework for this book—an ecosystems model built on notions of empowerment (refer to the later section on empowerment). Both systems and empowerment concepts spell out areas of power differentials that give meaning to the social work enterprise.

What Is the Contribution to Social Work?

As we move well into the twenty-first century, depletion and pollution of the physical environment threaten to become major influences on the social welfare of individuals and whole societies. Therefore, the *physical* environment is as much an issue for the social work profession as is the traditional focus on the social environment. Social work's unique method of multidimensional and multilevel intervention and person-in-environment configuration render this profession ideally suited to address the relationship between people and their physical environments. Social work, as Besthorn and McMillen (2002) suggest, must continue to broaden and clarify the way it conceptualizes its ecological/systems models and the professional responsibilities that flow from them.

Influenced by the upsurge in interest in globalization, and the impact of the recent recession on workers and their families, the social work profession requires a theoretical base that is comprehensive and relevant to issues embedded in the fabric of the larger macro environment.

Among the advantages to social work of the ecosystems formulations listed by Payne

(2005) are as follows: its ability to analyze circular connections in transaction between worker and client; its value in assessment; its integration with other social work theories; and its inclusion of social factors to balance individual casework. An ecosystems approach avoids linear, deterministic cause-and-effect explanations of behavior of the kind common in cognitive-behavioral practice. As such, it may not generate statistical data, but it is more representative of reality, in which the cause is so often the effect and vice versa. Social workers arrange, integrate, and systematize how people interrelate with each other and within their environments. And the approach is adaptable to all levels of intervention with which the social worker is involved.

Because of its wide applicability to various aspects of the *human* condition, in short, ecological theory provides an exceptionally good fit for social work practice in any given area. The key advantages of this framework are the breadth of the knowledge it encompasses, its malleability in terms of needs of various fields of study, and its stress on the factor of interactionism in all human affairs.

Regardless of our theoretical approach—behavioral, psychodynamic, materialist, or solution focused—this way of thinking about the interlinking of systems can help in our understanding of families, groups, and organizations. It can also help us direct our interventions accordingly. What systems or subsystems is our client a part of? How do other systems affect these systems? How is a child linked to his or her family members through his or her identity? In what ways is the family linked to the community? What is the decision-making process in the workplace? Are the boundaries among workers and their supervisors flexible or tightly drawn? What are the channels of communication across systems?

The ecosystems approach is especially relevant to the group process as explored in Chapter 3 and the study of family dynamics, the subject of Chapter 4. It is also relevant to the practicing social worker in his or her analysis of the client's social world, including friendship patterns and work relations. Peer group ties play a role in the development of everything,

ranging from language patterns and adaptation to attitudes and values. Organizational relations can be analyzed in terms of ecosystems concepts as well.

Social workers today are well aware of the impact of the global economic forces on the services they are providing and on those they are no longer able to offer. They are made aware of this fact on an almost daily basis as the gap between human needs and environmental resources is ever-widening and many of the standard solutions no longer suffice. The more extensive the economic crisis affecting people's work and their livelihoods, the weaker the safety net of community services. From an ecosystems standpoint, social workers must direct their efforts to influence the quality of life in the community, mobilize community resources, engage in client advocacy, agency fund raising, policy formation, and the development of new strategies and solutions for problems that are more structural than personal in origin.

Resilience is an ecological concept that has special meaning for people facing hardship in tough times. In providing services to such individuals, ecosystems-oriented social workers look to protective factors (dispositional, psychological, and social) that can serve as a buffer against life stressors and reduce their impact. Because the knowledge base of ecosystems theory is structural in nature and extremely broad, the concepts from this formulation are especially relevant for working with people at risk of losing their homes and livelihoods.

What Are the Major Criticisms of Ecosystems Theory?

The very comprehensiveness of ecosystems theory lends itself to criticism that it is overly inclusive, nonprescriptive, and expository rather than explanatory (Payne, 2005). The importance of integrating parts of the system within the whole seems to indicate a preference for stability over change. The idea of feedback implies slow and manageable adjustment but not real radical change. Ecological theory, besides, as Payne contends, has not concerned itself with sustainable ecological systems. This is an omission that this text hopes to correct.

Kondrat (2002) brings to our attention the inclusion of the concepts of power and empowerment as only afterthoughts in this theory, not as core concepts. Ignoring the fact that individuals shape social institutions through their social actions, as well as having their actions shaped by social institutions, is, according to Kondrat, a serious neglect. Along the same lines, Germain and Gitterman's (1996) life model is criticized for neglecting to provide an analysis of the social structures that produce the inequalities to which they refer and for its inattention to the social work strategies for broad social change (Lundy, 2004).

What Does the Theory Teach About Human Behavior?

Role is the behavior that goes with a position or status. Within the family system, roles develop and change as members mature and learn to form new families. Roles and lifestyles can change in an orderly fashion; or there may be a crisis, such as an illness or divorce, and the behavior of each member may change as circumstances change. The family, a micro system and microcosm of society, is the system perhaps most familiar to students of social science. Systems theory brings our attention to how the behavior of family members changes with *feedback*, the most obvious of which occurs through the socialization process. Systems theory also brings attention to the *boundaries* between family members and between the family and other systems. We also play roles, however, in school and in the workplace. Consider how labels attached to roles—the scholar, the nerd, the star athlete, class clown—reinforce behavior. Work roles, similarly, come with expectations, so that the same person may play one role throughout the day at work—a librarian—and another at home—a sports fan or athlete.

Systems concepts, in short, help us predict and understand aspects of human behavior that are socially determined and how one person can play many roles within the systems of which he or she is a part.

In its focus on interaction within the person-in-environment configuration, ecosystems theory places great emphasis on people's dynamic transactions with the environment and the way their behavior is embraced or inhibited in accordance with life-sustaining attributes of the environment. The concept of *adaptation* is useful in assessing the goodness of person-environment fit, or how well people cope with *stressors* in their surroundings (Greene, 2009a).

In its expanded version, ecosystems theory teaches about oppression and the need for structural change to provide personal growth and development. The expanded version also relates to human behavior in its conceptualization of human beings as a part of nature, the person in the physical environment. Systems concepts help us grasp these important interconnections.

Structural functionalism is a related theoretical framework, at least superficially, in that it includes systems perspectives and is also a macro social theory. This theoretical perspective derives from sociology and is considered a traditional sociological theory.

Structural Functionalism

People who have taken an introductory course in sociology will be familiar with functionalist theory, especially through the writings of Talcott Parsons. Parsons was ambitious. His goal was to construct a general theory, a grand theory, not just for sociology but for all the social sciences. His work, much of it written in the 1940s and 1950s, was generally considered, as any graduate student of sociology will attest, among the most tedious and verbose in sociology. For example:

> From this point of view, it is always important whether the primary reference is to the relation of the acting system to its environment *or* to its own internal properties and equilibrium. The situation, or object-world, is in the nature of the case organized differently from the actor as system. Hence, in orientation *directly* to the situation, the specificities of the differentiation among objects and their properties become salient. On the other

hand, where internal "needs" of the acting system are paramount, the salience of these specificities recede, and the orientation to objects becomes more diffuse. This is the setting in which the specificity-diffuseness variable fits. (Parsons, 1967, p. 199)

What Are the Basic Assumptions and Concepts?

The conservative slant in functionalism is revealed in the terminology as well as the focus of this theory. Parsons taught that a social system must have an *adaptive function* to allow it to relate to other systems: The system must act as a unit, it must maintain itself as a whole, and there must be *pattern maintenance* and *tension management* (Parsons & Shils, 1962).

Borrowed originally from biology, the functionalist perspective focused solely on the structure of an organism. The functionalist image of society is that of a system or structure with interdependent parts that work together to produce stability. Each of these parts is assumed to have positive consequences or functions. People are seen as occupying positions in the social structures. Each position has a role associated with it. Functionalist theory is not discussed by Mullaly (2007), but it is classified by him as an example of order theory. Few social work textbooks mention this macro macro-level theory at all, in fact, or only in passing. The reason is probably its seeming lack of relevance to social work practice and the conservative bent of most of the writing. Furthermore, it does not lend itself to interventions with clients or client systems. One exception in the social work literature that includes a chapter on sociological theories and therefore discusses functionalism is the human behavior book by Rogers (2006). In agreement with Mullaly, Rogers sees this perspective as concerned with maintaining stability in the society and how the norms of society contribute to the overall good of society.

An odd characteristic of functional analysis is that a social institution or behavior that is considered negative, such as organized crime, is typically argued, from this perspective, to

meet the needs of the people. Merton (1957), for example, has argued that the corrupt political machine performs many functions for marginalized people, if not for the society as a whole. Merton (1957) distinguished between manifest and latent functions of social phenomena. *Manifest* functions are the stated, obvious reasons for an activity, whereas *latent functions* are neither intended nor initially recognized. Sociologists who adhere to the functionalist perspective examine the parts of a system to see how they fit within the whole. They observe the results of the practice of social institutions such as schools, prisons, and the family in terms of manifest and latent functions. *Functional analysis* is a useful technique utilized in sociology and anthropology to reveal the community value of a cultural trait or institution (such as religious rituals). Viewing a cultural norm (e.g., punishing those who shirk responsibility) in terms of manifest and latent functions leads to new ways of thinking about social customs (van Wormer, 2006). Merton's addition of the consideration of *dysfunctions* of a behavior or practice was an important contribution. Coser (1956) showed in *The Functions of Social Conflict*, his thought-provoking book that was widely read in the 1960s, the ways in which social conflict can unite people and galvanize them to work toward social change. Coser effectively combined conflict theory with the technique of functional analysis. Gans (1995) and Mullaly (2007), similarly writing from radical perspectives, argued the case that poverty is tolerated by society because of its many latent functions, such as keeping wages low and providing foot soldiers for war.

Is the Theory Verifiable?

This theory has not been verified, because it is often in the eyes of the beholder whether a custom or social activity is functional. Actually, the effort could be made, through use of government statistics, to show the good or harm of a certain practice, such as organized crime, the death penalty, or poverty. The social theorists of this school of thought, however, have made no effort, to our knowledge, to quantify arguments. Most of the observations are fairly obvious (such as the manifest function of sending children to school in order to educate them for good citizenship), so statistical analysis would seem unnecessary. To prove the effects of other aspects of social life, such as the role of religion in a given society, would be more problematic, however.

Does the Theory Incorporate Issues of Diversity and Oppression?

Structural functionalism as conceptualized by Parsons always took the point of view of mainstream society. This conceptual approach is built on a belief that social structures in society prevail through consensus and conformity (Mullaly, 2007). Deviance was seen as negative, a threat to the smooth functioning of the system. Merton (1957) wrote of social deviance in the form of delinquency, and Coser (1956) and Gans (1995) researched social conflict and poverty, respectively, albeit with undertones of sarcasm. In the same vein, van Wormer, Wells, and Boes (2000) made the argument that homophobia fulfills certain functions, as well as dysfunctions, in society. Functionalism does not handle issues of diversity and oppression in any conventional way, yet functional analysis has been used to show why certain negative practices and attitudes are so hard to eliminate. Structural functionalism as expounded by Parsons locates the source of social problems within the person himself or herself. In general, poverty, mental illness, drug addiction, and criminal activity are blamed on supposed personal defects (Mullaly, 2007). So to answer the question, this theory does not satisfy the social work profession's need for a theory centered on social change to end oppression but rather provides a justification for the present social order.

What Is the Contribution to Social Work?

This section can be brief because the contributions to social work are not readily apparent. It is relevant at the societal level when the focus is on community structure and function (Kirst-Ashman, 2007). The advantage of learning about structural functionalism is that community workers can examine social institutions from a broad-based perspective. There is little practice relevance here. Rogers (2006) sees the notion of dysfunction as useful; also functionalist concepts can be used to explain to clients how a system works. Few social work theorists make use of functional analysis except for Piven and Cloward (1993) (see the section on conflict theory) and van Wormer (2006), who do so from a radical social change perspective.

What Is the Major Criticism of This Theory?

Structural functionalism, as originally formulated, is often criticized for its conservative bias and rigid acceptance of the status quo as natural and good and of conflict as alien, even pathological. This theoretical perspective, in its classical form, fails also to focus on the nature and meaning of the interaction among humans, a severe limitation, at least from a social work perspective, given that this is what social work is all about (Schriver, 2010).

What Does the Theory Teach About Human Behavior?

Structural functionalism, despite its conservative cast and focus on order as opposed to conflict, offers some pointers about human behavior that can promote our general understanding. When we ask the "why" questions—for example, why do homophobia, poverty, or lengthy education persist in a society and what are the dysfunctions—our attention is drawn to facts about human behavior that might otherwise be overlooked. The concept of *latent function* can be especially revealing in exposing unintended and hidden aspects of the activities and rituals under study. When policy analysts ask who the stakeholders are in retaining a certain policy that they would like to change, this is essentially a form of functional analysis.

Conflict and Structural Theory

Of much greater importance to the social work profession is this conceptual framework, which perceives societies in conflict rather than united in consensus and which is often juxtaposed with theories of order, such as functionalism, for the purpose of contrast. Like functionalism, conflict theory works at the macro-macro level, and it is one of the primary theories studied in sociology courses. Politically, it is at the opposite pole from theories based on notions of consensus.

What Are the Basic Assumptions and Concepts?

Whereas functionalists regard society as balanced and in a state of equilibrium, conflict theorists see a society torn by constraint and struggles for power.

Conflict theory (actually a combination of theories) has its origins in early sociology and radical economics, especially in the work of Karl Marx. The story of history from this perspective is the story of class struggle between the owners and workers, the powerful and exploited. Conflict models offer a critique of capitalist structures and the production of inequality and exploitation. Part of the ideological climate or hegemony established by the dominant group is the formulation of laws, creation of social institutions, and the distribution of ideas that form the dominant group (Mullaly, 2002). These models emphasize the importance of a critical consciousness, collective action, and a radical restructuring of society (Lundy, 2004). A key concept from Marxist analysis is *alienation* of the people, who feel a separation from the social system. The cause of the alienation is not in the people themselves but in the social structure. Unlike the functionalist approach, conflict theory has been widely absorbed into social work perspectives, so much so that its radical origins are at times obscured. Early social workers in the United States recognized the existence of structural inequality and oppression and began to draw on concepts from this perspective from that point on.

The contributions of C. Wright Mills (1956, 1959) are noteworthy. Mills added such concepts as *power elite* and *the sociological imagination* to the literature and was at the forefront of criticism of Parsons's voluminous writings. The most important political decisions, argued

Mills, are not made by regular citizens but by extremely wealthy individuals of the ruling class who have access to Congress. These actual leaders are likely to come from similar backgrounds and have similar beliefs and values. What Mills observed in the 1950s is even truer today given the influence of the lobbying groups on Congress. Through use of the sociological imagination, the individual can understand the larger historical scene and know his or her own fate, gauging his or her own chances of success within the context of the times. Mills made the distinction between "the personal troubles of milieu" and the "public issues of social structure" so widely cited in the literature. "To be aware of the idea of social structure," wrote Mills, "and to use it with sensibility is to be capable of tracing such linkages among a great variety of milieu. To be able to do that is to possess the sociological imagination" (p. 11). Van Wormer (2006) adapted Mills's concept to develop a parallel concept, "the social work imagination."

Conflict theorists Piven and Cloward (1993) utilized the functionalist analysis method borrowed from Merton (1957) to enhance our understanding of how the social welfare system serves as a societal device for "regulating the poor" in the interest of capitalism. The latent function of social services, from this perspective, thus becomes to preserve the establishment. Piven and Cloward's basic premise, based on their review of social change throughout U.S. history, was that "relief arrangements are initiated or expanded during outbreaks of civil disorder produced by mass unemployment and are then abolished or contracted when political stability is restored" (p. xv). In other words, the elites in society can be counted on to provide only enough aid, stigmatized at that, to prevent mass disorder and regulate labor. (Despite their use of functional analysis, Piven and Cloward's perspectives are far more closely aligned ideologically with Marxism than with Parsons's functionalist writings.)

In addition to the terms *alienation, power elite*, and *the sociological imagination*, the following concepts are also germane to conflict theory:

> *Structural* explanations for social and many personal problems

> *Oppression* of the people who are left out
>   of the power structure
> *Social control* seen as a function of much
>   of social work

Payne (2005) refers to conflict theory as radical and socialist-collectivist. Still, as Rogers (2006) points out, the application of conflict theory to family and health care and domestic violence is consistent with the values and ethics of social work. From this perspective, social workers can grasp the obstacles to effecting social change. Social workers need to be educated about how powerful forces in the society, such as the medical and insurance industries, can block helping efforts. Feminist, empowerment, and anti-oppressive perspectives are included under the rubric of radical, as well as the structural approaches. We discuss the structural approach here because it also utilizes the notions of conflict and places a strong emphasis on economic and social equality among people. These macro economic theories are highly consistent with social work and ethical principles. Feminist, empowerment, and anti-oppressive approaches are discussed in the next section. These structural approaches, so called because the source of social problems is located in the social structure rather than in the individual, were inspired by the radical thinking of the 1970s, but their influence waned, as Payne speculates, with the collapse of communism in the 1980s. Along with the neoconservatism of modern times and the concordant erosion of the welfare state, there is a renewed interest within social work in effecting social change.

Structural social work is associated today with and best articulated through the writings of Canadian social work theorist Bob Mullaly. This concept got its start in the 1970s at Ottawa's Carleton University; this university's social work department is still closely associated with this theoretical orientation. Much like his predecessors, Mullaly (2007), in his book *The New Structural Social Work*, which is now in its third edition, espouses a conflict-oriented view of society and recognizes that one's circumstances and difficulties are connected to one's economic and social position in society. Mullaly's formulation is recognized by Malcolm Payne as being the major statement of Marxist social work in the literature.

Mullaly's (2007) vision of social work practice is that it must be anti-capitalist. If as social workers we do nothing to bring about progressive and radical change, we fail the people we serve. Then we become part of the problem instead of the solution. Almost religiously, Mullaly calls for a commitment to carry out the task of social transformation: "Structural social work is more than a theory or a technique or a practice modality. It is a way of life" (p. 362).

The principles of structural social work, as articulated by Mullaly, can be briefly summarized in eight key points:

1. The personal is political—practice and policy should not be viewed as a dichotomy; "if the personal is political, then social work is political also" (p. 165).
2. Empowerment is a goal and a process that transcends the micro and macro levels of practice.
3. Consciousness raising is predicated on the belief that reflection must precede action.
4. Normalization refers to learning that many others are in the same boat.
5. Collectivization means organizing for action.
6. Redefining is a consciousness-raising activity in which personal troubles are redefined in political terms.
7. The latter three activities are carried out through dialogue.
8. Oppression exists in the forms of exploitation, marginalization, powerlessness, cultural imperialism, and violence.

Colleen Lundy (2004), a professor of social work at Carleton University, builds on the conceptual approach from her own university and on the ideas of Mullaly to lay out concrete social work practice skills for individual, group, and community interventions. Using a structural approach, Lundy pursues issues related to social justice, human rights, and cultural diversity. Capitalism she sees as the fundamental cause of much of the social and economic injustice that the poor experience, so the inequities of capitalism must be confronted. Within the context of privatization of social services and the erosion of social welfare programs, social workers are in a precarious position as they try to abide by principles of social justice.

Of the conflict and structural theorists mentioned in this section, only Lundy (2004) emphasizes the factor of the capitalist globalization process in oppression. The term *globalization* is relatively new; it was associated with optimism and much excitement in the early 1990s but brings a much more mixed reaction today. *Globalization* is defined by Kahn and Kamerman (2002) as "the current buzzword used to describe the growing internationalization of the production of goods and services and the flow of capital" (p. 488). Lundy's discussion of the "free trade" movement and the control of internal government policies by transnational corporations and banks is eerily reminiscent of Marx and Engel's (1848/1963) analysis of the destruction of local and national industries by new global industries:

> Instead of the old wants, satisfied by the production of native industry, new wants appear, wants which can only be satisfied by the products of distant lands and unfamiliar climes.... It (the bourgeoisie) forces all nations, under pain of extinction, to adopt the capitalist method of production. (p. 30)

Anup Shah (2008) summarizes the stringent world banking requirements for refinancing loans as follows: the elimination of restrictions on imports and exports; privatization of national resources and public utilities; and cutbacks in spending on health, education, and housing to ensure capital growth. According to Shah, these policies are leading to, rather than preventing, poverty. As Lundy correctly argues, knowledge of where the pressures placed on ordinary people are coming from is essential to effective social work practice. Social workers need to be aware of their own history of organizing and advocating for social change and social justice. Knowledge of such global economic truths enables us to tune in to the experience of oppression and to help raise the consciousness of our clients and of the general public. As you read Box 1.1, Stacey Palevksy's "House of Support" on homelessness in Iowa, consider

the following questions: What is the cause of this individual's homelessness? Which theoretical explanation best applies to his or her situation? Are there alternative explanations? Which ones might the public favor?

Box 1.1 House of Support: Transitional Housing Program Helps Homeless Men Return to Independence

Stacey Palevsky, Courier Staff Writer

WATERLOO—For 14 days last summer, Steve Greene, 37, had nowhere to go except his 10-by-20 storage unit. Methamphetamine had derailed his life and left him homeless. It was humiliating, he said. And it was entirely his fault.

But shortly thereafter, a time he calls his absolute lowest, he began to think about truly changing his life. No more spending his 401(k) on meth, he thought. He checked into the Catholic Worker House, where he stayed for 3 weeks before earning a spot at the Salvation Army's transitional housing facility for men.

"You've got to be so far down before you can come back up," Greene said. "I'm done learning the hard way. I don't ever want to repeat any of the bad mistakes I've made."

The transitional housing facility, which opened 1 year ago, is the only one of its kind for homeless men in Waterloo. It combines affordable housing with supportive services to help men achieve self-sufficiency. Residents can stay up to 2 years in the blue house on Argyle Street. It accommodates 10 men at a time, each of whom gets his own room with clean white walls, a twin bed, and a desk.

"Right now, I don't know where I'd be without this place," said Leif Horton, 47, who entered the program after a divorce and illness.

When men are ready to move out, director Barb Lamfers said, the hope is that they'll be ready to obtain a stable job and permanent housing.

Learning to Live Again

Life isn't miraculously new and shiny upon moving into the 10-bedroom transitional home. It requires a big lifestyle change, which is tough for men whose struggle with responsibility rendered them homeless in the first place. Most of the residents have a history of substance abuse and depression, and many have criminal records. They range in age from 20 to 54. Within 6 weeks of entering the program, men must have a full-time job and pay rent at a maximum of 30% of income. They must stay clean and sober, receive substance abuse or mental health treatment if needed, and meet with a caseworker at least once a week. They must also attend life skills and money management courses. Agreeing to random urinary analyses is also a requirement.

Curfew is 11 p.m. on weekdays and midnight on weekends. Nights away require permission from staff. Everyone has chores.

"A transitional shelter is sort of like going back home to your mother and father, who try to teach you the proper way to go through society, to make ends meet, to get in there and play ball," said Al Ausili, a homeless outreach coordinator for Peoples Clinic.

The structure can cause friction among the housemates. At a house meeting Friday, men complained for 45 minutes of people leaving dirty dishes in the sink, taking more than their fair share of food, and disrespecting each other's space.

"I treasure this place," Horton said. "When people act like this is a motel, it's irritating."

But, if the men can live by the rules, they usually succeed. Seven have already graduated from the program, including Brian Malloy, who says the facility was "like a first-class hotel."

Malloy, a recovering alcoholic, entered the program after several months at a substance abuse treatment center. He stayed at the transitional facility for 3 months before he felt ready to leave. With encouragement from Lamfers, he moved back home with his wife, then pregnant. Their son was born a month later. The family just moved to Missouri, where Malloy has a good job as a commercial electrician.

"It did wonders for me. It more or less changed my life," Malloy said. "It taught me how to live with and be patient with others."

Homeless in Waterloo

Ausili initiated the conversation about a transitional housing facility nearly a decade ago. The Local Homeless Coordinating Board—a group of representatives from numerous human service agencies, including the Salvation Army and Peoples Clinic—liked the idea and soon looked into logistics like funding and zoning.

The U.S. Department of Housing and Urban Development supplied most of the funding for the million-dollar project. An anonymous donation of $150,000 also helped.

Waterloo's homeless population continues to grow. In January, the coordinating board counted 201 homeless persons in the community, 36 more than 6 months earlier. Ausili believes there are at least 200 more unaccounted for.

Whereas emergency shelters offer someone in crisis a place to stay for up to 3 weeks, transitional housing aims to reduce and eventually eliminate chronic homelessness in America by giving men support and time to put their lives back together. Lamfers, who once directed the Salvation Army's emergency shelter, was excited to lead the new approach. "Major changes cannot be seen in 21 days," Lamfers said. "I loved the idea of working with fewer clients for a much longer time period… to see them make major changes and meet their goals."

HUD began funding these facilities in 1988, with the first Iowa programs beginning several years later. Today the state has 15 transitional housing facilities for men and 25 for women and children.

Mistakes Repeated

Lamfers has had to kick out three men, including one on Saturday. Three others left because they didn't want to follow the rules. "I'd like to say that everyone stops their self-destructive behavior when they come in, gets a job, completes the program and becomes self-sufficient. Of course that is not true," Lamfers said. But if a resident conveys remorse and motivation to change, she said, she'll do anything to keep them there.

"I always try to keep in mind what we're doing—we're trying to reduce homelessness. So I'm merciful," she added. "How wise would it be to send them away? They'll only return to the park bench or shelter."

Greene moved into the Salvation Army's facility in August. Once, he broke the house rules and got caught with crack. Lamfers reassigned him to live at the Salvation Army's emergency shelter. Shape up and you can come back, she said.

Four days later, he moved back in. Getting caught with drugs, he said, was the best thing that could have happened. It motivated him to kick the meth habit that led to homelessness, find a steady night-shift job, and save money in preparation for moving out this summer.

Malloy made a similar blunder. He got drunk, and during his morning hangover, felt ashamed he had given into the temptation. Making the same mistake twice was not an option if he wanted to change his life. "People don't go in there to stay sober to then let someone else walk through the doors drunk," Malloy said. "I felt like I let my whole family down when I did it."

A New Kind of Family

Everybody watches out for one another in the transitional housing facility.

Lamfers is the mother of the household, the men say. She encourages them during the job search and hangs newspaper classifieds on a bulletin board in the common room. She gives them second and third chances if they stumble or fall.

"We've all been down at rock bottom, so we make bonds," Greene said. "These are heart-to-heart friends that we'll take with us even when we go." Greene smokes Marlboro reds. He works for $7.50 an hour in the rough mill at Omega Cabinets and saves all his Pepsi cans for the 60¢ each 12-pack yields. His room is decorated with biblical posters and photographs of his 9-year-old daughter—his world, he said.

"These men want better for their children," Lamfers said.

Greene's biggest motivation to save money and stay off drugs is his daughter, Madison. Once he is independent, he will be once again eligible for joint custody.

Horton, the divorced 47-year-old, said the stability of the facility has anchored him during a rough time. He's a minority in the house, never having battled a drug addiction. He has had, however, a slew of debilitating health problems: degenerative arthritis, non-Hodgkins lymphoma, spinal stenosis.

He cannot work and, after 3 years of petitioning, has not yet been able to get disability benefits. He's nonetheless more motivated than ever to change his life. He attributes his drive to a renewed faith in God and the support he gets from Lamfers and other residents. "Once I'm out of here, I don't want to be away from it," Horton said. "It's meant so much to me that I want to volunteer and help other men."

"Sleeping in the storage unit seems long ago," Greene said. He's been down low but is at a point where he feels like he's got nowhere to go but up.

"This is for people who really want and need to change their life," Greene said. "If you're willing to adapt, this place can really change your life. It's up to you."

Waterloo/Cedar Falls Courier, Waterloo, IA, May 8, 2005. Reprinted with permission of *The Courier.*

Change efforts, as David Gil (1998) suggests, must be directed at entire policy systems rather than at more marginal adjustments. Similarly, Mullaly (2007) advocates a radical reorganization of society to achieve a truly just social order. A collective, participatory ideology, he suggests, is essential to the achievement of a just social order.

Both Gil and Mullaly are critical of mainstream social work. Gil (1998) urges social work to shift its focus from the symptoms of oppression and injustice to the actual causes. The challenge, as Gil convincingly argues, must be to the "systemic sources in capitalist dynamics" (p. 85). Such a paradigm shift, notes Gil, would be entirely consistent with the mandate of the profession's Code of Ethics to pursue social justice and resist oppression. Conventional policy analysis in social work, as Gil further argues, is erroneous in its treatment of single problems, single solutions. Elimination of social problems that are supposedly unrelated when viewed in isolation is unlikely, because they all derive from a common cause. Each problem can be regarded as symptomatic of a weakness in the social structure. Homelessness and poverty, accordingly, may be simply a given in a competitive capitalist society.

Writing from a structural perspective, Mullaly (2002, 2007) articulates a major limitation of welfare capitalism and conventional social work as the narrow focus on economic inequality while often ignoring the decision-making structures that determine economic relations in society. To truly understand the dynamics of oppression, as Mullaly asserts, we need to consider the role of exploitation in maintaining an unequal distribution of goods and services. At the practice level, social workers should avoid the role of expert and engage in a mutual learning process with clients.

Is the Theory Verifiable?

Evidence for such theoretical notions as those that make up these radical theories in social work could come from surveys of worker satisfaction and alienation within a globalized economy and from an analysis of historical events to determine the extent to which mass social unrest leads to government reforms to benefit the masses. Mills's (1956) concept of *the power elite* is verifiable through a simple listing of major contributors to political campaigns by organizations that represent the interests of the rich and those that represent the interests of the poor. The vague claims of conflict and structural theories concerning what is good for the society or how social workers should construe their roles are clearly more difficult to substantiate with empirical data.

Does the Theory Incorporate Issues of Diversity and Oppression?

The radical theories look at the status quo in a critical light; attention is necessarily drawn to areas in need of change and therefore to issues of diversity and oppression. Radical perspectives do more than incorporate these issues; they seek to explain them. Macro forces favoring big business coupled with weak government protections for vulnerable populations create a situation of extreme imbalance in which the weak will be exploited by the strong. The concept of oppression is a key element in these perspectives derived from Marxism.

What Is the Contribution to Social Work?

The contribution of these radical, thought-provoking concepts to social work theory and to the profession is considerable. In recent years the professional associations of social workers have revised their codes of ethics to include ethical responsibilities for social change (e.g., Canadian Association of Social Workers, 2005), ethical responsibilities to the broader society (NASW, 1996), and a revised definition of social work stressing principles of human rights and social justice (IFSW, 2004). Although only a small percentage of social workers identify themselves as practicing structural social work or as subscribing to the conflict model, the ideas from this model are reflected throughout the social work literature on social welfare and on social policy. The critiques of global capitalism provided by conflict models are essential today to an understanding of recent economic developments and their impact on communities and families. Principles of conflict theory can help guide one's critical thinking about the typical client's position within the macro environment and the social worker's position as well. Knowledge of how the system works under a neoconservative regime that is bigger and more powerful than the individual party that was elected to office can aid social workers in anticipating moves. What is happening in Britain, for example, is happening everywhere—new managerial imperatives on welfare provisions were achieved by using economics as ideology rather than by launching an outright attack on public welfare (Dominelli, 2004). From the writings of structuralists such as Dominelli (her theory is discussed in the following section), social work administrators can learn to be aware of concessions under the guise of efficiency and cost-effectiveness. Means-tested programs are the death knell of the programs, because they are stigmatized as programs for the poor when they apply only to those below a certain income level. Other strategies that social workers should be leery of are the profit-driven hiring of more part-time and temporary workers for greater cost efficiency, the continuing deinstitutionalization of clients, and mandates for single mothers to get off welfare and enter the workforce. These trends of global economic growth at the upper levels of society, in conjunction with deepening human poverty elsewhere, clearly undermine the mission of the social work profession. Accordingly, education on these realities must be integrated across the curriculum, including the HBSE sequence (Morell, 2002). Critical analysis of government policy mandates instituted from the top down can aid the profession in knowing which policies to support and which ones to approach warily.

As Piven and Cloward (1993) wisely note, the effects of segregating programs for the poor are far reaching, dampening support for other welfare state programs. Citizens resent paying taxes for services from which they themselves receive no benefits. The value of providing social welfare is diminished when fragmented programs reach only narrowly defined groups. Some affirmative action programs, limited as they are in magnitude, have similarly created resentment and hostility.

What Are the Major Criticisms of This Theory?

A summary of the major criticisms of this broad-based radical approach is offered by Payne (2005). First is the fact that this theory leans toward collective action, whereas social services agencies that employ social workers are geared toward individual treatment. This approach is weak in dealing with individuals with emotional problems. Second, evidence-based-oriented commentators fault social workers who operate from a radical perspective for failing to listen to the client's interpretation of his or her problem. Third, radical insight does not necessarily lead to change, and this viewpoint can seem, and often is, negative. Fourth, the view of clients as victimized is disempowering. Fifth, this approach is highly ideological and can lead to conflict, as most agencies represent ruling ideologies. Payne cautions against going too far with these criticisms, however. The insights can be invaluable as ends in themselves.

What Does the Theory Teach About Human Behavior?

Perhaps more than any other, the conflict/structural perspective guides students and practitioners to think critically about power imbalances in society and how they are sustained, about how legislation is passed, and about how the public often is duped into supporting policies that oppress the poor or even themselves by campaigning on some vague issues such as morals or crime. This theory offers an explanation for such social phenomena as why the rich are getting richer and the poor poorer, why social insurance policies are acceptable to the public whereas means-tested ones are resented,

and how social welfare practices regulate the poor and serve a social control function for society. Conflict theory, in short, explains aspects of human behavior that are less than honorable—greed, punitiveness, and the tendency to look down on persons who suffer hardship. Conflict/structural theory offers insights into the behavior of the masses and into motivations at all levels of society that might be readily apparent. Instead of viewing the source of personal problems—especially those related to poverty—in the individual, the source is located in the wider social structure.

Feminist, Empowerment, and Anti-Oppressive Perspectives

Stemming from the same historical period as structural theory—the mass movements of the late 1960s and 1970s—these perspectives about patriarchal and other oppressive structures have been absorbed into structural/conflict theory, in particular, and social work in general. These approaches are associated with social action in that they derive from political movements. However, they also represent a mode of analysis that has attracted extensive scholarship. Together, these perspectives offer an enormous source of information and link the political to the personal more effectively than any other theory. As theories about discrimination in society, they relate to micro, as well as macro, dynamics in showing the impact of discriminatory attitudes and practices. These theories say a lot about human behavior and the tendency of some people privileged by their race, gender, and so forth to fight to maintain that privilege. The feminist and other empowerment approaches also show how societies tend to maintain their institutionalized patterns of oppression through various means and how such patterns affect the behavior of the persons regarded as other. Although they all sprang from the same progressive roots, each theoretical orientation has its own proponents and terminology. Feminist theorists are primarily concerned with issues pertaining to women, although even here different analyses exist with respect to the fundamental source of oppression in society (Mullaly, 2007). In our critical analysis of these perspectives, therefore, we discuss them collectively or separately as indicated.

What Are the Basic Assumptions and Concepts?

Feminism

The *feminist* perspectives, of which there are several, are basically reactions to the vestiges of sex discrimination in society. *Feminism* is defined by Van den Bergh and Cooper (1995) as "a conceptual framework and mode of analysis that has analyzed the status of women (and other disempowered groups) cross-culturally and historically to explain dynamics and conditions undergirding disparities in socio-cultural status and power between majority and minority populations" (p. xii). The central definition of feminism entails the conscious, explicit awareness that women are denied equal rights, opportunities, and access to goods and services (Averett, 2009). Feminism, which sprang out of the women's movement, offers a woman-centered approach to understanding human behavior across the life span, from the treatment of infants and little girls to the challenges facing elderly women.

For the present generation of young people, the term *feminism* has fallen into disfavor. In the recent book *Girldrive: Criss-Crossing America, Redefining Feminism*, authors Nona Aronowitz and Emma Bernstein (2009) took a road trip across the United States to interview women from diverse backgrounds and ages about their attitudes toward feminism. Some, such as two Native American women who worked for domestic violence services, saw feminism as central to their lives. But most of the young women had negative associations with the term. They seemed unable to get past the term's loaded meanings, dwelling on its purported history rather than relating it to their own experiences. Maria, aged 24 and Mexican American, refused to call herself a feminist because "it boxes you in" (p. 8). A pair of Latina twins expressed a belief in equality for women but "people in my community," one of them explained, "never use

the word. Feminism is seen as a bourgeois thing" (p. 11). Some of the Native Americans and African Americans interviewed saw race as the big issue in their lives, not gender. One black woman remarked, for example, that when you "call out men as sexist, it's like betraying your race" (p. 12). Despite many of the interviewees' resistance to using the term *feminist*, these young women were resourceful, confident, and seemingly enjoying the benefits that were a legacy of the women's movement of the 1970s Second Wave.

The women's movement is often described in terms of three waves. The first occurred during the struggle for women's suffrage, which ended with the passage of the Nineteenth Amendment in 1920, giving women the right to vote. From the late 1960s onward, the second wave was concerned with equality of opportunity, an end to blatant sex discrimination, and an acknowledgment of the physical victimization of women whether on the street, in the workplace, or in the home.

The third wave, which refuted the focus on victimization, began in the 1990s and is associated with young people today. An interesting fact about the women's movement of the second wave was the extent to which it made (white middle-class and upper-class) women aware of their own powerlessness apart from their connection to a powerful man, which so many had never had, would never have. It made women aware for the first time that the word *man* and the pronoun *he* were not universal after all but mostly referred to just the male of the human race. For years "women's lib" was mocked in the media and by the general public as a joke. But the biggest joke was on the opponents of the women's movement who had taken an action designed to defeat the movement for civil rights legislation. This action had, in fact, happened several years earlier, when a southern senator who was a segregationist added sex to the list of protected groups under the 1964 Civil Rights Act. This was his way of making a mockery of the act and ensuring its defeat. Curiously, the fact that women actually could claim discrimination was given no legal notice until about a decade later. Box 1.2, "Cries From the Second Wave," presents a personal narrative of a woman whose consciousness was raised in both expected and surprising ways.

Box 1.2 Cries From the Second Wave

Nancy L. Roberts

The slogan was "Don't iron while the strike is hot." The strike was to be commemorated by a parade through midtown, culminating in Central Park, where we would hear speeches. Women's liberation? How silly. Black liberation, of course. I could see rights for mental patients, children's rights, the rights of migrant workers, civil rights, of course. But us? This was going too far. Even so, I tagged along with the mob of women striding toward Central Park, curious, as always.

What a bursting forth! Everything the speakers said rang out like bells, the kinds that go off inside the head. I was flung into a succession of exploding thoughts, each one setting off a new connection, and my mind was awhirl with fractals:… there were all those men buzzing around as if I were some sticky comb dripping with sweetness for them to feed on, and then telling me I was "too smart for my own good," the bosses giving more and more responsibility but not paying enough to free me from my cozy slum. And always, the great confusion of loving to be desired but suspecting I was a blank screen on which men could project their image of the ideal. It seemed that as soon as I began to assert who I was, they withdrew, disappointed at this shattering of their dreams. There was this odd polarization: Either you are sensitive and sweet, or you are strong and independent. Why, I'd always wondered, can't all these things exist, happily, within one person? During this Friedan-inspired epiphany in Central Park, I no longer felt alone in my bewilderment, and I joyfully embraced what is now called the Second Wave of Feminism.

Consciousness-raising groups were the order of the day…. We, who had little in common except being women, sat in a circle on the floor of someone's apartment, and each week we'd go round-robin on a given topic, without anyone leaping to advise or judge. One week the topic was Orgasms: "I was married five years before…. I am not sure I know what one is…. I don't know how….

I'm afraid to ask…. I have so many he says I'm a nympho." Another week: Mothers. We mourned our mothers, pitied their subjugation, sensed their jealousy of us, their attempts to teach us how to live without hope. And we celebrated their outbursts, the subterfuges they taught us, the wisdom they'd gained in having to understand, to work around, to carve out creative and intellectual outlets with limited mediums at hand.

No stopping me now. I read every feminist writer's works I could get my hands on: Shulamith Firestone, Phyllis Chestler, Judy Chicago, Germaine Greer, Robin Morgan, Uta West, Virginia Woolf, stacks of newsletters published by groups with names like Bread and Roses. I went to the party celebrating the inaugural issue of *Ms*, shook the hand of Gloria Steinem. Assigned by a small newspaper to do an interview of Betty Friedan in her Manhattan apartment, I wrote my first published writing.

No one was claiming that all (or even any) individual women exemplified these nurturing traits, or that men had them not at all, but the point was this: As a group men were in power, and the values associated with primarily masculine traits got the support and recognition. Feminine values were seen as "virtues," sentimentalized, preached, praised, but not practical enough to be supported monetarily or allowed to influence seriously our corporate and social Darwinism.

Hence, the feminist thinkers wrote, the evils that trample the helpless and stunt our mental and spiritual growth flourished unchecked, unbalanced by too much aggression, too much worship of power. This imbalance led to all the forms of oppression— slavery, colonialism, corporate exploitation, environmental abuse—all came down, it seemed, to the root, to the everyday template of the traditional family, which modeled and taught inequality in all its permutations.

Exploring these ideas felt rather like revising the Garden of Eden where we could finally rewrite that long, sad story of separation and fear. The Second Wave tumbled us into a time of tremendous hope. Perhaps the world was finally coming home.

I was riding high on this wave: gave speeches, wrote pamphlets (for Macmillan Publishing Company), published more articles, ushered our Women's Group into its "coming out" presentation to management, met weekly with the chairman of the board, the president, and lawyers. In deference to our cause, the management instituted a donut-and-coffee protocol alternating responsibility between the men and the women. Our meetings were friendly, polite, inclined to indulgent humor, not very substantial.

Then Macmillan decided to fight us, urged to do so by their woman lawyer, who evidently did not see herself as a woman. After years of slugging it out under new leadership, our ragged women's group won a modest settlement and a favorable ruling from the nice State Attorney General. But it had come down to money—as it must, many say—and not the bridge of trust and respect I'd held up as our group's purpose (and thereby won so many followers at the first).

I saw the women's movement becoming not the radical cause the best thinkers espoused—and had espoused before Suffrage, and time out of mind before then—but defined as the male establishment defined it: success by force. A dear friend went to law school, and it changed her into a hard, cold, narrow-thinking person who came to use me as her confessional for extra-marital affairs. This is not to suggest that all, or even very many women lawyers turn out this way. But soldiers or hired guns tolerate their work only if they buy into the worldview it represents—winning or losing.... My friend is, in the eyes of the world, a winner. Why, I wonder, must so many successful people seem to confuse self-serving cruelty with having actual strength? Virginia Woolf once speculated that someday what is called women's weakness would be recognized as a vital form of strength. We had our chance for that, I thought, but it didn't happen....

I am a tenured professor at a growing university. I have arrived, have I not? But I see in colleagues, in students, in myself, a strange fear, as if we're frozen in our lives like winter waterfalls. The specter of endless war, yes, that will do it. Corporate capitalism's increasing backlash to uppity workers, minorities, and yes, to pesky women, in the form of job losses and cutbacks in assistance to all but the rich; the noose tightening around reproductive freedom—all that will do it, too. We carry on, celebrate at least the idea that we are free to be whatever we want to be. But the very air around us feels like an ill wind, whether or not we acknowledge it....

It's as if we've been colonized in a new way, taken on the codes of the outwardly powerful as the only right rules, fallen in step with their designs

despite our best intentions. In this fearful time since September 11—and since before that, when we came to be the only Western nation that drives its workers almost unmercifully, and supports them not at all if they get down on their luck—it seems that we've fallen to the ground and exposed our throats, or tried to be alpha wolves ourselves....

I am now officially entering old age, though I don't feel that way at all. No more swarming men or wondering if I got a job because the boss likes how I look. That is a certain relief, a kind of peace, my mourning nearly done. I've accomplished more than I had any right to expect, given the way I tumbled ashore so bewildered, unguided, unfunded. This should be a time of joy and gratitude. It is such a time, actually, when I hear a mockingbird, ride a horse, cuddle with my dogs, when I hear a student say, "You've given me a whole new way of seeing." But the knives seem thicker, sharper, and the world is a lonely place. Too many people feel that their shelf life has expired in our market-oriented society. To feel valued, a woman my age seems to need at least one of these things: a family, wealth, fame, and established community, nearby friends. Social safety nets for people like me, and for people of color, the handicapped, the ill, the geographically dislocated, are being ripped away with astonishing speed. In terms of our membership in the wider American community, some of us feel in danger of extinction.

A friend, Martin, built with his wife a once-thriving small business. Now he's had to sell it at a loss just to get out from under debts. We speak of how this seems to be happening everywhere, and how this collapse seems oddly connected to the stunning demise of environmental protections, support for education, the assault on rights for women and minorities, and the specter of diminishing help for us, the aging. I tell him that being an American right now feels like living in a family whose father gets drunk and runs off to gamble away even the food money for some besotted, sentimental vision of glory.

Second-wave writer Sheila D. Collins coined the famous truism, "The Personal is Political." Perhaps it's no accident that we use the word "domestic" to describe both our personal and our national homes.

I tell Martin my optimistic notion that we're riding a last mad arc before we circle back to something like the second wave, a circle made richer with new research, technology, insights garnered.

Many say that some other principle, the primate instincts at the base of our brains, rules us, always will. Well, yes, but we're impelled, too, I hope, by the gifts of reason, creative vision, and intuition, by the memory of the sea, to begin to rise above ourselves at last.

Nancy L. Roberts is a former English professor who lives in Park City, Utah. Her book of short stories, *Woman and Other Bodies of Water*, was published in 1987. Her work has appeared in various literary journals. *Crossing the Great Divide* is her recent collection of short stories. Printed with permission of Nancy Roberts.

Roberts, N. (2004). Cries from the second wave. In E. Oaks & J. Olmstead (Eds.), *Life writing by Kentucky feminists*. Bowling Green, KY: Western Kentucky University.

Dominelli (2002b) and Payne (2005) have filtered out from the feminist literature the following five types of feminism or feminisms:

- *Liberal feminism* seeks equality between men and women mainly through legislation and socializing children to enjoy more flexible roles.
- *Radical feminism* focuses concern on patriarchy, celebrates the differences between men and women, and promotes women's own separate structures.
- *Socialist or Marxist feminism* emphasizes women's oppression as part of structural inequality within a class-based social system. All oppressions are seen as interconnected and stemming from the same source. Power and violence in relations between men and women are not emphasized.
- *Black feminism* starts with racism and draws parallels between racism and sexism. Black women's experience of oppression is heightened compared with that of white women.
- *Postmodern feminism* focuses on how society through language creates social assumptions about how women are and how they should be treated. There is little emphasis on oppression here. The personal narrative is a preferred form.

Of special relevance to macro social work and the study of human behavior from a collectivist standpoint is Socialist or Marxist feminism, and the feminisms associated with minority groups of the most recent period or Third Wave. Marxist feminists argue that as private property evolved, males dominated all social institutions. Proponents of this belief system emphasize women's oppression as arising from their structured inequality in society (Payne, 2005). From this perspective, gender and class inequalities are viewed as closely related.

According to Marxist ideology, capitalism profits from the low-wage work of women in factories and corporations, both in the United States and elsewhere. Under capitalism, women who do not work are seen as confined in the home to domestic slavery, a form of exploitation that parallels the exploitation of the women workers.

Marxist feminists have been criticized for their overuse of economic explanations of women's opportunity to the neglect of the effect of family relationships and socialization factors (Burke, 2005). The lack of scientific proof for Marxist assumptions is another major criticism of this belief system. To challenge this argument, Vieraitis, Britto, and Kovandzic (2007) examined female homicide victimization data across counties in the United States. Their finding that counties with the highest levels of poverty had the highest femicide rates lends some support to Marxist feminist theory.

Relevant to social work, Marxist feminists explain domestic violence against women in part as related to their lack of access to resources and their relationships with men who are frustrated because of their own low economic standing (Littlefield, 2003).

Black Feminist Thought by Patricia Collins (2000) articulates the African American feminist position. Social change will only come, argues Collins, when the consciousness of individuals is raised—consciousness about the domination of intersecting oppressions. The historical structure of these interlocking oppressions must be acknowledged in order to transform the institutions of domination for the people's empowerment. Following Collins, Lay and Daley (2007) describe the black feminist framework in terms of acknowledgment of the historical structure of institutions of dominance. Others such as

Potter (2006) have adopted a black feminist framework to focus on intimate-partner violence experiences of African American women. Drawing on Collins' (2000) conceptualization of critical race theory, Potter examines women's victimization from a combined gendered and racialized standpoint.

Many African Americans concerned with the treatment of women in society prefer the term *womanism* to *feminism*. Womanism, to Littlefield (2003), "is an emergent theoretical perspective that reforms and expands mainstream feminist theory to incorporate racial and cultural differences, with a particular focus on African American women" (p. 4). *Womanism*, according to Littlefield, focuses on three key themes: the interlocking nature of multiple oppressions, the meaning of self-determinism for African American women, and the importance of naming and claiming African American women's culture. Moreover, writers from this school emphasize the key role that personal spirituality and religion play in African American women's cultural and personal empowerment.

The impact of ethnicity, gender, and class are inextricably linked in the life of the Mexican American woman. Her socioeconomic class as a Spanish-speaking, low-income Chicana woman determines her political and social position. In this way, her challenges differ from those of poor African American women and Anglo white lower-class women. *Telling to Live: Latina Feminist Testimonios* is a more recent anthology selected and organized by the Latina Feminist Group (2001). Part I of this book is entitled "Genealogies of Empowerment" and includes vignettes and personal narratives of a diverse group of Latina women, for example, a Spanish-speaking Jewish woman, an academic, and a working-class Puerto Rican. A major theme is empowerment and the mapping of individual paths to achievement despite historical displacement. Collectively, these writers bear witness to social injustice related to social barriers and those derived from gender constraints.

Relevant to social work treatment, Lorraine Gutiérrez and Edith Lewis's (1999) edited volume *Empowering Women of Color* provides the foundation for a model of empowering practice with Latina women. The two major components for such work are an understanding of power and powerlessness, and the importance of the development of a sense of self-efficacy in conjunction with a connectedness to social networks. Organizations must be transformed so that they are primarily accountable to the communities they serve.

To this list of feminisms we wish to add ecofeminism. *Ecofeminism* is a radical environmental philosophy that starts with a view of the oppression of women and the oppression of nature as inextricably linked. The involvement of women in environmental policies bolstered this movement. Ecofeminism asserts that the dichotomy between human beings and nature is a false one and that famine and overpopulation are rooted in oppressive power structures.

Besthorn and McMillen (2002) extend ecological/systems constructs by incorporating this feminist environmental philosophy. This expanded ecological paradigm, which is the one favored in this book, joins ecosystems concepts with feminism and offers a critique of existing society for its tendency to dominate both nature and humanity. From this perspective, there is a connection between the oppression of women and the oppression of nature.

Related contemporary developments in feminism are the inclusion of the rights of women who choose to make their contribution in the home, a global consciousness of the repression of women in other cultures, a recognition of biological differences between the sexes that affect brain development, and a reinterpretation of feminism by the younger generation.

One constant from the second wave to the third wave is that feminists continue to view the legal field as a viable platform for effecting change (Farmer, 2008). Many activist women decide to become lawyers themselves. Gloria Steinem, the foremost leader of the second wave along with Betty Friedan, who was interviewed by Farmer for the article, states that the feminist movement today is now global with a focus on issues such as sex trafficking and environmental dangers that know no national boundaries. Politics is another arena of activism today; large numbers of young feminists were active supporters of Hillary Clinton's candidacy for president.

Third-wave feminism consists of the daughters (and in some instances, sons) of the second-wave feminists. Their contribution to women's history builds on the foundation of the second wave. As explained by 23-year-old master of social work student, Bridget Boehmer (personal correspondence, January 21, 2006), "A Third Wave approach is very empowering because it is inclusive of all women from housewife to tomboy to girlie and so on. The inclusiveness makes it a genre of feminism that is becoming important to young women as it can help all women to feel empowered without placing feminism's 'restrictions' on them." The somewhat negative view of the foremothers' contributions or activist style is typical of the younger generation, of both those who reject the movement and those who understandably wish to carve out their own definition of feminism without giving up the fight for equal rights.

In *Feminism Is for Everybody*, bell hooks (2000) applies her critical analysis to misconceptions about earlier feminism, the belief by many people that the movement was only about equality and that feminism was anti-male. "Their misunderstanding of feminist politics," she states, "reflects the reality that most folks learn about feminism from the patriarchal mass media" (p. 1). She goes on to further explain, however, that there was indeed a great deal of anti-male sentiment among some early feminist activists who were responding to male dominance with anger: "It was that anger at injustice that was the impetus for creating a women's liberation movement" (p. 2).

A popular book written for third-wave feminists is *Manifesta* by Baumgardner and Richards (2000). Writing for young people, these authors differentiate the various waves of feminism without deriding any of them. They define the new feminism as an expanding feminism that is reclaiming the word *girl*, but with a difference. "Girlies," they tell us, are girls in their 20s and 30s who are into manicures, hairstyles, and the color pink. They are "reacting to anti-feminine, anti-joy emphasis that they perceived as the legacy of Second Wave seriousness" (p. 80). Baumgardner and Richards, who are young themselves, believe that feminists should build on the legacy rather than rebuild it. All feminisms, they suggest, share a struggle for justice and equality and against paternalism or protection (or domination and violence). These authors see a common ground as the young women pursue their course, "pushing voter registration, organizing against date rape, becoming women in rock, blowing the whistle in sexual harassment, publishing zines, and fighting for women's reproductive rights" (p. 79).

Third-wave feminists, who are also called *women of color feminists*, *womanists*, and *critical race feminists*, object to white feminists defining "women's issues" from their own standpoint without including women of color and third-world concerns. At the same time, they object to the anti-racist theory that presumes that racial and ethnic minority women's experiences are the same as those of their male counterparts. These modern-day feminist theorists focus on the significant roles that sexism, racism, class bias, sexual orientation, age, and other forms of socially structured inequality have in women's lives. Central to their approach is the notion of *intersectionalities*, a term which calls our attention to the interlocking sites of oppression inherent in the categories of race, ethnicity, class, gender, sexuality, and age.

Feminists, for the most part, advocate individual choice when it comes to abortion. The priority is on women's right to have control over their bodies. Feminists for Life, however, a group that was thrust in the limelight when Sarah Palin, who was listed on the Feminists for Life Web site as an active member, was chosen to be John McCain's running mate in the 2008 presidential election. This group of feminists maintains that being pro-life is compatible with the feminist values of justice, non-discrimination, and working to end domestic violence against women.

Feminism in all its forms focuses on the empowerment of women. Empowerment is a basic theme, in fact, of all the macro theories discussed in this chapter except for structural functionalism in any of its iterations. Empowerment is a core concept of all social work practice, almost to the point of becoming a cliché term.

Empowerment

What is known as *the empowerment perspective* has its origins in Solomon's (1976) groundbreaking work *Black Empowerment*, on the history of the struggle for equality by black people. Solomon saw the process of empowerment as a means of increasing the personal, interpersonal, political, and economic power so that people could take action to improve their life situations. This concept quickly took hold in social work and is the subject of a number of books—for example, by Simon (1995), *The Empowerment Tradition in American Social Work: A History*; by Lee (2001), *The Empowerment Approach to Social Work Practice: Building the Beloved Community*; by Gutiérrez, Parsons, and Cox (2003), *Empowerment in Social Work Practice: A Sourcebook*; by Bussey and Wise (Eds.) (2007), *Trauma Transformed: An Empowerment Response*; by Kirst-Ashman (2007), *Human Behavior, Communities, Organizations, and Groups in the Macro Social Environment: An Empowerment Approach* (2nd ed.); and by Adams, (2008), *Empowerment, Participation, and Social Work* (4th ed.)

Judith Lee (2001) and Walsh (2009), following Solomon, provide an expanded definition of *empowerment* to relate not only to what is happening inside of people but to include political processes, objectives, and transformations, thereby restoring the term to its original meaning. Lee's theoretical framework is the same as the one chosen for this book: Framed within the ecological perspective that maintains a dual, simultaneous concern for people and environments is an empowerment approach to assist people to live life to the fullest. Empowerment is both a process and an outcome (Walsh, 2009). As a process it includes attitudes and beliefs, validation through collective experience, knowledge and skills for critical thinking, and social action. To practice this approach, Lee recommends adoption of a multifocal vision. This vision includes the following:

> ▶ An *ecological view*, including a stress-coping paradigm and other concepts related to coping
> ▶ A *historic* perspective, learning a group's history of oppression, including related social policy

> ▶ A *critical* perspective, a class perspective, and *multicultural* perspective
> ▶ A *global* perspective

We have chosen the empowerment perspective as an adjunct to the ecosystems framework for this book both because of its familiarity and because it speaks to issues of social justice and human rights. To "be empowered," a person or group requires an environment that provides options and ascribes authority to the individual to choose (Rapp & Goscha, 2006). An empowerment approach responds to the individual's and group's experience of oppression (Saleebey, 2006). Some empowering activities by groups of people are simply about individual expression and festivity. See Figure 1.4 of the annual Solstice parade in Seattle.

Central to the empowerment approach is the concept of *power*, not in the Weberian sense of the ability to coerce but in the sense of liberation, of seizing control. Implicit in this concept is an awareness that disadvantaged persons are threatened by powerful others in their lives. Their very economic hardships may stem from global forces over which they are powerless and of which they may even be unaware. To Gutiérrez (1991), gaining a sense of personal power can be a first step in assuming personal responsibility for change; as an emotional force, this sense of personal power can move us from emotional apathy and despair to positive social action. Empowerment practice requires social workers to be agents of change, to help people gain or regain power in their lives. This is the goal of counseling at the interpersonal level. Oppressed individuals are not viewed as devoid of personal or moral strengths or resources; help in tapping into those resources often is needed. *The empowerment perspective* encompasses the strengths approach in its focus on helping clients tap into their inner and cultural resources. It goes further, however, in focusing on oppression and power imbalances in the society. Empowering practice begins by acknowledging that structural injustices have prevented many individuals and groups from receiving the treatment and resources to which they are entitled. This approach blurs the lines between macro and

Figure 1.4. This Seattle solstice parade brings out human behavior in all forms. Photo by Rupert van Wormer.

micro theory and practice. Much the same can be said for the anti-oppressive model, a model that, being European, is both more politically radical—in essence a structural approach—and more globally focused than its U.S. counterpart.

Anti-Oppressive Approach

Anti-oppressive analysis takes as its starting point the view of the capitalist social system as generally oppressive, a fact that, according to this logic, it behooves social work to try to offset. The most widely cited formulations of this perspective are found in the writings of Dalrymple and Burke (1995) and Dominelli (2002a). *Anti-oppressive practice* is about minimizing power differences in society and maximizing the rights to which all people are entitled (Dalrymple & Burke, 1995). *In Anti-Oppressive Practice: Social Care and the Law*, Dalrymple and Burke developed a practice model that operates at the level of *ideas*, working to achieve a changed political consciousness, and at the level of *feelings*, reflecting the client's and worker's histories. Partnership between worker and client is a central aspect of this approach. Empowerment here consists of helping people grasp the links between their personal positions and structural inequalities.

The difference between anti-oppressive and empowerment theory is that the former has a socialist base, whereas the latter has its origin in work with minorities. Anti-oppressive practice is focused on social change; empowerment practice is geared to working within the present social system. The backdrop for any discussion of oppression must include, to paraphrase Bishop (2002), the amazingly powerful and well-coordinated web of control the multinational corporations and financial institutions have woven around the world. Political, military, and ideological powers all come together in the service of global economic integration. Anti-oppressive theory, because of its structural, Marxist base, would be expected to incorporate such realities that perpetuate lopsided economic growth of some classes and societies at the expense of others.

In her book, *Anti-Oppressive Social Work Theory and Practice*, Dominelli (2002a) advocates a human-rights-based social work as a means of effecting change at the personal, institutional, and cultural levels toward realizing the rights that attach to citizenship. Dominelli perceives the context of social work practice within a globalizing economy. From this perspective, anti-oppressive social work is concerned about the deleterious effects that macro-level forces can have on people's daily lives.

Anti-oppressive concepts are widely used in the United Kingdom, Israel, and Canada. A recent publication in the *British Journal of Social Work* is typical. In the article, "Developing Anti-Oppressive Services for the Poor," Strier and Binyamin (in press), who practice social work in Israel, examine the relationship between poverty and oppression, review the literature on anti-oppressive organizations, and challenge the neo-liberal and managerial ideologies that are associated with punitive welfare "reform." In Canadian social work education, the structural approach still predominates. At the University of Victoria, for example, the mission statement reads:

> The vision of the School of Social Work commits itself to social justice, anti-oppressive social work practices and to promoting critical inquiry.... In particular, we endeavor to prepare First Nations social workers and child welfare practitioners, and we emphasize structural, feminist, First Nations and anti-oppressive analyses. (University of Victoria School of Social Work, 2009)

Are the Empowerment Approaches Verifiable?

These theory formulations—feminism, empowerment, and anti-oppressive analysis—are verifiable to the extent that discrimination and oppression in society can be validated. The researcher can draw on statistical data from government and international sources to gauge poverty levels among the various social class and ethnic divisions in the society.

Empowerment research requires the involvement of service users in the research process. Empowerment, which arguably is the goal of feminist, empowerment, and anti-oppressive practice, can be achieved through process, as well as outcome (and even in spite of outcome). Payne (2005) cites evidence that group empowerment work with people from deprived communities can increase later citizen participation. He goes on to say that group work in

its very nature is empowering—for example, self-help groups (see Chapter 3) and group work in residential settings. Fleming and Ward (1999) contrast this client-centered approach with that of the positivist tradition in which data collection involves clients as passive research subjects. Successful application of this model has been demonstrated in the United Kingdom in work with the Somali community, in research in a Malaysian village, and in interviews of persons with disabilities. A detailed case example of a British inner-city health needs assessment that utilizes qualitative methods is provided (Fleming & Ward, 1999). Such methods obtain rich information from the people that would not have been discovered otherwise, information about the meaning of health, the need for translators when receiving medical services, and the impact of social isolation and discrimination. Moreover, participants can be involved at every stage of the project, including, as in this case example, the dissemination of the results. Although social action research such as this entails a demanding agenda and is time consuming, the findings are apt to be more meaningful than information gathered by standard research designs.

Do These Empowerment Approaches Incorporate Issues of Diversity and Oppression?

Empowerment theory involves challenging oppression and making it possible for people to take charge of matters that affect them (Payne, 2005). The feminist approach relies on the personal narrative, on hearing people speak in their own voices. Not only is an empowerment approach effective in regard to issues of diversity and oppression, but empowerment is also crucial so that oppressed persons are the subjects, not the objects, of the investigation. Anti-oppressive formulations are centered around challenging conditions of oppression and injustice, as the label of the approach implies. Feminist perspectives are inclusive of diverse populations and of global issues that pertain to sex discrimination as well. The early variety of feminism, however, was criticized as neglecting issues of race and class, as only pertaining to the interests of middle-class white women.

What Is the Contribution to Social Work?

Of the three theoretical perspectives discussed in this section, clearly feminism has had the most significant impact on social work—both indirectly, through the cultural paradigm shift in women's awareness that they deserved respect and access to the privileges and rights that men have, and directly, in social work as a predominantly female profession. For the profession of social work, the new thinking associated with the women's movement was a return to the profession's roots, when women had been at the helm of the leadership (Kendall, 1989). During the conservative period of the 1950s and early 1960s, however, women were mostly under male authority, and mothers and other women were encouraged to play subordinate roles. Then, when the second wave of feminism got under way, social workers, like other professionals, began to focus on women's needs and safety rather than on conformity to narrowly circumscribed roles. The redefinition of masculinity that came with consciousness raising has, to some extent, freed men from the rigid role expectations that have been the cause of so much personal misery. Black feminist perspectives have been especially helpful in directing attention to the oppression of black women in a racist, sexist society. Recognition that the struggle against sexism must be the struggle against racism, as well, is an important insight well articulated by bell hooks (1995).

Anti-oppression analysis helps us realize that the dynamics of oppression—exploitation, social isolation, marginalization, and backlash when rights are won—are the same regardless of the characteristics of the group in question. Instead of separating the various forms of oppression into a hierarchy according to each victimized group, anti—oppression theory correctly views gender, ethnicity, class, and so forth as having a potentiating or multiplying effect when combined (Payne, 2005). Empowerment can be viewed as a major goal of social work intervention, as a process through which people reduce their sense of powerlessness and

gain greater control over all aspects of their lives and their social environment (Mullaly, 2007). Empowerment concepts are highly applicable to social work in relating to all population sizes—individuals, groups, communities—and their strengths-based interventions are highly effective, building on the positive in people, helping people tap into their natural resources.

What Are the Major Criticisms of Empowerment Perspectives?

So ingrained are these theories in social work knowledge that little criticism is provided. Feminism has not always been inclusive of women from working-class backgrounds and of those who wished to remain at home as housewives. It has been widely criticized on that score. Liberal feminists are criticized by radicals for accepting the present social order and for overlooking serious power differences in society (Payne, 2005).

Despite, or maybe because of, the fact that the term *empowerment* is so highly acceptable, it has been co-opted, as Dominelli (2002b) cautions us, by unlikely, even disempowering sources. Others have described the term as so popularly used as to be relatively useless. There is some truth to the criticism; the best way around it is for theorists to be careful to define the term when they use it. Empowerment theorists often direct attention to helping people work within the system to the neglect of the need to change the system itself.

Anti-oppressive theory has been criticized for the opposite reason—seeking change within the wider system. Often the oppressed populations, however, do not accept the structural view of their own oppression and do not feel kinship with other oppressed groups (with gay and lesbians, for example). There is no good solution to the problem of one oppressed group devaluing the oppression of another (see van Wormer, 2004).

What Do These Approaches Teach About Human Behavior?

Feminism, empowerment, and anti-oppression models have a lot to say about gender relations and about the basis of oppression of all forms—sexism, racism, ageism, heterosexism, ethnocentrism, and so forth. These conceptual perspectives tell us not only about the nature of oppression but also about the uses of power in a positive way through consciousness raising. Principles of empowerment transcend all three formulations. Central to empowerment theory is the basic assumption that with help most people can gain power over their own lives, that the helping effort must be collaborative in terms of relationship and purpose, and that the highest level of empowerment comes with taking action against one's own or another's oppression (van Wormer, 2004).

These perspectives, like structural approaches that direct our attention to problem causation outside the self, have strong didactic power. At the idea level of which Dalrymple and Burke (1995) speak, these theories often produce great "aha!" moments of realization for both social workers and their clients. Examples of such "lightbulb" experiences are the battered woman who learns of the power games that were played to put her down, the batterer who recognizes his own sense of insecurity and obsessions, the rape victim who realizes it was not her fault, or the boy who comes out to himself as gay. In short, many insights about human behavior can be gleaned from empowerment theory, which is the reason we have chosen this theory to augment the ecosystems model that guides this human behavior macro-level text.

Practice Implications

The implications for social work practice for each of the various macro theoretical perspectives discussed have been included along with the critical analysis of each category. To summarize: the general systems model is invaluable in family therapy because it broadens our perspective and alerts us to patterns of interaction and interrelationship within the family unit and with systems on the outside. Ecological theory adds the notion of the social and physical environment and of a spiritual interconnectedness of all life. Structural functionalism has a

contribution to make as well: Social workers can enhance their practice by considering the social functions of such customs in the society as weddings, funerals, and ethnic celebrations.

Knowledge of power dynamics and the central role of conflict in social life is essential to a critical analysis of social welfare policy, which, in turn, is necessary to influence state and local policy. Feminist theory guides practitioners to deal with situations such as partner violence, gender identity crises, and child-rearing practices. For work with all oppressed groups and oppressions, empowerment and anti-oppressive approaches provide additional insights and enhance critical analysis.

In this chapter we have offered an ecosystems-empowerment framework for the study of human behavior in the macro environment. This formulation of all the models is the most closely related to macro-level practice because of its relevance to life in an increasingly profit-driven world. Yet inasmuch as different interventions are required for different situations, and given the complexity of human behavior, familiarity with a variety of theoretical perspectives can provide a repertoire from which to suit the action to the need. This is what development of a *social work imagination* is all about—to see multidimensionally and to choose interventions creatively—to be able to ask not only "Why?" but also "Why not?"

Summary and Conclusion

In accordance with Council on Social Work Education (CSWE; 2008) accreditation standards for educating social workers, course material on *human behavior and the social environment* will cover "the range of social systems in which people live; and the ways social systems promote or deter people in maintaining or achieving health and well-being." Social workers need to be able to "apply theories and knowledge from the liberal arts to understand biological, social, cultural, psychological, and spiritual development" and to "critique and apply knowledge to understand person and environment" (Standard 2.1.7, p. 6). Toward this end, this chapter has presented a critical analysis of some of the major theoretical frameworks that are the most relevant to an understanding of human behavior at the level of the family, group, organization, and community. The importance of theory to social work is two-fold. First, the practice nature of the social work profession requires a theoretical base to shape the treatment focus and goals; second, it is important as a means of interpreting the wider social reality within which the change effort occurs. A variety of theoretical models have been proposed to this end, some adopted from other disciplines, each setting forth to organize knowledge about people in interaction with their environments, each seeking to answer the profession's call for a unifying framework. That an understanding of the broader social dimension of human behavior is essential to social work practice is a basic assumption of this book. The social dimension with which we are concerned encompasses everything from group membership to workplace interaction to social action in the political-economic sphere.

The frameworks described in this chapter and book are those that relate to the macro level of human behavior. The following macro theories were selected for examination: ecosystems, structural functionalism, conflict/structural, and the empowerment approaches (feminist, empowerment, and anti-oppression). As the guiding framework for this book, ecosystems received the major emphasis. In this second edition of the book, in light of recent social and political developments, this model was expanded to include a consideration of environmental and economic sustainability.

To further our analysis, we drew up a set of questions to apply to each of the theoretical models. The questions concerned each theory's basic assumptions, empirical validation, handling of diversity, contribution to social work, study of human behavior, and major criticisms. This format for the theoretical analysis brought our attention to the underlying ideological assumptions of the various models, some of which were focused on order and others of which were directed toward conflict in pursuit of social change; some were geared to local concerns, and others included a global perspective.

From these macro-theory formulations, we have chosen for our organizing framework for this book an expanded ecosystems model built on principles of empowerment: Ecology provides the scope, systems the sense of interconnectedness, and empowerment the concepts and tools for practice. As adapted for our purposes in this study of human behavior, and to better reflect the values and ethics of social work, our ecosystems model incorporates two additional dimensions—the physical and the spiritual.

Please take note that this is not an ordinary ecosystems model that focuses on the person's adaptation to the social environment (the life-model formulation). The model used here is more radical and more inclusive than that. The expanded ecological approach encompasses, as mentioned earlier, the natural and spiritual realms of existence. Our vision is of global interconnectedness; we see a drastic need for a model of social change, one that recognizes differences in access to power in society. A model centered on change questions rather than accepts the established social order. Such questioning is important today given the current global imperatives for the benefit of corporations rather than people. Our ecosystems, empowerment-based model offers a foundation from which to work to end oppression in all its forms.

Thought Questions

1. Discuss the image the holon in relation to macro-level social work.
2. Read Standard 6 of the NASW Code of Ethics (p. ix). What are some of the dilemmas that may arise from this standard?
3. How are macro understandings important for social work practice? How are theory and practice intertwined?
4. Give some examples of macro-level social work practice.
5. What do the major social work perspectives have in common?

6. Give some examples of broad-based historical paradigm shifts.

7. What are some difficulties facing macro-level research?

8. What are some biases in conventional research designs and the funding process?

9. Check the discussion of the U.S. government's pie chart on where the tax dollars go at http://www.warresisters.org, and discuss how statistics can be used to advocate for more progressive social welfare policies.

10. Discuss the basic concepts of general systems theory. What are the major criticisms?

11. What does the ecosystems approach contribute to our understanding? What is the science of ecology?

12. What does ecosystems theory say about the physical environment? Is this a bio-psycho-social-spiritual theory?

13. Discuss the concept of sustainability in terms of your college campus. To what extent does your university curriculum address this topic? Are students actively involved in activities geared toward "saving the environment"? If so, what are they?

14. What can we learn from functional analysis? Give an example. How can structural functionalism be used by both conservatives and liberal-to-radical theorists?

15. What is unique about conflict and structural perspectives? How is this perspective considered radical? Relate the theory to a contemporary political development.

16. "Mullaly's (2007) vision of social work practice is that it must be anti-capitalist." Discuss. Relate the social change focus of Mullaly with that found in the NASW Code of Ethics.

17. Discuss Piven and Cloward's contributions to macro social work theory.

18. Discuss how feminism caused what can be considered a paradigm shift. What were some of the social changes? Relate to Nancy Roberts's "Cries From the Second Wave."

19. How can feminist and anti-oppression theories be considered empowerment perspectives?

20. In your opinion, which perspective is the most relevant to macro human behavior? Which one relates more clearly to practice?

References

Adams, R. (2008). *Empowerment, participation, and social work* (4th ed.). New York: Palgrave Macmillan.

Akerlof, G., & Shiller, J. (2009). *Animal spirits: How human psychology drives the economy, and why it matters for global capitalism*. Princeton, NJ: Princeton University Press.

Armstrong, K. (1993). *History of God*. New York: Ballantine.

Aronowitz, N., & Bernstein, E. (2009). *Girldrive: Criss-crossing America, redefining feminism*. Berkeley, CA: Seal Press.

Associated Press. (2008, October 12). Ohio shooting puts face on foreclosure crisis. *MSNBC*. Retrieved from http://www.msnbc.msn.com/id/27149774/

Averett, P. (2009). The search for wonder woman: An autoethnography of feminist identity. *Affilia*, 24(4), 360–368.

Barker, R. (2003). *The social work dictionary*. Washington, DC: National Association of Social Workers (NASW) Press.

Baumgardner, J., & Richards, A. (2000). *Manifesta: Young women, feminism, and the future*. New York: Farrar, Straus & Giroux.

Bazaar, E. (2009, May 4). Economic casualties pile into tent cities. *USA Today*. Retrieved from http://www.usatoday.com/news/nation/2009-05-04-new-homeless_N.htm

Berry, T. (1988). *The dream of the earth*. San Francisco: Sierra Club Books.

Berry, T. (2009). *The Christian future and the fate of the earth*. Maryknoll, New York: Orbis Books.

Besthorn, F. H. (2002, February 15). *Toward a deep ecological social work: Its environmental, spiritual, and political dimensions*. Paper presented at the Social Work Faculty Forum, University of Northern Iowa, Cedar Falls.

Besthorn, F. H. (2003). Radical ecologisms: Insights for educating social workers in ecological activism and social justice. *Critical Social Work*, 3, 66–106.

Besthorn, F. H., & McMillen, D. P. (2002). The oppression of women and nature: Ecofeminism as a framework for an expanded ecological social work. *Families in Society, 83*(3), 221–232.

Bishop, A. (2002). *Becoming an ally: Breaking the cycle of oppression—in people* (2nd ed.). Halifax, Nova Scotia, Canada: Fernwood.

Brueggemann, W. (2005). *Practice of macro social work* (2nd ed.). Belmont, CA: Wadsworth.

Brundtland, G. H. (1987). *Our common future.* New York: Oxford University Press.

Brundtland, G. H. (2002). *Madam PM: A life in power and politics.* New York: Farrar, Straus, and Giroux.

Buchinger, E. (2004, September 16–17). *What is theory for? On the relationship between social theory and empirical research.* Paper presented at the Conference of the Social Theory Committee of the European Sociological Association, Paris.

Burke, R. H. (2005). *An introduction to criminological theory* (2nd ed.). Devon, England: Willan Publishing.

Bussey, M., & Wise, J. (2007). *Trauma transformed: An empowerment response.* New York: Columbia University Press.

Canadian Association of Social Workers. (2005). *Social work code of ethics.* Ottawa, Ontario: Author.

Coates, J. (2003). *Ecology and social work: Towards a new paradigm.* Halifax, Nova Scotia, Canada: Fernwood.

Collins, P. H. (2000). *Black feminist thought* (2nd ed.). New York: Routledge.

Connolly, K. (2009, August 31). Socialism is the best medicine. *Newsweek,* p. 83.

Coser, L. (1956). *The functions of social conflict.* Boston: Routledge & Kegan Paul.

Council on Social Work Education. (2008). *Handbook of accreditation standards and procedures* (6th ed.). Alexandria, VA: Author.

Dalrymple, J., & Burke, B. (1995). *Anti-oppressive practice: Social care and the law.* Buckingham, England: Open University Press.

Dawkins, R. (2004). *The ancestor's tale: A pilgrimage to the dawn of evolution.* New York: Mariner Books.

Dominelli, L. (2002a). *Anti-oppressive social work theory and practice.* New York: Palgrave.

Dominelli, L. (2002b). *Feminist social work theory and practice.* New York: Palgrave.

Dominelli, L. (2004). *Social work: Theory and practice for a changing profession.* Cambridge, England: Polity Press.

Dover, M., & Joseph, B. H. (2008). Human needs: Overview. In National Association of Social Workers, *Encyclopedia of social work* (pp.398–406). New York: Oxford University Press.

Faiola, A. (2009, March 9). U.S. downturn dragging world into recession. *The Washington Post,* p. A01.

Farmer, A. (2008). Feminism today: The personal is still political. *Perspectives, 17*(1), 4–7.

Faulkner, W. (1950, December 10). Speech upon receiving the Nobel Prize for literature. Stockholm, Sweden. Retrieved May 1, 2006, from http://nobelprize.org/nobel_prizes/literature/laureates/1949/faulkner-speech.html

Fleming, J., & Ward, W. (1999). Research as empowerment: The social action approach. In W. Shera & L. Wells (Eds.), *Empowerment practice in social work: Developing richer conceptual foundations* (pp. 370–389). Toronto, Ontario: Canadian Scholars Press.

Freire, P. (1973). *Education for critical consciousness.* New York: Seabury Press.

Freud, S. (1975). *A general introduction to psychoanalysis.* New York: Pocket Books. (Original work published 1924)

Gans, H. (1995). *The war against the poor.* New York: Basic Books.

Germain, C. B. (Ed.). (1979). *Social work practice: People and environments: An ecological perspective.* New York: Columbia University Press.

Germain, C. B., & Gitterman, A. (1996). *The life model of social work practice: Advances in theory and practice* (2nd ed.). New York: Columbia University Press.

Gil, D. (1998). *Confronting injustice and oppression: Concepts and strategies for social workers.* New York: Columbia University Press.

Gore, A. (1988). *The earth in balance: Ecology and the human spirit.* New York: Rodale.

Gore, A. (2006). *An inconvenient truth.* New York: Rodale.

Gore, A. (2009). *Our choice: A plan to solve the climate crisis.* Emmaus, PA: Rodale Books.

Green, J. B. (2003). *Introduction to family theory and therapy: Exploring an evolving field.* Belmont, CA: Thomson.

Greene, R. (2009a). Ecological perspective: An eclectic theoretical framework for social work. In R. G. Greene (Ed.), *Human behavior theory and social work practice* (3rd ed., pp. 199–236). New York: Aldine de Gruyter.

Greene, R. (2009b). General systems theory. In R. G. Greene (Ed.), *Human behavior theory and social work practice* (3rd ed., pp. 165–197). New York: Aldine de Gruyter.

Grunwald, M. (2009, April 13). How Obama is using the science of change. *Time*, 26–32.

Gutiérrez, L. M. (1991). Empowering women of color: A feminist model. In M. Bricker-Jenkins, N. Hooyman, & N. Gottlieb (Eds.), *Feminist social work practice in clinical settings* (pp. 119–211). Newbury Park: Sage.

Gutiérrez, L., & Lewis, E. (1999). *Empowering women of color*. New York: Columbia University Press.

Gutiérrez, L. M., Parsons, R. J., & Cox, E. O. (2003). *Empowerment in social work practice: A sourcebook*. Pacific Grove, CA: Brooks/Cole.

Haight, W., & Taylor, E. (2007). *Human behavior for social work practice: A developmental-ecological framework*. Chicago: Lyceum.

Hartman, A., & Laird, J. (1983). *Family-centered social work practice*. New York: Free Press.

Hearn, G. (1969). *The general systems approach: Contributions toward a holistic conception of social work*. New York: Council on Social Work Education.

Hollis, F. (1965). *Casework: A psychosocial therapy*. New York: Random House.

hooks, b. (1995). *Teaching to transgress*. New York: Routledge.

hooks, b. (2000). *Feminism is for everybody*. Cambridge, MA: South End Press.

Hutchison, E. (2008). Aspects of human behavior: Person, environment, time. In E. Hutchison (Ed.), *Dimensions of human behavior: Person and environment* (pp. 3–36). Thousand Oaks, CA: Sage.

Hutchison, E., & Charlesworth, L. (2008). Theoretical perspectives on human behavior. In E. Hutchison (Ed.), *Dimensions of human behavior* (3rd ed., pp. 37–76). Thousand Oaks, CA: Sage.

International Federation of Social Workers. (2005). *Definitions of social work*. Retrieved from http://www.ifsw.org/f38000138.html

Kahn, A., & Kamerman, M. (2002). International aspects of social policy. In J. Midgely, M. Tracey, & M. Livermore (Eds.), *The handbook of social policy* (pp. 479–491). Thousand Oaks, CA: Sage.

Keefe, T. (1980). Empathy skill and critical consciousness. *Social Casework, 61*, 387–393.

Keefe, T. (2003). The bio-psycho-social-spiritual origins of environmental justice. *Critical Social Work, 3*(1), 1–17.

Kendall, K. (1989). Women at the helm: Three extraordinary leaders. *Affilia, 4*(1), 23–32.

Kirst-Ashman, K. (2007). *Human behavior, communities, organizations, and groups in the macro social environment: An empowerment approach*. (2nd ed.). Belmont, CA: Brooks/Cole.

Kondrat, M. E. (2002). Action-centered social work: Re-visioning "person-in-environment" through a critical theory lens. *Social Work, 47*(4), 435–446.

Korten, D. (2009). *Agenda for a new economy: From phantom wealth to real wealth*. San Francisco: Barrett-Koehler Publishers.

Kuhn, T. (1962). *The structure of scientific revolutions*. Chicago: University of Chicago Press.

Latina Feminist Group. (2001). *Telling to live: Latina feminist testimonios*. Durham, NC: Duke University Press.

Lay, K., & Daley, J. (2007). A critique of feminist theory. *Advances in Social Work, 8*(1), 49–61.

Lee, J. A. B. (2001). *The empowerment approach to social work practice: Building the beloved community* (2nd ed.). New York: Columbia University Press.

Leopold, A. (1949). *Sand county almanac*. New York: Oxford University Press.

Lewin, K. (1951). *Field theory in social science*. New York: Harper & Row.

Littlefield, M. (2003). A womanist perspective for social work with African American women. *Social Thought, 23*(4), 3–17.

Lundy, C. (2004). *Social work and social justice: A structural approach to practice*. Petersborough, Ontario, Canada: Broadview.

Malamud, M. (2009, November). NASW calls for action on CEDAW (Convention on the Elimination of All Forms of Discrimination Against Women). *NASW News, 54*(10), p. 7.

Mary, N. (2008). *Social work in a sustainable world*. Chicago: Lyceum.

Marx, K., & Engels, F. (1963). *The communist manifesto*. New York: Russell & Russell. (Original work published 1848)

Maslow, A. (1970). *Motivation and personality*. New York: Harper & Row.

Massey, D., & Denton, N. (1993). *American apartheid: Segregation and the making of the underclass*. Cambridge, MA: Harvard University Press.

Massey, D., & Fischer, M. (2006). The effect of childhood segregation on minority academic performance at selective colleges. *Ethnic and Racial Studies, 29*(1), 1–27.

Merton, R. K. (1957). *Social theory and social structure* (2nd ed.). New York: Free Press.

Mihm, S. (2009, September 13). Why capitalism fails: The man who saw the meltdown coming had another troubling insight: It will happen again. *Boston Globe*. Retrieved September 13, 2009, from http://www.boston.com/bostonglobe/ideas/articles/2009/09/13/why_capitalism_fails/

Mills, C. W. (1956). *The power elite*. New York: Oxford University Press.

Mills, C. W. (1959). *The sociological imagination*. New York: Oxford University Press.

Morales, A. T., Sheafor, B., & Scott, M. (2010). *Social work: A profession of many faces* (12th ed.). Boston: Allyn & Bacon.

Morell, C. (2002). Human behavior and commercial culture: Bringing the new global economy into HBSE. *Journal of Progressive Human Services*, *13*(2), 27–42.

Mosher, C. R. (2009, May 9). *A new paradigm for sustainability and social justice*. Paper presented at the International Conference on Ecological and Professional Helping, Calgary, Alberta.

Mullaly, B. (2002). *Challenging oppression: A critical social work approach*. Don Mills, Ontario, Canada: Oxford University Press.

Mullaly, B. (2007). *The new structural social work: Ideology, theory, and practice* (3rd ed.). Toronto, Ontario, Canada: Oxford University Press.

National Association of Social Workers. (1996). *NASW Code of Ethics*. Washington, DC: Author.

National Association of Social Workers. (2001). *NASW standards for cultural competence in social work practice*. Washington, DC: NASW. Retrieved, from http://www.socialworkers.org/practice/standards/NASWCulturalStandards.pdf

Paige, M. R. (2009). *Empowering women toward recovery: The use of language and metaphor with women who have experienced sexual assault*. Paper presented at the annual meeting of The Association for Women in Psychology. San Diego, CA. Retrieved, from http://www.allacademic.com/meta/p230895_index.html

Parsons, T. (1967). *Sociological theory and modern society*. New York: Free Press.

Parsons, T., & Shils, E. (1962). *Toward a general theory of action*. New York: Harper & Row.

Payne, M. (2005). *Modern social work theory* (3rd ed.). Chicago: Lyceum.

Piven, F., & Cloward, R. (1993). *Regulating the poor: The function of social welfare* (Updated ed.). New York: Vintage.

Popple, P. R., & Leighninger, L. (2010). *The policy-based profession: An introduction to social welfare policy analysis for social workers* (5th ed.). Boston: Allyn & Bacon.

Potter, H. (2006). An argument for black feminist criminology: Understanding African American women's experiences with intimate partner abuse using an integrated approach. *Feminist Criminologist*, *1*, 106–124.

Raheim, S. (2006). Promoting diversity and social and economic justice in social work education: A process of organizational transformation. *Social Work Education Reporter*, *54*(1), 1, 6–7.

Rapp, C., & Goscha, R. (2006). *The strengths model: Case management with people with psychiatric disabilities* (2nd ed.). New York: Oxford University Press.

Rapp, C., Shera, W., & Kirsthardt, W. (1993). Research strategies for consumer empowerment. *Social Work*, *38*(6), 727–735.

Rogers, A. T. (2006). *Human behavior in the social environment*. Boston: McGraw Hill.

Rosenberg, J. (2009, November 23). Economic literacy. Communication shared with the Baccalaureate Program Directors listserv.

Sager, J. S. (2008). Social planning. In the National Association of Social Workers (NASW), *Encyclopedia of social work* (pp. 56–61). New York: Oxford University Press.

Saleebey, D. (2006). Introduction: Power in the people. In D. Saleeby (Ed.), *The strengths perspective in social work practice* (4th ed., pp. 1–24). Boston: Allyn & Bacon.

Satir, V. (1972). *People making*. Palo Alto, CA: Science and Behavior Books.

Schriver, J. (2010). *Human behavior and the social environment: Shifting paradigms in essential knowledge for social work practice* (5th ed.). Boston: Allyn & Bacon.

Sfiligoj, H. (2009a). NASW, New York chapters file brief in same-sex parenting case. *NASW News*, *54*(9), p. 7.

Sfiligoj, H. (2009b). NASW weighs in on student strip search case. *NASW News*, *54*(9), p. 10.

Sfiligoj, H. (2009c). Social work day at the U.N. celebrated: Global poverty—challenges for social work practice was this year's theme. *NASW News*, *54*(7), p. 6.

Shah, A. (2008). Structural adjustment: A major cause of poverty. *Global Issues*. Retrieved from http://www.globalissues.org/article/3/structural-adjustment-a-major-cause-of-poverty

Shalowitz, M., Isacco, A., Barquin, N., Clark-Kauffman, E., Delger, P., Nelson, D., et al. (2009). Community-based participatory research: A review of the literature with strategies for community engagement. *Journal of*

Developmental and Behavioral Pediatrics, 30(4), 350–361.

Simon, B. L. (1995). *The empowerment tradition in American social work: A history.* New York: Columbia University Press.

Smith, D. (Producer). (2005). *America's lost landscape: The tall grass prairie* [Motion picture]. Iowa Public Television. Retrieved from http://www.iptv.org/series.cfm/13698/americas_lost_landscape

Solomon, B. (1976). *Black empowerment: Social work in oppressed communities.* New York: Columbia University Press.

Strier, R., & Binyamin, S. (in press). Developing anti-oppressive services for the poor: A theoretical organizational rationale. *British Journal of Social Work.*

Surface, D. (2009). Understanding evidence-based practice in behavioral health. *Social Work Today, 9*(4), 22–25.

Tavris, C., & Aronson, E. (2007). *Mistakes were made (but not by me).* Orlando, FL: Harcourt.

Tester, F. (1994). In an age of ecology: Limits to voluntarism and traditional theory in social work practice. In M. Hoff & J. McNutt (Eds.), *The global environmental crisis: Implications for social welfare and social work* (pp. 75–99). Aldershot, England: Ashbury.

Thomas, L. (2009, May 14). Thriving Norway provides an economic lesson. *The New York Times,* pp. A1, A4.

University of Victoria School of Social Work. (2009). *Mission statement.* Retrieved from http://socialwork.uvic.ca/mission.htm

Van Den Bergh, N., & Cooper, L. B. (1995). Intro-duction to feminist visions for social work. In J. E. Tropman, J. L. Erlich, & J. Rothman (Eds.), *Tactics and techniques of community intervention* (3rd ed., pp. 74–93). Itasca, IL: Peacock.

van Wormer, K. (2004). *Confronting oppression, restoring justice: From policy analysis to social action.* Alexandra, VA: CSWE.

van Wormer, K. (2006). *Introduction to social welfare and social work: The U.S. in global perspective.* Belmont, CA: Brooks/Cole.

van Wormer, K., Wells, J., & Boes, M. (2000). *Social work with lesbians, gays, and bisexuals: A strengths perspective.* Boston: Allyn & Bacon.

Vieraitis, L., Britto, S., & Kovandzic, T. V. (2007). The impact of women's status and gender inequality on female homicide victimization rates. *Feminist Criminology, 2*(1), 57–73.

von Bertalanffy, L. (1968). *General system theory: Foundations, development, applications.* New York: Braziller.

Walsh, J. (2009). *Theories for direct social work practice.* Belmont, CA: Cengage.

Witkin, S. (2001). Whose evidence and for what purpose? [Editorial]. *Social Work, 46*(4), 294.

Zastrow, C., & Kirst-Ashman, K. (2010). *Understanding human behavior and the social environment* (8th ed.). Belmont, CA: Brooks/Cole.

The Social Psychology of Group Behavior

Oh wad some power the giftie gie us to see oursels as others see us!

—ROBERT BURNS

To a Louse, 1786/1968

Are people sheep? How vulnerable are people to going along with the crowd? How about you, the reader? How would you answer the following questions? Have you:

▶ Stood up to join in a standing ovation for a performance or speech of which you were less than enthusiastic or even disapproved?
▶ Laughed at a joke to show you "caught on" when you didn't?
▶ Joined in laughter at a joke that you thought was offensive and later regretted it?
▶ Pledged allegiance to the flag even though it didn't make a lot of sense to you?
▶ As a teen followed the peer group into doing something that was hard to explain later?

People are social creatures; we crave rewards and dread ridicule. As social creatures we do what we have been socialized to do most of the time, and that keeps us out of trouble. But this same tendency to conform is our very weakness and a hindrance to courage. On a mass basis, social conformity is played out in everything from traffic regulation to the formation of fanatical religious cults and the heeding of a call to war.

Such social phenomena as the thrust toward conformity exist in their own right. They are stronger than any individual capacity to control them. Their power is such that they persuade, even control us whether we realize it or not. The more powerful the social forces are, the less equipped we are to recognize them. (For a photograph that depicts gender conformity in early childhood, see Figure 2.1.)

Our journey in this chapter leads us into the realm of group dynamics. First we get a sense of the power of the group in controlling the behavior of its members. Drawing on classic experiments from social psychology, we explore the impact of various contrived situations on human participants—children as well as adults. Attention is paid not only to ethical issues inherent in research but also to the possibility of political uses of the power of the group for social control. Related theories from social psychology concerning the psychology

Figure 2.1. Socialization into gender-role conformity starts early. Photo by Rupert van Wormer.

of group aggression, prejudice, victim blaming, and homophobia are discussed. Among the small-group experiments described are leadership studies in social conflict; a participant-observation venture into the heart of a UFO cult; Milgram's (1963) classic obedience demonstrations; and a pseudo-prison experiment that degenerated into an institutional madness. Such classic experiments are discussed in light of contemporary attempts at replications and relevant controversies of the present time. The personal narratives, both of which were written especially for this chapter on groups, should be of special interest to social workers. The first is the story of a man who experienced many turning points in his life on the long road from a commuted death sentence and lengthy imprisonment to professor of social work at a major university. The second relates to the 2005 natural disaster (Hurricane Katrina) and describes both political and personal responses to this tragedy.

Historical Development

One reason we, as well as other researchers on group behavior, rely on truths from the classic studies in social psychology has to do with

research ethics. Researchers today are required to obtain permission through the human participants'research board before the university or any external funding source will endorse the study. Institutional review boards have high standards; most acts or statements of deception, for example, are disallowed in experimental situations. The contemporary standards exist for the purpose of protecting all people used in research studies, from drug trials to psychology experiments. The kinds of studies that were conducted in the past, especially the most intriguing and memorable ones, would simply not be able to be performed today for both legal and ethical reasons.

Modern-day social psychologists face a dilemma when investigating such important issues as conformity, obedience, and helping behaviors in everyday life, because with issues with the greatest significance for society, the potential for harm is the greatest as well (Aronson, 2008). Although we cannot replicate some of the early studies, we can still read the journal articles and books that described them, and we can watch videos in some cases to follow the results. Some of these experiments, despite the ethical issues they raise, are educational in what they tell us about human nature. In this chapter, therefore, we review the findings of some of the most interesting and creative of these early experiments. To take one example, one social scientist turned his department's offices into a huge cage and locked participants up in it. That was the famous Zimbardo prison experiment. We also study some later, ethically acceptable research designs. Today's experimenters can gain approval of the human participants' research review board by ensuring that no psychological harm is done to the participants and that participants leave the experimental situation in a frame of mind similar to the one they were in before the experiment. Debriefing the participant later about the true purpose of the study is generally required.

Small-group research is said to have begun with Kurt Lewin, who started using empirical methods to study group dynamics in the 1940s. Lewin, who is a credited with contributing the idea that groups have a life of their own, launched a whole generation of research into group dynamics (a term that he coined). His own research widened the focus of psychology into the social realm and into the study of forces such as anti-Semitism and racism (Burnes, 2004). To Lewin, human behavior was not the product simply of personal forces within us but also of the complex dynamic environment we inhabit.

Having grown up as a Jew in authoritarian Germany and then being introduced to a more democratic political system in the United States, Lewin was inspired to study the impact of styles of leadership at the University of Iowa (Burnes, 2004). He directed an experimental study of 10-and 11-year-old boys who were organized in groups of five. Graduate students trained to provide democratic, autocratic, and laissez-faire styles of leadership were rotated among the three groups. Under the *democratic* leadership situation, decisions were made by majority rule. Under *autocratic* leadership, strict discipline was imposed. Under the *laissez-faire* style, the boys worked and played as they liked. The experiment took place as part of an after-school program and lasted 18 weeks. The most productive group was the one under autocratic leadership, but when the leader left the room, very little was accomplished. In the democratic-led group, the boys took the most initiative and had the most fun. The boys expressed the greatest satisfaction with the democratic leader; their work had continued even when the leader was out of the room. And the boys in the laissez-faire group were unproductive altogether (Lewin, Lippitt, & White, 1939).

In addition to demonstrating the impact of leadership styles on the behavior of group members, Lewin contributed to group theory. Uniquely, he viewed the group as a gestalt, as an evolving entity oriented toward goals (Toseland & Rivas, 2001).

Interest in group behavior mushroomed in the late 1940s and the 1950s. A primary impetus, directly or indirectly, was connected to events in prewar Germany and to the war itself. Studies conducted on combat units, for example, helped identify the powerful effects that small groups can have on the behavior of their members. A major finding was that soldiers' loyalty to their unit, their strong group ties, strengthened their morale and kept them fighting even against overwhelming odds (Shils & Janowitz, 1948; Stouffer, 1949).

When asked about sources of support during combat, the combat infantrymen listed prayer as first and loyalty to one's buddies—not wanting to let the other men down—as second. Ideology, as Stouffer (1949) suggested, was not a primary fighting motive. In another landmark study, Shils and Janowitz (1948) interviewed German prisoners of war in an attempt to discover why some continued to fight even after it had become obvious that their country would lose. Again, loyalty to the primary group of buddies emerged as the key factor. Follow-up research conducted by social scientists from the U.S. Army Strategic Studies Institute with U.S. soldiers in Iraq confirmed the importance of social cohesion among the troops. Soldiers interviewed often used the analogy of the family in referring to their ties. Spending a great deal of time together, usually in austere conditions and with nothing to do to pass the time but talk, soldiers develop close and trusting bonded relationships (Wong, Kolditz, Millen, & Polter, 2003).

Interest in group work as a form of social action also proliferated in the late 1940s. In her historical study of the growth and development of group work, Andrews (2001) chronicled the origins of group practice as rooted in liberalism and a zeal for democratic principles. U.S. group workers learned from immigrants the importance of community life and the strength of the group. In this movement, the influence of Jewish refugees, such as Gisela Konopka, who held strong humanistic beliefs, was pronounced. Just as American social work benefited from the forced emigration of social psychologists such as Lewin, so the teachings and practice of Konopka spawned the recognition of the efficacy of the group process. Konopka trained as a social worker and returned to postwar Germany at the request of the U.S. State Department to help rebuild the country. She played a significant role in developing West German social work in a humanistic direction as well. Konopka is credited by Germans for much of this development and is, in fact, today considered the mother of social group work in Germany (Andrews, 2002).

Konopka provided a theoretical grounding for group work practice that enhanced its prestige and professional image. Under skilled leadership, as Konopka taught and demonstrated, the group could and did become a powerful mechanism for interpersonal growth and development. Although in later years, the field was to professionalize, along with social work, and to become more associated with therapy than with social action, we can today appreciate group work of the postwar period as a field that attracted some of the best minds in social science and social work.

Two other developments of note about this time were numerous studies of Chicago street gang membership (for example, Thrasher's, 1936/1927, "the gang") and research on industrial work groups (Roethlisberger & Dickson, 1939). The theme of those observational investigations was how norms are enforced on errant members. For example, in the factory, informal group structure sets production norms against those who produce too little or too much within the time frame (Etzioni, 1964).

A student of Lewin, Muzafer Sherif, conducted small-group experiments with children in the late 1940s and early 50s. His experimental situations, the Robber's Cave experiments, took the form of three summer experiences.

The method used was participant observation. To the participants, who were the boys, the researchers appeared to be simply camp counselors. During the summer of 1954, the most famous of the Robber's Cave experiments took place. The goal of the experiment was to learn about the causes of intergroup conflict and resolution of the conflict. The experiment started with the encouragement of internal bonding in two separate teams. Next, the teams were encouraged to challenge each other to very rough, winner-take-all tug-of-war games. An in-group versus out-group mentality and much name calling ensued. Fights broke out, and team flags were stolen. Researchers then set out to create peace across the groups. They did this at first through religious ceremonies and negotiations, but the tension only got worse. Finally, a strategy emerged that worked: This was the strategy of *superordinate goals*. The about-turn was accomplished by setting up a series of situations in which the two groups had to cooperate to obtain their objective. For example, all the boys had to pull together to get a broken-down truck moving on one occasion and to locate a problem with the water supply on another. Gradually the warring ended to the extent that, at the end of the sessions, campers from mixed teams asked to go home on the same bus (see Sherif, 1956; Aron & Aron, 2005). The implications of this study extended the findings from the small-group situation to the global search for peace through unity.

Leon Festinger, who had also studied under Lewin, engaged in a naturalistic social psychological experiment that is highly controversial due to certain disturbing aspects of the research methodology, aspects that are honestly discussed by Festinger, Henry Riecken, and Stanley Schachter in the appendix to the book *When Prophecy Fails* (Festinger, 1956). The research, which was conducted through a research laboratory at the University of Minnesota, was an attempt to study how people respond to evidence that contradicts their deeply held beliefs, how people reconcile two contradicting pieces of evidence, for example. What fell into Festinger's hands was an opportunity to study a group of UFO religious fanatics who believed their leader had received a message that the world was coming to an end on a certain day. What would group members do when that day arrived and the world didn't come to an end? The opportunity was in the form of a local newspaper article announcing that Lake City (not its real name) would be destroyed by a flood on December 21; the prophecy had been sent by "superior beings" from another planet. The researchers then took advantage of the situation and managed through the use of ruses and false stories to become accepted as active members of the group.

Cognitive dissonance, a term coined by Festinger, was the concept that guided this research. This term refers to the state of two pieces of information in conflict. What the researchers found was that the pressures within the group for members to prove their faith in the prophecy were profound. Eight members went so far as to make irreversible decisions, such as to quit their jobs or sell their possessions. The group's expectation was that, because of their faith, they would be picked up by flying saucers on the appointed date. When the first date arrived without incident, surprisingly, the group cohesion strengthened, as members operated on the defensive. Proselytizing in search of additional converts increased. But when another failure of prediction that the world would end took place, some members drifted away. In general, the researchers found that group members who stayed together when disconfirmation occurred maintained their belief and accepted the rationalization that they were being spared, whereas persons who were isolated grew angry and disillusioned. The strength of group bonding, therefore, was confirmed in this study of cognitive dissonance. The study also confirmed the original hypothesis that the more the individual takes an action for the sake of his or her belief, the greater the individual's commitment to it. The dissonance arouses discomfort, so the person might try to change one or more of the beliefs, acquire new information, or come to feel that the discrepancies are not so important. But again, as Festinger and his colleagues concluded, social support in sustaining belief is crucial.

Social psychologists Tavris and Aronson (2007) see the significance in this experiment in revealing the principle of self-justification that operates in connection with the thrust to resolve the problem of dissonance. People will unconsciously distort their perceptions in a positive direction to justify their sacrifices toward a certain end, for example, obtaining group membership. Empirically based research on fraternity initiation shows that the tougher the initiation, the more loyal are group members to the fraternity. This occurs, as Tavris and Aronson indicate, because people don't want to think they suffered through excruciating trials and rituals for a goal that was worthless; they resolve the dissonance by convincing themselves their sacrifices were worthwhile.

Festinger had some dissonance to resolve himself in justifying an experiment that raised some ethical issues. The chief ethical question that the authors of *When Prophecy Fails* acknowledge (in the appendix methodology section) is the extent to which their joining the cult and pretending to be true believers reinforced the faith of cult members. The researchers admitted that, as plausible and well-educated "converts," they did have an impact on the movement, although they did not get involved in proselytizing. It seems quite obvious that no comparable study design today would receive academic backing due to the potential harm that could arise from such activity. The risk to the university's reputation by a sanctioned deception on this scale would be considerable. Nevertheless, Festinger resolved the dissonance by deciding the experiment was worthwhile for its didactic attributes, which indeed it was.

Tavris and Aronson (2007) review a moment in history when the will to resolve dissonance was strong in some segments of the American public. This moment took place when after initiating the war on Iraq weapons of mass destruction were not found. President George W. Bush and his supporters were forced to find other reasons for the war, for example, that the world was a safer place without Saddam Hussein. Many members of the public, in surveys, showed that they refuted the evidence provided in the media and insisted on believing that the weapons had been found. The phenomenon revealed in this episode has a scientific basis. Tavris and Aronson cite research by neuroscientists in a study on bias that monitored people by magnetic resonance imaging (MRI) while they were trying to process dissonant information about George W. Bush or John Kerry. Based on their political orientations, the experimenters found that when participants were confronted with dissonant information about their favored candidate that the reasoning areas of the brain shut down. Such findings show that there is a neurological basis for people's rejection of the facts when the facts go against what they want to believe. They also show the importance of soliciting opinions from sources that are unbiased for information that we can trust.

Studies of Social Conformity

Homans, who called himself a microsociologist, published *The Human Group* in 1950 and *Social Behavior: Its Elementary Forces* in 1961. Much of his small-group research centered around social conformity. Homans's basic assumption was that conformity is maintained in informal groups because people value approval by their family and friends and therefore will shape their behavior accordingly.

Aronson (2008) summarizes experimental research from the early days of Lewin's school to the present time that consistently shows that dissenters from group norms are disliked. *Conformity* is defined by Aronson as "a change in a person's behavior or opinions as a result of real or imagined pressure from a person or group of people" (2008, p. 19). Aronson directs our attention to the classic experimental design of Solomon Asch (1951). In what is one of the best known and least offensive of conformity studies, students in a small group participated in what they were told was a study on perceptual judgment. They were shown lines drawn on a poster and asked which of three other lines on an adjacent poster was the closest in length to another line. The students ("stooges") had been instructed to choose the obviously correct answer at first, then to select the same incorrect response on subsequent trials. In Asch's experiment, approximately one-third of the overall responses conformed with the incorrect judgments;

three-fourths of the participants gave incorrect responses at least once. Unlike some of the experiments done in the early days of social psychology, the Asch experiments do not raise ethical issues and have been successfully replicated. The results have been consistent over time.

The question that we, like the researchers, would want to ask is, "Why, in the absence of rewards or punishment, do so many of the participants conform?" Follow-up interviews revealed that a few of the participants actually said that they perceived the lines to be of the incorrect length that was indicated by the others. In other words, their perceptions were altered by group suggestion. Tavris and Aronson (2007) refer to this phenomenon as "believing is seeing" (p. 17). Others explained that they did not want to be different from the group. In an interesting variation of this experiment, one of the observers dissents and picks the correct answer. Here the pressure to conform is considerably reduced. When the study has been replicated in other countries, results have varied: Conformity is more prevalent in collectivist societies such as Japan, Norway, and China than in individualistic societies such as the United States and France.

The lesson here for administrators and group leaders who wish to reach decisions through the group is to ensure that all sides of an issue are expressed. The goal would be to prevent groupthink or dominance by one faction over the others who feel forced to conform. In *Sway: The Irresistible Pull of Irrational Behavior*, a book on decision making, Brafman and Brafman (2008) relate Asch's findings to strategies used by the Supreme Court for inclusive decision making. Since the 1880s, the Supreme Court has established a tradition to ensure that minority opinions are not suppressed. Each member reads the all the legal briefs, and after the testimony has been heard, a conference is held behind closed doors in which each member speaks in turn so that every viewpoint is considered.

Social Psychology of the Jury Trial

Because observers and cameras are not allowed in the jury room, social psychologists who wish to study decision making must rely on mock trials or on witness accounts at some later date. Mock trials have the advantage of revealing to lawyers before they try a case with actual jurors how the group dynamics will play out on the issue of concern. We can also learn of the role of group dynamics from reports after the fact by individual jurors.

The tendency to want to conform to group norms, which is an attribute found cross-culturally, explains why the jury system works as well as it does. This fact also explains why sometimes the justice system does not seem to reach a reasonable decision. Diversity in the jury pool is important to reduce the chances of groupthink. Empirical studies of jury deliberations have shown that reducing the size of the jury from 12 to 6 produces much faster decision making and less predictable amounts of awards in civil cases and that the pressures for conformity are even stronger in the small group because the chance of finding an ally in dissent is lessened (Waters, 2004). Even in the traditional jury of 12 members that was portrayed in the 1957 Hollywood movie, *12 Angry Men*, the one dissenter was able to convince all the other 11 to think his way. The group dynamics and the way one forceful and appealing personality can affect the dynamics of the group as a whole are brilliantly portrayed in this film. Thus, even then, they were able to come up with a unanimous verdict. How is this so? The reason is that citizens want to do the right thing, and, combined with sometimes overwhelming pressures to conform to the whole, members of the jury pool, even if they feel uncomfortable about the decision, will tend to conform their beliefs to the majority will. In real life, therefore, in the majority of jury trials, unanimous agreement is reached, sometimes after days or weeks of deliberation. In a simple vote in the absence of deliberation, the chances of unanimity would be minute.

A recent study by Bloom (2005) explored jury group dynamics in Japan. Japan has been studying how the system works as they prepare to move to a new system to incorporate citizen input. Significantly, the Japanese government chose a mixed system (to be instituted in 2009) in which judges joined the jurors for decision making. Because Japan is a collectivist, as opposed to individualist, society (see Chapter 5), the fear is that the jury system would not work there; the impetus to conform to the majority would impede critical thinking.

In the recent highly publicized trial of Michael Jackson, in which the jury found the defendant, Jackson, not guilty of sexual abuse of a minor, the jurors chose to hold a follow-up press conference and reveal how they reached their decision. The jurors, all 12 of them, spoke with one voice at this time and expressed agreement with the verdict. Much camaraderie was shown among the jurors who had spent so much time in each other's company. The former jurors' willingness to subject themselves to lengthy interviews about their thinking and behavior within the jury room is unprecedented in television history and provides us with a rare glimpse into actual jury room proceedings.

From reports that were given initially and broadcast on several cable TV stations, the picture that emerged was of a highly cohesive group of members who had bonded over the long months of the trial (Guest, 2006). Once in the jury room, according to the jurors' immediate reports, an anonymous poll was taken; most voted to acquit, but a few voted guilty. Discussions reportedly were congenial. Although there seemed to have been general agreement about Jackson's inappropriate conduct with the boys in his charge, there was also a general revulsion at the behavior of the mother of the alleged victim. Because the jurors had been allowed to take notes, they spent much time in deliberations poring over them. In the end, jury members decided to follow the judge's instructions to disregard evidence of other alleged offenses and to restrict their verdict to the one case in question. Accordingly, the jurors found the accused not guilty on all counts. When asked about the bonding that had developed, some of the jurors stated that they planned to maintain the friendships that had developed.

In later interviews, however, the image of congeniality broke down, and a very different picture of the behavior inside the jury room emerged. Reports of dissension and harsh sanctioning of two of the members who felt that Jackson was a child molester surfaced (Caruso, 2005).

One woman, Eleanor Cook, aged 79, stated in a TV broadcast that she was planning to write a tell-all book, *Guilty as Sin, Free as a Bird* to describe the harassment, including ageism, that had forced her to shut up (MSNBC, 2005). A fellow juror who now feels guilty about his compliance told how he was bullied into going along with the others and that, regrettably, he had caved in. These former jurors complained that they were firm believers in Jackson's guilt. We might conclude from this illustration that the pressure toward conformity is strong and that otherwise consensus could not be achieved. Keep in mind that even when disagreement occurs, hung juries are uncommon. As far as Eleanor Cook's planned book is concerned, its publication is increasingly unlikely given the passage of time and the Michael Jackson's untimely death in 2009.

Obedience Studies

Related to conformity research are the studies of obedience to authority conducted by Stanley Milgram in the early 1960s. Milgram had been Asch's graduate assistant in psychology at Yale, and he considered Asch his most important scientific influence (Blass, 2004). Milgram's (1963, 1974) research went far beyond that of his mentor and never could be repeated today because of the risk of psychological harm. This obedience research, which showed how far people would be willing to go to obey an authority figure, made the headlines all over the world and led to profound revisions in some of the fundamental assumptions about human nature.

Milgram's interest in the study of obedience emerged out of a continuing identification with the mistreatment of fellow Jews at the hands of the Nazis. The fact that seemingly average citizens had failed to speak out and had blindly followed orders preyed on his mind. As he advanced in his studies, Milgram wanted to determine whether what had happened in Germany could also happen here.

Later, as a researcher at Yale University, Milgram recruited a random sample of white-collar and blue-collar workers to participate in a "teaching" experiment. Volunteers were told that they would be testing the effects of punishment on learning. As each volunteer arrived, he or she was met by a stern-appearing man in a lab coat and introduced to the supposed subject of the experiment, the "learner," an older man who comments that he has a heart condition. The man was strapped to a machine. The volunteer was taken to another room with the man in the lab coat and shown the "shock generator," a machine that supposedly would induce up to 450 volts of electricity. By throwing the successive switches when wrong answers were given, the "teacher" believed that he or she was delivering increasingly intense shocks each time the "learner" missed the question. The shocks were said to be painful but not to cause permanent harm. As the experiment began, the "teacher" heard the "learner" scream (the shrieks were actually on tape) and shout, "Let me out of here!" until finally, after a series of shocks, there was complete silence in the other room. "You must continue," instructed the technician. And in most cases the "teacher" did what he or she was told.

Afraid that no one would believe his results, Milgram taped the experiment on the last day. Results showed that two-thirds of the participants followed instructions and kept raising the voltage—right up to the levels marked DANGER: SEVERE SHOCK. The participants were not sadistic, however. As demonstrated on the tape, most of the subjects hesitated and showed signs of extreme discomfort even while they administered the "shocks." Milgram found that compliance was greatest when participants could not see the face of their subject (Blass, 2004). In another variation of the study, when joined by two other people who defied the experimenter, the participant went along with the experiment in just 10 percent of cases (Aronson, 2008).

Tavris and Aronson (2007) offer an interpretation of the willingness of people to engage in such extreme, apparently harmful, behavior. This experiment is generally interpreted, they say, as a study of obedience to authority. But it is more than that, according to these researchers: It is also a demonstration of the results of *self-justification*. The phenomenon of self-justification is similar to that of chasing one's losses once an investment has been made in something; the tendency is to invest a little more. If the subjects had been told they were to inflict 500 volts of painful shocks to a slow learner, as Tavris and Aronson suggest, most would have refused. Yet when they had already administered 10 and 20 volts, they were lured in gradually to ever higher levels; they justify each step along the way, and once so implicated in committing these acts, they were less likely to quit. The insight into human nature that Tavris and Aronson provide can be generalized to a large number of situations, including participation in crime. Once you have compromised and taken one step in a certain direction, it is human nature to go on. How do you get an honest person to sacrifice his or her moral principles? You get him or her "to take one step at a time, and self-justification will do the rest" (p. 37).

Milgram's research and its implications—that a high percentage of people will cause pain to other people in obedience to authority and because they have been led into it gradually—have been widely cited recently due to public disturbance over what happened at the Abu Ghraib prison in Iraq. (In 2004, graphic photographs were published throughout the world showing Iraqi prisoners positioned by U.S. military police in humiliating poses.) Milgram's warning has much resonance today: "[When an individual] merges. . . into an organizational structure, a new creature replaces autonomous man, unhindered by the limitations of individual morality, freed of human inhibition, mindful only of the sanctions of authority" (1974, p. 188). The desire to conform to social expectations, coupled with the difficulty of going back once small steps have been taken in a certain direction rather than individual tendencies toward sadism, apparently is the key to explaining seemingly incomprehensible behavior.

Role Theory

Readers of Erving Goffman's writings, such as *The Presentation of Self in Everyday Life* (1959), *Asylums* (1961), and *Stigma* (1963), may find

the view of human relations represented in those books disturbing. The readers may disagree with the underlying theory, but they will probably never be able to look at human behavior—the rituals/roles—in quite the same way again once they are made aware of the roles we play in everyday life. Drawing on Shakespeare's famous metaphor—"All the world's a stage/And all the men and women merely players" (*As You Like It*, Act 2, Scene 7), Goffman's writing provides a dramatized model for understanding social interaction. In Goffman's world, the social imperative to impress other people, the struggle to manage impressions, is an abiding drive in human relations.

Goffman's (1959) contrast between frontstage and backstage behavior is perhaps his most memorable contribution. The performance that a person gives on the *front stage*, the presentation of self before the public, the dress, speech, manners, and props, marks a sharp contrast with the reality of *backstage behavior*. Everyone who has participated in a play or ballet can relate to this. The back region must be kept closed to members of the audience, or they might become disillusioned. The performances vary by time and place. For example:

> While in church, a woman may be permitted to sit, daydream, and even doze. However, as a saleswoman on the floor of a dress shop, she may be required to stand, keep alert, refrain from chewing gum, keep a fixed smile on her face even when not talking to anyone, and wear clothes she can ill afford. (1959, p. 109)

The Presentation of Self in Everyday Life is highlighted with memorable illustrations of role playing and role conflict from the home, hospital, factory, workplace, restaurant, church, and party. Because different performances may be required in different situations, audience segregation is a must. Suppose, for example, that a husband and wife are in the middle of a minor quarrel when an intruder appears. The couple most likely will play different roles and act as though nothing is amiss. Another possibility is to include the third party in the conversation as though it were not meant to be private.

Goffman describes impression management at a mental hospital in these terms:

> If a mental hospital staff is to give a good impression of the hospital to those who come to visit their committed kinfolk, then it will be important to be able to bar visitors from the wards, especially the chronic wards, restricting the outsiders to special visiting rooms. (1961, p. 114)

Asylums (Goffman, 1961) shows how human behavior is controlled in institutions—such as prisons, the military, the convent, and mental institutions—to serve social control functions. Newcomers are indoctrinated and deindividualized through initiation rituals that make them amenable to control.

Corrigan (2007) is concerned with the use of stigmatizing labels in diagnosing clients with mental disorders. Mental health providers, he suggests, are prone to using stigmatizing language and to focus on diagnosis and psychopathology rather than on individuals. Perhaps, he speculates, because professionals tend to see persons with mental illness when they are at their worst and come in for treatment, they are less inclined than others to use a dimensional perspective or to see their clients' problems along a continuum. As we turn to the topic of the social life of the nursing home, let us consider the extent to which stigma is involved and whether Goffman's theoretical conceptualization has any relevance in this institutional setting. (Further discussion of Goffman's work is found in Chapter 7.)

Social Life of the Nursing Home

In *Asylums* Goffman (1961) argued that institutionalization was a mortifying experience that included isolation, invasion of privacy, regimentation, and labeling (pp. 13–14). If Goffman wrote the book today, his focus might very well be on the nursing home rather than mental institutions, because most mental institutions closed down during the deinstitutionalization frenzy that took place in the 1970s. The nursing home, therefore, has become a much more familiar total institution to friends and family members than the mental asylum. Of Americans over age 65, more than 40 percent will spend time in a nursing home before they die, unless current trends change (Ulsperger & Paul, 2002). Figure 2.2 shows women in a nursing home engaging in a recreational activity.

A *total institution* is defined by Goffman as "a place of residence and work where a large number of like-situated individuals, cut off

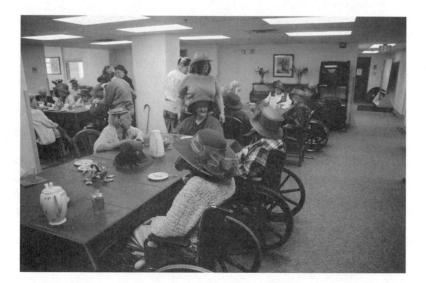

Figure 2.2. A group of residents at the "red hat ladies" tea party at the Western Assisted Care Center, Cedar Falls, Iowa. Photo by Rupert van Wormer.

from the wider society for an appreciable period of time, together lead an enclosed, formally administered round of life" (1961, p. xiii). Although Goffman does not focus on nursing homes, he does include homes for the aged under one of his categories of total institutions—those established to care for persons in need of such aid.

In common with other total institutions, the nursing home controls virtually every aspect of life. This includes meals, bathing, sleeping routine, dressing, visiting hours, the noise level, control over people coming in the room, and so forth. Because the vast majority of the nation's 17,000 nursing homes have too few workers (and pay is abysmally low), patients are at serious risk for such health problems as bedsores, blood-borne infections, dehydration, and malnutrition, according to a federal study headed by Connolly (2002) of the U.S. Justice Department that details staffing problems.

Inspired by Goffman's concept of "impression management" by public institutions, sociologist Jason Ulsperger conducted a participant-observation study in three for-profit nursing homes (Ulsperger & Paul, 2002). A priority was placed on creating a satisfying image in order to "pull in" prospective residents, as these researchers found. Impression management was achieved to the maximum degree through the services of a public relations representative, who covered up institutional problems when dealing with family members or the public.

The first rule of impression management is to rename the thing that has taken on negative connotations. Nursing homes, accordingly, have been renamed "assisted living centers" or "skilled care facilities." (They used to be called "old folks'" or "old people's" homes.) Front-stage appearance, in Ulsperger and Paul's (2002) study, was carefully managed—furniture and décor were chosen to be comfortable and homelike. Yet the residents interviewed by the researchers apparently did not feel at home; they expressed the belief that the security system operated to keep them confined.

This case study of the nursing home shows that Goffman's theory is as relevant today as it was in the 1950s, and not only for punitive or training institutions such as prisons or military boot camps but also for a caregiving facility such as a nursing home.

Stigma

In *Stigma*, Goffman's (1963) theory parallels sociological labeling theory, as he shows in his field notes and excerpts from literature how physical disabilities and official diagnosis come to take on a life of their own. The key factor here is role playing; people come to take on the roles assigned to them by society and to internalize those roles to the extent that they become a part of one's personality. Goffman's work is widely credited for conceptualizing and creating a framework for the study of disability in this regard. Often stigmatized people, as do all people, try to manage the impressions others have of that aspect of them that is socially disapproved so that they can pass as "normal." Goffman explained that stigma falls into three categories—abominations of the body, or physical deformities; blemishes of individual character, such as criminal records; and tribal stigma of race, nation, and religion. *Stigma* discusses gays trying to pass as straight, mentally ill and developmentally disabled persons embarrassed when audience segregation breaks down, and persons stigmatized in other ways who are striving for social acceptance. Among persons who have a disease or disability, the highest degree of stigma is accorded to persons whose symptoms cannot be concealed and who are seen as bearing responsibility for their own conditions.

Goffman's dramaturgical role theory is widely criticized for its presentation of only one aspect of human nature—our appearance and management of how we appear to others. He is further criticized for his failure to acknowledge the work of other sociologists and social psychologists on which his role theory is built. Yet Payne (2005) points to the value in these ideas in that some behavior can be understood as role conflicts and efforts to maintain one's performance. Moreover, role theory takes a social perspective on behavior, so it is a useful link between human actions and the social environment.

In Box 2.1, "Turning Points in the Life of Rudolph Alexander, Jr.," is an essay written by a man for whom Goffman's theories on stigma, labeling, and institutionalization would have much meaning. Alexander's experience epitomizes the worst aspects of the criminal justice system at every step of the way, from law enforcement through racist courtroom justice through maximum security imprisonment (see Figure 2.3). The narrative, written especially for this text on human behavior, is also about sheer human determination in overcoming a past of crime and punishment, including a brutal miscarriage of justice, and, above all, it is about resilience—an aspect of human behavior about which Goffman said very little.

Box 2.1 Turning Points in the Life of Rudolph Alexander, Jr.

Learning that a full professor of social work at a major university had a death sentence in Georgia's electric chair in the late 1960s and later a life sentence may pique the interest of most people. Immediately, some individuals might believe that the Georgia Department of Rehabilitation and Correction did a wonderful job in rehabilitating such a person. But this hypothesis of rehabilitation would be very far from the truth. Of course, such a story would have multiple critical points that ultimately routed such a person to an academic career. Subtly presented in my autobiography, *To Ascend Into the Shining World Again*, these critical points are described here. But I begin with what occurred in 1967 as a 17-year-old African American youth that propelled me into the legal system in Savannah, Georgia.

In 1967, within a span of 7 months, I went to the hospital 3 times as a result of 2 attacks. The first attack with a box-cutter required emergency surgery and left me with severe damage to my left eye to the point of blindness in that eye. The person who attacked me was found guilty of assault and received 4 months in jail and was fined. As a result of this attack, I had to wear an eye bandage from January 1967 to June 1967, alerting everyone that I had sustained a very serious injury. I had a second surgery in July 1967 to remove a cataract for my left eye. Two weeks after my second surgery, I was attacked by a gang that called themselves the Tornadoes. While one person held a gun on me, threatening to shoot me if I moved, another person cut me with a knife and I sustained a deep wound in my right eyebrows that required several stitches to close. Reportedly, this second attack was intended to put out my good eye. In both attacks, I never saw the weapon that injured me. Vowing that I had enough and would not be going to the hospital anymore, I armed myself and later shot and killed one member of this Tornado gang. However, this person was praised by a Catholic priest and the newspaper called him the "slain choir boy."

My parents hired and paid in full the top criminal defense attorney in Savannah—a man with 50 years of criminal trial experience. However, this attorney did not come to court and represent me and sent instead another lawyer who butchered me in the courtroom in the most treasonous and treacherous conduct imaginable. Specifically, no one interviewed me. I was put on the witness stand with no forewarning and not given the basic legal advice, such as what questions I would be asked on the witness stand, admonition to answer questions yes or no, what to expect on cross examination from the prosecution, or instruction to watch the jury when I testified. No evidence was presented in my favor—nothing about my previous injuries and surgeries, my background, and the prosecution of my first attacker. This defense attorney told the jury that I might be a hoodlum, although I had no criminal or juvenile record and had finished high school at 17 years of age. When I was a junior in high school, I worked at a restaurant washing dishes and was not getting home until 2 A.M. in the morning, but I was still getting up and going to school. Yet, I was presented to the jury as a bloodthirsty hoodlum who shot and killed someone for dubious reasons. In a trial that lasted a little more than 2 hours, I was convicted of murder and given a death sentence. The three prosecutors in my case did not ask the jury to return a death sentence. It was, in fact, the defense attorney who raised the issue of the death penalty. Later, my family was told that the deceased family, who initially tried to hire the same top criminal defense attorney to prosecute me, made a deal for my defense to be sabotaged and thrown. This defense attorney's explanation for why he did not go to court to represent me was that he had to suddenly go out of town about 16 hours before my trial began, but my family learned that he was in his office and was not out of town. Little could be done to correct this injustice because the legal system in Savannah was very corrupt and racist. The one judge who was responsible for trying all felony cases hated and despised all African Americans and was a racist to the marrow of his bones. Because of a fortuitous U.S. Supreme Court decision in an Illinois capital case involving jury selection that was rendered 2 months after my trial, my death sentence was overturned by the Georgia Supreme Court and I was resentenced to life imprisonment in 1969. Then 19 years old, I began this sentence at the maximum security prison in Reidsville, Georgia—one of the most violent prisons in the country. In 1975, I was paroled. Also, in 1975, I began college in my hometown and obtained an associate degree in criminal justice. Later, I left Savannah and moved to Texas for employment reasons. I obtained a BS degree in criminology and correction from Sam Houston State University. Shifting to the field of social work, I received a MSW from the University of Houston. In 1989, I received a PhD in social work from the University of Minnesota. Also, in 1989, I was hired as a social work professor at Ohio State University and earned tenure and promotion to associate professor in 1995. In 2000, I was promoted to full professor. Besides my autobiography, I have published four books— *Counseling, Treatment, and Intervention Methods With Juvenile and Adult Offenders* (2000), *Race and Justice* (2000), *Understanding Legal Concepts That Influence Social Welfare Policy and Practice* (2003), and *Racism, African Americans, and Social Justice* (2005). I have published about 55 articles in peer-reviewed social work and criminal justice journals.

A number of critical turning points have occurred in my life that helped me get where I am now. First, I totally reject the notion that I was rehabilitated by the Georgia prison system. I saw no mental health professional in prison and did not participate in programming. I believe that there was never anything wrong with me. But for the ways that I was betrayed and mistreated by the justice system, I never entertained the notion of mistreating innocent others. Frequently, many guys in prison who believe that they have been wronged state that they intend to make someone pay for their maltreatment. Thinking this way was never part of my character. I had very supportive parents. Although my dad was

powerless to deal legally with the corrupt criminal justice system in Savannah, he, shortly before I began the life sentence, made me the beneficiary of his life insurance so that if he died while I was in prison I would have some money that might help free me from the Georgia prison system. My parents frequently visited me in prison. In short, my parents and family were my first turning point. Another turning point for me occurred after I was made a trusty in prison, which made my prison stay somewhat easier. This decision was made by an official from the Georgia Department of Rehabilitation and Correction in Atlanta, Georgia. This trusty status made me a candidate for early parole. Trusties frequently serve less time in prison than other prisoners. In prison, I acquired an interest in the law and read constantly. I was able to teach myself some things about the law and later used this knowledge to propel me toward tenure. I frequently published academic articles that addressed legal issues in social work and criminal justice. Then, I have met some very good people who believed in giving individuals a chance to prove themselves. One person was the individual in Texas who gave me in 1978 my first counseling job working in a wilderness camp for boys after I told him about my background. His name is Lyndy Langford, and he and I have stayed in contact throughout the years. Later, the Dean of Social Work at Ohio State University, Richard Boettcher, hired me in 1989 after I informed him of my background and my intention to write my autobiography one day which would not make a lot of people happy. However, my religious friends tell me that I have been blessed by God, and God was my turning point although I am not religious.

Reprinted with permission of Rudolph Alexander, Jr., Professor of Social Work, Ohio State University.

Studies Involving Context

In 1971, an experiment with results equally as shocking as those of Milgram's earlier work and with perhaps even more relevance to Abu Ghraib was directed by Stanford University psychologist Philip Zimbardo. What Zimbardo

Figure 2.3. Rudolph Alexander, Jr., presenting his research findings at the University of Toledo, Ohio. Photo by Robert van Wormer.

did was to set up a mock prison. Gladwell (2002), author of *The Tipping Point*, classifies this experiment as an illustration of the power of *context*, or the social environment, to affect human behavior.

The prison that Zimbardo created out of university office space consisted of a cell block with a prefabricated wall and cells made from laboratory rooms. A closet was turned into a solitary confinement cell. The researchers then advertised for college students to volunteer and picked the most psychologically stable of the lot. Half the group members were chosen at random to be guards and were given uniforms and dark glasses. They were instructed to keep order. The other half were told that they were prisoners; they were actually "arrested" by the local police department, fingerprinted, and blindfolded. In the psychology department basement, they were stripped and given prison uniforms and numbers to wear.

What Zimbardo and his colleagues learned was shocking. In no time, the guards grew abusive and the inmates cowed. At night, when

Zimbardo was gone, guards put bags over inmates' heads, stripped them of clothing, and told them to simulate sex acts (see Haney, Banks, & Zimbardo, 1973). Years later, in an article written on parallels between the Stanford "prison" and Abu Ghraib, Zimbardo (2004) urged commentators and government to blame the system rather than the personalities of the abusive guards:

> Again, there is the same rush to the person-centered analysis of human behavior, which blames flawed or pathological individuals for evil and ignores the host of contributing factors in the situation in which they were embedded. Unless we learn the dynamics of *why*, we will never be able to counteract the powerful systemic forces that can transform ordinary people into evil perpetrators. . . .
>
> My guards soon began doing terrible things that were comparable to many of the horrors reportedly inflicted on the Iraqi citizens who were being held in "pre-trial detention," for vague security reasons, without recourse to legal counsel or family. My guards repeatedly stripped their prisoners naked, hooded them, chained them, denied them food or bedding privileges, put them in solitary for the least infractions of arbitrary rules, made them clean toilet bowls with their bare hands, and worse. As the boredom of the job got to some of the guards, they began using the prisoners as their playthings, devising ever more humiliating and degrading games for them to play. Over time, these amusements took a sexual turn, such as having the prisoners simulate sodomy on each other. Once aware of such deviant behavior, I closed down the Stanford prison. Perhaps the military should follow suit in Iraq. (2004, pp. 1–2)

Zimbardo closed his experiment down after 6 days. Zimbardo and other psychologists who have studied torture and sadism by prison guards and soldiers believe that most abuse can be traced to group dynamics and circumstances rather than to individual traits of character.

As Gladwell (2002) notes, when it comes to interpreting other people's behavior, human beings invariably make the mistake of overestimating the importance of fundamental character traits and underestimating the importance of situation and context. What is true of the prison environment is also true during warfare, in which epidemics of bad behavior can occur in situations without any clear common structure. Emulating what other people do—contagion—figures prominently in negative, as in positive, examples of collective behavior.

Dehumanization is a process that was evidenced among the children at the Robber's Cave summer camp with their intense in-group, out-group loyalties and the separation of people into categories of Us and Them. This behavior was displayed again in Zimbardo's laboratory research. The psychological process of dehumanization means that moral law does not apply to Them. From the Holocaust to the hunting of Bushmen by Boers to treatment of American Indians by Spanish conquerors to the lynching of African Americans to Bosnian ethnic cleansing, the psychological dynamics are relatively the same.

One aspect of group aggression that emerges in the experimental and real-life situations is the relationship between group size and level of aggressive behavior. Another key element is anonymity, which induces *deindividuation*, or a state of lessened self-awareness. Aronson (2008) describes the phenomenon in which female students who dressed in robes in a dimly lit room administered longer and more of what they thought were severe shocks to another student than they did when they had personal contact with the student. Studies of mob behavior in real life reveal the same phenomenon outside the laboratory. As size and emotions intensify, the groups can solidify into mobs (Goldstein, 2002). The larger the crowd is, as at a lynching, the greater the depersonalization, emotional contagion, and violence. American history is a chronicling of labor violence, feuding vigilante groups, massacres of American Indians, and riots. So, indeed, is much of the history of humankind (Goldstein, 2002). The fertile soil for the growth of mob violence, as Goldstein explains, is found in

certain sociocultural contexts, often economic, in combination with some immediate triggering event. In a crowd, the heightened state of arousal, combined with modeling of aggression by others, feeds on itself. The sheer excitement of the moment works like a drug, so much so that ordinary people "lose themselves" in the excitement of the crowd; the reasoning part of the brain is suppressed by pure emotion. In the near-lynching scene in the film based on the novel *To Kill a Mockingbird* (Lee, 1960/1988), for example, when the child, Scout, addresses the leader of the would-be lynch mob, Mr. Cunningham, by name and tells him she knows his son at school, his aggression is defused and he backs away.

The diffusion of responsibility that occurs in the crowd also explains another phenomenon of human behavior: When an individual is attacked before a crowd, bystander inhibition occurs. Each person assumes that someone else will call the police, for example, as in the stabbing of Kitty Genovese, who was attacked over a 30-minute period in New York City while 38 of her neighbors watched from their windows and did nothing. In staged emergencies, the one factor that emerged above all others in predicting helping behavior was how many witnesses there were to the event (Gladwell, 2002).

Helping is also more common, as Aronson (2008) indicates, when people share a sense of common fate and identity. The predominant explanation given by the 38 onlookers to the Genovese murder was "I didn't want to get involved." Although there is no reason to believe that prejudice played any role in this situation, one could hypothesize that, in general, racial differences between bystanders and persons in need of help would increase the sense of distance and motivation to intervene. We see this tendency to turn away from another's suffering as both a cause and an effect of prejudice and of the tendency to blame the victim.

Prejudice

Prejudice is a learned phenomenon, transmitted from generation to generation through socialization processes. *Prejudice*, a term that we use here in a negative sense, refers to a preconceived and unjustified negative attitude. Prejudice involves prejudgment on the basis of a defined characteristic, such as race, ethnicity, religion, or gender. Although prejudice is an attitude that is often associated with discrimination, the two terms are not synonymous. *Discrimination* involves a physical act, such as refusing to hire a person because the person is African American or Latino or a woman. Discrimination may arise from unofficial policy (such as admission policies at Russian universities designed to reduce the enrollment of Jews) or official policy (for example, by the U.S. military to remove openly gay and lesbian soldiers from service). Note that the individual who carries out the policy may discriminate without being prejudiced. Conversely, the individual may harbor his or her own prejudices but refuse, because of government regulations, to discriminate.

Prejudice is unjustified when an individual is unfairly judged based on observations about the group of which he or she is a member; for example, someone meeting a member of an outside group and having preconceived notions that are based on stereotyping. To *stereotype* is to assign identical characteristics to any person in a group, regardless of the actual variation among members of that group (Aronson, 2008). Sometimes stereotyping arises from direct experience with one or several members of a group; the negative characteristics of these individuals are then generalized to all group members. Sometimes an influx of newcomers to an area is met with resistance when the people are culturally different. A program at the University of Northern Iowa to create diversity through recruitment of Latino students from San Antonio, Texas, has worked out well and led to cross-cultural friendships. When an incident at a fraternity party involving an ethnically motivated assault of a Mexican American student was followed by the sight of a swastika chalked on the campus sidewalk, faculty and students joined together to stand up against the intolerance. Figures 2.4 and 2.5 are of the vigil that recently took place on the campus.

A history of war, of territorial disputes, of persecutions, and of economic exploitation exacerbates prejudice toward persons who are

Figure 2.4. Students and faculty turned out in large numbers to take a stand against racist and ethnocentric incidents that took place on the campus. Photo by Joanna Herrington.

Figure 2.5. Latina students hold up a sign that reads ¡Basta ya! (Enough is enough) at the campus vigil against hate crimes on the University of Northern Iowa campus. Photo by Joanna Herrington.

of the same ethnicity as those from the enemy camp. The victims will tend to stereotype others in the same category as their oppressors, a direct and understandable emotional response probably related to the psychological process of conditioning. What is less understandable is the process by which the persons who did the victimizing and exploiting of a given population turn against their victims with a hatred that is even more pronounced than that of the victims. Psychologically, this rejection can be understood as a defense mechanism against guilt feelings and as a way of justifying the group's misdeeds. (Refer to the later discussion of blaming the victim.)

No single theory can explain all the reasons for prejudice; prejudice actually involves a number of factors. It is important for social workers to have some general understanding about the nature of prejudice, because they can expect not only to work with diverse populations but also—and this is a fact rarely addressed in social work training—to work with people whom one could easily characterize as racial or personal bigots. Training in cultural competence, to the extent that this entails learning

about the cultural characteristics of a particular ethnic group, is of little value to the therapist when his or her client starts spouting racial or antigay epithets during the course of treatment, sometimes even in group therapy sessions. These expressions by a member of one marginalized group (a client with a disability) against another (a member of a racial minority) can come as a shock to the novice social worker. Some knowledge about the psychological and cultural origins of the bigotry and prejudice can help prepare the therapist for such an eventuality.

Psychological Explanations

Many of the earlier theorists located the cause of prejudice within the personal psyche. In his definitive study *The Nature of Prejudice*, Allport (1954/1981) investigated what he saw as the generalized aspect of out-group prejudice, the tendency for a given individual to be intolerant of all forms of diversity. Allport regarded prejudice as a trait of personality, one that is correlated with hostility and fear and related to an authoritarian upbringing.

Some empirical support for the existence of a personality dimension in prejudice was provided during the 1940s by a team of researchers who carried out an in-depth investigation into the dynamics of anti-Semitism. The study was inspired by events that had occurred in Nazi Germany. Adorno, Frankel-Brunswick, Devinson, and Sanford (1950) devised the F-Scale to measure fascist or authoritarian tendencies. Among items included in this scale are the following:

> Obedience and respect for authority are the most important virtues children should learn.
> There is hardly anything lower than a person who does not feel great love, gratitude, and respect for his parents.
> Sexual offenders ought to be publicly whipped or worse.
> The businessman and the manufacturer are much more important to society than the artist and the professor.

Scores on the F-Scale were found to be correlated quite strongly with scores on anti-Semitism, general ethnocentrism, and political conservatism (also dogmatic communism, as revealed in a later study). To explain the development of authoritarianism, Adorno and his associates looked at early child-rearing practices. Employing arbitrary and harsh methods of discipline, authoritarian parents may produce children whose feelings of frustration are repressed. This hostility may be displaced and directed instead toward powerless groups in society.

A highly unusual study utilized advanced statistical methods to detect personality patterns in politically conservative persons (Jost, Kruglanski, Glaser, & Sulloway, 2003). Data gathered by this team of psychologists were culled through 50 years of research literature and involved an unprecedented 22,818 cases. The material originated from 12 countries and included political speeches and interviews, opinions rendered by judges, and experimental field data. The findings, which were widely reported in international news reports and on the Internet, linked the following common psychological factors to political conservatism:

> Fear and aggression
> Dogmatism and intolerance of ambiguity
> Avoidance of uncertainty
> Need for cognitive closure and structure
> Resistance to change
> Endorsement of inequality
> View of reality in terms of black and white—no shades of gray
> Terror management—shunning or punishing outsiders

In a follow-up analysis of their findings, Dixit (2007) reviewed literature from psychology that showed that when people are prompted to think of death or terrorism, they tended to support conservative candidates. Conservatives tend to engage in more black-and-white thinking, and images of terrorism such as reminders of 9/11 awaken deep desires for reassurance and acceptance of the status quo. Strategies used in the 2004 election—playing a threatening Osama bin Laden tape and stepping up the government color-coded security threat levels right before the election—were highly effective in wooing voters. So what can be done to help insulate people from such manipulations? There is a lesson from one experimental situation that used a control group: The subjects who were cautioned to think rationally before they were exposed to the images of death did not shift their opinions into a right-wing direction compared to the control group who did so. Liberal politicians of course can use the same strategies to drum up support for military action. In a recent speech delivered at West Point to defend his plan to build up the number of troops in Afghanistan, for example, President Obama began with a grim reminder of the events of 9/11 and of the threats of terrorism that still apply today (Wilson, 2009). Intolerance of ambiguity is a trait that deserves more research, especially research on the issue of the relationship between such intolerance and a lashing out against people who are different. In any case, the linking of political ideology to personality dynamics helps to explain why so often members of the general public can be manipulated by slogans even when the slogans are based on untruths or half truths. These research findings by Jost et al. (2003) further help explain why relatively new ideas such as gay marriage or the creation of a world criminal court to enforce human rights standards are apt to be strongly resisted in far right-wing quarters. This study on rigid belief systems is reminiscent of Adorno et al.'s (1950) work in its attribution of political ideology to personality characteristics. The Adorno study used the term *authoritarianism* instead of *conservatism*, a usage that is more reflective of reality. Many conservative people, after all, are moderates in their thinking. We need to remember that authoritarian characteristics were prevalent among Russian communist party leaders, as well as among Ku Klux Klan members and German fascists (see van Wormer, 2006).

Projection and lack of empathy are two psychological tendencies that may have a bearing on prejudice. *Projection* is the psychological defense mechanism first described by Freud as the tendency to unconsciously attribute our own motives, attributes, or unacceptable ideas or impulses to another. This mechanism was believed by Freud and others of the psychoanalytical school to be part of the reason for the supposed link in men between homophobia and unconscious, suppressed homosexual desires. Men with forbidden tendencies were projecting these tendencies onto others. *Reaction formation* is a related concept in which people overreact to a tendency in themselves that they fiercely reject. For this proposition of the homophobia–gay hatred link, there was no evidence until fairly recently. Adams, Wright, and Lohr (1996), researchers at the University of Georgia, conducted a study to investigate experimentally the relationship between homophobia and latent homosexuality, to test the Freudian hypothesis that anxiety about the possibility of having homosexual tendencies might lead to an extreme overreaction and generalized hostility. The research question was this: Would homophobic men show more sexual arousal to homosexual cues than non-homophobic men?

In the laboratory study, a preselected sample of straight males was divided into two groups based on their levels of homophobic responses to items on a questionnaire. *Homophobia* was defined as having an irrational fear and hatred

of homosexuals and a dread of being close to them. When exposed to heterosexual, gay, and lesbian videos, over half the homophobic men evidenced arousal (measured by changes in penile circumference) to videos showing gay male sex. Less than a quarter of the non-homophobic group were similarly aroused. Although this experiment was limited to men and involved a small sample at that, it is the first presentation of scientific evidence on the nature of homophobia. The findings of a close correlation between physiological response to homoerotic stimuli and prejudice against homosexuals are consistent with the psychoanalytical concept of reaction formation. The implications for mental health professionals in these findings are that male clients who project anger and hostility onto gender-nonconforming males and gay men might need help in sorting out their own insecurities concerning sexuality.

Despite the compelling evidence of psychological maladjustment in some homophobic men, we would want to be cautious about relegating homophobia to a medical condition. This actually did happen in New Zealand while the country was embroiled in a homosexual law reform bill campaign. Homophobes were labeled as "sick" and "diseased," and such groups as the Mental Health Foundation called for the treatment of what was perceived as the morbid fear of homosexuals. Ironically, such a focus made the oppression of lesbians and gay men a personal issue, while the political aspects fell to the background (Atmore, 1995). Accordingly, the reform victory that took place was less complete than it might have been otherwise. A further risk is that, in court cases, the homophobic defense might serve as a legal defense in cases of hate crime violence.

Consider Freud's theory and other explanations for prejudice against gays and lesbians as you view the photograph of the antigay protest at the Blessed Sacrament Church in Waterloo, Iowa (see Figure 2.6). A memorial service was scheduled for the murder of Jason Gage, 29, an openly gay man who was beaten to death (Stanton, 2005). The case was reminiscent of the torture and murder of Matthew Shepard several years before. Members of an ultraconservative group led by the Reverend Fred

Figure 2.6. Protest at a gay man's funeral by anti-gay-lesbian cult members from Topeka, Kansas. Photo by Robert van Wormer.

Phelps from Topeka, Kansas, came to town to picket the mourners. Signs declared that gay people and their allies were going to hell. As parishioners arrived for the mass, they were greeted with signs such "AIDS Is God's Curse" and "Matthew Shepard Is in Hell."

Lack of empathy is the second psychological factor in prejudice, one that Danielson (2004) cites as a thinking error. This error in thinking often goes with a distorted self-image. If we believe that others are unfair to us, it reduces our motivation to consider how *they* might feel or might otherwise be affected by unequal treatment. Danielson likens these cognitive distortions to those attributed to the so-called criminal personality that are widely prevalent among prison inmates. Such distortions rebound around lack of insight, victimization, and blame of others; such attitudes proliferate in a pervasive atmosphere of distrust such as within a prison. Fueled by irrational fears and anger, such thinking tendencies can foster a racist mentality and can be used to justify the domination, exploitation, and control of people who differ in some way from the ones in power.

Because lack of empathy is closely associated with prejudice, it stands to reason that some sort of training of people to put themselves in the place of others would go far in alleviating prejudice. The more empathy a person has, the less he or she logically would resort to aggressive action.

Empathy-training activities with children have been shown to reduce their aggression against others considerably. This has been shown in laboratory experiments as well: Students who think they are delivering shocks to another tend to reduce the amount when they learn something personal about the person first. Recall the boys' camping experiments directed by Sherif (1956) and how the boys came to identify with each other and move from seeing the members of the opposing team as "them" to seeing everyone as "us." Aronson believes that a key factor in change is the development of empathy. Aronson's earlier work with children in the schools in situations of racial tension showed that group bonding could be promoted across racial lines through cooperative rather than competitive learning. In the exercise, a biography was given to the children to be read in pieces. Each child in the learning group had only one piece of the whole, and they had to communicate their knowledge to each other. This made each child an expert on one part, so, instead of taunting each other, students encouraged each other to achieve their mutual goals. The technique is called the *jigsaw technique*, and it is seen today as a highly effective practice for improving race relations in desegregated schools.

Xenophobia, a term derived from the Greek word for stranger, is used in modern English to refer to a fear and dislike of foreigners. Such a dislike seems to be relatively universal. Evolutionary psychologists assert that ethnocentrism— the belief that one's culture, nation, or religion is superior to all others—strengthens our group bonds and loyalty to persons "of our own kind" (Tavris and Aronson, 2009). A tendency toward xenophobia relates to dividing the world into "us" and "them" and to actions such as the mass internment of Japanese Americans (but not of German Americans) during World War II and to the fear of dark-skinned Muslim immigrants today. In an extensive survey of Detroit's Arabs and Chaldeans, 15 percent said that they personally had "had a bad experience" following the September 11th, 2001 attacks (University of Michigan, 2004). Abu-Ras and Suarez (2009) similarly found that Muslim men and women who were interviewed felt less safe after 9/11 and experienced a sharp change in the treatment they received following this day of horror. However, there was likely some prejudice against Arab Americans even before 9/11 as revealed in an experiment from the University of Nevada. Kemmelmeier and his team stamped letters with American flags addressed to both a fictitious Christian organization and a made-up Muslim group. The letters were left in public places across town. As one would expect, almost all the Christian letters were forwarded by passersby, but only half of the Muslim letters were mailed (Kemmelmeier & Winter, 2000). We can attribute such findings of discrimination to the tendency to identify with people who seem more like ourselves than different. Following the attack on the New York City Twin Towers the fear factor was clearly at work. Politicians have been able to

capitalize on this factor to sway voters and the general public to support war ventures. Half a century of research has shown that fear is one of the most politically powerful emotions a candidate or politician has to woo supporters to various causes as Drew Westen, author of *The Political Brain: The Role of Emotion in Deciding the Fate of the Nation* (2007), makes clear. Drawing on the power of fear that is evidenced in brain-imaging studies and research from evolutionary psychologists showing that alertness to danger is a carryover from our ancestral past that helped ensure the survival of the species. The memory of fear-provoking events is imprinted in the brain; for this reason, politicians and defense contractors can summon up the memory and associated fear reaction to serve their ends. Awareness of such strategies is essential to defeating them and the xenophobia the fear-mongering sometimes arouses.

Sociological Explanations

Herbert Blumer (1958) viewed racial prejudice through a sociological lens. His approach did not stress socialization into negative feelings about out-groups, in itself a viable approach to prejudice. Rather, Blumer's focus was on feelings of perceived threat by the dominant racial group, on the threat to its status, power, and livelihood should the minority group exercise its rights and enter into competition: This is, at its core, a theory about opportunity. Bobo (1999) builds on this classic model to include the notion of alienation of members of racial minority groups due to their social and economic disadvantages. His prediction is that members of more recently arrived minority groups would have lower expectations and feel less alienated. Their arrival would be resented, however, by the minority groups that had been in residence the longest. Bobo's analysis of extensive survey data from Los Angeles County revealed that, as predicted, both blacks and Latinos perceived greater competitive threat from Asians than from each other and that Asians felt the greatest threat from blacks. Whites felt the greatest threat from Asians and the least from blacks.

Politicians can and do use such feelings of resentment by one class against another and by working-class whites against the "liberal media" and liberal universities and same-sex marriage to get the votes (Frank, 2004). In the 2004 election, for example, people in rural America generally voted against their economic interests (such as obtaining health care) on the basis of "moral values" (see Chapter 5).

So what are the social functions of prejudice? In the best sociological tradition, we might ponder this question as an exercise in critical thinking. Possible functions of prejudice might be to solidify the group and encourage internal bonding. From the perspective of the "powers that be" in society, these power elites can manipulate the public's natural tendencies and thereby shield themselves from opposition to their policies of economic aggrandizement. In this way, the ruling classes can distract members of the general public from the true source of their problems.

Employment practices in hiring have a tremendous economic impact on the community. An extensive sociological investigation of job offers revealed that black men whose job applications stated that they had spent time in prison were only about one-third as likely as white men with similar applications to get a positive response. The research design was reminiscent of the best of the social psychological experiments of decades ago. Sociologist Devah Pager (2005) sent 13 white, black, and Latino men posing as ex-convicts to more than 3,500 job interviews throughout New York City to apply for a broad spectrum of blue-collar jobs. Applicants told employers that they had served 18 months in prison on a drug conviction and had a high school education, and they listed a parole officer as a reference. The study showed clear discrimination against black ex-convicts but revealed no conclusions about the Latino applicants. White ex-convicts, in comparison with black ex-convicts, were discriminated against to a much lesser extent. This finding concerning racial discrimination against poorly educated black ex-convicts shows that it may not be membership in one minority group alone but membership in two or three such categories (race plus class plus ex-convict status) in combination that is pivotal. The effect is a synergistic, or multiplying, one.

Scapegoat theories are sometimes called the frustration-aggression hypothesis or theories of displaced aggression. From this perspective, an individual who is mistreated or suffers averse conditions from one source, such as the school or economic system, may lash out against a less powerful source who just happens to be a convenient target. The term *scapegoat* refers to the ancient Hebrew atonement ritual in which a rabbi recited the sins of the people while placing his hands on the head of a goat. This ritual symbolically transferred the sin to the goat; the goat was then allowed to escape (Aronson, 2008). When large numbers of people are unemployed, scapegoating in the community is common. In Nazi Germany, it was the Jews, homosexuals, Romany (Gypsies), and other groups, the same groups that were scapegoated during the great European plague, the Black Death of 1348 in Europe. In nineteenth-century California it was Chinese immigrants, and in the Deep South, it was black people. A much-cited study in the sociological literature is the classic research on lynchings in the South, correlating the rise in the number of lynchings with a major drop in the price of cotton that year (see Blumer, 1958; Hovland & Sears, 1940; Tolnay & Beck, 1995).

Bullying in the schoolyard can be considered a representation of the same phenomenon on the micro scale. Interestingly, bullying is most common during the difficult junior high years. Youths who are seen as gender inappropriate are common targets (van Wormer, 2006). Group norms have a definite influence on bullying behavior, particularly of the kind that leads to exclusion from or ridicule by the peer group. Bullying, as Goldstein (2002) suggested, is most certainly appropriately viewed as a group process, with the group structural and functional properties shaping its course and consequences.

Blaming the victim has both psychological and sociological aspects, depending on what system level (the individual or society) one is talking about. Pervasive in the American psyche, the phenomenon of blaming the victim is a generic process applied to almost every social problem in the United States (Ryan, 1976). As a traditional ideology related to the work ethic, intellectual, scientific, and religious forces have all historically fed the mythology. Philosophically, the ethos of the Protestant ethic and social Darwinism each contributed to blaming the victim.

Lerner (1980), in *Belief in a Just World*, describes how people turn away from a loser, how vulnerable we are to the suffering of other people. We are vulnerable, however, only to the suffering of a hero. Condemning the victim (of crime, disease, a relationship) is a natural response that we apply without awareness so as to maintain our sense of justice in the world. The seemingly natural tendency is to believe that the unfortunate victim somehow merited his or her fate. This tendency might help explain the popularity of *The Bell Curve* by Herrnstein and Murray (1994). These authors boldly posited that the safety net of welfare aid was the cause of poverty and that the removal of this safety net would be best for all concerned. The thinking that guided this book and that was a force behind "welfare reform" arguably builds on the belief that people basically get what they deserve in life.

When Hurricane Katrina left over 100,000 people stranded in the center of New Orleans, some government officials were ready to cast blame on the individuals who did not heed the mayor's evacuation orders. By the same token, there was an outpouring of help and care by people all across the United States and the world for the displaced population. Read Box 2.2, "Hurricane Katrina and Human Behavior," for a discussion of the human side of one of the worst natural disasters in American history. An important fact to keep in mind as you read Box 2.2 is that in a groundbreaking decision, a federal judge ruled that the Army Corps of Engineers' mismanagement of maintenance at the Mississippi River-Gulf Outlet was directly responsible for flood damage in St. Bernard Parish and the Lower 9th Ward after Hurricane Katrina (Schleifstein, 2009). A second fact to bear in mind is that the lower 9th ward is largely African American and poor and St. Bernard Parish is a working-class area with a high minority population. The negligence of the Army Corps of Engineers in setting up the conditions for devastation of this area east of the Mississippi River is thus tainted with elements of racism and classism as was the treatment of the survivors of the storm who were so slow to be rescued.

Box 2.2 Hurricane Katrina and Human Behavior

Katherine van Wormer and Ardie Blakeney, both New Orleans natives

If you wanted to design a social psychological experiment for the observation of mass behavior, you would be hard pressed to find anything better than a natural disaster of a significant magnitude. Hurricane Katrina was a case in point. Because, unlike in recent wars, the reporters were not embedded, the world got to see the turmoil and suffering close up; the images, repeated in the media endlessly, were unforgettable. Through the prism of Katrina we saw the following:

From a *biological* perspective—people without food or water or sanitation stranded at the Superdome and Convention Centers, water swamping a city, the drowning of people in their houses, the catapulting of caskets from the above-ground tombs (in the St. Bernard Parish cemetery)— all this, the result of global warming, a failed levee-wall system, and poor emergency planning for a storm that was not only foreseeable; it was foreseen.

Psychologically—grief, anger, and heartache; the valuing of loved ones, including pets—over material possessions; victim blaming by some government officials of people who did not, could not evacuate.

Socially—the largest mass movement of people since Southerners fled the ravages of the Civil War; the salience of race and class in determining who got out ahead of the storm and, afterward, who could come back; the Coast Guard and doctors and nurses struggling against incredible odds to rescue people and preserve human life; the strength of family ties revealed in the search after the storm for loved ones; and the nursing of tattered photographs salvaged from the rubble.

Spiritually—the questioning of their religious faith by some, as, in Milton's (1667/2003) terms, people strived to justify "the ways of God to man" (book 1, line 22). Conversely, a resurgence of spiritual faith and gratitude took place in many.

At a social work conference that took place shortly after the disaster, I had the occasion to interview (on November 4, 2005) a survivor of Hurricane Katrina at the recruitment booth of Tulane University. Gail Brown, the admissions and recruitment coordinator for Tulane University School of Social Work, was "manning" the booth and passing out Mardi Gras beads. What an opportunity, I thought, to ask her to speak of her grief and loss. Gail Brown readily consented to an interview but, to my surprise, her mood was very upbeat. Like many others who had suffered housing damage, she still counted her blessings.

> My situation was different than other people because we had some place to go. We were leaving for Natchez, Mississippi, for a birthday party. We thought we would be gone a couple of days. We watched the news reports and realized the storm would be a category 4 or 5. I'm part of east New Orleans, not a part of the lower 9th ward. When we got to return, we found three or four feet of water in the house. And even though the water had receded, mud and slush were on everything; all furniture was turned upside down. We searched for anything salvageable. . . . We had been there 30 years so there are lots of memories. Scrapbooks and pictures were lost. One scrapbook had pictures of us as little children, of picnics we went on. We were able to save a few items from my father from 12 years ago, pictures of vacations we took. My son grew up in that house. I've lost a lot of memories but I'm fortunate. My mother who's 90 years old is alive and well. Furniture to me is stuff. My family and friends are all safe. I feel very fortunate and blessed. We're going to survive. Tulane will survive.

A second testimonial is provided by a hurricane survivor (provided in personal correspondence of September 15, 2008 by Ardie Blakeney) who left the state and decided to become a social worker:

> On August of 2005, my life was directly impacted by the devastating effects of Hurricane Katrina. My family members and I were trapped in our shotgun wooden-frame house for approximately six days. On the first day of the ordeal, the flood waters began to gradually rise into the house. As the waters rose, we tried to place valuable items on the tallest furniture. The water slowly began to recede but we were forced into the attic because the house was still submerged in a considerable amount of water. On the days that followed, we did not receive any assistance from state or government officials. We listened to a battery operated radio and were told by the mayor and other officials that help would arrive soon but this information did not give us any reassurance because on the fifth day help had not arrived and we were running out of food and water. On the sixth day, a rescue boat arrived at the house and we were told to take only small and basic necessities. We were taken to the end of a bridge where we were informed that buses were going to arrive to bring us to a shelter in Texas. The buses that were promised to us never arrived and we were forced to spend the night on the bridge.
>
> On the bridge, there were families with members of all ages from infants to the elderly. The images that I saw were horrific and disheartening. Many of the families set up tent-like areas where their possessions were placed. There were a few portable toilets but they were filthy and were loaded with mounds of fecal material so individuals were forced to relieve themselves in an unoccupied area that was up the road. Food supplies were dropped from helicopters. The women who had babies and toddlers tried their best efforts to make the children as comfortable as possible in the scorching heat on the concrete bridge. My family and I eventually boarded a helicopter and we were given the assistance that we needed.

Printed with permission of
Ardie Blakeney, MSW.

The event of Hurricane Katrina says a lot about people in crisis and what they really care about. Economists weighed the effect of the oil and transportation crisis in the Gulf region as it rippled through the rest of the nation, and political pundits reflected upon the latent cruelty in twenty-first-century capitalism now exposed for the world to see. At the same time, the media in their extensive, unrehearsed interviews revealed that what people cherish the most are not material things at all, but their ties to one another, and their memories. Live coverage of the rescue missions showed this

The Social Psychology of Group Behavior 79

universal reaction. A revelation that seemed to surprise the reporters was the lengths to which many people would go to keep from abandoning their pets. In short, through the catastrophe of a late summer storm, the invisible was made visible— about our social system and about ourselves.

So aptly described by William Faulkner (1936/1964) as "that city, foreign and paradoxical, with its atmosphere at once fatal and languorous, at once feminine and steel-hard" (pp. 108–109) and by tradition as "the city that care forgot," New Orleans, at the time of this writing, faces a second catastrophe. This time the threat is oil. As livelihoods are destroyed, more people will flee. Many will do better elsewhere. But their love of this beautiful but damaged city will stay with them always.

Reference

Faulkner, W. (1964). *Absalom, Absalom!* New York: The American Library. (Original work published 1936).
Milton, J. (2003). *Paradise lost*. London: Penguin Classics. (Original work published 1667).

Progressive Aspects of Collective Behavior

The very aspect of dehumanization in a crowd can lead to an almost intoxicating sense of oneness. Billy Graham Crusades, like earlier tent revivals and the very Mardi Gras gatherings that Billy Graham himself once denounced, can be powerful participant experiences. The thrill of sports events has been equated with our tribal ancestry in our tendency to root like maniacs for our team. Such emotionally charged rooting for one's side makes perfect sense from an evolutionary standpoint, when each clan had members who foraged for food and fought as warriors to protect the group (Cialdini, 1998). Football can be viewed, from the evolutionary perspective, as a metaphor for war, as a territorial struggle with shifting front lines and ball-throwing quarterbacks. Conroy's (2002) graphic depiction of triumph and despair on the basketball court captures this same, almost ineffable phenomenon (see Chapter 3).

Involvement in a protest demonstration, such as one of the periodic marches on Washington, provides a similar sense of solidarity and power. Music and chanting by the crowd bring people of all ages and backgrounds together in wonderful ways. Whether the mobilization of troops is from the left or the right, the sense of exhilaration is one and the same. In rallying and protesting, there is much camaraderie and much humor. Consider this description of "the Raging Grannies," a group of mostly elderly women who use satire and hilarious skits to ridicule government policies of which they disapprove. As described in *Canadian Dimension:*

> With their disarming smells, outlandish hats, arousal of witty, spunky lyrics and outrageous actions, the Raging Grannies have become an institution in protest circles. They tap into an unending stream of creative ideas for songs and stunts to express their views on peace, environment, social and economic justice, women's issues and human rights. They challenge authorities and stereotypes, bring new approach to activism.
> (Roy, 2004, p. 22)

Two social movements that draw on collective organization and social action to achieve positive goals are the sustainable environmental movement and the social-work-led Kensington Action Alliance. Both issues have a great deal of relevance to macro-level social work. The sustainability movement not only strives for replenishment of natural resources and "saving the Earth" but also, beyond that, moves in the direction of a human rights focus—the rights to potable water, nutritious food, and arable land.

The link between sustainability and women's issues has now been recognized. This link was articulated for the first time by an international body at the Population Conference in 1994 and later at the World Summit for Social Development held in Copenhagen in 1995. At these conferences, the terms of the discourse shifted, and the link between women's issues and sustainability was formally recognized.

Not only were women on the agenda, but women also helped to set the agenda (United Nations, 1995; Worldwatch Institute, 2002).

The involvement of women in environmental politics has bolstered this movement considerably. *Ecofeminism* is a term used to describe the link between the "twin oppressions of women and nature within the dominance structure of patriarchal social conventions" (Besthorn & McMillen, 2002, p. 224). Besthorn and McMillen (2002) assert that the dualistic division between humankind and nature is a false one and that famine and overpopulation are rooted in oppressive power structures.

Tying human rights, health, access, lifestyle, and equitable distribution of resources to the natural environment and its conditions and management enhances our concept of social justice (Keefe, 2003). The well-publicized involvement of the world's citizenry at each recent international forum has bolstered the understanding of the human dimension of the environmental crisis. In Rio, for example, 20,000 concerned citizens and environmental activists from around the world outnumbered official representatives by at least two to one. The same was true at Cairo and was even more striking at the Women's Conference in Beijing. At these conferences, members of nongovernmental organizations (NGOs), rather than official delegates, captured the imagination of the world. Many of the organizations represented— for example, Greenpeace, Amnesty International, International Planned Parenthood, and Friends of the Earth—are themselves international. This participation of the world scientific community has been crucial in providing the data to inform the world of the need for renewable energy sources, a very important development to counterbalance the lobbying efforts of oil and coal companies.

Moving from the global to the local, the Kensington Welfare Rights Union (KWRU), based in Philadelphia, has been actively building a mass movement to end poverty since 1991. Social workers involved in the movement see themselves not as advocates but as allies, seeking collaboration in all dimensions of the necessary work in organizing to end economic oppression. One of the highlights of KWRU

was the "New Freedom Bus Ride" that crossed the country. At each stop along the route, local groups joined members of the radical social work organization SWAA (Social Welfare Action Alliance) for rallies and teach-ins to focus on ways the United States was in violation of the U.N. Declaration of Human Rights (Lee, 2001). Today, KWRU is one of more than 50 groups that have come together in a network called the Poor People's Economic Human Rights Campaign. An unprecedented victory was achieved when, under the leadership of two masters of social work students who worked through Pennsylvania State Representative Lawrence Curry, the Curry Resolution was passed. This resolution called for the legislature to hold hearings on economic human rights in the state (see http://www.kwru.org). Social work educator and social activist Mary Bricker-Jenkins (2002) describes the mission as follows:

> We are working to fulfill an often-ignored dream of Martin Luther King—that the poor of America would unite across racial and ethnic lines to become an "unsettling force" that would challenge and change a system that would not feed and clothe and house its people. (p. 8)

Read Boxes 2.3 and 2.4 for an update on KWRU activities and to learn of a unique experience that is offered at the University of Iowa for social work majors. This program is controversial because students are working in an urban area with a high crime rate, and they are helping poor families move into unoccupied, abandoned buildings and take them over.

Box 2.3 *Working With the Kensington Welfare Rights Union: Teaching Social Work Students About Macro-Level Practice*

Sara Sanders, Ph.D, and Joelle Osterhaus, LMSW

The Kensington Welfare Rights Union (KWRU), located in the Kensington district of North Philadelphia, is "a multiracial organization led by poor and homeless families organizing for Economic Human Rights..." (Kensington Welfare Rights Union,

2008). KWRU works to build leaders among the poor to address economic human rights violations. Through projects of survival, such as tent cities, food distributions, political education, as well as protests, lobbying, and acts of civil disobedience, members of the KWRU seek to build awareness about the way that the poor are impacted by local, state, and national economic, educational, and health care policies. KWRU is part of the Poor Peoples Economic Human Rights Campaign (http://www. economichumanrights.org) (PPEHRC) led by Cheri Honkala, a welfare mom who has been organizing around issues of poverty for over 20 years. The PPEHRC is a national organization that works to unite individuals impacted by poverty and organizes around Articles 23, 25, and 26 of the Universal Declaration of Human Rights (right to health care, education, housing, and a living wage). Member organizations of the PPEHRC are present at state and national political campaigns; provide support to unions; hold marches, sit-ins, and protests throughout the country; and work to provide education and a vision on how poverty can be ended in the United States.

Since 2005, the University of Iowa, School of Social Work has offered an immersion experience for social work students to learn about macro-level work and organizing from the Kensington Welfare Rights Union in Philadelphia. Students are taken out of their comfort zone and placed into the lives of the poor and homeless in one of the poorest communities in Pennsylvania and the United States. From the time students arrive in North Philadelphia, they begin to feel the plight of the poor. Drug dealers and prostitutes are positioned on each street corner. Young women with their children hustle down the streets to school, the grocery store, or to catch a bus. Young men loiter outside stores. Old men and women peer outside of their windows wondering what happened to their community that was once booming with factories and jobs. People with vacant eyes slip in and out of fences as they look for heroin and crack. Police drive quickly with sirens blaring, passing drug deals that are occurring in broad daylight to get to a more pressing issue in the community. This is a picture of a community that is struggling. Trash is everywhere, but it seems unnoticed by those living in the community. The streets of North Philadelphia are lined with dilapidated row homes, abandoned lots, and

struggling stores, but also areas that are slowing being torn down to build expensive luxury apartments. It is clear that no one from North Philadelphia will be able to afford these homes, raising questions about where the poor will go when the more affluent move in. There are not businesses in the area that can employ a large number of individuals from the community; instead hundreds of individuals line up for a small number of positions at local fast food stores or gas stations.

As the immersion trip unfolds, students have the opportunity to learn about the lives of the poor from people who are trying to survive in these conditions. Students learn that the main source of income in North Philadelphia is drugs followed closely by prostitution and welfare. Students hear from women and families about what it is like to try to survive on the welfare system and about the daily struggles of trying to feed, cloth, and protect their children given the environment in which they live. The phrase "we fear social workers more than the police" is frequently stated and forces students to consider the amount of power that social workers from child welfare agencies, the public welfare system, and other agencies can have over the lives of the poor. Students hear from individuals addicted to crack and heroin about what it is like to live in an environment where drugs are readily available and are used to medicate feelings of depression and hopelessness that are common in the community. Mothers share about the struggle that their children face in trying to obtain a quality education in schools that spend the majority of their time addressing behavioral issues that occur in and out of the classroom.

Students interface with organizations that support the work of the KWRU. Organizations, such as drug treatment centers, advocacy groups for the disabled, school systems, and other member groups of the PPEHRC from neighboring cities, share about how they also work to address the issues of poverty and the social problems that come with being poor. While each organization has a different focus, all are intertwined to help change the social climate of not only North Philadelphia but also similar communities in the United States. Students witness life in a public school and the struggle of teachers to teach students who have been passed from grade to grade without having the necessary knowledge and skills to move forward. Students observe violence in the halls of the schools and conversely hear from students who are succeeding about how they try to isolate themselves from others who may try to divert them away from their studies and into situations that will get them into trouble. Additionally, students have a chance to interact with community members through food distributions and observe how thankful people are for fresh fruits and vegetables, which are considered delicacies given how expensive they are to purchase. Finally, students also have the opportunity to hear from the police and social workers who are also trying to manage working within the system but also trying to change the system concurrently. Police share that the volume of problems in North Philadelphia is so immense that they often have to prioritize calls, taking the most significant, such as homicides and others issues of violence, first and leaving lesser issues, like dealing drugs and minor assaults, to wait for hours or days. Social workers share the challenges of trying to empower individuals to change their circumstances even though they are impacted by a very disempowering system and environment. Both the police and social workers identify that large-scale community-based interventions are needed to improve the conditions of this community.

Students leave this immersion trip recognizing that the works like that of the KWRU and the PPEHRC campaign are essential to create community-level change. They learn the importance of movements being led by those individuals who are most impacted by the problems. Students see how they can be part of the process of strengthening a community regardless of the type of social work practice they choose to pursue. Also important, students on this immersion experience learn that effective change takes *assessment*, *strategy* with *incremental* steps, *labor*, *time*, and must also involve *evaluation*. Identifying leaders of a problem-affected community, such as the poor, is also essential, as is pulling together a group of both concerned professionals and citizens to serve as both resources and community advocates. Finally, students also learn that while addressing the volume of issues that are present in the communities they may practice in may seem daunting, social issues need individuals like themselves who are concerned and dedicated to working with others to produce systemic change.

Original contribution. Printed with permission of Sara Sanders and Joelle Osterhaus, University of Iowa, Department of Social Work.

Box 2.4 My Immersion Experience: A Student Account

Amanda Miller, MSW

In my senior year of college I had the privilege of traveling to Kensington in North Philadelphia to work with a grassroots welfare rights organization. The Kensington Welfare Rights Union is comprised of poor people who have decided to take a stand against the systematic oppression that is being inflicted due to their economic or minority status. My role as a student was to experience how an agency such as the KWRU works to effect change for individuals, the community, and the state and national governments.

When we left for Kensington, we all knew that the impending experience would impact our lives dramatically, but none of us knew just how profound that impact would be. At the time I left for North Philly I had done some travelling, but I had never been expected to leave my comfort zone. This trip was drastically different. The ten of us students and our three faculty chaperones/facilitators stayed in a dilapidated church with no heat or beds. In the beginning, we, as social work students, were primed and ready to effect change in this community we knew nothing about. As the week went on, and we interacted with community members (both affluent and poor), social service agencies, schools, drug rehab facilities, and police departments, we found that our views of poverty and discrimination were changing. Overt discrimination was not always prevalent, but the effects of discrimination were seen throughout each facet of the poor peoples' lives.

There were several activities that we participated in while we were in North Philadelphia, but a few stood out. We met with a few families that were living in homes that had been abandoned then "taken-over" by the KWRU. I should add that many groups nationwide, such as PPEHRC, are moving people into abandoned homes and are engaged in reclaiming foreclosed properties with their owners. Another major activity for our group was food distribution to people on the streets of Philly. Early in the morning we travelled to what we called the "food docks," a market-like area where restaurants and the like can purchase fresh food each morning. We went to the docks for a different purpose; our intent was to get vendors to provide us food for free, which we would later sort and distribute to individuals on the street in downtown Philly. Because most of the vendors are hard working, pull-yourself-up-by-the-bootstraps kind of men, the trick to obtaining high quantities of fruits and vegetables was to tell the vendors that the food would be used in a soup kitchen. We were warned that if the vendors were told that the food was going to be given away to homeless people on the street, we would be denied food. The plan worked and we loaded vans with fresh food. Later in the day, the food was sorted and taken downtown for distribution. The effect that giving food to people, with no strings attached, had on me was profound; I had been sharing things with individuals my entire life, but never had I met so many people that were taken aback by receiving something as a gift with no expectations on behalf of the giver. The gratitude, and sometimes confusion, was amazing.

While the activities, protests, and meetings in which we partook were fascinating, the really measurable change came when we who had gone on the trip came home. We found ourselves overcome with the desire to begin creating change in our own communities. Perhaps the most important impact was the poor people's perspectives and experiences on our own lives. We, as social work students, had left Iowa with the belief that we were the "good" people. What we learned is that social workers, police, and other public servants in these areas are often feared. The ultimate lesson for me is that while we may be able to effect change at a micro level (through food distribution), and at a mezzo level (through protesting companies that exploit minority workers), we must address the perpetuation of oppression through our practices at a macro level. We as social workers can no longer allow our prejudices, biases, and siloed perspectives to govern our work with people in need. We must address the issue of oppression by thoroughly and critically analyzing the systems in which we practice. Change can happen, poor people can be empowered, and social workers can make this happen. These processes are painful, terrifying, and require mountains of hard work, but ultimately the systemic change required for the betterment of individual lives lies in the hands of those who have the ability to make it happen. And that is why I am a social worker; it just so happens that it took a trip to

a rough neighborhood in Philadelphia for me to understand the impact that one person can have on her environment.

Printed with permission of Amanda Miller, LBSW, MSW student, University of Northern Iowa.

Practice Implications

Why should social workers study these old theories and experiments from social psychology? The reason is that social work is about social change, helping people with problems—with relationships, with addictions—to turn their lives around. Social work is also about working for social justice and social change. The insights from social psychology are invaluable toward achieving these ends. Knowledge of social psychology provides us with a multidimensional understanding of people, of their social constructions of reality, and of the attitudes and behaviors that are learned; these are basic truths that have relevance for both the personal and political dimensions of life.

A theme that runs through a number of the experiments we discussed in this chapter and especially Milgram's shock experiment and Festinger's investigation of dissonance in a religious cult is the theme of self-justification or the tendency to resist losing one's investment in some enterprise. This phenomenon was shown to explain how people who are lured into committing small acts that are illegal can be much more easily lured into committing progressively more serious crimes, or taking harder drugs. Social workers can learn from this insight of Tavris and Aronson (2009) to better understand some of their clients' decisions. But they can also use this same insight to encourage clients to take just one step toward a positive treatment goal such as attending a therapy group. One important principle of motivational enhancement therapy, for example, is that if you can get a client to just take one step in the direction of recovery, the person is increasingly motivated to take another step.

Knowledge about the impact of group cohesion on identity and decision making and how to avoid groupthink, the role of empathy in curbing prejudice, the twin phenomena of bullying and scapegoating, and the tendency to blame the victim and ourselves when we are victimized—all of these are aspects of human nature, the knowledge of which is vital to the pursuit of standard social work goals. There is knowledge here, also, in this summary of findings from the science of social psychology that can help members of the social work profession pursue leadership roles, whether in working outside the system through involvement in a social movement or working within the system through policy planning and initiation.

Summary and Conclusion

Our review of classic studies in social psychology revealed an interesting theme—that, disproportionately, the directors of the small-group experiments and group therapies were refugees from Nazi Germany and/or of Jewish descent. The studies, not surprisingly, concerned obedience and conformity and how far ordinary people would go to obey orders. From Kurt Lewin, whose work and leadership were inspirational to so many others, we learned the effects of authoritarian leadership on the performance of a group of preadolescent boys. Sherif, a student of Lewin, uncovered some truths about conflict and group bonding against an enemy with his summer camp experiments; a major finding was how ruthless competition can lead to dehumanization of the enemy, whereas pulling together for common goals can lead to friendship. The famous studies of American and German soldiers similarly revealed how social cohesion among troops fighting a common enemy is associated with all kinds of acts of heroism in a war.

Lewin inspired Festinger's work as well. When Festinger and his colleagues infiltrated a cult whose members believed the world was coming to an end on a particular day, they had the unique opportunity to study how group members would handle their disappointment when nothing happened. Their study had a lot to say about group cohesion, the importance of togetherness in the face of cognitive dissonance.

From Asch's social perception of the length of lines we saw how norms of conformity affect human behavior and even, in some cases, our visual perception. Milgram's obedience study was, of course, much more dramatic, with its rigged-up shock treatment equipment that made participants think they were torturing someone if they obeyed orders; the majority did so, even though they themselves were under duress. This and Zimbardo's simulated prison experiment have been recently highlighted in mass media reports because of the lessons they contain concerning prisoner abuse such as occurred at Abu Ghraib.

Students of interpersonal behavior can learn much from these mid-twentieth-century studies and from the theoretical model of role playing as contributed by Goffman. Goffman's work is rich in metaphor and lively illustration from the home, mental asylum, and place of work. That his work on impression management is still meaningful today is seen in the popularity of such situation comedies as the British television series *Keeping Up Appearances*, which depicts scenes of social pretense and personal embarrassment when the audience sees a show that was not intended for them. Goffman's study of the person's suffering because he or she has been given a negative label by society led into an autobiographical sketch by a man whose life journey led him all the way from maximum security prison after receiving a death sentence to a successful career in higher education.

A phenomenon of human behavior that has received a substantial degree of study is prejudice. We explored psychological and sociological explanations of the nature of prejudice. Empathy and the lack thereof were discussed as key factors that bear on individual and group collective behavior. Behavior that may arise from strong feelings of prejudice and resentment of persons of another race or religion may take the form of mob activity. On the other hand, from the exhilaration of the crowd can come many positive experiences, whether at a carnival event, a political rally, or a mass protest activity.

The research reviewed in this chapter shows that, whether groups are used for good or ill, the processes are relatively the same. Social norms develop in a group and community, and the nature of the human being is pretty much to "go along with the crowd." So why do people conform to the group and even follow orders that go against their personal beliefs? The best explanation seems to be that we are socialized from the earliest days to like to please people, whereas the peer pressure of schooldays can take its toll on our individuality. The next chapter further explores the small group as an important resource for social workers in enhancing the empowerment and change efforts that are at the core of all social work intervention.

Thought Questions

1. Give some examples of overconformity in everyday life.
2. Discuss some ethical dilemmas for the social science researcher. What kinds of social experiments that were done in the past never could be repeated today? Why not?
3. What is the contribution of Kurt Lewin? How did his background help inspire his research?
4. Discuss some similarities in the lives and work of Lewin and Konopka.
5. What have researchers learned about why soldiers fight?
6. What can we learn from the Robber's Cave experiment?
7. Discuss some of the ethical problems that Festinger's naturalistic study raised. What do the results say about cognitive dissonance?
8. How do the results from Asch's experiment on visual perception hold up in other countries?
9. Relate findings on group conformity to the process of jury deliberation.
10. Briefly describe Milgram's experiment and discuss its implications. Consider the insights provided by Tavris and Aronson.
11. Relate Zimbardo's prison simulation experiment to the scandal at the Iraq detention center at Abu Ghraib.
12. Discuss the basic theme of Goffman's *Presentation of Self in Everyday Life*.
13. Describe some of the turning points in the life of Rudolph Alexander.
14. Discuss the processes of dehumanization and deindividuation, themes that run through this chapter.
15. What are some factors that account for mob violence?
16. How is Allport's understanding of prejudice largely psychological?
17. What are some characteristics of political conservatism as set forth in Jost et al.'s study?
18. How can empathy-training help reduce prejudice? Describe the jigsaw techniques as well.
19. What can we learn from the modern experiment on hiring ex-convicts?
20. Relate scapegoat theory to bullying at school.
21. Discuss the tendency to blame the victim in U.S. society.
22. What are some goals and strategies of the Kensington Welfare Rights Union? React to the personal narrative by the student of her experience doing community organization work. Is this an experience that would appeal to you? Why or why not?
23. Discuss the principle of self-justification in terms of uses in social work practice.

References

Abu-Ras, W., & Suarez, A. (2009). Muslim men and women's perception of discrimination, hate crimes, and PTSD symptoms post 9/11. *Traumatology, 15*(3), 48–63.

Adams, H. E., Wright, L., & Lohr, B. A. (1996). Is homophobia associated with homosexual arousal?. *Journal of Abnormal Psychology, 105*(3), 440–445.

Adorno, T., Frankel-Brunswick, E., Devinson, D., & Sanford, N. (1950). *The authoritarian personality*. New York: Harper & Brothers.

Allport, G. (1981). *The nature of prejudice*. Reading, MA: Addison-Wesley. (Original work published 1954)

Andrews, J. (2001). Group work's place in social work: A historical analysis. *Journal of Sociology and Social Welfare, 28*(4), 45–65.

Andrews, J. (2002, Fall). Reflections on writing a biography of a living hero: Gisela Konopka. *Reflections*, 11–22.

Aron, A., & Aron, E. (2005). Chutzpah: Social psychology takes on the big issues. In J. Nier (Ed.), *Taking sides: Clashing views on controversial issues in social psychology* (pp. 30–37). Dubuque, IA: McGraw-Hill.

Aronson, E. (2008). The social animal (10th ed.). New York: Worth.

Asch, S. (1951). Effects of group pressure upon the modification and distortion of judgment. In M. H. Guetskow (Ed.), *Groups, leadership and men* (pp. 117–190). Pittsburgh, PA: Carnegie.

Atmore, C. (1995). Drawing the line: Issues of boundary and the homosexual law reform bill in New Zealand, 1985–1986. *Journal of Homosexuality, 30*(1), 23–52.

Besthorn, F., & McMillen, D. P. (2002). The oppression of women and natives: Ecofeminism as a framework for an expanded social work. *Families in Society, 83*(3), 221–232.

Blass, T. (2004). *The man who shocked the world: The life and legacy of Stanley Milgram*. New York: Basic Books.

Bloom, R. M. (2005, March 16). *Jury trials in Japan*. (Boston College Law School Faculty Paper No. 41). Retrieved March 14, 2010, from http://lsr.nellco.org/bc/bclsfp/papers/41

Blumer, H. (1958). Race prejudice as a sense of group position. *Pacific Sociological Review, 1*, 3–7.

Bobo, L. (1999). Prejudice as group position: Microfoundations of a sociological approach to racism and race relations. *Journal of Social Issues, 55*(3), 445–472.

Brafman, O., & Brafman, R. (2008). *Sway: The irresistible pull of irrational behavior*. New York: Doubleday.

Bricker-Jenkins, M. (2002). Organizing to end poverty: A story of strategy and tactics. *BCR Reports, 13*(20), 8–9.

Burnes, B. (2004). Kurt Lewin and the planned approach to change: A reappraisal. *Journal of Management Studies, 41*(6), 977–1002.

Burns, R. (1968). To a louse. In J. Bartlett (Ed.), *Familiar quotations* (4th ed) (p. 493). Boston: Little, Brown. (Original work published 1786)

Cialdini, R. B. (1998). *Influence: The psychology of persuasion*. Glasgow, Scotland: Collins.

Caruso, M. (2005, August 4). *Jackson jurors bank on flip-flop*. New York Daily News, p. 1A.

Connolly, M-T. (2002). Federal law enforcement in long term care. *Journal of Health Care Law and Policy, 4*, 230–293.

Conroy, P. (2002). *My losing season*. New York: Doubleday.

Corrigan, P. (2007). How clinical diagnosis might exacerbate the stigma of mental illness. *Social Work, 52*(1), 31–39.

Danielson, P. (2004). Is racial discrimination based on criminal thinking?. In C. Zastrow & L. Kirst-Ashman (Eds.), *Understanding human behavior and the social environment* (6th ed., pp. 194–195). Belmont, CA: Brooks/Cole.

Dixit, J. (2007, January/February). The ideological animal. *Psychology Today, 40*(1), pp. 81–86.

Etzioni, A. (1964). *Modern organizations*. Englewood Cliffs, NJ: Prentice-Hall.

Festinger, L. (1956). *When prophecy fails*. New York: Harper & Row.

Frank, T. (2004). *What's the matter with Kansas?* New York: Henry Holt.

Gladwell, M. (2002). *The tipping point: How little things can make a big difference*. Boston: Little, Brown.

Goffman, E. (1959). *The presentation of self in everyday life*. New York: Doubleday.

Goffman, E. (1961). *Asylum: Essays on the social situations of mental patients and other inmates*. Garden City, NY: Doubleday.

Goffman, E. (1963). *Stigma: Notes on the management of a spoiled identity*. New York: Prentice-Hall.

Goldstein, A. (2002). *The psychology of group aggression*. Hoboken, NJ: Wiley.

Guest, L. (2006). *The trials of Michael Jackson*. Vale of Glamorgan, Wales, UK: Aureus Publishing.

Haney, C., Banks, W. C., & Zimbardo, P. (1973). Interpersonal dynamics in a simulated prison. *International Journal of Criminology and Penology, 1*, 69–97.

Herrnstein, R., & Murray, C. (1994). *The bell curve*. New York: Free Press.

Homans, G. C. (1950). *The human group*. New York: Harcourt, Brace & World.

Homans, G. C. (1961). *Social behavior: Its elementary forces*. New York: Harcourt, Brace & World.

Hovland, C., & Sears, R. R. (1940). Minor studies of aggression: Correlations of economic indices with lynchings. *Journal of Psychology, 9*, 301–310.

Jost, J. T., Kruglanski, A. W., Glaser, J., & Sulloway, F. J. (2003). Political conservatism as motivated social cognition. *Psychological Bulletin, 129*(3), 339–376.

Keefe, T. W. (2003). The bio-psycho-social-spiritual origins of environmental justice. *Critical Social Work, 3*(1), 1–17.

Kemmelmeier, M. & Winter, D. (2000). Putting threat into perspective: Experimental studies on perceptual distortion in conflict. *Personality and Social Psychology Bulletin, 26* (7), 795–809.

Lee, H. (1988). *To kill a mockingbird*. New York: Warner Books. (Original work published 1960)

Lee, J. (2001). *The empowerment approach to social work practice: Building the beloved community* (2nd ed.). New York: Columbia University Press.

Lerner, M. (1980). *Belief in a just world: A fundamental delusion*. New York: Plenum Press.

Lewin, K., Lippitt, R., & White, R. (1939). Patterns of aggressive behavior in experimentally created social climates. *Journal of Social Psychology, 10*, 271–301.

Milgram, S. (1963). Behavioral study of obedience. *Journal of Abnormal and Social Psychology, 67*, 371–378.

Milgram, S. (1974). *Obedience to authority*. New York: Harper & Row.

Pager, D. (2005). Double jeopardy: Race, crime and getting a job. *Wisconsin Law Review, 2005*(2), 617–660.

Payne, M. (2005). *Modern social theory* (3rd ed.). Chicago: Lyceum Books.

Roethlisberger, F., & Dickson, W. (1939). *Management and the worker*. Cambridge, MA: Harvard University Press.

Roy, C. (2004, November/December). The Raging Grannies. *Canadian Dimension, 37*(6), 22–26.

Ryan, W. (1976). *Blaming the victim*. New York: Random House.

Schleifstein, M. (2009, November 19). Corps' operation of MR-GO doomed homes in St. Bernard, Lower 9th ward, judge rules. *New Orleans Times-Picayune*. Retrieved from http://www.nola.com/hurricane/index.ssf/2009/11/post_16.html

Sherif, M. (1956). Experiments in group conflict. *Scientific American, 195*, 54–58.

Shils, E. A., & Janowitz, M. (1948). Cohesion and disintegration in the Wehrmacht in World War II. *Public Opinion Quarterly, 12*, 280–292.

Stanton, J. (2005, April 10). Community fights back at Gage protesters. *Waterloo/Cedar Falls Courier*, p. 1A.

Stouffer, S. (1949). *The American soldier: Combat and its aftermath*. Princeton, NJ: Princeton University Press.

Tavris, C., & Aronson, E. (2007). *Mistakes were made (but not by me)*. Orlando, FL: Harcourt.

Thrasher, F. M. (1936). *The gang: A study of 1,313 gangs in Chicago*. Chicago: University of Chicago Press. (Original work published 1927)

Tolnay, S., & Beck, E. M. (1995). *A festival of violence: An analysis of the lynching of African Americans in the American South 1882–1930*. Champaign: University of Illinois Press.

Toseland, R., & Rivas, R. (2001). *An introduction to group work practice* (4th ed.). Boston: Allyn & Bacon.

Ulsperger, J., & Paul, J. (2002). The presentation of paradise: Impression management and the contemporary nursing home. *Qualitative Report, 7*(4). Retrieved from Nova Southeastern University website: http://www.nova.edu/ssss/QR/QR7-4/ulsperger.html

United Nations. (1995). *The world's women 1995*. New York: United Nations Development Programs.

University of Michigan. (2004, July 29). University of Michigan, Detroit Arab American Study. *University of Michigan News Service*. Retrieved from http://www.umich.edu/news/index

van Wormer, K. (2006). *Introduction to social welfare and social work: The U.S. in global perspective*. Belmont, CA: Brooks/Cole.

Waters, N. (2004). *Does jury size matter? A review of the literature*. San Francisco: Administrative Office of the Courts.

Westen, D. (2007). *The political brain: The role of emotion in deciding the fate of the nation*. Cambridge, MA: Public Affairs.

Wilson, S. (2009, December 2). Obama: U.S. security is still at stake. *Washington Post*. Retrieved from http://www.washingtonpost.com/wp-dyn/content/story/2009/12/01/ST2009120100456.html

Wong, L., Kolditz, T., Millen, R., & Potter, T. (2003). Why they fight: Combat motivation in the Iraq war (Strategic Studies Institute Monographs). Retrieved March 1, 2006, from the U.S. Army website: http://www.army.mil/professionalwriting/volumes/volume1/september_2003/9_03_1.html

Worldwatch Institute. (2002). *State of the world 2002*. New York: Norton.

Zimbardo, P. (2004, May 17). Pathological power of prisons: Parallel paths at Stanford and Abu Ghraib. Retrieved, from http://antiwar.com/orig/zimbardo.php?articleid=2590

The Small Group as a Social System

Thomas Keefe and
Katherine van Wormer

*There is a strength in the union even
of very sorry men.*
—HOMER

The Iliad

With our curiosity and ability to make things, humankind has adapted to and inhabited many of the Earth's diverse physical environments. However, as important as these natural environments have been, the ever-present and ubiquitous environment of human evolution has been the small group. Whether in the form of an arboreal company of primates, an early hominid troupe, or a hunting and gathering band, the small group of extended families has existed in conjunction with both nature and human nature. Although this notion ultimately may not be provable, we must wonder to what extent our vision, hearing, sense of smell, recognition of the human face, and apparatus for speech are the selected qualities of a social environment consisting of a small group of our own kind. If, for the period of human evolution, the small group—the first one of which is the one we are born into—has been important in shaping who we are, there may be cause for concern if the social and economic forces of our contemporary historical period prevents or stunts this aspect of human experience. George Homans, the social scientist and systems theorist who pioneered the study of the small group (1950), noted that forces of modern civilization, such as centralized bureaucracy, continually tear at the cohesiveness of the small group but that the group still remains at the core of social experience.

Groups, as we have seen, do have a powerful influence on human behavior. Think back to the small-group experiments and participant observations of researchers such as Lewin and his colleagues (1939), Asch (1952), and Festinger (1956; see Chapter 2). Such classical studies of individual and group conformity graphically illustrated this powerful influence in real-life situations. In recognition of the insights provided in these pioneering studies, it is no surprise that social workers and others concerned with helping people to modify their behavior in some way have drawn on the power of the group.

The Social Work Dictionary defines a group as a "collection of people, brought together by mutual interests, who are capable of consistent and uniform action" (Barker, 2003, p. 185). The small group is the primary formal or informal unit of social organization. Entities as diverse as families and corporate boards can be seen as small groups. Social workers might be involved with community activist groups, student organizations, church social action committees, or formal or informal networks of people working for social goals, such as corporate boards, professional organizations, or staffs of political organizations. In addition, knowing the ways in which groups can influence social decisions of communities can lead to meaningful group social action. Social action groups that might consist of professionals working to strengthen relevant legislation or involve agency workers and clients in a joint campaign can empower members in several ways. Kirst-Ashman (2007) lists the following five ways that such groups are empowering: through increasing understanding of the issues; in inspiring others to act; through consciousness raising; by providing mutual support; and in simply working together as a team. When in a public setting, people often feel more comfortable as a member of a group than being alone (see Figure 3.1 which shows children sitting together as they enjoy a celebration). Joining others in group activities can lead to a lot of fun and even some dare

devil behavior as seen in the photo of the young men in Figure 3.2.

Perhaps more familiar to readers of this book is the social worker's role in conducting treatment groups. Treatment groups vary greatly in process and structure; included in this category are support groups designed for people who are coping with a certain disease such as AIDS, therapy groups to help members with emotional problems, substance abuse treatment groups, and bereavement groups.

Task groups often form in pursuit of a certain goal, such as preparation for an agency site visit by an accreditation dean or funding source. Social workers also periodically meet for client staffing and to attend to administrative matters. Finally, in their private capacity, social workers might participate as members of self-help groups such as Alcoholics Anonymous (AA) or Parents, Family, and Friends of Lesbians and Gays (PFLAG). There are literally thousands of such self-help groups across the country that provide critical social support to persons who might otherwise be trying to function in isolation (White & Madara, 2002).

Understanding small-group structure, processes, and development is crucial to social

Figure 3.1. Children at a Cinco de Mayo celebration. Children of the same age often relate to each other in groups. Photo by Rupert van Wormer.

work practice in that it boosts practice skills. In addition to the classical and important theory that harks back to the settlement house movement and to community leaders such as Jane Addams, social scientists, psychologists, group psychotherapists, group social workers, managers, coaches, and political activists are among the contributors to the vast base of knowledge and skills related to work with small groups.

The theme of this chapter is the study of the structure and function of the small group—the group as a social system. Moving from the general to the specific, we look at such social phenomena as groupthink, the organizing strategies of the megachurch, and the contribution of self-help groups. Readings from a former member of a religious cult, on group empowerment practice, and visits to 12-Step meetings highlight the chapter. What we present here is not a comprehensive survey of the vast body of research, knowledge, and skills, but rather what we hope is a useful distillation from practice experience for beginning work with groups at multiple levels.

Compared with other branches of the helping professions, the argument can be made that the skills of group work come quite naturally to members of the social work profession. First, because of their background in systems theory and their grounding in principles of the person and the environment in dynamic interaction, social workers tend to think in the plural rather than singular in terms of relationships. Second, client behavior is often understood as occurring not in a vacuum but in terms of forces in the social environment. The social work perspective, in short, can be conceived of as a collective or group perspective.

Why Study the Small Group?

In contrast to micro practice, which involves working with an individual one-on-one to enhance his or her social functioning, mezzo, or micro-macro practice, is oriented toward the family and other small groups. Group work is a major part of social work, and social work practitioners need to understand human behavior in groups for several reasons. First, the agencies in which practitioners work often expect staff to counsel their clients in a group setting. This is done for reasons of cost-effectiveness and efficiency, as well as for therapeutic reasons. Second, the group leader can acquire a wealth of information about how the client carries himself or herself in a social setting, how

Figure 3.2. Some groups form spontaneously, such as this one at the Seattle Gas Works Park. Photo by Rupert van Wormer.

he or she relates to a variety of types of people. Self-destructive patterns, for example, can be observed as the group leader sits back and watches. Third, social workers, in the political aspect of their work—community organizing, for example—typically work through group meetings to gather information and to build support for a cause or action. Through such empowering experiences as consciousness raising, the group process helps members, individually and collectively, become aware of mutual interests, goals, and the need for social change. Fourth, and this is the matter that concerns us here, the group process as a therapy device is highly productive in effecting individual change and encouraging mature decision making. Treatment groups provide vicarious learning opportunities and peer feedback that cannot be replicated in individual treatment (Toseland & Rivas, 2001).

A Psychodynamic Approach

In his groundbreaking book, *The Theory and Practice of Group Psychotherapy*, now in its fifth edition, psychiatrist Irvin Yalom (2005) identified 11 primary elements or curative or therapeutic factors involved in therapeutic change through group therapy. They are as follows:

1. Instillation of hope through support and encouragement
2. Universality, or awareness that one is not alone in feeling a certain way or in having a particular problem
3. Imparting information, the educational factor that is often singled out by participants as the aspect of group therapy that was most valuable
4. Altruism, or helping one another
5. The corrective recapitulation of the primary family group, or reenacting roles played in one's family of origin and improving on them
6. Development of socializing techniques, or helping people through feedback and role plays to develop social skills

7. Imitative behavior, or the unconscious process in which group members model the behavior of others
8. Interpersonal learning, or learning through the relationship that develops
9. Group cohesiveness, or sense of unity, that ideally takes place over time
10. Catharsis, or emotional release
11. Existential factors related to the here and now of the group process

In his review of the literature on groups and his own follow-up research, Yalom found that inpatient group members put more of a premium on instillation of hope than did members of outpatient groups, presumably because their situations were more desperate. Groups of elderly patients, not wanting to think too much of the future, placed the highest value on existential factors, or those intrinsic to the group process at that moment. The provision of information was singled out by partner abuse members and participants in groups for spouses of persons with life-threatening illness.

Yalom's ninth element, cohesiveness, is singled out by Goldstein (2002) as primary among the characteristics of group development, both in determining the nature of interaction patterns and in the group's success in achieving its goals. Cohesiveness can be said to occur when group members are highly attracted to the group, not only feeling close to individual members but also, beyond that, to feeling bonded to the group as a whole. The group literature, as summarized by Goldstein (2002), indicates that group cohesiveness may be enhanced by rigorous initiation rituals for entry into the group (best exemplified by delinquent gangs and fraternities and sororities), status homogeneity, acceptance by others, cooperative interaction, similarity in values and attitudes, and an externally imposed threat. The latter characteristic is one of the most interesting. Unity in the face of opposition ensures that emotions are strong and that pressure toward conformity within the group is high. A strong sense of "we're all in this together" emerges. So strong is the group bonding in combat situations, for example, that members of the fighting unit will fight to the death, and survivors may feel that bonding throughout their life-times (Stouffer, 1949). On a less extreme scale, politically focused groups, whether of the left or the right, often divert a great deal of emotional energy in reporting and reacting to external threats, real or imagined.

Yalom's notion of the therapy group as social microcosm is helpful in our understanding of its power and potential to be used or abused. Yalom's basic argument is that the treatment group is not only real but given the depth of the relationships that develop and the personal level of the sharing, the therapy group can be far more real than the world out there. As Yalom elaborates:

> The group attempts to identify and eliminate social, prestige, or sexual games; members go through vital life experiences together; the reality-distorting facades are doffed as members try hard to be honest with one another. How many times have I heard a group member say, "This is the first time I have ever told this to anyone"? These people are not strangers. Quite the contrary: they know one another deeply and fully. Yes, it is true that members spend only a small fraction of their lives together. But psychological reality is not equivalent to physical reality. Psychologically, group members spend infinitely more time together than the one or two meetings a week when they physically occupy the same office. (2005, p. 47)

The therapy group serves as a microcosm in that, through the feedback participants receive for their positive and maladaptive behaviors, members are made aware of how they come across to others. The more real and emotional the group experience, notes Yalom, the more potent its impact. By risking new ways of being with others in the group, the client is enabled to carry them over in his or her social environment and, in the same way, to extinguish negative or conflict-generating behaviors.

Keep Yalom's therapeutic factors in mind as we move into a more abstract level of analysis and explore the dynamics of the group process. Because one of the skills useful in facilitating

groups involves understanding their structure and processes, we now look to sociological insights into the general shape and workings of small groups. After examining the stages of growth and development that small groups typically pass through, we examine some principles of group leadership.

Small-Group Structure and Process

One of the characteristics of small human groups is that they tend to organize themselves into particular structures. Both clinicians and scientists have noted the propensity of small groups to structure themselves hierarchically. Over half a century ago, Bales (1950), in his scientific observation of small-group interaction, noted that one dimension of group social structure is the relative status of group members. Much of what happens in small groups is conditioned by the stratification of its membership.

Consequently, skillful work with groups requires the understanding of the dynamic of hierarchical ordering of members in the group's life. At first, the notion of human groups naturally stratifying into hierarchies may seem alien to persons who hold values of equality and democratic governance. Yet if we look closely at the determinants of group hierarchy formation, we find in this natural propensity the source of these very values.

Internal Group Hierarchy

Two members of a group may continually argue. The topic or "bone of contention" may be any of a thousand things. But behind the literal content of their argument may be an interpersonal dynamic. This is the jockeying for position in the status ordering of the group. Sometimes the decision of the group to go with one person's point of view rather than another's may help to determine the interpersonal outcome of the relative status of the two members. Sometimes the leader of the group will choose whose point will prevail and at the same time determine the relative status of the two members. Much of the process or interaction that takes place in small groups can be seen as motivated by the quest for position in the hierarchy of the group.

Our experience with small groups suggests that the hierarchical ordering is fluid and seldom a rigid ladder or pecking order. But we must be conscious of this phenomenon if we are to fully understand much of what is taking place in the groups we work in and with. Leaders tend to hold positions at the top of the status order. Sometimes there are coalitions of individuals who constitute the higher status members. Adherence to group norms and working toward group goals help to ensure a member's place in the group's hierarchy. The talents and resources that a member has that assist the group in meeting the environmental demands also seem to contribute to a member's relative status. New members are checked out by old members as to the characteristics they have that will be compatible with the group's norms and goals. New members also may constitute a threat to the ordering of the membership.

Leaders usually have a vested interest in maintaining the status quo in their groups. A radical reordering of the group hierarchy may bring a reordering of leadership as well. Hence, leaders are seen to resolve disputes and act in ways that help to maintain group order. The advantage to the group of this traditional structuring of the membership is the efficient ordering of group tasks, responsibilities, and rewards. (See Figure 3.3 which captured a moment of consultation among members of a professional team.) A basketball coach had best know his or her starting lineup before the season is well under way so that he or she may put the best team players on the court to face the opponents. The coach must also know the virtue of having some stability in the lineup to allow players to learn each other's capabilities and shortcomings.

Hierarchy, Equality, and Democratic Functioning

Where in this hierarchical view of the small group is there room for egalitarian and democratic values? Are such values really useful to the functioning of small groups?

Let us return to the example of the basketball team. Sometimes the team will face opponents of very diverse talents. One night they may face a tall, skilled team that will play slowly and deliberately. On another night they may face a shorter, quicker team that will run

Figure 3.3. Social services leaders consult at an open-house presentation for the opening of a new supportive housing complex, Seattle. Photo by Rupert van Wormer.

the length of the court on most plays. If the team can change its lineup and put the players most likely to cope with the different opponents on the court, they may stand a better chance of winning than if they simply started the same players each night. In short, the team has to adapt to its changing environment. Sometimes the leadership is so restrictive, however, that the team is unable to adapt to changing circumstances; sometimes the only way to achieve one's goals is to overthrow the formal leadership and rely on a folk or internal leader.

In his autobiography of a harsh Southern upbringing, *My Losing Season*, Pat Conroy (2002) presents an astute study of the inner workings of a fiercely competitive basketball team at the Citadel. This coming-of-age story could also be taken as a portrait of the small group in action, a group under the *formal* authority of an authoritarian and bungling coach (Mel) but under the *informal* leadership of Conroy, the team captain. In the following selection, Conroy experiences a turning point in the sudden realization that to find his voice, he must defy his coach's orders:

> In the circle of hell where we now sat in agony, I watched my broken teammates trying to gather inward strength that could combat the awesome forces of Mel's negativity. Our coach could yell and rage and throw chairs and yell obscenities and make us run laps until we dropped and suicide drills until we vomited—but in the well of this existential moment among boys suffering from the ferocity of Mel's pitiless charge, I heard a voice scream out inside me, an actual voice—embryonic and unsure—cry out from within me in alarm: "Mel can destroy us and loathe us and demean everything about us, but he cannot and never will coach us. He cannot make us into a team. He cannot teach us to be the thing we need to be."
>
> With this strange and disloyal insight in a gym in New Orleans, I think I was born to myself in the world. That night in New Orleans a voice was born inside me, and I had never heard it before in my entire life. (pp. 186–187)

As Conroy defies the coach, the team emerges as a team: "Wildly, we played that night because of our wordless, ineffable, and unstealable love of each other" (p. 187). In analyzing Conroy's team, the Green Weenies, as a social system, we see how as a whole, in one glorious defiant night, united against their enemy—the opposing team—but more so against their coach, team members rose to a victory that went beyond the numbers on the scoreboard. From a systems perspective, their solidarity can be seen as a product of external conflict, internal bonding, and a cooperation that drew on the individual talents of all the members. What we can learn from this illustration is the principle of adaptation; often the group has to break through a rigidity in pattern in order to adapt to circumstances. Further, we can learn from Conroy's detailed narrative that sometimes goals that are achieved are not the tangible, manifest goals at all but something that was not even anticipated at the outset. So it is that, paradoxically, the losing season became not a losing season at all.

In contrast to the hierarchal structure of the traditional sports team, Schriver (2010) describes an alternative perspective on leadership that recognizes the potential for anyone in the group to be a leader. This style of leadership relies on the relevant expertise of individual members to pursue group goals and is called *functional* leadership. A rotating rather than a fixed structure of leadership serves to break down the reliance on one person for decision making. Self-help groups such as Alcoholics Anonymous (AA) effectively use a rotating style to reduce tendencies toward hierarchy.

Schriver (2010) further turns our attention to the alternative paradigm thinking embodied in the teachings of feminism. Feminist philosophy replaces hierarchy with equality and replaces notions of "power over" with a position of shared power. The stress on personal empowerment requires the contributions of all group members. The American Indian customary use of the "talking stick," which gives the floor to the holder of the stick or feather as it is passed around the group of people seated in a circle, is a highly effective equalizing strategy that has been widely adopted by discussion and treatment groups of various sorts.

Internal and External Systems

In his classic observations of groups, George Homans detected two overlapping systems at work. The first is an external system of sentiment, activity, and interaction aimed primarily at the environment of the group that enables the group to survive. The second is an internal system of sentiment that group members develop toward one another in the process of the group's interactions (Homans, 1950). Crudely stated, the external system is concerned with the tasks of the group, and the internal system is concerned with the social and emotional factors among group members. These systems interact and mutually influence each other.

Leaders can develop within each of the two systems. A task leader may set goals, keep the members on task, or help the group stay focused. Social workers call this *gatekeeping*. A socioemotional leader may provide a model for sentiment and abet the group's morale. Sometimes the task leadership and the socioemotional leadership can come from the same person. Sensitivity to the two systems within a small group can both facilitate the understanding of what is going on and help the group work toward its goals.

Group Norms

Small groups develop certain patterns and expectations of behavior for their members. Homans (1950) observed that industrial work groups develop expectations about the level of output of manufactured product expected from each worker. When a worker exceeded this level of output, he was open to group censure for violating the group's norms. As Homans observed, "A norm, then, is an idea in the minds of the members of a group, an idea that can be put in the form of a statement specifying what the members or other men should do, ought to do, are expected to do, under given circumstances" (1950, p. 123). Homans saw norms as affecting the member's social ranking. Group norms and individual member's needs and desires to match the behavior, attitudes, and perceptions of the group are powerful determinants of human behavior. Although some group

members are easily intimidated by the norms that arise and pick up on them, other, less sensitive souls grow more aware of them in the breach. A recent example happened in a small adult Sunday-school class that met regularly. (This example, provided by van Wormer, occurred at a southern Unitarian church.) Although it was clear to all those present that one newly transgendered member, Roseanne—the only woman who was really dressed in truly feminine attire, in fact—was now an identified woman, one elderly class member inadvertently (or stubbornly) referred to her as "he." Roseanne firmly said, "I want to talk to you later," and then took her aside and straightened the matter out. In this way, one politically incorrect individual was brought in line with the group norms.

The specific nature of the roles and norms that structure a group may serve either to maintain power inequality and restrict diversity or, conversely, to guide groups toward acceptance and respect of all the members (Schriver, 2010). Sensitivity to the processes of small groups enriches our understanding and effectiveness when working in and with small groups.

Group Processes

Scientists and clinicians who have studied and worked with small groups have observed a variety of behaviors of individual group members and of the membership of groups as a whole that seem to augur stability and maintenance of the group. These traits are most apparent when the group has entered the working stage. From a systems perspective, group members can be seen to be engaged in constant interaction through body language or verbally giving feedback to others. Such responses seem to have the effect of restoring the group to a kind of homeostasis and stability when a disruption occurs. When group members develop more anxiety than they can sustain, one member may help relieve the tension by commenting on the interaction in such as way as to reduce the anxiety to tolerable levels so that the group can continue to function. The most common such response is the collective laughter that comes after and relieves a moment of tension. When one member begins to monopolize the group, participants might provide helpful feedback through restless body language. The person who is sensitive to the needs of others will pick up this feedback unconsciously and beckon to someone else to speak. Sometimes, however, with involuntary clients, if too little structure is provided, the group turns into a gripe session. In such cases, the leader has to intervene quickly to put a stop to such negativism before it becomes a pattern that is hard to break.

Transference

Psychotherapists, especially those of the psychodynamic school, have long observed the phenomenon of transference (Corey, 2008). Originally, Sigmund Freud identified transference neurosis as the regressive behavior observed in his patients in which they would hold intense feelings about him as the therapist that they had originally experienced toward their parents (Freud, 1924/1975). Clinicians have observed that members of therapy groups sometimes react to one another in distorted ways. They see traits in another member through the mechanism of projection (Corey, 2008). Or they react with intense feelings that are partly based on similarities between group members and important persons in their pasts. The roles that group members choose to play or unwittingly end up playing are often reminiscent of the way they once interacted with family members. Yalom (2005), reflecting on his years of group psychotherapy experience, observes:

> There is an enormous variety of patterns: some members become helplessly dependent on the leaders, whom they imbue with unrealistic knowledge and power; others blindly defy the leaders, who are perceived as infantilizing and controlling the others; others are wary of the leaders, whom they believe attempt to strip members of their individuality; some members try to split the cotherapists in an attempt to incite parental disagreements and rivalry; some compete bitterly with

other members, hoping to accumulate units of attention and caring from the therapists; others expend energy in a search for allies among the other patients, in order to topple the therapists; still others neglect their own interests in a seemingly selfless effort to appease the leaders and the other members. (p. 15)

To some extent transference is present in all small groups. Although it is all too convenient to attribute all otherwise unexplainable feelings or behaviors among group members to transference, it is worth keeping in mind as a possible dynamic in group interaction. The group leader might address this phenomenon directly in a therapy group. In a support or task group, the leader might approach this issue in a tentative way out of concern for the group's effectiveness and well-being. Helping a member or members to check out their perceptions with others in a deliberate way can alleviate problems or problematic feelings born of past relationships and carried into the group.

Acting Out

In our experience, behavior that has the characteristics of being destructive and repetitive and that is not under the conscious control or will of the person carrying it out often occurs in therapy groups. When it does occur, it is a problem for the group. Such annoying or even antisocial behavior can be called *acting out* because it is seen as springing from conflicted psychological tensions (Yalom, 2007). Hence, when a group member repeatedly is late to the meetings and enters in a disruptive way, or when a member persistently fails to carry out tasks vital to the group's goals after promising to do so, he or she may be seen as deliberately acting out.

Because the behavior is not under rational control, the person acting out cannot usually respond to reasoned arguments or suggestions. Unless the small group in which the behavior is taking place is a psychotherapy group, the person who is engaging in this destructive behavior is best referred for professional counseling. If this is not possible, reassignment to tasks unrelated to the person's conflicts or a new role for the person in the group may be in order. Acting-out behavior is nettlesome and may prevent the group from being effective in achieving its goals. Sometimes small groups will ostracize or isolate individuals whose behavior is so destructive that it harms the group purpose. So although tolerance is the sign of a group with a flexible, adaptive structure, there are limits to tolerance—most especially when the existence and major goals of the group are defeated by acting-out behavior.

It is often interesting when working with a group to have the various members describe the roles that they play in the group. Typical labels that might emerge are as follows: the information giver, the enabler, the initiator, the clown, the true confessor, the confronter, the cynic, and the nurturer. After members have claimed their roles, an interesting task is to explore how the roles played today are carryovers from those played in the family.

From a psychodynamic perspective, the group leader might use transference and countertransference (the therapist's tendency to emotionally respond to a client based on interactions with a significant individual in his or her past) reactions to help members work through unresolved conflicts. The group leader, for example, might interpret the behavior of two group members who are struggling for the leader's attention as unresolved sibling rivalry (Toseland & Rivas, 2001). As members develop insight into their own behavior, they are on the road to changing behavior patterns outside the group as well.

In the traditional psychotherapy group, the leader, who typically plays the role of expert, may take advantage of the situations that arise naturally in the group to help clients work through unfinished business from long ago. Yalom (2005) refers to the therapy group as providing a vast array of "recapitulative possibilities" (p. 15), as, for example, in the case of Betty, a woman who revealed her resentment at sharing the group leader with others. Yalom saw the group format as particularly valuable in allowing the client's own insecurities and craving for personal attention to emerge. This format provided Betty with the chance to test out new behaviors as her old patterns were challenged and to relive the patterns "correctively."

Solutions-focused group therapy is not concerned with issues such as transference because it is geared toward preparation for future living, not on bringing up problems. Corey (2008) draws a sharp contrast between the psychodynamic approach as that advocated by Yalom and an approach based on solutions. Central to brief solutions-focused group therapy are the following precepts:

- Group members, not the group leader, are the experts; the group leader is more of a consultant than a therapist.
- The past should only be addressed in terms of ways group members were able to overcome difficulties; otherwise members are apt to get mired in unresolved past conflicts.
- Empathy for the group member, who is not generally referred to as a client or patient, is favored over assessment and use of labels.
- Goals should be set by individual members that are achievable and short term; the group process is short term.
- The group process is grounded in the assumption that members are resilient and can take control of their own lives.
- In sum, a focus on personal resources, strengths, and possibilities should help motivate members to move toward positive change.

The strengths-based philosophy behind the solutions approach is revealed in the questions asked. These questions are designed to produce responses that move the individual and group into positive directions, questions about successes and joys. Corey offers this illustration: The leader may start the group session by asking, "Who wants to begin today by telling us what has gone better for you since our last meeting?" (p. 430).

Scapegoats and Out-Groups

It is frequently observed that political leaders can consolidate the support of their followers if they can direct attention toward an enemy.

An enemy constitutes a threat to the nation, the team, or the group. Patriots rally to protect, whereas persons seen to undermine the status quo, especially in threatening times, are subversives.

As we mentioned earlier, the membership hierarchy in a small group can serve the group's processes. From our practice observations of small groups, we offer as working hypotheses some dynamics associated with scapegoats and out-groups. An external threat can cause the group to rally as individual members subordinate their own agendas to help meet the needs of the group. When this consolidates the current status quo, the leader's position, as well as the positions of other group members, is secured.

Identifying a scapegoat within a group can have a similar function. A scapegoat is the target of the group's rage, hostility, or teasing (Corey, 2008). Often the characteristics that group members do not find attractive in themselves are projected on the scapegoat, who is then persecuted by the group for harboring them. But behind the convenient psychological payoff to group members of treating a member as a scapegoat, the group's response serves a deeper social function.

A scapegoat is not always the most inept member. Sometimes it is a person who has considerable ability or resources relative to other group members who also violates or flaunts the group's norms. Such a person may constitute a threat to each member's status in that he or she could displace any member should he or she suddenly conform to the norms of the group. That person might also be a threat to the group leadership if he or she were not a scapegoat. So in an ironic way the scapegoat threatens the group's pecking order but also forces it to consolidate and support the leader. If a small group that engages in scapegoating behavior can come to an understanding of this pattern of behavior, it will develop a more conscious understanding of its own structure and dynamics. We can postulate that a group that is more tolerant and less inclined to scapegoat members is one with a flexible structure. In any case, the group leader can curb scapegoating through open and honest discussion of the process. The targeted individual can be encouraged to share his or her feelings with the group. Empathy can be encouraged thereby.

Groupthink

Excessive emphasis on group conformity can interfere with critical thought and lead to susceptibility to the phenomenon of groupthink. Groupthink arises when one or two members express certain opinions and others go along without voicing disagreement (Barsky, 2010). The group process may encourage this outcome that suppresses dissent in the interests of group cohesion and to avoid conflict. On the subject of foreign policy that backfired, Janis (1982), who first labeled the process, identified the problem as stemming from mindless conformity or groupthink. Research into group dynamics shows, as Janis indicates, the tendency of groups to stereotype out-groups and to take a riskier course of action than any individual member would do. Parallels in contemporary foreign policy are evident. One has only to read the history that is currently emerging on the decision to go to war against Iraq. (See, for example, Bob Woodward's *Plan of Attack*, 2004; Richard Clarke's *Against All Enemies: Inside America's War on Terror*, 2004; or the British Government's secret document, the "Downing Street Memo," Manning, 2005. Together these sources relate how the decision to go to war in Iraq was made first, then the facts "fixed around" that decision.) Consider recent decisions pertaining to foreign policy from the standpoint of Janis's criteria:

▶ Belief in the group's inherent moral superiority
▶ Sharing stereotypes, demonizing the enemy
▶ Examining few alternatives or contingency plans for any action
▶ Protecting the group from negative views or information that would contradict members' basic assumptions
▶ Having the illusion of invulnerability

Schriver (2010) adds to the list:

▶ Direct social pressure placed on a member who argues against the group's shared beliefs

> Members' self-censorship of their own dissenting thoughts

Groupthink was graphically exemplified in Festinger's (1956) *When Prophecy Fails*, which illustrates how group members were pushed to show their faith in the group by quitting their jobs (see Chapter 2). Sometimes the leaders deliberately create a situation for groupthink so that they can use the group for their own selfish ends. Some religious cult movements, for example, have this characteristic.

Cults

Perhaps the most notorious cult in recent memory is the one that led to the mass slaughter of 900 people at Jonestown, Guyana. People joined this religious cult, which started in Indianapolis, when the religious leader, Jim Jones, provided food, clothing, and shelter to poor people of all races. Jones' preaching was mesmerizing and the group rapidly grew. After the magazine exposé that revealed Jones was a drug addict who performed fake healings and tricked his flock out of their savings, he took hundreds of members to Guyana and established a communist-style collective farm on land leased from the government (Cavendish, 2008). The settlers there became virtual slaves and the punishments for minor transgressions were severe. Growing increasingly paranoid, Jones preached that if the group was surrounded they had to be prepared to commit mass suicide. When a Congressman came to investigate, he and several reporters were killed and Jones and his loyalists forced the cult members to poison their children with cyanide and then themselves. Nine hundred dead bodies were found laid out the next day.

Cult is defined in *The Social Work Dictionary* (Barker, 2003) as:

1. A group in which members hold strong beliefs associated with the teachings of a leader;
2. A body of beliefs and rites practiced by a group that usually attributes religious, mystical, or magical powers to its leader.

Some cults are pathological in nature such as "The People's Temple" or the Jonestown settlement. Others are much closer to mainstream. But all have a tradition of charismatic leadership to whom followers are blindly devoted. The small religious group of true believers who waited for the world to come to an end as investigated by Festinger (1956) and summarized in Chapter 2 is one such example.

Preaching that the world is soon coming to an end is apparently common among cult groups. A remarkable first-hand account of an abusive religious cult experience that was shared with van Wormer in personal correspondence is included as Box 3.1. The survivor, Rose Janssen, utilized the consciousness-raising format—I heard, I saw, I smelled, etc. that she had learned in class.

Box 3.1 My Life at End Time Religious Camp

Rose Janssen

I heard: You will go to hell if you leave this camp that God has sent you to. Remember all of you that in the Bible it is written that the dead rose and walked the streets after Jesus' resurrection. Those same people will come and kill you for disobedience to me. We are in the last, of the last days, and right up there, in the clouds, is where Jesus will split the eastern sky, and come back to get this group of people here, and take us to heaven.

I saw: Faces that were full of fear and I saw faces that were full of joy. I saw control from the apostle in charge as he stood and faced this group of people I had joined, who as I, were wanting to be pleasing to God.

I smelled: The sweat of those that were standing closely beside me because we had just come from working in the garden from sun up to almost sun down. I was tired and my body ached, my feet hurt, and my head was pounding fiercely.

I tasted: My bad breath because I was in thirst for water and my mouth was parched wanting to be cool once again.

I felt: Fear as he said that he was going to take the Bibles from the women because only the men needed to read the word of God.

That to me was: Injustice, control, and intimidation. I wanted to read the word of God. I had just prior to coming to this place in the mountains of Smithville, Arkansas, given my life to Jesus. I knew I was to submit, but is this right? Why do I feel sick to my stomach and want to run from this place? Am I dreaming or is this really happening? I cannot be experiencing such terror. Is this my future, some man calling himself an apostle of God ruling over me, not even allowing me to contact my family or leave this place?

I said: No! I packed a small bag and headed down the long winding road to the highway to make my escape to the nearest town.

Printed with permission of Rose Janssen, BASW.

The general public caught a rare glimpse into the inner workings of a fanatical religious group in April 2008 and for several months following. Cameras descended on the Texas compound of the Fundamentalist Church of Latter Day Saints (FLDS) when a false report was given to the police by a woman who claimed to be a captive of this group. Temporarily, the children were removed from the compound and placed in foster care until the investigation was completed. In response to the mothers of the children who conducted a public relations campaign when their children were removed, feminists and others were stunned when the submissive roles the women were playing came to light.

According to cult expert Rick Ross (interviewed by Cross, 2008), there are around 50,000 members of these fundamentalist groups which fit the classic definition of the cult. The Texas FLDS polygamous group, according to Ross, fits the classic definition of a cult. Some of the most horrific complaints of sexual and physical abuse of which Ross is aware have come from these polygamist groups.

According to *God's Brothel* by Moore-Emmett (2004), who interviewed 18 women who had escaped the FLDS cult:

> With few roles in the world other than as "vessels to be worn out in childbirth," women in polygamy are often told it is their duty to deliver a child per year. Domestic violence and spousal rape are not acknowledged as such....In the FLDS religion, men can be excommunicated from their church....while their wives and children are given to another man. (p. 49)

A very different and more frightening form of cult-like behavior is reportedly emerging in the form of bands of homegrown terrorists. Such groups, although small in scale, are springing up across Europe and the United States in response to military action by the United States and its allies against Muslim terrorists in the Middle East. Members of these militant bands tend to be alienated young men whose extremist Muslim beliefs and violent schemes feed off of each other. Organizing and recruitment are taking place through the Internet (Sheridan & Hsu, 2009). Previously it had been believed that because of the high degree of assimilation of American Muslims and their relative prosperity compared to European Muslims, recruitment efforts by forces loyal to Al Qaeda would have little effect. How much of a threat these activities are in the United States is not clear, but counter-terrorism officials are sounding a warning. And while underlining that only a tiny minority has become radicalized, two major mainstream groups—the Muslim Public Affairs Council and the Council on American-Islamic Relations—have launched counter-radicalization programs aimed at young people.

To summarize this section: Our earlier discussion of groupthink has led us to delve into this consideration of extreme and extremist behavior. We switch gears now as we return to the major theme of this chapter, which is group facilitation and leadership. Keep in mind as we explore the workings of the therapy group that the group experience is very powerful, and, as we saw earlier, potentially dangerous. Groups have been used by enemies in wartime and by religious fanatics to brainwash people; inherently they have the capacity to be used for good or for ill. Now let us focus on the good.

New Members and Status Changes

In an active, working group, the addition of a new member to a group requires some adaptation on the part of old members. They have to size up the new member as to his or her relative status and other characteristics. Perhaps just as important, the old members have to assure themselves that the new member can and will make similar investments in the group to those that they have made. Will the new member share sensitive feelings? Will he or she keep sensitive information within the group? Will the newcomer make the same investments of time, money, or effort as older members have made? Will the new member conform to the group's norms?

Groups sometimes seem to reach a plateau relative to the pursuit of their stated purposes and goals. They sometimes seem to go nowhere. The addition of a new member or new members will cause a period of seeming stagnation while the new member is checked out. In fact, the group is engaged in a very important process of monitoring its boundaries of membership. For members and leaders who are conscious of this process, it may present an opportunity to move things along. New members can be described before they arrive, can be introduced, invited to talk or to participate, and given tasks that will demonstrate competence and involvement.

Open and Closed Groups

A group whose membership constantly changes is called an *open group*. An open group has the disadvantage of not progressing to levels of trust and involvement that it might if the membership was relatively closed. Some groups for substance abuse and batterers, for example, are open ended and last up to 24 weeks (Lundy, 2004). The content is planned in such a way that no matter when a person enters, he or she will rotate through all topic areas in the course of six months. A *closed group* is one in which the membership does not turn over very rapidly. Indeed, some groups have the same membership for the life of the group and, in rare cases, for the lives of the group members. The result is a cohesiveness and sense of safety that works well for persons who feel particularly vulnerable and are struggling with sensitive concerns such as sexual abuse (Lundy, 2004). Sometimes, especially with community action groups and other citizen groups, it may be beneficial for the group to consider at some point limiting its membership in order to allow the trust and involvement to develop beyond that which is allowed by an open membership.

Changes in the status of a group member, such as losing a job or getting married, can affect the other members of a group. It may change the configuration of the group or affect the level of anxiety as members identify with the affected person. Status change may also lead to a period of apparent stagnation or sorting out. Open communication about feelings is the best way to handle such situations. One of the co-authors of this book (van Wormer), in her alcoholism treatment group, had to spend time processing feelings with group members when one of the members committed suicide. On another occasion, her elderly co-therapist suffered a near-fatal, incapacitating stroke following a difficult group session in which members confronted him about the group therapy. Such situations arise, and no matter how much you prepare for such eventualities, emotional reactions by all parties are apt to be intense.

Stages of Group Development

Observers of small groups and practitioners with small groups often develop their versions of how the small group passes through stages or phases in the course of its existence. Such a framework is helpful in order to appreciate how a collection of strangers can come to constitute a micro social system in which the participants play roles that complement each other's. Our rendition of the stages of group development is not meant to apply universally. The stages roughly coincide with Tuckman's (1965) developmental sequence: forming, storming, norming, performing, and adjourning. Some groups may depart from the stages we suggest. Groups intentionally formed to last a specified length of time or that are controlled in their structure and development may differ, especially in the later stages, from the pattern we suggest. Some groups will never achieve the later stages. But being able to recognize typical stages of group development will enable members or leaders to help move the group to a more mature stage and thus closer to the goals of the group.

Orientation Stage

In the initial gathering, people usually do not constitute a group. They are a collection of individuals. They do not identify with one another; they do not take one another into account. They do not share a significant commonality.

A collection of people on an elevator will become a group if they become stuck between floors for an extended period. The reason is that the ingredients and experiences necessary for them to become a group can develop from their enforced proximity, shared experience, and communication.

Usually, when people get together for the first time, they begin to question one another about their respective backgrounds and interests. The unspoken interpersonal agenda is to determine each other's relative initial status and to discover mutual interests. Prospective group members are determining whether they can identify with one another. If, during this orientation stage, there is sufficient affinity and mutual interest, a group may develop, which is signified by the start of the second stage.

The Mutuality Stage

In the mutuality stage, the group consolidates its identity and aligns its member hierarchy with the group's requirements. Members of the group will recognize and identify with each other as members of the group even at times when the group is not formally meeting. Members begin to show their respective abilities and resources. Patterns of communication, alliances, and subgroups emerge, as do roles and responsibilities. As members jockey for position, a status hierarchy may arise and group leadership develop. There is a great deal of testing; members may feel anxious because they fear looking foolish if they take risks.

The Drama Stage

Each member of a group brings to the group his or her experiences and ways of perceiving and relating. Seldom is there total harmony among members from start to finish. Because of different personal needs, agendas, or hang-ups, conflict, squabbles, emotional intensity, transference, acting out, status hunger, jealousies, and other human proclivities emerge. Sibling rivalry crops

up as a higher level of intimacy is reached (Yalom, 2005). The resemblance that the small group bears to family, especially in the intensity of a therapy group, is strong. As these complexities develop in the group's life, they can be seen, if one develops some distance, as dramatic interactions. Hence, this stage of small-group development is seen as the drama stage. Much of what takes place in this stage is a testing of old patterns of behavior in the context of the group. Ideals about the goals of the group and the nature or character of the members meet the realities and are not always easily accepted. In some groups, even nontherapy groups, feelings and conflict can become intense and may involve competition for status and the acting out of deep transference problems. In groups that are not of a therapeutic or counseling nature, such dramatic problems must cool out on their own through continuing communication and work toward overall goals.

Love Ties

Successful marriages weather an initial romantic period of intense positive and negative feelings related to the collision of images of an ideal partner and the daily reality of an actual partner. Resolution and survival of this infatuation period lead to a conjugal affection between the partners in which the other is accepted with his or her shortcomings, foibles, and warts and is valued for the real person he or she is. A similar process occurs among members of a small group as it weathers the drama stage and members begin to accept each other despite shortcomings and foibles and develop affectionate ties, love ties, with each other. How does such a group appear from the outside? Van Wormer (1995) describes a love-ties stage alcoholism treatment group as if viewed by an invisible outsider:

> A working therapy group has about it a certain glow, an aura that is infectious. One person speaks; sometimes several speak at once; all heads nod in unison. Eyes move, too, from speaker to speaker. And the expression on one member's face, whether a grin or a look of pain, is

mirrored on all the faces. A oneness of feeling and mood permeates the air. Should the group progress falter, the group leader prompts the players and helps get the group back on track. The leader's hardest work was done earlier, however. Now it is time to sit back and enjoy the performance. (p. 239)

This stage of a group is usually marked by a good fit with the environment. Sometimes such groups persist for the lifetimes of the members. In small-town rural America, farmers still gather at the diner on Saturday morning to discuss the market, the weather, and other news. Their ties are strong, their manner is mellow, and their group will persist while they farm their land. Such groups are rare in mass industrial urban society, but they can be found. Some sports teams reach this stage, as well as some business elites or churches. We see no reason why groups must automatically disband when such a stage of homeostasis is achieved. But sometimes changes in members or the environment causes the group members to move on.

Blossoming

In some groups that have achieved a stage of love ties, members continue to grow and change due to other influences in their lives, such as continuing education or occupational development. For such members, this change and growth may bring a decline in involvement in the group as activities beyond the group compete for the member's time or meet the member's needs better than the group does. In clinical groups, members may achieve a remission of depression, learn new and effective ways to manage anxiety or anxiety-provoking thoughts, or gain a more secure sense of identity and of personal boundaries. With their personal goals met, they may no longer wish to continue in the group. Indeed, the experiences of the members in the group may precipitate such growth, give rise to new goals beyond the group, and help elicit the confidence to pursue them.

If substantial numbers of the group begin to change and grow in other directions, the group may come to an end, not so much through stagnation of the group as through blossoming that scatters the seeds of new involvements as members move on.

At this point we must sound a cautionary note to our discussion of small groups as emotionally bonded groups of people seeking, let us say, social justice. Michael Harrington (1973), a laborer in those fields of justice all of his adult life, wrote about the creation of small groups in the 1960s for the purpose of seeking social change.

To Harrington's mind, communities of people seeking social justice in that decade were destroyed after the death of Martin Luther King, Jr. "The movement," he says, "also died because the dream of a beloved community was and had to be an illusion. In a country profoundly suffused with economic, social, and psychological racism, it is possible to build a little island of love for a while; then the exigencies of struggle intervene, and one must choose from among competing bills, decide between politicians, deal with egos—and the community turns on itself" (1973, p. 263).

In other words, small groups can be enormous sources of personal growth and satisfaction, or, if they are groups with social rather than clinical goals, they can give the emotional lift and sense of solidarity needed to work on issues such as justice. Nevertheless, the real business of politics is compromise, tactics, and partial victories and defeats. This is the way progress is made, but it is also the way in which tightly knit groups are torn apart.

Group Leadership

From the advice of Niccolo Machiavelli (1532/1980) to Lorenzo de Medici to modern research, much has been made of the skills for leadership. We share a few of the more useful insights into the nature of small-group leadership and facilitation skills after making the important distinction between leadership and group facilitation.

Early social workers used small groups as a means to effect social goals in the settlement houses of our larger cities. These groups worked for the mutual benefit of their members, working to improve their lot and the quality of life in their communities. Such groups developed their own leadership from among their members. The social workers working with such groups consciously cultivated the group's leadership without becoming leaders of each group themselves. They facilitated the groups and their leaders, who were seen collectively as their clients. This basic notion of professionals facilitating a group's development, goals, and leadership is now a part of many approaches to work with small groups. Some psychotherapists, counselors, community organizers, and other professionals see themselves as group facilitators rather than as group leaders. For many such professionals, especially social workers, the group itself is their "client," and its leadership is developed from the membership.

Some of the skills of facilitators and of group leaders disclosed in now-classic small-group research are directly parallel. We review a few of these.

Group Facilitation

In the classic study of group leadership described previous in the chapter, we learned of the impact on group members of different leadership styles—authoritarian, democratic, and laissez-faire.

George Homans enunciated some behaviors for leaders based on studies of small groups (Homans, 1950). These seem somewhat authoritarian today in that they were based on an industrial management model. In short, Homans stated that a leader will maintain his or her position; his or her orders will be carried out. And in every group there is a zone of indifference or a certain latitude that a group will allow for a leader to give orders without consciously challenging them. A leader will abide by the norms of the group and look out for the interests of the members. A leader will not give orders that will not be obeyed.

Today, group theorists have refined the desired roles of the group leader in a much more democratic fashion since Homans presented his ideas. Corey and Corey (2006) list the following as desirable group leader characteristics: courage, willingness to model, presence, goodwill, belief in group process, nondefensiveness, awareness of one's culture, willingness to seek new experience, personal power, stamina, self-awareness, sense of humor, inventiveness, dedication, and commitment. These personal characteristics need to be complemented with professional skills such as active listening, reflecting, summarizing, clarifying, and facilitating, among others.

According to Kenneth Reid (2002), the group facilitator:

- Encourages members to share and to actively participate
- Links interrelated issues, ideas, feelings, and thoughts
- Blocks the expression of inappropriate behaviors by members or by the group as a whole
- Limits behaviors and actions by holding to boundaries and structure
- Parcels problems or concerns into manageable units
- Reframes problems and situations

Diversity Issues

Schriver (2010) makes some interesting points concerning group composition. African Americans, he notes, have been found to prefer group composition to be approximately half white and half nonwhite. Whites, in contrast, appear to prefer that African Americans make up no more than 20 percent of the members. It is important to avoid tokenism by either race or gender. In his review of the relevant research, Schriver indicates that an important means of addressing women's inequality in a mixed group is to have women in visible positions of leadership at all levels of the organization.

Often in the course of group treatment, members come out with a racial slur or with bigoted remarks about persons of other races or cultures; usually representatives of those groups are not present. The dilemma for the group leader is whether to let the speaker continue without interruption or to break in immediately with a response. Pence and Paynar (1993) provide the following example based on their work with battering men. In the illustration presented, the speaker, a Vietnam veteran, describes a woman as "going out with a gook." "Why do you use the term 'gook'?" asks the facilitator. The group member explains that this was the term used by soldiers who had served in Vietnam. First, the leader responds to the content of the discussion but later addresses the issue of derogatory terms that are used in the group. He invites group members to think critically about such name calling (cited in Lundy, 2004).

Group members can be encouraged through reinforcement to confront others with an appropriate statement when they are offended. The person might say, for example, "When you talk that way about the Mexicans taking your jobs, I think of my own grandchildren who are Mexican American. . . ." (This incident occurred in one of van Wormer's groups of alcoholics; as the woman passed around the pictures of her grandchildren, the man who had made the angry remark apologized profusely.)

Generally, leaders, group counselors, and facilitators want a group to develop an identity and a group feeling of affinity. They want the group to develop through the early stages into an effective entity. To do so, they can make use of pragmatic procedural skills.

Procedural Skills

If the group is to conduct most of its business in a face-to-face setting, as in a planning group, setting up the physical meeting place is important. A circular arrangement of chairs that allows each member to have easy eye contact with each other member facilitates group interaction. This is especially true if the group consists of between 5 and 10 members. Groups of larger membership than 10 tend to break up into small subgroups if the topic of discussion does not command full attention. A room that prevents frequent interruption and that has a door that can be closed to signify the start of business is best.

Often in groups that meet face to face and require discussion, the simple technique of going around can be helpful in ensuring the participation of each member and in giving each a voice (Lundy, 2004). With the group arranged in a circle, with each member within the circle as opposed to "hiding out" behind other members, the leader or facilitator can suggest that each person comment on the issue or topic. Such a procedure can help new members to get into the habit of talking. It can allow opinions and feelings that might otherwise go unexpressed to be expressed. Sometimes it can get things started at a first meeting, especially if prospective members are asked to share why they have come to the group's meeting and what they expect or hope to gain from membership in the prospective group.

If the group has specific external tasks and is divisive, as citizen action groups can be, use of parliamentary rules is advised when appropriate to the group's purpose. This would include the taking of minutes of the meeting. Minutes can allow members to refer back to past meetings to check decisions or group policy.

If one is in a facilitator role and wishes to help the group develop its own leadership, it is best to be quite active at first. This activity can involve getting discussion started, keeping the group focused on tasks relative to its goals, inviting participation from quiet people, demonstrating appropriate participation, and so on. As the group begins to take on an identity and enter a mutuality stage, the facilitator can withdraw more and more, allowing the natural leadership of the group to develop.

Some techniques that come from group therapy may be appropriate and useful in other kinds of groups. For instance, if one senses that a member is dissatisfied with a plan of action, encouraging that member to share his or her concerns could give voice to feelings other members have as well. Judicious use of such a skill may help the members work more in concert with the group's goals.

Keeping in mind the motivational power of the group's structure and the competition that can develop for position in the group's order, a leader or facilitator may wish to stop destructive disputes. This may entail supporting the existing hierarchy. Or it may be better managed by changing the group environment sufficiently to force the group to have to rely on the talents or resources of low-ranking members. Eventually a more flexible view of the group's order and a more egalitarian mode of functioning may develop. As we indicated earlier, these attributes of a mature group allow it to function in a variety of environments.

Sometimes a member or several members will repeatedly drift into topics or activities that are tangential to the goals of the group. If the group is still agreed on the goals, gatekeeping may be in order. This skill is manifested by leaders, facilitators, and other group members alike. Essentially, it is any action or communication that serves to limit the group's divergence from the goals and tasks and that returns the group to its purposes. For example, communications preceded by such phrases as "Let's get back to the subject," or "Can we deal with that later and get on with business?" or "I think we should be focusing on . . ." are examples of gatekeeping. Rounding up group members, enlisting the aid of high-status members to enforce the group's norms, calling members personally to come to meetings, or gently cutting off or blocking communications from members who are disruptive are activities that also serve a gatekeeping function.

In the initial meetings of a group, when a facilitator wishes to encourage group identity and participation prior to the development of a group leader, summarizing the events of the meeting and anticipating the next and future meetings, coupled with sharing honestly felt positive feelings about the group and its prospects, are all helpful skills.

Small Groups, Social Decisions, and Action

Many efforts to realize social justice involve influencing social decisions. In a democratic society, these decisions may be of a political or economic nature and quite contentious. Small groups of people can help influence the social decisions of a community or larger social system through activities skillfully directed toward sources of power and appropriate strategies and tactics for change. In *The Tipping Point*, Gladwell (2002) traces the growth of social movements through the networking of groups that are linked to other groups. This is how, Gladwell reminds us, Wesley's Methodism spread all across England and America through the rise of small close-knit groups. If we are interested in starting an "epidemic" or reaching a tipping point with an idea or product, as Gladwell advises, the way would be to mobilize small groups with real social power; they would be the means by which the message would be spread. Today, the phenomenon of the megachurch, spreading as rapidly as these enormous buildings on the outskirts of town can be constructed, owes its exponential growth to small groups or "cells" that maintain a high level of intimacy and probably social control (Sharlet, 2005).

Power and Empowerment

The primary role of the social worker is to assist the client to develop a sense of control and power. A community's shared values can be a source of power. Consensual values can rally support for a cause—such as peace—when the relationship of values to the decisions at hand are articulated. In addition, solidarity groups such as ethnic groups, churches, and unions can generate enormous power and influence over social decisions as their numbers and activism allow. Creative activities that can enlist these sources of power in a community to influence peace-related decisions can become a meaningful and fruitful activity for groups working for peace.

Empowerment-based work in the community requires an understanding of the sources of power just described and knowledge of group dynamics and processes as a means of mobilizing energy. The challenge, as Browne and Mills (2001) suggest, is to politicize and educate consumers, as well as social workers, to the value and political uses of power. Within the agency, as well, when social workers have access to resources and a say in decision making, their practice tends to be more effective. To the extent that in the economic crisis that occurred at the end of the George W. Bush administration and into the Obama administration, the urgency toward cost containment is disempowering to social service organizations from the top down, and feelings of hopelessness and powerlessness can infiltrate down to the lowest level, the treatment group. The significance of ecosystems theory for social work group practice with oppressed and vulnerable populations is in directing the social worker's attention to environmental forces that diminish personal power and to the need to develop strategies, ideally through worker–client collaboration, that get to the roots of the problem. As a strategy of empowerment, group leaders can facilitate such understandings by helping clients differentiate between difficulties that stem from the larger external environment and those that are manifested at the individual level (Browne & Mills, 2001). What we are talking about here is consciousness raising.

Critical thinking is essential to consciousness raising as individuals place the events of their lives within a social and economic context and identify ways of working toward solutions to the problems. This process of awareness, or consciousness raising, helps clients move from a position of powerlessness, internalized oppression, and alienation to one of empowerment and liberation (Lundy, 2004).

Often because of court mandates, social workers lead groups of individuals who are considered more the oppressors than the oppressed. Uniquely, Colleen Lundy applies the concept to consciousness raising to the groups of battering men she has led. As she tells us:

In my own groups, I have suggested that members draw a picture of a situation in which they used violence. Many of these pictures portray the man as larger than everyone else and holding his fist in the air; his partner has a look of horror and pain; and there are children hovering in the background. This has proved to be a particularly moving experience for the men as they describe their practice to the group. (p. 162)

Groups that have decided to form peaceful communities separate from the rest of society, such as the Amish or the counterculture groups of the 1960s, realign the values and behaviors of their own communities, disassociating from the larger society to varying degrees. They attempt to develop autonomy and separate identity in keeping with their group's values. Conflict and even persecution by the larger society may follow. But their example may educate others about the value of decisions for social and environmental justice or peace and peaceful lifestyles.

To see how ecological systems theory meets empowerment practice and consciousness raising, read Box 3.2, "Empowering Group Practice."

Box 3.2 Empowering Group Practice

Kalleen Ragan-Pepper, MSW

Human beings strive throughout life for the best person:environment "fit" possible between their needs, rights, capacities, and aspirations, on one hand, and the quality of their environment on the other.
—Carel Germain, 1991

Drawing from Germain's (1991) work, which clarified and contemporized the ecological perspective for social work education, several inferences can be made about the relationship of empowerment to human behavior in the social environment. The lens of the ecological perspective and a systems theory point of view are two tools workers can employ to identify disempowering, as well as empowering, transactions between people and their environment.

Judith A. B. Lee (2001) built on the work of Germain to construct a model for empowerment practice to "release the potentialities of people and environments" (p. 24). Further, she notes that oppressed people rarely experience a "goodness of fit" between themselves and their environment. Oppressed people must "name, face, and challenge the forces of oppression as they have been internalized and encountered in external power structures that exist at close range, mid range, and wide range in our society" (p. 24).

The process of empowerment is like a system in flux seeking equilibrium. A disempowered person or community seeking empowerment is a system seeking balance. The model in Figure 3.1 presents the steps in the empowerment process as they relate to the ecological perspective and systems theory.

Step 1: The individual is alone in oppression. The individual cannot name the oppressor.

The person/system's boundaries with other systems are rigid. If energy is exchanged between systems, it does not serve to enhance the well-being of the person. There may be subcultural/subsystem support from family, but essentially the person is not able to control the environment in any significant way. In addition, the person has little access to environmental resources. Stress for this individual/system is both external and internal. The person may develop coping mechanisms. By definition, the oppressed person will have difficulty with human relatedness, lack a sense of self-confidence, and have low self-esteem. It is important to note that the oppressor is also disempowered completely in this phase.

Step 2: The oppressed person begins to associate with others of the same oppressed group and their collective consciousness is raised. They are able to name the oppressor.

In this step the boundaries of the focal system become permeable. Group members begin to exchange energy in the form of consciousness raising. The group may be getting outside help in the form of an ally who provides crucial knowledge about how the oppressive system operates. The ally adds yet another dimension to the exchange of energy. The group learns that knowledge is power and not all power is negative. As this energy exchange increases in scope and intensity, the individual will still feel stress, but now the stress begins to take on a more positive, affirming, zestful quality. This exchange becomes a method of coping for the individual that therefore reduces negative stress, but it will also—at least temporarily—increase anger in the person and the group. This is the juncture at which the group begins to collectively suspect that they are able to affect the power, oppression, and toxicity that informs their world. They relate (and will disagree, jockey for power, etc.) and begin to have an intuitive sense of their self-direction and increased level of competence.

Step 3: The oppressed group initiates the process of reflection. Members use their collective intelligence to grasp a broad view of their oppression.

The group begins to understand how the holon functions. They see how systems interact and think about the big picture, like fitting the pieces of a puzzle together to make a picture. Using their intellectual capacities to learn creates a new worldview. Individuals begin to have a sense of adaptedness. The power, oppression, and pollution are still present, but the group can think, talk about, and envision other realities. As they relate to each other, the individuals feel a sense of relatedness, their self-esteem is increasing, and they feel a higher level of competence. It is at this point that the oppressor will begin to feel negative stress because the oppressed system is encroaching upon the oppressor's boundaries hoping to exchange energy.

Step 4: The group takes action to alleviate the oppression.

In this step the group of oppressed individuals functions together in solidarity and is ready to take action, effectively challenging the limits of their oppression. They intuitively know their oppressed system boundaries and stand in readiness to press back against the system that oppresses to attain homeostasis. They have adapted to their new sense of self and have the competence that comes from self-conceived/self-directed action. Their action is not characterized by anger but by a righteous sense of justice.

Step 5: The group uses the process of reflection again, this time to evaluate the action taken and its relative success or failure.

Liberation! The individuals have acted to change the environment. Feedback from the oppressor system reaches the oppressed system. Members now know they can exert at least a moderate amount of control over their transactions with the environment. They have minimized life stressors by gaining power. Returning to their respective systems, they reflect on the action taken to end oppression and change their environment. The interesting reality is that their action against oppression serves the entire holon by balancing the component systems. The oppressor is now free of the stress of oppressing. The other members of the subsystem are inspired by the exchange of energy across a formerly rigid boundary. This is empowerment, and it will begin again as soon as the individuals in the group complete this reflection phase because empowerment is not an end product, rather a process that occurs over time.

References

Adams, R. (2003). *Social work and empowerment* (J. Campling, Ed., 3rd ed.). Hampshire, UK: Palgrave Macmillan.

Bishop, A. (2002). *Becoming an ally, breaking the cycle of oppression* (2nd ed.). New York: ZedBooks.

Freire, P. (2000). *Pedagogy of the oppressed* (M. B. Ramos, Trans.). New York: Continuum. (Original work published 1970).

Germain, C. B. (1991). *Human behavior in the social environment an ecological view*. New York: Columbia University Press.

Gutiérrez, L. M., Parsons, R. J., & Cox, E. O. (1998). *Empowerment in social work practice*. Belmont, CA: Brooks/Cole.

Lee, J. A. (2001). *The empowerment approach to social work practice: Building the beloved community* (2nd ed.). New York: Columbia University Press.

Schriver, J. M. (2004). *Human behavior and the social environment: Shifting paradigms in essential knowledge for social work practice* (4th ed.). Boston: Allyn & Bacon.

See Figure 3.4 for an example of a direct action group that was empowering in terms of the solidarity that it generated on the part of the participants.

Values and Group Work

Small groups, with their normative attitudes and behaviors, inevitably create a spoken or unspoken value set. Those who work with small groups need a set of professional values to guide their work in this value-laden context. For group work, social workers Helen Northen and Roselle Kurland (2001) identified a set of basic values—namely, dignity and worth of the individual; social justice, including rights and self-determination; and mutual responsibility. These values spring from the reality of our need to survive and meet basic needs. In addition,

Northen and Kurland identified the following global ethical principles for those who work with small groups:

- Professional relationship, including trust, warmth, empathy, genuineness, and use of power for the client
- Group relationship, interdependence, mutuality
- Multiculturalism, respect for diversity and commonalities
- Empowerment, through imparting knowledge and opportunity to reach goals
- Confidentiality and privacy, which means controlling information about oneself
- Self-determination balanced with group consensus
- Professional competence, doing what is in one's sphere of expertise

Given the power and influence of the small group in our lives and the lives of those who we seek to help, a set of values and ethics is an important anchor to our understanding and work with groups (Barsky, 2010). In *Ethics and Values in Social Work*, Barsky devotes a chapter to social work with groups. The ethical principles in group practice vary depending on the type of group we are talking about, whether we are talking about task groups consisting of colleagues or community members or whether we are talking about treatment groups. With client groups, ethical issues such as informed consent, confidentiality, and maintaining appropriate boundaries will arise. The ethic of informed consent means that the facilitator will engage clients at the outset of providing services to explain the purpose of the group, the risks and benefits, and other important information such as the worker's credentials, theoretical orientation, and expected roles of the group members. Based on the ethic of confidentiality, facilitators disclose the degree to which information obtained about individuals in and out of the group setting will be shared or not shared. Barsky recommends having a consent form to formalize the confidentiality agreement. Clients need to be advised of duties to report child abuse or to respond to court

Figure 3.4. March for human rights organized by the Women's Economic Agenda Project, which joined the Poor People's Economic Human Rights Campaign in mid-July in Louisville, Kentucky, 2009 for a solidarity rally. Photo provided by the Women's Economic Agenda Project, Oakland, CA, Nicole Martin, photographer.

orders and what kind of information will be recorded in personal files. The purpose of the ethic of maintaining appropriate boundaries is to ensure that everyone feels safe in the group, what types of touch if any are permitted in the group, to what extent group members will contact each other outside of the group, and a rule against sexual relationships among group members.

At the policy level, an ethical issue raised by Reid (2002) concerns the practice, in this era of managed care and third-party-payer restrictions, of routinely placing clients into groups as a means of expediency and cost-effectiveness. In such instances, little thought is given to the individual's therapeutic well-being, not to mention the impact that a person will have on the group as a whole. For the new member unsuited for group work, this treatment modality may be nontherapeutic and may lead to active resistance or withdrawal. The group members may have feelings of frustration and a sense of having little or no control over the treatment process.

Some individuals, by their very nature and behavior, have difficulty in small, intimate groups.

Examples provided by Reid (2002) include individuals who:

‣ Are extremely labile and for whom a low-stimulation environment is desirable
‣ Are acutely agitated and cannot tolerate sitting in a room or attending to what is going on
‣ Are characteristically suspicious and hypervigilant toward the environment
‣ Have a well-documented history of antisocial behavior problems
‣ Have a history of decompensation or self-destructive behavior after being frustrated
‣ Have a documented history of violence

What the Research Tells Us

Anecdotal reports of the power of the group to help motivate clients to change abound. We have all heard of cases in which even the most recalcitrant of individuals were moved into making life transitions due to the influence of group persuasion. And you might remember from the wealth of historical data in the previous chapter how whole epidemics—commercial, political, or religious—can arise through the interlinking of individuals in small groups. Once there is a tipping point, contagion often sets in.

Nevertheless, as far as evidence-based research that compares individual and group treatment modalities is concerned, Meier and Comer (2005) inform us that empirically based outcome studies are relatively rare. Few studies achieve the statistical power needed to detect treatment effects, in part because researchers have problems obtaining and retaining sufficiently large samples. Group workers, therefore, have difficulty in obtaining systematic evidence on the efficacy of small-group interventions. Meier and Comer recommend instead that agencies sponsor pilot projects and get feedback at every stage from participants, then, following treatment, that they assess former members to see whether their participation in the group helped them achieve their desired goals. Results would be compared with the results of clients with similar presenting problems who received individual therapy instead. Yalom's (2005) research, described earlier in the chapter, offered confirmation of group psychotherapy effectiveness in this manner. And Toseland and Rivas (2001), in their review of the literature on comparative treatment modalities, concluded that group treatment may be more effective for enhancing social supports and less effective for dealing with highly personal, psychological problems.

Focus Groups

One type of group that macro social workers can be expected to use increasingly is the focus or discussion group. Dating back to the 1920s, focus groups have been used by sociologists for research on such topics as propaganda efforts and worker productivity (Stewart, Shandasani, & Rook, 2007). After a period of decreased use, focus groups have emerged as a tool for marketing and discovery, as well as other research interests.

The focus group is a popular research technique that collects information on a given topic by submitting questions for discussion to participants. Seated with a moderator who directs questions, the focus group approach affords the researcher the opportunity to interact with respondents, thus allowing for greater elaboration of views and values (Pinaire, 2004). Participants (generally 8–10 adults) may be asked to discuss an issue and to give their degree of support for various policies or positions and the reasoning that led them to such conclusions. With the opportunity to ask for clarification, scholars who use focus groups can, argues Pinaire, arrive at a "truer" and more nuanced sense of public opinion on issues of consequence, as compared to public opinion surveys. There are numerous focus group formats: the self-contained group as an end in itself, the focus-group format as a principal source of data, and the focus-group format as a supplementary source of data to validate empirical research. Such a format, therefore, is more directed than a simple open-ended discussion while still providing the opportunity for interaction on the topic. And it can be done in more depth than simply interviewing each individual one at a time. Focus groups produce qualitative data that can be extremely useful to guide program planning, for monitoring studies, and in treatment evaluation. Researchers might use four to six focus groups on a topic, although sometimes they might find that that many focus groups become redundant and are not necessary (Stewart et al., 2007).

Casey and Krueger (2004) recommend that the moderator come equipped with no more than 12 questions and that the questions be introduced informally in a logical flow from general to more specific. Sample questions that they provide to evaluate a service for children include the following instructions and questions:

> Introduce yourself and tell how you learned about these services.
> Think back to when you first became involved with these services. What were your first impressions of the service?
> What has been particularly helpful about the services your family has received?
> What has been frustrating? (p. 65)

A remarkable piece of research was conducted by Denham, Meyer, Toborg, and Mande (2004) with women from rural Appalachia. The purpose of the study was to find out how to shape health education efforts and how to pitch prevention programming to one hard-to-reach and culturally distinct community. Fifty-two focus groups consisting of females, males, and adolescents were set up exclusively for the purpose of recording attitudes on various aspects of health education, such as preventing tobacco use among teenagers. Group sessions were tape-recorded and simultaneously observed and later analyzed by researchers. Results were used to shape health education strategies that hopefully would be more effective than those used in the past.

What the researchers learned was significant: an emphasis on the whole family and especially on female family members who traditionally provided informal health education inside their families. The men and adolescents favored factual, concrete messages about health care. Some women were possible community leaders; others, however, were found to be fatalistic; this was evidenced in statements that revealed a sense of futility about life and in regard to raising children. The analysts recommended one-on-one counseling to establish trust and boost the women's coping skills. Another finding was that in response to specific anti-drug-use messages, participants were extremely negative toward messages that were insulting to individuals for using drugs; they showed this through responses that defended users who were attacked or made fun of in some way. Denham et al. (2004) concluded from their study that to be effective in this mountain area, health education services must be culturally sensitive and tailored to the traditions of the people involved.

Part of the present popularity of focus groups may indeed be due to their unique advantages for addressing such contemporary issues as empowerment and diversity (Morgan, 1996). Participants in a focus group spontaneously conversing with each other share information that would not come across in a straight questionnaire-interview format. For this reason, focus groups are widely used to help lawyers in difficult civil or criminal trials learn how to pitch their arguments so that favorable results may be obtained for their clients (see Ball, 2001). Politicians rely on this setup as well to provide feedback from average citizens on issues of the day; the findings then serve to keep the politicians abreast of issues of concern and solutions (such as a cigarette tax) that are acceptable. Marketers of commercial products use this method extensively to help them design their products and discover which messages are appealing and to which populations.

Of relevance to the social work profession, the focus-group format holds promise for social work researchers in developing knowledge for practice. Graduate students of social work, as in the social sciences, increasingly use this research design in studying attitudes toward a social problem or treatment intervention. Community organization workers can learn much about the needs of a community and the acceptability of new ideas through this information-gathering strategy. Another possible use of focus groups for the profession may be the measurement of outcomes—both student learning outcomes in social work education and the treatment outcomes of social service delivery systems and agencies.

The remainder of this chapter describes some examples of the transformative power of the group process, first in professional circles and then in situations of self-help.

Innovative Group Work in Women's Prisons

Despite the notorious treatment of men and women in the criminal justice system, starting with harsh sentencing laws, there is some innovative programming, especially in women's prisons, that meets the criteria for empowerment therapy. Among examples of innovative, gender-specific programming are as follows: an art therapy program at the Kingston prison in Canada that provides incarcerated women with a voice to deal with trauma; the indigenously based Sycamore Tree project, which follows the principle of restorative justice in helping female inmates in New Zealand reintegrate with the community; and a bereavement and loss group in an English women's prison for those who needed to mourn the death of a loved one (see van Wormer, 2010). Central to all these program innovations is the theme of personal empowerment—empowerment through self-expression of a fulfilling, yet enjoyable sort. The learning of life skills, such as parenting, can flow naturally and spontaneously through involvement in mutual aid or support groups focused on a common, all-absorbing task. The hallmark of the effective group leader is enthusiasm and unshakeable confidence in the women's latent talents and abilities. The leader's or social worker's role, as described by Gutiérrez and Suarez (1999), should be that of consultant and facilitator rather than instructor, so as not to reinforce the sense of powerlessness that these women need to overcome. Small groups, according to these authors, have special relevance for empowerment practice with Latinas because they offer an effective means for raising consciousness and because it is in keeping with the Latinos' history of working with one another to provide mutual aid. African American culture is similarly oriented more toward family and community systems than toward individual achievement.

The importance of such group work for all the participants is that gaining competency in one area—writing poetry, drawing, parenting—leads to skills in performing adult roles valued by society. The socially empowering group, even within the confines of the stark prison setting, can be individually transformative, the more so among women who have been removed from and punished by society, estranged from loved ones, and forced into lockstep with institutional demands. The actively working, fun-loving group can thus represent a strange and powerful anomaly given where it is and the personal history of its members. Such a group can serve as a bridge to the cultural milieu of the larger society.

Self-Help Groups

The practice of group work is regularly applied to persons in treatment with a wide variety of problems. The populations are defined by a particular physical or psychological condition, by a social identity, by an unmet need for a service or form of help, or by a challenge that arises from their stage of life or personal history (Ephross and Vassil, 2005). Such individuals, in general, can benefit from participating in a group through which they can gain skills and understandings and, as Yalom (2005) points out, develop confidence through risking new behaviors that can carry over into their social environment.

Participation in a self-help group offers many of the same benefits. A major advantage of a self-help group is the freedom pertaining to group membership: A person can attend each week or whenever he or she feels like it; there is no red tape, no problem with payment or insurance reimbursement; and friendships that develop are not restricted in any way by agency rules. For these reasons, many people attend such mutual aid or support groups. Their wide variety is revealed in a scanning of any local newspaper. Thus, there are groups for people with addiction problems, family members of people with all the major diseases, single-parent groups, and groups for newly divorced people.

The difference between a self-help group and a professionally led treatment group can be compared to the difference between a church with a minister and one that is congregation led, such as is found among Quakers and Unitarian groups. In these cases, responsibility for the functioning of the groups is dispersed among the fellowship.

Many self-help groups stress (1) a confession by members to the group that they have a problem; (2) testimonials by members of the group recounting their past experiences with the problem, expressing their gratitude, and describing their plans for handling the problem in the future; and (3) support (Zastrow & Kirst-Ashman, 2010). A major theme of addictions-related or 12-step groups is contained in the 12th step: "Having had a spiritual awakening as the result of these steps, we tried to carry this message to alcoholics, and to practice these principles in all our affairs" (Alcoholics Anonymous, 1939/1976). Through helping others, the helper maintains his or her own sobriety. A student visitor who attended an Alcoholics Anonymous (AA) meeting in small-town Iowa effectively describes the extent of this helping effort in "A Visit to an AA Meeting" in Box 3.3. Box 3.4 describes an earlier experience that a social work student had at an Al-Anon meeting for concerned families and friends of alcoholics.

had similar feelings to his. The most astounding of all was at the end of the meeting when several group members hugged the man and gave him their phone numbers, and expressed to him the value he held in their hearts. They told him to call anytime, and especially to avoid relapsing. The members giving their phone numbers ranged from all ages.

Personal communication from Victoria Filzer of Fayette, Iowa. Printed with permission of the writer.

Box 3.3 A Visit to an AA Meeting

Victoria Filzer

I attended an AA meeting at the hospital where I did my internship in chemical dependency. After a reading of the 12 Steps and 12 Traditions of AA, the two group leaders presented their personal stories of recovery ("drunkalogs") and then opened the floor for questions, concerns, and/or anything that any of the members present would like to discuss. . . .

It just seemed really overwhelming to me and virtually impossible for someone to be dealing with all of the problems that they discussed at once. One good example was given by an older man. His wife had just been placed in a nursing home after she had had an operation. She thought that she was just going to be staying for a few days, but the nursing home staff called the man and told him that she would not be able to return home in her condition. He knew that he would not be able to care for her anyway, as he was having enough difficulties in working through his own recovery or taking care of himself. He discussed his feelings of loneliness and despair, which were feelings that had been triggers for his drinking previously. He was very worried about telling his wife that she could not come home and very concerned about the possibility of his relapsing. Tears came to his eyes as he talked; his story was heartbreaking.

Members of the group chimed right in to give him reassurance in his time of great need. It was amazing; it seemed like they knew everything, more even than a therapist could have done for him. Group members told him about care meetings where he could discuss with the nursing home staff how he or they together could tell his wife that she would not be able to return home. He was given tips for his relapse prevention plan, and people gave examples of coping techniques they used when they

Box 3.4 Visit to an Al-Anon Meeting

Jaclyn Randolph

I attended a 12-Step program about a year ago, and I remember it very well. I went there during the time my ex-boyfriend who was my boyfriend then was acting strange. His behavior had changed after he moved to Iowa City for school. I had been dreading it since I had been suspicious of him being an alcoholic. He had once claimed he was and then claimed he wasn't and said his parents only ever saw him drunk. I wanted to believe him but I never truly did. While he had been living in town he did not have many opportunities to drink since he was living at home. That is why when he did move to Iowa City and his behavior changed I knew something was up. He would not talk to me as much and when he did that in town here it was when he was drinking and when he moved it was an everyday thing. I hardly got a hold of him. I kept trying to find someone to talk to about it and it seemed no one was able to tell me what I needed or make me feel better. That is when his mother told me that I should attend a 12-Step program. I was scared to go because I did not know what to expect. I am not a very outgoing person.

When I got there I was surprised it was in a tiny little building and all the people there were women. The chairs were in a circle, which I expected, but what surprised me was how everyone acted like they were friends. I saw people running over to another and hugging and laughing and I was a little confused. I was expecting to see people sad and not very happy to be there. When the meeting began to start they noticed I was new; I must have stuck out like a sore thumb. I was the youngest there everyone—else was probably in their 40s or older.

Right away they had a list going around and the people were putting down their numbers for me. I did not realize this until later when it was handed to me. Everyone had books and I was curious why. I knew nothing of the 12-Step program and really before I went I did not really know it existed. One person led the group and read a passage before people shared things about themselves. All the people at this program were suffering from an alcoholic; they themselves were not alcoholics.

The group focused on one of the 12 Steps for that day. The one they happened to be on was an eye opener for me. I did not realize it until they came across to one woman who I felt I was a lot alike. She explained about how she had been mean to the man in her life who as an alcoholic. She would threaten him and things that were not very helpful for the alcoholic. It made me realize I had not been very helpful to him. I criticized him, got mad at him when he drank, and threatened to leave if he did not change. For me it was frustrating because he would say he was in control but his actions never showed that and I would always point that out. Our last fight had been about his drinking. I reminded him of his dad. Something I never wanted to be compared to. He said I made him feel terrible and when he told me that I felt awful and told him I would work on it, me going to this program was that. I thought to myself that even if he does not admit he is an alcoholic I need to do something for myself. I never really wanted to leave him. I loved him and knew he could be a good guy when he was not drinking. I was willing to accept that and I knew I was not perfect. When that lady said the things she said emotions just flooded for me and when they came to me I broke down. I was embarrassed but it was then I realized just how mean I had been. I had been claiming to be there for him but I wasn't really. I was hurting him.

This program only lasted 30 minutes, but those 30 minutes changed my life. I did not attend a meeting after that even though I said I would. The reason was he broke up with me. I was going to go to another meeting for healing, but I saw that he had moved on with another girl right after we broke up and that is a long story in itself. For me during that time other things were bothering me more than his addiction.

Paper written for Katherine van Wormer as a class assignment on November 7, 2009. Printed with permission of Jaclyn Randolph.

Self-help groups, compared with professionally run therapy groups, are much more standardized in format. In AA, for example, the focus is on total abstinence, learned use of labels, ritualized readings at the start of each meeting, rotating leadership, and the structural use of the personal narrative. It is a narrative structure because it is more comparable to other voluntary associations of people "living lives"—such as religious organizations, political parties, even families—than it is to a social service agency setting in which clients come to receive services from professional helpers (van Wormer & Davis, 2008). In the narrative framework, people joining AA are not help seekers in search of treatment but storytellers who, through telling and listening, transform their lives. The professionally run group, on the other hand, relies on the expertise of the credentialed leader, is built on the development of group cohesiveness and relative stability of membership, is geared toward expressing feelings even when clients want to hold back, and often organizes a discussion around a theme, such as anger management. Members who do not abide by the rules can be removed from the treatment group by the agency or the group leader or graduated from one group to the other. Confidentiality is often stronger in the 12-Step group, because in so many of the professionally run groups records are kept and progress is reported to other agencies, such as a court or the Department of Human Services, once the necessary release forms are signed. Three things these two types of group meetings have in common are a focus on sharing relevant information, instilling hope by offering solutions to the problem, and building relationships and trust.

Some self-help groups advocate for the rights and lifestyles of people whose members are viewed by society as being different (Zastrow & Kirst-Ashman, 2010). One such group is PFLAG. PFLAG is a vast grassroots network of more than 250,000 members and 500 affiliates in the United States. It has a large following in Canada as well and exists in 11 other countries. PFLAG has a self-help component in that it is a place to which parents and spouses of gays and lesbians come to get support, initially on the shock of learning a family member is gay or lesbian. Because some of the most active members are gays and lesbians themselves, many of the questions a family member has can be answered directly by the gay or lesbian member. PFLAG is also an advocacy group that works for safe schools and that is responsible for the passage of protective legislation and for influencing the Department of Education policy (see http://www.pflag.org). Meetings often start with members introducing themselves and briefly telling their individual stories. The following dialogue was recorded by van Wormer from an actual PFLAG meeting in which she participated in Waterloo, Iowa:

First Man: We have a son who's gay and a son who's a Promise Keeper.
Woman No. 1: Our daughter's a lesbian. She's in her thirties.
Her Husband: She's very much in the closet and living in Washington state. So we have to keep quiet too.
Woman No. 1: She's a very private person, you see.
Woman No. 2: Our daughter's a lesbian also. We just never suspected a thing.
Paul: I never suspected my children were straight! But when I came out to them, they announced they were straight. [Laughter.] Recently John [his partner] and I, this was a first; we stayed over at my daughter's home. Everything seemed to be fine. She let us sleep in her bed. But when we got home, I got a letter. The letter said, "I love you Dad, but these things are off limits." Then she wrote a list—things such as no physical contact between John and me, no lovemaking when we are at her home, no gay lingo or risqué gay novels. No remarks about good looking men you pass on the street. . . . We won't go back. I don't know if it influenced her, but my ex-wife once told me that her psychologist said, "Just don't have anything to do with someone you disapprove of. . . ."
All: Oh, no!
Paul: I guess my wife never really got over it. . . . There's never a good time to tell your wife you're gay. And it was a

difficult time telling the kids. I've been to my son's home in Dallas only twice. When I used to visit, his house was always full of his friends. He hasn't told his friends about me, and he never brings them around.
Man No. 1: People are so afraid of homosexuality. . . . We were asked to leave the church as our son was dying of AIDS.
His Wife: Yes, it all started when I went in to tell our minister about our son. And he said he would have to check with some others if we would be welcome back at the church. Later I got a call asking our family to leave the church.
Man No. 1: So we found another church. . . . They were wonderful. But then I discovered I was discriminated against at the factory.
Group Member: Why?
Man (angrily): I'm the father of a FAGGOT. . . . Even after my son died. . . . I've never had the kind of work I got before. Now I'm on the road crew. [Sympathetic moans from the group.] (van Wormer, Wells, & Boes, 2000; pp. 166–167)

Groups such as AA and PFLAG are excellent resources for social workers. Al-Anon and Alateen deserve special mention, as well, as places where family members of substance abusers can receive group support and advice, mostly in the form of the Serenity Prayer: to change the things you can and accept the things that you can't do anything about.

Practice Implications

The challenge to the social work profession is to continue the tradition of group work that goes back to the early days of social work and reached its heyday under the leadership of Gisela Konopka and others. Nevertheless, social workers today rely heavily on group strategies, whether in conducting staff meetings, establishing task groups, or running treatment groups for clients with an array of problems. Equipped with an ecosystems understanding of how the group functions as a whole—a whole that is more than the sum of its parts but within which each part has a role to play—and an empowerment approach, social workers have a contribution to make in partnership with clients toward solving problems in living.

From the study of the small group as outlined in this chapter, social workers can be aware of the power of the group itself as a force for change and of power relations within the group and the need for racial ethnic and gender balance as opposed to tokenism. Challenging stereotypes and biases that crop up within the group is important for ethical reasons—in that such comments should always be challenged—but also as an opportunity, in collaboration with group members, to provide some education. Recall that, in Yalom's (2005) study of the curative factors in the therapy group, receiving information and education were cited by participants as the most valuable thing that they had gained from the group experience.

Summary and Conclusion

In light of Homans's (1950) theory of the small group, we have described numerous types of groups of relevance. Yalom's (2005) extensive work as a group practitioner provided insights from a psychodynamic perspective, insights on how roles that clients play in the group recapitulates roles they played earlier in the family. These insights help inform the ecosystems approach to small-group work. We introduced an integrated model for empowerment practice (Kalleen Ragan-Pepper's "Empowering Group Practice"). The group process can be negative, as well as positive, as demonstrated in the mechanisms of scapegoating and groupthink. We concluded with an in-depth description of two self-help groups, one a group for recovering alcoholics, the other a pro-gay-lesbian advocacy group. Much of the theory and information about group dynamics provided in Chapters 2 and 3 is interconnected with our exploration of macro-level family dynamics, which follows in Chapter 4.

Those interested in working for oppressed populations and toward individual potential, social support, and social justice may find some form of small group to be their medium. Many social workers have for many decades. Working with small groups has been a part of the history of the social work profession since its earliest years. After recounting the history of social group work and social work, Janice Andrews concluded, "Group work ideology has stood up well over time because it is rooted in a clear understanding of the realities of human lives and the human condition. Concepts of citizenship, participation, community, mutual aid, and democracy are still powerful" (Andrews, 2001, p. 62). An understanding of small-group structure, process, and development, coupled with pragmatic leadership and facilitating skills, will continue to enhance effectiveness. Innovative new research approaches will inform practitioners regarding interventions and about what works (see, for example, Comer, Meier, & Galinsky, 2004). Yet much of what is effective in work with small groups of people still must come from practical experience. Such experiences can be gained only through being involved with other people in some form of small groups and influencing their development and potential or their social decisions in the larger community.

Thought Questions

1. "The small group has been important in shaping who we are." Discuss.
2. Discuss some key reasons that people in the helping professions need to know about groups.
3. Which are the most important of the "curative factors" that Yalom has identified that stem from the group process?
4. Give some of your examples of the role that universality can play in therapy.
5. What does Goldstein (2002) say about the importance of cohesiveness in the group?

 6. Discuss the notion of the social microcosm.
 7. Describe the group as a system in terms of statuses, roles, and interactive feedback.
 8. What do we learn of team play from Pat Conroy's *My Losing Season*?
 9. How does feminism present an alternative paradigm for group structure?
10. Explain how group norms arise and are reinforced in a group.
11. Discuss how Ragan-Pepper ("Empowering Group Practice") combines ecological and empowerment concepts.
12. Discuss the matter of transference in the group setting. How might "sibling rivalry" play into this?
13. "Political leaders can consolidate the support of their followers if they can direct attention toward an enemy." Discuss.
14. Describe some of the roles that individuals play in the small group. Which role or roles do you tend to play when you have been a group participant (in a class seminar, discussion, group, etc.)?
15. What is the danger of scapegoating in the group? How can the group leader confront this problem?
16. Discuss the phenomenon of group think. Give some examples of your own.
17. Consider the characteristics of a cult and the FLDS phenomenon in light of these characteristics. Compare the religious cult with those that have a military, terroristic purpose.
18. Imagine a group of drug addicts and take them through the group stages.
19. Discuss difficulties that may arise related to race and gender composition.
20. Describe the process by which groups can form networks that lead to a social movement.
21. Identify the basic sources of power in the community listed by Rossi (1969). What is their relevance to social action groups?
22. Discuss social work ethics related to group work.
23. Design an imaginary focus group on a topic related to community-wide research. What kinds of questions would you ask? What might you learn?
24. What does empirical research say about the effectiveness of group treatment?
25. Compare self-help and therapy groups.
26. Describe how the AA group helped the man whose wife was in a nursing home (Victoria Filzer's "A Visit to an AA Meeting"). Do you personally know of a similar instance when a self-help group made a difference in someone's life?
27. Why is it important for social workers to know about PFLAG?

References

Alcoholics Anonymous. (1976). *Alcoholics Anonymous: The story of how many thousands of men and women have recovered from alcoholism*. New York: Alcoholics Anonymous World Services. (Original work published 1939).

Andrews, J. (2001). Group work's place in social work: A historical analysis. *Journal of Sociology and Social Welfare, 28*(4), 45–65.

Asch, S. E. (1952). *Social psychology*. Englewood Cliffs, NJ: Prentice-Hall.

Bales, R. F. (1950). *Interaction process analysis*. Cambridge, MA: Addison-Wesley.

Ball, D. (2001). *How to do your own focus groups: A guide for trial attorneys*. South Bend, IN: National Institute for Trial Attorneys.

Barker, R. (2003). *The social work dictionary* (5th ed.). Washington, DC: NASW Press.

Barsky, A. E. (2010). *Ethics and values in social work: An integrated approach for a comprehensive curriculum*. New York: Oxford University Press.

Browne, C., & Mills, C. (2001). Theoretical frameworks: Ecological model, strengths perspective, and empowerment theory. In R. Fong & S. Furuto (Eds.), *Culturally competent practice: Skills, interventions, and evaluations* (pp. 10–32). Boston: Allyn & Bacon.

Casey, M. A., & Krueger, R. (2004). An overview of focus group interviewing. In A. Roberts & K. Yeager (Eds.), *Evidence-based practice manual: Research and outcome measures in health and human services* (pp. 61–69). New York: Oxford University Press.

Cavendish, R. (2008). November 29, 1978: The Jonestown mass suicide. *History Today*, *58*(11), 13–14.

Clarke, R. (2004). *Against all enemies: Inside America's war on terror*. New York: Free Press.

Comer, E., Meier, A., & Galinsky, M. (2004). Development of innovative group work practice using the intervention research paradigm. *Social Work*, *49*(2), 250–259.

Conroy, P. (2002). *My losing season*. New York: Doubleday.

Corey, G. (2008). *Theory and practice of group counseling* (7th ed.). Belmont, CA: Brooks/Cole.

Corey, M. S., & Corey, G. (2006). *Groups: Process and practice* (7th ed). Belmont, CA: Brooks/Cole.

Cross, J. (2008, April 11). Expert: FLDS polygamous group is a classic cult. *Free Republic*. Retrieved from http://www.freerepublic.com/focus/news/2001395/posts

Denham, S., Meyer, M., Toborg, M., & Mande, M. (2004). Providing health education to Appalachia populations. *Holistic Nursing Practice*, *18*(6), 293–312.

Ephross, P., & Vassil, T. (2005). *Groups that work: Structure and process*. New York: Columbia University Press.

Festinger, L. (1956). *When prophecy fails*. New York: Harper & Row.

Freud, S. (1975). *A general introduction to psychoanalysis*. Riverside, NJ: Simon & Schuster. (Original work published 1924).

Gladwell, M. (2002). *The tipping point: How little things can make a big difference*. Boston: Little, Brown.

Goldstein, A. P. (2002). *The psychology of group aggression*. Chichester, England: Wiley.

Gutiérrez, L., & Suarez, Z. (1999). Empowerment with Latinas. In L. A. Gutiérrez & E. A. Lewis (Eds.), *Empowerment of women of color* (pp. 167–186). New York: Columbia University Press.

Harrington, M. (1973). *Socialism*. New York: Bantam Books.

Homans, C. (1950). *The human group*. New York: Harcourt, Brace and World.

Homer. (1968). Iliad. In J. Bartlett (Ed.), *Familiar quotations* (4th ed) (p. 63). Boston: Little, John, Brown. Originally circa 700 BC.

Janis, I. (1982). *Victims of groupthink: A psychology of foreign-policy decisions and fiascoes*. Boston: Houghton Mifflin.

Kirst-Ashman, K. (2007). *Human behavior, communities, organizations, and groups in the macro social perspective* (2nd ed.). Belmont, CA: Brooks/Cole.

Lewin, K., Lippitt, R., & White, R. (1939). Patterns of aggressive behavior in experimentally created social climates. *Journal of Social Psychology*, *10*, 271–301.

Lundy, C. (2004). *Social work and social justice: A structural approach to practice*. Petersborough, Ontario: Broadview.

Machiavelli, N. (1980). *The prince*. New York: New American Library. (Original work published 1532).

Manning, D. (2005, May 1). The secret Downing Street memo. *London Sunday Times*. Retrieved from http://www.timesonline.co.uk/tol/news/uk/article387374.ece

Meier, A., & Comer, E. (2005). Using evidence-based practice and intervention research with treatment groups for populations at risk. In G. Greif & P. Ephross (Eds.), *Group work with populations at risk* (2nd ed., pp. 413–439). New York: Oxford University Press.

Moore-Emmett, A. (2004). *God's brothel: The extortion of sex for salvation in contemporary Mormon and Christian fundamentalist polygamy and the stories of 18 women who escaped*. San Francisco: Pince-Nez Press.

Northen, H., & Kurland, R. O. (2001). *Social work with groups*. New York: Columbia University Press.

Pence, E., & Paynar, M. (1993). *Education groups for men who batter: The Duluth model*. New York: Springer.

Pinaire, B. K. (2004, May 27). *The focus group method: Observation, elaboration, and deliberation*. Paper presented at the Annual Meeting of the The Law and Society Association, Chicago, Illinois. Retrieved from http://www.allacademic.com/meta/p116856_index.html

Reid, K. (2002). Clinical social work with groups. In A. Roberts & G. Greene (Eds.), *Social workers' desk reference* (pp. 432–436). New York: Oxford University Press.

Schriver, J. M. (2010). *Human behavior in the social environment: Shifting paradigms in essential knowledge for social work practice*. (5th ed.). Boston: Prentice Hall.

Sharlet, J. (2005, May). Soldiers of Christ: Inside America's most powerful megachurch. *Harper's*, 41–54.

Sheridan, M., & Hsu, S. (2009, December 12). Arrests suggest U.S. Muslims, like those in Europe, can be radicalized abroad. *Washington*

Post. Retrieved from http://www.washingtonpost.com/wp-dyn/content/article/2009/12/11/AR2009121104404.html?wpisrc=newsletter

Stewart, D., Shamdasani, P., & Rook, D. (2007). *Focus groups: Theory and practice* (2nd ed.). Thousand Oaks, CA: Sage.

Stouffer, S. (1949). *The American soldier: Combat and its aftermath*. Princeton, NJ: Princeton University Press.

Toseland, R., & Rivas, R. (2001). *An introduction to group practice* (4th ed.). Boston: Allyn & Bacon.

Tuckman, B. W. (1965). Developmental sequences in small groups. *Psychological Bulletin, 63,* 384–399.

van Wormer, K. (1995). *Alcoholism treatment: A social work perspective*. Belmont, CA: Brooks/Cole.

van Wormer, K. (2010). *Working with female offenders: A gender-sensitive approach*. Hoboken, NJ: Wiley & Sons.

van Wormer, K., & Davis, D. R. (2008). *Addiction treatment: A strengths perspective.* (2nd ed.). Belmont, CA: Brooks/Cole.

van Wormer, K., Wells, J., & Boes, M. (2000). *Social work with lesbians, gays, and bisexuals: A strengths-based perspective*. Boston: Allyn & Bacon.

White, B. J., & Madara, E. (Eds.). (2002). *The self-help group source book: Your guide to community and online support groups* (7th ed.). Denville, NJ: St Clare's Health Services.

Woodward, B. (2004). *Plan of attack*. Riverside, NJ: Simon & Schuster.

Yalom, I. (2005). *The theory and practice of group psychotherapy* (5th ed.). New York: Basic Books.

Zastrow, C., & Kirst-Ashman, K. (2010). *Understanding human behavior and the social environment* (8th ed.). Belmont, CA: Wadsworth.

Families in Society

The family is the natural and fundamental group unit of society and is entitled to protection by society and the state.

—UN UNIVERSAL DECLARATION OF HUMAN RIGHTS

1948, Article 16(3)

4

This chapter bears a close connection to Chapter 7 in *Human Behavior and the Social Environment, Micro Level*, "The Individual in the Family" (van Wormer, 2011). This chapter, like this book, focuses on macro-level understandings and on empowerment at the macro level and addresses questions such as the following: What are the functions of families for the society? How does a society ensure family values? What is the impact of globalization?

Our starting point is a brief review of eco-systems concepts as first discussed in Chapter 1. Our emphasis in this chapter is on the process of family adaptation and family resilience under conditions of stress. For immigrant families, as we show in this chapter, adaptation is essential on multiple levels related to relocation, a past of loss and displacement, and cultural misunderstandings. We consider also in a related section diverse family patterns based on such factors as ethnicity and sexual orientation.

Policy relevant to family life is a major theme of this chapter. Policies in the United States are briefly compared with more family-friendly policies such as those provided by the European model. Globalization has a major impact on the family, in part indirectly through work pressures on the adults of the family. We discuss the impact of global competition on the family unit.

Although all aspects of the world's victimization of girls and women are not related to economics or to the increasing gap between the rich and the poor, sex trafficking and the luring of poor girls and women into the sex trade undoubtedly are. We consider this and other forms of exploitation and suppression of women across the globe. Mindful that the United States has its share of family violence, we examine gender-based violence internationally from a human rights perspective. Genital mutilation and honor killings are among the practices discussed. The chapter concludes with a global view of a different sort, an overview of family-centered innovations such as kinship care and family group conferencing. Such practices provide models of empowerment that can serve as a guide for social work with families at risk. The first boxed reading is a personal narrative of a hearing woman raised by loving deaf parents; the second presents the testimonial of a 9-year-old boy who lost his parents to the state correctional system; the third and fourth are contributions from young women who grew up wrestling with bicultural identities; and the fifth contains interviews with members of a lesbian-headed household.

Family ethnicity is far more diverse today than formerly, as we know from first hand experience and from the census data which we discuss later in the chapter. See Figure 4.1 for a delightfully happy family; the father is from Jamaica and the mother from the Midwest.

The Family as an Ecosystem

When we say that the family is an ecosystem, we are joining two concepts: one from the science of ecology, which views the organism in the environment; the other from systems theory and family systems theory, in which the focus is on how the parts together form a whole that is greater than the sum of the parts. Both Murray

Bowen (1978) and Salvadore Minuchin (1974) were pioneers in regarding the family as a unit and in arguing for treatment of individual problems through an understanding of family scripts or patterns that were intergenerational and that induced symptoms in individuals with problems. These theorists revolutionized psychotherapy by including families in therapy and extending family concepts to the understanding of any family (Green, 2003).

At the macro level, we want to think about the family, rather than the individual, as the organism, and we want to see the family as linked to other families and other systems in the universe. The family in the environment is thus our basic concern. And by environment we mean the house or other place we live in, the air we breathe, the conditions for travel to work and to school, the neighborhood, and the politicoeconomic system. The focus on how families adapt to environmental factors is central to the ecological framework.

The systems concept calls our attention to the way a family is constructed in terms of boundaries and role relationships. From this

Figure 4.1. A close-knit family. The family is a system of roles and relationships that are at once predictable and unique. Photo by Rupert van Wormer.

perspective, the family can be conceived as an open system that constantly receives and reacts to feedback from the environment. Boundaries are permeable to the extent that messages freely flow back and forth. Think of neighborhood kids coming in and out of the house to play and the kids in your house spending time in various homes across the neighborhoods. This brings the adults in the families together so that the links become ever wider and more complex. Some families, however, are closed systems, either in themselves or as a part of another closed system such as a religious cult. By definition, the cult shields itself from the outside world for protection and to exert control over the thinking and loyalties of its members. Some families try to operate the same way—erecting barriers to halt the flow of information from the outside world.

Because ecosystems concepts are reality based, they can serve as a guide for practitioners who work with individuals, for school social workers who work with families, or for community organizers who work with multiple groupings of people. (See Chapter 1 for a detailed look at this theoretical construct.) Perception, goals, and patterns are the principal concerns of this approach. Attention is paid to the complex ways in which individual persons and families are reciprocally linked. (Observe the family dynamics in Figure 4.2 which follows.)

The formulation of the family as a system in the environment and of the individual as a subsystem in the family is one of the most dynamic and useful developments in mental health counseling. The family systems concept, although sometimes presented as a separate theory, is a natural fit with ecological concepts, as both approaches are built on the notion of interrelationships. Ecological theory adds a key element to our study of the family system in that it reminds us to include in our understanding both the physical and the wider social environment; these are essential components in the quality of life pertaining to the basic unit of society, the family. The view of the family in the wider environment expands the concept of the social environment to include the family's ability to meet the members' physical needs, as well as the impact of such forces as natural disasters, government policy, and macro economics.

The ecosystems framework, in short, extends our focus beyond relationships among family members and links between families and community resources into an even higher plane of interconnectedness. The ecosystems approach makes clear the need to see the family in its mediating or bridging role between individuals and society. Central to the ecosystems family perspective are four fundamental concepts: interactionism, stress, coping, and adaptation. Each of these concepts is relevant to macro-level theory and practice. *Interactionism* tells us of the interconnectedness of things, how each participant in an exchange is affected by the other's actions. Interaction, in other words, encompasses the give and take of feedback. All relationships are conceived as reciprocal, not only at the moment but over time as the history of the interaction builds. As Germain (1991) explained, transactional causality occurs in a circular loop. Cause and effect are intertwined. An event or process may be a cause at one point and an effect at another in the ongoing flow of information and actions. Germain's conceptualization is often contrasted with the traditional linear or cause-and-effect models in which a cause (such as mental illness) is seen as preceding an effect (such as abusive drinking). Interactive or transactional in its approach, the ecological model has important implications for social work intervention into the world of the family, a world that is the *shaper of* the family even as it is *shaped by* the family. This process of environmental interactionism is not static but ongoing.

Stress is the second key concept of ecosystems theory. In contrast to interaction, which tells us how relationships work, stress is about external forces, forces that may be derived from biological factors—for example, from disease or nature—over which people often have little control. A related ecological concept that is useful in thinking about family dynamics is adaptation to the stress stemming from the environment. *Adaptation* is defined by Germain (1991) as an active process of self-change or environmental change or both. It is not, she informs us, a mere passive adjustment to circumstance. Adaptation comes about as human beings strive for the best person-environment "fit" possible between their needs and capacities and the requirements of the environment.

Following Germain's logic, people may adapt to stress in the physical environment, such as a shortage in the usual food supply, or to the cultural realm, for instance, lack of fluency in the host language. Adaptation in the first instance may mean finding a food substitute, such as grain or fish instead of meat. Adaptation in the second instance may entail geographical relocation and/or learning the language of the dominant culture. The family's adaptation may be positive in reducing the stress, consistent with Germain's positive formulation; or adaptation, as we see it, may be stress inducing and counterproductive. An example of an unhealthy adjustment to change would be an adolescent joining a gang to fit in with new surroundings. Parents may take to drinking as a means of self-medication in regard to pressures of their own. Whether productive or not, these reactions are ways of coping, and that brings us to the fourth of the key concepts that we have filtered out from the theory.

Coping behavior, as we have seen, may either reduce the stress or exacerbate it. Sometimes what seems like stress to the outsider—such as growing up bilingual or in a narrow religious community—is seen as an advantage to family members, and often it does provide the individual with an advantage that few outsiders would realize. Social workers, who are trained to look for strengths in the ways individuals and families learn to cope through adaptation, will often uncover such truths. In Box 4.1, "Growing Up 'Deaf,'" Barbara Rindels describes coping and adaptation within a deaf family as told from the viewpoint of a hearing woman who grew up within that family. (See Chapter 6 for a description of the Deaf community as a self-contained and viable community.)

Germain's ecosystems paradigm, with its interrelated concepts of adaptation, stress, and coping, provides a framework through which to view various situations that are external to the family but that have important ramifications for the family holon. (The holon, as described

Box 4.1 Growing Up "Deaf"

Barbara Rindels

People assume that growing up with deaf parents, my family life must have been different, the dynamics strange. It *was* different in that I grew up in a different culture, a different environment. Many things were similar to any other "normal" family, though.

My father was the patriarchal figure, the "head" of the household. My mother was submissive to my father, but kind. And then there were the children . . . all of us were different. I am the oldest of four. I am hearing. In Deaf culture that means I am a CODA—a Child of Deaf Adults.

My siblings, in order, are: Sandy (hearing), Tracy (Deaf), and Emily (hard of hearing). Our first language was American Sign Language. Our first culture was Deaf culture. One of my earliest memories was being told by my mom, in sign language, that I needed to tell my sister she was wrong for playing with the TV. My sister, who was about 2 years old, bit me when I told her, "No, don't touch the TV!" I told her "no" because I was told to do so. Somehow, because I was the firstborn hearing child, the first CODA of the family, this means I am the "voice" of the family, of my parents.

Many people assume that my house, growing up, must have been very quiet. On the contrary, it was often very loud. Since my parents couldn't hear me, I could blast my stereo, talk on the phone late at night, and yell and scream at my little sisters. The TV volume was always turned way up so my hard-of-hearing sister could hear it.

My parents also contributed to the noise level. It surprises people that Deaf people do use their voices. Many Deaf children were taught to form words in their mouths through feeling the vibrations on someone else's throat, cheeks, and lips. My mother had a very high-pitched voice, cultivated through years of speech therapy when she was growing up. If people got used to my mother's voice, she was generally intelligible. My dad's speech wasn't as good as my mother's. He was raised in a household with a Deaf brother who never learned to use his voice.

I find most people are very ignorant about deafness, deaf people, and Deaf culture. Many people I have met over the years ask me questions like, "How do your parents drive?" I think that is the most common, annoying question I get, and the answer is simple: "Like everyone else, with their feet, eyes, and hands." Deaf people often have keen eyesight and use the mirrors in a car diligently.

People also ask me, "How did you learn to talk?" I don't know exactly, but I always had hearing people around me, like my grandmothers and babysitters. I could hear the TV. I guess I just picked up the language, English. That was my second language.

The first language I learned, the language of my birth, is American Sign Language (ASL). ASL isn't English. It isn't structured like English at all. It is a language in its own right; I would say the structure is closer to Spanish than English. I grew up in the Deaf culture. I went to the Deaf club on Friday and Saturday nights. I dated Deaf boys I met at the Deaf club and went to a Deaf Bible camp in the summer. English was more difficult for me because the structural rules were so different from *my* language.

Some things were very different for me at home. We didn't have a phone at my house until I was 13 years old. I always had to ask the neighbors if I could use their phone to make phone calls for my parents.

As the oldest CODA, I had to interpret for my parents in many situations: at the store, at my grandfather's funeral, at school meetings. I remember my dad telling me to interpret the 5 o'clock news. I sat next to the TV trying very hard to interpret things I couldn't always understand.

Sometimes I took advantage of my position as the "voice" of the family. At school meetings, I would often tell my parents what I wanted them to hear and tell the teacher what I wanted her to believe my parents had said. Once I was suspended from school for 3 days. I had to bring a parent in with me after my suspension to meet with the principal. I took my father with me for the Monday morning meeting because I knew my father wasn't very good at reading lips. When the principal said, "Your daughter was suspended for smoking pot," I told my dad I had gotten caught smoking a cigarette. I then told the principal that I was in terrible trouble and that my father was very angry and had grounded me for a month. Of course my dad had done no such thing. He was actually surprised the principal was making such a big deal out of a cigarette.

I'm still surprised that I got away with that one.

Twenty-five years later, even though I moved to a different community from the one I grew up in, I still attend the Deaf club in my area. I feel more at home among Deaf people, and they always welcome me. Being bilingual (ASL-English) and bicultural (Deaf-hearing) has given me a variety of opportunities in my life, and taught me many life lessons.

Printed with permission of Barbara Rindels, Waterloo, Iowa.

in Chapter 1, is a whole "entire of itself" and, at the same time, a part of a wider whole.) By way of illustration of this theoretical construct, consider the impact of a natural disaster. Earthquakes and hurricanes are recent events highlighted in the news that illustrate the viability of the family unit. In Hurricane Katrina, media reports revealed images of an extraordinary intergenerational caretaking and sometimes a refusal to leave a flooded area if the group could not stay intact or if pets were to be left behind. The sequence is as follows: from stress (loss of housing) to steps to counter stress (removal to safe quarters) to adaptation (regrouping as an expanded or reduced family unit). *Biologically*, urgent physical adaptations to flood conditions are required in the absence of shelter, food, and drinkable water. Both short-term and long-term adaptations may occur. *Psychologically*, mental health (for example, trauma) is linked to responses (whether healthy or unhealthy). Psychological stress may lead to alcohol abuse. *Socially*, adaptation to a pattern of drinking determines the company one keeps; likewise, the society reinforces one's chance of survival (for example, through aid from the Red Cross or the federal government). In short, psychological and environmental factors have a powerful influence on the experience of stress and efforts to deal with it. It is not the magnitude of the stressor itself but the perception of its magnitude that is important.

In times of crisis, each family will have its own peculiar style of adaptation—coping through blaming, denying, and protecting. In a national economic downturn, for example, the emotional and financial resources of the family may be almost entirely depleted. The concept of *coping* refers to the special adaptations that are

Figure 4.2. Family members watch and march in the Seattle solstice parade. Photo by Rupert van Wormer.

made in response to internal stress (Holland & Kilpatrick, 2003). Problem solving and managing negative feelings are two major aspects of coping. The concept of coping implies that some sort of crisis has occurred. A macro-level crisis that is societal (such as a major flood) does not affect every family in the same way. Generally, families that were marginalized and highly vulnerable, devoid of backup plans, savings in the bank, and marketable skills even before the crisis, bear the brunt of the pain. Hurricane Katrina made that reality evident in images of suffering and helplessness that were projected around the world.

We can visualize the family in the world with the help of an ecomap. The *ecomap* is a didactic and assessment tool for depicting the relationships and interactions between a client family and the social environment (Zastrow & Kirst-Ashman, 2010). Figure 4.3 shows the interlocking nature of systems in the community within the context of wider environmental forces, including factors related to global economic competition and the forces of nature—the air, soil, and water—and the spiritual realm. The former are represented inside the concentric rings and are included as external global forces. The outer level represents the natural

and spiritual realm, the world we know and the world we don't know.

From an empowerment perspective, Gutiérrez and Suarez (1999) recommend the use of eco-mapping to identify the relative power of individuals, families, and other systems in the social environment. The ecomap can be drawn to show school–family interactions at the community level; these relationships are the most familiar and easy to visualize. The child can be shown to be both a member of the family and of a class cohort at school. If there are problems at school, the effect can be felt at home through the child's acting-out behavior. Conversely, problems internal to the family, such as alcoholism, can create a stress that extends across systems. The stress related to out-of-control drinking can have a synergistic or multiplying effect throughout the family system and related environmental network.

In a collaborative effort between therapist and family members, special markers, such as dotted lines, can be placed on the arrows that extend among the various systems to indicate tension or closeness in the relationship. The direction in which the arrow is pointed represents the flow of energy, which is often both ways. For example, trouble in the family may

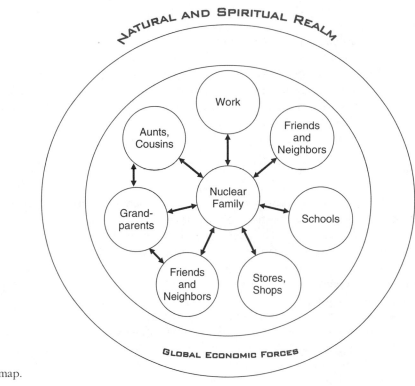

Figure 4.3. Family ecomap.

affect a person's productivity and relationships at work, and trouble at work can have a bearing on home life. Therapists can use their imaginations in what they want the lines to represent and what symbols are used. Figure 4.3 is just a basic outline. When this drawing of the family ecosystem is completed, as Gutiérrez and Suarez (1999) suggest, the ecomap can serve as an assessment tool to indicate to the social worker and clients areas in which an increase of personal, interpersonal, or political power may be lacking and areas in need of attention. (See the genogram in *HBSE, Micro Level*, Chapter 4 [van Wormer, 2011], for a diagram that reveals the internal dynamics of the family.)

The family may come to serve in a mediating role between the individual member with an illness, such as alcoholism, and other systems—work, school, larger family. But gradually, as the illness progresses, the bridges between the alcoholic and his or her social world will be broken. The family may then adapt to social isolation and the continual stress

of the progressing alcoholism, or members may regroup and form a reconstituted family without the alcoholic. A third alternative, of course, is treatment for the "alcoholic family" as a family. Treatment considerations would focus on healthy adaptation to the demands of familial sobriety. Work with the family from an ecosystems and empowerment perspective facilitates the process of recovery through attention to support systems and interrelationships among the participants (Goldenberg & Goldenberg, 2002). The twin notions of interactionism and adaptation to stress inform the family treatment process.

Unlike the *psychodynamic* approach in social work, which stresses personality or intrapsychic variables, the *ecological* approach tends to perceive personality and environmental characteristics in dynamic interaction with each other. The latter view is more complicated and psychologically demanding than the former; it goes against the natural tendency to simplify human experience. The ecological approach also goes against another tendency, which is to attribute another person's actions solely to *innate* personality characteristics rather than to a combination of factors.

To the study of the family, the ecosystems approach offers, as stated earlier, a nonlinear view of causation, a circular chain of acts and reactions. Each member in the family group may be seen as at once a nurturer and a recipient of nurturing by the others; conversely, each member may be victim and victimizer of the others, or a combination of these roles. Ecological theory is a framework for action directed at the here-and-now interactions of individuals and families; work focuses on altering the basic structure of those interactions to enhance functioning. To help the family negotiate the system, the family therapist may join the family unit temporarily, acting as a pseudo-family member to help shape a way for healthy and adaptive family functioning. The family therapist must forever be cognizant of the impact of issues in the macro environment, such as welfare policies, that impinge on family development and even on family survival. The family therapist must also maintain a high level of sensitivity to unique family forms, whether stemming from cultural or sexual patterns. From a strengths perspective, we now explore a few of the most common ethnic family patterns. Mainstream cultural value orientations, which generally are considered the conventional pattern in Anglo-Saxon North America, are described in Chapter 5.

Sustainability is an ecosystems term that lends itself to a policy-level consideration. Two basic questions that guide this chapter are these: What are the major threats to the sustainability of the modern family? And to what extent is American society truly family friendly? Imagine as you read the sections that follow a world united in its investment in families. Such a world would include greater equalization of the wealth and a network of social supports to enhance the well-being of all children and their parents. Imagine employment practices that guaranteed a living wage and working hours and conditions that are compatible with family life. We need to keep sustainability in mind as we contemplate the impact of employee layoffs, foreclosures of the family home, immigration

raids (a topic for Chapter 6 on the community), the extremely high imprisonment rate of mothers and fathers caught up in the war on drugs, and benefits denied to gay- and lesbian-headed households. This consideration of sustainability is relevant to all the discussions on the following pages but especially to the sections on economic globalization and violence against women globally.

Ethnic Family Patterns

Immigrant families invariably bring their cultural values with them as they migrate to the new land. Social work educators Snyder, May, Zulcic, and Gabbard (2005) have written of Bosnian Muslim culture. Their description is drawn from their familiarity with Bosnian refugees who have settled in Bowling Green, Kentucky, as well as with the research literature. These researchers call our attention to the following cultural norms:

> Bosnian men and women tend to adhere to traditional gender roles; connected with this issue is the intense stigma attached to the sexual violation of women. Bosnian Muslims typically act in ways that preserve the positive image of the family's identity.
>
> Family is the most important social structure across the urban and rural regions of Bosnia. Up until the 1970s it was common for adult children to live with their parents and for multiple generations to live within the same house, but now nuclear families predominate with extended family members living nearby. A cluster of shoes can often be found outside a Bosnian home; it is customary to remove street shoes and leave them at the door. Bosnians maintain a strong social tradition of neighborliness. The drinking of strong coffee or the sharing of food, which is accompanied by the essential element of conversation, is an important aspect of social life. Traditional music and folks dances are an important part of cultural celebrations. (p. 621)

Snyder et al. (2005) further note that strong family ties have fostered resiliency among Bosnians and helped them adapt to relocation in the aftermath of war trauma. Possessing a strong cultural identity, performing cultural rituals, and maintaining a sense of connectedness to others are characteristics of healthy outcomes. The authors make the case that the Western approach to trauma treatment tends to be based on the individual as the primary system of focus. The theoretical emphasis is on intrapersonal rather than interpersonal processes, to the neglect of the cultural context and ethnic source of empowerment.

U.S. society is increasingly multicultural, not only as a society but also within families due to intermarriage across cultural and racial groups. The cross-cultural mingling of heritage, including language, religion, and value systems, enriches America and acquaints us with multiple approaches to similar situations (greater reliance on kinship care, for example). In conceptualizing multiculturalism, it is helpful to think in terms of cultural pluralism, or what Canadians term a cultural mosaic, instead of a melting pot. The concept of the mosaic encourages us to respect rather than deny differences and to understand each family within the meaning of cultural context. The following descriptions are provided to outline common characteristics of four sets of minority families: American Indians, African Americans, Latino Americans, and Asian Americans. These brief descriptions cannot do justice to diversity within the cultural groups, but they do bring our attention to the fact that mainstream (especially white Anglo-Saxon Protestant and German American) values that prioritize needs of the nuclear family, often to the neglect of extended family members within the global context, are, in fact, not mainstream at all. Throughout the world, the definition of family tends to be more inclusive than in certain regions of the Global North.

American Indians

American Indians as a group have resisted assimilation as much as possible. This is evidenced through the maintenance of a distinct culture, language, and worldview, despite the many efforts by the government to eradicate American Indian culture and practices (Day, 2007). Although tribal differences are pronounced, we can filter out several themes that transcend the variations in American Indian practices. Among the traditional values singled out by Coyhis (2000) are as follows: a strong emphasis on *being*, not doing; cooperation over competition; a group focus; working only to meet one's needs; nonmaterialism; right-brain orientation; the importance of extended family; a flexible concept of time; individual freedom; living in harmony with nature; and a pervasive sense of spirituality. Although the dual focus on the extended family and the individual may appear contradictory, as Zastrow and Kirst-Ashman (2010) indicate, children in Native American families are reared to pursue their own interests and to make their own decisions. Much of their learning comes through their own observations; they are taught to rely on nonverbal rather than verbal cues (Gesino, 2007). This cultural tradition was very surprising to European explorers and settlers who encountered the custom of *berdache*. This custom allowed for culturally prescribed roles by which effeminate gay men and masculine-acting women could follow their innate proclivities in dress and in marriage (van Wormer, Wells, & Boes, 2000). Today, in acknowledgment of the existence of people whose spirits are neither entirely male nor entirely female, the term *two spirit* is preferred by many North American indigenous peoples.

In American Indian, as in African American, families, family life has a history of existing within a context of racial and economic oppression. Forced to continually move westward and to live on reservations on lands that were undesirable for cultivation, families were uprooted again and again. The Christian missionary effort further eroded native tradition while undermining forms of family life that did not correspond to the patriarchal nuclear family (Longres, 2000; Morales, Sheafor, & Scott, 2010). Nevertheless, matriarchal norms have persisted, and women have occupied positions of tribal leadership. Respect for kinship continues, though to a much lesser degree than formerly (Morales et al., 2010). The Indian way of life is much more prominent on reservations than in cities. Even on reservations, though, tribal elders have witnessed the deterioration of cultural traditions, ancient beliefs, and respect for elders. Despite the financial gains from casinos on some reservations, social problems, such as high unemployment rates, low school completion rates, high alcoholism rates, and widespread domestic violence, persist (Koppelman, 2005). These problems have a strong impact on family life, directly through violence and suicide and indirectly through a high prevalence of health problems (Morales et al., 2010).

In the cities, Indian groups do not cluster in certain neighborhoods but are integrated; high rates of intermarriage with members of different tribes and with non-Native Americans is enhancing a loss of cultural identity in urban areas (Longres, 2000). Still, as Day (2007) points out, members of tribes in urban areas maintain indigenous customs through community gatherings, tribal education for the children, and tribal social services.

One of us (van Wormer), in her alcoholism treatment counseling with Native Americans from Washington State, discovered strengths unique to this cultural group, strengths related to cultural pride and tradition. The "harmony with nature" theme provided a sense of hope in difficulty and guidance for maintaining a balance in life. Spirituality and the understanding of life as a circular process gave meaning to people's existence, and death was accepted as a return of the person's spirit to the life beyond. In individual therapy, Native American clients found meaning and solace in the symbolism contained in dreams. They also had knowledge of herbal remedies for various ailments, as well as of herbs that could be used in hallucinogenic rituals.

In high-functioning American Indian families, extended family members include parents, children, cousins, aunts, uncles, and grandparents. Grandparents remain, as formerly, an important influence in the Native American family (Gesino, 2007). In fact, according to the 2000 U.S. Census (U.S. Census Bureau, 2003), 8 percent of American Indian families, compared with 2 percent of white families, include grandparents in the household. Children receive

instruction from relatives of several generations, as well as from their parents (Zastrow & Kirst-Ashman, 2010). Parents are thus freed to have less pressured relationships with their children compared with parents in the dominant culture. Fuller-Thomson and Minkler (2005), however, in their analysis of U.S. Census data on American Indian grandparenting, offer a somber note in that one-third of the grandparent caregivers were found to be living below the poverty line and that only one-quarter of these were receiving the kind of public assistance that they needed. Compared with non-caregiving grandparents from the same ethnic group, these caregivers were disproportionately female, poor, living with a functional disability, and living in overcrowded conditions.

Priscilla Day (2007), who is of Ojibwe heritage herself, describes how the strength of the extended family among American Indians leads to the expectation that frail Indian elders will be cared for by family members. In her discussion of the nursing home, she advises social workers and other staff in nursing homes that knowledge of the historical and contemporary context of American Indian life is essential. In a moving passage, Day quotes an Ojibwe elder who talked about how American Indian people are unique because we "look through the eyes of elders when we look at the world" (p. 49). American Indian children are taught from an early age to respect and care for their elders. These elders are the links to the past, to the time when the tribes lived close to the land and with all creatures. The elders are also the link to the upheaval that came with conquest and that is conceived as "the wounding of the soul" in which the spirit was injured. The wisdom of the elders and their carrying on of the oral storytelling tradition are sources of strength and pride in the Native American community.

In working with Native American and Canadian families, and most families for that matter, the metaphor of the Medicine Wheel, which exemplifies the wholeness of life, is useful. The Medicine Wheel teaches about the cycle of life, a cycle that encompasses infancy through old age, the seasons, and four directions of human growth—the realms of the emotional, mental, physical, and spiritual. From this perspective, all parts of the universe are inextricably related. In Indian country, as explained by Coyhis (2000), there is a movement to return to cultural values and folkways, to reestablish the sense of social interconnectedness. The Indian belief is that those things that have been will be again, that history repeats itself in never-ending cycles.

African American Families

Over the past few decades, single-parent households, almost all of them headed by women, have become increasingly common throughout American society. Among African Americans, 69.3 percent of births were to unmarried women in 2005 (the white rate was also strikingly high at 31.7 percent; U.S. Census Bureau, 2009a). The share of the nation's children living in single-parent households actually declined in the late 1990s. This seemingly positive result was soon viewed in a new light, however, as researchers at the Urban Institute discovered, through a closer analysis, that due to the loss of welfare benefits and the irregular hours of low-wage jobs children increasingly are being moved into the homes of relatives, friends, and foster families (Bernstein, 2002). The change in family living arrangements was most pronounced in African American families. Joblessness, poverty, reluctance to marry, and family breakup are all highly interrelated. These enduring conditions help explain why blacks marry at much lower rates than other groups in the United States (Coontz & Folbre, 2003).

Many scholars have emphasized the importance of the African cultural heritage in understanding the functioning of contemporary African American families (Black & Jackson, 2005; Scheele, 2007). Capture and forced migration, enslavement followed by segregation, racism, and oppression create a need for reflecting on historical losses even while accomplishments should be celebrated (Black & Jackson, 2005). Some people of African origin, accordingly, have an internalized rage that can be the result of a lifetime accumulation of real and perceived slights and insults, as Black and Jackson (2005) indicate. Yet Schiele (2007) notes that many of the positive attributes of today's black families, such as strong religious orientation, flexible

family roles, extended family networks, and informal adoption processes, are a legacy of African cultural patterns and the black experience on this continent.

The important caretaking role accorded to women in the family is a cultural strength derived from blacks' African legacy and reinforced during the period of slavery, as Scheel (2007) and See, Bowles, and Darlington (2007) suggest. This fact provides resilience to the black family given the decline in high-paying manufacturing jobs and the associated decline in the earning power or even employment for working-class men. Sex-role flexibility, although a source of strength and survival for many African American families, nevertheless has often been viewed as a deficit because it differs from the white middle-class nuclear family model (Schriver, 2010).

Black single-parent families, moreover have a major advantage over white single-parent families that statistics fail to reveal. In these families, the image of the lone woman in social isolation struggling to rear her children does not apply. Usually a number of kin, including a mother, aunt, or brother, from a number of households make up a domestic network of supportive relations (Longres, 2000). Despite an upsurge in the number of births to single mothers among white women and a decline in the birthrate for unmarried black women, this pattern is still disproportionately found among blacks. This pattern may be more a reflection of the shortage of marriageable males and of women's willingness to delay marriage until a suitable partner comes along than the result of any devaluation of the institution of marriage, however.

The high mortality rate among young black men—many die as a result of homicide—combined with the fact that many are in the military or married to women of another race or caught up legally in the war on drugs has depleted the numbers of eligible men. Here is an astonishing statistic: around 11 percent of African American males, compared with around 3.5 percent of Latino males and 1.7 percent of white males in their late 20s and early 30s, are behind bars (Bureau of Justice Statistics [BJS], 2009). About 37 percent of all male inmates at midyear 2008 were black, down from 41 percent for midyear 2000. Part of the reason most likely is a decrease in arrests for crack cocaine. African Americans constitute 59 percent of those convicted of drug offenses, despite the fact that their drug use is not substantially higher than that of other racial groups (Drug Policy Alliance, 2009). As a result of racist sentencing practices and the low numbers of black males attending college, today more African Americans are serving time in prison than in programs of higher education (Green, Ensminger, Robertson, & Juon, 2006).

The racial disparities in drug arrests and convictions have had a devastating effect on families. According to a special BJS (2008) report on children of incarcerated parents, black and Hispanic children are about eight and three times, respectively, more likely than white children to have a parent in prison. Among minor children in the U.S. resident population, 6.7 percent of black children, 2.4 percent of Hispanic children, and 0.9 percent of white children have a parent in prison. The toll on the children in inner-city families has been enormous—first in the loss of the father and second in terms of bearing the stigma of having a father in prison. Without intervention, children of incarcerated fathers are five times more likely than other children to be sent to prison themselves (Mazza, 2002).

Class differences affect opportunities and family lifestyles among blacks as among all ethnic groups. Affirmative action programs in higher education and the professions, which were stronger over the past decade than they are today, have helped many members of minority groups achieve the "American dream." Enrollment of black women in college increased significantly in all levels of higher education, and according to a recent report from *The Journal of Blacks in Higher Education* ("African Americans Show Positive Gains at All Academic Levels," 2009), black males as well are graduating from college in record numbers. African Americans received 9.6 percent of all bachelor's degrees in 2007, 10.3 percent of all master's degrees, 7.2 percent of all professional degrees, and 6.6 percent of all doctorates. The gender breakdown at the bachelor's level is that women received 63 percent of the degrees

awarded to African Americans in 2007. Although historically class differences within the black community were based on skin pigmentation (a legacy of plantation life and white supremacy), today educational achievement is a primary factor in social mobility. Relatively high incomes are attributable to two-parent families with dual incomes, professional opportunity, and, of course, hard work.

The black church cannot be overlooked as a major source of support and strength to the African American community. Providing numerous functions, the black church—socially, politically, culturally, and even economically—offers a refuge in a troubled world. Much like the extended family, the church provides help to the needy and bereaved and role models for the young, to say nothing of the aesthetic contribution through music. The church brings the community together and provides an outlet for leadership and creative talents. A wide variety of social activities—trips, dinners, church socials, and Sunday-school classes—bring people of all classes together in connection with the church (Goldenberg & Goldenberg, 2002). The religious teachings themselves are powerful; the focus on faith, forgiveness, clean living, and tolerance help strengthen the moral fiber of the community. The Black Muslim movement deserves special mention for the "lives turned around" and the family stability encouraged by this religious group.

A major impediment to successful work with families of color and to reinforcing their strengths is the fact that public policies are targeted to individuals and not families. One notable innovation, however, is the institutionalization of foster kinship care, which encourages relatives to become foster parents and under which the state provides financial help to make this care possible (see the discussion of kinship care later in the chapter).

In one of our (van Wormer) courses on injustice and oppression, the 9-year-old grandson of an M.S.W. student was sitting in on class one day and heard some oral reports. He later announced that he would like to do a report for the class. He returned to class with his grandmother on the day her report was due and read his paper (see Box 4.2, William Burt's

"A Nine-Year-Old Boy's Story")—his own story of oppression and injustice, in his own words. Following the reading, the students broke into enthusiastic applause.

Box 4.2 A Nine-Year-Old Boy's Story

William Burt, Waterloo, Iowa

Justice is fairness, fair treatment, and sound reason.

Injustice is the violation of another person's rights and unfair treatment. It is also a wrong and unjust act.

What I am going to tell you about today is the injustice that I have had in my life.

Injustice is very common in the black race. There is lots of prejudice directed toward all people of color.

A couple of years ago, my two sisters, my brother, and I had to live with my granny because, first, my dad went to prison for fighting with my mom too many times and a couple of months later my mom was taken to prison because my cousin lived with us and had drugs in our house, but my mom got in trouble because it was her house. If I did not have my granny I would have been an oppressed kid living in a foster home away from my family.

When my mom and dad was in prison I was very sad because the police had taken them away from me and I couldn't see them. I could only talk to them on the phone.

Whenever I talked to them they would both tell me how bad it was in prison and how they did not have good food to eat, or if they were sick there was no good doctor, and how they stayed locked in their cells most of the time.

They finally got out and came home, first my mom and then my dad. I was very happy. But the happiness did not last because somehow my dad became a target for the Waterloo Police Department. The police would stop him when he was driving down the street just to harass him and search his car.

About 1 year ago, my aunt and I was driving to the grocery store when we seen my dad walking down East 4th Street. My aunt pulled over to ask my dad if he needed a ride and up drove a police car and a police [officer] jumped out and pulled my dad

to his car and put him in handcuffs. He was accused of selling drugs to us, and neither me or my aunt even use drugs or alcohol.

I think that just because my dad was a young black man walking down the street, that he was automatically [thought to be] selling drugs. They never found any drugs on my dad or searched my aunt's car, but they took my dad away.

Then 2 months ago, they stopped my dad in his car while he was going to work. They searched his car and said they found a weed seed and took my dad to jail again. My dad said that he could have found a fly that was bigger than the seed the police claimed to find.

But I guess this kind of treatment is thought to be okay if you are black and poor. (Life is not fair.)

And now you have heard my story of injustice. The End.

Printed with permission of William Burt and Angela Burt, MSW. Presented to social work class, summer of 2005.

Latino Families

When the number of Latino Americans reached 13 percent of the population (U.S. Census Bureau, 2001), Latinos replaced African Americans as the largest minority in the United States. Their birthrate, although declining, is significantly higher than that of other groups.

Familism, or *familismo*, is the term used to refer to the central role of the family in Latino communities. Among Mexican Americans, the term includes immediate family, extended kin, and coparents, or godparents. In Puerto Rican culture, although the nuclear family pattern is increasingly apparent, value is also attached to kin and godparents (Longres, 2000). About twice as many Latinos live in extended family situations as do European Americans ("Older Americans 2004," 2005). More than a quarter of Latinos live in families of five or more, compared with 11 percent of whites. Families of Mexican origin are the largest in size, and Cubans the smallest.

The diversity that exists among Latino groups is underscored by the history of Latino migration to the United States. The largest concentration consists of Mexicans in the South and West, Puerto Ricans in the East, and Cubans in Florida. The increase in the number of Dominicans, Central Americans, and some South American groups such as Colombians and Brazilians has been pronounced in recent years. The term *Latino*, therefore, refers to various diverse populations whose presence within the United States is changing the face of U.S. society. One-third of all Hispanics in this country are under the age of 18, so their influence, political and social, will even be more marked in the future. Although Latinos come from many different countries, and although some were here before their territory was conquered by the United States, some generalizations are possible. Most are Roman Catholic and have in common values and beliefs rooted in a history of conquest and colonization. Most are dark-complexioned with a similarity in physical features as a result of the mixing of races that has occurred in most of these countries (Garcia-Preto, 2005a). From the literature, the most commonly cited characteristics are close family ties, *personalismo* (relating to people in a personal manner), traditional sex-role behavior, and care and respect for the elderly (e.g., Colon, 2007; Garcia-Preto, 2005a; Goldenberg & Goldenberg, 2002; Longres, 2000).

Family ties, as mentioned earlier, are strong. Although, as revealed in census data, 48 percent of Latino births are to young, single mothers (just over one-third of all births are of this type), and although the poverty rate is quite high within this population, the infant mortality rates and low-birth-weight rates for Hispanics compared with African Americans and all other low-income groups are strikingly low. This phenomenon is termed the *epidemiological paradox*. There is an extensive literature on this point. McGlade, Saha, and Dahlstrom (2004) explain this paradox in terms of dietary practices; less use of substances, including tobacco; and positive attitudes toward childbearing, as well as social support factors. Close family ties, the likely presence of older relatives in the home, and the nurturance provided to pregnant women likely are the protective factors that ensure the health of infants born in such families. The active role of the maternal grandmother in the care for the pregnant woman and the newborn infant is pronounced. An additional paradox, however, occurs with acculturation into U.S. society, when the infant mortality rate goes up. Reasons given for this phenomenon relate to such lifestyle factors as use of tobacco and illicit drugs and heavy drinking, which are more characteristic of assimilated than immigrant Latinas (Delgado, 2007; Peak & Weeks, 2002).

The difference in the pace of life north and south of the border is a commonly noted phenomenon. The often tight time schedules that many families in the United States and Canada endure are less in evidence in most minority households, in fact. As described by one student:

> The Mexican mother of a friend of mine has told me that Americans greatly value time. She pointed out that this especially affects family values. Whereas in Mexico, the family has a long dinner together every night no matter what, here in the U.S. everyone is rushing to the next event. In Mexico, each person is more a member of a family than an individual. (Elizabeth Kenney, personal communication with van Wormer, June 2002)

Personalismo is a Latino value that denotes the importance of relating to people in a warm, friendly manner; for example, not racing through negotiations in a business deal but taking the time to establish some sort of personal relationship first (Colon, 2007). The personal touch is expressed physically in that members of this cultural group are more comfortable standing in close proximity to each other than are members of the European American ethnic group. *Respeto* and *dignidad* are related concepts singled out by Colon that denote values evidenced in interactions between Latinos and professionals.

Traditional Latino culture is marked by a strict delineation of sex-role behavior. This sexual division, which has been labeled *machismo* for men and *marianismo* (after the Blessed Virgin Mary) for women, is associated with a patriarchal family arrangement (Delgado, 2007). Higher standards of morality are required of the married woman than of the man, and women are expected to sacrifice their personal interests for the family as a whole; a sense of martyrdom may result (Colon, 2007). Still, as Longres (2000) indicates, male authority is never absolute, and middle-class Mexican American families and relationships are more egalitarian than are those among lower-class households.

Rituals are integral to Latino family life, often connected to passages related to age. The Catholic Church (and increasingly, Pentecostal churches) and religious worship and festivities figure prominently in these rituals. Women are seen as more spiritually inclined than men, yet the whole community participates in these celebrations. Most Latinos tend to emphasize spirituality and to express a willingness to sacrifice material satisfactions for spiritual goals (Garcia-Preto, 2005a). Godparents, created through a Catholic baptism custom, may share responsibilities for the children's welfare (Goldenberg & Goldenberg, 2002).

Care for the elderly is a preeminent value in Latino culture. Elderly family members are highly respected and are believed to have an inner strength that can be a resource for the younger generation (Gardiner & Kosmitzki, 2005). As important links to the past and tradition, elders do not feel useless or like a burden and are not ashamed to ask for help. Children, especially daughters, play a major role in providing such care. Many of the older immigrants, however, suffer feelings of loss for the social status and connections in their country of origin, for the smells and sounds of their former surroundings, and for their friends and neighbors (Delgado, 2007; Garcia-Preto, 2005a).

Although many pursue the American dream, most, as Garcia-Preto (2005a) indicates, "come looking for a place in the sun, but are burned by the scalding rays of oppression" (p. 157). The unemployment rate is high, most who work are trapped in low-wage service jobs with little chance for advancement, the high school dropout rate is extremely high, and housing is substandard and unaffordable. Those who are educated, fluent in English, and have financial resources are in a better position to live out the dreams, and they experience a greater connection to the society in which they live.

Latinos who enter counseling generally come because of court-ordered addiction treatment

or cultural conflicts in the home. Because of their familial orientation, Mexican Americans easily accept family therapy (Falicov, 2005). Many Mexican Americans believe that emotional problems are rooted in family interactions, particularly between the nuclear and the extended family. Garcia-Petro (2005b) discusses conflict in gender roles among Puerto Ricans on the mainland and how this might bring them to the attention of therapists. Puerto Rican men, as Garcia-Petro suggests, tend to have difficulty in dealing with the stress caused by migration and acculturation because of negative stereotypes associated with them in this culture. The more oppressed and helpless they feel, the greater the risk is of their engaging in alcoholism, addiction, and violence in the home. In contrast, the experience of Puerto Rican women tends to be more positive; often they gain in status working outside of the home while men lose status. Women who come to treatment often exhibit depression and anxiety about having lost control over their children or about their husbands' drinking. Gays and lesbians have much difficulty coming out to their families because of the emphasis placed on having children and, for men, the emphasis on manhood and the playing of traditional roles. However, perceptions are gradually changing due to gay and lesbian activism.

In working with Puerto Rican families, Morales et al. (2010) recommend conducting an ecosystems focus to bring to the forefront of the treatment process facts that relate to the social structure. First and foremost, when working with families who are disempowered, the social worker should take into account environmental circumstances such as job loss and the creative ways that such families have found to cope with these challenges. Two case studies provided by Morales and his colleagues describe low-income migrant families who regard qualifying for disability payments as the best solution to their economic difficulties. The therapist helped the family member in case one that qualified for financial aid to do so and the client from case two to work on his self-efficacy and prepare to enter a job training program. In working with Mexican and Mexican American families, Morales and his colleagues provide micro and macro case examples. Drawing on an ecosystems assessment, these social work educators show how the documentation status and exploring strengths in the ethnosystem are essential to effective treatment. Their reference is to the *barrio*, which typically is composed of indigenous social support systems such as churches, neighbors, friends, barber shops, and families. Social network intervention means the inclusion of extended family members and other concerned persons to provide emotional strength to the family.

Asian American Families

Although there is a great deal of diversity within the Asian American population, the U.S. Census Bureau (2004) shows that Asian Americans exceed the national average on all positive categories (for example, education, income, longevity) except for home ownership and English-speaking ability. The divorce rate, for example, is half the national average; the average income level is above that of the national average; and the rate of single motherhood is the lowest of any racial ethnic group listed (U.S. Census Bureau, 2009a).

The importance of family life in Chinese culture cannot be overemphasized, and Japanese Americans show great concern for family reputation and go to great lengths not to bring shame on the family line (Longres, 2000). Personal ambitions and desires are sacrificed for the needs of the family, a value expressed in the term *kenshin*, which refers to renunciation of selfish interests. In both groups, the family is multigenerational.

Asian cultures place high value on hierarchical organization of the family, stressing responsibility for family obligations based on status and role in the extended family (Lee & Mock, 2005). Males are more highly valued than females, and daughters in traditional Asian families are expected to be absorbed into their husband's families (Goldenberg & Goldenberg, 2002; Yoo, 2004). In her interviews with 100 pairs of young Korean adult daughters and their mothers, Yoo (2004) found strong attachment bonds. As daughters entered marital relationships, however, the level of attachment

weakened somewhat. The mothers' levels of attachment did not diminish, however; their love was unconditional even when daughters pulled away. Yoo (2004) refers to a Korean maternal tradition of unconditional love. Acculturation into American society, however, has brought about changes for the younger population. The rate of racial intermarriage is very high, especially among Asian American women.

Gardiner and Kosmitzki (2005), in reviewing the literature on fathers' roles in the family, concluded that whereas Chinese fathers have played more active roles, Japanese and Korean fathers have often reduced their involvement in family matters to providing financial support and enforcing the family rules. The mother is the nurturer and caretaker of the children among all the Asian American groups (Lee & Mock, 2005).

The Confucian Doctrine of the Mean, which emphasizes a balance in all things, has influenced Japanese, as well as Chinese, culture. Personality is seen as a result of interaction of two forces—yin (passive, feminine) and yang (active and masculine). People are expected to be active or passive according to the situation. Indirect communication of feelings and the appearance of extreme modesty are cultivated traits in Japanese and Chinese culture (Gardiner & Kosmitzki, 2005).

The Asian population in the United States is now 4.2 percent of the total population and is growing as rapidly as the Latino population (U.S. Census Bureau, 2004). The largest group is those of Chinese descent, at 23.8 percent; next come Filipino, Asian Indian, and Vietnamese. Sixty-nine percent of all Asians are foreign born.

The striking success of Asian Americans who trace their heritage to China, India, and Japan contrasts sharply with data showing struggles among Cambodian, Laotian, and Hmong immigrants. A close look at the data for these latter three groups paints a picture far different from the image of Asian Americans as the "model minority." The plight of refugees from Cambodia, Laos, and Vietnam, who make up less than 14 percent of Asian Americans, gets lost in the statistical averages. Yet these Southeast Asians came to the United States fleeing wartime persecution; many were mountain people who could not read or write (Thrupkaew, 2002). Their unemployment rates, especially among the Cambodian and Hmong populations, have been especially high, and so is their poverty rate. Largely as a result of the "killing fields" that wiped out large portions of the population, nearly one-fourth of Cambodian households are headed by women. Many have relied on welfare, but the 1996 welfare reform act has removed this source of income from most of these immigrants. Children born to Cambodian and Hmong parents have adopted the materialistic values and the language of the American nation, and they resist taking the menial jobs that their parents have endured (Portes, 2002). Yet the younger generation lacks the education and resources for upward mobility, so their futures are problematic. Hmong women are expected to marry young and rarely attend college. About 60 percent have less than a high school education (U.S. Census Bureau, 2004).

Asian family values can be differentiated from Western family values. Traditional Western values of independence and autonomy for children are not valued or desired. Educational expectations can be extremely high, especially in Japanese American and Korean American families. Successful education of children can become an all-consuming enterprise in these households. Family loyalty is paramount, and within the family talking about difficulties such as discrimination in the society might be seen as a sign of weakness (Shibusawa, 2005). In Asian cultures the family unit is highly valued and emphasized throughout the life cycle (Lee & Mock, 2005). Rather than an "I" identity, Asians are taught to think in terms of "we."

Cooperation and sharing among siblings are expected; the parents usually delegate child-care functions to older siblings, usually a girl (Lee & Mock, 2005). Respect and care for the elderly is a value that transcends all these diverse Asian groups. Living together in common households with dependent elderly relatives is common. The mother–son bond is especially strong, a fact that ensures security for the mother's old age, when her son's wife, according to traditional arrangements, will care for her (Goldenberg & Goldenberg, 2002; Lee & Mock, 2005).

Instead of generalizing about all Asian Americans in terms of their needs, family counselors working with Asian American groups need to be familiar with the history of that particular group. Whether the family members, their parents, or their ancestors came to America as refugees or as highly skilled professionals and whether they came from a country ravaged by war or from a peaceful nation can have a significant impact on one's ability to adapt to life in a modern, industrialized society. Family therapists need to know also the cultural traditions of that particular group and for how many generations the family has been in the United States. Because family pride often means not sharing personal troubles with an outsider, practitioners are advised to be sensitive to the cultural norms in this regard. In working with Chinese Americans, Lai (2001) recommends individual over group or family counseling and a focus on concrete services until trust is established. With Asian Indian Americans, Sandhu and Malik (2001) similarly caution the social worker to be very sensitive and careful not to embarrass family members in front of each other, as shame plays a prominent role in interpersonal relations. (For a detailed discussion of cultural norms related to working with Asian Indian families, see Almeida, 2005).

Lee and Mock (2005) recommend that therapists incorporate the Eastern holistic way of thinking into clinical practice, viewing the mind and body as integrally connected. Family therapy may not be feasible, as individual problems such as mental illness or depression are not often seen as family related. Traditional Asian husbands are usually reluctant to participate. If family therapy is feasible and desired, conflict should be handled in an indirect way to minimize feelings of shame and self-blame. In working with Japanese families, Shibusawa (2005) advises against giving directives to family members to talk to each other—which can hinder communication—but has found that nonverbal activities such as family sculpting and drawing can be effective. Role reversals, such as relying on English-speaking children to serve as culture brokers and interpreters, can cause anger and resentment. Careful use of a genogram is often helpful as an objective means of exploring family heritage and immigration status and the history of each member. Educational approaches based on social learning principles work well and are compatible with Asian values and beliefs (Lee & Mock, 2005). Migration and postmigration experiences should be explored. Strengths of Asian American families can be found in the strong work ethic, emphasis on education in most of these groups, parental sacrifice for their children, resilience in the face of cultural conflict with Western values, and the pooling of family resources for the greater good of all.

The intermarriage rate among Asian Americans is significantly high. According to the U.S. Census (2002) report, "The Asian Population," around 30 percent of persons who identified as at least part Japanese are multiracial, and around 15 percent of Chinese Americans claim to be of more than one race. This means many children are growing up with mixed identities, where the grandparents on both sides of the family have very different cultural and language traditions. Because of their increasing numbers in the population, social workers can expect to be working with families with mixed cultural traditions.

Multicultural Families

The number of people who identify themselves as multiracial people rose 3.4 percent last year to about 5.2 million, according to the latest U.S. Census estimates (Yen, 2009). Since 2000, the number of Americans who check more than one box for race on census surveys has risen by 33 percent to comprise 5 percent of the minority population—with millions more believed to be uncounted. About 1 in 13 marriages are mixed race, with the most prevalent being white-Hispanic, white-American Indian, and white-Asian. Demographers attributed the recent population growth to more social acceptance of mixed-race couples and slowing immigration (Yen, 2009). They cited in particular the high public profiles of Tiger Woods as of President Barack Obama, a self-described "mutt," who are having an effect on those who might self-identify as multiracial.Read Boxes 4.3 and 4.4 to appreciate how one Latina woman of mixed

heritage and one woman of mixed German African American heritage developed strong ethnic identities and a sense of determination that are major assets as they pursue their career goals.

Box 4.3 How I Resolved My Ethnic Identity Crisis

My ethnic identity is Mexican American, or Latina.I was born first-generation Mexican American on my mom's side of the family and fourth-generation Irish American on my dad's side. All I knew growing up was that we spoke Spanish in my household, and it was the culture we celebrated even though my dad did not fit the stereotypical mold because he had bright red hair.

My dad was enamored with the Mexican culture; he grew up in a small town in Missouri which he escaped as soon as he could to become a professor in Mexico. In Mexico he became acculturated; there was much he discovered of the Mexican culture that couldn't be acquired in years of Spanish classes. My *padrino* (godfather), Oscar Reyes, adopted my dad into his family of six kids and from then on Mexico was home. My dad met my mom while they were both working at a *Universidad* in Mexico. My mom crossed the border on their wedding day, accompanied by one of her five siblings. My *Mama* (Grandma), wasn't allowed to attend the wedding by her second husband because my mom was marrying a *gringo*. On that day my mom went from being Maria Patricia Reyes to Pat Shaney.

When I was born, my mother still was not fluent in English, so Spanish was my first language. As a toddler my *mama* that lived across the border in Reynosa, would take care of me. Every morning my dad crossed the border to drop me off before he went to work at Pan American University. My paternal grandparents lived in Missouri, so I did not see them often. When I did see them I remember their frustration at my lack of English vocabulary. When I asked for milk, I said *leche*. They used to ask my Dad "Why doesn't this child speak English?" To which my Dad would purport some answer like "because Mexico is part of her culture." My grandparents were never too thrilled that my Dad had married a Mexican woman, not to mention one that didn't speak English. Microaggressions were very common during the entirety of my Mom's relationship with my grandparents.

In my own personal experience my Mexican American identity crisis came in junior high when a substitute teacher asked the class which students spoke Spanish. I feel this particular substitute was fascinated at the number of brown-skinned Mexicans that didn't speak Spanish. When I raised my hand and informed this substitute that I spoke Spanish he took one look at the color of my skin and my name Sarah Shaney and said, "You can't speak Spanish, you are white." I began to turn away at this point from my Mexican, Spanish-speaking identity and identify with the white (or "American") side of my identity. After all, my "white" identity was what the world told me I was, and the box that I was supposed to check on ethnicity questionnaires.

In high school I realized how quickly I was losing my Spanish and my accent. It was in a conversation with my *mama* who I remained close to that I discovered how saddened she was by my choice. I was the oldest grandchild, and she feared that if I continued denying my culture one day I would deny her and the rest of my family, "*tus raices son Mexicanas* (your roots are Mexican)" she said. In that moment I realized that maintaining my connection to my family and my cultural roots was more important than the color of my skin, my name, and any stereotypical ideas about what my culture should be.

In college I decided that I wanted to become a bilingual educator. By this time my dad had passed away, and I chose this path as a legacy to him and my *familia mexicana* (Mexican family) in celebration of our Mexican culture. I only hoped that I could use my passion and experience as a bi-cultural person to make a difference in the lives of others. Today being Latina defines me to my core. Although judgment of others is an everyday occurrence, *mis raices* (my roots) in the Mexican culture are what remind me "This is who I am."

Printed with permission of Sarah Reeves, who teaches fourth grade as a bilingual elementary school teacher.

Box 4.4 *Not Black Enough*

Saskia Dula-Klontz

I am the product of a multicultural couple: My father is African American and my mother is German. I was born in the United States and lived there for nine years before the Army sent us to Germany where we lived for six years. Before we moved, I identified myself as "black" simply because I was around the black part of my family. When we moved, I met my German family and started to spend time with them. It was during this time that I started to have an internal struggle. Who was I? What was I? Did I have to choose just one culture or could I be proud of both?

The text [previous edition of the HBSE text] states that society is organized around a tendency to categorize people in either/or categories, placing pressure on children of mixed backgrounds to identify with just one racial-ethnic group. There may also be rejection from one community or family or the other. Besides the constant fascination with my skin color, my German family was very accepting of me. Race was never an issue between us. However, the black children in my Army community were a different story. Even though I still identified myself as black, it seemed as if I wasn't "black enough." Yes, my closest friends were black, but the black children who didn't know me would make snide comments, such as "look at that heifer with good hair. She thinks she is all that just because her skin is lighter." These words were hurtful and I felt that I needed to prove myself as worthy of being called black. I started to become ashamed of the fact that I was half German. When my German grandparents would pick me up from school, I would desperately try to avoid them. I even became embarrassed of my mother. Unfortunately these feelings lasted for 5 years. When I found out that we were moving to Oklahoma, I embraced my German culture and became proud of it and myself. I now have great relationships with both my mother and my grandparents. Even though they never experienced cultural identity challenges, they somehow knew what I was going through and knew that someday I would figure it out. Thank God that I did and today my children are educated and raised with the traditions of both cultures.

Printed with permission of Saskia Dula-Lontz, MSW student, University of Texas.

Family therapists need to be prepared to work not only with ethnically diverse families but also with diversity in the form of sexual orientation. A discussion of some of the attributes of gay and lesbian families follows.

Gay and Lesbian Families

Learning that an adolescent child is gay or lesbian can be a tremendous shock to parents for a number of reasons. Awareness of disparaging messages in the society about homosexuality, a wrench thrown in plans for later grandparenting and carrying on the family line, fear that the child will be subjected to ridicule and later career failure, and a feeling of having failed as a parent to raise a gender-appropriate and well-adjusted child are just a few of the factors that affect parental response on learning of a gay or lesbian child's sexual orientation. Drawing on interviews with a sample of PFLAG (Parents, Families and Friends of Lesbians and Gays) members, Saltzburg (2004) explored the meanings that parents ascribe to disclosure by their adolescent that he or she is gay or lesbian. She found, in analysis of the parents' reports, that although they were initially stunned, they had had some awareness at a semiconscious level that this child was different. Nevertheless, a period of denial ensued. This was followed by a time of panic for many. As described by one parent, "It's like the death of a child that you thought was going to grow up and be the way you always thought about. All your dreams for this kid—you know, marriage, the whole bit—none of that is going to happen" (Saltzburg, 2004, p. 113). Finally, after a period of estrangement, the parents typically adjusted to the new image presented to them, the reality of a nonnormative sexual orientation. As members of PFLAG, they found strength in connecting with other parents. Gay couples also find support in involvement with this advocacy and self-help group, chapters of which are active all over North America.

Reardon (2009) brings our attention to the importance of taking a family-centered, systems-centered view of the home environment in which gay, lesbian, and transgendered youth live. There are now hard data, as Reardon indicates, to prove the extent to which family rejection increases the risk of poor health and mental health outcomes over the life span. The Family Acceptance Project (FAP) provides research-based educational material and interventions to strengthen families in their support of their coming-out youths. Interviews that were a part of this research showed a correlation between rejecting behaviors in the families and attempted suicide, high levels of depression, use of alcohol and other drugs, and engaging in unprotected sex. The FAP's experience is that when families are given this information, many of them want to make changes to limit the risk to their children.Same-sex marriage is an issue that has occupied the consciousness of the nation since the late 1990s, an issue that has been used by conservative politicians as a ploy to distract voters from pursuing their own economic interests. An analysis of postelection exit polls showed that the presence of amendments to ban same-sex legal rights on states' election ballots brought out conservatives to vote in droves (Greenberger, 2004). The Republican Party picked up an enormous number of votes by putting measures to "preserve marriage" for heterosexuals on the ballot. Such measures attracted voters disproportionately from the right wing. The deciding factor in the 2004 election seems to have been so-called moral values.

People with gay or lesbian sexual orientations seek to form families, the same as everybody else. Many are deprived of the right, however—not only through legal means but also because an individual with a live-in partner of the same sex may arouse suspicion that the relationship is homosexual. Many gays and lesbians who would like to have families remain outside of committed relationships in order not to be spurned by their families of origin and society or fired from their jobs. The outcry over the demand of sexual minorities for full marriage rights is indicative both of the degree of nonacceptance of homosexuality in U.S. society and of the degree of gradual acceptance of gay and lesbian marriage rights as human rights.

Denmark, Norway, Sweden, the Netherlands, Belgium, Canada, Spain, and, most recently, Britain and South Africa allow gay marriages on roughly the same basis as heterosexual mar-riages, and many other countries allow regis-tered partnerships ("Gay marriage around the world," 2009). By 2010, five U.S. states and Washington, D.C. granted marriage licenses to same-sex partners while three additional states recognized homosexual marriage but did not grant licenses.In 1990 the U.S. Census for the first time included a question in their survey about unmarried partner couples. Because gender was included also, information became available on gay male and lesbian couples nationwide. The 2000 Census revealed that there were 594,391 same-sex couples (301,026 male couples and 293,365 female couples) in the United States (Gates & Ost, 2004). Vermont had the highest concentration, followed by California and Washington. Nearly a quarter of same-sex couples are raising children, and these families live in 96 percent of U.S. counties. Interestingly, more than 1 in 10 same-sex couples includes a partner age 65 or older.

Demographer Gary Gates of the Williams Institute provides a highly detailed analysis of the 2008 American Community Survey on family living arrangements. Significantly, the survey differentiates between gays and lesbians who are in partnerships and those who see them-selves as married, even if not legally wed. Based on the new data, Gates found that more than one in four (nearly 150,000) same-sex couples designated themselves as spouses, and that 31 percent of same-sex couples who identify themselves as spouses are raising children com-pared to 43 percent of heterosexual spouses. Other findings of the report are that same-sex couples who identified themselves as spouses differed from same-sex couples who identified themselves as unmarried partners in the fol-lowing ways:

‣ Same-sex spouses were more likely to be female; 56 percent of same-sex spouses were female, while unmarried same-sex partners were evenly split between the sexes.
‣ This characteristic mirrors the higher rate of actual marriages by female couples in states that have extended marriage to same-sex couples.

‣ Same-sex spouses were twice as likely to be raising children.

The National Association of Social Workers (NASW; 2009), in its policy statement on the subject of same-sex marriage, states that NASW "supports the adoption of local, state, federal, and international policies/legislation that ban all forms of discrimination based on sexual ori-entation. LGB people must be granted all rights, privileges, and responsibilities that are granted to heterosexual people, including but not lim-ited to inheritance rights, insurance, marriage, child custody, employment, credit, and immigra-tion" (p. 220). The denial of marital rights to same-sex partners has grave social and economic consequences. These consequences involve the denial of a range of rights and benefits, includ-ing income tax deductions, family health ben-efits in most companies, the right to have a say in medical emergencies, and child custody and visitation rights. Alienation from the traditional teachings of church, mosque, or synagogue additionally closes the door on a support system that may have played a part in one's upbringing.

Census data estimates are almost certainly an underestimate, as many gay and lesbian families seek privacy for obvious reasons (Gates & Ost, 2004; Johnson & Piore, 2004). Even so, the survey showed that at least 150,000 same-sex couples have one or more children in the home. Two-mother families, as Graff (2002) suggests, are popping up everywhere. The les-bian baby boom began in Boston and San Francisco in the mid-1980s. In both cities, after mainstream doctors refused to offer donor insemination services to unmarried women, les-bians started their own sperm banks and clin-ics. Gay dads are following, though in smaller numbers; some by hiring surrogates, others by assuming custody of their children from a pre-vious heterosexual marriage, and still others by being foster parents. Television shows such as *Modern Family* in which a gay couple adopt a baby from Vietnam reflect the trend.

One aspect of the gay-lesbian marriage debate that has been largely overlooked in the media concerns the children. What is it like for children growing up with parents of only one gender? How do they turn out? In her new book, *Lesbian and Gay Parents and Their Children*, psychologist Abbie Goldberg bases her conclusions on an analysis of more than 100 academic studies, most using large samples of lesbian mothers and a few with research on gay fathers.

Among Goldberg's findings are that, compared to children of heterosexual parents, children of same-sex parents show no greater incidence of psychiatric disorders, are just as popular at school, and have just as many friends. While girls raised by lesbian mothers seem slightly more likely to be more sexually active, and boys less so, than those raised by heterosexual mothers, neither sex is more likely to suffer from gender confusion nor to identify themselves as gay. There are some marked differences in that these children, as one would expect, are less conventional and more flexible than others in their gender roles, while over twice as many of the daughters of lesbian mothers are more likely to engage in rough-and-tumble play in childhood and to aspire to work in professions such as medicine and law.

For the stability of all children (foster children, adopted children, and biological children of one partner) brought up by same-sex parents, one would think that the benefits of marriage and the legal rights pertaining thereto would be endorsed by supporters of family values. One positive recent development is that 10 states now allow gay and lesbian parents to adopt children as couples. After winning constitutional amendments in 11 states banning gay marriage in 2004, opponents of gay-lesbian rights put gay adoption on the state ballots in the next election. These initiatives backfired and now gay adoption is allowed in practically all the states (Padgett, 2007). Gay and lesbian couples can now adopt each others' children or adopt children in the custody of the state. Much of the impetus has been by child welfare authorities anxious to find homes for children in need of care. Social workers and others such as juvenile judges have worked to get legislatures to remove the barriers to gay-lesbian adoption. The advocacy has taken the form of a child-friendly rather than a gay-friendly focus and that apparently has made a difference.

Canada recently followed the Netherlands and Belgium in providing full-fledged marital rights for gays and lesbians. Now Massachusetts and other states, barring the passage of federal legislation against it, are following suit. Norms are changing rapidly. The majority of people age 30 and younger see gay marriage as inevitable and acceptable (Sullivan, 2003). In agreement with Sullivan, lifelong Republican Theodore Olson (2010) makes the conservative case for gay marriage—that marriage will change gay subculture by strengthening commitment between partners, encouraging monogamous relationships and family stability through the sanction of the state. Legalizing same-sex marriage as Olson further argues, represents the culmination of America's historic commitment to equality and justice for all. Karen Heinselman's "Family Adventure" (see Box 4.5) contains a description of a two-mother family in Cedar Falls, Iowa.

Box 4.5 Family Adventure

Karen Heinselman, Courier Staff Writer

WATERLOO—Three not-so-serious contestants sit around a kitchen table. A game of Sequence is in full swing. Brittany Flokstra glances at her cards, at the board, then back at her cards.

"Where am I going to go? None of these are good for me," she exclaims.

Her 11-year-old son, Colton Questra, giggles at his mom's frustration. Susan Hill smiles at the banter and places a chip.

It's not hard to see why board games, complete with good-natured teasing, are a favorite family pastime for Flokstra, Hill, and Colton. What is more likely to catch strangers off guard is that the threesome is a family.

"The unique and interesting thing about our family is that we are a lesbian couple with a son," Flokstra wrote in a letter to the *Courier*. "However, we are definitely an 'everyday family' in as many ways as any other family in the Cedar Valley."

Colton describes a family as relationships based on love and commitment rather than gender.

"They give me a lot of attention and they discipline me," said the cheerful youth who wants to be a famous actor. The Waterloo household includes a gerbil, Dangler, and two cats—Thea, the mean feline (please don't pet) and Fizban, the nice one (do pet).

Work, school, and activities keep this family hopping. But they find time to do life together. The three eat dinner together every night. They go to church at the Unitarian Universalists Society of Black Hawk County, attend arts and music events at the Gallagher-Bluedorn Performing Arts Center, and read Harry Potter books. They worry about retirement, complain about taxes, volunteer in the community, and take special trips. Flokstra and Hill watch Colton play football.

"I think we are adventurous," Hill said.

Flokstra, 35, originally from Missouri, met Hill, 43, at a spiritual retreat in the summer of 1999. She and her then-5-year-old son had moved to Indiana for a graduate program. They moved to Iowa on the coldest day of December 2000 to live with Hill.

Flokstra and Hill exchanged vows July 14, 2002, in Missouri.

"It was not an 'official' marriage with paperwork, etcetera," said Flokstra. "It was a commitment between two people done intentionally within our community of friends. It included a section of joining us together as a family, with Colton, Sue, and I pouring different colored sand into a bowl and mixing our 'lives' together.

". . . The essential point is that marriage is an acknowledgment to yourselves and to your community that you are entering a different stage of relationship to one another. That this commitment is witnessed by others is part of what makes it important. This is not a private, closed commitment, it is an intention we stated to our community that we are joined together. It doesn't matter whether or not the states recognize it. We do and our community does."

Flokstra, Hill, and Colton appear comfortable with their family unit, sometimes forgetting that others are puzzled by the women with matching rings who discuss money issues and home decorating like any other couple.

"We are not the only lesbian family in this town. We are not the only gay family in this town," Hill said. "They tend to be invisible because people don't want to notice or because they want to be invisible."

There are those who would question or condemn the same-sex relationship. Both women worry that Colton will be teased because of their relationship or parenting style that shies away from gender stereotypes.

"We try to tell him it's not a very fair or just world," Flokstra said. "Maybe he can make it better." But many others have demonstrated support or indifference. That Flokstra and Hill walk in academic circles erases some of their fears about job security and community backlash—but not all. Flokstra is a doctorate student in environmental engineering at the University of Iowa. Hill is a professor of religion and philosophy at the University of Northern Iowa.

As in any close relationships, the trio experiences occasional breakdowns in communication. "Sue I call Sue," Colton said.

"And sometimes he calls me Brittany," Flokstra said.

"And sometimes he calls me Mom," Hill said.

Sometimes Colton isn't specific when he calls for help and the "wrong" person comes to his aid. Colton, displaying his acting skills, mimics his frustration.

"'Ugh. The other mom,'" he said.

The Courier, Waterloo, Iowa. September 17, 2005. "Family Adventure" by Karen Heinselman. Reprinted with permission of *The Courier.* Copyright © 2005 *Waterloo/Cedar Falls Courier*.

Macro Policy Issues

One of the most important challenges for policy makers is to gain more understanding of why some families are not able to meet their own expectations, achieve their own goals, and discharge all of their duties—despite their desires to do so (Briar-Lawson, Lawson, & Hennon, 2001). It is time, as Briar-Lawson et al. (2001) suggest, to discard language and practices that are deficit- and problem-oriented, ones that label and stigmatize families in need as "dysfunctional" or "pathological." Family-centered policies can enhance family functioning and self-actualization of its members. We are not referring to piecemeal, means-tested policies for families who have lost everything or who live at the margins. We are referring rather to universal policies that prevent such occurrences (such as loss of housing and health care) from happening in the first place.

Before looking at the European model as a case example of the institutional approach to enhancing family functioning, let us consider why families are so important to society. The family, we could easily argue, is the backbone of society. From a global and historical perspective, the family has always performed a number of functions, from providing food, clothing, and shelter to procreation, socialization, education, and production of goods and services (Logan, 2008). Additionally, families address the health, emotional, and spiritual needs of its members. Families, as Briar-Lawson et al. (2001) indicate, constitute the largest social welfare institution in the world. A healthy community depends for its sustenance on healthy family life, and vice versa.

The quality of people's social relationships is crucial to their well-being. People need social bonds in committed taken-for-granted relationships, not simply interactions with strangers, to experience well-being, as psychologists Diener and Seligman (2004) point out. In their research study of happiness, Diener and Seligman found that every single respondent in the happiest group had excellent social relationships. And these researchers confirmed the old cliché that it is better to give than to receive. Giving social support to others was shown on longevity measures to be more important than receiving social support. Their recommendation is for government policies that bolster the level of well-being in a society, such as those that lower unemployment and indirectly reinforce relationships. Similarly, Boushey's (2005) research on family-friendly policies stressed the importance of workplace flexibility to allow for the caregiving responsibilities of employees.

Sometimes families in the nonindustrialized world, perhaps because of the collectivist orientation or perhaps because of strong extended family ties, do better by their loved ones than families in the wealthier nations. An interesting

and unexpected finding of the International Pilot Study of Schizophrenia launched by the World Health Organization (WHO) was that patients in countries in less developed parts of the world have a more favorable course of the diseases that were studied than patients in Europe and North America (Sartorius, Gulbinat, Harrison, Laska, & Siegel, 1996). The original study was done in the 1960s, and the results have been confirmed in later replications ever since.

This is not to say, however, that government policy is not important. Government policies can go a long way, in fact, toward insulating families from the everyday vicissitudes of life—health problems, disability, and loss of jobs, for example. The best measure of how successful countries are in this regard is revealed in the United Nations' annual human development report. The human development report presents a composite of statistics related to poverty, literacy and education, child welfare, health care, and clean environment from international data-gathering sources. Norway consistently holds its position as number 1; in 2009 Norway was followed immediately by Australia, Iceland, Canada, and Ireland. The United States has fallen to the number 13 position and to number 26 in life expectancy, far behind Japan, which was number one (United Nations, 2009). Those countries ranked higher than the United States have family-friendly and child-friendly policies. Social scientists Meyers and Gornick (2003) describe how such policies in France, Sweden, and other European countries make the link between family and work systems a compatible one. Extensive paid maternity and paternity leaves allow parents to care for infants and still retain their jobs. In Sweden, parents have the right to work reduced hours until their children are 8 years of age. High-quality government-subsidized child care is available for all parents; child-care workers are highly paid and well qualified in the Nordic countries. Workers in all the industrialized nations, in fact, have more vacation time than do U.S. workers. (The Japanese often refuse to take their vacations, but that is another story.) Most of these countries provide 30 to 40 vacation days per year, compared with 12 days on average in the

United States (Brady, 2002). Still, the impact of the global market and of the global competition among workers is increasing the pressure on families everywhere.

The Impact of Globalization Worldwide

Globalization can be looked at in a number of contexts, both positive and negative, that are relevant to the lives of women. First, as noted by Dominelli (2002), increasing global interconnectedness has resulted in social problems that transcend national boundaries. Among these problems are the following: the plight of women refugees escaping the ravages of war; the mass emigration of people escaping personal and political violence; sex trafficking; and women being used as "mules" to transport illegal drugs across borders. The war on drugs is a war of global proportions, and its impact falls sharply on the shoulders of women. Second, from an economic perspective, is the impact of market-driven measures of capitalism to reduce social services through cutbacks, privatization of services, and the deprofessionalization of workers. The loss of welfare benefits and services from the state, in conjunction with deinstitutionalization of mental patients, in turn, has increased the numbers of homeless young people roaming the streets; this fact has intensified the vulnerability of girls and women to sexual victimization, sexual exploitation, and drug use. Consider also the reduction in funding for victim assistance services and women's shelters. Third, global market forces pave the way for agency consolidation and corporate management techniques, with the result that men displace women managers (Dominelli, 2002). This fact is seen in connection with the masculinization of correctional services and standardization of treatment philosophies. The bulk of the funding has gone to high-tech security systems and to surveillance rather than to educational and counseling services. The fourth aspect of globalization relates to the clash of civilizations through the communications revolution. The fear in certain quarters across the globe is that, if women's consciousness is raised, they will demand their rights. A counter-reaction, therefore, has taken place, a backlash

by entrenched forces with a vested interest in the status quo. This backlash is especially pronounced in regions of the world in which religious fundamentalism has been used to threaten women and suppress them. Economic competition undoubtedly plays a role in what has been termed the "world's war against women" as well.

Worldwide, as competition for well-paying and secure jobs in a global economy heats up, dangerous right-wing extremist movements are seizing political power. The mistreatment of women globally tends to be expressed in the guise of an attack on modernization, including the threatened liberation of women (van Wormer, 2004). We return to the topic of the connection between raw economics and the trafficking in girls and women in the section on family violence.

Impact on the Family

It is well known that poor communities disproportionately experience the stress of balancing family and work demands, as well as the impact of environmental pollution and other health problems, homelessness, and the crackdown associated with the war on drugs. The burdens of increasing global competition have contributed to the heavy load of stress already experienced by low-income families (Franze, Foster, Abbott-Shim, McCarty, & Lambert, 2002). A spike in homeless families has accompanied the economic upheaval that began in 2008; the number of people in homeless families—typically a mother and two children—increased by nine percent overall within a year's time and rose by more than 50 percent in the suburban and rural areas ("A spike", 2009). The joblessness rate for 16-to-24 year-old black men has reached Great Depression proportions or over 34 percent, more than three times the rate for the general U.S. population (Haynes, 2009). For black male teens the rate is even higher. Construction, manufacturing, and retail experienced the most severe job losses, having a huge impact on immigrant workers. Such joblessness is here to stay, argues Foroohar (2009). In a low-wage service economy, with manufacturing declining and rents soaring, families with children have become the fastest growing segment of the homeless population. In 2005, for the first time, the government (through Housing and Urban Development [HUD]) conducted an actual street count of homeless people. (Previous surveys had taken their number counts in the shelters.) The final tally has not been released yet by HUD, but a preliminary tabulation of the results reveals that families account for 42 percent of the approximately 700,000 persons found to be homeless in the survey (Kasindorf, 2005).

The impact on the family of the mounting work pressures is of sufficient magnitude to be a concern of all those in the helping professions. Workers at low income levels often find that one job is not enough; some even take on second jobs (Ehrenreich, 2005). University students typically attend the university full time while holding down full-time jobs, at the expense of the educational experience.

Grueling work schedules, coupled with increasing job insecurity, are taking a toll on working-class families. When there is a shortage of money, tensions mount, and conflict often develops among individual members. Depressed wages, a frenetic pace set at the workplace, the rapid rise in temporary work, decreased long-term employment, the growing disparity between the haves and have-nots, and the dramatic shrinking of the middle class are placing unprecedented stress on the American workforce (Korten, 2009). As jobs have been eliminated, the survivors are now doing the tasks of two or three people. In *Bait and Switch: The (Futile) Pursuit of the American Dream*, Ehrenreich (2005) chronicles corporate America's indifference to the needs of its workers. This book focuses on white-collar work; Ehrenreich's (2002) *Nickel and Dimed* reveals the daily grind of blue-collar work as the author went undercover to work as a waitress, a nursing home aide, and a cleaning lady. "Something is wrong, very wrong," she concluded, in her earlier book, "when a single person in good health, a person who in addition possesses a working car, can barely support herself by the sweat of her brow. You don't need a degree in economics to see that wages are too low and rents too high" (2002, p. 199).

Unable to maintain a home, pay for higher education for their children, save for retirement, or maintain their purchasing power, the working poor endure a major crisis at every turn—for example, a car breakdown or personal illness. People often blame themselves for problems that are structural in nature. Ehrenreich (2009) argues that the American tendency for optimism explains the reckless buildup of bad debt and unrealistic loans and spending that finally caught up with the nation. The big banks ultimately were spared but many people lost everything.Preliminary reports are that the suicide rates rose during the worst recession in decades, according to a *Wall Street Journal* survey of data in 19 states. In 2008, calls to suicide hotlines were way up, and suicides in the workplace (Murray & McKay, 2009). More troubling are the spate of whole family murder-suicides that have taken place in early 2009. Although the exact motives are always complex, unemployment and economic difficulties are often a part of the pattern in situations where a man has killed his whole family and then himself (Britt, 2009). Contagion undoubtedly plays a role, as such cases tend to occur in clusters.

As hard as Americans work, the Japanese dedicate themselves to their work with a sense of obligation that is difficult for the Westerner to understand. The boundaries between work and after-hours recreation (often at a karaoke bar) are not clearly drawn. In Japan, overwork leading to death is common enough to have been given a name—*karoshi*—meaning dropping dead at one's desk (Kanai, 2009).

Work-related family crises are occurring not only in North America and East Asia but universally. In Mexico City, small children without siblings are often left alone or brought to work; daughters often stay home from school to care for the younger children. This lack of child care in the global economy is a worldwide phenomenon, according to a report on world trends released by the United Nations (2010) in a policy brief on early childhood. Increasingly, according to this report, mothers are raising children alone and also working outside the home; fathers are absent because they have migrated for work and/or formed new families; and children are at high risk of being poor and left to fend for themselves.

At the opposite end of the work continuum among industrialized nations is the attitude toward work in Scandinavia. A guide to business customs in Sweden describes business meetings as formal and goal oriented. At the same time, the business person is advised to do the following:

> Arrange the timing of meetings thoughtfully. Offices are often deserted on Friday afternoons, particularly in the summer, and the whole country seems to close down from July to August and during the winter school half-term holiday. Try to fix meetings for early morning. Late afternoon is equally unpopular due to thoughts of going home, as are the few days before a public holiday such as Easter, when executives want to clear their desks. (Hutchings & Hatchwell, 2002, p. 328)

In her experience working as a program director at a Norwegian alcoholism treatment center, van Wormer found that Norwegians worked hard during their short work days but that their leisure time was more highly valued. Workers thought nothing of taking the day off for a dental appointment, and a year's (paid) leave for pregnancy was provided. Sick leave for emotional problems related to work stress could last a year as well. Employers, therefore, made considerable effort to treat the workers well and not to get into trouble with the unions. Family ties were close within the nuclear family, and family life was enhanced through shared activities, most of which were outdoors, especially in the winter and early spring. Elderly Norwegians were well taken care of by the state rather than by their grown sons and daughters, however (see van Wormer, 2006), and reports were that they felt relatively isolated.

We come now to a discussion of situations in which the treatment of people by society is discriminatory and oppressive and in which victimization and exploitation of girls and women is structural, both in its causes and in its consequences.

Family Violence in Global Perspective

To appreciate how susceptible girls and young women within the family are to sexual exploitation, we need to look again at forces in the global and regional markets. *Economic globalization*, or the macro economic policies associated with the global economy, has important human rights implications. Such policies require that the nonindustrialized nations reduce their indebtedness to the world banks through reducing social welfare spending of the kind that makes life livable. Relevant to economic inequities, women perform two-thirds of the world's work but earn only one-tenth of all income; women own less than one-tenth of the world's property (Human Rights Watch, 2002). People in a position of economic servitude to others who have control over the resources are generally vulnerable to mistreatment, and they have little recourse for justice. Economic destitution makes a young woman ripe for sexual exploitation, including being tricked into prostitution with the promise of a lucrative job abroad.

It stands to reason that as the economy improves in a country, more girls are educated, birth control is practiced more widely, women move into the workforce, and the lives of women improve. In a recent address to the United Nations Commission on the Status of Women, The UN Deputy Secretary-General Asha-Rose Migiro, (2010) reversed the proposition that reducing poverty reduces violence against women in arguing that stopping violence against women is the key to economic sustainability and eliminating poverty. The reason is that, under circumstances of gender equality, women who are not terrorized by violence are free to make decisions concerning family size and to access health care for themselves and for their children, including girls, and to reduce the incidence of harmful traditional practices. Studies show that when women control the family spending, they are more likely than men to invest a higher percentage of their earnings in family needs. Such inequality as exists today in many countries is in itself a violation of human rights.

The adoption of a human rights framework is increasingly relevant today, given the realities of the global market. A human rights discourse can provide a basis for awareness of, and alternatives to, the global regime that reinforces structures of disadvantage "through blatantly undemocratic processes which result in benefits for the few rather than the many" (Ife, 2001, p. 202). Human rights violations directed at women occur at three levels—the family (domestic violence, genital mutilation of girls, honor killings), the community (sex trafficking and sexual slavery), and the state (rape in war, abuse of immigrants in detention, and torture of women in prison; Erez, 2000). All these human rights abuses have serious implications for family survival and the ability of the family to achieve its functions.

Edna Erez listed sex trafficking as an example of gender-based violence that stems from economic forces in the community, forces related to the big business of transnational, organized crime. *Sex trafficking* is defined simply by Kathryn Farr (2005) as "a business venture in which traffickers trade the sexualized bodies of others for money" (p. 2). As defined by the WHO (2002), sexual trafficking "encompasses the organized movement of people, usually women, between countries and within countries for sex work" (p. 150). More than 1 million women and children are trafficked each year, often resulting in vast amounts of money for the industry. Girls and women are bought or kidnapped from poor countries such as Thailand, Nepal, or countries of the former Soviet Union and transported into countries where their services can fetch the highest price.

Around the globe, sexual slavery in Thailand, dowry deaths in India and Pakistan, and other forms of violence against women less directly related to economics continue to proliferate. Among them are death by stoning in Iran and Nigeria; genital mutilation in 28 African nations; rape of young girls in South Africa in the belief that sex with a virgin will cure AIDS; and wife abuse in all countries. In its annual reports, Amnesty International continues to outline the mechanism by which hundreds of

women a year are smuggled, imprisoned, exploited, raped continuously, blackmailed, and physically and sexually abused, and documents attempts made to combat this human rights violation. Some promising steps are being taken, according to Amnesty International (2007), in the founding of the Council of Europe Convention Against Trafficking. This organization has formed to offer a concerted effort to end sex and labor trafficking and to protect the victims of these international operations. Israel had been criticized earlier for its failure to protect women from the former Soviet Union and Eastern Europe who were brought in for purposes of sexual exploitation. Probably in reaction to the criticism, Israel has since passed laws outlawing human trafficking, punishing traffickers, and aiding victims of this human trade ("Knesset approves," 2006).

In an investigation of sex trafficking in the United States, *The Kansas Star* found that many people are brought into the United States under false pretenses and worked as virtual slaves, not only in the sex industry but in other lines of work as well (McGraw & Bauer, 2009). In fact, the government estimates that since 2002, up to 140,000 trafficking victims have been brought into the United States. But only 1 percent of them, about 1,600 people, have been given visas meant for trafficking victims. Instead, they are deported back to their home countries. As the report concludes, despite rhetoric about cracking down on human trafficking in the United States, very little is being done to encourage the victims to come forward or to help them when they do.

Domestic Abuse

The savage suppression of women by the Taliban in Afghanistan received enormous media attention in the 1990s. It was only after September 11, 2001, however, that the U.S. government, which had previously looked the other way, called for the liberation of these women. Today, under a new regime in Afghanistan, many women are still forced to hide their bodies in the *burqa*, and girls' schools are subject to burning. The treatment of women in the United States, although undeniably better than in some parts of the world, is not exempt from international concern. According to an Amnesty International (2001) investigation, *Broken Bodies, Shattered Minds*, family violence against women is a common occurrence.

The United Nations (2008) provides the following facts concerning family violence against girls and women:

- Dowry murder is a brutal practice where a woman is killed by her husband or in-laws because her family cannot meet their demands for dowry—a payment made to a woman's in-laws upon her marriage as a gift to her new family. While dowries or similar payments are prevalent worldwide, dowry murder occurs predominantly in South Asia.
- The practice of early marriage is common worldwide, especially in Africa and South Asia. This is a form of sexual violence, for young girls are often forced into the marriage and into sexual relations, causing health risks, including exposure to HIV/AIDS, and limiting their attendance in school.

In contrast to the American pattern in which the weapon of choice was a gun, in India, a large number of deaths among women, as mentioned earlier, were "bride burnings" and officially recorded as accidental burns. Indian feminists use the term *femicide* to fit the reality of such female killing in their country. This term also includes the common practice of elimination of female fetuses through abortion or of female infants through neglect. Such killing of females is considered femicide, according to the United Nations (2007) definition, inasmuch as it is the gender-based murder of women. In China, the number of "missing females" is the highest in the world. At birth, the sex ratio is 117 boys to 100 girls (Banister, 2004). The Chinese "one-child" policy, coupled with modern technology (ultrasound tests), favors the selection of male over female children because parents, for economic reasons and tradition, favor having sons over daughters.

In traditional societies, wife beating is largely regarded as a consequence of a man's right to inflict physical punishment on his

wife—something indicated by studies from Bangladesh, Cambodia, India, Mexico, Nigeria, Pakistan, Papua New Guinea, and Zimbabwe (WHO, 2002). Research from industrialized and nonindustrialized nations alike shows that partner violence is justified by the perpetrator on the following grounds: the woman's arguing with him, refusing sex, not having a meal ready, suspected infidelity, and disobedience. In many nations, women who were interviewed agreed that beatings were justified under certain circumstances. A much more extensive investigation by the WHO (2005) confirmed the earlier findings of widespread acceptance of intimate violence against women. Reports of physical or sexual violence over the course of the relationship ranged from a low of 15 percent in Japan to over 60 percent in Peru, Ethiopia, and Bangladesh. The abused women reported many health problems as a result.

A 10-country study on women's health and domestic violence conducted by the World Health Organization (WHO) (2009) based on interviews with over 24,000 women found that:

- Between 15 and 71 percent of women reported physical or sexual violence by a husband or partner.
- Many women said that their first sexual experience was not consensual. (Twenty-four percent in rural Peru, 28 percent in Tanzania, 30 percent in rural Bangladesh, and 40 percent in South Africa).
- Between 4 and 12 percent of women reported being physically abused during pregnancy.
- Worldwide, about 5,000 women are murdered by family members in the name of honor each year.

Studies reviewed by the WHO suggest that women stay in abusive situations because of fear of retribution, lack of means of economic support, concern for the children, and the stigma attached to being unmarried. Research also showed that leaving such a relationship was not a one-time thing—that most women leave and return several times before making the final break (LaFraniere, 2005). Because maintaining shelters is expensive, many poor nations have set up an informal network of "safe houses" to deal with the emergency of domestic abuse. Nongovernmental organizations often offer specialized services for victims of abuse in countries in which they are active (WHO, 2002).

Sexual abuse is a common co-occurring component of partner violence. In most countries, in fact, marital rape is considered an oxymoron. In Ethiopia, until recently, a man who wanted to marry a girl or woman could kidnap and rape her, then agree to marry her and escape punishment (Women's Action, 2005). Because the girl or woman was defiled, the family had to agree to the arrangement. Recent legal reform removed the exemption from the crime of rape as abduction for forced marriage. So far, the new rape law has not been enforced.

In Pakistan, especially in the southern Punjab province, women who are raped typically experience rejection by their families and society. Tribal traditions dictate that a raped woman is dishonored, cannot marry, and should be discarded, if not killed, by her family (see Human Rights Watch, 2008). Suicide among the women is common. The following case is representative: Dr. Shazia, a 32-year-old Pakistani physician, was raped in her home by an intruder (Equality Now, 2005). When she reported the crime to the police, her employers and the government pressured her to keep silent. Her husband was supportive, but her father-in-law declared that she was a stain on the family honor. When she pursued the case, the president announced on television that her life was in danger. Shazia contemplated suicide but then decided to emigrate instead in hopes of getting political asylum somewhere. At the time when the article was written, she still had not been granted asylum in any country.

Although, in this case, it was probably not her family members who threatened her life, women in Pakistan who have been raped are at risk of honor killing by a male relative for a perceived violation to the family honor. An estimated 1,000 honor killings take place each year in Pakistan.

This report shows that women at risk of violence require protection, whether through refugee services that grant them the right of political asylum or safe places such as women's shelters in their own countries. Escape through emigration may be the only recourse. This brings us to the topic of immigration and the kind of domestic violence to which immigrants are uniquely subject.

Immigration and Domestic Violence

Many factors, notes Hochschild (2003), contribute to what she calls "the growing feminization of migration" (p. 17). Economic opportunity is one such factor; romantic attachments and the promise of happiness in a land where women have more freedom undoubtedly are others. In her discussion of battered immigrant women, Gilfus (2002) describes how immigration status can be used as a weapon of abuse by husbands who threaten to destroy vital documents or to turn their wives over to the Immigration and Naturalization Service for deportation. A power imbalance takes place here because immigration laws allow men to sponsor their wives and thus to control their wives' immigration status. Many women also fear that the batterer himself, due to his violent behavior, might be deported or leave the country, taking the children with him.

A study of the experience of domestic violence among Cambodian refugee women (who met in focus groups) revealed that within this group such violence was often viewed as the woman's fault (Bhuyan, Mell, Senturia, Sullivan, & Shiu-Thornton, 2005). Divorced women faced disapproval within the community. The participants in the focus groups described extensive verbal abuse, including put-downs. Some described their husband's affairs with other women as a form of abuse. The women's wish for the future was support from their spouses and friends, not to end the marriage.

Bui (2003), in her study of Vietnamese immigrants, stressed the role of resettlement in the man's sense of control and the impact of exposure to racism and classism in the new society. Downward mobility, changes in gender-role practices, and role reversals may cause family conflict and lead to aggression in immigrant families. Data drawn from interviews with the women in Bui's study showed that wife abuse occurred within the context of adjustment to life in a new and frustrating environment. Loss of status emerged as a key aspect in the men's personal adjustment. Moreover, when Vietnamese American women changed their attitudes toward gender equality but their husbands did not, the men sometimes tried to assert their control through violence. Foreign wives of military men often have difficulties as well. Erez and Bach (2003) conducted in-depth interviews of 10 immigrant women who were intimate partners of U.S. servicemen. Abuse of these "military brides" was a common occurrence, and when it was too late for them to escape the relationship, the women's immigrant status and the military context and culture compounded the abuse. Although we know that military men, especially those returning from war, often have problems with violence at home (Zamichow & Perry, 2003), foreign women are especially vulnerable. They may not speak the language, may lack familiarity with American cultural norms and the law, and may tend to be socially isolated and dependent for their immigration status on the man. Military men who choose to marry foreign women may be atypical Americans, as Zamichow and Perry (2003) suggest, in the sense that they may expect that a foreign woman would be submissive, as well as extremely grateful for the opportunity to have material comforts not available at home. Such men may be totally unprepared for interpersonal conflicts that arise in intercultural marriages. And if they are combat veterans, these men may be suffering the aftereffects of warfare, besides. Let us now look more closely at what the experience of combat does to a relationship.

The Legacy of the Iraq/Afghanistan Wars

Unique to the military is the training of men (and women) to kill. In combat conditions, the soldier is in danger and kills almost as a protective reflex. Military socialization "to make a man out of the boy" not only attempts to obliterate all that is feminine but also breeds misogynous heterosexism in the soldier (Farr, 2005). The degradation of traits such as weakness in battle, squeamishness, and compassion—traits associated with femininity—helps create or preserve the masculine detachment and aggression that are desirable for battle. Such conditioning can be devastating for later family functioning, however.

On the home front, a condition such as posttraumatic stress disorder (PTSD) or a state of intoxication (even being suddenly aroused from sleep) can trigger violence. Depression related to PTSD can lead to suicide. Anderson (2005) studied the seven homicides and three suicides that have been committed in western Washington State by returning soldiers from the war in Iraq. Five wives, one girlfriend, and one child have all been killed. Two of the suicides were committed after murder. These cases and others like them reported across the United States seem to suggest that, as an antiwar slogan popular in the 1960s said, "War is not good for people or other living things." War is definitely not good for families.

The year 2008 saw a record number of suicide cases in the army—140; and the number was expected to rise again in 2009 (Hall, 2009). Fort Campbell, Kentucky, alone has had 18 confirmed or suspected suicides since the beginning of the year, while other installations are dealing with a rash of violent acts such as homicide. A study of the first 100,000 Iraq and Afghanistan veterans seen at VA facilities showed that 25 percent of them received mental health diagnoses (Roehr, 2007). Of these, 56 percent had two or more mental health diagnoses. Today in response to these incidents and a spurt in domestic violence and homicide, the Army has bolstered suicide prevention (Hall, 2009). The new prevention program uses a strategy called "motorpool counseling," which entails hanging around with the soldiers and meeting them outside of the office, at a coffee shop or at the motorpool. Battalion leaders will get training in how to handle behavioral health issues.

In summary, families are harmed when government policies deny the rights of women, their education, earning power, and political participation. A society arming itself for war or fighting a war is a society in which money that could help to empower families (whether through providing health care, housing, and nutrition) instead gets diverted into military training and the manufacture of technologies for mass slaughter. (See http://www.warresisters. org for the latest update on where the U.S. tax dollar really goes.) Let us now consider some promising developments from home and abroad.

Promising Initiatives

Kinship Care

Over 2.5 million children are living with relative caregivers today; these include grandparents, aunts, uncles, and older siblings (Casey Family Programs, 2008; Children's Defense Fund, 2008). Much of this care is informal. In the past, relatives could not qualify to be foster parents so they faced the prospect of having to send the children away if they could not afford to care for them. The practice of subsidizing family members to provide care for children in need, which was written into law in New Zealand, has had a significant influence on U.S. and British foster care policies. Accordingly, in both countries, kinship care has become the fastest growing child placement program in child welfare (Hawkins & Bland, 2002). The idea for this formalized system of care rapidly gained ground in the 1980s as the demand for homes in which to place children in need of care far exceeded the number of available registered foster homes. A key incentive for the increase in kincare arrangements came with the new federal law requiring that the states allow relative caregivers to be paid foster parents (Hegar & Rosenthal, 2009). A second factor that contributed to the promotion of relative foster care was the growing recognition of the benefits of family care and the stabilizing effect that extended family can have on placement. An additional incentive for providing kinship care is the desire of all parties to avoid placement of children outside of their own racial or ethnic communities. Now all states require that workers give priority consideration to relatives when making decisions about a child's out-of-home placement (Samantrai, 2004).

Formal kinship care often involves placement, generally of an African American child, with his or her grandmother. Often, the grandmother is in need of financial assistance to help

in this way, and assistance is provided with this program. Key advantages of such an arrangement are its relative permanence and stability, the familiarity of the child with the setting and relatives, continuity in schooling, and the absence of stigmatizing family removal. Research indicates that children in kinship care remain longer in the homes than children in other forms of care. Hegar and Rosenthal (2009) confirmed the importance of sibling relationships and of keeping siblings together in foster care. In their examination of kinship care relationships among kinship foster care, sibling placement, and child welfare outcomes, based on 2,488 observations of 1,415 different children, they concluded that maintaining kin ties generally was associated with more favorable outcomes than was placement outside of the family. Consistent with the kinship care literature, children were more satisfied with this form of care and elicited fewer behavior problems at school.

So how widespread is the use of kinship care? As we learn from the White Paper from Casey Family Programs (2008), around 24 percent are formally placed with relatives; of these around three-fourths are racial and ethnic minorities; the children are rarely infants and are often in their teens. The caregivers are more likely than non-kin caregivers to be older, living without a partner, and to be below the poverty level. The White Paper presents a strong case for more active federal support of these struggling families.

Relative caregivers report that one of their greatest challenges in raising children is getting accurate information about the benefits and services that are available to their families. As a result, many of the caregivers are overwhelmed and lack the resources to properly provide for the children. This is the picture provided by researchers Simpson and Lawrence-Webb (2007), who interviewed women who provided informal kinship care. Combining ecological and womanist perspectives, these researchers used an ecological approach to look at the family system within the larger context of neighborhood and other potential support systems, and a womanist approach to draw attention to issues of gender, class, race, and power arrangements. From this perspective, Simpson and Lawrence-Webb describe the situation facing the grandmother caretakers who were sometimes pushed into providing informal care to their grandchildren when the social services department threatened to otherwise take the kids away. The financial resources available to these grandmothers through Temporary Assistance to Needy Families (TANF) were inferior to those that would have been provided to foster parents. One interviewee later qualified to be a kinship foster parent, but the obstacles to these poor, often uneducated women were many.

Fortunately, major improvements in the system are underway thanks to a new act of Congress geared to make services more readily available to family caregivers and to raise their standards of living. The Fostering Connections to Success and Increasing Adoptions Act of 2008 (P.L. 110-351) offers help to children raised by relatives by establishing a Kinship Navigator Program, which would fund grants to help link relative caregivers, both inside and outside of the formal child welfare system, to a broad range of services and supports needed for their children and themselves. The bill also establishes a Kinship Guardian Assistance Program, which would help to ensure permanent homes for some children living with relatives (Children's Defense Fund, 2008). As time will probably tell, this programming should help caring relatives provide the best care possible for the children in their charge. A very different child-care arrangement is described next, one that is more preventive in focus.

Shared Family Care

Inspired by the Danish whole-family placement program, in which troubled families receive 6 to 8 weeks of constant supervision and guidance, the Shared Family Care Program, which was established in Colorado Springs, is whole-family placement program (National Abandoned Infants Assistance Resource Center [AIA], 2009). In addition, today Families First, Inc., in Contra Costa County, CA, serves families in the child welfare system who are at risk of having their children removed or in the process of reunifying with them. And in St. Paul, Minnesota,

Growing Home has a Whole Family Placement Program, recently restructured to serve adolescent mothers with severe emotional disturbances and their children. Shared family care programs are now available in 10 states. Instead of splitting up the family while it gets help, the local social service agency moves entire families into foster care. Unlike Denmark's foster care arrangement, in which families are mentored by professionally trained social workers, these families move in with a mentor family, hopefully to absorb parenting skills from their hosts. The beauty of this program is that it enables families that have minimal support systems to get the resources and skills they need to move toward self-sufficiency. It ensures that children are protected while parents learn the parenting skills they need (Samantrai, 2004). This practice of opening one's home to unrelated dependent adults has been in operation for centuries in Europe.

Five types of shared family care arrangements in the United States singled out by the Child Welfare Information Gateway (2008) are as follows: *(1)* residential programs for children that also offer residence and treatment for their parents; *(2)* drug and alcohol treatment programs for adults that also provide treatment for children; *(3)* drug treatment programs for mothers and children; *(4)* residential programs for pregnant and parenting mothers; and *(5)* foster family homes that offer care for a teen parent and child. Although funding for such whole-family program designs has not been widely available in America, as in Europe, this form of family presentation holds much promise for future development. Results from the small studies that have been done are promising: Children whose parents complete the program are only half as likely to reenter the child welfare system as are those families reunited after foster care (Samantrai, 2004).

Other Empowering Approaches

The universal paradox is whether to risk erring on the side of the child or on the side of the family. Perhaps the question is not "either/or" but "both/and." Highly critical of the way the present child welfare system holds single mothers responsible for their children without regard for the circumstances affecting their lives and child care, Brian Wharf (2002) directs our attention to community work approaches to child welfare. Maybe it is not an issue of whether one should either protect the child or support the family, as Wharf suggests, but rather how to provide a means of empowerment for all persons in the equation. Such a balance can be achieved, he further suggests, through the building of mutual aid associations and group and community approaches to provide the maximum benefit for all family members.

Formulated on the North American continent and originally directed toward women and minority groups, the principle of empowerment is the cornerstone of the community-centered innovations. Jenkins (2006), for example, describes how culturally specific family services and the use of a strengths perspective can protect children and empower families within the natural context of their home communities. Incorporating natural networks that exist within African American communities (for example, the church and child-care cooperatives) can

strengthen high-risk families and prevent removal of children by child welfare authorities.

A rare find in the literature is the description of an artificially designed community now called "Generations of Hope" that houses about 30 children who currently live with adoptive parents in 10 homes. The community is also home to 42 older people who have subsidized rent in exchange for their volunteer work with the children, acting as tutors and often playing grandparent roles (Eheart et al., 2009; Johnson, 2008). The "village" is located on a former Air Force base in Rantoul, Illinois. Generously funded by the state of Illinois, this experiment in community living has led to much media attention as a model that works. It is soon to be replicated in 11 other states with support of about $7 million from the Kellogg Foundation. While children and adoptive parents are carefully matched, the youngsters form alliances with the older residents more informally, over time.

Another model of child protection that is premised on increasing partnerships with families through community involvement is found

Figure 4.4. Head Start provides family-centered day care to help prepare children for school. Photo by Rupert van Wormer.

in Iowa (Iowa Department of Human Services, 2008). Placing less emphasis on the incident in question and more on the family's strengths and concerns, social workers who work for the Iowa DHS learn competencies for strength-based assessment in workshops and trainings that are offered statewide. Assessments are done in collaboration with family members. Instead of a problem-solving focus, workers are encouraged to ask solution-focused questions. Questions of the form "After all you've been through, how did you find enough strength to keep pushing on?" as opposed to "What could you have done differently?" are geared toward extracting positive responses. (Figure 4.4 exemplifies strengths-based social work practice.)

In Oregon, similarly, the casework assessments shifted from looking at problems to focusing on how to help families (National Center on Family, 2000). The Family Unity Meeting evolved as a partnership between professionals and family members. The Oregon model has many similarities with family group conferencing but developed independently of it.

Hawaii, with its universal health care and its generously funded programs, is a leader in providing nurturing care to families. Called Healthy Start, this federally funded program is basically an early-intervention program that helps parents provide good care for their children. It achieves this through providing public health instruction and guidance for the whole family (Hawaii State Department of Health, 2005).

Common to all these innovations is their reliance on the strengths and empowerment framework in working with, not against, families in the fulfillment of mutual goals. The strengths perspective, as conceptualized by Saleebey (2006), combined with the empowerment perspective, as formulated by Simon (1994) and Gutiérrez and Lewis (1999), is rapidly emerging as the most powerful framework for counseling and other interventions in North America.

Family Group Conferencing

Family group conferencing (FGC) involves the extended family in a solution-focused, strengths-based approach to solving problems (Walton,

Roby, Frandsen, & Davidson, 2003). We have the Maori people and social services authorities of New Zealand to thank for the introduction of the innovative programming known as family group conferencing. This model of restoring justice is an outgrowth of both aboriginal and feminist practice concerns stemming from the international women's and children's rights movements of the late 1980s and beyond. Evoking the family-group decision-making model in order to try to stop family violence, FGC made its mainstream criminal justice debut in New Zealand in 1989 and somewhat later in England and Oregon. This model is currently being tested in Newfoundland and Labrador, as well as in communities in New Zealand, Austria, England, Wales, Canada, and the United States (Pennell, 2005). Despite differences among jurisdictions, one common theme is overriding: Family group conferences are more likely than traditional forms of dispute resolution to give effective voice to those who are traditionally disadvantaged.

Interlocking demands of previous poverty, social exclusion, weak community linkages, and troubled extended-family relationships are typical challenges that face families seen in child welfare practice. We have filtered out from the literature a number of characteristics of FGC that are relevant to child welfare practice. Compared with traditional practices in family work, the philosophy of family group conferencing entails the following:

- The sharing of decision-making responsibilities with families
- The role of the social worker becoming partner/collaborator rather than expert
- Decision making by general consensus
- Process and decision making that are more likely to reflect the culture, traditions, and needs of the participants
- Stress on the *quality* of relationships, not family structures
- Beginning with a broad definition of what constitutes a family
- Acknowledgement of the value of kinship care over stranger care for children in need of care

▶ A solutions- rather than problem-focused framework

▶ A proactive rather than investigative model for addressing child mistreatment

▶ A focus on building up social networks while not being blind to the risks to children in an unhealthy social environment

Unlike FGC that concerns the welfare of an abused or neglected child, FGC for youthful offender situations involves a slightly different cast of characters and a focus on "deed, not need." The focus, in other words, is on the offense and the harm done. Compared with traditional forms of juvenile justice, FGC has the following characteristics (as described by Bazemore and Umbreit, 2001):

▶ It entails an informal, "around the table" nonadversarial process.

▶ It includes a trained facilitator as discussion leader.

▶ It directly involves the victim and the community who were affected by the wrongdoing in the discussion of the offense.

▶ It involves the victim and the victim's family directly in decisions regarding appropriate sanctions.

▶ It stresses offender awareness of the human impact of his or her behavior.

▶ It provides the opportunity for the offender to take full responsibility for his or her behavior.

▶ It uses a narrative approach, as each person involved tells how he or she is affected by the behavior in question.

▶ It engages the offender's family members and support system in the conference.

▶ It solicits the families' support in the process of the offender's making amends and repairing the harm.

In New Zealand, the whole-child welfare system has come to rely on FGC as a means of drawing on community and the extended family for help in cases of child abuse and neglect (Centre for Justice and Reconciliation, 2002). With the passage of the Sentencing Act of 2002, New Zealand enacted new legislation to make restorative justice processes that had formerly been used with juveniles and families in the child welfare system also available for adult offenders.

In their work with families, social workers will find that the spirituality components, non-bureaucratic processes, and reliance on mutual aid that characterize family conferencing are compatible with the values and traditions of the Latino community (Gutiérrez & Suarez, 1999), as well as with African-centered principles (Jenkins, 2006). Indigenous populations, such as North American Native tribes, incorporate spiritual leaders into the healing process. In aboriginal culture, all life is viewed as sacred; disruptive acts typically are viewed as signals of relational disharmonies.

Social workers in Hawaii have been quietly incorporating native Hawaiian culturally based tradition into their human service interventions. The impetus for introducing the culturally specific programming came in the 1970s when it was noted that native children were not responding to the standard forms of psycho-therapy provided. Hurdle (2002) chronicles the ways social workers, in collaboration with Hawaiian elders, worked to revitalize the use of *ho'oponopono*, an ancient Hawaiian conflict resolution process. This model is embedded in the traditional Hawaiian values of extended family, respect of elders, need for harmonious relationships, and restoration of good will, or *aloha*. The process is ritualistic and follows a definite protocol. With the leader in tight control of communication, the opening prayer leads to an open discussion of the problem at hand. The resolution phase begins with a confession of wrongdoing and the seeking of forgiveness. Uniquely, as Hurdle (2002) relates, all parties to the conflict ask forgiveness of each other; this equalizes the status of participants. This process effectively promotes spiritual healing and can be used in many contexts.

Pennell (2006) describes a successful child welfare program in North Carolina that advances family participation in child welfare planning. Conferences were held across the state to resolve situations where child protection was required. Meetings took place in churches and other community buildings and followed the

New Zealand model of giving the extended family members private time to reach a decision. A sample of 27 conferences involving 221 family group members revealed a high level of satisfaction with the conference process and decision. Respondents saw the plans as primarily reached through consensus, following a trusted leader, and bargaining. Conference preparation was an important part in the success of the process.

Walton et al. (2003) evaluated the FGC model through extensive interviews with family members, including children, and professionals who participated in 21 conferences in Utah. The participants reported many benefits from the conferencing, including feeling closer to other family members. Significantly, the researchers noted that "the practice of involving extended family in problem solving and decision making is natural for Polynesians and many minority cultures but is foreign for most Caucasian Americans" (Walton et al., 2003, pp. 18–19). Their recommendation is for additional preparation for these families to help them get beyond their individualistic outlook. Above all, the FGC process would benefit from a mandate by the government, as is the case in New Zealand, for greater use and the development of standard procedures.

Former Iowa child welfare worker Christina Hussey (in personal correspondence with van Wormer of July 27, 2009) recalls her participation in at least 20 family group decision-making meetings:

> These meetings included family members, friends of the family, and professional team members. During these meetings, the case manager and other professionals discuss the case status with the family and ask the family to determine what the best plan should be for the children. In nearly every case, the plan that the family came up with was successfully carried out, even when the family supported adoption by foster parents. I feel that the family group meetings really empowered families, helped to build trust, and resolved a very difficult problem for their loved ones. Sometimes family members were flown in

from all over the country. Once a teenaged girl was successfully placed with her father who she had not seen for seven years.

The FGC process is a prime example of the creative use of network meetings to reconnect estranged members to the family circle. In communities across North America, the extended family is gaining attention in child welfare as an invaluable resource for strengthening families and protecting children from neglect and mistreatment. We can expect to hear a great deal more about FGC initiatives in the future (see http://www. restorativejustice.org. to learn more about this family conferencing process).

Summary and Conclusion

The theme of this chapter can be defined by the word *adaptation:* the adaptation of one system, the family, to forces, natural and humanmade, in the environment. Thus, we considered the impact of various stresses such as natural disasters, population displacement, and macro economic upheaval on the family. Because our focus was on macro forces, we used the ecosystems framework to organize our understanding of how families cope in a time of sweeping social change. For our macro family analysis, we expanded the usual ecosystems formulation to pertain to the family in the environment to incorporate both elements—the family and the environment—in reciprocity. We extended the ecosystems metaphor into the political and economic arenas.

A major assumption of this chapter is that the quality of people's social relationships is fundamental to their ability to adapt and to their sense of well-being. Sustainable government policies can enhance these relationships. For example, policies can establish and support a comfortable standard of living and provide affordable housing, high-quality child care for all children, paid family leave when needed, health care, and a safety net in times of need. We reviewed models of family-friendly policies found in Europe. We also ventured into less familiar terrain, into places where family survival is threatened through cultural practices that degrade and exploit girls and women. Among the tragedies described is the big business of sex trafficking cross-continentally from poor nations to rich nations.

The global market and globalization are the major forces for social change in today's world. From an economic standpoint, globalization affects families in manifold ways—from survival issues related to work and pressures on the worker from global competition to social welfare provisions that bolster family care and provide a safety net in times of crisis to the push for migration and immigration that increases diversity within the society.

But, as we have demonstrated in this chapter, globalization is not just about economics. Globalization is about every aspect of family life. As all systems increasingly are brought into closer interconnectedness through the communications revolution, the impact is felt across the board—in our work, at school, and through information we get from the media and the Internet. Such communication brings news from one part of the world to everywhere in the world almost instantaneously. Perhaps this is one reason that human rights considerations have come into greater prominence in recent years. As described in this chapter, with reference to violations worldwide, the template for human rights and international law is the U.N. Declaration of Human Rights that was presented to the world in 1948.

Consistent with the central focus of this chapter on families and family functioning and in deference to the reality of globalization, we surveyed diverse family forms at home (Native American, Bosnian refugee, African American, Asian American, gay and lesbian). Resilience was evidenced in the cultural traditions and bonding of these disparate groups. The boxed readings also provided personal narratives of resilience: an interview with a woman who navigated the worlds of the Deaf and the hearing, a prison-orphaned child in his grandmother's care, and an interview with a thriving lesbian household. The dark side of life was addressed, as stated earlier, in the description of human rights violations against girls and women, some within the family itself and some emanating from cultural and economic forces. These include sex trafficking, genital mutilation, and honor killings. Our discussion of global domestic violence parallels the discussion of family partner violence in *Human Behavior and the Social Environment, Micro Level* (van Wormer, 2011). Ending on a positive note, this chapter described empowering policy initiatives from around the world that reinforce family strengths. Family group conferencing was presented as a means of decision making in situations of crises in which social service agencies collaborate with extended family members on solutions to problems. Family sharing and kinship care are other policies that were explored from a multicultural perspective. The next chapter concerns culture and society.

Thought Questions

1. Referring to the opening quotation, how is protection of the family a human rights issue? How successful is the U.S. government in abiding by this article from the United Nations?
2. Relate ecosystems concepts such as adaptation to the study of the family.
3. Discuss the family dynamics of life in a family in which the parents are deaf.
4. Construct an ecomap for your own family of origin or your present family and analyze the person-in-environment configuration that emerges.
5. What can we learn from American Indian tribes that can be incorporated into family counseling?
6. Discuss African American family patterns in light of the legacy of the past. What is your reaction to the story of the 9-year-old boy?
7. Define the *epidemiological paradox* regarding Latino death rates. What factors do you think account for this phenomenon?
8. Describe the diversity within the Asian American population in terms of history and culture.

9. Describe the lesbian-headed household described in the insert (Box 4.5) and what life would be like growing up in such a family. What kinds of government policies could protect the family members from discrimination?

10. Which of the progressive European policies do you think would boost family life if adopted in the United States?

11. Explain how Norway came out number 1 on the UN human development index.

12. "The victimization of girls and women is structural both in its causes and its consequences." Discuss.

13. How do grueling work schedules affect family life? What is the message of books such as *Nickel and Dimed?*

14. According to the United Nations Deputy Secretary-General, stopping violence against women is the key to eliminating poverty. Discuss this claim.

15. Relate honor killings to women's roles in some societies.

16. What is the correlation between immigration and domestic violence?

17. Explain the relationship, if any, between engagement in military combat and committing violence at home.

18. Describe the kinship care and shared family care initiatives and how they can serve the needs of children.

19. What are the roots of family group conferencing and what is it relevance to child protection?

References

Adoption and Safe Families Act of 1997, Pub. L. No. 105–189.

"African Americans show solid gains at all academic degree levels". (2009). *The Journal of Blacks in Higher Education*. Retrieved from http://www.jbhe.com/features/64_degreelevels.html

Almeida, R. (2005). Asian Indian families: An overview. In M. McGoldrick, J. Giordano, & N. Garcia-Preto (Eds.), *Ethnicity and family therapy* (3rd ed., pp. 377–394). New York: Guilford Press.

Amnesty International. (2007). Council of Europe convention against trafficking. New York: Author.

Anderson, R. (2005, August 31). Home front casualties. *Seattle Weekly*. Retrieved from http://www.seattleweekly.com/news/0535/050831

"A spike in homeless families". (2009, July 22). *Christian Science Monitor*, p. 08.

Banister, J. (2004). Shortage of girls in China today. *Journal of Population Research*, *21*(1), 19–45.

Bazemore, G., & Umbreit, M. (2001). *A comparison of four restorative conferencing models.* Washington, DC: U.S. Department of Justice.

Bernstein, N. (2002, July 29). Side effect of welfare law: The no-parent family. *The New York Times*, A1.

Bhuyan, R., Mell, M., Senturia, K., Sullivan, M., & Shiu-Thornton, S. (2005, August). Women must endure according to their karma. *Journal of Interpersonal Violence*, *20*(8), 902–921.

Black, L., & Jackson, V. (2005). Families of African origin: An overview. In M. McGoldrick, J. Giordano, & N. Garcia-Preto (Eds.), *Ethnicity and family therapy* (3rd ed., pp. 77–100). New York: Guilford Press.

Boushey, H. (2005). *Family-friendly policies: Boosting mothers' wages.* Washington, DC: Center for Economic and Policy Research.

Bowen, M. (1978). *Family therapy in clinical practice.* New York: Aronson.

Brady, D. (2002, August 26). Rethinking the rat race. *Business Week*, 142–143.

Briar-Lawson, K., Lawson, H. A., & Hennon, C. B. (2001). *Family-centered policies and practices: International implications.* New York: Columbia University Press.

Britt, R. (2009, February 2). Recession to fuel more family murder, suicide. *Live Science*. Retrieved from http://www.livescience.com/culture/090202-recession-suicide.html

Bui, H. (2003). Immigration context of wife abuse: A case of Vietnamese immigrants in the United States. In R. Muraskin (Ed.), *It's a crime: Women and justice* (pp. 394–410). Upper Saddle River, NJ: Prentice-Hall.

Bureau of Justice Statistics (BJS). (2008). Immediate press release: An estimated 809,800 of inmates in the nation's prisons were parents to 1,706,600 minor children. Retrieved from http://www.ojp.usdoj.gov/bjs/pub/press/pptmcpr.htm

Bureau of Justice Statistics (BJS). (2009). *Prison and jail inmates at midyear 2008.* Washington, DC:

U.S. Department of Justice. Retrieved from http://www.ojp.usdoj.gov/bjs/pub/pdf/pim08st.pdf

Casey Family Programs. (2008, May). *White paper: Kinship care*. Seattle, WA: author. Retrieved from http://www.casey.org/resources/publications/pdf/WhitePaper_KinshipCare_FR.pdf

Centre for Justice and Reconciliation. (2005). New Zealand expands official recognition of restorative justice. *Restorative Justice Online*. Retrieved from Prison Fellowship International Web site, http://www.restorativejustice.org/search?searcharableText

Child Welfare Information Gateway. (2008, September 18). Children's Bureau. Retrieved from http://www.childwefare.gov

Children's Defense Fund (2008, May 7). *Children's Defense Fund celebrates third national grand rally*. Retrieved from http://www.cdftexas.org/attached/advisories/GRally2008.pdf

Colon, E. (2007). A multidiversity perspective on Latinos: Issues of oppression and social functioning. In G. A. Appleby, E. Colon, & J. Hamilton (Eds.), *Diversity, oppression, and social functioning: Person-in-environment, assessment and intervention* (2nd ed., pp. 115–134). Boston: Allyn & Bacon.

Coontz, S., & Folbre, N. (2003, April 26–28). Marriage, poverty, and public policy. *American Prospect*. Retrieved from http://www.prospect.org/webfeatures/200403/c

Coyhis, D. (2000). Substance abuse and cultural issues in Indian country. In J.-A. Krestan (Ed.), *Bridge to recovery: Addiction, family therapy, and multicultural treatment* (pp. 79–114). New York: Free Press.

Crockett, S. A. (2002, August 30). Study: More African-American men incarcerated than in college. Retrieved from Black Entertainment Television Web site: http://www.bet.com/articles

Day, P. (2007). American Indians in nursing homes. In P. Kolb (Ed.), *Social work practice with racially and ethnically diverse nursing home residents and their families* (pp. 41–71). New York: Columbia University Press.

Delgado, M. (2007). *Social work with Latinos: A cultural assets paradigm*. New York: Oxford University Press.

Diener, E., & Seligman, E. (2004). Beyond money: Toward an economy of well-being. *Psychological Science in the Public Interest, 5*(1), 1–31.

Dominelli, L. (2002). *Feminist social work theory and practice*. Hampshire, England: Palgrave.

Drug Policy Alliance. (2009). *Race and the drug war*. Retrieved from http://www.drugpolicy.org/communities/race/

Eheart, B. K., Hopping, D., Power, M. B., Mitchell, E. & Racine, D. (2009). Generations of Hope Communities: An intergenerational neighborhood model of support and service. *Children and Youth Services Review, 31*(1), 47–52.

Ehrenreich, B. (2002). *Nickel and dimed: On not getting by in America*. New York: Owl Books.

Ehrenreich, B. (2005). *Bait and switch: The (futile) pursuit of the American dream*. New York: Metropolitan Books.

Ehrenreich, B. (2009). *Bright-sided: How the relentless promotion of positive thinking has undermined America*. New York: Metropolitian Books.

Equality Now. (2005, August). Pakistan: The Hudood ordinances—Denial of justice for rape. Retrieved from http://www.equalitynow.org/english/actions/action_2601_en.html

Erez, E. (2000, April 10–17). Women as victims and survivors in the context of transnational crime. Paper presented at the United Nations Congress on Crime Prevention and the Treatment of Offenders, Vienna, Austria.

Erez, E., & Bach, S. (2003). Immigration, domestic violence, and the military: The case of "military brides." *Violence Against Women, 9*(9), 1093–1117.

Falicov, C. (2005). Mexican families. In M. McGoldrick, J. Giordano, & N. Garcia-Petro (Eds.), *Ethnicity and family therapy* (3rd ed., pp. 229–241). New York: Guilford Press.

Farr, K. (2005). *Sex trafficking: The global market in women and children*. New York: Worth.

Foroohar, R. (2009, December 21). Joblessness is here to stay. *Newsweek*, p. 53.

Franze, S., Foster, M., Abbott-Shim, M., McCarty, F., & Lambert, R. (2002). Describing Head Start family service workers: An examination of factors related to job satisfaction, empowerment, and multiculturalism. *Families in Society, 83*(3), 257–264.

Fuller-Thomson, E., & Minkler, M. (2005). American Indian/Alaskan Native grandparents raising grandchildren: Findings from the Census 2000 supplementary survey. *Social Work, 50*(2), 131–139.

Garcia-Preto, N. (2005a). Latino families: An overview. In M. McGoldrick, J. Giordano, & N. Garcia-Preto (Eds.), *Ethnicity and family therapy* (3rd ed., pp. 153–165). New York: Guilford Press.

Garcia-Preto, N. (2005b). Puerto Rican families. In M. McGoldrick, J. Giordano, & N. Garcia- Petro (Eds.), *Ethnicity and family therapy* (3rd ed., pp. 242–255). New York: Guilford Press.

Gardiner, H. W., & Kosmitzki, C. (2005). *Lives across cultures: Cross-cultural human development* (3rd ed.). Boston: Allyn & Bacon.

Gates, G., & Ost, J. (2004). *The gay and lesbian atlas*. Washington, DC: Urban Institute Press.

Gares, G. (2009, October). *Same-sex spouses and unmarried partners in the American Community Survey, 2008*. The Williams Institute. Retrieved from the Williams Institute at UCLA Web site http://www.law.ucla.edu/williamsinstitute/pdf/ACS2008_Final(2).pdf

Gay marriage around the world. (2005, December 5). *Daily Times-Pakistan*, 9.

Germain, C. (1991). *Human behavior in the social environment: An ecological view*. New York: Columbia University Press.

Gesino, J. P. (2007). Native Americans: Oppression and social work practice. In G. A. Appleby, E. Colon, & J. Hamilton (Eds.), *Diversity, oppression and social functioning: Person-in-environment assessment and intervention* (2nd ed., pp. 134–156). Boston: Allyn & Bacon.

Gilfus, M. (2002). Women's experiences of abuse as a risk factor for incarceration. *National Electronic Network on Violence against Women*. Retrieved May 1, 2006, from http://www.vawnet.org/DomesticViolence/Research/VAWnetDocs

Goldenberg, I., & Goldenberg, H. (2002). *Counseling today's families* (4th ed.). Belmont, CA: Brooks/Cole.

Graff, E. J. (2002, April 8). The other marriage war. *American Prospect*. Retrieved from http://www.prospect.org/print/V13/7/graff-e.html

Green, J. B. (2003). *Introduction to family theory and therapy: Exploring an evolving field*. Belmont, CA: Thomson.

Green, K., Ensminger, M., Robertson, J., & Juon, H-S. (2006). Impact of adult sons' incarceration on African American mothers' psychological distress. *Journal of Marriage and Family, 68*(2), 430–450.

Greenberger, S. (2004, November 7). Gay-marriage ruling pushed voters. *Boston Sunday Globe*, B1, B7.

Gutiérrez, L., & Lewis, E. A. (Eds.). (1999). *Empowering women of color*. New York: Columbia University Press.

Gutiérrez, L., & Suarez, Z. (1999). Empowerment with Latinas. In L. M. Gutiérrez & E. A. Lewis (Eds.), *Empowering women of color* (pp.167–186). New York: Columbia University Press.

Hall, K. (2009, November 30). Brigade teams bring mental health to Fort Campbell. Associated Press. The Guardian. Retrieved from http://www.guardian.co.uk/world/feedarticle/8833272

Blacks hit hard by economy's punch. *Washington Post*. Retrieved from http://www.washingtonpost.com/wp-dyn/content/article/2009/11/23/AR2009112304092.html

Hawkins, C., & Bland, T. (2002, March/April). Program evaluation of the CREST project: Empirical support for kinship care as an effective approach to permanency planning. *Child Welfare 81*(2), 271–292.

Hawaii State Department of Health. (2005). *Early intervention*. Retrieved from http://www.hawaii.gov/health/family-child-health/eis/index.html

Hegar, R., & Rosenthal, J. (2009). Kinship care and sibling placement: Child behavior, family relationships, and school outcomes. *Children and Youth Services Review, 31*(6), 670–679.

Hochschild, A. (2003). Love and gold. In B. Ehrenreich & A. Hochschild (Eds.), *Global woman: Nannies, maids, and sex workers in the new economy* (pp. 15–30). New York: Metropolitan Books.

Holland, T., & Kilpatrick, A. (2003). An ecological systems–social constructionism approach to family practice. In A. Kilpatrick & T. Holland (Eds.), *Working with families: An integrative model by level of need* (pp. 14–32). Boston: Allyn & Bacon.

Human Rights Watch. (2002). *International Justice for Women: The ICC marks a new era*. Retrieved from http://www.hrw.org/legacy/campaigns/icc/icc-women.htm

Human Rights Watch (2008, May 4).Universal periodic review of Pakistan. Retrieved from http://www.hrw.org/en/news/2008/05/04/universal-periodic-review-pakistan

Hurdle, D. (2002). Native Hawaiian traditional healing: Culturally based interventions for social work practice. *Social Work, 47*, 183–192.

Hutchings, J., & Hatchwell, E. (Eds.). (2002). *Insight guide: Sweden*. Masapath, NY: Langenscheidt.

Ife, J. (2001). *Human rights and social work: Towards rights-based practice*. Cambridge, England: Cambridge University Press.

Iowa Department of Human Services. (2008, April). Children in child welfare: Comprehensive functional family assessment. Retrieved from http://www.dhs.iowa.gov/docs/Assessment.pdf

Jenkins, M. (2006). Gullah Island dispute resolution: An example of Afrocentric restorative justice. *Journal of Black Studies, 37*(2), 299–319.

Johnson, D., & Piore, A. (2004, October 18). At home in two worlds. *Newsweek,* 52–54.

Johnson, D. (2008, September 15). For distant generations in Illinois, unrelated but oh so close. *New York Times,* p. A17.

Kanai, A. (2009). Karoshi (work to death) in Japan. *Journal of Business Ethics, 84*(2), 209-216.

Kasindorf, M. (2005, October12). National count of homeless puts issue in human terms. *USA Today,* 1A, 6A.

"Knesset approves harsh punishments for human trade". (2006, October, 17). *Y Net News.* Retrieved from http://www.ynetnews.com/articles/0,7340,L-3316286,00.html

Koppelman, K. L. (2005). *Understanding human differences: Multicultural education for a diverse America.* Boston: Allyn & Bacon.

Korten, D.C. (2009). *Agenda for a new economy: From phantom wealth to real wealth.* San Francisco: Berrett-Koehler.

LaFraniere, S. (2005, August 11). Entrenched epidemic: Wife-beatings in Africa. *New York Times,* A1.

Lai, T-F. (2001). Ethnocultural background and substance abuse treatment of Chinese Americans. In S. L. Straussner (Ed.), *Ethnocultural factors in substance abuse treatment* (pp. 368–392). New York: Guilford Press.

Lee, E., & Mock, M. (2005). Asian families: An overview. In M. McGoldrick, J. Giordano, & N. Garcia-Preto (Eds.), *Ethnicity and family therapy* (3rd ed., pp. 269–289). New York: Guilford Press.

Logan, S. L. (2008). Family: Overview. In National Association of Social Workers (NASW), *Encyclopedia of Social Work* (20th ed., pp. 175–182). New York: Oxford University Press.

Longres, J. (2000). *Human behavior in the social environment* (3rd ed., pp. 109–130). Boston: Allyn & Bacon.

Mazza, C. (2002) And then the world fell apart: Children of incarcerated fathers. *Families in Society, 83*(5–6), 521–529.

McGlade, M., Saha, S., & Dahlstrom, M. (2004). The Latina paradox: An opportunity for restructuring prenatal care delivery. *American Journal of Public Health, 94*(12), 2062–2065.

McGraw, M., & Bauer, L. (2009, December 12). U.S. system to find, help victims of human trafficking is broken. *Kansas City Star.* Retrieved from http://www.kansascity.com/105/story/1626936.html

Meyers, M., & Gornick, J. (2003). *Families that work: Policies for reconciling parenthood and employment.* New York: Russell Sage Foundation.

Migiro, A.-R. (2010, March 1). Address to the UN Commission on the Status of Women. New York. Address by the United Nations Deputy Secretary-General. News and Media Division. Retrieved from http://www.un.org/News/Press/docs/2010/dsgsm489.doc.htm

Minuchin, S. (1974). *Families and family therapy.* Cambridge, MA: Harvard University Press.

Morales, A.T., Sheafor, B., & Scott, M. (2010). *Social work: A profession of many faces* (12th ed.). Boston: Allyn & Bacon.

Murray, S., & McKay, B. (2009, November 23). Early data suggest suicides are rising. *The Wall Street Journal.* Retrieved from http://online.wsj.com/article/SB125892118623059701.html

National Abandoned Infants Assistance Resource Center. (2006). Shared family care, abandoned infants assistance. Retrieved, from http://aia.berkeley.edu/information_resources/shared_family

National Association of Social Workers. (2008). Lesbian, gay, and bisexual issues. In *Social work speaks: NASW policy statements* (8th ed., pp. 218–222). Washington, DC: NASW Press.

Older Americans 2004. (2005). *Population: Older Americans 2000: Key indicators of well- being.* Federal Interagency on Aging. Retrieved from http://www.aoa.gov/agingstatsdotnet/Main_Site/Data/2004_Documents/Aboutthisreport.aspx

Olson, T. (2010, January 18). The conservative case for gay marriage. Cover story, *Newsweek,* pp. 47–54.

Padgett, T. (2007, June 5). Gay family values. *Time,* pp. 51–52.

Peak, C., & Weeks, J. R. (2002), Does community context influence reproductive outcomes of Mexican origin women in San Diego, California? *Journal of Immigrant Health, 4*(3), 125–137.

Pennell, J. (2005). Widening the circle. In J. Pennell & G. Anderson (Eds.), *Widening the circle: The practice and evaluation of family group conferencing with children, youths, and their families* (pp. 1–8). Washington, DC: NASW Press.

Pennell, J. (2006). Restorative practices and child welfare: Toward an inclusive civil society [Special issue]. *Journal of Social Issues, 62*(2), 257–277.

Portes, A. (2002, April 8). Immigration's aftermath. *American Prospect,* 35–37.

Reardon, C. (2009, October/November). Family acceptance project. *Social Work Today, 9*(6), 6–7.

Roehr, B. (2007, November 6). High rate of PTSD in returning Iraq war veterans. *Medscape Medical News.* Retrieved from http://www.medscape.com/viewarticle/565407

Saleebey, D. (Ed.). (2006). *The strengths perspective in social work practice* (4th ed.). Boston: Allyn & Bacon.

Saltzburg, S. (2004). Learning that an adolescent child is gay or lesbian: The parent experience. *Social Work, 49*(1), 109–118.

Samantrai, K. (2004). *Culturally competent public child welfare practice.* Belmont, CA: Wadsworth.

Sandhu, D. S., & Malik, R. (2001). Ethnocultural background and substance abuse treatment of Asian Indian Americans. In S. L. Straussner (Ed.), *Ethnocultural factors in substance abuse treatment* (pp. 368–392). New York: Guilford Press.

Sartorius, N., Gulbinat, W., Harrison, G., Laska, E., & Siegel, C. (1996, September). Long-term follow-up of schizophrenia in 16 countries: A description of the International Study of Schizophrenia conducted by the World Health Organization. *Social Psychiatry and Psychiatric Epidemiology, 31*(5), 249–258.

See, L.A., Bowles, D., & Darlington, M. (2007). In L.A. See (Ed.), *Human Behavior in the Social Environment from an African American Perspective* (pp. 631–656). Binghamton, NY: Haworth.

Schiele, J. (2007). Strength behaviors for African Americans socialization and survival. In L.A. See (Ed.), *Human Behavior in the Social Environment from an African American Perspective* (pp. 91–116). Binghamton, NY: Haworth.

Schriver, J. (2010). *Human behavior in the social environment: Shifting paradigms and essential knowledge for social work practice* (5th ed.). Boston: Prentice Hall.

Shibusawa, T. (2005). Japanese families. In M. McGoldrick, J. Giordano, & N. Garcia-Petro (Eds.), *Ethnicity and family therapy* (3rd ed., pp. 339–348). New York: Guilford Press.

Simon, B. (1994). *The empowerment tradition in American social work: A history.* New York: Columbia University Press.

Simpson, G., & Lawrence-Webb, C. (2007). Responsibility without community resources: Informal kinship care among low-income African American grandmother caregivers. *Journal of Black Studies, 39*(6), 825–847.

Snyder, C. S., May, J. D., Zulcic, N. N., & Gabbard, W. J. (2005). Social work with Bosnian Muslim children and families: A review of literature. *Child Welfare, 84*(5), 607–630.

Sullivan, A. (2003, June 30). The conservative case for gay marriage. *Time,* p. 76.

Thrupkaew, N. (2002, April 8). The myth of the model minority. *American Prospect, 23*(7), 38–41.

United Nations. (1948). *Universal declaration of human rights.* New York: United Nations.

United Nations (2008, February). *Unite to end violence against women.* Retrieved February 1, 2009, from http://www.un.org/women/endviolence/docs/VAW.pdf

United Nations. (2009). *Human development report 2009.* United Nations Development Programme. Retrieved from http://hdr.undp.org/en/statistics/

United Nations (2010, March). Care and education: Building the wealth of nations. Concept paper. World Conference on Early Childhood. United Nations Educational, Scientific and Cultural Organization. Retrieved from http://unesdoc.unesco.org/images/0018/001873/187376E.pdf

U.S. Census Bureau. (2001). *Overview of race and Hispanic origin.* Retrieved from http://www.census.gov/prod/2001pubs/cenbr01-1.pdf

U.S. Census Bureau (2002). *The Asian population: 2000.* Retrieved from http://www.census.gov/prod/2002pubs/c2kbr01-16.pdf

U.S. Census Bureau. (2003). *U.S. Census 2000: One-third of grandparents who care for grandchildren live in households with no parents present.* Retrieved from http://www.census.gov/PressRelease/www/releases/archives/census_2000/001442.html

U.S. Census Bureau. (2004). *We the people: Asians in the United States.* Washington, DC: U.S. Department of Commerce.

U.S. Census Bureau. (2009a). *Births to teens and unmarried women [table 85]. The 2009 Statistical Abstract.* Retrieved from http://www.census.gov/compendia/statab/tables/09s0085.pdf

U.S. Census Bureau. (2009b). *Population estimates. Annual estimates of the resident population by sex, race, and Hispanic origin.* Retrieved from

http://www.census.gov/popest/national/asrh/NC-EST2008-srh.html

van Wormer, K. (2004). *Confronting oppression, restoring justice: From policy analysis to social action*. Alexandria, VA: Council on Social Work Education.

van Wormer, K. (2006). *Introduction to social welfare and social work: The U.S. in global perspective*. Belmont, CA: Brooks/Cole.

van Wormer, K. (2011). *Human behavior and the social environment, micro level: Individuals and families*. New York: Oxford University Press.

van Wormer, K., Wells, J., & Boes, M. (2000). *Social work practice with lesbians, gays, and bisexuals: A strengths perspective*. Boston: Allyn & Bacon.

Walton, E., Roby, J., Frandsen, A., & Davidson, R. (2003). Strengthening at-risk families by involving the extended family. *Journal of Family Social Work, 7*(4), 1–21.

Wharf, B. (2002). Introduction. In B. Wharf (Ed.), *Community work approaches to child welfare* (pp. 9–28). Toronto: Broadview Press.

Women's Action. (2005, June). *Ethiopia: Abduction and rape*. Retrieved May 1, 2006, from Equality Now Web site: http://www.equalitynow.org/english/actions/action_2204_en.html

World Health Organization. (2002). *World report on violence and health*. Geneva, Switzerland: Author.

World Health Organization. (2005). *Multi-country study on women's health and domestic violence against women*. Geneva, Switzerland: Author.

World Health Organization. (2009, November). *Violence against women*. Retrieved from http://www.who.int/mediacentre/factsheets/fs239/en/index.html

Yen, H. (2009, May 28). Multiracial people become fastest growing U.S. group. *Project Race*. Retrieved from http://www.projectrace.com/inthenews/archive/inthenews-052809.php

Yoo, G. (2004). Attachment relationships between Korean young adult daughters and their mothers. *Journal of Comparative Family Studies, 35*(1), 1–15.

Zamichow, N., & Perry, T. (2003, June 25). Home is where the hurt is. *Los Angeles Times*, A1.

Zastrow, C., & Kirst-Ashman, K. (2010). *Understanding human behavior and the social environment* (8th ed.). Belmont, CA: Brooks/Cole.

Culture and Society

He was not a being, an entity, he was a commonwealth.

—WILLIAM FAULKNER

(1936/1964)

5

The term *culture* is often used with respect to the macro social environmental (Kirst-Ashman, 2008). As we move from the topic of families in society in the previous chapter to the related topic of culture, the shift in focus represents a progression into a wider and more abstract social realm—from mezzo, or middle-level, considerations into the macro-level territory of sociology and anthropology. *Culture*, which we can define as the sum total of social patterns passed from generation to generation, is a topic that is vast and very abstract. "Cultural legacies," writes Malcolm Gladwell, the author of *Outliers: The Story of Success*, "are powerful forces. They have deep roots and long lives. They persist generation after generation, virtually intact, even as the economic and social conditions that spawned them have vanished" (2008, p. 175). Sometimes later generations celebrate the symbols of the legacy, such as the Norwegian Americans participating in the town parade as shown in Figure 5.1.

Culture and community are intertwined. Many minority cultures, for example, exist within a given community or location; others maintain a sense of community that transcends geographical boundaries. Such communities may be set apart from mainstream society by customs and linguistic styles that are culturally distinct. There are many other types of communities, however, that are not culturally homogenous, that are bonded in ways that have little bearing on culture. Culture and community, therefore, are not one and the same. Hence, we have separated these concepts into two chapters, focusing on culture in this chapter, whereas community is the subject of Chapter 6.

The study of culture is the study of a people's social heredity, or a way of thinking, feeling, and believing that sets one group apart from another. From the food we eat and how we eat it to our tastes in music to much of what people think of as personality, the individual's behavior is shaped by his or her culture in many deep and pervasive ways. Think of traits such as manners, humor, gender roles, pitch of voice, and use of hand gestures while speaking. These are just a few of the forms of human behavior that are seen as personality in the individual yet may be prescribed by culture.

Figure 5.1. Norwegian Americans celebrate their Viking heritage in this Cedar Falls, Iowa, summer parade. Photo by Robert van Wormer.

Following an introduction into the whys and wherefores of studying culture and of developing cultural sensitivity, this chapter delves into a discussion of cultural values from a systems perspective. What are the dominant American beliefs and values? Are the values reflected in behavior and social policy? These are among the questions considered against the backdrop of international perspectives. The nine cultural dimensions that have been filtered out from the literature provide the organizational scheme for the major portion of this chapter. The chapter concludes with a boxed reading on Appalachian folkways, inspired by the PBS special *Country Boys.*

We are all cultural beings; how much so is little noted until an encounter with other cultural traditions takes place. Only then do we begin to realize how large a role culture plays in who we are and what we do. Knowledge of culture and cultural history, as Saleebey (2001) suggests, provides important perspectives for understanding human behavior. A recent study of language brings home this point convincingly: Psychologists at the University of Texas, Austin, asked bilingual Mexican Americans a set of questions designed to assess personality (Ramirez-Esparza, Gosling, Benet-Martínez, Potter, & Pennebaker, 2006). Questions included "Are

you talkative?" and "Do you tend to be disorganized?" Many participants changed their answers when the questioners switched languages. When participants spoke English, their responses emphasized assertiveness and achievement— responses that correspond with the individualist traits of U.S. culture. These findings, according to the authors, confirm the tendency that people have to change their interpretations of the world in response to cues in their environment, cues that trigger their internalized norms of behavior. Similarly, research on Chinese Canadians showed that Chinese-born students reported more collectively oriented self-statements in open-ended self-descriptions when writing in Chinese than did a randomly assigned group who answered in English (Ross, Xun, & Wilson, 2002). Ross et al. (2002) also reported in the article that for Chinese participants, cultural cues such as a picture of the Great Wall of China brought forth an expression of Eastern values and attributes, whereas pictures of Superman or of an American flag evoked more self-centered statements.

Members of minority groups are not the only ones who must navigate more than one culture. In our complex and diverse society, individuals who work with the public, such as health care workers and mental health professionals, regularly encounter multiple cultures with diverse customs and value systems. In working cross-culturally, the social worker from the dominant group will need to recognize how his or her style of interacting and conducting business is culturally bound and how this style might come across to others from different backgrounds.

Language is our camera on the world, as Appleby (2007) suggests; the particular words we use reflect our worldview and living conditions. The Inuit language, for example, distinguishes among different types of snow, while the English language has multiple terms for different types of housing, among them—duplex, apartment, bungalow, shot-gun house, ranch house, and condo. And as Appleby further indicates, the language we speak predisposes us to interpret life in specific ways. Some languages do not distinguish among past, present, and future; masculine and feminine divisions are more prominent in some languages than in others, and some cultures have formal and informal forms of address that denote age and class positions as well. Variations within a linguistic group often designate differences in social class; this is in terms of accent and/or grammar.

Language, as Mullaly (2002) suggests, does more than simply reflect social phenomena; it can also be used to construct and maintain oppression of a subordinate group. Efficient and straight-to-the-point means of gathering relevant information, for example, may be seen as officious and uncaring. The interviewer's body language may be taken as intrusive or cold and distant, depending on the ethnic norms of the people with whom he or she is communicating.

Most social workers can expect to deal with such differences on a daily basis. Today, even in many rural areas, America is a pluralistic, multicultural society. The influx of immigrants, mostly from Latin America, is not only changing the face of the United States but is forming sharp age and race divisions (Frey, 2001). Estimates from the U.S. Census Bureau (2005) show that the Hispanic and Asian populations are growing at more than 10 times the pace of whites who are not Hispanic. By 2008 nearly one in six residents was Hispanic, while almost half of children under age 18 are minorities (U.S. Census Bureau, 2009). (See Figure 5.2 which

Figure 5.2. Peruvian band, Seattle. Every ethnic group in the United States has its own unique musical traditions that can be shared and enjoyed by everyone. Photo by Rupert van Wormer.

captures a Peruvian street band and Figure 5.3 of Mexican day laborers.) Because immigrants tend to be young and to arrive with several children, they are becoming a larger part of the nation's younger population. Interethnic and interracial marriage is becoming increasingly common as well (Lee & Edmonston, 2005).

Research on treatment effectiveness reveals that a culturally focused prevention approach is more effective in reaching the population at risk than are standardized approaches. One controlled study of inner-city minority adolescents, for example, indicates that participants given a culturally focused prevention approach currently used less alcohol and had lower intention to drink beer or wine than those in a generic skills group (Botvin, Schinke, Epstein, Diaz, & Botvin, 1995). Similarly, a study that compared a multicultural smoking curriculum for adolescents with a generic curriculum that lacked cultural references found that the multicultural curriculum proved more effective in preventing smoking initiation among Hispanic boys (Unger et al., 2004). A research design using focus groups to discuss health issues demonstrates that culturally sensitive and individualized health care education is vital for the delivery of health messages to residents in rural Appalachian regions (Denham, Meyer, Toborg,

& Mande, 2004). We can infer from these findings that shared cultural understandings and role expectations can enhance treatment effectiveness and lead to the adoption of desired behavioral changes.

Any serious attempts at formulating and/or practicing anti-oppressive social work must incorporate the concept of culture, which means being informed by research and literature from cultural studies (Mullaly, 2002). In working with persons from distinct cultures and backgrounds, knowledge of their group's culture and customs is essential. This includes knowledge of explanations for illness and folk remedies rooted in traditional culture, as well as familiarity with indigenous styles of communication and with leadership roles within the family and community. Given the increasing exposure of social workers to situations involving interracial marriage, international adoption, and cross-cultural foster care arrangements, the task of multicultural social work practice is to consider the cultural milieu when designing treatment approaches. The task, as Fong (2001) suggests, is to shape assessments and interventions to be consistent with the beliefs and practices of the community and to acknowledge the multiethnic identities and differing environments of clients. Formal bureaucratic methods (as often required by

Figure 5.3. Immigrant day labor, Seattle. Photo by Rupert van Wormer.

third-party payers for social services rendered) and a professional frame of reference are often anathema to the treatment mission (see Mullaly, 2002, and his discussion of professionalism, p. 95).

Cultural Competence

Cultural competence is the social work term for the knowledge and skills that one needs for effective work with clients from diverse cultural backgrounds. Cultural competence, as Weaver (2005) indicates, goes beyond cultural sensitivity by integrating appreciation of difference with relevant skills. Cultural competence embodies at least three elements that require that we *(1)* understand and take responsibility for our own beliefs and attitudes, *(2)* learn about and expand multicultural experiences, and *(3)* use our knowledge to become proponents of multiculturalism (Marsh, 2004). Exposure to other cultures can open our eyes to realities not seen before.

The 2004 Spanish-language film *Motorcycle Diaries* (a biography of the early life of Che Guevara), for example, recounts the political awakening that can come with travel. Following his motorcycle journey all across South America, the narrator tells us: "It's changed me more than I thought. I am not me anymore, at least not the same me I was."

Cultural competence entails recognition of society's prejudices—ethnocentrism, sexism, classism, heterosexism, and racism—and of our own possession of many of these traits. To fully appreciate cultural differences, self-awareness is a must. Social workers must recognize the influence of their own culture, family, and peers on how they think and act. Cultural competence requires continuous efforts to gain more knowledge about the client's culture—the norms, vocabulary, symbols, and strengths—and to view the client's value and belief systems not as tangential but as central to the client's functioning. This latter point is underscored by Rowena Fong (2001), who urges a shift in perspective from a mere awareness of cultural differences to acquiring a bifocal vision, or, as she

terms it, a "biculturalization or multiculturalization" of practice methods (p. 7). To be culturally competent, from Fong's perspective, is to learn the cultural values of the client system as a means of identifying resources for intervention. Strategies of helping must be chosen that are congruent with the customs and values of the cultural group in question.

McGoldrick, Giordano, and Garcia-Preto (2005) argue that discussing cultural generalizations is as important as discussing any other norms of behavior. Without some inkling of the norms of the cultural group we are dealing with, as they further suggest, we would have no compass for doing clinical work at all. Their edited book *Ethnicity and Family Therapy* contains 54 chapters, 53 of which each describe the norms and folkways of one specific ethnic group in U.S. society, written by a member of that group who is also a mental health practitioner. In their overview chapter, they discuss differences in communication styles as an illustration of the type of knowledge that can help prepare us for culturally competent family counseling:

> The dominant assumption is that talk is good and can heal a person. . . . A high level of verbal interaction is expected in Jewish, Italian, and Greek families, whereas Anglo, Irish, and Scandinavian families have much less intense interaction and are more likely to deal with problems by distancing. (p. 29)

The colorblind and gender-blind notions of many European American social workers are a denial of a person's whole being. Through accepting that significant differences do exist between people of different ethnic backgrounds, professionals are recognizing a person's wholeness and individuality. To tell a lesbian or gay person to "just stay in the closet and you'll be all right" or "don't ask, don't tell" is to deny that person an important part of him- or herself. Multicultural social welfare education exposes people to divergent thinking as they are forced to examine formerly taken-for-granted assumptions. The University of Minnesota-Duluth has shaped an American Indian culturally specific program that relies on learning circles for non-Indian students to help them serve the needs of American Indian clients (Jackson, 2003). Culture and language institutes are provided for American Indian students to address their different needs. Their M.S.W. program can be seen as a model of education for competence in one particular area.

Canda and Furman (2010) regard cultural competence as an essential quality of spiritual understanding. Their concept of a *transcultural approach* to spiritual diversity connects the social worker's particular spiritual and cultural experiences with those of the client and the helping process. Diversity and commonality are both embraced from this perspective, which goes beyond mere tolerance.

In working with diverse cultural groups, support and adoption of indigenous interventions is crucial. What we learn from effective indigenous customs and strategies, in fact, can be adopted and integrated within standard social work models. This has happened in New Zealand with family group conferencing learned from the Maori people and with restorative justice initiatives borrowed from Canadian aboriginal tribes (discussed in Chapters 4 and 6, respectively).

Cultural competence becomes more and more critical to effective social work practice as global interdependency increases. Professional developments in other countries are becoming especially relevant to those in the United States, as social problems become universal. Much as nations of the Global South have looked to nations of the Global North for models of social work education, truly reciprocal exchanges are becoming the focus today to prepare graduates for the increasingly global nature of social work practice—for example, with clients of diverse national ethnic, religious, social, and cultural backgrounds and with persons from other countries. Otherwise, instead of cultural sensitivity, ethnocentrism would prevail.

The National Association of Social Workers' (NASW; 1996) Code of Ethics includes a special section on cultural competence and social diversity (section 1.05):

(a) Social workers should understand culture and its function in human behavior and society, recognizing the strengths that exist in all cultures.

(b) Social workers should have a knowledge base of their clients' cultures and be able to demonstrate competence in the provisions of services that are sensitive to clients' cultures and to differences among people and cultural groups.

(c) Social workers should obtain education about and seek to understand the nature of social diversity and oppression with respect to race, ethnicity, national origin, color, sex, sexual orientation, age, marital status, political belief, religion, and mental or physical disability.

Generally the preceding ethical mandate is interpreted to mean learning about cultures other than mainstream culture. Taken at its face value, however, section 1.05 speaks of understanding of culture in general and of its function in human behavior and society. Such is the basic perspective of this chapter and this book. The study of culture, inasmuch as it affects social work practice, is far more than a familiarity with the customs, music, religious beliefs, and rituals of a people; it is the study of worldview and ideology. Often the social worker must interpret the norms and beliefs of mainstream society to clients who have been brought up with different values and perhaps devoid of opportunities for personal achievement. Women from foreign countries, in particular, may not see the need to take language classes or driving lessons because there was little stress on women's independence in their home countries. Within this context, it is critical that the social worker be able to approach these and other issues from a dual perspective, to be empathetic to the client's reality while seeking solutions within the wider system that are compatible with the client's wishes and needs.

From a macro ecosystems perspective, we need to examine our human service organizations. To be culturally competent, a human service organization must acknowledge the importance of culture throughout the system and be vigilant in addressing and welcoming cultural differences. Services must be adapted so that they are congruent with community norms or, better yet, adopted from the community and institutionalized throughout the system.

As Raheim (2006) correctly indicates, the NASW standards as listed earlier and as endorsed by our schools of social work tend to focus on individual, in contrast to organizational, cultural competence. At the systems or organizational level, cultural competence development involves valuing diversity as an asset rather than a problem and regular self-assessment by organizational leaders to identify areas in need of strengthening or change. Both forms of cultural competence are essential today when even in the heartland, in Iowa, rural areas that were slowly dying have come to be connected to the global economy through widespread immigration (Adams, 2009). When 20 years ago "diversity" meant your antecedents were German or Scandinavian, the much more significant ethnic differences today require major adjustments by the more homogeneous rural populations and by the human service organizations in these areas.

Ethnocentrism

The opposite of cultural competence is *ethnocentrism*, or the taken-for-granted assumption that one's culture, religion, and so forth are superior to those of other groups. The paradox of culture is that as we humans learn to accept our own cultural beliefs and values, we unconsciously learn to reject those of other people.

Mullaly (2002) conceptualizes ethnocentrism as a form of oppression that, in its extreme form, is played out as *cultural imperialism*. Cultural imperialism, he suggests, comes about when the dominant group universalizes its experience and culture and uses them as the norm. This injustice is experienced in varying degrees by all oppressed groups. The stereotypes applied to oppressed people, which brand them as deviant and inferior, are so pervasive in society that they are seldom questioned.

Immigration and war are two activities that often, through cultural clash, heighten the sense of ethnocentrism in a community. Immigration provides an example of potential conflict as disparate value systems exist side by side. Boundaries between groups can become increasingly thick and exclusionary. Neighborhoods are affected by an influx of immigrants; the workplace is affected also as newcomers flock to accept jobs that locals would find undesirable.

The impact of war is infinitely much worse, as the enemy and all members of the enemy group come to be identified as "other." Feeling threatened, people in the society lash out. The psychological phenomenon of guilt comes into play as well—the more we inflict pain and suffering on the enemy, the more we are prone to attach blame to justify our actions. (The defense mechanism of dehumanization of the enemy was discussed in Chapter 2.)

Religion, like patriotism, can take on aspects of ethnocentrism. Karen Armstrong (1993), in her history of Judaism, Christianity, and Islam—the God-based religions—explains:

One of the most characteristic new developments since the 1970s has been the rise of a type of religiosity that we usually call "fundamentalism" in most of the major world religions, including the three religions of god. A highly political spirituality, it is literal and intolerant in its vision. In the United States, which has always been prone to extremist and apocalyptic enthusiasm, Christian fundamentalism has attached itself to the New Right. . . . Jews, Christians, and Muslims who punctiliously attend divine services yet denigrate people who belong to different ethnic and ideological camps deny one of the basic truths of their religion. It is equally inappropriate for people who call themselves Jews, Christian, and Muslims to condone an inequitable social system. The God of historical monotheism demands mercy not sacrifice, compassion rather than decorous liturgy. (pp. 290, 292)

The war in Iraq epitomizes the kind of ethnocentrism that such conflict induces. The terrorism and suicide bombings have a decidedly fanatical religious cast. Based on extensive interviews with jailed Islamist militants, Khosrokhavar (2005) explores the notion of sacred death in various Islamic countries. Significantly, in interviews the would-be suicide bombers spoke of a divine mission and of martyrdom rather than suicide.

The United States has participated in many wars as memorialized in Figure 5.4. In the wake of the September 11, 2001 terrorist attacks several well publicized surveys of world opinion revealed shocking evidence that America indeed was not well liked, not even by average people in friendly countries (Davis & Silver, 2004). Since 2002, interviewers have polled over 175,000 people in 54 nations and the Palestinian territories to compare and contrast public opinion around the world on a large variety of subjects. The surveys have shown that under the Bush administration, the way America used its power—militarily and economically—to dominate the world was widely resented. In the Pew Global Attitudes Project (2005), for example, greed and violence figured prominently as purported American traits. The most positive assessments came from India and Eastern Europe, the lowest from the Muslim countries. Whereas the European respondents and many others in the sample saw Americans as too religious, Americans saw themselves as not religious enough. The negative results were thought by the pollsters to be correlated with opposition to the war in Iraq. With the election of President Barack Obama, U.S. favorability ratings soared throughout the western world, Asia, and Africa nations (Pew Global Attitudes Project, 2009). Only in the predominantly Muslim countries of the Middle East were the ratings still low. Confidence that the United States would do the right thing in foreign policy declined in Israel and remain abysmally low in Pakistan under the Obama administration.

These contrasting mass media portrayals can be expected to reflect and also generate different attitudes about social welfare policies as well. Here, again, a great divide between American and much more liberal European attitudes concerning the role of the government in providing social benefits is apparent.

Figure 5.4. This statue in downtown Bowling Green, Kentucky, honors combat veterans from past and recent wars who fought and died, as the plaque says, "for our freedom." Photo by Robert van Wormer.

These differences, of course, relate to historic and cultural distinctions as well.

In an article originally published in German in Berlin, Schneider (2004) contrasts European and American viewpoints and makes the following points—American commentators who warn about the new fundamentalism focus only on the Islamic variety of fundamentalism—Islamism. This viewpoint, according to Schneider, was revealed in its most extreme terms by the U.S. President at that time, George W. Bush, who used such terms as "crusade" and "axis of evil" to define the mission. This approach, as Schneider argues, reveals "the assumption of a religious mantle by a secular power, which in Europe has become unthinkable" (p. 1).

Interestingly, Ruby and Smith (2007), in their analysis of public opinion surveys by the Pew Research Center, find striking similarities in the intensity of religious belief among Muslim Americans, white evangelicals and black Protestants. Within all three groups, large majorities

(72% of Muslim Americans, 79% of white evangelicals and 85% of black Protestants) say religion is "very important" in their own lives. This is in contrast about one-half of Catholics and just over a third of white mainline Protestants who state that religion is very important.

Social workers often work with clients who are evangelical in their personal beliefs or who are influenced by family members who adhere to a strict religious code. Interpersonal conflict may arise when young people wish to date or marry outside of their narrow religious circle or in struggles over gender identity issues. Accordingly, practitioners need an awareness of the psychological hold that fundamentalist indoctrination has over people and of the internalization of a sense of sin in those who were reared in strict religious households. The young person may experience serious conflict in being torn between the need to pursue his or her own happiness and the desire to please family members. Sometimes the cultural clash is between values of an immigrant older generation and their offspring who have been assimilated into the wider society.

Speaking of negative aspects of American mainstream culture, Saleebey (2001) issues a cautionary note: All cultural groups, he argues "are subsumed under a dominating steamroller of an overriding culture: advanced capitalism ruled by the marketplace and spread through the media" (p. 56). Critical analysis of the cultural ethos, in short, is a vital aspect of social work education. As an introduction to the discussion on American values, the values "on which this nation was built," let us apply the ecosystems model to the notion of culture.

Culture as Macro System

Margaret Mead (1972), in her autobiography *Blackberry Winter*, provided us with instructions for unraveling the intricacies of a new culture. The approach Mead took was to view individual cultural traits within the context of the whole. Our goal must be to "understand a myriad of acts, words, glances, and silences as they are integrated into a pattern one had no

way of working out as yet, and finally, to 'get' the structure of the whole culture" (p. 275).

Margaret Mead's daughter, Mary Catherine Bateson (1984), uses the metaphor of finding four-leaf clovers to describe the anthropological task. "A four-leaf clover," writes Bateson, "is a break in pattern, a light dissonance, that can only be seen against an awareness of the orderly configuration in the grass" (pp. 202–203). Approaching an unfamiliar culture, one seeks regularity in behavior. Over time, the details that seem so chaotic at first do hang together. "Often a dissonance," says Bateson, "the interruption in one pattern you have learned to expect, is the key to a larger pattern" (p. 204).

The view of culture as an integrated whole borrows a concept from the biological sciences in which the organs of the body complement each other in remarkable ways to make up a functioning system. Like an organism, culture has form and pattern. There is a degree of order and a system that is greater than the sum of its parts. To the anthropologist, the related patterns of the environment, the resources, the people's beliefs about what they do, and the relationships between the larger group and themselves are all part of the system out of which individuals structure their behaviors (Esber, 1989).

The critical analysis of culture as a system requires a consideration of issues of power, including belief systems that produce or allow for structural inequalities and the social class hierarchy. Because every individual is a part of two systems, the larger societal system and the smaller world of the immediate social environment, the social worker must rely on a dual perspective to be aware of both worlds simultaneously. A dual perspective provides an alternative lens to the social worker so that he or she can work in the immediate environment while grasping the reality of the structural barriers in the dominant system erected against people that belong to a certain group. Such barriers are more often cultural than physical, keeping oppressed classes of people from tapping into their collective power. Women's socialization, for example, often leads to a sense of inadequacy and discouragement that precludes organizing for collective sharing of experience (Weick, 2001).

Cultural Values

Common social heritage passed from generation to generation is what makes for cohesion and solidarity that helps ensure the continuity of group life. This same heritage provides for each new generation a value system and a sense of what is right and what is wrong. In our study of any item of behavior or belief, following Margaret Mead, our view is that such a behavior or belief can be evaluated correctly only in the light of its meaning to the people who practice it or subscribe to it, its relation to other elements of the culture, and the part it plays in the adaptation of the person in the environment.

Every society has a system of values or set of interrelated beliefs that their members hold dear and on which their social structure is built. Mostly the values are not spelled out, and they are so obvious to members of the society as to not even be realized.

The study of cultural values explains a lot about human behavior at both the individual and societal levels. When people move from one culture to another, they tend to adopt the perspectives of the new culture in which they are immersed. The psychologist Richard Nisbett (2004), author of *The Geography of Thought*, has measured perceptual changes in people who switch between Western and Eastern cultures. From the Eastern perspective influenced by Confucianism, there could be no self in isolation, so self-control was paramount in order to suppress one's selfish desires. To a Westerner, relations are different, including relations with nature and the universe; nature was viewed, in the Greek tradition, as separate from humans—"man versus nature." Keep in mind such contrasts in worldview as we explore the dominant U.S. cultural orientation.

Building on the most widely quoted commentary on early U.S. society—Alexis de Tocqueville's (1835/1951) observations of nineteenth-century American social life—and on sociologist Robin Williams's (1979) widely cited array of crucial American values (work ethic, equality, individualism, democracy, etc.), van Wormer (2006) delineated nine value dimensions of most direct relevance to social work. These value dimensions are as follows:

- Work versus leisure
- Equal opportunity versus equality
- Mobility versus stability
- Competition versus cooperation
- Individualism versus collectivism
- Independence versus interconnectedness
- Materialism versus spirituality
- Nuclear family versus extended family
- Moralism versus compassion

If you view this set of value dimensions as two columns, the items in the left-hand column are closely interrelated; they represent the essence of American values, values closely tied in with capitalism and industrialization. These value dimensions must be understood not in terms of voiced ideals and proclamations but in terms of actions and policies. Any American you would ask, in all probability, would proclaim that he or she held the values in the right column—leisure and equality, for example. People in other nations, including many industrialized nations and minority groups within the United States, in contrast, might show, by their actions, priorities that one would consider less individualistic and less moralistic. Keep in mind, however, as you study the various cultural characteristics that, in reality, there are no pure forms of such phenomena but only degrees of one thing or another.

When we speak of American values, we are speaking of something tangible and unique (as de Tocqueville observed in his contrast between the New World and the old aristocratic societies). And yet, for every value or characteristic that can be spelled out, there is evidence of its opposite. Along with tolerance, there is punitiveness; with raw optimism, despair; and with warm generosity, greed. The inherent conflicts, many of which appeared before the nation was a nation, are with us still. As in any society, there is always the conflict between the value and the practice, between ideology and reality, and between how a people describe themselves and how others see them. In the United States, the contradiction can be seen in the espousal of beliefs that, as discussed later, conflict; for example, individualism and family values, materialism and the stress on religion. We are, as political scientist Seymour Martin Lipset (1997) writes, "the most religious, optimistic, patriotic, rights-oriented, and individualistic" country in the world (p. 26). At the same time, however, we are also, as a nation, the "wealthiest in real income terms, the most productive as reflected in worker output, the highest in proportions of people who graduate from or enroll in higher education but the least egalitarian among developed nations with respect to income distribution" (p. 26).

Let us look at some of these value dimensions more closely.

Work Versus Leisure

A focal point of American culture is work and preparation for work. Through one's occupation or profession, an individual gains status and a sense of self-importance. A huge wage and salary gap exists between the higher and lower echelons of a company, as well as in society as a whole. Equality of incomes from work would be seen as undesirable because of the feared deleterious effects on educational and work incentives.

Few ideas, as Wagner (1994) indicates, dominate Western political and social discourse as much as the idealized work ethic—"the view that all who are able-bodied and of working age have a moral obligation to work and that they are slothful or pathological if they do not" (p. 718). Indeed, the work ethic is one of the oldest and most enduring (if not endearing) of the American cultural attributes. The value placed on hard work is closely tied to moralism. The notion of the work ethic encompasses the traits that the typical employer desires: punctuality, efficiency, and productivity. Workers deficient in these qualities will be eliminated. Today, as a result of the Welfare Reform Act of 1996, all able-bodied welfare recipients, mostly mothers with young children who previously were eligible for welfare, are being forced to leave the welfare rolls once they have completed job training and to take a full-time job. Child-care reimbursement has been severely limited.

One way to gauge the strength of the work ethic is to analyze data on leisure time pursuits.

As far as leisure is concerned, a right embodied in the United Nations Declaration on Human Rights but not recognized in the U.S. Constitution, Americans have the fewest number of paid vacation days per year in the industrialized world. According to government statistics from a variety of sources, German and Spanish workers get 30 days, the British and Australians get 25 days, the Japanese 18, Chinese 15, and Americans 10 (Snapshot of America, 2004). Compared to other industrialized nations, U.S. workers generally work longer hours and have no guaranteed vacations. Germans work 1,436 hours, Norwegians, 1,400 hours, while the United States and Japan clock up over 1,800 hours (Fleck, 2009). Norway, the country in which people work the fewest hours of any industrialized democracy, has seen a significant increase in the purchase of vacation homes and boats (Thomas, 2009). The sick leave policies are among the world's most generous.

So how is it that Americans believe so religiously in the value of work? The word *religiously* provides a clue. The American emphasis on work is derived from a Puritan heritage that valued work for its own sake (Johnson & Rhodes, 2009). Work for economic gain was considered the key to success, and success was viewed as important from the very beginning. Renowned German sociologist Max Weber (1958/1905), in his classic *The Protestant Ethic and the Spirit of Capitalism*, compared work productivity levels in Protestant and Catholic regions of Germany and elsewhere as evidence for his theory correlating Protestantism and capitalism. Protestantism emphasized the autonomy of the individual and repudiated dependence on the Church, priesthood, and ritual, according to Weber. The qualities of self-discipline, hard work, and communal service were viewed as a likely sign of salvation. Martin Luther's belief in work as a "calling" gave Protestantism a singularly practical bent. Taking Luther's argument one step further, John Calvin, who was Luther's counterpart in France and later Switzerland, introduced the notion of predestination into the Protestant vocabulary.

Predestination is the doctrine of God's election or choice of souls to salvation or damnation. The interpretation of predestination carried by way of England and Scotland (through the preaching of John Knox) to America was that those predestined to salvation could be identified in this life through the evidence of their wealth. Although one's fate was sealed, in a sense, Calvinist philosophy posited that indications of this fate could be detected on earth. Using this line of reasoning, the wealthy could justify not only their wealth but also their exploitation of workers to accumulate it (Day, 2008). The belief system also legitimated forcing people to work for their own good. Max Weber described Calvinism as that which was not leisure and enjoyment but activity that served to increase the glory of God. Waste of time thus was perceived as a deadly sin. And condemnation of the sinner was justified. With its emphasis on individual achievement, frugality, and opportunity, the creed of Calvinism has very much affected the American character, even long after the direct religious connection has been lost. In this vein, the eighteenth-century inventor and acknowledged atheist Benjamin Franklin espoused the principles of the Protestant work ethic in his often quoted sayings, such as "early to bed, early to rise makes a man healthy, wealthy, and wise," "the early bird catches the worm," "time is money," and "a penny saved is a penny earned."

The Protestant work ethic, according to Zimbardo (2008), generated a new hardworking class of entrepreneurs. Even today, he asserts, the gross national product of predominantly Protestant nations is greater than that of Catholic nations. As well, the Jewish tradition, because of an emphasis on scholarship, and education, is associated with a work ethic rooted in an orientation toward the future and future planning.

How about a "Catholic ethic?" John Tropman (2002), author of *The Catholic Ethic and the Spirit of Community*, draws on social surveys, opinion polls, and insights from sociology to contrast the Protestant esteem for individualism and a reluctance to provide social welfare with Catholic cultural values. Religion and culture he sees as inextricably linked. Tropman perceives the Protestant ethic as achievement oriented and the Catholic ethic as helping oriented, as stressing "salvation through work" as opposed to "salvation through works" (p. 42). It is not

that Catholics don't value work, as Tropman suggests, but that work is not ritualized as it is in the Protestant tradition, and how people earn a living is not necessary to social acceptance. Even the concept of time differs by religious belief in that Catholic culture is built on a here-and-now orientation, in other words, live for the moment. In his presentation of the "ideal type" of a Catholic belief system, Tropman acknowledges there are strong ethnic differences, and related to his generalizations on Protestantism, he indicates that there are important differences among the various denominations, and that African Americans have a strong helping ethic borne out of their historic experiences.

In locating the roots of the American work ethic, we need to take into account geography, as well as ideology. As settlers arrived on the bountiful American landscape, there was no limit to the possibilities for work that needed to be done. So the work ethic was continually rewarded at every turn; in the American colonies, unemployment was unknown. Just how intransigent was the religious-economic ideology is seen in its ability to outlast its religious roots and to influence welfare policy to this very day.

Are there any other places on earth where the work ethic is as strong? Yes; in South Korea and Japan, in fact, the work ethic goes beyond anything we could imagine. In a visit to Korea, van Wormer was impressed and somewhat appalled to learn of a land so competitive that children rarely play and are tutored during most waking hours until their education culminates in rigorous university entrance exams. In late adolescence, students return home from crash courses at midnight, only to be awakened, according to her Korean hosts, for school in the wee hours of the next morning (van Wormer, 2006). And Chinese children, according to a report by the Asia Society, spend twice as many hours doing homework as do their U.S. peers (Powell, 2009). The Chinese educational system, however, stresses rote memorization although change is underway. The Japanese work ethic, according to all reports, is similar. Like Americans, many Japanese citizens "live to work." So serious is this problem that the Japanese government is writing new rules to force workers to take their vacations. (Over 90 percent of Japanese workers use only part of their vacation days [Hall, 2009].) The new rules will penalize companies whose employees fail to take their annual leave. The goal is to stimulate the economy and generate jobs. The suicide rate, which is highest in the countries of the former Soviet Union, is still quite high in Japan and South Korea, according to the World Health Organization (WHO, 2009). In these Asian countries suicide tends to be linked to personal failure and a sense of shame.

Equal Opportunity Versus Equality

The current state slogan of Iowa, which visitors see as they arrive on the Mississippi River bridge, is "Welcome to Iowa: Fields of Opportunities." This slogan, which recently was selected following a much publicized statewide contest, succinctly sums up the value that Americans place on possibility, the possibility that is born again in each generation of the fulfillment of the American dream.

In keeping with the ethos of opportunity, the United States, Canada, and, for the most part, Australia are the three nations in the world with relatively open and supportive immigration policies. The United States prides itself on being a "nation of immigrants," and Canada similarly exults in its multicultural mosaic patterns of appreciation of differences. This is not to say that the treatment of immigrants does not leave much to be desired, only that opportunity for asylum seekers and those in special occupational categories is better in the less crowded countries with strong traditions of resettlement. (Europe's policy is geared toward temporary asylum rather than assimilation of refugees.)

Consistent with the North American opportunity ethos are early education programs such as Head Start, job training, and higher educational "opportunity-enhancing programs" to help disadvantaged individuals compete on an equal footing with more privileged youths. Such opportunity-enhancing programs, unlike quotas or preferential initiatives, are less likely to be perceived as challenging the values of

individualism and the work ethic. In their comprehensive opinion survey, Page and Jacobs (2009) found that most Americans strongly favor government actions that greatly increase such opportunities, as, for example, college scholarships and early childhood education programming. Such government-sponsored overtures, in themselves, provide substance to the widely held belief that the road to upward mobility is open to those who "play by the rules."

Opportunity is the counterpart not of equality but of inequality. The more freedom there is, theoretically, the more opportunity exists for the rich to get richer, as they invest their earnings and profits. The lower the taxes, the higher the economic incentives for individuals to invest in business and buy up the property and resources; income and wealth disparities increase. Opportunity thus opens up the possibility for some to achieve enormous success and others to fail miserably.

But how about people within modern society who have lost faith in the system and do not perceive that there is an opportunity to advance according to the norms of society? Some, as we know, place their energy in the criminal underground; they achieve material success at least for a period of time. Still other groups of people opt out of the competition altogether, crushed by personal failure early in life or by the failure of preceding generations. The hope of becoming a part of the affluent society around them ceases to be a reality; it becomes a taunt. This is what Michael Harrington (1962) said in his classic work on poverty, *The Other America*. People who no longer believe that they have a stake in the system, such as the long-term unemployed, can sink into passivity and rely on deceit and manipulation of the system as a way of surviving in a competitive society. Their anti-achievement values may be imparted to their children and their children's children. Such cultural traits exist in regions of the country that are economically backward, where the goals of achieving social and economic equality appear elusive at best.

Equality basically means sharing the wealth between the haves and the have-nots. There is less opportunity to get rich and superrich in a nation with a strong social welfare system.

Equality is used here in the European sense of equalizing social benefits and living standards "from the cradle to the grave."

Americans have a formal commitment to equality before the law, as Johnson and Rhodes (2009) indicate. The focus on equality is consistent with the American system of mass education, the informality in language and dress, absence of aristocracy or titles, fairly standard speech patterns except by region (in contrast to British class distinctions in accent), and admiration for the "self-made man," for persons who manage to go "from rags to riches."

Among the advanced industrialized nations of the world, the United States leads in the proportion of income going to the wealthiest fifth (Boshara, 2003). As the federal minimum wage has remained flat for years, the disparity between rich and poor continues to grow. According to a report by the Center on Budget and Policy Priorities (2006), the incomes of the poorest 20 percent of families nationally grew by an average of 19 percent over the past 20 years, whereas the incomes of the richest fifth of families grew by almost 60 percent (figures were based on U.S. Census data). Looking at overall wealth rather than income, the discrepancy is even greater. In the United States, the richest 1 percent of households own a third of the nation's wealth, whereas the bottom 80 percent have just 16 percent. This gap has been growing for at least two decades (Mishel, Bernstein, & Allegretto, 2005). The racial gap is startling. About 31 percent of black households have zero or negative net wealth, whereas just over 13 percent of white households do. Consisting of savings, real estate, stocks and bonds, and related property, assets, can be liquidated during periods of adversity, thus offering the owner a buffer against poverty (Karger & Stoesz, 2009). They also appreciate in value, thus generating additional wealth. The tax structure, moreover, is set up to tax dividends related to wealth at lower rates than earned income. Similarly, earned income by persons on fixed salaries, such as teachers, are taxed at rates higher than incomes of those, such as lawyers and realtors, who engage in private practice. The latter rely on deductions that keep the amount of taxes paid down. In all

these ways, the rich tend to get richer across the life span.

An important distinction needs to be made between values of equality of opportunity (the North American value orientation) and equality of living standards (the Nordic model; see Nelson & Shavitt, 2002). Often the impetus toward equality means differential treatment of unlike people to equalize the result. In Finland, for example, as in other Scandinavian countries, the fines for speeding are imposed based on a person's earnings and net wealth, data that can be retrieved readily due to the thoroughness of government records (British Broadcasting Company, 2002; "Norway: Rich Man Fined $109,000 for Drunk Driving," [2009]). The purpose of this approach is to ensure that the penalty will hurt as much whether you are rich or poor.

Societies that pride themselves on egalitarianism take an *institutional* approach to social welfare provision. At the opposite end of the continuum is the *residual*, or so-called safety-net, approach characteristic of what we have in the United States. In the residually oriented society, of which the United States and Japan are prime examples, a stigma is attached to receiving welfare aid. The causes of welfare clients' difficulties are often seen as rooted in their own malfunctioning—the persons themselves are blamed for problems perceived as stemming from their own inadequacies (Zastrow, 2010). The values that underpin residual thinking are capitalism, independence, and belief in opportunity.

An *institutional*, or social insurance, approach to public welfare would provide a very different scenario with regard to aid. The institutional approach is preventive rather than curative and universal rather than means-tested. (Means-tested programs, which are only available to people below a certain income level, tend to become stigmatized and to lose popular support over time.) David Wagner (2000) contrasts the U.S. system of "charity, therapy, and correction" (p. 178) with the model of most European nations that provide all their citizens with basic health care, subsidized child care, extensive paid vacations, and automatic pensions.

In the United States, Social Security and public education are two of the nation's few universal social programs. Both these programs are regarded as rights or entitlements for all the people. As a result, they are willingly funded. Programs associated with the poor, in contrast, can be abolished in the next political campaign.

Economic globalization makes a much better fit with the value of equal opportunity than with equality, as is discussed later. Under the economic pressures of globalization, there is a tendency of convergence in regard to social welfare provisions. Alber and Gilbert (2010) argue that under the new European Union (EU) constitution the postcommunist countries, which look more to the United States than to western Europe for their social and political models, will lead to the adoption of market economy concepts, including the restructuring of the social security systems and an emphasis on rapid privatization. Drawing on earlier European income data, Fritzell (2001) determined that in the United Kingdom income inequality has increased; this gap between the rich and the poor is evidenced in mounting rates of child poverty. In the Scandinavian countries, however, despite a rise in levels of unemployment, income inequality remains relatively low. To such a great extent is equality a Nordic and particularly a Norwegian value, that even up against the pressures of the global economy, associated as it is with higher unemployment, the Nordic countries still manage to maintain a high level of equality in the distribution of income (Thomas, 2009).

Mobility Versus Stability

A value related to work is the desire to "get ahead," to move upward and onward. A significant proportion of Americans are geographically mobile, as well, moving their households every 5 years. Children will often have attended school in several school systems before they graduate. The American ideology promotes a belief in progress. Workers are expected to climb the corporate ladder and to be willing to relocate if necessary for career advancement. Persons receiving government aid are expected to get training and to quickly gain their independence. Because the United States has been a land of unparalleled resources and opportunity,

people who are downwardly mobile or who remain at the bottom are often held responsible for their lowly status.

From the middle teen years, Americans often get jobs so that they can buy their first automobiles for personal freedom and mobility, as the word *automobile* implies. The United States is unique among industrialized nations in not providing adequate mass transportation; in the 1950s and 1960s, public spending on streetcars was greatly reduced, and money was put into highways instead; those who could afford it moved to the suburbs, leaving the urban poor behind (Johnson & Rhodes, 2009).

We use the term *mobility* here to describe more than social and geographical mobility and to get at the kind of restlessness that often has been said to typify the American character. Thus, from the French commentator de Tocqueville (1835/1951), we hear, "America is a land of wonders, in which everything is in constant motion and every change seems an improvement. The idea of novelty there is indissolubly connected with the idea of amelioration" (p. 18).

Europeans tend to view Americans and Australians as "brash and risk-taking," as Hartmann (1997) suggests. Consider the types of people who would have fled the Old World to take a dangerous journey across the Atlantic. These adventurers presumably would have carried with them the genetic material that might have caused their descendants to crave mobility over a more routine lifestyle and competition over cooperation.

The urge to move, which has so dominated American society, has been a cultural attribute in times of economic recession as well as in economic booms. There are two threats today to these mass migrations ("Labour Mobility: The Road Not Taken," 2009). The first is the housing bust. Housing prices have collapsed, so homeowners with mortgages are unable or unwilling to sell their homes and thus stay put. The second factor is the high unemployment; youths who are seeking employment and eager to move out into their own homes are often forced to stay where they are. These observations are borne out in a report from the Census Bureau that found that the number of people who changed residences in 2007 to 2008 was the lowest since 1962, when the nation had a much smaller population (Roberts, 2009).

Competition Versus Cooperation

One need not search far in the American popular press for evidence of competition. (Just glance through the advertisements.) Typically, in any given week stories celebrate personal and team victories in events ranging from sports to spelling bees; the win-or-lose outcomes of courtroom battles; TV reality shows that feature survival exploits or intense dating competitions; and intense pressure among youth to gain entrance into certain elite colleges. In other words, sharp competition is everywhere in a society that prides itself on being the world's superpower. (This ethos is captured in the bike race shown in Figure 5.5)

Achievement may be more the goal than competition, but in order to win, Americans from childhood are taught to compete (Gladwell, 2008). Writing on the U.S. system of education, Ediger (2000) likens the emphasis on pupil competition as a spur to learning to the beliefs of the marketplace economy. "The free enterprise system in education," as Ediger notes, "has always stated that the United States became

great due to competition in the market place where goods and services are bought and sold" (p. 14). Proposals for a voucher system of schooling, for example, pits charter schools against regular public schools in attracting students. Many services in these new schools are privatized to reduce costs. Free technological equipment may be provided, along with programs containing advertising, which students then watch in class.

Mass testing programs compare individual children, schools, and whole school systems on the basis of standardized measures of achievement. Ediger (2000) compares this approach with one of cooperation. Advocates of cooperation favor helping students individually to proceed at their own pace to learn what they need to learn and want to learn.

Often the competition, as enshrined in the courtroom's adversary system, is played out as "winner take all." Contrast this attitude with the following Arabic principle, as described by Moore (2004) in his study of words from different cultures that are untranslatable: The term *taarradhin* is a happy concept related to compromise but that means "I win, you win." It's a way of resolving a problem, as Moore notes, without losing face. Anthropologists Gardiner and Kosmitzki (2005) bring our attention to the

Figure 5.5. Competitors in a city bike race. Photo by Rupert van Wormer.

fact that the Chinese have no equivalent word for personality. The American absorption with self is unknown in most Asian cultures.

Another value system is found in Norway and other Scandinavian countries, where the cultural ethos can be summed up in the word *egalitarianism*. In daily life, Scandinavians believe in the staunch egalitarian value that no person is either better or worse than anyone else, even while acknowledging, for example, that the other person coincidentally may have more money or lower status (Erickson, 2005). On the competition-to-cooperation continuum, the Norwegians are far toward the cooperation end. This value (*samarbeid*, literally "to work together") is instilled in the family in early childhood and reinforced throughout school life; it permeates every aspect of culture. The school anti-bullying programs that are now being instituted across the globe originated in Norway, perhaps because bullying on the school playground was rare and out of sync with Norwegian values of caretaking (van Wormer, 2006).

Nelson and Shavitt (2002) provide the kind of empirical verification of cross-cultural differences concerning individual achievement that is a rare find in the literature. The comparison is between American and Danish students. Danes, as the authors indicate, share a similar language and culture with Swedes and Norwegians; all three groups look down on conspicuous success and bragging. Denmark and Norway additionally share a ubiquitous, unwritten social modesty code; this code is reflected in interpersonal norms, as well as in benevolent social welfare policies toward the least fortunate in society. Nelson and Shavitt (2002) term this code "horizontal" as opposed to "vertical" values. The social structure in the United States, in contrast, is vertically oriented, a phenomenon, as the authors note, that is likely a reflection of the frontier spirit of exploration, in combination with the Protestant work ethic. The American notion of equality is actually equal opportunity. This notion is reflected in the tax system and resource allocation, as Nelson and Shavitt (2002) further suggest.

In their research findings based on in-depth interviews with a small sample of Americans

and Danes, Nelson and Shavitt (2002) found that, whereas a majority of Americans mentioned achievement in relation to happiness, none of the Danes did. The Danes' first priority was family; second was work. Single American men almost unanimously mentioned work goals alone. These findings from the interviews were confirmed in the second portion of this study (Nelson & Shavitt, 2002), which compared answers to 60 items related to achievement. Questionnaires were administered to 82 communications students in Denmark and to 152 comparable students in the United States. Results confirmed that Danes scored much higher on values related to protecting the environment, social justice, equality, and peace than did their U.S. counterparts. Americans were oriented toward success, ambition, and gaining influence.

Bishop (2002) conceptualizes competition in the collective sense, especially in regard to which group is the most oppressed:

> We are fighting over who has more value, who has less, instead of asking why we must be valued as more or less. . . . How can we take back our world and reorganize it to benefit everyone if we cannot even talk about our different forms of oppression without getting tangled up in the net of competition? (p. 19)

This brings us to an appreciation of the sense that "we are all in this together," the need to think collectively.

Individualism Versus Collectivism

A value dimension closely related to competition is individualism or self-reliance, a trait for which Americans are noted today and one that de Tocqueville found a risk to the national interest. A legacy of the Protestant Revolution, this ethos was carried across the Atlantic by the Puritans, who believed that their "City on the Hill" in Massachusetts was divinely inspired and would serve as a model of religious faith (Baldwin, 2005). During the first century or so of the Puritan settlement, loyalty was to the group and community, but later the belief in the right to liberty and the pursuit of happiness took over. The writings of this later period hailed individual freedom and private experience as the virtues to be cherished.

Individualism, probably the most sacrosanct of the America philosophical beliefs, is related to and revealed in capitalism and a reliance on charity to provide help to the poor. This is not to say that a collective spirit has not prevailed at various key periods in American history. Kaplan and Kaplan (1993) provide careful documentation to show that public opinion in the post-World War II era favored strong government intervention; surveys of that time reveal that a substantial portion of the population thought in collectivist terms. The contradiction in values between a focus on building character—the ability to stand up to the group—and conformity to the corporation and the peer group captivated the mass media during the 1950s and early 1960s. Out of this fear of conformity were born heroes such as the Lone Ranger and characters played by Alan Ladd in *Shane*, Gary Cooper in *High Noon*, and James Dean in *Rebel without a Cause*. And then for a short period in the mid-1960s and 1970s, the national fervor for social and economic equity was pervasive.

At the same time, within homogenous contexts, such as in high school and the military, conformity to group norms is the standard and has been for some time. In social psychological experiments, as has been discussed (see Chapter 2), Americans generally emerge as conformists, though less so than the Norwegians or Japanese.

Collectivist ideology accords prime importance to collective forms of association in which people share resources and decision making (Midgley, 2000). If you hold a collectivist orientation, you are more likely to put aside your individual goals for the well-being of the group (Seiler & Beall, 2008). As a European manifestation, collectivists believe that the state is jointly owned by its citizens and that the state is the most effective agent for meeting social needs. Among indigenous populations, such as certain African tribes, collectivism takes the form of traditional ways of knowing and a sense of intrinsic unity between individuals and communities (Kreitzer, 2002). Wright (2001) describes value themes carried from Africa that

are still in evidence among African Americans today. Among the themes singled out by Wright are oneness with nature and spirituality, mutual aid aimed at survival of the group, a present orientation and a spiral concept of time, and intergenerational bonding.

Anthropologist Alvin Wolfe (2002) contrasts the collective spirit of progressive periods in U.S. history with the social climate surrounding the welfare reform movement of today. The belief that each person shapes his or her own destiny, denial of structural causes of poverty, blaming of victims, and acclaim of the wealthy as heroes are all a part of this cultural ethos. This ethos sums up the cultural climate in the United States, this sense of "I" rather than "we." The focus on self at the personal level is matched on the political level by unilateral foreign policy and a refusal to join the nations at the International Criminal Court or to abide by decisions of international law.

The implications of these cultural differences are seen in social welfare policy in the various nations. On this side of the Atlantic, welfare programs are geared to specific individuals or groups who are functioning poorly. In Europe, the focus is more on the population as a whole. In the United States, social welfare programs that focus on changing the internal person rather than the external system have been favored.

The collective spirit in Norway combined with a moral belief in preserving the nation's wealth for future generations has brought major dividends in helping this nation withstand the economic collapse that has impacted the United States and the United Kingdom (Thomas, 2009). Instead of spending its oil riches lavishly, Norway set up a wealth fund to guard against future losses. Meanwhile, tight public oversight over bank lending practices has protected the banks from high-risk investments. There has been no real estate crash in Norway, accordingly.

Weiss's (2005) discussion of cultural differences among social workers in various countries is enlightening. The profession in the United States places a strong emphasis on self-determination, in contrast to Danish social work, which stresses integration. In Asia and Africa, the contrast is even greater, with social workers viewing self-determination as problematic. Van Wormer, during her sojourn in Norway, was struck by the strident group solidarity, the overriding sense of "we-ness" (van Wormer, 2006). The fortitude of this value is confirmed in a recent news report that the Norwegian court has decided that it is a punishable offense to prevent a spouse from being integrated into Norwegian society (No Abuse, 2004). The case involved a middle-aged immigrant who had been brought to Norway by her Algerian husband and who was forced to dress in traditional Algerian attire and was not allowed to speak with other classmates at the end of her class. (The child welfare department had ordered the woman to take a language course in Norwegian.) Although the prosecutor asked for a sentence of 1½ years for the husband, who was charged with abuse, the court doubled the sentence to 3 years, a long sentence by Norwegian standards.

In their study of South Asian immigrant mothers in Canada, Maiter and George (2003) noted the strength of the collectivist culture in their mothering roles and their expectations for their children. The internalization of group values, such as respect for elders and for their authority, and transmitting a sense of belonging to a cultural group were emphasized. Hirayama (1999), similarly, draws a sharp contrast between the American emphasis on fostering a competitive spirit in the child and encouraging self-sufficiency from an early age with the Japanese cultivation of a sense of group identity and solidarity. Social structure is hierarchical, and loyalty to family and the wider culture are primary. Self-control, piety, avoidance of shame, and emphasis on consensus are key cultural values (Gardiner & Kosmitzki, 2005).

Japanese society is generally understood to be highly consensual: "The fondness for group activity means most Japanese travel in groups, a habit that is said to date back centuries to the days when they flocked from temple to temple to hear Buddhist teachers" ("Consensus and Contraction," 2002, p. 8). In Japan, as the article continues, foreigners are tolerated more than welcomed and often held responsible for the rising crime rate. In the absence of sizable minority populations, Japan is culturally homogeneous

and devoid of much social disruption—a largely egalitarian society of which the unifying principle is termed *wa*.

From a global perspective, American individualism comes across as rather extreme, even offensive. The use of the word *I* is commonly heard throughout any conversation in which North Americans participate (Seiler & Beall, 2008). Sikeena Karmali (2003), who was born in Africa to Indian parents but who was educated in Canada, describes the East-West divide. As she observes:

> The self is the orienting principle of the West, perhaps even of modernity as a whole. All things—community, the nation, religion, spirituality, even God—are subordinated to the individual, which is the highest form of good. If we take a cursory glance at contemporary Western media, we find that the self is the supreme subject of conversation—my mind, my body, my home, my fashion, my spirit. There seems to be an earnest endeavor—in talk shows like *Oprah* and sitcoms like *Friends*, in the proliferation of lifestyle coaches, personal trainers, nutritionists, and shrinks—to perfect the individual. . . .
>
> The East, with its heavy hand of tradition, functions through consensus. Loyalties and duties are ascribed by birth. Community, and not self, is the orienting principle. (p. 2)

Karmali's hope is that East and West will come together as soul mates and that she herself, as a product of both worlds, somehow will be able to "integrate these values where they are needed" (p. 2).

Independence Versus Interconnectedness

Independence is closely related to individualism in the same way that interconnectedness is related to collectivism. Within the family, as well as in society, Americans strive to be fiercely independent. The word *codependency*, which signifies a too-close emotional dependence, accordingly has taken on extremely negative connotations. Parents train their children to be independent and to one day leave the "nest."

The myth of independence suggests that each individual is singularly in control of his or her own destiny, according to Tropman (1989). As people age, they fight to hang on to their independence for as long as possible. The value of independence has important implications for social welfare. Prolonged dependence on government help is actively discouraged, and many Americans refuse to accept benefits because of personal pride. "The Lord helps those who help themselves" is a commonly heard refrain.

At the international level, the United States has a strong propensity to lead or to "go it alone," but rarely to collaborate in international decision making. This propensity also figures in the governmental refusal to sign international accords on behalf of human rights or conventions banning chemical and biological weapons or land mines. In comparison with the United States, the nations of Europe, for example, appear to be far more interdependent in their dealings with each other. If we agree with Midgley (2000) that globalization can serve to provide sustainable development and enhance people's welfare, then we need to advocate for a perspective more in keeping with the demands of this global age.

The sense of interconnectedness is a staple of traditional indigenous culture. The First Nations peoples in North America rely on the metaphor of the Medicine Wheel, which exemplifies the wholeness of all life. The Medicine Wheel teaches about the cycle of life, a cycle that encompasses infancy through old age, the seasons, and four directions of human growth—the emotional, mental, physical, and spiritual. This is not a linear system, and all the parts are interconnected. American Indian teachings are traditionally presented as narratives and shared within a talking circle. Don Coyhis (2000), the director of White Bison, a substance abuse treatment center, incorporates the wisdom of the Medicine Wheel in his treatment programming. In Indian country, the heart of the sobriety movement, as explained by Coyhis, revolves around a return to cultural values and folkways. Among these values are a strong emphasis on *being*, not doing, and on cooperation over competition; group emphasis; working only to meet one's needs; nonmaterialism; right-brain

orientation; and living in harmony with nature. The theme of these values is social interconnectedness. This is one of the many insights offered by Coyhis:

> The elders have shared with us the Native understanding that all things are related and connected. There is a level in the unseen world where we are all connected to one another. . . . For example, one of the teachings of the Medicine Wheel says that the Honor of One is the Honor of All. And if that is true, then the Pain of One is the Pain of All. (pp. 90–91)

Materialism Versus Spirituality

America is viewed with distain in many parts of the world for its perceived embrace of godless and value-free materialism and for its imposition of the same on the rest of the world, for putting profits ahead of people (Davis & Silver, 2004). In fact, materialism should not, strictly speaking, be considered a value, because the term is laden with undesirable connotations. But the United States is clearly a capitalist nation, and status is accorded to those with high earning power or, in upper-upper class settings, to those who have access to inherited wealth. Americans may be accused on occasion of flaunting their wealth. The number of toys that many American children have would be considered in some circles to be almost obscene. And at the macro level, American capitalism is a cause of both resentment and emulation in every part of the globe.

Throughout her writings, bell hooks captures the essence of the search for meaning that sadly has caused so many to worship at the throne of money. In *Salvation: Black People and Love*, hooks (2001) describes how the focus on material gain has affected the black family: "Like the culture as a whole, masses of black people now look to material success as the sole measure of value and meaning in life. Gaining access to material privilege will never satisfy needs of the spirit. Those hungers persist and haunt us" (p. 15).

In an article entitled "Through New Eyes," Ron Marks (2003), the dean of the Tulane

University School of Social Work, describes how a group of American social work students adapted to the special rhythm of a Tibetan community in India. He writes:

> Whether witnessing a cremation or interacting with a person with leprosy, we discovered a spiritual richness among the Tibetan refugee community in Dharamsala, despite the material poverty. We, in turn, learned to measure modernity in a more humble way. (pp. 36–37)

Alexander (2005) describes his amazement in discovering the good life in the South Indian state of Kerala. Much has been written of this part of India, where poverty does not mean high infant mortality or short life spans or lack of education for girls and women. Aware of these facts, Alexander traveled to Kerala to live for several years among the people and uncover the secret of their success. What he found was a modest level of consumption, sustainability of available resources, and a high level of well-being. Women's leadership in the society and values of simplicity, as opposed to consumerism, were characteristics of this culture from which Americans have much to learn.

Value conflict between old (tribal) and new ways are commonplace across the globe. Social work educators from the University of Guam (Schwab & Dames, 2006), for example, write of cultural clash on their small Pacific island of Guam. The Chamorro, an indigenous people believed to be of Mayo-Polynesian descent, are the preservers of the ancient Guam culture, a culture that was historically matrilineal and matriarchal. During the Spanish occupation, the culture was preserved by the women, women whose influence was ignored by the Spaniards. Today, accordingly, many of the traditions remain—the belief that the land and its produce belongs to everyone, a powerful concern for mutuality rather than individualism, spirituality rather than material values, and reverence for elders (Government of Guam, 2004). A strong military presence, however, threatens to overwhelm the native cultural ethos.

The United States as a nation has a strong religious character. In a Gallup poll survey on religious beliefs, more than 85 percent said that religion was important in their lives (Newport, 2004). About two-thirds reported membership in a specific church or synagogue. About one-third attend every week. African Americans and women are the subgroups for whom religion is most important. Evangelical Christianity has made a strong comeback before and during the Bush administration, and plans for funding of faith-based initiatives for social services gained wide acceptance. The national thrust toward religiosity is confirmed in a worldwide survey undertaken by the Pew Research Center (2005a) in which three-fourths of the respondents said that religion was a very important part of their lives. An earlier worldwide survey in 2002 found that among wealthy nations such as Britain, Germany, Italy, and Korea, the United States is the only one in which a majority of the people say that religion plays an important role in their lives (Pew Research Center, 2005b)). A recent survey shows that young people are less religiously active than previous generations, but that their beliefs are fairly traditional. Pew Research Center (2010) surveys show, for instance, that young adults' beliefs about life after death and the existence of heaven, hell and miracles closely resemble the beliefs of older people today. The key factor may be aging rather than difference across the decades.

Organized religion is often much more visible in the United States than is spirituality. Spirituality, as described by Canda and Furman (2010), "orients the person and groups toward meaning, purpose, connectedness, and transcendence. This spiritual aspect is fundamental to human nature and infuses the other bio-psycho-social aspects" (p. 87). Spirituality, in short, relates to a universal and fundamental aspect of what it is to be human. Relevant to the family, the rituals and ceremonies associated with spirituality and religion mark important transitions and unite the generations in shared worship and reinforce feelings of gratitude and caring. (See Chapter 9 for a discussion of social work's rekindled focus on spirituality.)

Nuclear Family Versus Extended Family

"The Incredible Shrinking Family" is the title of a chapter in Robert Reich's (2000) *The Future of Success.* Although Reich's concern is the impact of the new working arrangements in the postindustrial society, the result is fewer children and longer working hours for both partners. Geographical mobility to "where the jobs are" leaves the older generation and aunts and uncles behind. In terms of economic support, the vulnerable members of the family, such as the elderly and the disabled, are more likely to be supported through social welfare provisions than by their kinfolk.

Throughout the nonindustrialized world, kinship arrangements are very different. Marriage may be viewed as a union between families rather than individuals. Residences may be shared intergenerationally. In India, for example, the social institution that is key to Hindu life is the joint family (Nimmagadda & Cowger, 1999). Social workers who provide counseling to troubled family members, such as to those in an alcoholic family, often find, according to Nimmagadda and Cowger, that acceptance of one's fate and fierce loyalty by wife to husband may prevent the alcoholic from changing but also may provide a strong support system. Although trained in Western models of individualism, social workers routinely adapt these foreign models to the norms of the local culture. For a compelling description of a Bedouin-Arab social worker's role as conflict mediator in a complicated marital situation, see Al-Krenawi and Graham (2001). The emphasis in the intervention, consistent with Arab cultural norms, was on the good of the family rather than the good of the individual.

Elizabeth Kenny (personal communication, June 2002) compares concepts of time in Mexico and the United States and the impact of the time dimension on family life:

> The Mexican mother of a friend of mine has told me that Americans greatly value time. She pointed out that this especially affects family values. Whereas in Mexico, the family has a long dinner together every night no matter what, here in the U.S. everyone is rushing to the next event. In Mexico, each person is more a member of a family than an individual.

Moralism Versus Compassion

A carryover from Puritanism, moralism is indeed one of the singular features of American society. As described by political scientist Seymour Lipset (1997), "America is the most moralistic country in the developed world. That moralism flows in large part from the country's unique Protestant sectarian and ideological commitments" (p. 26). Of all the U.S. value dimensions, this one, in our view, is primary. Tropman (1989) defined *moralism* as the tendency to be judgmental about affairs and events. This notion to Americans, according to Tropman, is sufficiently pervasive that poverty becomes a moral issue and money becomes the focus of moral judgment. Johnson and Rhodes (2009) concur: A narrow Puritanism that seeks reasons for disapproval of others leads to viewing the dependent state of the chronically poor and unsuccessful as immoral rather than simply unfortunate. Time and again, concerns of personal responsibility and fault have dominated the discourse on issues such as social welfare needs, including affordable housing, and, of course, problems with drug misuse and addiction. To please the people, politicians very often come down on the side of harsh treatment and punishment rather than compassion.

So entrenched is moralism in American discourse that, as an article from the conservative British magazine *The Economist* ("Living With a Superpower," 2003) argues, domestic issues, even technical matters such as stem-cell research and gun control, become moral questions. There may also be a link between moralism and militarism, as the article speculates. Data to support the article's contention that Americans and Europeans view the world differently come from the Pew Research Center's (2008) international poll on national attitudes across in Europe and the United States. Consider the contrast, as well, in the longstanding reluctance to accept gays and lesbians in the military compared to policies in European countries and the resistance of Americans to outlaw all forms of corporal punishment used with children. (See Chapter 4, *HBSE*, micro level.) (For international comparisons on a number of issues, see http://www.worldvaluessurvey.org.)

Punitiveness is a cardinal American value that is difficult for U.S. citizens to explain to outsiders (see Figure 5.6). The death penalty, harsh sentencing laws for drug users and dealers, the exposure of inmates to violence in prison—these are just a few examples that come to mind. Retribution rather than rehabilitation is still a major focus in the sentencing laws although more progressive programming is being introduced across the states. Over the past decade we have seen the construction of new jails and prisons expand exponentially; the war on drugs and the war on welfare have accompanied the prison growth. A record-breaking two million-plus people are in U.S. jails and prisons, one million of whom are incarcerated for violations related to drug use (Bureau of Justice Statistics [BJS], 2005). Although minorities are disproportionately serving time in prison, a shift in the drug of choice from crack cocaine to methamphetamines has resulted in more whites receiving prison sentences and a decline in the percentage of black inmates (BJS, 2009). Imprisonment and the prison industrial complex, which means jobs for construction workers and correctional officers and more federal and state funding to the community due to the population growth of inmates, ensures that the prison

network is now deeply ingrained in American life (Daniels, 2004). There is always the hope that, with the steady decline in the crime rate, political sentiment will shift and that, as Grimsrud and Zehr (2002) envision, present-day alternatives to retributive criminal justice will emerge that reflect the general thrust of compassionate justice. Such initiatives, which are at the compassionate end of the continuum, include victim-offender reconciliation programs and healing circles, which are discussed later in Chapter 6.

Is this pervasive moralism unique to American society? Indeed not. Remember the reaction in Japan to the Japanese hostages who were captured in Iraq and later released? Because their travel to Iraq had been in defiance of the Japanese government, which had discouraged such travel, they were greeted at the airport with abuse. The government condemned the former hostages and billed them for the airfare. According to an article by Onishi (2004), their sin was to defy *okami*, literally, "what is higher." Treated as criminals by the population and publicly rebuked by government officials for their irresponsible and selfish behavior, they were forced to go into hiding. Their families were the recipients of hate mail.

Figure 5.6. The United States incarcerates the highest percentage of prisoners in the world; life in the maximum security prison is especially harsh. Photo by Rupert van Wormer.

This incident reveals a moralism that relates the norm of obedience to higher authority, to sanctions against sticking out in the crowd, and to victim blaming in the extreme.

In summary, there is much that is unique about American society and, despite an amalgam of cultural characteristics in a heterogeneous nation, we have laid out some of the most obvious value dimensions, foremost among them moralism, individualism, and the work ethic. Keep these themes in mind during the discussion of community and community development in the chapter that follows.

The Political Manipulation of Cultural Values

A paradox that few have been able to explain is why, in the poorest counties in America, the voters consistently vote against their own economic and political interests for the political party of big business. Formerly, this phenomenon was explained as a consequence of racism—poor whites afraid of job loss to blacks and angry over policies of affirmative action. Thomas Frank (2004) updated this argument in his book *What's the Matter With Kansas? How Conservatives Won the Heart of America*. The paradox of which Frank writes is that of the working class voting for people who, as Frank dramatically puts it, "may talk Christ, but they walk corporate" (p. 6). Frank explains this phenomenon in terms of what he calls the Great Backlash. The primary contradiction of the backlash he sees is that it is a working-class movement that has done incalculable, historic harm to working-class people. While the backlash leaders downplay economics and tout traditional values, Frank further asserts, what they will actually deliver will be an economic regimen of low wages and lax regulations for industry.

Similarly, political scientist Peter Starke (2008) looks at what he calls "radical welfare state retrenchment" in global context. The recent health care debate in Congress provided a rare look into the inner workings of Congress and of forces that progressive politicians had to overcome. These forces were both economic

and cultural. Extensive lobbying by insurance companies and pharmaceutical companies effectively stymied passage of a health care bill that contained a public option to compete with private corporations. Culturally, as T. R. Reid, the author of *The Healing of America: A Global Quest for Better, Cheaper, and Fairer Health Care* (2009), indicates, countries with universal government-run health care differ from the United States in a striking way—they accept health care as a right and that one system should be available for all. The moral impetus to guarantee health care is seemingly too weak to overcome the power of the major corporations. Resistance to change undoubtedly is another major factor that came into play as the health care reform efforts consistently were scaled back in order to get the needed number of Congressional votes. Meanwhile, use of fear tactics by conservative politicians were highly effective in reducing what public support there might have been for a real overhaul of the health care system. Chapter 7 analyzes the policy making process involved in the passage of the 2010 health care reform act in more detail.

Economics affects cultural values, and cultural values have a strong bearing on human behavior. What we are talking about here is a belief system that arises in a time and place of prosperity, that feeds confidence in the system, and that is also associated with generations of failure, out migration, and endemic poverty. (See Box 5.1, "Appalachia: A Study in Contrasts.")

Box 5.1 Appalachia: A Study in Contrasts

Katherine van Wormer

The past is not dead; it's not even past.
—William Faulkner, *Requiem for a Nun*

Appalachia, which extends across the southeast mountain region of the United States, held a great fascination for sociologists and journalists in the middle of the last century. Much of the focus was on the history and culture of the region. The titles of some of the popular books of the day proclaimed the predominant sentiment that there was much wrong with this region: *Night Comes to the Cumberlands: A Biography of a Depressed Area* (Caudill, 1962); *Yesterday's People* (Weller, 1965); *The Other America* (Harrington, 1962). These were not books that spoke of strengths or resilience in the face of hardship. Caudill referred to these people as the failures of the failures. The War on Poverty launched by Lyndon Johnson in the 1960s was spawned in part by Harrison's book and focused on this area of the United States. The government sent workers through the Volunteers in Service to America (VISTA) program, which was likened to the Peace Corps in the kind of community work that was done and funded.

But then the national interest in the region suddenly subsided. Perhaps it was the war in Vietnam that drew attention away or the discrediting of the "culture of poverty" theories that were now considered examples of victim blaming and stereotyping. In any case, the focus went elsewhere, and the idiosyncrasies of the region were largely forgotten by the media and general public.

In the 1970s I lived in southern West Virginia and taught sociology at Bluefield State. What impressed me most about the culture was the people's easy sense of humor, combined with cynicism, that made teaching a delight; their distrust of authority; and their natural sympathy for the underdog. One does not find the usual kind of victim blaming that is associated with a belief in a just world. In my personal losing struggle against a corrupt and callous academic bureaucracy, the commiseration I received was wonderfully comforting. On the negative side, I remember that cheating on exams was relatively common, a fact I learned the hard way. Religious experiences, as described to me by students, were highly emotional, characterized by frighteningly vivid images of the devil and hell, and often disturbing to children. Earlier, before I ever went to Appalachia, I had taught school for several years in Northern Ireland, so the impact of extreme fundamentalism on children was familiar to me. That was not the only connection here; the roots of the Appalachian people (the so-called Scotch Irish) actually are in Northern Ireland.

The American term *Scotch-Irish*, or, more correctly, *Scots-Irish*, refers to the zealous Protestants who migrated first from Britain to Northern Ireland and then from Northern Ireland to America (Gladwell, 2008). This was in the 1700s.

Because these emigrants did not fit in with Tidewater Virginia society, they migrated westward to till the land nobody wanted and otherwise eked out a living in the "hills" of Kentucky and West Virginia.

According to Northern Ireland native Morris Taggart (2005), the customs and values that defined life for the Scots-Irish still persist across a vast region of Appalachia today. Even long after the challenges and hardships that directed attitudes and behavior had vanished, the cultural legacies persist. This is how Gladwell explains the form of violence that is characteristic of Harlan, Kentucky, violence that is not related to economic gain but to attacks on one's honor. The unique cultural ethos that Gladwell found in Harlan, Kentucky, is what it is because of where the original inhabitants of the region came from.

Sociologist Harry Caudill (1962), himself a descendant of the mountain people, graphically describes the early settlers as "a population born of embittered rejects and outcasts from the shores of Europe—as cynical, hardened and bitter a lot as can be imagined outside prison walls" (p. 13). Despite his harsh words, however, Caudill very much sees these people as the victims of history, especially related to the exploitation of the land and of its people by the coal companies. The operators of these companies preferred to keep the workers ignorant and dependent on them for their livelihood and in a state of near serfdom in terms of what they could buy and even in their community life. Then, once the land was depleted of resources, the companies moved on, leaving the people with a despoiled landscape and without a livelihood. This continuing experience with the power elites, many of whom came from the outside, has left the native inhabitants dejected and demoralized.

My fascination with the culture of this unique region of the United States was rekindled recently, as was that of much of the nation, with the airing on PBS of David Sutherland's gripping and disturbing documentary, *Country Boys* (PBS, 2006). This three-part documentary concerned the growing pains of two teenage boys, Chris and Cody, both of whom attend a high school for behaviorally disturbed kids in Floyd County in eastern Kentucky. Cameras follow the boys everywhere and record intimate details of their lives over a 3-year period. Chris's family lives in "the hollers" in a run-down trailer with his rough-spoken mother and chronically drunken father. Chris, who narrates much of the story in a melodious, almost theatrical voice, encounters defeat after defeat, a fact that he attributes to his own self-destructiveness. Despite the personal attention he gets from school counselors and the principal, he cheats the system with excuses and sham mental health problems that qualify him for disability payments that his mother needs to live on. Although he finally manages to graduate and makes a powerful graduation speech, the epilogue indicates that he has gotten nowhere in his life and is mired in poverty and a minimum-wage job.

Cody is rebellious in another way. His house is clean and attractive; his stepmother's well-spoken mother is his caretaker. Cody sees himself as one of the "haves" as opposed to "have nots." His background is clouded, however. His mother committed suicide, and his father later killed his stepmother and then himself. The tragedy of his early childhood hangs over him, but in the end, the unconditional love of his step-grandmother sustains him, and he makes plans to go to college.

The story of *Country Boys* is the story of resilience in the one case and defeat in the other. It is also the story of a culture and way of life in an area of grinding poverty. Does culture come into play in holding adolescents such as Chris back, and if so, is it, as defined by Harrington (1962) and Sarnoff (2003), the culture of poverty? To the extent that the culture of poverty is defined as the cause rather than the effect of poverty, this explanation is fallacious. Sarnoff's focus on the systemic nature of poverty is appropriate, however, because it puts the responsibility for ending the poverty where it belongs, with the social structure that must provide opportunities for people before the people can develop aspirations and confidence that their actions will make a difference.

Because the culture-of-poverty theory is so often misused or misunderstood, I use the term *culturally based theory* to cover the same ground. Culturally based theory can serve to explain many of the problems that oppressed people have in abiding by the norms of society, especially regarding achievement and self-sufficiency. Such a theoretical perspective locates the source of oppression within the values, norms, and attitudes of the oppressed group, but only as a legacy of earlier mistreatment, for example, conquest or enslavement. Like individual history, the history cannot be neglected. People who have been socially excluded and whose ancestors have been subjected to social exclusion over long periods of time develop survival mechanisms that may no longer be functional.

Illustrative of this approach is Cattell-Gordon's (1990) analysis of the traumatic effects of the loss and absence of work over generations in southern Appalachia. Utilizing the concept of culturally transmitted traumatic stress syndrome to describe the character of the mountain people, Cattell-Gordon, a native of Bluefield, West Virginia, records the long history of economic exploitation and government abandonment over the years. Such mistreatment can leave a land and its people broken and bruised. According to Cattell-Gordon, "These particular cultural traits—an enduring sense of resignation, deep depression, disrupted relationships and hurtful forms of dependency—appear, again and again, in the culture as each new generation faces unemployment" (p. 43). This is the legacy of economic oppression. If we accept that economic oppression is the cause of certain attitudes, then the solution, too, must be economic—not handouts but mass community organization efforts to establish programs, an investment in communities, as well as in people. This is our responsibility to the Codys and the Chrises of the world, to invest in them with real commitment so that they can see that they and their children will have a future. Grassroots power is of course important as well. Read about the work in supporting grassroots leadership efforts against economic injustice of the Highlander Research and Education Center at http://www.highlandercenter.org.

Social worker Ed Miner (in personal correspondence of March 2007) responded to Cattell-Gordon's observations from the vantage point of having worked with impoverished Appalachian and African American populations in Columbus, Ohio:

> The long history of suffering and oppression among Appalachian people causes a grinding down of the people that becomes ingrained in daily life. People who have been oppressed can develop a sense of resignation, deep depression, and other symptoms that lead to dysfunction. I witness the evidence of this everyday. I work with many families who, during their mental health history, tell about legal, economic, and psychological struggles that go back generations. Most of them have families who were coal miners. They relate stories of death from black

lung disease, companies that did not care for employee health, and acceptance of disasters such as mine accidents. I see the sense of resignation in an interesting phenomenon in one mostly Appalachian neighborhood called "the Bottoms." Several of my families move all the time, sometimes two or three times a year. However, they never move out of the Bottoms. They will live in the same two or three mile square area for years never even considering living anywhere else. This is different from a broader "culture of poverty" idea in that it recognizes that the psychology and values of a particular population have unique causes. Appalachians and African Americans in the inner city of Columbus seem, on the surface, to have similar problems related to poverty. But they are not as monolithic as the "culture of poverty" idea would indicate. I see subtle differences all of the time. These are generalizations but seem to hold true over my experience. My African American clients are more likely to value education and less likely to have truancy problems. My Appalachian clients are generally more willing to work with a psychiatrist and are less suspicious of mental health services. Appalachian clients are also more likely to have extended family connections in the city as they often move to the city "together." My African American clients tend to be transplants from other inner-city locations; Detroit, Cleveland, and Chicago are the most common. But this is to say that I agree that "culture of poverty" thinking can cause us to be blind to subtle differences in the situations of our people. These subtle differences need to be recognized in the way we work with families.

References

Cattell-Gordon, D. (1990). The Appalachian inheritance: A culturally transmitted traumatic stress syndrome? *Journal of Progressive Human Services, 1*, 41–57.

Caudill, H. (1962). *Night comes to the Cumberlands: A biography of a depressed area*. Boston: Little, Brown.

Faulkner, W. (1951). *Requiem for a nun*. New York: Random House.

Gladwell, M. (2008). *Outliers: The story of success*. New York: Little, Brown and Co.

Harrington, M. (1962). *The other America: Poverty in the United States*. Baltimore: Penguin Books.

Public Broadcasting Service. (2006, January 9–11). Country boys. David Sutherland, producer. *Frontline*. Retrieved May 2006, from http://www.pbs.org/countryboys

Sarnoff, S. (2003). Central Appalachia: Still the other America. *Journal of Poverty, 7*(1/2), 123–140.

Taggart, M. (2005). Scots-Irish families. In M. McGoldrick, J. Giordano, & N. Garcia-Preto (Eds.), *Ethnicity and family therapy* (3rd ed., pp. 654–663). New York: Guilford Press.

Practice Implications

In 1996, the National Association of Social Workers' (NASW) Code of Ethics was revised to include a global mandate. Social workers are now enjoined to "promote the general welfare of society, from local to global levels" (section 6.01). In light of the current globalization of the economy and the high rate of immigration over the past decade, social workers inevitably will be working with people of diverse cultural backgrounds. An awareness of aspects of North American cultural norms and values that might seem odd or uncaring to an outsider is essential. Once we learn about our own cultural values, we can come to have an awareness and appreciation of values of representatives of diverse populations.

Realistically speaking, cultural competence is something to strive for but not something that is ever completely achieved (Weaver, 2005). Every client experiences his or her culture differently, and factors of age, degree of acculturation, education, and class always must be factored in. Preparation for intervention in a system in which mixed racial and ethnic identity issues are potentially volatile is imperative (Daly, 2001). A basic technique for crossing the cultural barrier recommended by Daly (2001) is the communication skill of active listening, in which the listener repeats what he or she has heard and what his or her perceptions are of circumstances, decisions, and so on. In this way, any misunderstandings can be cleared up. In paying close attention to the client's definition of the situation, social workers, moreover, show a willingness to listen and learn.

An essential ingredient of multicultural social work is empowerment. Empowerment may be manifested at the community level through the inclusion of the community group in the change effort and in the development of macro-level interventions. Above all, empowerment practice requires taking identity issues and a group's cultural identities into account, because these are integral to the group member's sense of worth.

Attention to the social and cultural context of clients' lives must be included in culturally competent service provision for optimal results. Research from public health work in the area of substance abuse prevention bears this out (Botvin et al., 1995; Unger et al., 2004). For work with refugee communities such as Cambodian or Bosnian residents as well, service offerings need to be readily accessible, equipped with language translators and practitioners who are sensitive to their unique histories (such as conflict among rival ethnic groups) and cultural rituals (see Fong & Furuto, 2001). In striving toward the goal of cultural competence, we need to recognize how various behavior patterns that may seem dysfunctional within a safe and secure setting might have been functional for survival in a hostile social environment. Social workers working with refugees from war-torn areas, for example, should have a working knowledge of the history of a people and how they survived in the midst of mass violence and ethnic conflict. Attendance at professional workshops on the dynamics and symptoms of posttraumatic stress disorder can be helpful. Finally, ethnic-specific treatment modalities must be adapted for work with the various population groups.

Above all, an emphasis on empowerment—personal and cultural—is important. Daly, Jennings, Beckett, and Leashore (1996) recommend that social workers be cognizant of African American cultural perspectives and approach these from a nondeficit model of empowerment. Evidence indicates, for example, that African American women coping with domestic violence are apt to be particularly sensitive to the influence of family and support systems. It has been found, as Daly et al. (1996) indicate, that social supports from the extended family, in fact, serve to decrease spouse assaults in African American homes. Increasingly, social workers trained in a strengths perspective look to the wider family as a major resource and recognize the importance of honoring all different kinds of family forms; for example, those that are blended with children from previous marriages, nonkin families, and same-sex parented families. Kinship care, as described in Chapter 4, is preferred over adoption by nonfamily members by the National Association of Black Social Workers for children in need of care (Suppes & Wells, 2008). This traditional, informal arrangement has become a model for all families in need of care. Child welfare workers increasingly rely on kinship care arrangements in cases of parental absence or neglect.

Summary and Conclusion

The purpose of this chapter was to provide an overview of cultural norms and expectations as relevant for macro-level generalist practice. Culture has a significant influence on an individual's and a group's values, beliefs, worldview, and child-rearing practices. Filtered from the literature of international social work and anthropology, nine value dimensions emerge with relevance to cultural values. These are work versus leisure, equal opportunity versus equality, mobility versus stability, competition versus cooperation, individualism versus collectivism, independence versus interconnectedness, materialism versus spirituality, nuclear family versus extended family, and moralism versus compassion. Comparative analysis shows that, except for the family construct that is associated with modern industrialization and globalization, the attributes on the left side of the continua are characteristically American, whereas some of those characteristics on the right-hand side—equality, cooperation, and collectivism—are representative of advanced welfare states such as those found in the Nordic countries. The message here is at the macro level—how social service provisions can be improved to prevent poverty and disease and meet the needs of all the people. Other cultural orientations on the right side of the continua that have a bearing on the personal level of social work—interconnectedness, spirituality, and extended family orientations—are characteristic of traditional cultures and have implications for how social work protocols will be received by such minority populations. This discussion of cultural values and cultural sensitivities to difference provides a backdrop for the following chapter on community and community development.

Thought Questions

1. Discuss some ways that culture and community are intertwined.
2. "We are all cultural beings." Discuss.
3. How can knowing another culture give us awareness about our own?
4. Review NASW's Code of Ethics, section 1.05, and what it says about culture.
5. Consider ways that religion can take on aspects of ethnocentrism.
6. Discuss the metaphor of finding four-leaf clovers with regard to the study of a new culture.
7. Which of the values listed in the nine value dimensions, in your opinion, best encapsulates the "American way of life"?
8. Trace the historical roots of the work ethic. What was Max Weber's theory?
9. Relate the teachings of Calvinism and Benjamin Franklin to any personal teachings in your family or educational background.
10. Today we are a secular nation. To what extent do you think the Protestant work ethic applies or does not apply at this time?
11. Discuss the value put on work in several different countries.
12. Differentiate equal opportunity from equality.
13. To destroy a social welfare program, make it means tested. Discuss this claim. Consider recent changes in Medicare.
14. Argue that mobility is a key characteristic of U.S. society.
15. Describe a society in which the social climate is cooperation-based rather than competition-based.
16. Contrast the concept of the Indian Medicine Wheel with the mainstream U.S. focus on independence.
17. Relate the force of moralism to punitiveness in American society.
18. Discuss the underlying thesis of the book *What's the Matter With Kansas?* What is its contemporary relevance?
19. How can social workers be better prepared to work with people from diverse backgrounds? Relate the discussion to recent presidential elections.
20. Using culturally based theory, account for the persistent poverty in parts of Appalachia.

References

Adams, P. (2009, April 11). Immigrants in the American heartland. *BBC News*. Retrieved from http://news.bbc.co.uk/2/hi/americas/8339249.stm

Alber, J., & Gilbert, N. (2010). Introduction. In J. Alber & N. Gilbert (Eds.), *United in diversity? Comparing social models in Europe and America* (pp. 3–18). New York: Oxford University Press.

Alexander, W. M. (2005, May). Simplicity, poverty, and gender in the Indian state of Kerala. *Friends Journal, 51*(4), 14–17.

Al-Krenawi, A., & Graham, J. R. (2001). The cultural mediator: Bridging the gap between a non-western community and professional social work practice. *British Journal of Social Work, 31*, 665–685.

Appleby, G. (2007). Culture, social class, and social identity development. In G. A. Appleby, E. Colon, & J. Hamilton (Eds.), *Diversity, oppression, and social functioning* (pp. 16–35). Boston: Allyn & Bacon.

Armstrong, K. (1993). *A history of God: The 4,000-year quest of Judaism, Christianity, and Islam*. New York: Ballantine Books.

Baldwin, N. (2005). *The American revelation: Ten ideals that shaped our country from the Puritans to the cold war*. New York: St. Martin's Press.

Bateson, M. C. (1984). *With a daughter's eye: A memoir of Margaret Mead and Gregory Bateson*. New York: Pocket Books.

Bishop, A. (2002). *Becoming an ally: Breaking the cycle of oppression in people* (2nd ed.). Halifax, Nova Scotia, Canada: Fernwood Press.

Boshara, R. (2003, January/February). The $6,000 solution. *Atlantic Monthly*, 91–95.

Botvin, G., Schinke, S., Epstein, J., Diaz, T., & Botvin, E. (1995). Effectiveness of culturally focused and generic skills training approaches to alcohol and drug abuse prevention among minority adolescents: Two-year follow-up results. *Psychology of Addictive Behaviors, 9*(3), 183–194.

British Broadcasting Company (BBC). (2002, January 14). *Nokia boss gets record speeding fine.* Retrieved, from http://news.bbc.co.uk/1/hi/business

Bureau of Justice Statistics. (2005). *Prison statistics.* Washington, DC: U.S. Department of Justice.

Bureau of Justice Statistics. (2009, December). *Prisoners in 2008.* Washington, DC: U.S. Department of Justice.

Canda, E. R., & Furman, L. D. (2010). *Spiritual diversity in social work practice: The heart of helping* (2nd ed.).New York: Free Press.

Center on Budget and Policy Priorities. (2006, January 26). *Income inequality grew across the country over the past two decades.* Retrieved from http://www.cbpp.org/cms/?fa=view&id=978 t

Consensus and Contraction. (2002, April 20). *Economist* (Suppl.), 8–10.

Coyhis, D. (2000). Substance abuse and cultural issues in Indian country. In J. Krestam (Ed.), *Bridges to recovery: Addiction, family therapy, and multicultural treatment* (pp. 79–114). New York: Free Press.

Daly, A. (2001). A heuristic perspective of strengths when intervening with an African American community. In R. Fong & S. Furuto (Eds.), *Culturally competent practice: Skills, interventions and evaluations* (pp. 241–254). Boston: Allyn & Bacon.

Daly, A., Jennings, J., Beckett, J., & Leashore, B. (1996). Effective coping strategies of African Americans. In P. Ewalt, E. Freeman, S. Kirk, & D. Poole (Eds.), *Multicultural issues in social work* (pp. 189–203). Washington, DC: NASW.

Daniels, P. (2004, May 13). U.S. prison boom creates an Orwellian world. *World Socialist WebSite.* Retrieved M from http://www.wsws.org/articles/2004/May2004/pris-m13.shtml

Davis, D. W., & Silver, B. D. (2004). Americans' perceptions of the causes of terrorism: Why do they hate us? *American Journal of Political Science, 48*(1), 28–46.

Day, P. (2008)). *A new history of social welfare* (6th ed.). Boston: Allyn & Bacon.

Denham, S., Meyer, M., Toborg, M., & Mande, M. (2004). Providing health education to Appalachia populations. *Holistic Nursing Practice, 18*(6), 293–312.

de Tocqueville, A. (1951). *Democracy in America* (P. Bradley, Trans.). New York: Knopf. (Original work published 1835).

Ediger, M. (2000, March). Competition versus cooperation and pupil achievement. *College Student Journal, 34,* 14–21.

Erickson, B. (2005). Scandinavian families: Plain and simple. In M. McGoldrick, J. Giordano, & N. Garcia-Preto (Eds.), *Ethnicity and family therapy* (3rd ed., pp. 641–653). New York: Guilford Press.

Esber, G. (1989). Anthropological contributions for social work education. *Practicing Anthropology, 11*(3), 4–11.

Faulkner, W. (1964). *Absalom, Absalom!* New York: Random House. (Originally published in 1936).

Fleck, S. (2009, May). International comparisons of hours worked: An assessment of the statistics. *Monthly Labor Review,* 3–31.

Fong, R. (2001). Culturally competent social work practice: Past and present. In R. Fong & S. Furuto (Eds.), *Culturally competent practice: Skills interventions, and evaluations* (pp. 1–9). Boston: Allyn & Bacon.

Fong, R., & Furuto, S. (Eds.). (2001). *Culturally competent practice: Skills, interventions, and evaluations.* Boston: Allyn & Bacon.

Frank, T. (2004). *What's the matter with Kansas? How conservatives won the heart of America.* New York: Metropolitan Books.

Frey, W. (2001). *America by the numbers.* New York: New Press.

Fritzell, J. (2001). Still different? Income distribution in the Nordic countries in European comparison. In M. Kautto, J. Fritzell, B. Hvinden, J. Kvist, & H. Uustalo (Eds.), *Nordic welfare states in the European context* (pp. 18–41). London: Routledge.

Gardiner, H. W., & Kosmitzki, C. (2005). *Uses across cultures: Cross-cultural human development* (3rd ed.). Boston: Allyn & Bacon.

Gladwell, M. (2008). *Outliers: The story of success.* New York: Little, Brown and Co.

Government of Guam. (2004). *The culture of Guam.* Retrieved March 20, 2004, from http://ns.gov.gu/culture.html

Grimsrud, T., & Zehr, H. (2002). Rethinking God, justice and treatment of offenders. In T. O'Connor (Ed.), *Religion, the community, and the rehabilitation of criminal offenders* (pp. 259–285). New York: Haworth.

Hall, K. (2009, May 11). Take a break, or else. *Business Week*, p.O14.

Harrington, M. (1962). *The other America: Poverty in the United States*. Baltimore, MD: Penguin Books.

Hartmann, T. (1997). *Attention deficit disorder: A different perception*. Grass Valley, CA: Under Wood Books.

Hirayama, H., & Hirayama, K. (1999). Cross-cultural application of empowerment practice: A comparison between American and Japanese groups. In W. Shera & L. Wells (Eds.), *Empowerment practice in social work: Developing richer conceptual foundations* (pp. 246–258). Toronto, Ontario: Canadian Scholars' Press.

hooks, b. (2001). *Salvation: Black people and love*. New York: Harper Collins.

Jackson, K. (2003, November). Meeting the needs of American Indian communities: Focus on a unique program. *Social Work Today*, pp.14–31.

Johnson, M., & Rhodes, R. (2009). *Human behavior and the larger social environment: A new synthesis* (2nd ed.).Boston: Allyn & Bacon.

Kaplan, C., & Kaplan, L. (1993). Public opinion and the "economic bill of rights." *Journal of Progressive Human Services, 4*(1), 43–58.

Karger, H. J., & Stoesz, D. (2009). *American social welfare policy: A pluralist approach* (6th ed.). Boston: Allyn & Bacon.

Karmali, S. (2003, January-February). Unraveling the East-West myth. Utne Magazine. Retrieved from http://www.utne.com/2003-01-01/unraveling-the-east-west-myth.aspx?page=2.

Khosrokhavar, F. (2005)). *Suicide bombers: Allah's new martyrs*. London: Pluto Press.

Kirst-Ashman, K. (2008)). *Human behavior, communities, organizations and groups in the macro social environment: An empowerment approach* (2nd ed.). Belmont, CA: Brooks/Cole.

Kreitzer, L. (2002, June). *Globalization and indigenization: Power issues in social work knowledge*. Unpublished thesis, University of Calgary, Alberta, Canada.

"Labour Mobility: The Road Not Taken". (2009, March 21). *Economist*, p. 31.

Lee, S., & Edmonston, B. (2005). New marriages, new families: U.S. racial and Hispanic intermarriage. *Population Bulletin, 60*(2), 3.

Lipset, S. M. (1997). *American exceptionalism: A double-edged sword*. New York: Norton.

Living with a superpower. (2003, January 2). *Economist*. Retrieved May 1, 2006, from http://www.economist.com/displaystory.cfm?story_id=1511812

Maiter, S., & George, U. (2003). Understanding context and culture in the parenting approaches of immigrant South Asian mothers. *Affilia, 18*(4), 411–428.

Marks, R. (2003, Spring). Through new eyes. *Tulanian*, 28–37.

Marsh, J. (2004). Social work in a multicultural society. *Social Work, 49*(1), 5–6.

McGoldrick, M., Giordano, J., & Garcia-Petro, N. (2005). Overview: Ethnicity and family therapy. In M. McGoldrick, J. Giordano, & N. Garcia-Petro (Eds.), *Ethnicity and family therapy* (3rd ed., pp. 1–40). New York: Guilford Press.

Mead, M. (1972). *Blackberry winter: My earlier years*. New York: Morrow.

Midgley, J. (2000). The institutional approach to social policy. In J. Midgley, M. B. Tracey, & M. Livermore (Eds.), *The handbook of social policy* (pp. 365–376). Thousand Oaks, CA: Sage.

Mishel, L., Bernstein, J., & Allegretto, S. (2005).*The state of working America*. Ithaca, NY: Cornell University Press.

Moisi, D. (2009, May 12). *Le fossé des émotions transatlantique* [The gap in transatlantic emotions]. *Les Echos* Retrieved from http://www.lesechos.fr/info/analyses/4862342-le-fosse-des-emotions-transatlantique.htm

Moore, C. J. (2004). *In other words: A language lover's guide to the most intriguing words around the world*. Los Angeles: Walker.

Mullaly, B. (2002). *Challenging oppression: A critical social work approach*. Don Mills, Ontario, Canada: Oxford University Press.

National Association of Social Workers. (1996). *Code of ethics*. Washington, DC: NASW Press.

Nelson, M. R., & Shavitt, S. (2002, September). Horizontal and vertical individualism and achievement values. *Journal of Cross-Cultural Psychology, 33*(5), 439–458.

Newport, F. (Ed.). (2004). *A look at Americans and religion today* [Poll]. Princeton, NJ: Gallup Organization.

Nimmagadda, J., & Cowger, C. D. (1999). Cross-cultural practice: Social worker ingenuity in the indigenization of practice knowledge. *International Social Work, 42*(3), 261–276.

Nisbett, R. E. (2004). *The geography of thought: How Asians and Westerners think differently and why*. New York: Free Press.

No Abuse. (2004, February 27). Dømt for å nekte integrering [Sentenced for refusing to integrate]. Retrieved from http://www.noabuse.no/avis/vo/2004/arkiv35.htm

"Norway: Rich man fined $109,000 for drunk driving" (2009, May 13). *Waterloo-Cedar Falls Courier* (Iowa), p.A5.

Onishi, N. (2004, April 23). Freed from captivity in Iraq, Japanese return to more pain. Retrieved, from http://www.nytimes.com/2004/04/23/international/asia/23JAPA.html?pagewanted=1

Page, B., & Jacobs, L. (2009). No class war: Economic inequality and the American public. In L. Jacobs and D. King (Eds.), *The unsustainable American state* (pp. 135–166). New York: Oxford University Press.

Pew Global Attitudes Project. (2005, June 23). *U.S. image up slightly, but still negative.* Retrieved from http://pewglobal.org/reports/display.php?ReportID=247

Pew Global Attitudes Project (2009, July 23). Confidence in Obama lifts U.S. image around the world. Retrieved from http://pewresearch.org/pubs/1289/global-attitudes-survey-2009-obama-lifts-america-image

Pew Research Center. (2005a). The American public: Trends 2005. *Pew Forum on Religion and Public Life.* Washington, DC: Pew Research Center.

Pew Research Center (2005b, April 21). Secular Europe and religious America: Implications for transatlantic relations. Retrieved from http://pewforum.org/Politics-and-Elections/Secular-Europe-and-Religious-America-Implications-for-Transatlantic-Relations.aspx

Pew Research Center (2008, December 18). Global public opinion in the Bush years (2001-2008). Retrieved from http://pewresearch.org/pubs/1059/global-opinion-bush-years

Pew Research Center (2010, February 17). Religion among the millenials. Washington, DC: The Pew Forum. Retrieved from http://pewforum.org/Age/Religion-Among-the-Millennials.aspx

Powell, B. (2009, November 23). Things we can learn from China. *Time*, pp.35–43.

Raheim, S. (2006). Promoting diversity and social and economic justice in social work education: A process of organizational transformation. *Social Work Education Reporter, 54*(1), 1, 6, 11.

Ramirez-Esparza, N., Gosling, S., Benet-Martínez, V., Potter, J., & Pennebaker, J. (2006). Do bilinguals have two personalities? A special case of cultural frame switching. *Journal of Research in Personality, 40*(2), 99–120.

Reich, R. (2000). *The future of success: Working and living in the new economy.* New York: Vintage.

Reid, T. R. (2009, August 31). The healing of America: A global quest for better, cheaper, and fairer health care. *Time*, p.14.

Roberts, S. (2009, April 23). Slump creates lack of mobility for Americans. *The New York Times,* p.A1.

Ross, M., Xun, W. Q., & Wilson, A. E. (2002). Language and the bicultural self. *Personality and Social Psychology Bulletin, 28*(8), 1040–1050.

Ruby, R.& Smith, G. (2007). How Muslims compare with other religious Americans. *Pew Forum on Religion and Public Life.* Retrieved from http://pewforum.org/Muslim/How-Muslims-Compare-With-Other-Religious-Americans.aspx

Saleebey, D. (2001). *Human behavior and social environments: A biopsychosocial approach.* New York: Columbia University Press.

Schneider, P. (2004). Separated by civilization. *International Herald Tribune, p.4.*

Schwab, G. J., & Dames, V. L. (2006). U.S. military and U.S. welfare: Partners in (de)colonizing Mironesian islands. Boxed reading in K. van Wormer,, *Introduction to social welfare and social work* (pp. 62–63). Belmont, CA: Cengage.

Seiler, W. & Beall, M. (2008). *Community: Making connections* (7th ed.). Boston: Allyn & Bacon.

Snapshot of America. (2004, June 28). *U.S. News & World Report*, p. 41.

Starke, P. (2008). *Radical welfare state retrenchment in comparative perspective.* New York: Palgrave Macmillan.

Suppes, M., & Wells, C. (2008). *The social work experience: An introduction to social work and social welfare* (5th ed.). New York: McGraw-Hill.

Thomas, L. (2009, May 14). Thriving Norway provides an economics lesson. *The New York Times*, pp. A1, A4.

Tropman, J. (1989). *American values and social welfare: Cultural contradictions in the welfare state.* Englewood Cliffs, NJ: Prentice Hall.

Tropman, J. (2002). *The Catholic ethic and the spirit of community.* Washington, DC: Georgetown University.

Unger, J., Chou, C., Palmer, P., Ritt-Olson, A., Gallaher, P., Cen, S., et al. (2004). Project FLAVOR: One-year outcomes of a multicultural, school-based smoking prevention curriculum for adolescents. *American Journal of Public Health, 94*(2), 263–265.

U.S. Census Bureau. (2005). *Facts for features.* Washington, DC: Government Printing Office.

U.S. Census Bureau News (2009, May). Census bureau estimates nearly half of children under age 6 are minorities. *U.S. Department of Commerce.* Retrieved from http://www.census.gov/Press-Release/www/releases/archives/population/013733.html

van Wormer, K. (2006) *Introduction to social welfare and social work: The U. S. in global perspective.* Belmont, CA: Brooks/Cole.

Wagner, D. (1994, November). Beyond the pathologizing of nonwork: Alternative activities in a street community. *Social Work, 39,* 718–727.

Wagner, D. (2000). *What's love got to do with it?* New York: New Press.

Weaver, H. (2005). *Explanations in cultural competence: Journeys to the four directions.* Belmont, CA: Brooks/Cole.

Weber, M. (1958). *The Protestant ethic and the spirit of capitalism.* New York: Scribner. (Original work published 1905)

Weick, A. (2001). Overturning oppression: An analysis of emancipatory change. In K. J. Peterson & A. Lieberman (Eds.), *Building on women's strengths: A social work agenda for the 21st century* (pp. 253–269). New York: Haworth.

Weiss, I. (2005). Is there a global common core to social work? A cross-national comparative study of BSW graduate students. *Social Work, 50*(2), 101–110.

Williams, R. (1979). Change and stability in values and values systems: A sociological perspective. In M. Rokeach (Ed.), *Understanding human values: Individual and societal* (pp. 15–46). New York: Free Press.

Wolfe, A. W. (2002). Welfare reform: Self-sufficiency or what? In A. Podolefsky & P. J. Brown (Eds.), *Applying cultural anthropology: An introductory reader* (pp. 282–285). Mountain View, CA: Mayfield.

World Health Organization (WHO). (2009). *Suicide rates per 100,000 by country.* Retrieved from http://www.who.int/mental_health/prevention/suicide_rates/en/index.html

Wright, E. M. (2001). Substance abuse in African American communities. In S. L. A. Straussner (Ed.), *Ethnoculutural factors in substance abuse treatment* (pp. 31–51). New York: Guilford Press.

Zastrow, C. (2010). *Introduction to social work and social welfare* (10th ed.). Belmont, CA: Brooks/Cole.

Zimbardo, P. (2008). *The time paradox: The new psychology of time that will change your life.* New York: Free Press.

Community and Community Development

A community is more than a social habitat in which people fill ecological niches. The community becomes the bearer of the self.

—WILLIAM BRUEGGEMANN

(1996, p. 117)

Community is defined in the *Social Work Dictionary* as "a group of individuals or families that share certain values, services, institutions, interests, or geographic proximity" (Barker, 2003). The kinds of community we are dealing with here in this book and this chapter are groupings of people based on a perceived common characteristic such as tribe, ethnicity, or religion, groupings that are not necessarily geographical. Community in this sense, accordingly, refers to a state of mind, a common identity. Most such communities have relatively the same cultural characteristics, whereas a geographical community, or community of place, can include a great deal of cultural diversity. One exception is discussed in the section on rural communities; even there, however, the focus is on interconnectedness in addition to place.

Thinking back to the cultural dimensions that framed most of the discussion in the previous chapter, recall the qualities that formed the right side of the continua—leisure, equality, stability, cooperation, collectivism, interconnectedness, spirituality, extended family, and compassion. These qualities are the ones that are associated more with happiness and a sense of wholeness than with the accumulation of wealth; they are also the very qualities that make for community and belongingness. Maslow (1968) included belongingness as the third level in his hierarchy of needs. Belonging to something—to a family, a peer group, a religion, an interest group—gives meaning and substance to human lives (Gilgun, 2004). Parker Palmer's (1998) definition of community corresponds to the one used here:

> Community cannot take root in a divided life. Long before community assumes external shape and form it must be present as seed in the undivided self: only as we are in communion with ourselves can we find community with others. Community is an outward and visible sign of an inward and invisible grace, the flowing of personal identity into the world of relationships. (p. 90)

The beauty of living in a community is that your friends are also friends with each other, and they share in the raising of children. Relationships extend over time rather than for just one purpose only. Cities and towns can enhance the sense of community by drawing people together for parades and band concerts such as shown in Figure 6.1.

Spatial units with clearly defined geographic boundaries are seemingly becoming less necessary to communities because of rapid electronic communication, ease of physical mobility, and globalization (Hardcastle & Powers, 2004). The community can be regarded as a social system, a system of values, expectations, and obligations; in such a community the child learns to be social and also learns who he or she is.

The Shorter Oxford English Dictionary (2007) differentiates three types of communities on the basis of *location*; having a common *identity*, religious or otherwise; and *shared* interest in pursuing common goals, professional or political. There may be overlap among these types of communities, such as when members of a close-knit ethnic community share a common living area. From the science of ecology, according to *The Shorter Oxford English Dictionary*, a community is a group of interdependent plants or animals growing together in natural conditions or inhabiting a specified locality.

Consistent with this book's theme of sustainability, a major consideration in our analysis of community is to what extent a community is sustainable. According to the UK government, which held the largest summit on the sustainable community ever in 2005, a sustainable community is a place where people want to live and work now and in the future. In his opening address to the summit, the Deputy Prime Minister (2005) presented a vision of future communities that are safer, cleaner, and greener than at present. Such communities connect the people with the places in which they live. Such places are inclusive; they provide housing that is adapted to people's needs and disabilities. Point number 20 of the Deputy Prime Minister's address is to "to link housing, transport and economic development at the regional level, help narrow the economic gap, create mixed communities, use land more efficiently, help protect the countryside, reverse the growth of out of town retail, and encourage people and retailers back into our city centres."

Is the sense of community being lost in today's world? In some ways, the answer is yes and in some ways, no. Communication technology facilitates community and social action organizing. So, of course, does location—being

Figure 6.1. Band concert, Cedar Falls, Iowa. Community events such as this weekly summer concert are enjoyed by people of all ages. Photo by Rupert van Wormer.

together at communal events, living nearby, sharing a common heritage. We begin this discussion with the major leading arguments that there is community breakdown, that community bonding is no longer what it was. Then we consider forces in today's world that reinforce the sense of community, including rural, religious, and minority forces and modern-day initiatives in community building.

Theories of Community Breakdown

Durkheim (1897/1952) coined the term *anomie*, or normlessness, to describe breakdowns in social norms in the social system caused by the industrial economic order. Congruently, under industrialization, the appetite for goods replaced the constraint put on people's earthly desires by the church. In his empirically based study of suicide rates, Durkheim found that the suicide rate in Protestant areas of Europe was higher than in Catholic areas and higher in times of economic shifts than in periods of stability. His prediction was that industrialized nations would have higher suicide rates than less industrialized nations. Indeed, this hypothesis holds today in contemporary international comparisons— several eastern European countries and Japan and Taiwan top the list (World Health Organization [WHO], 2009) as we learned in the previous chapter). Somewhat related studies on subjective well-being states, as reported by citizens of countries across the world, found that for a given nation, the level of happiness generally rises in accordance with economic development. Latin Americans expressed a relatively high level of happiness, however, that was out of proportion to their level of prosperity, while the former communist nations scored disproportionately low (Inglehart, Foa, & Peterson, 2008). The researchers speculated that strong spiritual beliefs and religious bonding in the high-scoring states help insulate them from economic hardship. Leading British economist Richard Layard (2005) concludes, based on his analysis of economic data from an earlier survey that reported similar results, that capitalism's emphasis on individualism and competition

has helped to diminish a feeling of a common good among people of various classes and societies. In summary, what the suicide and happiness studies seem to indicate is that, although prosperity brings security, some aspects of modernization are associated with a weakening of community ties.

A book that has received much press coverage, *Bowling Alone* by sociologist Robert Putnam (2001), uses the sport of bowling to serve as a metaphor for community togetherness. Years ago, as Putnam suggests, thousands of people belonged to bowling leagues, whereas today they are likely to bowl alone. That our community bonds have weakened is Putnam's basic claim, a claim bolstered by statistics showing that Americans attend public meetings less often than they used to and that they are more geographically mobile. He writes:

> Television, two-career families, suburban sprawl, generational changes in values— these and other changes in American society have meant that fewer and fewer of us find that the League of Women Voters, or the United Way, or the Shriners, or the monthly bridge club, or even a Sunday picnic with friends fits the way we have come to live. Our growing social-capital deficit threatens educational performance, safe neighborhoods, equitable tax collection, democratic responsiveness, everyday honesty, and even our health and happiness. (p. 367)

To the extent that this is true, the longer working hours and pressures on married couples to work two and even three jobs to support their families, combined with the high divorce rate, are likely causes. Counterarguments against Putnam's thesis are the large numbers of self-help groups that meet regularly across this nation and the revitalization of evangelical church communities. The wave of immigration over the past decade has brought new forms of community, besides, that might be replacing some of the older forms. More research is needed before the argument that our social life is diminishing can be made.

On one point we can probably all agree— modern technology has transformed the way people relate to each other and reduced the amount of or need for face-to-face interaction. First was the invention of the radio. The transformation of family life that came with this invention was graphically portrayed in Woody Allen's semiautobiographical 1987 movie, *Radio Days*. Families who would have gone out to stage shows and live music performances huddled around the radio set. Television was, of course, more captivating, even in its early black-and-white version, with a picture that had to be continuously monitored to prevent skipping. At least with only a few channels, the public all tended to be glued to the same programs. A common culture of sorts developed, a culture that was shared communally. This would all change, however, with the introduction of cable TV, with its possibility of dozens of choices around the clock. We gain as individuals through the proliferation of all these entertainment options, but we lose as a family and as a society. Programs that once were viewed by multiple generations are now targeted to specific age groups and interests. Family members often retreat to their own TV viewing; specialization has thus led to fragmentation and isolation.

In *Interpersonal Divide: The Search for Community in a Technological Age*, Bugeja (2005) examines the impact of the Internet, e-mail, computer games, TV, and cell phones on the sense of community in American life. His thesis, in a nutshell, is that the global village that was once anticipated has been replaced by a global shopping mall, that entertainment is now solitary as people rent DVDs to take home, that the few idolized entertainers are elevated to the status of icons, and that people are advised by self-help gurus to look inward for satisfaction. Bugeja (2005) urges that we spend less time hooked to technological equipment and more time conversing with people. Let us pursue this line of investigation with a consideration of the effect of some other aspects of globalization on community life.

The Impact of Globalization

Globalization is defined by the International Federation of Social Workers (IFSW, 2005) as "the process by which all peoples and communities come to experience an increasingly common economic, social, and cultural environment." Globalization, according to Hardcastle (2004), breaks down community. A global nonregulated market encourages a form of capitalism that is exploitative of both the social and the physical environment. Community cohesion is eroded, in Hardcastle's (2004) opinion, because corporations have no stake in any particular community or any reason to make investments in social welfare programs. What gains exist are concentrated at the top of the income distribution. Hardcastle (2004) writes from a social work perspective, a fact that Midgley (2004) indicates may be significant, inasmuch as globalization has often been defined in social work circles in narrow economic terms. This conceptualization is to the neglect of the larger trend toward greater international interdependence and integration, which are positives.

Globalization in itself is neither good nor bad; or, broadly speaking, it is both good and bad. To the extent that we are talking of enhanced global interconnectedness and exchange of products and ideas, the concept is positive. Concepts such as human rights, including women's rights and international law, are enlightening many areas in the world. From a community standpoint, the Internet itself is creating communities, even across continents, in cyberspace. People who are afflicted with certain diseases, for example, confide personal stories and exchange information through regular e-mail correspondence. And even across continents, such communication has brought people together in personal and meaningful ways, sometimes for dating and marriage. It has led to reunions among people who have found each other through a search engine and renewed long-lost friendships from years before.

Patterson (2004), a coordinator of social services in Romania, provides the example of the good that international nongovernmental organizations can do by working at the community level with abandoned children to find them homes. The new openness to the West, however, has led to a tremendous brain drain of professionals and paraprofessionals; this is splitting up communities, as many elderly persons are left behind. Sewpaul (2004), a social work educator from South Africa, speaks much more strongly of the effects of the demands of the global market with its bias in favor of corporate welfare over the welfare of citizens. The threat to community life in South Africa takes the form of "structural adjustments" by the world banks, which require reduction in social welfare spending to reserve capital. Gaps between the rich and the poor are increased thereby; this is divisive within the black population and constitutes a source of much discontent.

Some have argued that one reaction to the process of globalization, including the resentment of the world banks and the World Trade Organization for the harsh policies they impose on nations, has been an escalation of tensions and conflicts that escalate rapidly around the world (IFSW, 2005). War and violence, in turn, are associated with ecological destruction, as witnessed in the anticapitalist attacks on the World Trade Center in New York but also in the retaliatory bombings by the United States on Afghanistan and, later, Iraq. War and violence in any country, moreover, are associated with the erosion of the rights of dissenters, minority groups, and women. In a national military crisis, military spending takes precedence over all other spending. War wrecks families and produces an atmosphere of hate and distrust and divisions in the community that may never heal.

Let us now briefly consider one aspect of globalization—the corporation.

The Corporation and Community

The community is built on the personal relationship, the relationship as an end in itself, not a means to an end—such as is found in an exchange relationship or, as in business, a use of friendship for the sake of lining up prospects. Trust and intimacy, the cornerstones of community, are broken down when relationships are thus commodified.

Historically, the corporation arose as an entity subordinate to the state; corporations were chartered by the government to serve a certain function, such as building a bridge. Bakan (2004), in *The Corporation: The Pathological Pursuit of Profit and Power*, records the

history of the corporation. In brief, the corporation, which was set up to provide a public service, came to control the government that created it, mostly by rewriting the laws in calculated and ingenious ways. The *raison d'être* of the corporation is profit, not the common good (see Chapter 7 for further discussion of the corporate role in U.S. politics).

Corporate control of community life is represented in the community tax structure that favors big business and building construction (for example, of new jails and megaschools). Three key themes related to corporate growth—privatization, intensified productivity levels, and the technological revolution—have important implications for the community. The thrust toward privatization—the goal of which is cost savings through reliance on a low-paid workforce—is a factor that affects the human service work environment and service provision in hospitals, mental health clinics, prisons, nursing homes, and child welfare agencies. The services that make the community livable are gradually being eroded in this way. At the workplace itself, much of the easy socialization with members of the public has given way in the push for maximum worker output. The location of such work itself is less likely to be the local, family-owned grocery store or drugstore counter than the highly efficient chain, such as Wal-Mart or Target. Finally, the technological revolution can be considered a mixed blessing; much time is lost from the family through use of the Internet, but at the same time, the ease with which we can communicate and reunite with friends from childhood and organize through coalitions for political change enhances community ties by creating virtual communities.

Trends in Transportation and Education

A comparison of cities in terms of livability and sustainability reveals that towns laced with lakes, parkways, and accessible transportation systems are the most desirable places to live. Despite their destruction in the 1950s by the automobile industry, light-rail systems are making a comeback today in many cities that once had streetcars (Driehaus, 2008). San Diego started this trend some 20 years ago, but it continues in many large to mid-sized cities today. Baltimore, Maryland; Charlotte, North Carolina; Houston, Texas; and St. Louis, Missouri, for example, all have new light-rail and streetcar systems which are making a major contribution to the urban community. This form of mass transit offers an ideal way to get to work, while it reduces the environmental damage of automobile pollution. In terms of environmental impact, urban planners confirm that a rail line uses only one-quarter of the land needed for a six-lane freeway. The freeways, which slice through neighborhoods, filling the air with noise and pollution and devastating any sense of community, have already done irreparable damage to most American cities. However, any reduction in traffic on these highways can be an enormous benefit to the air as well as to the people.

Environmental health scientists Jackson, Wiland, and Bell (2009) relate the use of public space as a result of urban sprawl and the growth of highways with the state of public health in a society. In the twentieth century, as these researchers recall, federal funding of highway construction enabled the growth of the outer rings of cities and suburbs, while inner-city urban rail and trolley lines declined for lack of similar support. Government incentives that subsidized mortgages and highways encouraged home building subdivisions further out from the urban core. In conjunction with the construction of mega-malls, mega-schools, and mega-subdivisions, natural watersheds and vast stretches of forests and farmland have been lost. Many of the new subdivisions lack public parks, playgrounds, libraries, and nearby stores or cafés to bring people together. Among the relevant statistics gathered by Jackson et al. are as follows:

❥ Typical American families earn in real dollars roughly what they earned in the 1970s, but we spend much more now on motorized transportation.
❥ Since 1970, the U.S. population has increased 37 percent, but the distance traveled by the nation's fleet of personal automobiles and motorcycles increased 143 percent.

❥ From 1982 to 2000, the annual hours of highway traffic delay per person in urban areas increased from 16 hours to 62 hours per year.
❥ And Americans now work more hours than people in any other major industrial nation in the world. (p. 5)

Reviewing these data, it is easy to understand how time and resources are consumed by the distance between where people live and where they need to be to carry out their daily activities. The construction of major highways is not only a threat by allowing for mass mobility but also in breaking up established urban neighborhoods. When planning for a highway to pass through the heart of Greenwich Village in New York City, only the activism and community organizing efforts of a single woman saved the day for the community. *Wrestling With Moses: How Jane Jacobs Took on New York's Master Builder and Transformed the American City* by Anthony Flint (2009) documents the story of how one woman managed to defeat power broker Robert Moses's plans for urban renewal of her community. Her local battle soon grew into a local grassroots movement to protest projects that would displace thousands of families and businesses for the sake of "progress." Preventing the construction of the Lower Manhattan Expressway, a ten-lane elevated superhighway was a major triumph that inspired citizens across the country to protest similar projects in their own communities.

Related to transportation is the absence of sidewalks in many suburban communities. Sidewalks can be construed as a path among houses in a neighborhood. The presence of sidewalks encourages friends to walk to each other's houses and children to explore their neighborhood; and the sidewalks make safe the use of skates, scooters, and bicycles—even by the very young. Without sidewalks, for example, children are unable to walk or bicycle safely to and from neighborhood schools. But then, maybe there is no neighborhood school.

This brings us to a second destabilizing trend: the consolidation of our public schools. The consolidation means larger schools that are removed from the local community. This trend gains support from construction companies that build the mega-schools and support from politicians desperate for cost-saving measures and the belief that bigger is best. The trend toward large, distant schools began in the 1950s as people moved to the suburbs. School districts sought lower land costs and space for sports fields. The elimination of the schools that had glued "walkable" neighborhoods together was one unforeseen consequence (see Kaplan & Kaplan, 2003). The number of children who walked or biked to school dropped from nearly half in 1960 to 1 in 13 today, a contributing factor to obesity in children, along with reduced time spent in physical education (Centers for Disease Control and Prevention [CDC], 2005). The Institute of Medicine calls for the need for safe routes for walking and biking to schools (Committee on Prevention of Obesity in Children and Youth, 2004, p. 213).

Some advantages of small schools are that attention can be provided to kids who engage in bullying; that drug use is reduced as there are fewer drug users who can establish their own peer groups; and that greater opportunities for school leadership and athletic accomplishments exist. Catholic schools have served diverse populations in low-income areas with success for years.

Studies show that small public schools have higher attendance rates and lower dropout rates, benefits that are especially pronounced in lower-income communities (Ark, 2003). The Met High School in Providence, Rhode Island, has reduced the dropout rate significantly and helped motivate children to learn. Schools in Chicago and Philadelphia have seen equally promising results. Ark (2003) describes results in midtown Manhattan, which has reorganized its structure into a consortium of small schools, each with no more than 300 students: "Metal detectors have been replaced with teachers who know every student's name, and incidents of violence have plummeted" (p. 56).

The neighborhood school pulls the community together; families are united as their children make friends. Through involvement in extracurricular activities, students enrich the community and the pride that people take in the local talent. In Appalachia, for example, the community school plays a central role in the life of the community. Once the school is removed through centralization, which is now the trend, community life is shattered, as former Vermont school superintendent William Mathis (2009) asserts. In Iowa, the debate over the proposed elimination of small neighborhood and rural schools has been met with strong opposition, as reflected in a heated exchange in letters to the editor, the majority of which are along these lines:

> I taught in a school that required teachers to wear identity badges and there was at least one fight a day. We were also told not to work in the building after dark. Students at larger schools have more chances to fall through the cracks and not succeed because no one notices. Iowa is concerned about losing people. The more schools you consolidate and close, the more towns will die. How many people will move to a community that doesn't have a school? How many hours do you want students to ride a bus to get to that larger school so they could take Japanese because it is offered? Let's look at the quality and not the quantity of education. (Geitz, 2005, p. 20)

In many states, an effort to save older neighborhood schools and to build the new ones smaller is gaining strength (CDC, 2005). Thanks to the Bill and Melinda Gates Foundation, over $1 billion has been put into incentives to create small schools. Now we look at the other side of the argument that community ties are eroding and see to what extent they are thriving.

The Community Is Alive and Well

An antidote against alienation in modern, industrialized, globalized society is active involvement in a social network. Community has often been viewed as a kind of middle ground or context in which people's primary relationships, such as those in family and close friendship groups, come together with their secondary relationships, which are more specialized associations such as those in formal organizations (work, school, religion; Schriver, (2010)).

Five years after the publication of *Bowling Alone*, which documented the decline of community involvement, there are some signs of a new spirit of civic involvement (CDC, 2005; El Nasser, 2005). Among the signs of the new spirit are the increased rate of parent–school involvement; the large numbers of older parents with children; active neighborhood associations; American Association of Retired Persons (AARP) reports of increased rates of volunteer services offered by seniors; the huge expansion of membership in the mega-churches; and high rates of volunteering and low-paid community service work among today's youth.

The Virtual Community

People might be less involved in clubs and stay at home more, but there are other ways of connecting and relating. Rheingold (2003), author of *Smart Mobs*, documents the global influence of the Internet and other technology in enabling people to keep connected even when on the move from place to place. This capability is especially helpful for organizing and participating in political activities and street demonstrations. The Web site http://www.moveon.org, for example, has become a big factor in liberal political organizing. Mobile telephones are transforming youth culture, as is the availability of "WiFi" areas that create for the young a virtual social scene.

Rather than lament the loss of pub-culture camaraderie and the reduction in the number of bowling leagues, Hardcastle and Powers (2004) suggest that we appreciate the new models of community that are being formed. Through virtual organizations such as Internet support groups, social isolation is reduced, especially for persons with unusual self-identities such as transgendered people who can find others like themselves from across the globe.

Empirically based evidence from the Pew Internet Personal Networks and Community survey provides solid evidence in a comparison of individuals who actively use the new communication technologies with individuals of the same socioeconomic levels that do not (Hampton, Sessions, Ja Her, & Raine, 2009). Survey findings show that Americans are not as isolated as has been previously reported and that the use of the mobile phone and Internet is associated with larger and more diverse discussion networks. Long-term comparisons revealed that the extent of social isolation has hardly changed since 1985, and that only six percent of the adult population has no one with whom they can discuss important matters or whom they consider to be especially significant in their lives. A broader examination of people's full personal network—their strong and weak ties—found that Internet use in general and use of social networking services such as Facebook are associated with more diverse (racially and ethnically) social networks.

Technology continues to advance at exponential rates. In the fields of genetics, nanotechnology, and robotics, advances hold the promise of positive as well as negative changes in human life. Ultimately, the linking of humans to machines—such as with medical advances, memory enhancement, or learning—will lead to the development of a pairing of our biological selves and digital machines that radically expands our consciousness. As this book is written, we stand on the edge of technological changes that will affect our entire experience of community and other aspects of our social life.

Rural Communities

Bonding emerges from togetherness; as people see a lot of each other over time, attachments form, as do interdependencies—the teenager down the road does the babysitting; one man's wife takes care of his friend's wife, who has Alzheimer's. A child is lost in a cornfield, and the entire community is out searching. Relationships in one place—the local store—overlap with relationships elsewhere—as at church.

In studies of the rural community, the most oft-cited conceptualization is that of Tönnies (1887/1963). His division into ideal types of rural and urban is helpful because it focuses on ways of relating and also offers a theoretical, ideal typical scheme built on fairly universal characteristics. The ideal types that Tönnies delineated were the *Gemeinschaft* and *Gesellschaft*. *Gesellschaft* relationships are ways of relating defined by contract, such as those involved in exchange of needed goods, money, or services. Relationships that develop here are pragmatic, goal oriented, and formal within a bureaucratic system. Such relationships characterize life in the urban community. *Gemeinschaft* relationships, according to this formulation, are just the opposite, based on shared experiences, traditions, and a sense of mutual responsibility that arises from that tradition. The tradition of mutual aid is one that transcends the rural consciousness and that is especially pronounced in farm communities.

Farmers of all races and ethnicities historically have maintained their common welfare through offering mutual aid in times of need—crop failures, barn burnings, illness. Men have generally been responsible for the heavy labor, and women have bonded together for childbirth, child care, cooking, and other nurturing activities. Such traditional communities are almost a thing of the past in today's highly mobile society. Many countries of the Global South, Native American tribes who live on reservations, and the kibbutzim of Israel follow this way of life. Such communities are characterized by commonality of belief, rituals, and social bonding beyond what is found in most of contemporary society (Meenaghan & Gibbons, 2000). This sense of communalism is preserved to some extent in many rural areas and maintains its pure form among the Amish today and among some organic farmers. Both the Amish (or Mennonites) and organic farmers often have fresh farm produce for sale at farmers' markets (see Figure 6.2 for a typical example).

Tönnies shared the view of other early sociologists that modernization was leading us away from *Gemeinschaft* and into an urbanized social order. Often a clash of values occurs as urbanization and suburbanization lead to a cultural conflict between what Becker (1957) termed the *sacred* (rural reluctance to change) and the *secular* (urban acceptance of more flexible moral standards). Thomas Frank (2004) wrote of this same phenomenon in his explanation of conservative rural voting patterns in *What's the Matter With Kansas?*

According to the U.S. Census Bureau (2001), just under 20 percent of the population is rural,

Figure 6.2. This farmers' market is a popular social gathering place that also supports the small farm and boosts the sale of organic produce. Photo by Rupert van Wormer.

a slight decrease from 1990. The Canadian breakdown is comparable. Poverty is a constant in rural parts of North America; most of the poor counties in the United States, in fact, are rural (Hardcastle & Powers, 2004). Most of the rural poor are white, in contrast to the United States as a whole, in which a disproportionate number of poor families are African American and Latino. Predictions are that rural localities will continue to lose population as the natural resource base continues to decline and low-skill workers face increasing competition for well-paying jobs.

Problems from industrial competition that lead to factory outsourcing and problems in the farm economy are largely responsible for the kind of devastation seen in rural America. Rural factories cut 4.6 percent of their payrolls in 2002 and closed about 140 plants (U.S. Bureau of Labor Statistics, 2003). But things were only to get much worse. In Iowa in Boone, Mount Pleasant, Ottumwa, and other places with fewer than 30,000, for example, residents have lost nearly 20,000 factory jobs since 2007, when the current recession first began (Eller & Eckhoff, 2009). The hope is that the loss in manufacturing jobs will be replaced by employment in renewable energy enterprises. Earlier competition from cheap labor in other parts of the world continues to take a toll as well.

Eighty percent of the farmlands in Iowa, a state in which 90 percent of the land is farmed, is owned by people who live in the state (Rood, 2005). Farm families support the schools and local businesses, and people who live on and work the land could be expected to take better care of it than absentee landlords. For generations in Iowa, farmland has been not just a source of livelihood for rural Iowans; "it was their foundation, their roots" (Rood, 2005, p. 1AA). Unfortunately, according to agriculture experts, a transition is occurring in favor of large farms owned by landlords who live out of state. Modern technologies, related indebtedness, and increased global competition weigh heavily on the aging generation of farmers. This shift in ownership is expected to have serious repercussions on the farm community. Children will no longer grow up on the farm.

"Stress Pushes Rural Iowans to the Brink," as a headline in *The Des Moines Register* announced (Fitzgerald, 2003). Even though crop yields are excellent, "economic pressures are pushing farmers to the brink emotionally and financially and stymieing the next generation of farmers" (p. A1). Evidence is in the form of the number of calls to Iowa Concern, a hotline established during the 1980s farm crisis, which has now set a record, with 951 rural residents seeking legal, financial, and mental health advice. The one industry that makes a difference to some rural communities is the massive prison expansion that is creating jobs for local residents and helping keep the population statistics up. (Counties that can keep their population numbers up in this way receive better representation in Congress and qualify for funding passed on such statistics.)

The focus of this section is not on poverty, however, but on community bonding. Even under the circumstances of out-migration and the farm crisis, the natural helping networks survive. A community survey called Voices of Rural America, for example, found that rural residents were more likely to view their civic and service clubs as more effective problem solvers—sources of information about health care, jobs, and so forth—than did those in urban communities (Hardcastle & Powers, 2004). Other studies have found, similarly, that when rural families have problems, they may first go to clergy, family, and friends, and only then to social services (Strickland, Welshimer, & Sarvela, 2008).

Racial and Ethnic Communities

Think again of the community as a system, a whole that in essence almost takes on a personality, a character, of its own. In such a configuration a network of social relations links the members of the group. When people are of the same ethnicity, especially one that differs from the mainstream culture, they often construct boundaries around themselves to enhance their ethnic identity and to protect themselves and their identity from absorption into the mainstream culture. The ethnic community further can help members to meet economic needs through the sharing of resources and to preserve their cultural values. Often members of such minority groups are accused of being unfriendly or "always hanging around together."

The African American community is a diverse and multidimensional community that includes subgroups from countries in Africa and the Caribbean, people of a variety of shades of skin color, and the same class differences found in all racial and ethnic groups. Billingsley and Morrison-Rodiguez (2007) examine the black community as a social system of roles bound together in a pattern of mutual interrelatedness. The black church and the black family, from this perspective, are units that work in harmony to sustain the sense of community, church, and family, thus becoming mediating structures between African Americans and the mainstream society that often functions as a barrier to full integration. Black traditions, customs, and values are rooted in a rich African heritage, and they play a significant role in uniting African American families, communities, and organizations (Manning, 2001).

Mutual aid among African Americans is based on a cultural heritage that has stressed strong extended family ties and the tradition of adopting nonrelatives into the family network. Individual interests were not placed above those of the group; cooperation and sense of community prevailed. Before the Civil War, there were half a million free persons of African descent in the United States (and 4 million slaves); half of the freed slaves lived in the South (Day, 2008). A great deal of charity work was done by these free blacks; they had churches, relief associations, and societies for mutual aid. Among the slaves, obligations to kin and a general altruistic behavior promoted the collective survival of a people in a cruel and racist society.

Earlier we read of the Native American sense of interconnectedness with all other creatures of the universe and their reliance in ceremonies on the metaphor of the Medicine Wheel to represent the circle of life. Sacred landscapes, rivers, forests, stories, songs, medicinal plants, dances, and symbols are often at the center of indigenous spirituality and play a role in helping First Nations peoples find wholeness and healing their cultures (Yellow Bird, 2001). In a sentence, Brave Heart (2001) defines what she

calls the collective ego ideal: This ideal member of the Lakota tribe "is an interdependent and generous person who places the good of the Nation before oneself, can manifest bravery and endure suffering for the good of others, embraces the sacredness of women and children, communicates with the spirit world, and has compassion for the animal world" (p. 164).

Japanese society is generally understood to be highly consensual and collectivist. In Japanese, *sekentei* consists of two words: *seken* and *tei*. *Seken* means society, community, and the public, and *tei* refers to reputation and honor (Asai & Kameoka, 2005). In Japanese culture, there is constant concern about others' evaluations of one's behavior. Relevant to social work, there is often a sense of shame when family caregivers use formal services.

Within the Latin American subgroups— Mexicans, Puerto Ricans, Cubans, and others— who often live in the same neighborhoods, the sense of community is strong. Perhaps for this reason, Puerto Rico, affectionately referred to as the "Island of Enchantment," is the region that is home to the people in the world with the highest level of subjective sense of well-being (World Values Survey, 2004). Despite their low socioeconomic status in the United States and their lack of sufficient access to health care services, the health of Latinos is similar to or better than that of non-Hispanic whites (Morales, Kington, Valdez, & Escarce, 2002). The only possible explanation for this phenomenon is the strength that comes from family caring and interdependency. The tradition of folk healing among Latino families is a major source of empowerment as well.

A major issue today in some rural communities is the impact of mass immigration. Postville, Iowa, is a town that was settled primarily by German Americans, a homogeneous farming community. When a kosher meatpacking plant moved to the town, the culture of the town became more complex with the influx of Hassidic Jews. Employing over 800 workers at its peak, Agriprocessors became the nation's largest kosher meat producer (Grey, Devlin, & Goldsmith, 2009). Workers at the plant were recruited from Guatemala and Mexico. After some difficult adjustments, these new immigrants with their young families became active participants in community life. Then the federal government moved in, conducted a raid, and forced the plant to close. Read Box 6.1 to learn of the impact of these now historic events that took place in Postville, Iowa in 2008.

Box 6.1 The Impact of an Immigration Raid on a Small Town: The Case of Postville, Iowa

Cindy Juby and Laura Kaplan

Meatpacking plants have developed a tremendous dependence on immigrant workers in the United States. Because many immigrants are desperate for any kind of job, they are willing to work at these dangerous and physically demanding occupations that generally attract few locals (Grey, Devlin, & Goldsmith, 2009). As a result of the high number of unauthorized immigrants employed at meatpacking plants, they are often the target of worksite raids.

On May 12, 2008, one such raid occurred in the small town of Postville, Iowa, and was, at that time, the largest worksite raid in U.S. history. Three hundred and eighty-nine (389) unauthorized workers, the majority from Guatemala and Mexico, were arrested at the Agriprocessors kosher meat processing plant by Immigration and Customs Enforcement (ICE), the primary investigative arm of Homeland Security. Charges against these workers included identity theft and Social Security fraud (Schulte, Jacobs, & Strong, 2008).

While individuals were significantly impacted by the raid—many of the children were severely traumatized when their parents were taken away— the community suffered as well. The community effects could be categorized into two areas: structural and economic. Prior to the raid, Postville was structurally different from the rest of the state; it was a diverse town in a largely homogeneous, predominantly European American state.

The Hassidic Jewish owners of the meat processing plant moved to Postville, challenging the town. These new community members were completely unfamiliar and confusing. For example, these new people had unusual appearances; would not eat food their neighbors offered in welcome; had very different behaviors around Sabbath rituals;

they brought an unknown lifestyle to Postville. As the 2001 PBS documentary *Multiculturalism in Postville Iowa: When Cultures Collide* points out, the Hassidic Jews set up their own school and held their own celebrations, including a parade. The addition of the workers from Guatemala and Mexico was met with initial hostility by the town. But as the documentary pointed out, the local businesses thrived and the townspeople gradually adjusted to being a mosaic of diversity. Postville has received much national recognition, and university courses on diversity commonly show the PBS documentary. Now there is a new 2009 PBS documentary to show, this one concerning the upheaval caused by the raid—*Frontline: Guatemala: A Tale of Two Villages: U.S. Immigration Raid Leaves History Mark*.

The fact that a large portion of the minority groups in Postville were unauthorized immigrants and that the owners of the meatpacking plant had hired them illegally made the newcomers vulnerable to prosecution. The fact that they had falsified documents made them vulnerable to more severe penalties than other undocumented workers. Following the raid, in which arrested workers were detained far away from their homes, a dramatic change took place that affected the entire community. Children were taken out of school by scared parents who feared they would be arrested next. The removal of the workers meant that Agriprocessors had to seek workers elsewhere because few locals sought employment at the plant. What resulted was another influx of minorities into the town. The addition of homeless people from the South, and a whole new group of immigrants, many still of Latino descent but now including Africans, Bosnians, and others, challenged the small town once again. While Postville is resilient and has demonstrated an ability to adapt to changes in demographics, this dramatic transformation in a short period of time is requiring substantial adjustment for the community to assimilate to the differing cultures.

One interesting aspect of the immigration raid has been the role that the Catholic church has played in providing community support and help to the many families that were left homeless and with no means of earning a living. While some of the immigrants were immediately deported, several more were mandated to remain in the United States to attend future court hearings. Some of those hearings were not scheduled to take place until the following year. Because the immigrants were not allowed to work during that time but were required to remain in the area, many families were left homeless and jobless. In the meantime, the local church had taken on the major responsibility of ensuring the basic needs of those involved. A priest from the church reported:

> It seems like now we're more of a social services agency, in that we have so many people in our community that are really dependent on contributions that are coming in from all over the country, and some even from outside the country, from which we have to provide for all of their needs—all the way from rent all the way up to utilities, food, emergency medical situations sometimes, emergency dental. They pretty much depend on us.

While there was a great deal of support from the community, the resources were limited and began running out within a few months of the raid. Additionally, the raid had negatively affected the economy of Postville, sending the community spiraling toward economic collapse, the closing of local businesses, and the threat of closing the local school. Although the economy of the town may be preserved in the future with the opening of a newly managed Kosher meatpacking plant, the community of Postville will never be the same.

References

Grey, M.A., Devlin, M., & Goldsmith, A. (2009). *Postville, U.S.A.: Surviving diversity in small-town America*. Waukesha, WI: Ingram Publishing.
Shulte, G., Jacobs, J., & Strong, J. (2008, May 14). Town of 2273 wonders: What happens to us now? *The Des Moines Register* (Iowa), p. 1A.

Printed with permission of Cindy Juby, Assistant Professor of Social Work, University of Northern Iowa and Laura Kaplan, Associate Professor of Social Work, University of Northern Iowa.

To what extent is diversity an asset to the community and to what extent does it hurt civic life? As we learned from the history of Postville, diversity enriches a community once trust is built up as the townspeople get used to the differences and come to appreciate the benefits that the newcomers bring to the community.

The newcomers, for their part, need to become acculturated to a certain extent and to conform their behavior to the community's norms. Sometimes as is happening all across Europe, however, ethnic diversity has brought conflict, discrimination by the natives, crime, and distrust within the community. A controversial study by Robert Putnam (2007) that was based on interviews of nearly 30,000 people across the United States concludes that the greater the diversity in a community, the fewer people vote and the less they volunteer to work on community projects. Putnam did not find that the increased contact with people of different backgrounds led to greater understanding and harmony nor did he find increased conflict among the residents. Rather, what impressed Putnam in his interviews was the apathy of the people living in the diversified neighborhoods and their lack of community involvement. To offset such tendencies, Putnam recommends government projects such as expanding English-language instruction and investing in community centers and other places for meaningful interaction across ethnic lines.

The Gay/Lesbian Community

June is the unofficial month for celebrating gay pride throughout the United States and many other countries. The rainbow-colored balloons symbolize the diversity among people and also the bonding among people who are gay, lesbian, bisexual, and transgendered. To get a sense of the community spirit of members of this group, read this letter by the head of Capital City Pride (of Des Moines, Iowa) that was addressed to the Iowa gay community concerning the reason for pride fests:

> What do we have to be proud of? Our community . . . our family . . . our lives? In order to have pride in ourselves we have to understand what defines us, and what we like about ourselves. . . . Our community, which is our family, has plenty to be proud of. We have accomplishments, we have creativity, we have diversity, and most of all, we have spirit. That is a spirit that cannot be

broken. A spirit that binds us together into a community to be proud of. (*Accessline*, p. 1)

In Iowa, *Accessline: Iowa's Gay Newspaper*, which is published monthly, provides relevant news coverage and announces to the community such events as the pride celebrations, the Matthew Shepard Scholarship Awards, and gay- and lesbian-friendly churches in the area. The paper is distributed free of charge at coffee shops, counseling centers, churches, and other gathering places across the state. It is sponsored by law firms, realtors, and restaurants who welcome business from gay and lesbian patrons.

The Deaf Community

Among communities of persons who are considered disabled, the Deaf community stands alone in having its own language, American Sign Language (ASL; Johnson & Rhodes, 2009). Language denotes culture, as it automatically sets up a boundary around group members based on communication. The use of ASL, often taught in residential schools, has the effect of cementing the culture and creating a special worldview. To define deafness totally in terms of a hearing impairment is to deny the existence of a whole community and culture. In contrast to persons who label themselves "hard of hearing," those who identify as Deaf do not view themselves as handicapped or disabled but as members of a close-knit group (Baruch, Kaufman, & Hudson, 2008). In fact, a recent survey of over 100 medical clinics specializing in fertility treatment through embryo implantation found that 3 percent used genetic testing to select an embryo for the presence of a disability—deafness or dwarfism. The reason is to have children who resemble their parents. Members of the Deaf community define deafness as a cultural rather than an audiological term. Some deaf parents adamantly resist having their children receive a cochlear implant, a small electronic device that helps children with little or no hearing to pick up sounds. The conflict among extended and nuclear family members over whether to have this surgery perfomed is the theme of the remarkable 2001 public

broadcasting service (PBS) documentary *Sound and Fury*. As revealed in this emotionally charged film, a common language, shared experiences of alienation from the larger, hearing society, social participation, and a sense of cultural identity are recognized criteria for membership in this unique group. (For a relevant personal narrative, see "Growing Up 'Deaf'" in Chapter 4).

Religious Communities

The United States, historically, as we saw earlier, has always been one of the most religious of the industrialized nations, a fact that has persisted over the years. Whereas attendance has slipped in many mainstream Protestant churches, the upsurge in evangelical and fundamentalist worshippers—especially in mega-churches—is of historic proportions. According to Rick Warren (2002), a Southern Baptist pastor of a mega-church with a weekly attendance of over 15,000, more Americans will attend a religious service than all the Americans who attend sporting events over an entire year—combined. Johnson and Rhodes (2009) discuss the consequences for the society and for the individual members in terms of the negatives and the positives. On the negative side, "how religion obstructs well-being" (p. 76), the authors list the subordination of women in the three monotheistic religions, the "hate the sin, love the sinner" response to homosexuality, and the overzealous proselytizing by some sects. On the positive side, in discussing "how religion promotes well-being," the authors single out a number of factors conducive to community integration. Religion:

▶ Establishes values of cooperation, altruism, and often social justice
▶ Provides help for the poor, immigrant asylum seekers, the sick and disabled, orphans, and so forth
▶ Refers members of the church, synagogue, or mosque to social services, jobs, and training opportunities as needed
▶ Provides meeting space to nonprofit organizations
▶ Helps members retain a sense of ethnic identity in many cases

▶ Provides a refuge for specific populations shut out of some mainstream churches, such as gays and lesbians

▶ Can serve as a cradle for the civil rights movement, as did the African American churches (pp. 76–77)

Jewish people share both an ethnic and religious heritage. Judith Lee (2001) cites Elie Wiesel, who, in speaking of the importance of community to people who have weathered centuries of oppression, says that a Jew would be like a withered branch without his or her community. Faith, community, and a shared value system, as Lee further notes, enabled Jews to survive generations of continuing discrimination, including the mass genocide of the Holocaust.

Billingsley and Morrison-Rodriguez (2007) look at the historic leadership role of the black church for the African American community in times of crisis. The church has been not only a spiritual resource but also a social institution with the capacity to touch all aspects of family life. In structurally impoverished rural areas, as the authors indicate, smaller churches offer an alternative resource for black families when other social institutions fail to meet their needs. Apart from providing what aid they could to needy families, their focus would be to organize media campaigns on behalf of social policy influence and to partner with the government in providing faith-based programming and other essential services. Continuing in this same vein, let us explore some other avenues of community development.

Building Community Bonds

Mutual aid groups often have a community development component as they are drawn to some form of social action directed at the source of the problem. For persons who have been oppressed, as bell hooks (2001) tells us, healing occurs through collective organization and personal testimony. This is what empowerment is all about. Empowerment practice follows a basic premise: Change the world, change yourself. At the societal level, the goal of empowerment practice is social justice and a

reduction of social inequality (Gutiérrez & Lewis, 1999).

Community building is achieved, as Lee (2001) suggests, "through increased participation and the enlivening of people to respond to the needs of all members of the community" (p. 399). Ideally all citizens are included in the process, even the most marginalized or socially excluded. *Conflict resolution*, which is concerned with efforts directed at reducing grievances between persons and groups, often when there are power imbalances, may be a starting point or parallel process to contributing toward building what Lee calls—following Gandhi and Martin Luther King, Jr.—"the beloved community."

Sometimes a part of the goal of building community bonds might include humanizing existing institutions. A case example from Black Hawk County, Iowa, involved a small group of people whose actions seemed futile at the time but that were to bear fruit almost a decade later. The small group consisted of former staff members of the women's shelter, 13 people who were fired or forced to resign due to their feminist leanings. The court watch, "take back the night" and other public informational drives against violence toward women, and hospital and policy advocacy programs all came to an abrupt end. The former employees went to the press; a series of articles followed accusing the agency of mismanagement. After joining with interested social work faculty, a social action group was formed. An alternative hotline for battered women and rape victims was formed and staffed with volunteers.

The goal of the grassroots activity was to obtain funding from the state. For years, the established organization received the bulk of the funding, however, while group members got involved in related small-scale, statewide grant-funded services. Ten years later, according to news accounts, the women's shelter and their parent organization were denied grant money due to a series of violations and omissions; these included inadequate staff training, fiscal irresponsibility, and lack of assistance to victims ("Problems at Women's Shelter," 2005). The original group, semidormant for years but not forgotten by authorities, was invited to reapply for the grant money and did so under the auspices of an established abuse, prevention, and advocacy organization from a nearby town. This organization, Seeds of Hope, which relies on aggressive outreach, safe houses, court advocacy, and so on, received the entire annual grant of $200,000 (Downs, 2005). Successful ingredients in this story included whistle-blowing to authorities about inadequate services, group solidarity, reliance on extensive press coverage during key periods in decision making, and patience in waiting for the investigative bodies and funding sources to do their work.

A second example of grassroots activity that paid off over time concerns policy reform at the state level. This movement got its impetus through alliances between the African American community and state legislators. The issue was the restoration of voting rights for more than 50,000 disenfranchised persons who had been convicted of felonies upon completion of their prison and parole terms. As social worker David Goodson (2005) explains:

> I was hosting a radio show, and the general counsel to the (Iowa) governor was a guest on the show to talk of African Americans who were essentially disenfranchised. I (as an ex-convict) was working on a seven- or eight-page application at the time for the lengthy process of obtaining a pardon so I could have my rights restored. Many of the ex-prisoners are illiterate or uneducated and never could fill out these forms without help. The general counsel took the information back to the governor, and the process was simplified. That was the first step in making for change. Then I worked with local legislators to keep the voting issue on the front burner. When I talked to Howard Dean in his campaign in Iowa for president, he reminded me that voting was not a privilege but a right. In Vermont, because voting is considered a civic duty, inmates are encouraged to vote while they are incarcerated.

In July 2005, Governor Tom Vilsack of Iowa issued an executive order restoring voting rights to Iowans with criminal convictions. Many are

hailing the action as a civil rights victory (Eby, 2005). From the community's standpoint, such successful grassroots activity contributes to empowerment of the people and provides proof that through organization, long-term planning, and unity, structural roadblocks to the expression of one's civil rights can be overcome. Not only was the community's sense of powerlessness diminished but the organizing also raised their stake in and connection with the rest of society.

The next example is of a community effort that involves a whole town, and an unlikely one at that—Tupelo, Mississippi. In *Better Together*, the authors (Putnam, Feldstein, & Cohen, 2003) sought to find what Putnam (2001) had earlier claimed was so rare in today's world—social capital, or *communitarianism*. They found their example in rural Mississippi. What is so remarkable about the Tupelo story is that, with so few resources (except for wood), this once poor, rural segregated Mississippi town grew to become an internationally recognized magnet for industrial investment. The town even managed to lure a company from Mexico to relocate in Tupelo. The roots of Tupelo's transformation can be traced to a man with a mission—George McLean—who had sufficient wealth and connections to make things happen. Buying the local newspaper was the first step in shaping public opinion and building trust. Other strategies included financing educational and vocational initiatives, promoting consensus through organizing town meetings, and enticing business leaders to invest in local enterprises. Collum (2004) attributes much of the economic success to the city's development of social consciousness; this included interracial cooperation and collaboration, consensus building, charitable giving, and the support of the locally owned media. The town newspaper openly states its dedication "to the service of God and mankind" and takes this proclamation literally. The progressiveness of the paper surprised Collum, who wrote of his discovery in this Deep South state of "a thoroughly professional small city paper that, when it betrayed a bias seemed firmly in favor of public education, racial reconciliation, and a bottom-up vision of economic development" (2004, p. 33). A rare alliance of capitalists and workers, combined with participatory involvement at every level of this booming community, has put the town of Tupelo on the map, a map that goes beyond rural Mississippi (Putnam et al., 2003).

In May 2007, a monster tornado flattened the town of Greensburg, Kansas; barely a house or building was left standing. Today, thanks to the leadership of one persistent environmentalist, Greensburg is taking its name to heart and striving to become a green community of the future (Shattuck, 2008). Crisis became an opportunity, and within weeks, residents were riding a wave of environmentalism that had been stirring even before the storm. Today the city leaders are using solar and wind technologies to harness power and geothermal heat. They're also conserving energy by building with solid concrete, using more natural light, and installing better insulation and state-of-the-art windows. According to a media story entitled "The Greenest Town in America," Greensburg is fast becoming the most energy-efficient, environmentally sensitive municipality in the United States, a sustainable development laboratory that is creating interest worldwide (Graham, 2009). Eco-friendly industries are moving in. Greensburg is rising from the rubble environmentally and psychologically.

To the extent that the Tupelo and Greensburg stories illustrate consensus in decision making, the next example illustrates the viability of conflict theory. This is about the struggle for social justice against resistance by the state; it is a meeting of resistance with resistance. The Philadelphia-based Kensington Welfare Rights Union (KWRU) began as a movement of the people in 1991 to end poverty. It is a return to the tactics of mass social activism characterized by well-organized and publicized marches, the demand for rights under the law (international law), and other forms of public protest, including freedom bus rides across the nation. This is a movement that has turned welfare recipients and former welfare recipients into social activists. Much of the focus is on the need for housing for homeless families in Philadelphia.

Social workers involved in the movement see themselves not as advocates but as allies, seeking collaboration in all dimensions of the necessary work in organizing to end economic oppression. Rallies and teach-ins focused on ways the United States was in violation of the U.N. Declaration of Human Rights (Leland, 2009). The KWRU, as described in Chapter 2, is one of more than 50 groups that have come together in a network called the Poor People's Economic Rights Campaign that focuses on the need for affordable housing. Taking advantage of the huge number of homes that are unoccupied due to foreclosures, members of this and other well-organized groups operate openly, screening residents for potential problems such as drug addiction and willingness to work doing repairs around the house. Most of the homes are in poor neighborhoods where the neighbors are more accepting of the squatters (Leland, 2009). (For information about the campaign, see http://www.kwru.org.)

The involvement of social workers and students of social work in such mass organizing efforts is consistent with the educational policy of the Council on Social Work Education (CSWE, 2008), which stipulates that "social work's purpose is actualized through its quest for social and economic justice, the prevention of conditions that limit human rights, the elimination of poverty, and the enhancement of the quality of life for all persons" (p.1). Especially relevant to the quest for social justice is the indigenously derived movement known as restorative justice.

Restorative Justice as Community Justice

A major macro-level concern to any community is the presence (or fear) of crime. Crime and criminality within any social group break the sense of trust among the group members and contribute to estrangement of people on either side of the law. The standard criminal justice process often exacerbates community divisions. The restorative justice movement often works in conjunction with established institutions, in some cases to undo the damage of the standard processes, especially from the standpoint of the victim of crime. What restorative justice does is to bring parties to a dispute together for some form of resolution or peacemaking and thereby, it is hoped, to unite opposing elements.

Restorative justice is a form of community justice that reflects community values. One of its major goals is to restore the torn fabric of community and to restore a sense of wholeness to all those affected by crime. Repairing the harm done to the victim and community is an important part of the process, to make the offender accountable to both the victim and community. Victims, offenders, and communities are the three central parties in restorative justice. Part of this process of reconciliation enables victims to express and offenders to understand the harm done by criminal acts. Family group conferencing is one of the major forms of restorative justice, as was discussed in Chapter 4. Other commonly used forms are: *victim-offender conferencing*, which may take place in a prison as victims and/or their families meet with the offender in a ritualized session to learn details of the crime and reach an understanding; *circle sentencing*, a First Nations people's custom to promote peacemaking and healing and to determine the appropriate sanction for a wrongdoing; and *community reparations*, which offers reparations for violations of human rights, often for historical wrongs.

Restorative justice operates at the macro level to help whole societies heal in the aftermath of mass injustice. The international community has struggled to find acceptable and sustainable ways to help societies recover from violent conflicts so that future generations can find peace. Androff (in press) traces the new global trend of restitution for historical injustices, a trend based on the belief that nations as moral beings must acknowledge their past wrongdoing if they are ever to get beyond it. Examples are reparations made in 1988 by the U.S. Congress to Japanese Americans for revoking their freedom in World War II and the truth telling and public confessions for crimes committed under the apartheid regime in South Africa. The United Nations has been a prime mover in endorsing the principles of restorative justice. Social workers who have stayed on the sidelines of such great developments can contribute to Truth and Reconciliation Commissions by eliciting testimonials from victims of mass violence and advocacy for compensation for the survivors of war crimes. (See relevant documents on truth and reconciliation commissions at http://www.restorativejustice.org.)

Common to all these forms of restorative justice is an emphasis on face-to-face communication, truth telling, personal empowerment, and healing by all parties to the wrongdoing. Around the globe, such restorative processes are offering hope for more constructive responses to harm inflicted by humans on one another. Rooted in the rituals of indigenous populations and Canadian Mennonite forms of resolving conflict, restorative justice advocates nonadversarial means of settling disputes; the goal is to restore individual lawbreakers to the community rather than isolating them from it. The active involvement of family members of both the offending and injured parties is one of the most striking aspects of this form of peacemaking. Today, across North America, Britain, Northern Ireland, and Australia, restorative justice is emerging quietly to take its place alongside mainstream criminal justice. In the United States, Vermont and Minnesota have been the most committed to system-wide endorsement of restorative principles. Among cultural groups, Native Americans, like their Canadian counterparts, have done the most to bring this peacemaking process to their people. This trend is a movement back to the old ways, such as Navajo traditions in which issues were resolved through process and not by rules but through relationships (Mirsky, 2004). "Tribal courts are important to community and to nation building," according to Judge Joseph Flies-Away (Mirsky, 2004, p. 5). Central to Indian justice is the role of the sacred; the ritual of prayer helps create a safe atmosphere conducive to trust and truth telling.

Restorative justice, at its core, is a community-building enterprise, the outcomes of which should be an increased sense of community by its members. Karp, Lane, and Turner (2002) provide a case study from Ventura County, California, of a community victim-offender model designed to help juvenile offenders on probation be integrated into the community. An onsite restorative justice advocate-mediator works to get victims to participate in the process. In one example in which a youth stole something from a department store, the mediator set up a meeting in the store manager's office. In this meeting, the manager asked for an apology and scolded the boy but then agreed to let him work in the store for 8 hours to help pay his restitution. This program depends largely on community support and involvement in this predominantly Latino community with an extremely high crime rate among young people. Services are located within the heart of the community; services include job searches, tutoring, and sports for high-risk youths. Probation services are informal, so there are no bulletproof glass, metal detectors, and so forth. Community volunteers are involved in the various projects. As the authors define community justice:

> We do not only ask, "Why is the individual misbehaving?" But also, "What are the social influences or pressures that make people in one community more likely to offend but people in another community less likely to offend?" We do not just ask, "What kind of person are you?" but "What kind of place is this?" (Karp et al., 2002, pp. 1–2)

With this holistic approach, the focus is on neighborhoods and comprehensive strategies for improving the social environment. Ohmer, Beck, and DeMasi (2008) discuss how restorative strategies can serve to build collective efficacy in a high-crime neighborhood. Research shows that by means of community trainings of residents, consensus building, and organizing, violence prevention efforts can be successful. Peacemaking circles were used to resolve conflict and build community bonding.

What does empirical research show about the effectiveness of these alternative forms of justice? Most evaluations have been done in relation to victim-offender conferencing. The findings, both of victim satisfaction and reduced rates of offender recidivism, have been highly favorable (Umbreit, Vos, Coates, & Brown, 2003). The social work profession in the United Sates (acting years behind social workers in New Zealand and Canada) is beginning to take notice of this far more humane form of meeting victims' and offenders' needs than standard Anglo-American criminal justice practices. (In Box 6.2, "Restorative Justice: A Model of Healing," Sheryl Fred recognizes these dynamic restorative initiatives.)

Box 6.2 Restorative Justice: A Model of Healing—Philosophy Consistent With Social Work Values

Sheryl Fred, News Staff

Paula Kurland has said that she died on September 13, 1986, the day her 21-year-old daughter Mitzi was brutally stabbed to death in Austin, Texas.

It wasn't until she met her daughter's killer 2 weeks before his execution in 1998 that she admitted to feeling alive again. Although she could never forgive Jonathan Nobles's actions, after a 5–hour discussion with him, Kurland was surprised to feel not only relief but also some level of compassion for the man about to face lethal injection.

"I walked out of death row a new person," she told PBS in a 2003 report on the death penalty.

This widely publicized case is one of the more striking examples of the power of restorative justice—a relatively nascent movement that turns the traditional criminal justice model on its head. Instead of focusing solely on retribution, restorative justice emphasizes truth, accountability, and, most important, healing for the victim, offender, and community.

Restorative justice, the roots of which lie largely in indigenous traditions, comes in many forms. Family group conferencing, derived from the Maori people of New Zealand, is an alternate form of sentencing that involves the victim, offender, and the family and friends of both in resolving a criminal or delinquent incident. Peacemaking circles, based on Native American talking circles, bring people together to speak as equals about troubling issues in their communities.

What Kurland and Nobles engaged in is called victim-offender mediation (VOM), also referred to as victim-offender dialogue, reconciliation, or conferencing. Generally used post-adjudication in cases of everything from petty crime to rape and murder, VOM involves counseling victims and offenders and then bringing them together for a frank discussion. Usually run by nonprofit groups, criminal justice systems, and faith-based organizations, it is the most common and most studied form of restorative justice in the country today.

With a focus on social justice, empowerment, and holistic practice, it is no great surprise that social workers were among the first to engage in restorative justice. In the late 1970s, NASW member Mark Umbreit, now the director of the Center for Restorative Justice and Peacemaking at the University of Minnesota School of Social Work, helped launch the country's first victim-offender reconciliation program in Elkhart, Ind. (The first-ever of these programs was launched in Ontario in 1974.) Since then, Umbreit and a handful of other social workers across the country have made restorative justice the centerpiece of their practice and research. But according to many of these same experts, social work as a profession still has a lot of room to get involved in the restorative justice movement in the United States.

Some say restorative justice cannot evolve without social workers' support; others say social workers cannot continue their tradition of serving in correctional settings without embracing restorative justice. All seem to agree that social workers would be natural leaders in the restorative justice movement.

The Philosophy

"Restorative justice and social work are a match made in heaven," said NASW member Mark Chupp, a project manager with the Center for Neighborhood Development in Cleveland, who also got his start working at an early victim-offender reconciliation program. "The philosophy of restorative justice and values of social work are very consistent."

Restorative justice, and VOM in particular, often fills the enormous voids left by the criminal justice system. It does so by incorporating some of social work's core values as laid out in NASW's Code of Ethics: service, social justice, dignity and worth of a person, and importance of human relationships.

At its core, restorative justice is focused on serving victims, whose needs often get overlooked in this country's retributive criminal justice system. In the early days of the movement, victim advocacy organizations balked at the idea of bringing victims and offenders together. Today, these same groups see VOM as an invaluable service.

Despite its victim-centered approach, restorative justice is also meant to heal the wounds of other parties affected by conflict, including offenders.

"Restorative justice very closely relates to social justice or fairness in that the victims and offenders each have their interests represented in the proceedings," NASW member Katherine van Wormer, a professor of social work at the University of Northern Iowa, wrote in an article for *Families in Society: The Journal of Contemporary Human Services* in 2003.

As van Wormer pointed out, the dignity and worth of an individual—as well as the related person-in-environment perspective—are also central components of this process.

"With restorative justice," she wrote, "the dignity of both offender and victim are maintained through a process that is diametrically opposite to customary criminal justice proceedings—the orange suit, the publicity attached to the arrest and trial, the opposing lawyers' indignities and accusations, especially of witnesses. . . . The focus on the offender is on the offender's whole personality, not on only the act or acts that have caused the harm."

VOM similarly focuses on human relationships by allowing the victim and offender to see how the offender's actions have affected them both, as well as their communities.

"Restorative justice looks at the interpersonal and societal dimensions of crime," said NASW member Edward Gumz, associate professor and chair of the undergraduate social work program at Loyola University in Chicago.

The Evidence

Of course, restorative justice has its critics. The most common complaint about VOMs and other similar programs is that they go too easy on offenders. But in his latest book, *Facing Violence: The Path of Restorative Justice and Dialogue*, Umbreit counters this argument.

In his extensive interviews for the book, offender after offender (including Jonathan Nobles) told Umbreit that facing their victims or victims' family members and being held accountable for their actions by those who were most affected by them was the hardest thing they'd ever had to do—far harder than serving time in prison.

Umbreit said other research in the field of restorative justice—the most extensive of which focuses on VOM—should also be encouraging to the social work profession, especially with its recent emphasis on evidence-based practice.

"There are few better examples of evidence-based practices in corrections than in victim-offender mediation," Umbreit said.

In *Facing Violence*, which focuses on VOM programs in Texas and Ohio that deal exclusively with cases of severe violence, Umbreit found that 8 out of 10 participants (victims and offenders) in the dialogue sessions reported major life changes occurring.

"The most frequent statements related to their overall outlook on life being more positive and being more at peace with the circumstances they are faced with," he wrote.

An article by Umbreit, Robert B. Coates, and Betty Vos, published in the Fall-Winter 2004 issue of *Conflict Resolution Quarterly*, surveyed three decades of research on VOM's application in property crimes and minor assaults in thousands of cases across the world.

"Expression of satisfaction with VOM is consistently high for both victims and offenders across sites, cultures and seriousness of offenses," they wrote. "Typically, nine out of 10 participants report being satisfied with the process and with the resulting agreement."

In this same article, the authors reviewed three meta-analyses of restorative justice. In each case, these studies found that offenders who participated in VOM typically had lower rates of recidivism than those who did not.

"This is a concept that works," said Luisa Lopez, manager of NASW's Human Rights and International Affairs Department. "If your end goal is justice—righting a wrong—this practice can have a lasting impact."

The Opportunity

Beginning with Jane Addams's efforts to reform Chicago's juvenile justice system in the early twentieth century, social workers long have been involved in corrections. But according to Gumz, the profession has been somewhat turned off in recent years by the criminal justice system's retributive approach.

"Social workers in the criminal justice system have been greatly affected by a trend away from rehabilitation and toward retribution," he said.

In a 2004 article for the *International Journal of Offender Therapy and Comparative Criminology*, Gumz noted that "current evidence indicates that

the social work presence in corrections has recently declined." He pointed to a 2001 study showing that an average of only 0.7% of graduate students in schools of social work listed corrections/criminal justice as their primary specialty.

Social workers currently at the helm of the restorative justice movement say restorative practices represent an exciting opportunity for the profession to return to its roots in corrections. Once social workers buy into restorative justice and its many possibilities, they add, there will be plenty of work waiting for them.

"In restorative justice, the social worker's role is to bring people together at the community level who want to see a holistic approach taken," said NASW member Gale Burford, a professor and former director of the Social Work Department at the University of Vermont.

More specifically, Burford said, social workers would be particularly adept at preparing both victims and offenders for mediation.

"Social workers are in a unique position to give their clients the good preparation they need to participate in these very emotional meetings," Burford said.

Case referral, intake, dialogue facilitation, case follow-up, advocating restorative justice initiatives, and working with local, state, and federal governments to reevaluate the nature of their criminal justice systems are some other ways social workers could get involved.

"Restorative justice is one area where we can bring a helpful perspective to bear," Gumz said.

NASW News, February, 2005, p. 4. Reprinted with permission of NASW.

Practice Implications

Social workers can play a key role in helping to organize their local communities and in engaging in legislative advocacy for social justice and policy change. Many social service programs evolved in such a way, as an outgrowth of grassroots action and consciousness raising of the public. For example, feminist mobilization of the community led to the design of prevention and safe-space domestic violence programming, including the establishment of shelters for the protection of women from family violence. Mandatory treatment for batterers was an outgrowth of the original campaign for the end of violence, as well.

The task of the social worker, as described by Lundy (2004), is to engage community members in the struggle for economic and social justice and thereby to advance the overall goal of enhancing overall community functioning. Increasingly, in a time of massive cuts in funding for social services, social workers are realizing the importance of coalition building, political lobbying for cost-effective initiatives, and community organizing for solutions to the designated problems.

The understanding of the community as an ecosystem can aid the social worker in appreciating the fit between the individual and his or her social environment. Many of an individual's or family's problems are related to or stem from broader issues in communities, and many of an individual's attitudes and patterns of behavior are derived from his or her everyday experiences in the community. An empowerment perspective is essential in helping communities and community members build on their strengths and recognize the structural origin of many of their problems.

Rapp and Goscha (2006), in their new volume on case management with people with psychiatric disabilities, detail innovative community strategies consistent with the strengths model. The strengths model, as they suggest, calls for a return of community to our work. To separate community mental health from community has stifled the integration and quality of life of people with psychiatric disabilities. The kind of community support initiatives that Rapp and Goscha (2006) recommend are based on a profound recognition that to enhance successful community living for people requires attention not only to their medical (psychiatric) needs but also to housing, employment, income, food and clothing, socialization, and other factors. Supported housing services are far preferable to total institutional settings for persons with mental illness because, when high-quality case management is provided, consumers can live independently and achieve stability in

housing. The quality of life of these consumers is therefore improved and their recovery is enhanced even as their interaction with others in the community is normalized.

In criminal justice, as well, community support systems can be brought into play to ensure that social justice is achieved. Only recently gaining recognition by the U.S. social work profession is the empowering practice for settling disputes known as restorative justice. Collectively, the initiatives that go under the rubric of this form of justice have been inspired by community-centered processes for meting out justice. These initiatives are compatible with the values and teachings of social work. Restorative justice brings empowerment to the kind of situations that often involve shame and disempowerment for all parties. Much more needs to be done in this regard to help meet the needs of offenders and victims and whole communities whose rights have been violated. We conclude this chapter with an inspiring piece of writing by a recent college graduate who describes her work as a Peace Corps community organizer in Eastern Europe (see Box 6.3, "Community Development in Moldova" by Krista Mahler).

Box 6.3 Community Development in Moldova

Krista Mahler

Introduction

People ask me what I do and I say that I'm a community development consultant. That is vague. So is the job. This job can be anything you want it to be, but first you must have a vision for the prospective community—and the community must have the same vision. How hard can working in a community really be? Hard. But once you understand a bit about communities and people and once you have the right approach, success will come!

My name is Krista Mahler and I am 24 years old. I graduated from Luther College, a small liberal arts college in Decorah, Iowa, with a bachelor's degree in social work. I immediately joined the Peace Corps, a program run by the United States Government that places and supports citizens of the United States in developing countries for a time commitment of 2 years.

My education in social work prepared me for working in the field of community development—but there is so much that we never heard about in school that I learned while working within a village community. I hope to share those insights with you now. A social work education teaches you many things about working with people, about empathy, and about communication between individuals, groups, and communities. I thought I was prepared when I was placed with a nongovernmental organization (NGO) that works with socially vulnerable children of the village, as well as orphan girls. I was prepared to listen and to share my ideas about their programs, but there were also things that I was not prepared for. I was not prepared to fail. I was not prepared to be as patient as I have been, and I was not prepared to feel lost. But one thing I have learned is that you can never be quite prepared for what you might encounter as a community developer.

I am a community developer in the full sense of the word. I had no idea what I was getting into, but I have been given a grand opportunity to work in a village community in the Republic of Moldova (in between Ukraine and Romania in Eastern Europe). As I studied social work, I was drawn to the community aspects of my classes. In my perspective, development of individuals is directly related to their environment. As social workers, we study human behavior in the social environment because there is an inevitable relationship between one single person and that person's surrounding environment. This is actually what attracts me to social work. I have studied some psychology and some sociology. Both are extremely important in understanding people and their behaviors, but as a social worker I can take the middle ground between these two important domains and I can understand why people are the way they are, as well as understand why and how their environment has affected them. Also, changes in behavior often require changes in social environment. This connection between human behavior and social environments started out as an important theory for me in my social work education, but during my service in Peace Corps as a social work volunteer, my conviction regarding this theory has been strengthened and solidified and, most important, been put into practical use.

Definition

Community development is a hard thing to define. There are so many ways to aid in the development of a community, but I will do my best to explain my experience within this aspect of social work.

To begin with, the word "development" has many connotations and has come to mean different things to different people. You can talk about "housing developments," development of infrastructure (such as building bridges and roads), and you can refer to "economic development" as well. But to me, development in its broadest sense is: any process that promotes the dignity of a people and their capacity to improve their own lives. The goal of any development project is to see a community learn to help itself.

Aspects of Community Development

To be a community developer—to have success being a community organizer—you must fully *submerge yourself into the community*. You must live there (or spend *lots* of time there) and participate in the activities; you must be aware of the laws, the problems, the people in charge, and the people of influence. You must also be aware of the people who have no influence and the children who have no voice. You must be aware of the happiness that exists and you must find out why it exists, but you need to be aware of the fear and pain that exist and know the reasons for their existence as well. You must be prepared to become a community member. If you are not a community member, you will not find out about the community's problems, issues, or its strengths. You will hear the superficial things that are every community's issues. But you will not understand the issues until you are a part of them. But as a social worker you must also keep your boundaries and a distant perspective to be able to assess the issues of a community.

One must remember that development can be big, but many times it is smaller than we think. One might think of development as a huge campaign to fight AIDS, as a large corporation that has come out with a new, useful product, as launching rockets into space to land on and explore Mars, or as the passing of a new law.

After having experience in community development, I can say that most of the time *development is not big—it is small*. Some small examples I have of community development in my village are as follows: circulating announcements to the community a few days before an event at the school instead of the day of the event; the fact that the accountant in the NGO doesn't argue with people anymore but has a discussion and finds a solution to the problem rather then slamming doors and yelling at others; celebrating the children's birthdays at the After School Center during their free lunch in the soup kitchen, giving them something to look forward to and also helping them have some self-esteem; or a clean toilet campaign teaching kids and families the importance of keeping toilets (indoor or backyard outhouses) clean and the importance of washing hands after use.

These are just a few examples of things that were done in my village. Other people here in Moldova have other ideas of community development, such as getting the community businesses and citizens to donate money to a project that will benefit the people, putting trash cans along the roads so that people can be environmentally conscious, creating a women's group where friends can chat about their troubles and laugh with each other to relieve the stress created by the workload and responsibility in the village.

All of these things can be considered community development, but there is one more thing that makes a community develop—and that is *community participation*. In all of the examples that I have given you, none can be accomplished without the aid of community participation. Some of these are obvious to us; for example, the AIDS campaign—people who make up this community are very involved (i.e., patients, families, and other interested supports). I can say that the accountant wouldn't have changed the atmosphere of the office if he had not been willing to talk with me for hours and hours on many different occasions to realize that he was not problem solving but creating the problems himself. And regarding the trash can installation, it wouldn't have made a difference if the community developer had put trash cans alongside the road—no one would have used them—but if that developer had the help of community members who also wanted to promote the use of trash cans, more villagers would hear the message about why they should use them; and it also helps that they saw their neighbors installing the cans themselves.

Many times as a community developer you have great ideas and you think they will work, but you are

not successful. First, this is because you have failed to reach and understand the community; second, this is because the community doesn't understand you. You need strong links and clear communication with people from the community to create successful results.

Case Study #1

Here in my village of Tintareni, I work for an organization called Bethania. This is a relief organization founded and run by a group of Moldovan Baptists. They have created many projects through this organization that help support and give relief and aid to people from their village. The two main projects are the After School Center for children and the Transit House for orphan girls. The After School Center provides free lunch, activities, and homework help and tutoring for 50 socially vulnerable children of this village. This service is provided free of charge. The center is funded by international donations and grants, as well as a few small income-generation projects (i.e., a greenhouse that provides income from the sale of vegetables at the local market). The Transit House is a place where eight orphan girls of ages 16–17 live for 2 years while learning life skills (cooking, cleaning, conflict resolution, self-esteem, participation, self-initiative, etc.), as well as finishing their high school education. This project has been very successful in many ways. Twenty-five girls have participated or are currently participating in the project, and five of these girls are currently attending the state university, studying courses ranging from foreign languages to social work to law. Also we have accomplished the main goal of the project, which is to protect girls from human trafficking, a large problem in Eastern Europe.

One very clear example of the relationship between human behavior and the social environment is shown through one of the projects that I work with. This is the Transit House for orphan girls. Most of the girls we work with are truly orphans or have parents that cannot take care of them (alcoholism, working abroad, etc.). These girls are given a choice about their participation in the project. Once they accept the project, they are brought to the Transit House in the village. They start their 2 years in the village during the summer. During this time they adjust to the home and to the people of the village. They are encouraged to make friends and attend the youth group at the Baptist church. They also have individual and group sessions with social workers and mostly discuss issues related to adjustment. In the fall they start 10th grade in the village school. The first semester is very hard for them because they have been moved out of their old school environment where they were comfortable.

The girls are not successful at first because their teachers expect much more of them than was expected at the orphanage. They struggle and often times act out because they are not succeeding and are not comfortable. After their environment becomes something normal to them, they realize that they can succeed and be happy. Of course, through their 2 years in the group house they learn and grow and struggle often. But this is what changes them. Once their environment has changed around them, it isn't long until these girls are changing themselves. They now have more respect for themselves and for others, and they do their best to work hard. Their self-esteem and self-confidence are high, and they laugh much more often than they cry. Sometimes the girls go home and visit relatives or parents in their villages. But upon their return we can immediately tell that they were out of the environment that they are now used to. They come back with tempers and negative attitudes, and they often bring other peoples' problems home with them. It takes a few days for them to readjust to the transit house's safe atmosphere. In one overnight trip they can oftentimes revert to their old habits and forget much that they have learned at the transit house. But with persistence and a positive surrounding environment, this project has managed to change the behavior of many orphan girls in Moldova. As a result of these behavioral changes, we now have girls studying in the university and working in the capital city. These girls chose to make behavioral changes over time, but none of it would have happened if their environment hadn't changed, too. Behavior and environment go hand in hand, and as a social worker one must never forget this.

Case Study #2

Here is a typical day working in community development in a small village in an Eastern European country.

I usually check in with my community partner at 9 a.m. We will have coffee and chat about the day

and what needs to be accomplished within the organization. Then we check our e-mail and the news. We are lucky because we have the Internet in our office. Then we will respond to any of our sponsors/donors. I have learned to speak and write in Romanian, so I'm usually the translator of these letters back and forth between our foreign supporters. I will often be translating a potential project or grant proposal so that we can continue funding our current projects. Money is hard to come by, and it is a topic of daily discussion. "How will we fund this activity?" or "How will we pay for meat this month for the children's soup kitchen?" are common questions asked. As a consultant I discuss other options with my partner. We look at our budgets and see where we can cut money out so that we can pay for something else. We are always in search of financers and donations. But in my 2-year experience, we haven't ever had to terminate a project or activity because of lack of funding. Termination does happen, but if you are creative with money and with your current resources, you can make lots of things happen. You can even do many projects without money.

After this type of discussion, I will usually work on translations. Then before lunch I will walk over to the school to see how the day is for the teachers and the children of the village. I will have tea with the director of the school and try to discuss new ideas with him for different activities. Perhaps a Penny War at school between grades or a Disco that makes money by charging only 1 leu at the entrance (8 U.S. cents). After I work with the director and some of the teachers in developing one of our ideas, I go back to my NGO. I might stop by the town hall and chat with the mayor about village concerns, problems, or activities. Later I might work on planning a Training of Trainers (TOT) about giving a health seminar or a business planning seminar. Then sometimes we will evaluate the NGO and its development as an organization. We have some different methods of measuring and evaluating the progress of development in an NGO. We look at the NGO and see if it has all the characteristics of a developed NGO, such as an employees' handbook, sick policies, employee contracts; if they have a board of directors and the responsibilities of that board; and so forth. My NGO has some of these things and doesn't have others. It is my goal to help the director of the NGO to develop the organizational structure, the efficiency, and the organization's management structure. This is the hardest part for me. I was not trained in this type of work while studying social work.

While being a community developer, you will encounter anything to everything, and you can't be timid about doing some things just because you don't have the experience. People will come to you with ideas or complaints about some aspect of the community functioning, and you must work with that person until something is resolved. Hopefully, by using the social work strengths perspective, you can aid the community into helping itself, but most communities can't help themselves alone. They need a *facilitator (you) who acts as a catalyst in their development*.

In the evenings, I will play with children and try to organize a soccer game or a discussion group. I cook dinner with families or visit people for chat sessions, which always seem to cover the topics of the problems in the village. While doing this I try to encourage people to think of their own solutions.

This is just a small portion of my community development experience here in Moldova. I hope to enhance my knowledge in development even further when I come back to the United States in the spring of 2006. I hope to find a job working within the aspects of community development mentioned above.

Summary

Development is any process that promotes the dignity of a people and their capacity to improve their own lives. And to have success in community development one must remember:

- Submerge oneself in the community.
- Development is not big—it is small.
- Community participation is necessary for success.
- Be a facilitator who acts as a catalyst in a community's development.

Original essay by Krista Mahler, B.A., social work. Christian Relief Association, "Bethania." Peace Corps, Moldova. Printed with permission of Krista Mahler.

Summary and Conclusion

This discussion on community began with a consideration of theories and facts concerning whether community in the sense of belongingness is on the decline in today's world. As in other matters, the conclusion one reaches depends on the questions asked and the data examined. Studies of the impact of communications technology, religious gatherings, and rural and minority group mutual aid activities favored the positive side of the argument. Conversely, studies based on surveys of TV viewing habits, the new technologies, corporate control of modern life, school consolidation, pressure in the workplace for ever-higher levels of productivity over personal fulfillment, and the expansion of solitary as opposed to team sports pronounced the demise of community life. The truth, in all likelihood, is somewhere in the middle. There have been losses that have accompanied the invention of computer technology, but there have also been gains attached to this instantaneous form of communication. Consider the reuniting of old friends and relatives through the medium of Facebook, for example.

The sustainable community as described in this chapter is one that is safe, open, and health preserving for people of all ages and abilities to contribute to the functioning of the whole. A planned environment holds the potential for addressing many of the nation's greatest current public health concerns, including obesity, cardiovascular disease, diabetes, asthma, injury, depression, violence, and social inequities. To achieve this public health ideal, as Jackson et al. (2009) inform us, requires increasing green space, reinventing our buildings and settlements, improving public transportation, limiting carbon emissions, and actively promoting a reasonable, active, healthy lifestyle for all. The building of a more sustainable physical habitat is a major public health consideration.

At the societal level, the goal of empowerment practice is social justice and a reduction in social inequality. Community building, as in the examples included in this chapter, is geared toward the key social work value of social justice. Such community building efforts call on an empowerment perspective to help people organize and tap into the strengths of their particular culture and traditions. Knowledge of the wider cultural ethos is essential, as well, and a part of the critical analysis needed for effective community-based social action. The next chapters extend this cultural understanding into the organizational and environmental realms.

Thought Questions

1. Following theories such as that offered in *Bowling Alone*, make the case that sense of community is in a state of decline.
2. "Globalization breaks down community." Discuss.
3. Describe what is meant by the corporate media and the extent of the influence. Relate to the war in Iraq.
4. Describe the impact of the technological revolution on human service operations.
5. Debate the advantages and disadvantages of small schools. What is the latest trend in your area? Who benefits?
6. Argue that the community is alive and well. What is the virtual community?
7. What are the basic characteristics of *Gemeinschaft* relationships? Relate to the rural community.
8. Discuss the tradition of mutual aid among African Americans.
9. Discuss measures of subjective well-being in various nations.
10. Compare the philosophy of restorative justice with that of standard justice.
11. Discuss community development work as described in Mahler's "Community Development in Moldova." Would you like to join the Peace Corps and engage in this kind of work?

References

Accessline. (2005, July/August). Iowans celebrate gay pride. *Accessline: Iowa's Gay Newspaper*, pp. 1, 3.

Androff, D. (in press). Truth and reconciliation commissions: An international human rights intervention and its connection to social work. *British Journal of Social Work*.

Ark, T. V. (2003, February). The case for small high schools. *Educational Leadership, 59*(5), 55–59.

Asai, M., & Kameoka, V. (2005). The influence of *Sek entei* on family caregiving and underutilization of social services among Japanese caregivers. *Social Work, 50*(2), 111–118.

Bakan, J. (2004). *The corporation: The pathological pursuit of profit and power*. New York: Free Press.

Barker, R. (2003). *The social work dictionary* (5th ed.). Washington, DC: NASW Press.

Baruch, S., Kaufman, D., & Hudson, K. (2008). Genetic testing of embryos: Practices and perspectives of U.S. IVF clinics. *Fertility and sterility, 89*(5), 1053–1058.

Becker, H. (1957). Current sacred-secular theory and its development. In H. Becker & A. Boskoff (Eds.), *Modern sociological theory in continuity and change* (pp. 137–185). New York: Free Press.

Billingsley, A., & Morrison-Rodriguez, B. (2007). The black family in the 21st century and the church as an action system: A macro perspective. In L. A. See (Ed.), *Human behavior in the social environment from an African American perspective*. (pp.57–74). Binghamton, NY: Haworth.

Brave Heart, M.Y. (2001a). Culturally and historically congruent clinical social work assessment with Native clients. In R. Fong & S. Furuto (Eds.), *Culturally competent practice: Skills, interventions and evaluations* (pp. 163–177). Boston: Allyn & Bacon.

Brueggemann, W. (2005). *Practice of macro social work* (2nd ed.). Belmont, CA: Wadsworth.

Bugeja, M. (2005). *Interpersonal divide: The search for community in a technological age*. New York: Oxford University Press.

Centers for Disease Control and Prevention. (2005). *Kids walk-to-school resources*. Retrieved May 1, 2006, from http://www.cdc.gov/nccdphp/dnpa/kidswalk

Collum, D. (2004). The Tupelo miracle. *Sojourners Magazine, 33*(10), 32–37.

Committee on Prevention of Obesity in Children and Youth. (2004). *Preventing childhood obesity: Health in the balance*. Washington, DC: Academic Press.

Council on Social Work Education (CSWE). (2008). *Educational policy and accreditation standards*. Alexandria, VA: Author.

Day, P. J. (2008). *A new history of social welfare* (6th ed.). Boston: Allyn & Bacon.

Deputy Prime Minister. (2005, February 1). *Opening address to the Delivering Sustainable Communities Summit*. Manchester, England.

Retrieved, from http://archive.cabinetoffice.gov.
uk/dpm/speeches/050201_delivering_sustainable_
communities_summit_manchester.html

Diehaus, B. (2008, August 14). Downtowns across
the U.S. see streetcars in their future. *New York
Times*, p. A17.

Downs, W. (2005, May 14). *Seeds of Hope targets
domestic violence. Waterloo-Cedar Falls Courier*.
Retrieved from http://wcfcourier.com/
columnists/guest_column/article_29fe6ad8-bdd4-
5242-87ff-fde8e649efce.html

Durkheim, E. (1952). *Suicide* (J. Spaulding &
G. Simpson, Trans.). New York: Free Press.
(Original work published 1897).

Eby, C. (2005, July 4). Governor restores the vote to
felons. *Waterloo Cedar Falls Courier*. Retrieved,
from http://wcfcourier.com/news/politics/article_
eacaec84-03bf-58a7-86df-101daaaee4a4.html

El Nasser, H. (2005, June 2). Beyond Kiwanis: Internet
builds new communities. *USA Today*, 1A, 2A.

Eller, D., & Eckhoff, J. (2009, November 8). *Factory
losses strike deepest in rural Iowa. Des Moines
Register*. Retrieved from http://www.
desmoinesregister.com/article/20091108/
BUSINESS/911080344/Factory-losses-strike-
deepest-in-rural-Iowa

Fitzgerald, A. (2003, January 19). Stress pushes rural
Iowans to the brink. *Des Moines Register*, p. A1.

Flint, A. (2009). *Wrestling with Moses: How Jane
Jacobs took on New York's master builder and
transformed the American city*. New York:
Random House.

Frank, T. (2004). *What's the matter with Kansas?
How conservatives won the heart of America*.
New York: Metropolitan Books.

Geitz, S. (2005). Small schools think big [Letter to
the editor]. *Des Moines Register*, p. 2.

Gilgun, J. (2004). The 4-D: Strengths-based
assessment instruments for youth, their families,
and communities. *Journal of Human Behavior
in the Social Environment, 10*(4), 51–73.

Goodson, D. (2005, July 20). Social action.
Presentation made at the University of Northern
Iowa, Social Work Department.

Graham, L. (2009, April 19). The greenest town in
America. *Parade*, pp. 6–8.

Gutiérrez, L., & Lewis, E. (1999). Preface. In
L. M. Gutiérrez (Ed.), *Empowering women of
color* (pp. xi–xix). New York: Columbia
University Press.

Hampton, K., Sessions, L., Ja Her, E., & Rainie, L.
(2009, November). *Social isolation and new
technology. Pew Internet Personal Networks and
Community Survey*. Retrieved March 16, 2010,
from http://www.pewinternet.org/~/media//

Files/Reports/2009/PIP_Tech_and_Social_
Isolation.pdf

Hardcastle, D. (2004). Globalization, welfare states
and social work. In N-T. Tan & A. Rowlands
(Eds.), *Social work around the world* (Vol. 3,
pp. 95–112). Berne, Switzerland: International
Federation of Social Workers.

Hardcastle, D., & Powers, P. (2004). *Community
practice: Theories and skills for social workers*
(2nd ed.). New York: Oxford University Press.

hooks, b. (2001). *Salvation: Black people and love*.
New York: William Morrow.

Inglehart, R., Foa, R., Peterson, C., & Welzel, C.
(2008). Development, freedom, and rising
happiness: A global perspective. *Perspectives on
Psychological Science, 3*(4), 264–285.

International Federation of Social Workers. (2005).
*International policy statement on globalization
and the environment*. Retrieved May 1, 2006,
from http://www.ifsw.org/en/p38000222.html

Jackson, R., Wiland, H., & Bell, D. (2009). *Public
space/public health: How the built environment
impacts our health*. Retrieved from the Media
and Policy Center Foundation Web site:
http://mpcdev.miramontes.com/docs/american-
cities.pdf

Johnson, M. N., & Rhodes, R. (2009). *Human
behavior and the larger social environment:
A new synthesis*. Upper Saddle River, NJ:
Prentice Hall.

Kaplan, S., & Kaplan, R. (2003). Health, supportive
environments and the reasonable person model.
American Journal of Public Health, 9(9),
1484–1489.

Karp, D., Lane, J., & Turner, S. (2002). Ventura
County and the theory of community justice. In
D. Daye & T. Clear (Eds.), *What is community
justice?* (pp. 1–33). Thousand Oaks, CA: Sage.

Layard, R. (2005). *Happiness: Lessons from a new
science*. New York: Penguin.

Lee, J. (2001). *The empowerment approach to social
work practice: Building the beloved community*
(2nd ed.). New York: Columbia University Press.

Leland, J. (2009, April 9). With advocates' help,
squatters call foreclosures home. *New York
Times*, p. A1.

Lundy, C. (2004). *Social work and social justice:
A structural approach to practice*. Peterborough,
Ontario: Broadview Press.

Manning, M. (2001). Culturally competent
assessments of African American communities
and organizations. In R. Fong & S. Furuto (Eds.),
*Culturally competent practice: Skills,
interventions, and solutions* (pp. 119–131).
Boston: Allyn & Bacon.

Mathis, W. (2009, December 21). School consolidation: Money, democracy and community. *Vermont Tiger*. Retrieved from http://www.vermonttiger.com/content/2009/12/school-consolidation-money-democracy-and-community.html

Meenaghan, T. M., & Gibbons, W. (2000). *Generalist practice in larger settings*. Chicago: Lyceum.

Maslow, A. H. (1968). *Toward a psychology of being*. Princeton, NJ: Van Nostrand.

Midgley, J. (2004). The complexities of globalization: Challenges to social work. In N-T. Tan & A. Rowlands (Eds.), *Social work around the world* (Vol. 3, pp. 13–29). Berne, Switzerland: International Federation of Social Workers.

Mirsky, L. (2004, April 27). *Restorative justice practices of Native American, First Nation and other indigenous people of North America. Restorative Practices E-Forum*, 1–7. Retrieved from http://restorativejustice.org/articlesdb/articles/4230/?searchterm=Native%20American,%20First%20Nation%20indigenous%20people.

Morales, L., Kington, L., Valdez, M., & Escarce, J. (2002). Socioeconomic, cultural, and behavioral factors affecting Hispanic health outcomes. *Journal of Health Care for the Poor and Underserved*, 13(4), 477–503.

Ohmer, M., Beck, E. M., & DeMasi, K. (2008, November 1). Building collective efficacy to prevent violence: Using restorative justice and consensus organizing. Paper presentation at the 54th Annual Program Meeting of CSWE, Philadelphia, Pennsylvania.

Palmer, P. (1998). *The courage to teach: Exploring the inner landscape of a teacher's life*. San Francisco: Jossey-Bass.

Patterson, E. (2004). The impact of globalization in social work practice in Romania. In N-T. Tan & A. Rowland (Eds.), *Social work around the world* (Vol. 3, pp. 95–112). Berne, Switzerland: International Federation of Social Workers.

Problems at women's shelter didn't happen overnight. (2005, May 24). Editorial. *Waterloo-Cedar Falls Courier.*, p.A6.

Putnam, R. (2001). *Bowling alone: The collapse and revival of American community*. New York: Simon & Schuster.

Putnam, R. (2007). E pluribus unum: Diversity and community in the twenty-first century. *Scandinavian Political Studies*, 30(2), 137–174.

Putnam, R., Feldstein, D., & Cohen, D. (2003). *Better together: Restoring the American community*. New York: Simon & Schuster.

Rapp, C., & Goscha, R. (2006). *The strengths model: Case management with people with psychiatric disabilities* (2nd ed.). New York: Oxford University Press.

Rheingold, H. (2003). *Smart mobs: The new revolution*. New York: Basic Books.

Rood, L. (2005, July 17). Uprooting a way of life. *Des Moines Register*, 1AA, 6AA.

Schriver, J. (2010). *Human behavior and the social environment: Shifting paradigms in essential knowledge for social work practice* (5th ed.). Boston: Allyn & Bacon.

Sewpaul, V. (2004). Globalization, African governance and the partnership for Africa's development. In N-T. Tan & A. Rowland (Eds.), *Social work around the world* (Vol. 3, pp. 30–47). Berne, Switzerland: International Federation of Social Workers.

Shattuck, K. (2008, June 10). *Playing a leading role in the ruins of a tornado. New York Times*. Retrieved from http://www.nytimes.com/2008/06/10/arts/television/10green.html

Shorter Oxford English Dictionary. (2007). New York: Oxford University Press.

Strickland, G., Welshimer, K., Sarvela, P. (2008). Clergy perspectives and practices regarding intimate violence: A rural view. *The Journal of Rural Health*, 14(4), 305–311.

Tönnies, F. (1963). *Community and society*. New York: Harper & Row. (Original work published 1887).

Umbreit, M., Vos, B., Coates, R., & Brown, K. (2003). *Facing violence: The path of restorative justice and dialogue*. Monsey, NY: Criminal Justice Press.

U.S. Bureau of Labor Statistics. (2003). *Displaced workers summary*. Retrieved May 1, 2006, from http://www.bls.gov/news.release/disp.nr0.htm

U.S. Census Bureau (2001). *Statistical abstract of the United States: 2001*. Washington, DC: Government Printing Office.

Warren, R. (2002). *The purpose-driven life: What on earth am I here for?* Grand Rapids, MI: Zondervan.

World Health Organization (WHO). (2009). *Suicide rates per 100,000 by country*. Retrieved from http://www.who.int/mental_health/prevention/suicide_rates/en/index.html

World Values Survey. (2004, November). *Subjective well-being rankings of 82 societies*. Retrieved from http://www.worldvaluessurvey.org/Upload/5_wellbeingrankings.doc

Yellow Bird, M. (2001). Critical values and First Nations peoples. In R. Fong & S. Furuto (Eds.), *Culturally competent practice: Skills, interventions, and evaluations* (pp. 61–74). Boston: Allyn & Bacon.

Human Behavior and the Organizational Environment

The Community of Work

Organizational politics is a powerful force for misery, especially in social work. However, organizations are a critically important area of empowerment practice.

—JUDITH LEE

(personal communication, 2005)

When you see the word *organization*, what images come to mind? Consider your different responses to each of the following situations:

- The well-defined roles of the staff in a modern hospital
- The chaos of decision making and management in the crisis as the giant oil spill reaches the Gulf Coast
- Factory workers on an assembly line performing mindless tasks in unison
- The bureaucracy requirements—endless paperwork—for the economic functioning of the county mental health agency
- The turf fights that take place among professions at a human service organization

Your image probably depends, in Goffman's (1959) terms, on whether your perspective is from the outside looking in (*front stage*) or from the inside looking out (*backstage*). Often what the insider sees and what the general public sees are two different things. When the public sees more than is intended, a crisis may occur. Such a breakdown in boundaries can reveal too much and be disturbing to management and disillusioning to the average citizen. Still, members of the public are often genuinely curious about what goes on behind closed doors of major organizations. One can often hear workers in hospitals or restaurants say to their friends, "If only you knew what goes on behind the scenes." Books about the inner workings of the various branches of government are often especially compelling. From a human behavior standpoint, organizational crisis is intriguing. Students of the organization can learn as much, and often more, from the study of behavior that breaks the norms as they can from behavior that is normative and predictable.

This chapter explores the formal organization in both of these dimensions—the deviant and the normative. The emphasis is on settings of special relevance to social work practice—human service organizations. This chapter introduces readers to the organizational setting as a context for the delivery of social services and as a target of economic and political interest groups. The emphasis is on settings of special relevance to social work practice—human service organizations—and on styles of leadership relevant to such organizations. We give attention to historical and theoretical perspectives and to more highly developed theory—classic and modern. Alienation theory from classic formulations is shown to have much resonance today as workers' rights fall to the wayside in the competition of the global market. Workers compete with workers across the globe, and companies struggle to survive in what has been called the "third industrial revolution" (Rifkin, 1996, 2002). By the middle decade of the twenty-first century, argues Rifkin (2002), we will likely be able to produce goods and services for everyone with only a small fraction of the human workforce we now employ, thanks to the breakthroughs in computer and telecommunications technologies. Meanwhile the economic urgencies create incentives for businesses and human service organizations to do more with less. These organizations react to the pressure through the initiation of strategies to increase productivity, cost-effectiveness, and accountability to funding sources while struggling to maintain quality in the provision of services.

A basic underlying assumption from ecosystems theory is that the organization is not an entity *sui generis* (entirely of itself) but, rather, that it exists alongside and in connection with other agencies and organizations as a part of a wider whole. A related fundamental assumption is that, as humans shape organizations, so organizations shape human behavior. This chapter, accordingly, explores the human service agency in terms of internal agency climate, as well as external interconnections.

Unique to this book, as compared with others in this field of human behavior, is the attention paid to the effect of a confluence of external forces—namely, pressures that stem from the global market and that are played out as competitive business practices—on the human service organization. Parallels are drawn between pressures on the ordinary worker in an age of increasingly global competition and the pressures placed on the social worker in his or her treatment center. One form of organization

that we take a close look at is the business corporation, an entity that has come to assume unprecedented power in today's world. The boxed reading for this chapter is a social worker's description of empowerment practice in an unlikely place for empowerment practice—a state prison.

What Is an Organization?

Organization denotes structure, hierarchy, channels of communication, a working environment in which there are proper designated chains of command. For smooth functioning, organizations are built on a designated leadership structure of hierarchy and a bureaucracy of rules and regulations. From the mission statement to the goals to the rules and responsibilities to rights, everything must be documented and in writing. Communication is often done through the memorandum, so that the writers, usually from management, can "cover their tracks." As in all social systems, the occupier of a position or status within the organization plays a clearly defined role. Roles are behaviors that accrue to the positions. Because the individuals who occupy these positions are by definition replaceable, their role performances are continually evaluated, often by consumers, as well as by those higher up the ladder of the hierarchy. The formal organization is built on documentation rather than trust. Of all the types of organizations, the total institution is the most rigid and forbidding. Goffman, in *Asylums* (1961), defined the total institution as a place in which all activities, including sleeping and eating, occur in the same place (pp. 5–6). The most familiar examples are the prison, mental hospital, military camp, or convent. Within such institutions, there is a split between staff and inmates, and inmates typically follow a clear "moral career." The individual's moral career progresses from deprivation of the symbols of his or her former life—clothing, hairstyle, and so forth—to the possession of new symbols and a new identity in the new life. Authorities control the recruits through strict monitoring and use of rewards and punishments. In short, the organization controls the whole life of the resident in a total institution. Decision making is entirely in the hands of the staff; dictates flow from top to bottom of the chain of command.

Most organizations in the society are less authoritarian. Each one, as anyone who has attended a staff meeting or been a member of a board of directors knows, tends to develop its own set way of doing things. Each organization, in other words, develops its own culture, a culture that depends in part on tradition but also in part on the personalities of the major players. *Organizational culture* is defined as the "shared norms, beliefs, values, symbols, and rituals" that guide social behavior (Hanson, 2002). This term refers to the qualities of the overall atmosphere that makes the difference between group satisfaction and longevity and a situation of high turnover. Some examples of characteristics that can define the organizational culture of an unsustainable organization are as follows:

- An overall climate of intensity; relationships are tension driven
- Keen competition and jealousy among the key players
- An atmosphere of almost religious loyalty to the ideals of the organization and intolerance of dissent
- Conflict at upper levels that leads to burnout and cynicism at lower levels
- Hierarchy built on favoritism and friendship rather than designated roles
- Intolerance of critical thinking and proposals for change

However, one might also find:

- Open communication at all levels of engagement
- Democratic decision making coupled with organizational loyalty
- Members who have a shared sense of mission in what they do
- Camaraderie among staff members, a true sharing of joys and concerns

What we are talking about here is the human factor in organizational functioning. Whether the organization is a church or a workplace,

power is determined not necessarily by authority but by influence. This means being heard by people in decision-making positions at the top. ("Ground-up" decision making is ideal but relatively rare.)

Human service organizations are defined here, following Brager and Holloway (1978), as "the vast array of formal organizations that have as their stated purpose enhancement of the social, emotional, physical, and/or intellectual well-being of some component of the population" (p. 2). Examples are mental health clinics, schools, nursing homes, hospitals, and correctional institutions such as halfway houses. These organizations differ from other bureaucracies in that they function within a social mandate to "serve" people and/or to mold their behavior in some way. Unlike other work organizations, their "raw products" are not things but people. The people who become clients are transformed, processed, or assisted in some specified manner (Hanson, 2002). The societal mandate, as Brager and Holloway (1978) argue, is contradictory and reflects the equivocal pattern of values of the society. On the one hand is the value of care and provision of services for the needy; on the other hand is the belief that the behavior of the needy must be controlled. Human service organizations thus serve a social control function for society. Professional values and societal values often conflict in this regard; professionals focus on helping the client, and the society imposes restrictions on the help that is given.

Environmental factors, such as a changing political climate and economic conditions, influence agency operations profoundly (Hanson, 2002). The realities of a new globalized social and economic order also have a profound impact on organizations and agency function (Massey, 2009). Under a conservative political administration, management can become so preoccupied with agency survival, and individual social workers with cost-containment mandates from third-party payers, that the interests of the clients can be lost. Front-line workers are the closest to hearing and seeing how agency services empower or disempower clients (Lee, 2001; Somers & Block, 2005), and such an experience in a time of externally imposed budget cuts can be disheartening. A sense of perspective can often help the worker understand agency policy and anticipate policy initiatives.

In their critique of prominent social work theories and their proposal of the just-practice framework, Finn and Jacobson (2003) raise questions about the relationship between social work theory and real-life practice. Sometimes social work students on their first field practice experiences are disturbed or even disillusioned by organizational functioning and external pressures. Social work major Sara Leahy (in private correspondence with van Wormer of August 18, 2009) shares with readers her thoughts on reconciling classroom theory with practice:

> I can definitely relate to the topic of reconciling theory and practice. I remember my first social work field experience during my sophomore year of college. This consisted of 40-hour weeks for three and a half weeks at a rural hospital, where I shadowed for two different social workers. I tried to pay so much attention to the ways in which the social workers interviewed the patients and other clients. It was not until the next semester in my Practice I class where I learned different interviewing and counseling techniques, that I realized they were rarely ever used in the hospital setting in which I observed. Looking back on it, the pressure to see all of the patients combined with the loads of paperwork made spending extra time with a client almost impossible. I also experienced the introduction of new technology for the social workers, as while I was there they were learning how to enter data on computers instead of on paper. I think the stress of learning how to do this, for people who are not extremely familiar with computers, was so great that they could hardly focus on the work they should be doing with their clients. Although I learned a great deal about social work in a hospital setting, I also came to realize the frustration of placing theory into practice.

Adopting a Critical Perspective

Judith Lee (2001) discusses critical thinking in terms of envisioning organizational response to the needs of clients. A critical perspective, she notes, goes beyond the observation and description of social conditions and transactions. "This entails," as Lee notes, "questioning all forms of oppression and assisting in the development of alternative social forms" (p. 183). A critical view requires sensitivity to institutional racism, sexism, and classism as expressed through organizational structures. Sometimes the structures themselves will be objects, as well as vehicles, of change efforts. In our change efforts, we cannot shy away from conflict, though, as Lee asserts, neither do we court it. We need to be careful to avoid all deterministic thinking. A commitment to questioning how an organization fits into the wider social context is the essence of a critical perspective.

A reading or rereading of C. Wright Mills's (1959) classic, *The Sociological Imagination*, especially its Chapter 1, is useful in this regard. Mills's words on the use of a critical mind to connect private troubles with public issues have as much meaning today as formerly. See Figure 7.1 to appreciate the cost paid by individuals for contemporary government policies. The late 1950s, like the early twenty-first century, was a period of rapid social change and political retrogression as reflected in Mills's definition of the sociological imagination as follows:

> (It) is the capacity to shift from one perspective to another—from the political to the psychological; from examination of a simple family to a comparative assessment of the national budgets of the world; from the theological school to the military establishment. . . . To be aware of the idea of social structure and to use it with sensibility is to be capable of tracing such linkages among a great variety of milieux. To be able to do that is to possess the sociological imagination. (pp. 7, 10–11)

Social workers can draw on their *social work imaginations* (in the tradition of Jane Addams and Bertha Reynolds) in a similar vein.

Figure 7.1. When organizations fail, human beings suffer. An unidentified homeless woman with a cart of her belongings stands on a San Francisco street. Photo by Rupert van Wormer.

In this spirit, we pursue our investigation of the organization. Critical inquiry from the social worker's perspective involves viewing the problems that people have in relation to their environment and in drawing on the sources of power to which social workers in organizations have access (Lee, 2001). But, unfortunately, as Brager and Holloway (1978) pointed out, and is still true, the mental health professional typically holds a position of limited influence and lacks the authority to change the client's situation for the better. These authors recommended a method of "bottom-up" change using organizational knowledge and practice skills. Their focus was more on internal organizational politics than on situational factors, however. We return to the topic of effecting substantive change later in the chapter.

Historical Perspectives: An Overview

The dominant ways in which humans have organized themselves to perform social and economic activities have varied in different societies and in different historical eras (Hasenfeld, 2010). The nature of human relationships was and is conditioned by these ways of organizing

our socioeconomic activities. The primary relationships in a hunting and gathering society, for example, were different from those in an agricultural society with its peasantry and aristocracy, and both were very different from the relationships of industrial wage workers in a capitalist-industrial society. Although there certainly have been examples of formal organizations and bureaucracy in earlier civilizations whose material reflections can be seen in the pyramid-building societies, it is in the era of industrial production that we find the large-scale formal organization and bureaucracy as a dominant form of organization and a ubiquitous presence around the globe.

Much of social work direct practice is directed toward the primary, personal relationships that people maintain apart from formal organizations. At the same time, social workers practice in the context of formal organizations that employ them. So the client system may be exemplified by an individual receiving therapy for a personal problem or a family being helped with boundary issues. The agency in which the social worker is employed may be a local family services organization—a formal organization. If the worker is employed by the city or the state, the employing organization may be a complex formal organization, a bureaucracy.

Social workers often stand at the intersection between the small personal group such as a family and the large bureaucratic organization that employs them. The contrast between these organizational entities is instructive.

Max Weber observed that large-scale bureaucracies exist for a purpose—now often referred to as a mission. He observed their characteristics as having specialized roles or duties; valuing competence; having offices with a hierarchical, pyramid ordering; forming rules to guide actions; taking a detached impersonal approach; using formal written communications; and selecting workers on the basis of specified qualifications who are rewarded by salary, pensions, and seniority (Weber, 1924/1947; Macionis, 2004). By contrast, the family is a small primary group in which members share personal and enduring relationships (Macionis, 2004). Social workers are in the position of working in and with both kinds of systems. The contrasts, however, include relationships that are personal, emotional, and subjective versus those that are impersonal, detached, and objective.

One way the contrast can create strain for the social work practitioner is in the conduct of his or her professional role. The employing bureaucracy may expect efficient processing of cases and associated paperwork, which may interfere with a more personal and involved relationship with client families. Often the professional code of ethics provides some guidance in addressing these kinds of conflicting expectations.

Leadership in Organizational Settings

Perhaps one of the most neglected aspects of social work research and education is the role that leadership plays in good social work practice. In 1986 social work researcher Elizabeth Brilliant suggested that leadership preparation was a missing ingredient in social work education and charged that leadership "is essentially a non-theme in social work training" (Brilliant, 1986, p. 325). Similarly, Stoesz (1997) also lamented that social work tends to celebrate and extol the leadership virtues of its prominent historical figures, such as Jane Addams, Bertha Cappen Reynolds, and Florence Kelley, while at the same time giving little or no attention to the development of leadership potential in its young professionals. In recent years, there has been a call for social workers to assume more leadership roles in interdisciplinary collaboration in several fields, including developmental disabilities, legal services, and child protection and health care. Indeed, Rank and Hutchison (2000) note the very pressing need "for social work leadership in the new millennium to position the profession in a more positive and productive capacity, not only with political leaders and American society, but with the professional's own membership as well" (p. 488).

Canda and Furman (2010) urge an envisioning of the helping role and its organizational context for long-term sustainability for future generations. Their vision is of a spiritually sensitive administration, the mission and productivity goals of which would be designed primarily to serve the goals of personal well-being of clients and staff in the interests of social justice.

What, then, is leadership? It is not an easy task to define a series of traits, functions, and capacities that most of us take for granted but that few of us have taken little time to fully comprehend. Such is the case in attempting to define leadership. Despite a lack of definitional precision, it is possible to agree on some broad parameters. Bass (1990) provides this general and useful definition:

> Leadership is an interaction between two or more members of a group that often involves a structuring or restructuring of the situation and the perceptions and expectations of the members. . . . Leadership occurs when one group member modifies the motivation or competencies of others in the group. Any member of a group can exhibit some amount of leadership. . . . (pp. 19–20)

As this definition suggests, leadership involves a participatory process that includes two or more people and that, in some manner, changes the nature of the interaction between these parties. In other words, at its most basic level, leadership is the manner in which a group of people, or some person, influences another. Leadership, according to Hutchison (2008), is a process whereby an individual influences a group, rather than a particular characteristic of an individual. The most difficult part of leadership studies has turned out to be not how to define the construct but rather how to determine what constitutes a good leader. Everyone seems to know, almost instinctively, what a bad leader is or how a bad leader acts. Few are as clear about what a good leader is and how a good leader leads. Hutchison (2008) identifies core competencies of effective social work leaders of formal organizations. These are problem solving; flexibility; self-awareness of one's beliefs and attitudes; ability to articulate a vision and a plan; good oral and written communication skills; and knowledge of how to handle conflict and maneuver bureaucracies and complex systems. To this list, we would add good listening skills and a sense of humor. Hutchison differentiates between assigned and emergent leadership. Assigned leaders have formal authority; an emergent leader is one whose influence is recognized.

Traditional Leadership Theories

Since the beginning of the twentieth century, social theorists, psychologists, management experts, and political devotees have endeavored to describe the magical and often furtive ingredient or ingredients that make for good leadership. Many theories have been propounded, and many more have evolved over time as refinements and extensions of some original theoretical formulation (Netting & O'Connor, 2003; Schmid, 2010). We look at several of the most well known of these traditional leadership theories.

Trait Theory

This theory of leadership suggests that leaders have certain personality traits that qualify them for leadership positions. It is sometimes referred as the *great man* or *great person* theory of leadership. It is what many of us have been

accustomed to think of when we ponder leadership. These personality traits, or certain attitudinal and behavior qualities, have included such things as unflappability, the capacity to make quick decisions, rationality, emotional stability, analytical skill, and any of a number of several hundred other traits that have been suggested as representative of good leaders. This theory tends to imply that great leaders are born and not created and that they are somehow destined to find their leadership positions. In other words, the traits so characteristic of good leaders are so complex and so multifarious that only a person who has had these qualities since birth is likely to raise to positions of leadership in the short space of a single lifetime. Captains of industry, military leaders, political figures, religious leaders, and entertainment personalities are often cited as prominent examples of the reality of this trait-based perspective on leadership. One problem is that there is no possibility of coming up with a standard set of leadership traits that can be generalized across time and cultures. The possibilities are endless, and, in the end, it is likely that we will fail to produce even one personality trait or set of qualities that can be used unequivocally to demarcate leaders from non-leaders. A second problem with trait theory, as indicated by Lazzari, Colarossi, and Collins (2009), is that these designated traits are decidedly masculine in nature and their correlation with greatness is not substantiated.

Positional Theory

The positional theory of leadership is based on the idea that leaders are not necessarily born but are, rather, created by virtue of the positions of authority they may hold at a given time. The position of chief executive officer (CEO), president, or chairperson will elicit from a person holding that position those qualities necessary to serve as an effective leader. The positional theory infers that the authority and influence necessary to function as an effective leader is vested in the position or the title. For instance, a police officer has no natural or inherent authority except that which is granted her by virtue of the position she holds.

Situational Theory

The situational or contingency theory of leadership is based on the premise that leadership is a function of the behavior of the leader in relationship to behaviors of followers as well as to changing organizational situations (Schmid, 2010). Hersey and Blanchard (1969), who are the best-known proponents of this view, believed that leadership is not inherent to the personality of the leader—as trait theory would suggest—but is a flexible quality developed over time that is sensitive to change. With appropriate training, leaders can be developed in a manner that allows them to adapt their individual leadership capacities to their followers' needs; it is really followers who dictate what kinds of leaders and leadership emerge. Good leadership depends on how ready members are to be led and how capable they are of accomplishing specified group tasks. Hersey and Blanchard (1988) defined four levels of member readiness: those who are able and willing, those who are able but unwilling, those who are unable but willing, and those who are unable and unwilling. The most effective kinds of leaders are those who are able to recognize these predominant follower styles and to adjust their own leadership skills in light of these.

Style Theory

The style theory of leadership attempts to understand leadership by looking at the various styles of leadership that characterize certain leaders. Lewin, Lippitt, and White (1938) summarized hundreds of qualities that seemed to characterize good leadership and came up with a cluster of traits that were said to form one of three predominant leadership styles. In other words, instead of looking at individual traits, Lewin et al. (1938) created a typology of leadership styles that were made up of related traits that seemed to provide a general description of leadership that was simpler and easier to understand.

The *authoritarian leader* is very directive and nonparticipatory, takes personal charge of decision making, is concerned with the instrumental needs of the organization, and demands strict compliance from subordinates. In a crisis, this kind of leadership style is much approved of, but it often fails to win the hearts and minds of staff members during day-to-day operations of the organization. The *laissez-faire leader* is much the opposite of the authoritarian leader. He or she tends to be very nondirective and permissive and to allow subordinates to function more or less independently. Although staff members may appreciate the freedom this style of leadership provides, they also may be very uncomfortable with the perceived failure of the leader to "take charge" during protracted and/or thorny organizational problems. The *democratic leader* is more expressive and is focused on including everyone in the decision-making process. He or she tends to prize active member participation, honest and constructive feedback, and the ability to formulate consensual decisions. We look at democratic leadership in greater detail shortly.

Theory X, Theory Y, and Theory Z Leadership

In early 1960, Douglas McGregor proposed two types of leadership style that were largely dependent on how the leader understood his or her subordinates' general character and how they (the workers) viewed themselves in relationship to the work environment. These two leadership styles—one referred to as *people oriented* and the other as *production oriented*—were tied very closely to so-called Theory X and Theory Y perspectives on human nature, management, and work. Later, in the early 1980s, William Ouchi (1981) developed what came to be known as a Theory Z perspective on the character of leadership and management.

Theory X assumed that the "average human has an inherent dislike of work and will avoid it. Individuals must be coerced, controlled, directed, or threatened to produce. People avoid responsibility and take the route of least resistance" (Brueggemann, 2006, p. 89). Theory Y, on the other hand, assumed that people want to accept responsibility for their life and their work. They are willing to learn, experience change, and to work toward a common task. External inducements such as sanctions, punishments, and denial of privileges are not always effective and may, in fact, be counterproductive. Instead, people have the capacity for self-direction, self-growth, independence, self-determination, and self-reliance. This understanding of human capacity, inherent strength, and cultural-based knowledge shares similarities with Gardner's (1993) ideas that human beings possess a multiplicity of skills or intelligences rather than an abstract, kind of monolithic intelligent quotient. These multiple intelligences (e.g., emotional skills, musical skills, bodily-kinesthetic skills, interpersonal skills) are shared by all people to various degrees and prepare each to clearly assess and creatively solve life's problems.

Theory X leaders tend to be pessimistic, authoritarian, static, task oriented, and closed to new information or new strategies. Their focus tends to be solely on production quotas and on maintaining an efficient organizational operation in order to maximize these production goals. Theory Y leaders tend to be optimistic, flexible, growth oriented, open to new information and strategies, and nonauthoritarian. Their focus tends to be on how well employees are doing—emotional, physically, and relationally—in the process of meeting organization goals and objectives. They are concerned with human relationships rather than bureaucratic rules.

Theory Z models are a kind of hybrid of the more familiar Theory X and Theory Y perspectives. Theory Z looks less at the values of individual leaders and focuses rather on how to apply humanistic and collectivist management philosophies within the deeply engrained individualistic orientation of modern U.S. culture. The resulting approach to both leadership and management has changed the level of analysis from the employer–employee relationship to that of the person contextualized within the entire organization (Draft, 2004). Theory Z models emphasize a strong homogeneous set of shared values and are drawn loosely from a traditional Japanese cultural milieu. The primary features of Theory Z are a commitment to long-term employment, consensual decision making, individual responsibility, slow evaluative processes and promotional criteria, informal control mechanisms with formalized performance measures, moderately specialized career

paths, and a holistic concern for employees beyond the workplace.

Religion/Spirituality and Leadership

Historically, leadership studies tended to focus on external, visible, and action-oriented traits, which were believed to lead to tangible and measurable results such as individual accomplishment and material success. Spirituality, on the other hand, focused on internal, invisible traits, insights, and motivations. Traditional leadership studies have often equated the successful leader with the external and measurable—suggesting that these factors were more significant determinants of achievement than internal realities (Palmer, 2000; Vaughan, 1995).

Over time, leadership researchers began to discover that leaders who relied solely on external motivations often experienced significant feelings of incongruity between their professional roles and their personal values. This incongruity manifested itself in feelings of despondency and alienation, and it sometimes led to addictive behaviors, obsessive preoccupations, and personality changes (Bolman & Deal, 2008; Moxley, 2000). On the other hand, leaders who developed a level of congruency between their deeply held inner values and their outer actions experienced a greater sense of authenticity and equilibrium between their personal and professional lives (Moxley, 2000; Vaughan, 1995). Myran, Myran, and Galand (2004) confirmed that paying attention to the transpersonal dimensions of leadership resulted in a balanced connection between a leader's inner beliefs and his or her outward actions.

As a consequence of this new focus to find ways for leaders to be fully genuine in their professional responsibilities, leadership education began to acknowledge the value of religion and spirituality to both personal development and in the creation of authentic leaders (Chickering, Dalton, & Stamm, 2006; Palmer, 2000, 2004). Indeed, authentic leadership came to be defined, in part, as referring to those persons who had found ways to acknowledge and integrate transpersonal values into their professional leadership responsibilities. Authentic leaders were found to be strong advocates for an inclusive culture with a more holistic perspective on knowledge development and transmission, as well as a more globally inspired sense of community (Bolman & Deal, 2008; Rendon, 2006). Elsner (2006), for example, suggested that one of the major responsibilities of authentic leaders is to help others in the organization integrate their work with their inner lives. In some respects the essence of many leadership challenges are spiritual challenges: a leader's primary role includes a spiritual dimension. Chickering et al. (2006) and Tisdell (2003) report that authentic leaders who consistently modeled authenticity created a more multicultural and democratic organizational environment.

Democratic Leadership

In recent years, new perspectives on leadership have also emerged that focus more on the processes of leadership than on leadership style or leadership qualities (Bordas, 2007). One such perspective is sometimes referred to as *democratic leadership*. Democratic leadership is a response to classical leadership theory, which has traditionally identified the *great person* as the quintessence of leadership (Kane, Patapan, & Hart, 2009). This perspective has been identified by Gemmil and Oakley (1992) as an alienating social myth. The great-person model is a myth in the sense that, although we unconsciously believe in the need for great leaders and even unconsciously desire them, in the end this orientation leaves people feeling dependent, apathetic, and alienated from both their leaders and themselves.

The democratic leadership model is based on a paradigm of mutuality and interrelationship in which the organization—in this case a grouping of members referred to as the *demos*—is seen as an arena in which people find and express their identity, meaning, and values. The priority of the democratic leader is to support members of the *demos* in being active and creative agents who have the capacity to make choices about what kinds of actions or responses are necessary. In other words, the overarching purpose of the democratic leader is to function in a manner that sustains the

democratic process (Gastil, 1994). This overarching purpose is carried out through three subsidiary functions: *(1)* distributing responsibility within the *demos*, *(2)* empowering the membership, and *(3)* aiding the *demos* in its deliberations.

Distributing responsibility within the *demos* refers to the leader's task to elicit maximum involvement of every member in organizational processes. This suggests that the leader is always attempting to spread responsibility rather than to concentrate it. The essence of democracy is to encourage as much participation on the part of the citizenry as possible. Effective leaders, as Canda and Furman (2010) suggest, listen closely to staff, regard them as coworkers rather than subordinates, encourage joint decision making, and provide strengths-based evaluative feedback. Democracy cannot survive long when citizens relinquish their responsibility to be fully engaged in the activities and decisions of their government. Unfortunately, our representative form of democracy has, over time, conditioned us to believe that democracy is simply about voting, perhaps once or twice every four years. But true participatory democracy requires active contribution by each citizen in an ongoing process of consensus building. In the same manner, democratic leadership not only asks, but in some cases demands, that members take on their collective responsibility to the processes of governance and decision making in the organization.

Another vital function for the democratic leader is to provide an atmosphere of empowerment for members of the *demos*. In this context, empowerment refers to the leader creating contexts for members to develop their own decision-making abilities. Empowerment means encouraging members to become practiced in the critical skills necessary for an effective participatory democracy. These skills might include comfort with speaking in public, critical thinking, healthy self-esteem, organizing skills, and a belief in one's own political efficacy. Empowerment also presupposes that the democratic leader takes special care not to become paternalistic with members and avoids behaviors associated with the great-person model of leadership (Schriver, 2010). Finally, empowerment also means that democratic leaders believe in the capacity of members to be leaders themselves and to actively find ways to turn members into leaders.

One of the most important subsidiary functions of a democratic leader is to aid the deliberative processes of the *demos*. Indeed, the bulk of a democratic leader's time is devoted to ensuring productive and democratic decision making. Deliberation, debate, disagreement, compromise, and critique are at the heart of democracy. "Democratic leadership aids the deliberative process through constructive participation, facilitation, and the maintenance of healthy relationships and a positive emotional setting" (Gastil, 1994, p. 961). Practically, this means several things. It presumes that the democratic leader is strategically placed not to determine *what* the members of the *demos* shall think but rather *how* the members will go about the process of thinking and deciding. The democratic leader is the model, mentor, and monitor of a full, inclusionary democratic decision-making process. The democratic leader facilitates democratic decision making by keeping the deliberations on track, encouraging free discussion and broad participation, reminding members to observe the norms and rules adopted by the *demos*, and encouraging healthy emotional interactions and member relationships.

Putting all these theoretical perspectives on leadership together, Schmid (2010) argues that, because organizations vary in their ideologies, goals, and organizational cultures, they will behave differently in their selection of leaders. Leaders are selected and socialized not solely on their personality traits, as Schmid further indicates, but according to the extent that their abilities and qualifications fit different and changing organizational situations. Based on these assumptions, one can predict that in an economic crisis and period of threatened budget cuts to human service organizations the organizational leaders who will emerge will tend to be what Schmid terms "task oriented-external." The focus on attaining external resources and improving the organization's competitive ability will be stressed over people skills.

Multiple Theoretical Perspectives on Organizations

Whereas the robust theory of Weber (1924/1947) lays out the "skeletal bones" of bureaucracy, other perspectives have enriched our understanding of formal organizations, including the loosely defined "human service organizations," which may be so designated because they employ social work professionals, are designated by government, and are part of a network of organizations (Stein, 2003).

Every organization is shaped by the environment in which it is nested (Hasenfeld, 2010). We have looked at how one might define an organization, at organizational leadership, and at how organizations both influence and are influenced by their core constituents: human beings. We have also looked at adopting a critical perspective in our analysis of organizations and organizational structures. In the following brief overview, we sketch several major theoretical perspectives on organizations that have, at one time or another, been very influential in understanding our own organizational culture better (Aldrich & Ruef, 2006; Bolman & Deal, 2008). These theoretical perspectives represent both traditional and alternative perspectives on organizations that may appear quite familiar to the student or that may represent a significant departure from the ways in which organizations have been traditionally understood.

The Classic Bureaucratic Model

The classic bureaucratic model is what most people think of when their minds happen to wander onto the topic of organizations. It is what we all know and have experienced firsthand in our relationships with organizations. Indeed, we may think it is the only, the *true* model of not only how organizations function but also of how they *must* function (Netting & O'Connor, 2003). This theory of organization had its genesis in the mid-nineteenth century as the new tide of industrialism was beginning to wield its influence over Western culture. In the United States, the period of time just after the Civil War was a watershed in both social and organizational terms. There was a proliferation of great industrial enterprises and large corporations, and powerful magnates of the business class were beginning to exert considerable influence on every aspect of American life. By the late nineteenth century, heavy industry and manufacturing were in full swing. America was becoming the world leader in every manner of production and consumption.

At the heart of the industrial revolution was a belief in and reliance on mechanical systems, which were the engines that drove this new revolution. The machine—the steam engine, the cotton gin, the railroad locomotive, the water turbine, the automobile, the mechanical clock—became metaphors for nearly every aspect of modern life. Public and private organizations, corporations, and business were really nothing more than large machines whose parts—rather than being cogs, gears, and pendulums—were humans. Human machines were nothing more than interchangeable parts that fit together to contribute to the smooth and efficient running of the overall mechanism— the bureaucratic organization. This model was very hierarchical, much like a pyramid—a boss, middle managers, and, at the bottom, the worker. Communication generally flowed from top to bottom and decisions were, by and large, calculated based on principles adopted from the new natural sciences and their exquisite methods of data gathering and analysis, which we have come to call the scientific method. The structure of the organization was not generally democratic but, rather, monocratic. It had one person or small group in control—the CEO, managers, administrators—who aimed the organization in one direction to perform one essential function. Those at the bottom were to have few ideas or values and were simply to exchange their quiet acquiescence and labor for a paycheck.

The classic bureaucratic model of organizational structure was probably most effectively illustrated in the work of Frederick Winslow Taylor (1967), who in the early twentieth century developed what he called the *principles of scientific management*. It was Taylor who gave apparent scientific rigor and professional credibility to the increasingly austere and autocratic

principles of organizational structure that had already been in operation for over a quarter century (Brueggemann, 2006). For Taylor, most businesses in the United States were terribly inefficient. Most managers had little idea how to change this, and most workers could not be moved from utilizing the same tired and inefficient skills of earlier generations. For many, scientific management brought optimism to the field of organizational theory and organizational structure that seemed hopelessly outdated and inept. The goal of scientific management was to reduce every single act to a science and thereby increase productivity. Rooted in the "scientific management" concepts of Taylor, performance-based or merit pay plans have evolved as tools for improving individual and organizational productivity by linking organizational goals, performance, pay, and promotion (Rusaw, 2009).

Although the private sector has used various forms of performance-based pay for some time, only recently has the government come to rely on such incentives. According to Rusaw, employee motivation is not enhanced in this manner, and it can lead to a high degree of staff jealousy and reduction in morale. To improve morale, Rusaw recommends a shift to providing opportunities for continuous learning and a reliance on mentoring networks, and jobs that require uses of metacompetencies, particularly critical and creative thinking and their applications to particular social situations. Feminist critiques perceive an inherent conflict between values that women bring to their work environment and the competitive norms of bureaucracy (Hasenfeld, 2010). The risk attached to the bureaucratic management model, according to Canda and Furman (2010), is that the power hierarchy may engender exploitation of workers, remoteness of administrators from clients, and direct service staff, and inflexibility of rules and roles. Conformity rather than creativity may be stressed.

The Human Relations Model

The human relations model of organizations was a reaction to the rationality, the machine-like character, and the alienation and disempowerment often associated with scientific management and bureaucratic theory. With the onset of the worldwide Great Depression of the early 1930s, government officials and average citizens alike began to question the unrestrained power and god-like mastery associated with laissez-faire corporate capitalism. People could no longer believe that the *invisible hand* of the market would create just and prosperous social and economic conditions. Rich, as well as poor, were struck down by the Great Depression. Private philanthropy, corporate largesse, and government intervention seemed incapable of dealing with the mounting economic problems and social upheavals. Organizations were thrown into disarray as mass layoffs, union strikes, and sinking consumer confidence threatened to undermine the very idea that efficient, well-managed, and rational organizations were possible.

Human relations thinking began as a result of several seminal research studies—referred to as the Hawthorne studies—conducted by Elton Mayo and Fritz Roethlisberger at the Western Electric Company. In their research, Mayo and colleagues were looking to analyze ways that could make organizations more efficient and more rational. They were very much in the mindset of the bureaucratic-scientific management model. What Mayo discovered, to his surprise, was that organizational members often function and exert control over organizational dynamics in ways that diverge considerably from the goals of the organization and from what might be predicted from the principles of bureaucratic theory. Along with the outward, functional components of an organization, one could observe an informal, secondary social system that was formed out of the very human needs, feelings, and interests of the members of the organization (Hutchison, 2008). In other words, Mayo came to recognize that, contrary to common belief, organizations function best when managers pay positive attention to workers and when they honor the interests and expectations of the informal networks that workers create within the larger organizational structure. This has come to be known as the *Hawthorne effect*. These may not seem like important insights today, in our much more diverse and egalitarian organizational thinking,

but in the early 1930s these insights began to fundamentally change the way organizations were understood. So pervasive was the influence of these so-called *Hawthorne effect* factors that the metaphors for describing organizations shifted away from the mechanistic, natural scientific, and machine-like symbols; instead, organizations began to be understood as human-like, open systems that are adaptable to their world and that can grow, think, and evolve over time. Persons within this conceptualization of organizations were viewed as contributing members who had needs that must be met and who had creative contributions to make to the organization. The function of management was to understand what made individuals feel needed and what constituted satisfaction.

General Systems Models

General systems models of organizations began to emerge in the United States during the 1960s and 1970s, when the country was entering a new era of optimism, expansion, and growth. New information technologies were beginning to become more commonplace as televisions, early computers, and high-tech wizardry of all types were pushing Americans into the space age and into a new information revolution that would rival the industrial revolution of the previous 100 years. The new metaphor for this period came not from the machine or from human relations but from biology. General system theories have been used to construct models and conduct research on complex organizations in which the organization is viewed as an open system that interacts with the environment. It is affected by the environment, and, conversely, it affects the environment while maintaining its functions in proper states (Takahashi, Kijima, & Sato, 2004). System approaches to organizations focus on the integration of processes and outcomes and on the evolution of a holistic perspective on organizational structure and governance. For example, the interactional processes of staff members in a human service organization and the outcomes established for clients can be modeled and studied from a system's perspective—examining responses to the environment and the changes people experience over time.

One of the most notable examples of the application of a general systems theory to organizations is the *contingency school*. This theory accepts the premise that organizations are in constant movement—that they vary and are contingent on a number of different factors. The contingency model does not see the organization as a static entity but rather as a kind of living system in which everything is situational and in which there are no absolute truths of universal principles (Schriver, 2010). From this perspective, there is no best way to run an organization. Its size, structure, leadership, location, and mission are all dependent on unique variables that can differ from one organization to the next and from time to time. Just as no two human beings are exactly alike, no two organizations are exactly alike. Each one, the biological human being and the organization, must find for itself a unique niche, must adapt to those conditions that it cannot modify, and must seek to influence those conditions that it can change. The bureaucratic school created an organizational image that was static, abstract, and rational. The human relations school focused on including the human element in its understanding of the function of organizations. The contingency perspectives took these theories a step further toward an understanding that organizations are growing entities that both exploit and change their environments. Schriver (2010) draws on the work of Shafritz and Ott (1987) to suggest nine characteristics of contingent systems as they apply to organizations. The following is an adaptation of those nine characteristics:

1. *Importation of Energy*: Organizations must bring in energy from the external environment in the form of material and human resources. Organizations are neither self-sufficient nor self-contained.
2. *Throughput*: Organizations use their energy to produce products or services.
3. *Output*: Organizations send products or services into the environment.
4. *Systems as Cycles of Events*: The pattern of energy exchange that results in output is cyclical. An organization takes in raw materials (energy), uses them to produce a product or service (throughput), and returns that product or service to the environment (output) in exchange for money to purchase additional raw materials with which to begin the process over again

5. *Negative Entropy*: The processes an organization uses to stave off energy loss and decay, also known as entropy. Every organization, like everything in the universe, tends to break down and decay over time. Without concerted and timely effort to slow entropy, organizations will deteriorate. Synergy is the process whereby an organization uses some of the energy it creates in order to maintain and maximize itself.
6. *Information Input, Negative Feedback, and the Coding Process*. These are processes through which organizations develop mechanisms to receive information on their performance. Organizations develop selective coding processes to filter out unnecessary or extraneous information that may not be useful to the organization.
7. *Steady State and Homeostasis*: Organizations strive for a kind of flexible balance whereby they take in energy and information, use it, then export it back to the environment for other needed resources. This is a flexible or movable balance in the sense that it represents a continuous but dynamic state of change rather than a static condition.
8. *Differentiation*: The tendency of the organization to develop greater complexity and specialization of function.
9. *Equifinality*: The possibility of a system to attain its goals through a variety of different processes or paths.

Nonhierarchical, or Consensual, Models

Nonhierarchical, or consensual, models of organizations posit an alternative to traditional models of organizational structure (Bolman & Deal, 2008; Netting & O'Connor, 2003). Traditional perspectives often assume that a top-down hierarchical structure is the norm for an organization and that, indeed, it is a fundamental prerequisite for the efficient functioning of the organization. Even more broadly defined system perspectives assume some degree of hierarchical functioning, although the specific dynamics of this process may change to fit environmental contingencies. The hierarchical assumption dictates that power can and must be divided unequally among the members of the organization. The organization functions best when power is distributed in this manner. Generally, this means that powers rests with administrators and upper- to mid-level management, while workers have little power. These hierarchical structures reinforce a destructive and self-fulfilling source of social control that has the tendency to create organizations that are abusive, retaliatory, and in many cases deceitful both to their workers and to the larger society. Recent examples of these kinds of realities, from large corporate organizations such as Wal-Mart, Nike, and Exxon, serve to illustrate the potential negative impacts of tightly controlled hierarchical, top-down organizational structures.

Consensual models, on the other hand, assume that alternatives to hierarchy are possible in any organization. Indeed, a critical perspective would suggest that one must not accept the absolute necessity and inherent nature of hierarchy to organizational structure. We have seen that nonhierarchical models are not necessarily new. Human relations theory began to focus attention on these concerns well over 70 years ago. However, human relations theory and similar efforts to flatten hierarchical structures have always had a minority voice in organizational studies. Saying that, however, does not suggest that nonhierarchical models have no place in a social worker's understanding of organizations. Indeed, one might argue that in light of social work values that emphasize self-determination, empowerment, and social justice, consensual models are the best fit for social work managers and administrators.

Nonhierarchical models of organizations have been defined as "any enterprise in which control rests ultimately and overwhelmingly with the members-employee-owners, regardless of the particular legal framework through which it is achieved" (Iannello, 1992, p. 31). Nonhierarchical, or consensual, organizations have very different missions and goals for the organization and for its members. A primary goal is to prevent or to minimize the alienation that is experienced by most workers in larger, complex hierarchical organizations. As we have seen, alienation is minimized when workers feel that they have a stake in decision making and in the day-to-day operation of the organization. Hutchison (2008, pp. 429–430), following Iannello (1992), suggests seven traits of non-hierarchical, or consensual, organizations. These include the following:

1. Authority vested in the membership rather than in elite at the top of a hierarchy
2. Decisions made only after issues have been widely discussed by the membership
3. Rules kept to minimum
4. Personal rather than formal relationships among members
5. Leadership based on election, with rotations of leadership positions
6. Nonfinancial reward for leadership roles
7. No winners and losers in decision making—decisions made based on unchallenged prevailing sentiment or consensus

One of the most prominent recent examples of organizations that have been routinely based on nonhierarchical principles is the so-called *Japanese organization* (Macionis, 2004). Of course, there is no single or monolithic Japanese organization, but rather a composite of traits and emphases that have been defined as characteristic of many Japanese organizations. Western interest in the Japanese model grew out of the economic crisis of the 1980s, when American and Europe manufacturing hegemony was under severe threat. In the auto industry particularly, Japanese automobiles set a world standard for quality, reliability, and competitive pricing. The question arose: How could such a small country, still recovering from the destruction of World War II and having had a bad reputation for manufacturing cheap, poorly made products, suddenly become a world powerhouse in the auto industry? Part of the answer was found to be in the organizational structure of Japanese businesses. Japanese organizations often reflect the strong collectivist and collaborative spirit of Japanese culture. In the West, rugged individualism and personal responsibility are prized cultural values. The Japanese value cooperation and collective decision making. To a large extent Japanese organizations had become primary social and cultural group experiences, in addition to being primary economic units. William Ouchi (1981) highlighted five differences between formal organization in Japan and in the United States. We have touched on these in our previous discussion. We also need to be mindful that Ouchi's analysis, given recent economic downturns and corporate structural adjustments, may not completely reflect current Japanese organization practices. They do, however, serve to illustrate some of the general differences.

1. *Hiring and Advancement.* U.S. organizations hold out promotions and salary raises as prizes to be won through individual competition. In Japanese organizations, however, companies hire new school graduates together, and all employees in the group receive the same salary and responsibilities. Only after several years is anyone likely to be singled out for special advancement.

2. *Lifetime Security.* Employees in the United States expect to move from one company to another to advance their careers. U.S. companies are also quick to lay off employees during an economic setback. By contrast, most Japanese firms hire workers for life, fostering strong mutual loyalties. If jobs become obsolete, Japanese companies avoid layoffs by retraining workers for new positions.

3. *Holistic Involvement.* Whereas we tend to see the home and the workplace as distinct spheres, Japanese companies play a much larger role in workers' lives. They provide home mortgages, sponsor recreational activities, and schedule social events. Such interactions beyond the workplace strengthen collective identity and offer the respectful Japanese

employee a chance to voice suggestions and criticisms informally.

4. *Broad-Based Training.* U.S. workers are highly specialized, and many spend an entire career doing one thing. But a Japanese organization trains workers in all phases of its operation, again with the idea that employees will remain with the company for life.

5. *Collective Decision Making.* In the United States, key executives make the important decisions. Although Japanese leaders also take ultimate responsibility for their organization's performance, they involve workers in "quality circles" to discuss decisions that affect them. A closer working relationship is also encouraged by Japan's smaller salary difference between executives and workers—about 10 percent of the difference that is typical in the United States. (Macionis, 2004)

So how does the typical Japanese worker in a large firm or company fare today, given the global economic crisis? Rising sporadic employment and job loss by part-timers, which also means the loss of company housing, has been highlighted in the Japanese press. Yet, as Heinrich and Kohlbacher (2009) suggest, the traditional Japanese lifelong employment, seniority pay, and corporate welfare appears very much intact. The large Japanese companies fear the stigma of being a bad employer, so the Anglo-Saxon "hire and fire environment" seems unlikely to gain much traction in Japan.

Other Nontraditional Theories of Organizations

In addition to the theories we have discussed thus far, other nontraditional theories of organizations have emerged over the last quarter century. We only briefly mention a couple of these. At a less abstract level of analysis, organizations have been observed as reflecting and resulting from the basic *neurogenetic* structure of the brain (Silverman, 2000). So, for example, the rituals carried out in complex organizations are seen as partly a product of the reptilian brain, which wants repetition of behaviors as a survival mechanism. Employing a *psychoanalytic perspective*, Gabriel (1999) provides a host of insights into the workings of organizations. One, a contribution to administration, is the idea that organizations provide control, which is the opposite of chaos. However, control both within the person and in the organization is essentially an illusion.

Anti-Oppressive Analysis

Each of these definitions and theoretical perspectives of organizations, the traditional and the nonhierarchical models, provides an important, albeit incomplete, image of reality (Hanson, 2002). Missing from these representations of organizational theory is attention to political and economic forces that impinge on all organizations, but especially the human service organization (Minkoff, 2010). For a broader and more sociological understanding, we can turn to anti-oppressive analysis. Anti-oppressive theory of organizations, as formulated by Dominelli (2002), provides the provocative, indeed jolting, assessment of what she aptly terms the "new managerialism" (p. 143). Dominelli contrasts a people-oriented system that relies on relationship building with the new bureaucratic imperatives of the global age. Clients, now called consumers, have "become incorporated into a profit-making enterprise that private entrepreneurs can exploit" (p. 143). The profession of social work in the welfare state in Western countries has been subjected to market-oriented regulatory schemes to ensure cost-effective practices. The use of competency-based approaches further curtails professional power.

In summary, traditional theories and perspectives tell us much about the formal structure of organizations. They provide a framework by which we can analyze the organization within which we work. Based on our understanding of organizational structure, for example, we can map out the standard institutional hierarchy, layer by layer, and in this way visualize the chain of command from top to bottom. And we can analyze the flow of communication—for example, asking who are the first and last to

know of institutional changes—in this way to trace the process by which decisions are made. Using systems analysis, we can analyze inputs and outputs across positions within the social structure. Viewing the organization as an open system, environmental exchanges can be traced to reveal the patterns of interaction and the flow of information. Proponents of new conceptualizations integrate new knowledge and offer new metaphors for our understanding of the workings of organizations.

How does organization style relate to sustainability? Research generally shows that open and honest communication and shared decision making are correlates of organizations that thrive and are profitable (Canda & Furman, 2010). Some highly hierarchical organizations, however, such as military establishments may be considered sustainable in the sense that they achieve their recruitment goals and endure. Other highly democratic organization, in ecosystems terms, suffer entropy or shut down. Consider a fair-trade-oriented food cooperative that is forced to close down in a recession. Or a grassroots-run domestic violence shelter that has lost its funding and can no longer meet the needs of victims. The success of some authoritarian, even oppressive, enterprises over some empowering, consensus-based ones often has to do with financing and political support. Without government backing, human service organizations engage in community fund raising, while military and correctional establishments can count on government support. In short, for organizations to be viable they must be economically sustainable and have additional external backing to be capable of fulfilling their goals.

From our perspective, the ecosystems framework, which embodies anti-oppressive notions, extends our vision into the realm of external, political forces. These forces have their origins in "free market" economics and in an ethos that promotes the health of corporations over the health of the people. To understand the workings of the hospital, the mental health center, or the places in which our clients work—in the fast-food industry or the car factory—we need to consult sources such as Prigoff's (2000) *Economics for Social Workers* and Stiglitz's (2003)

Globalization and Its Discontents. One can learn a lot from the economics news magazines *Business Week* and *The Economist* as well. Knowledge from such sources helps us understand how institutions (whether they are in the public or private sector) work in terms of the close link between politics and market economics. Because politics shapes the policies that are the life blood of the social service organization, we start our discussion of the modern organization with a consideration of a key player in global economics—the corporation.

The Corporation

In his critique of American capitalism, Thom Hartmann (2009) argues that our democratic system today is threatened in the light of short-sighted policies and the unregulated reign of free market politics. He pinpoints the influence of the military industrial complex in encouraging production of unnecessary weapons systems, the $15 million the 30,000 corporate lobbyists spend weekly when Congress is in session, and the $1 trillion dollar war budget—as examples of waste. The economic sustainability of the nation, as Korten (2009) writes in his *Agenda for a New Economy*, is threatened by the dominance of economic theories that serve the narrow interests of a few at the expense of the many. These economic theories give the corporations unmitigated power over government policies. For recent examples of practices that have come to public light, consider these recent headlines:

- "Big Tobacco's New Targets" (Kluger, 2009, *Time*)
- "Why Health Care Insurers Are Winning" (Terhune & Epstein, 2009, *Business Week*)
- "Market-Driven Health Care Doesn't Work" (Henry, 2009, *Des Moines Register*)
- "Fannie Mae/Freddie Mac Bailed Out Again; CEO Pay Set for Huge Boost" (Horowitz, 2010, *Legal and Policy Center*)
- "Exploitation of Disabled at Turkey Plant" (Andrews, 2009, *Pro Publica*)

- "Monsanto's Dominance Draws Antitrust Inquiry" (Whoriskey, 2009, *Washington Post*)
- "Document Details Plan to Promote Costly Drug" (Harris, 2009, *New York Times*)
- "Accused Killer's Father: 'The Army Broke Him'" (Wiseman, Stone, & Zoroya, 2009, *Business Week*)

Linking the above headlines is the theme of exploitation of workers, taxpayers, and the general public. All the media headlines are self-explanatory except perhaps for the final one that relates to the killer's father. After being forced to serve three tours of duty in Iraq, this man's son killed five of his fellow servicemen. Stunned by the tragedy, the father lashed out at the army. Other headlines above relate to flaws in free market economics and the need for tighter regulation. At the Texas-owned turkey plant, for example, mentally disabled workers had become virtual slaves to the company that housed and fed them. Social workers employed at Exceptional Persons Incorporated assisted in the rescue of these men who were then placed in halfway houses in a neighboring community.

Resistance to this corporate control of social policies is indicated in Figure 7.2 of a public protest and Figure 7.3 in an information-gathering meeting and planning session by concerned members of an activist organization.

What is the connection of this topic of corporate power to social work? First of all, many social workers work in corporations such as hospitals or private treatment centers or in employee assistance programs (EAPs) under contract to private businesses. But the main effect of the corporate influence ties in with government policy. The effect is evidenced in minimal government funding for social welfare programming but maximum benefits for the business community, including the military-industrial complex (but not for the men and women in the military). Furthermore, the social work profession and the community it serves increasingly are scapegoated as causing social problems in the community. The corporate media compound the business influence. Economics plays into all of this, as political action committees are the source of financing for

Figure 7.2. The negative influence of corporate power is a concern of many. Photo by Rupert van Wormer.

political campaigns. Let us begin with the history of the corporation.

Historical Origins

The history of how the major corporations came to have so much control over American life is a story rarely told in the history books. The award-winning 2003 Canadian documentary *The Corporation* (written by Joel Bakan, who also published the facts in book form the following year; Bakan, 2004) charts the development of the corporation as a legal entity. Available on DVD, the film is highly entertaining, as

Figure 7.3. Seated around a table, members of the Poor People's Economic Human Rights Campaign listen to a presentation on the social contract between the people and the government and how corporate power is eroding the government's ability to honor this contract. Photo by Nicole Martin.

well as informative; the humor is derived from cartoons, background sound effects such as the Wal-Mart employee song, and old news clips from the 1950s. The film features not only interviews with prominent critics of the global economy but also opinions from company CEOs and researchers from conservative think tanks.

The corporation, as we learn, started out as a benign association chartered by governments to carry out public functions of limited duration. This organization rose to become a vast economic enterprise when the Fourteenth Amendment was interpreted to give the corporation the legal rights of a person. This fact shields it from the kind of governmental control one would expect to occur.

Satire is introduced into the film when the fact that the corporation is legally considered a person is taken to the lengths of justifying an official diagnosis. As each of the symptoms of antisocial personality disorder (psychopathy) from the *Diagnostic and Statistical Manual of Mental Disorders* (*DSM*) is listed, a description of behaviors of the corporation is given that match the criteria. For example, given its single-minded drive for profit, the corporation easily meets the criteria for this diagnosis because the corporation has no conscience. Through such use of humor, the film makes the point that the perils of big business have an impact on communities across the globe. Wal-Mart is singled out here and elsewhere as the prime example of the huge chain store that has driven local clothing stores, grocery stores, and pharmacies out of business by using a highly productive formula that involves low wages, poor benefits, and the manufacture of goods in Asia (Greenhouse, 2005).

As indicated in the film, *The Corporation*, as well as the 2008 film on the food industry, *Food, Inc.*, farming is an area of increasing corporate control. Today, Monsanto, for example, controls the production of genetically altered seeds. The vast majority of the nation's two primary crops grow from seeds that are genetically altered to withstand the assault from herbicides produced and patented by the same company (Whoriskey, 2009). Monsanto thus controls 93 percent of the soybeans and 80 percent of the corn produced, so they have the privilege of raising the prices at will. See Chapter 8 on the environment for more information on the impact of the genetically engineered plants on plant and animal life.

Renowned poet and farmer Wendell Berry (2009) deplores these technological developments. He argues for a return to a national consciousness that values farmers and the planting and consuming of the food that is raised. "But," he says, "we…. have decided as a nation and by policy not to love farming, have escaped it, for a while at least, by turning it into an 'agri-industry.'" He continues:

> Agri-industry is a package containing far more than its label confesses. In addition to an array of labor-saving or people-replacing devices and potions, it has given us massive soil erosion and degradation, water pollution, maritime hypoxic zones; destroyed rural communities and cultures; reduced our farming population almost to disappearance; yielded toxic food; and instilled an absolute dependence on a despised and exploited force of migrant workers. (p. 16)

Capitalism is supposed to work because of competition whereby the best companies—the ones that are the most people-friendly and that produce the best products for the money—win out. In the absence of tight regulation, however, monopolies such as Monsanto can enforce policies to eliminate competition and name their price. The pharmaceutical and health insurance companies operate in the same cut-throat fashion. All these corporations invest great resources in ensuring the legislation that is passed is favorable to big business. The automobile industry was one of the earliest of the major American corporations to conspire and lobby for the promotion of their products at the expense of the public good.

People today sometimes ask, What happened to the streetcars? Why did cities tear up their rail tracks? The story all goes back to General Motors, tire companies, and related corporations with an interest in killing off the competition to cars. The first step in getting incentives for Congress to build what would become the world's most extensive and expensive highway system was to replace the popular trolleys and streetcars that operated in the city centers and linked uptown to downtown with noisy, smelly buses. The destruction of the electric streetcar lines was carried out most ruthlessly in California between 1946 and 1958. This in conjunction with urban sprawl created a huge market for privately owned cars and a bonanza for the automobile industry. America's addiction to oil stems from this history (Rutledge, 2006). Today, at great expense, cities all across the United States, following Portland, Oregon's successful example, are investing in light rail. A surge in property values has resulted in housing within walking distance of the rail lines (Driehaus, 2008). The national investment in mass transit, however, is severely limited in comparison with the money placed in highway construction, and General Motors, Ford, and car dealers provide a major source of the revenues to mass media outlets.

In American politics, the role of the corporate media is primary. In a parliamentary system of government, in contrast, the political party controls the votes on key issues, so members of parliament are not dependent on private financing. The United States, in contrast, has a political system in which the individuals who run for office rely heavily on special-interest groups to finance their very lengthy campaigns. According to public records filed with the Senate, industry groups spent $1.1 billion on lobbyists and advertising for the first half of 2004. The top spenders were the Chamber of Commerce and the American Medical Association. General Electric Company spent over $8 million on issues such as gaining Iraq contracts, and the pharmaceutical companies spent a similar amount on legislation affecting Medicare and other health matters ("Lobbying Bill," 2004). Then along came the 2008 election campaign, which resulted in a record $2.4 billion as the most expensive presidential election in history drew to a close (Page, 2008).

The Corporate Media

Corporations are in a position to exert tremendous pressure on the media, which they virtually finance through their advertisements. The extent to which this is so came to light recently when the *Washington Post* (Noon, 2005) carried a story pertaining to an advertising boycott of the *Los Angeles Times* by General Motors. The boycott of the newspaper, which lasted four months and involved approximately $7 million in revenue, was brought about when a *Los Angeles Times* columnist wrote a scathing description of a new General Motors model. A settlement was reached, according to the article, once the *Times* "understood" the automakers' concerns about their coverage. The story of this boycott and subsequent backing down by the newspaper management reveal the extent to which even a progressive newspaper such as the *Los Angeles Times* is forced to cater to advertisers' interests. What is unusual about the case is that it came to light at all and that the newspaper even dared to print the critical column in the first place.

The political influence of the corporate media should not be underestimated. Given the popularity of TV news broadcasts and their power to shape attitudes and therefore human behavior, it is reasonable to examine the factors that go into selecting items for coverage. Social psychologist Elliot Aronson (2007) emphasizes the factor of entertainment value. To attract an audience and therefore corporate sponsorship, film footage of violent crime, celebrity trials, fires, kidnappings, floods, and bombings can be expected to be played at length. The repeated vivid imagery of this sort (as opposed to extensive coverage of the speeches at a peace rally) can create a slanted and false image of the extent of personal risk of victimization. Politicians have a symbiotic relationship with the media; they can generate news stories, but mostly they must (or think they must) reflect the public sentiment in order to win votes. Sometimes, accordingly, their powers of critical thinking are not evident.

To sway the public to protect the interests of the corporations, propaganda strategies are often highly sophisticated and of proven effectiveness. Propaganda ads on TV use such ploys as misrepresenting opposing positions, overgeneralizing and appeals to fear, special interests, and scarcity (Gibbs & Gambrill, 2009).

In the national health care debates, for example, such ads (sponsored by insurance companies and other groups with vested interests in preventing change) have used fear-arousing techniques to defeat initiatives for a public option to compete with private providers of health care. Meanwhile, there was a clamor among members of the public for the passage of some form of universal health care coverage (see Figure 7.4). In the end, manipulations of public fears of euthanasia of old people, creeping socialism, funding for abortion, and rationing of health care, all had an effect to bear on the policy that was shaped. Politicians, for their part, were reluctant to defy the insurance and pharmaceutical companies that they rely on for campaign finance. Republican Senator John McCain deserves credit for fighting over the years for campaign finance reform, for the most part, unsuccessfully, because such reform would have removed some of the clout of the special interest groups.

On March 23, Democrats in Congress celebrated as President Obama signed into law The Health Care and Education Affordability Reconciliation Act of 2010. As described by the *New York Times*, this is "the most expansive social legislation enacted in decades" (Stolberg & Pear, p. A19). A second article from the same source referred to the health care bill as "the federal government's biggest attack on economic inequality" since the enactment of Medicaid in the 1960s (Lenhardt, 2010, p. 1A). Millions of people will have health care insurance and therefore access to health care who did not have it before, and there are new restrictions on insurance companies to keep them from refusing to insure people who had chronic health conditions. And yet The Center for Public Integrity (2010), an organization that conducts investigative journalism, indicates that the true victors in the epic battle for national health care are the pharmaceutical companies and the health care industry. Corporations from these interest groups invested unprecedented amounts of money lobbying Congress, as high as $1.2 billion, according to early estimates (Eaton, Pell, & Mehta, 2010). Judging by the outcome, their money was well spent and preserved the interest of the corporations that had the most to lose from real health care reform. In contrast to Medicare and Social Security which were built on the concept of Franklin Roosevelt's New Deal in which the government

Figure 7.4. As the health care debate took place in Congress, some people gathered on a busy street in Cedar Falls, Iowa, to register their concern. Photo by Robert van Wormer.

was the insurer, health care reform relies on privatized, for-profit corporations to provide the required services for the people.

Critics from the right wing have been much more vociferous than critics of the left. Their focus has been largely on the cost and the mandate placed on individuals to buy health insurance if they are of sufficient means. In the tirade that was expressed against government controls of health care, curiously, the passage of one section of the health care legislation was largely overlooked. This was the section of the bill concerning educational grants for students. In order to save money, the government has removed the middleman and the banks as lenders of the federal student-loan program. Now the Department of Education is to handle the loans directly (Cruz, 2010) for a reported savings of $61 million over 10 years. Had the same approach been taken to health care, the savings could have been considerable as well.

Once the politician is in office, corporations and the corporate media maintain their influence, as Aronson (2007) correctly indicates. The repeated imagery, in conjunction with the bellicose slogans commonly seen on cable news channels—for example, "America Fights Back"—mobilizes the general public for war and for support of massive expenditures to this end. Other issues, such as health care, can then be put on the back burner. Such psychological manipulation has been used by political leaders for centuries to divert the people from a focus on their own economic interests. Patriotic media serve these ends very nicely.

The power of the media to mold public opinion was explored by journalist Paul Krugman (2003) in a *New York Times* opinion piece, "Behind the Great Divide." The great divide at issue is the difference in views toward what was then the pending war against Iraq. Krugman compared U.S. TV news headlines that proclaimed "Antiwar Rallies Delight Iraq" with a very different, much more positive portrayal on the other side of the Atlantic of the huge rallies that took place throughout the world. This difference in reporting, as Krugman speculates, may relate to different perceptions internationally in the role of the media. The American perception may be that it is the job of the media to prepare the public for a coming war. The European media, apparently having a different agenda, are far more critical of U.S. foreign policy. Accordingly, opinion polls, even in Britain, show that citizens there ranked the United States as the world's most dangerous nation.

Following the attacks of September 11, 2001, the government at every level began to restrict the information available to the public, including the holding of suspected terrorists at Guantanamo Bay, Cuba. Television news simply followed the orders of its corporate owners and political advisors in the service of patriotism.

As Chalmers Johnson (2004) suggests in his provocative look at American militarism, the military has become expert at managing the news. To sell the war in Iraq, some 6,000 male and female reporters and television crews were "embedded" with combat units on whom they were dependent for their safety (Johnson, 2004). The goodwill that was shared all round among the reporters and their protectors and comrades guaranteed positive and sanitized stories.

It's not just the government that's squeezing out the news, said journalist Bill Moyers (2004) in an address before the Newspaper Guild. Some of the media giants, he said, are doing it themselves in the form of monopolies—news chains are devouring other chains and reducing local ownership. About 80 percent of the daily newspaper circulation in the United States belongs to a few giant chains such as Gannett and Knight-Ridder, and the trend in owner concentration continues unabated (Parenti, 2002). Media owners do not hesitate to exercise control over news content. This development makes for a conformity of opinions that serves a partisan worldview and one that leaves the dictates of capitalism unquestioned. Clearly capitalism is here to stay; what is needed is greater regulation for the protection of the citizens.

The Need for Tighter Regulations

Much criticism in the printed media and left-wing radio talk shows has been leveled against corporate indulgence and how the big banks and credit card companies get away with deceptive practices and overcharges. Moreover, the explosion in the gifts in the form of extremely generous stock options by executives, huge severance packages of CEOs leaving in disgrace, and CEO pay that is at levels considered by many to be obscene has brought unwanted attention to how the major corporations do business. In recent years, as Mullaly (2007) observes, there has been a barrage of criticism aimed at corporate leadership for the failure to maintain high ethical standards and behavior that has sometimes spilled over into fraud.

A conflict of interest sometimes occurs as representatives of financial interests of one for-profit group are also on the payroll as consultants to political decision makers. A recent cover story in *USA Today*, for example, highlights the situation of corruption by defense contractors who employ retired military generals to help win Pentagon contracts and administrate them at the same time that they serve as advisors to the politicians who help decide on the military budget (Dilanian, Vanden Brook, & Locker, 2009). The popularity of Michael Moore's 2009 satirical documentary, *Capitalism: A Love Story*, which doesn't just go after some of the shoddy practices of major corporations such as Wal-Mart but also questions the nature of the modern U.S. political economy itself, says something about the level of public dissatisfaction. Students of social work and social workers will be interested in a historical flashback to Franklin Roosevelt's 1944 speech in which he endorsed an "economic bill of rights." This bill of rights included a job with a living wage, housing, medical care, and education.

The Corporate Work Model

Downsizing, outsourcing, wage flexibility, cost efficiency, accountability, and productivity—these are just a few of the buzzwords that cause workers in many parts of the world to cringe. Commentators study the impact of Wal-Mart, the $244-billion-a-year retailer, to highlight ruthless tactics in wiping out its rivals and in threatening the economies of small towns through driving small companies out of business. Wal-Mart has excited attention of another kind, however. According to the *New York Times* (Hays, 2003), this retailer has become a best-selling topic for the Harvard Business School, which sells Wal-Mart case studies to business schools around the world. Wal-Mart has become the company to watch and the company to emulate. Its policies—everything from its fight against the unions to its providing partner benefits to gays and lesbians—are highly influential and receive close scrutiny by economists. Wal-Mart's use of new technologies is closely scrutinized by economists as well. Scrutiny of a different sort is provided in the hard-hitting Robert Greenwald (2005) documentary *Wal-Mart: The High Cost of Low Price*. This film, which builds its case relentlessly through interview after interview with former employees of all levels and former small business owners, has received a lot of attention in the press (Burr, 2005).

Today, Wal-Mart employs some 1.4 million people in the United States. To keep the spirits of the workers up, three short rallies take place three times a day when employees let out cheers for Wal-Mart. Not only do the workers have to work fast under enormous pressure to shelve the merchandise but they have to engage in cult-like rites and rituals. As described by Rosenbloom (2009), when asked by the boss, "How do we feel?" the correct response is "Fired up!" (p. BU1). .

In a chapter titled "The Obsolescence of Loyalty" in his book on work, *The Future of Success*, Reich (2000) notes that not only is company loyalty to workers a relic of the past but so also is any sense of responsibility to the hometown. The focus of businesses in what Reich terms "the new economy" is singularly on earnings, on maximizing the value of their investors' shares, not on making contributions to the arts in the hometown community. Today's corporate headquarters can be anywhere near international airports, suppliers and partners, or nowhere in particular, and they continually change as the market changes. The commercial relationships are fleeting; it is hard to talk of social responsibility by organizations. As Reich argues, "in this emerging cyber-landscape it will be odd to speak of institutional loyalty because there will be fewer clear boundaries around any institution" (p. 84).

Interchangeable workers, homogenization of the product, standardized work routines, and technologies that take care of most of the "brain" work (such as making change)—these are among the characteristics of the fast-food restaurant singled out by sociologist George Ritzer (2004) in his popular (especially in Britain) *The McDonaldization of Society.* The process by which the principles of the fast-food restaurant "are coming to dominate more and more sections of American society as well as of the rest of the world" (p. 1) is epitomized in the global McDonald's chain, according to Ritzer. Not just characteristic of the restaurant business, the process is also affecting education, travel, organized leisure-time activities, politics, the family, and, of course, work itself. The McDonald's model has succeeded because time is at a premium in a work-crazed society. This model offers the consumer efficiency, predictability, and food for little money. For the worker, however, the setting is often dehumanizing; the average fast-food worker lasts only 3 months.

Most of the gains in efficiency, as Ritzer (2004) observes, are on the side of those who are pushing rationalization on us. Is it more efficient, for instance, to pump your own gas or to use exact change on a bus? Are prerecorded voices on the telephone responsive to our needs? Borrowing from Max Weber, Ritzer shows how, with greater and greater bureaucratization, the rational has become *irrational.*

Social work is affected by the psychological toll taken on individuals, by the toll on the American family, and by changes in the nature of social work itself. Many social workers now work for private agencies or hospitals, where the bottom line is profit rather than service.

Certainly much of the frustration that social workers feel working in large-scale organizations is a lack of control over the work and the often uninformed mandates from a central office or political entity. It may just be that people know best what they do and that central authority may be more concerned with control than with the original goals of the organization. It could be also that central authority is equally frustrated over the areas in which their influence is waning. In the next section,

we examine some of the pressures from above that affect management, workers down the line, and ultimately clients or consumers.

Impact of the Market Economy on Social Work

In a highly competitive society built on a creed of independence and inequality, the tendency is to cast aspersions on persons who are unsuccessful. The social work profession, which is associated with providing care for persons at the bottom tier of society, is stigmatized along with the population it serves (van Wormer, 2004). In marked contrast to the situation in a more advanced social welfare state such as Norway, where social workers play an active role in shaping policy, American social workers find themselves politically in a more reactive than a proactive role. Many aspects of the neoliberal ethos have only exacerbated the profession's sense of powerlessness in this regard.

The three key themes from the previous section that are related to globalization—privatization, intensified productivity levels, and the technological revolution—have important implications for every area of U.S. social work. The dismantling of social welfare programs is consistent with capitalist incentives to force more workers onto the labor market and increase the pool of cheap labor. The capital that is saved is freed up for future business investment. At the same time that social welfare programs are being dismantled, with drastic consequences for the general public, the social service agencies themselves are operating under harsh mandates that impede protections and reduce benefits for their workers.

The thrust toward *privatization* is a factor that affects the human service work environment in hospitals, mental health clinics, prisons, nursing homes, and child welfare agencies (Mullaly, 2007). Both public (for example, child welfare) agencies and private, not-for-profit organizations increasingly rely today on subcontracting services out as a cost-cutting measure. In northeastern Iowa, for example, much frontline family counseling for child neglect/abuse cases is provided by an outfit called Alternative Services. Employees of the latter organization typically are hired at hourly wages without health and retirement benefits. The pressure for such county and state level cost-cutting measures relates to funding cuts from the federal government. In the present neoliberal climate, there is intense competition among workers for the remaining public-sector social work jobs in local, state, and federal agencies. Competition for such secure, full-time work, in turn, removes the bargaining position of employees. A key casualty of such competition is that unions have become as scarce as the traditional public service jobs.

One result of the downsizing of social service agencies and of funding streams to support social programs, as Besthorn (2003) indicates, is a severe reduction in the number of appropriate field placement opportunities for students of social work. The quality of placements as avenues of first-rate learning experience and socialization into the profession has been seriously reduced thereby. Part of the problem stems from the market economy's emphasis on ever-heightened productivity standards for the worker.

Productivity in the global economy can be conceived as the push for the maximum worker output with the fewest number of workers. With productivity as the goal, worker output must be constantly measured in terms of speed and profitability. Lawyers at a law firm, for example, are required to produce a high number of "billable hours" for the firm. From the standpoint of human service organizations, pursuits such as intense field supervision of interns and public service work are thus sacrificed in order to "balance the books." Services that are not demonstrably cost-effective may no longer be provided. Speaking from his personal experience as student field placement liaison, Besthorn (2003) observes:

> Much more emphasis is now being placed on rapid assessment (problem focused), rapid treatment planning, targeted service delivery, specific and measurable outcome evaluation skills, brief treatment methodologies, and comprehensive recording of treatment progress. (p. 12)

Keep in mind, as Besthorn (2003) further informs us, that management in privatized service delivery is increasingly coming not from social work, not from other helping professions, but from business and public administration. This observation is validated in a recent article in *NASW News* that notes that an astonishing number of businesspeople are now taking the top posts in human services management (Slavin, 2004).

Consistent with the profit-over-treatment, efficiency-over-effectiveness focus of work today, the most often heard buzzwords in social work practice are *accountability, managed care, cost-effectiveness, downsizing, subcontracting, technology transfer*, and *evidence-based practice*. Most of these terms are self-evident, but managed care and evidence-based treatment can use some further clarification. Kirst-Ashman (2008) defines managed care as a changing mix of health insurance, assistance, and payment programs that seek to maintain quality while controlling the cost of the services provided. Financial concerns nevertheless have taken priority over quality. This can create an ethical dilemma for social workers in their advocacy for the best possible treatment for their clients, as Kirst-Ashman suggests. Managed care, typically restricts the choice of available treatment. Patients admitted to the hospital may be released sooner than is medically appropriate.

Although the term *evidence-based practice* is appealing from the standpoint of professionalism and credibility of social work interventions, the exclusion of non-evidence-based treatments means that many forms of traditional therapy (for example, family counseling and conflict-resolution techniques) may lose funding in favor of the easier-to-validate behavioral/cognitive strategies. Social work students skilled in strengths-based, client-centered, and motivational approaches that they were taught in graduate school may feel ill prepared for the reality of social work practice in today's world.

Even in a setting as public as child welfare, the pressures on the social worker (to get more done with fewer resources) are overwhelming. As the federal government puts the bulk of the tax dollars into an ever-expanding war machine, the military-industrial complex (official cost estimates for the war on Iraq are $9 billion per month), the burden for welfare spending falls increasingly on the individual states. And because politicians must be forever concerned with their reelection, they generally vote against the raising of state taxes, so that budget cuts become inevitable at all state-funded institutions. Child welfare is just one area in which much-needed services are now desperately underfunded. Yet reports of child abuse and child neglect are as frequent as ever.

Through the *modern technologies* that produce the shrinking of the world, accountants in India can check income tax forms for the Internal Revenue Service, and hundreds of thousands of Indian and Chinese technicians, programmers, and software engineers are working for U.S. and British companies from their own computers in Asia. Tax incentives provided by the U.S. government ease the burden of relocation abroad.

Paralleling developments elsewhere, the technological revolution is having a major impact on all human service operations. Practitioners now are instructed to use the new computer technology not only to store and access clinical data but also, through the Internet, to retrieve professional papers and medical and technical information and even to participate in continuing education courses offered through distance learning programs. Administrative uses of the computer include the recording of data online, especially data on services provided and even data concerning agency personnel.

Computer technologies do lend themselves to exploitation by managers in their close surveillance of individual workers and of the volume of work performed (Dominelli, 2002). And although office efficiency is enhanced through use of the new technologies, the typical worker's time is now spent more and more in isolation on the computer and less and less in face-to-face interaction with others. And where does the time go? The time goes into filling out multiple forms—forms related to accountability to funding sources, forms for the assessment of mental and/or substance abuse disorders, forms for child abuse investigation findings, and so on. The forms are often standardized, a part of what is called technology transfer; such transfer may or may not accommodate regional or

ethnic differences in populations. Dominelli (2002) sums up the impact of these corporate management forces, as she terms it, in a nutshell:

> Together they have: turned qualitative professional relationships into commodities that can be measured and quantified; subjected service provision to market forces via privatization, and de-professionalized labor through an outcome-based competence approach that converts professional work into a low-paid "proletarianized" activity described as economically productive. (p. 46)

By way of introduction to worker alienation in larger scale organizations within contemporary society, let us review what some of major thinkers have had to say on the subject of alienation and then relate these ideas to social work in today's world.

Classic Views on Alienation

A materialist view of alienation ties the experience of alienation to human activity, and it is this feature that makes alienation an important link between the individual and the social environment, particularly the organizational work environment. Alienation is defined in contemporary contexts as powerlessness, meaninglessness, normlessness, isolation, and self-estrangement (Brueggemann, 2006; Keefe, 1984; Seeman, 1959).

Alienation creates or contributes to tension and stress within the individual and between social systems such as organizational social classes. A variety of insightful conceptualizations of alienation have been articulated. Alienation, noted C. W. Mills (1959), is a major theme of the human condition in both the classic and contemporary literature of economics and sociology. Hegel (1817/1991) saw alienation as derived from the difference between the subjective self of experience and the objective self that is observed, realized, and identified in society. His work was to have a major influence in the development of the ideas of Karl Marx.

For Marx (1867/1967), our work is one important way we human beings relate to the material world. We organize ourselves socially to manage that relationship. Marx did not see alienation as being the same in all societies for all time. Rather, the kinds of alienation changed as society developed through historical periods: from primitive communal tribes to slave states, the feudal order, industrial capitalism, and, in the future, socialism. The ideal human condition, not yet evolved, would be an absence of alienation. This would occur, hypothetically, in an industrial economy in which those who produce wealth also control how it is produced and the wealth it generates. Under these conditions, the sources of alienation, such as social class domination, will be eliminated. One important criticism of this latter idea is that replacing private ownership of production with bureaucratic control of the formal organization may generate similar alienation experiences.

Durkheim (1897/1951) believed that alienation resulted from isolation in a disintegrating society; he introduced the term *anomie*, or normlessness. Weber's (1924/1947) form of alienation was more directly related to work; he saw alienation as arising as a result of bureaucratic centralization and rationalization. But it was Karl Marx who made alienation a powerful theoretical tool for sociological inquiry.

For Marx, alienation is expressed most forcefully in the world of work. Industrial wage workers, the *working class*, seldom own their own tools, control the working conditions, or determine the ultimate destiny of the commodities they produce. Factory work can be stultifying, and actualization needs and talents not useful to production can go unmet and unused. Indeed, one source of alienation and tension in this mode of production is the perception and/or reality that those who make the commodities do not recoup the value of the labor that they put into the manufacture of the commodities. The alienation, however, is not with nature or the local land baron but lies in the productive role itself. And yet there is an even deeper source of alienation in the industrial mode of production.

The Need to Create New Markets

It is in the nature of the capitalist-industrial mode of production, which dominates our historical era, that an economy must *expand to survive*. Competition among producers drives the quest for efficiencies that will secure profit. We are very good at becoming better and better in the production of commodities. We can become so good, in fact, that we may saturate available markets. In this situation, the demand for what we produce may fall and precipitate a *crisis of overproduction*. Workers may see themselves as working themselves out of a job: "The harder and more efficiently I work, the more likely I am to make too much or too many and have to be laid off." Price cuts, layoffs, and economic depression may follow unless greater efficiency can be realized or new markets created.

For a part of our history, Third-World countries served as potential new markets. However, various means of creating new needs and wants in existing markets are constantly devised. Today the predominant strategy is to set up industrial sites abroad in the hopes of selling to the markets in those industrializing nations. Status comes with the purchase of cars, boats, and technological devices—all to be used in the period of rest and recuperation from one's production role at work. All this pressure to consume adds to the alienation already being experienced in production roles.

It is in the nature of capitalist industrial economy to have its ups and downs. This we well know today. The significant downs mean unemployment for some. In a recession, the stresses, anxieties, and sense of losing control over one's life challenge almost anyone, but they can be devastating for some people who may be more vulnerable. Marx did not believe that a welfare society could exist under capitalism, because the dominance of the market would always gain precedence over the needs of the people (Mullaly, 2007). From this perspective, coercion and competition rather than solidarity and cooperation were the bases of capitalist social organization. Social democrats, in contrast, maintain that capitalism can be transformed through conflict among various constituencies and aided by a progressive democratic government. To Mullaly, Marxism is relevant to social work given its insights on the welfare state and its theoretical truths about the conflict between the needs of the people and the needs of profit-making companies. Marxism is also relevant in explaining the alienation of youth who internalize the materialistic goals of society but who fail to achieve these goals except by violating the norms of society.

In her study on political alienation in black youth, Cathy Cohen (2009) analyzes data from a comprehensive survey on political beliefs. While she found that the majority of representatives from African American, Latino, and white groups believed that equality of opportunity exists in the United States, Cohen found more alienation in older than among younger black youth. The most likely explanation is that the younger kids still had their dreams of accomplishment, while the more mature youth had hit the reality of the competitive job market. Cohen did find a gender difference among Latinos with Latina girls expressing more faith in the system than did the Latino boys.

Extending Critical, Material Perspectives: Structuration Theory

These interactions between the individual's identity, attitudes, and behaviors and the larger economic and political systems can be extended when joined with emerging *structuration theory* (see, for example, Giddens's, 1984, model as adapted by Kondrat, 2002). Among other components, structuration theory sees each individual in concert with others as active agents that shape, as well as being shaped by, social structures and institutions. Power is seen as the allocation of rules and resources. Humans are able to observe their own actions and outcomes and adjust accordingly.

The concepts of alienation, anomie, and commodity identity can assist in this observation and action process. In her discussion of structuration theory and research in social work, Kondrat (2002) says:

> According to structuration theory, individual actors construct, maintain, or alter social structures, whereas those same structures shape individual action. A good deal of social work research has focused on the effect of the social environment on

outcomes for individuals. However, by and large, the profession and its researchers have seldom asked the critical corresponding question: How and by what mechanisms are larger structural outcomes constructed and maintained by the interactions of individuals and groups over time? (p. 445)

Critical, material perspectives can contribute to the answer to this important question.

Now we turn to the opposite end of the worker satisfaction continuum—from burnout to empowerment—with a look at the qualities of the empowering organization. Before reading about such organizations, see Box 7.1, "Social Worker Incognito: Empowerment Behind the Wire," in which Ardyth Duhatschek-Krause describes a strengths-based approach by a social worker working within a setting in which humiliation and authoritarian treatment are a part of the routine—a women's state prison.

Box 7.1 Social Worker Incognito: Empowerment Behind the Wire

Ardyth Duhatschek-Krause, MSW, PhD

Even though I am a social worker by profession, the women I work with do not think of me as a social worker. Instead, I am known by the titles of "Director" and "Professor." Conversely, my students are not solely students to me. Because the university program in which I administer and teach is in a state prison for women, I must also view my students as "offenders."

A metal fence topped with circles of electrical barbed wire surrounds my students and me. Even though I am lucky enough to go home each night, my students and I are still literally and figuratively behind this wire together when it comes to our freedoms. My students have certain limitations on their basic freedoms of speech and action. For example, they cannot refuse the orders of authority figures, and there are strict limitations on what they can do, wear, or own. I, too, am limited by the procedural requirements of the prison in both my power to make educationally focused decisions in my formal university roles and in my ability to incorporate social work principles and values in my work with the students. For example, I am required to place "security" as the highest priority in my educational programming. Although crucial to prevent escapes and maintain order for the thousand-plus people living and working within the prison, security is also in direct opposition with one of the most cherished social work principles, that of self-determination. Thus, if a student is planning a class presentation or research paper, I must restrict her from certain topic choices that might in any way promote prison violence or a proclivity toward gang activity or facilitate an escape or a prison uprising. Or, if a student would rather miss class and sleep in with a scratchy throat on a blustery morning, unless she has been formally "laid in" by the medical department, I must "call out" that student and insist that she come to class immediately.

These limitations notwithstanding, I still manage to insert social work principles into my work insofar as it is possible. Drawing on Wilson and Anderson's (1997) five dimensions of empowerment (educational, economic, personal, social, and political), I will briefly show how I shape my instruction and programming accordingly.

Educational and *economic* empowerment come into play as my students work toward the goal of earning a college degree. Often, on graduation day, the students shed the tears of a very special joy. One student seemed to speak for many when she said: "I'm so happy! I have finally done something right!" When she said this, I realized that walking down that aisle of the prison chapel to "Pomp and Circumstance" might be the first time ever for some of the women to achieve societal accolades for an accomplishment.

In my role of instructor in courses on psychology and sociology, I have multiple opportunities to facilitate *personal empowerment*. Keep in mind that these inmates, battered as they have been by life's cruelties and by any regrets they may feel at their own behavior, typically have low self-esteem. The degrading treatment they receive as prisoners compounds this phenomenon. This low self-esteem is evidenced in inmate writings for class assignments. Whether due to earlier substance abuse or personal trauma or poor education, many of the writings are strikingly superficial. In my psychology class, one strategy to help students realize they are special is to

have them choose from a list of adjectives to describe their individual interests, views, and characteristics. A second strategy is to elicit group affirmation. For example, if we are discussing group membership and a student says: "I tend to keep to myself until I know people pretty well," I might ask the class something like: "Why might that be a good idea?" If another student then pipes up and says: "I'm different—I like to ask lots of questions to get to know people on my own," I might then ask the class: "How is asking questions another good way to fit into a group?" Finally, I try to further reinforce the students' sense of competence (as well as the value of individuality) by observing: "Isn't it neat how we can have two entirely different styles, and yet both of them are equally effective ways to relate?"

As both a teacher and an administrator in this environment, I try to provide as many choice-making opportunities as are practical. I do not just say "it is your choice" when I present these opportunities. Instead, I advise the student that a part of the process of deciding whether or not to drop a class, for example, or put extra work into a research paper involves a careful consideration of the pros and cons of all options, plus acknowledging the potential short- and long-term consequences of a choice.

The fourth form of empowerment identified by Wilson and Anderson (1997), *social empowerment*, involves a sense of group identity as a platform from which to influence mezzo and macro systems. Group identity is already well developed within the walls of a prison. The women are very cognizant of their common identity as "offenders." Even though this label seems at first blush to be kinder than the older terms of "prisoner" or "inmate," in my opinion, it is more abhorrent. Being called an "offender" is being told that you continually offend. Most of the women are painfully aware of how they have harmed society with their criminal offenses, or rather how they have "offended." Accordingly, I refer to the women, simply, as students.

My favorite method of social empowerment is therefore to insert content from feminist and women's studies literature into my course content whenever appropriate. Helping these women to develop a group identity as women serves two purposes. First, as opposed to their group identity as offenders, being "women" places them in membership in a group that is in many ways viewed positively by society. Second, women as a group also share oppression as a commonality with offenders. By creating an awareness of the meaning and impact of and coping strategies for the social injustices experienced by women as a minority, I hope to simultaneously instruct them in ways to deal with their other minority group status, that of "offenders."

The final type of empowerment is *political*. This type is actualized by knowledge of and participation in the democratic system. My senior seminar, a course which prepares students for life "outside the wire," includes material on the major political parties. I tell my students that I would like them to understand the political system so that when they get out, they can have an impact on it. I impart my desire that when they are legally able, at the very least, they will vote. (Our state—Indiana—is one of a limited number that eventually allows ex-felons to resume this right.)

A second way that I attempt to facilitate power is to give the students an opportunity to participate in an actual democratic system. Recently, we held an election for a student advisory committee. The students voted for which self-selected candidate they wanted to represent their degree program. The function of this committee is to advise our university program in the self-study that we are doing for accreditation purposes. We are hopeful that, if successful, this committee will become an ongoing opportunity for our students to have a voice in their educational experience.

In summary, it is true that the wire boundary that reduces the liberty of the ones who I serve also partially incarcerates the social worker in me. But what I tell my students, and what I remind myself daily, is that a fence is only a fence. Once we have tapped into the power of our internal wings, we are free to soar together to the remarkable heights of our own potentials.

Reference

Wilson, M. K., & Anderson, S. C. (1997). Empowering female offenders: Removing barriers to community. *Affilia: Journal of Women and Social Work, 12*, 342–369.

Printed with permission of Ardyth Duhatschek-Krause, University of Wisconsin–Eau Clair.

Organizations That Empower

Empowerment is generally conceptualized as a way of increasing power in personal, interpersonal, and political spheres. The change effort must be directed toward both large and small systems. To help clients feel empowered, a human services organization must first maintain a working environment in which the staff members engage in collaborative decision making. As social workers come to play active roles in their agency or other organization, their supervisors are modeling for them the roles they will take with their clients. The values of self-determination, collaborative decision making, shared values that promote multiculturalism, social justice, and a concern for client and worker welfare, all help create a supportive climate for all participants. Attention is paid to staff development, and education in organizational empowerment.is a work in progress. Because most large social service organizations are hierarchical in nature, persons who wish to create empowering organizations must look beyond the status quo to alternative models (Lazzari et al., 2009). In the alternative model described by Gutiérrez and Lewis (1999), the board of directors and administrators, as well as staff members, develop an organizational culture that is strengths-based. Because so few such organizations exist, organizational change is often necessary. Change efforts can start with data gathering, the rounding up of supporters, and presentation of a proposal for change at a staff meeting. Organizers should introduce ideas one at a time, be flexible and open to suggestions, and not invest too much power in one individual.

Long, Tice, and Morrison (2006) recommend a strengths-based assessment of the organization that parallels such an assessment of clients. Such an assessment helps macro social workers and consumers to focus on present conditions and discover areas of concern. Such an exercise is empowering in itself, as it promotes communication at all levels, including with constituents in the community. The ultimate goal is to give people, even those who are seemingly incompetent, more control over their own lives. New policies and programs can be designed not *to use on* consumers but *in conjunction with* consumers.

Sondra Doe (2004) suggests a link between strategy-based social work values and empowerment strategies within organizations to foster an effective work and treatment environment. Doe advocates a leadership style that is guided by a belief in the possibilities of the human spirit and egalitarian work relationships. Doe urges social work researchers to investigate the relationships when organizational effectiveness and spiritually based values are operationalized in a human service organization.

Practice Implications

The impact of extensive budget cuts at the state and local levels, a response to pressures from the global economy, in fields that specialize in working with people, such as teaching, nursing, and social work, is pronounced. There are fewer people today doing more and more work. And standards for university degrees, licensing, and so forth help preserve jobs for professionally qualified people. Talk of burnout is common, often due to work strain or the need for a long vacation from work in general or from dealing with a specific difficult population. Hutchison (2008) advises that social workers need to be attuned to symptoms of job-related burnout in their clients and in themselves. The social worker otherwise might feel alienated or estranged from the place of work when:

- The goals and aims of the organization conflict with social work values.
- The practices of the organization conflict with the agency mission.
- Client welfare is ignored or threatened.
- The social worker has authority to make certain decisions but lacks the power to do so.
- The worker encounters prejudice of some sort, for example, based on race, gender, age, sexual orientation, or style of dress.
- Pressures external to the organization hinder creativity and good use of individual talents.
- Personality conflicts and/or turf disputes produce an atmosphere of tension.

- Personal and family obligations cannot be met because of a heavy workload.
- The client caseload is too high to do an adequate job.

Summary and Conclusion

The ever-widening gap between the rich and the poor in our society is reflected in the huge social distance among different kinds of organizations in the social structure. Whereas the major corporations generally are thriving in the market economy and have a great deal of political clout, organizations such as health care facilities, nursing homes, and even higher education are struggling to maintain an acceptable level of services in the face of cutbacks. The corporation, as we have seen in this chapter, influences politics directly through contributions to politicians and indirectly through the corporate media to mobilize public opinion in favor of programs that benefit big business; for example, the privatization of services.

Organizations can be formal or informal, for profit or nonprofit, private or government owned. All are bureaucratic to various degrees, with a clear designation of authority. Human service organizations tend to be more humane, or at least more people-centered, than many others, such as industrial plants or technical companies, that exist solely for the purpose of generating business. In social work fields, the moral meaning of human relationships and the mission of helping people have been primary (Doe, 2004). Today, increasingly, however, the business model has come to serve as a model for social service agencies, with a focus on accountability of the agency to the funding sources, downsizing of staff, budget cuts, and cost-effectiveness of programming.

The same global forces of heightened competition among workers in manufacturing, farming, and white-collar work that are the cause of so much anguish to our clients are the cause of much distress throughout the social welfare system. As the power of the corporation has increased in every aspect of life in the welfare state, the power of the ordinary worker to control the conditions of his or her work has decreased commensurately. The providers of social services are affected similarly through ever-expanding workloads, in conjunction with shrinking funding. Competing mandates to control costs and to offer high-quality services can create feelings of alienation among members of the helping professions. Pressures from above are matched from pressures from below when client needs fail to be met.

The agency's working climate or culture reflects these societal pressures in terms of workload, lack of job security, and a general atmosphere of tension. But beyond that, the organizational culture of each agency is unique. This uniqueness derives in large part from such elements as the personalities of the cast of characters who occupy key positions. Facts related to the clientele and their level of motivation for treatment, of course, have an impact on agency culture as well.

The leadership style can have a crucial impact on worker morale. This chapter explored leadership theories in answer to the question, What makes a good leader? The theories variously posited personality traits, situational factors, and placement in a position of authority as factors in effective leadership. Our discussion of democratic leadership spelled out the qualities and functions of leadership that are associated with empowerment of members of the organization.

Two opposite themes emerged in this chapter: alienation and empowerment. The forces of alienation were seen as stemming from pressures in the global economy and focus on technologies more than on people. Within this economic climate, however, many social workers and their organizations have managed to remain faithful to the mission of social work. This mission is based on the concepts of social justice and client empowerment. When applied to an organization, empowerment derives from a democratic structure in which process is stressed as much as goals. Social workers committed to empowerment in their agencies work to meet the needs of the community and to help the agency move from a top-down decision-making process to one that is more collaborative. Social workers who are thus empowered

in their profession are better able to model this attribute with their clients.

As we conclude this chapter, we move from a consideration of social justice in the economic sphere to a consideration of environmental justice. The focus shifts from economic and social equity to sustainability of the earth's resources, from the social worker as organizational reformer to the social worker as ecoparticipant. Human behavior in the natural or physical environment is the subject of Chapter 8.

Thought Questions

1. Consider an organization with which you are familiar. Using Goffman's terminology, discuss the image management of this organization.

2. Name and describe some comedy shows that take their comedy from breakdowns of one sort or another of the smooth running of an organization.

3. Define the terms *organization* and *organizational culture*.

4. Discuss the boxed reading student testimonial which describes the rift between her idealism and the realities attached to clinical social work at an agency.

5. What makes a good leader? Is it personality, position in the organization, circumstances, or style of leadership? Consider whether the qualities can be learned or are innate. Have you ever had a boss who fulfilled the characteristics of a Theory X leader? If so, discuss his or her effectiveness or ineffectiveness in running the organization. If not, interview a worker who has had such an experience.

6. List and discuss the characteristics of bureaucracy as spelled out in classic theory. Contrast these principles with those of human relations theory of organizations. Which aspects of the bureaucracy might you have difficulties adjusting to, if any?

7. Contrast company management styles in Japan with those in the

United States. Which style do you prefer and why?

8. What is the anti-oppressive viewpoint regarding organizational theory?
9. Record the history of the corporation, how it was created by politicians but gradually came to call the shots in American politics.
10. Some say we have a liberal press; others say we have a corporate press. Using facts at your disposal, argue one or the other or both of these propositions.
11. What is meant by the corporate work model? Relate this model to the giant corporations.
12. What is the meaning to you of the "obsolescence of loyalty" regarding work?
13. Relate forces in the global market economy to social welfare and social work.
14. What does the stress on productivity mean to the average social worker? Relate it to your own experience in the field, or conduct relevant interviews with social workers. Can you think of any areas of work that are not affected by the new productivity standards? How about accountability? Cost-effectiveness?
15. Discuss alienation theory as espoused by classic theorists and relate it to the pressures on the worker in today's world.
16. List some of the causes of worker burnout. How can these factors be avoided?
17. Describe how one social worker within a nonprogressive institution—a women's prison—was able to draw on her social work imagination and philosophy of empowerment to help the women in her charge.
18. Describe the essence of an empowering organization in which social workers might be able to pursue their social justice orientation and thereby feel empowered themselves.

References

Aldrich, H., & Ruef, R. (2006). *Organizations evolving*. Thousand Oaks, CA: Sage.

Andrews, A. (2009, February 9). Exploitation of disabled at turkey plant. *Pro Publica*. Retrieved from http://www.propublica.org/article/afternoon-quick-pick-exploitation-of-disabled-at-turkey-plant

Aronson, E. (2007). *The social animal* (10th ed.). New York: Worth.

Bakan, J. (2004). *The corporation: The pathological pursuit of profit and power*. New York: Free Press.

Bass, B. (1990). *Bass and Stogdill's handbook of leadership*. New York: Free Press.

Berry, W. (2009, December). The necessity of agriculture. *Harper's Magazine*, pp. 15–16.

Besthorn, F. H. (2003, April). Globalization, privatization and the devolution of the social safety net: A U.S. perspective on the implications for practice teaching. Paper presented at the International Conference of the *Journal of Practice Teaching in Health and Social Care*, Imperial College, London.

Bolman, L., & Deal, T. (2008). *Reframing organizations: Artistry, choice and leadership*. Hoboken, NJ: Jossey-Bass.

Bordas, J. (2007). *Salsa, soul, and spirit: Leadership in a multi-cultural age*. New York: Berrett-Koehler Publishers.

Brager, G., & Holloway, S. (1978). *Changing human service organizations: Politics and practice*. New York: Free Press.

Brilliant, E. (1986). Social work leadership: A missing ingredient? *Social Work, 31*, 325–330.

Brueggemann, W. (2006). *The practice of macro social work* (3rd ed.). Belmont, CA: Brooks/Cole.

Burr, T. (2005, November 11). Dogged documentary presents a damning case against Wal-Mart. *Boston Globe*. Retrieved from http://www.boston.com/ae/movies/articles/2005/11/11/dogged_documentary_presents_a_damning_case_against_wal_mart/

Canda, E. R., & Furman, L. D. (2010). *Spiritual diversity in social work practice*. New York: Oxford.

Chickering, A., Dalton, J., & Stamm, L. (2006). *Encouraging authenticity and spirituality in higher education*. San Francisco: Jossey-Bass.

Cohen, C. J. (2009). From Kanye West to Barack Obama: Black youth, the state, and political alienation. In L. Jacobs & D. King (Eds.), *The unsustainable American state* (pp. 255–295). New York: Oxford University Press.

Cruz, G. (2010, April 5). Student loans get a government takeover. *Time*, p.12.

Dilanian, K., Vanden Brook, T., & Locker, R. (2009, December, 29). At Colorado firm, a cluster of retired brass is raking it in. *USA Today*, p. 1A.

Doe, S. S. (2004). Spiritually based social work values for empowering human service organizations. *Journal of Religion and Spirituality in Social Work, 23*(3), 45–65.

Dominelli, L. (2002). *Anti-oppressive social work theory and practice*. Hampshire, UK: Palgrave.

Draft, R. (2004). Theory Z: Opening the corporate door for participative management. *Academy of Management Executives, 18*(4), 117–122.

Driehaus, B. (2008, August 14). Downtowns across the U.S. see streetcars in their future. *New York Times*, p.A17.

Durkheim, E. (1951). *Suicide: A study in sociology*. Glencoe, IL: Free Press. (Original work published 1897).

Eaton, J., Pell, M., & Mehta, A. (2010, March 26). Washington lobbying grants cash in on health care reform debate. *New York Times*, p. A10.

Elsner, P. (2006, January 5). Authenticity and leadership: Integrating our inner lives with our work. Retrieved from http://www.paulelsner.com/pdf/2AUTHENTICITY.pdf

Finn, J., & Jacobson, M. (2003). Just practice: Steps toward a new social work paradigm. *Journal of Social Work Education, 39*(1), 57–79.

Gabriel, Y. (1999). *Organizations in depth*. Thousand Oaks, CA: Sage.

Gardner, J. (1993). *On leadership*. New York: Free Press.

Gastil, J. (1994). A definition and illustration of democratic leadership. *Human Relations, 47,* 953–975.

Gemmil, G., & Oakley, J. (1992). Leadership: An alienating social myth. *Human Relations, 45,* 113–129.

Gibbs, L., & Gambrill, E. (2009). *Critical thinking for helping professionals: A skills-based workbook* (3rd ed.). New York: Oxford University Press.

Giddens, A. (1984). *The constitution of society*. Oxford, UK: Polity Press.

Goffman, E. (1959). *The presentation of self in everyday life*. New York: Doubleday.

Goffman, E. (1961). *Asylums: Essays on the social structure of mental patients and other inmates*. London: Anchor Books.

Greenhouse, S. (2005, November 5). Wal-Mart gets report card and gets a "C." *The New York Times*, B4.

Greenwald, R. (2005). *Wal-Mart: The high cost of low price*. Brave New Films. Retrieved March 18, 2010, from http://www.walmartmovie.com

Gutiérrez, L., & Lewis, E. (1999). *The empowerment approach to practice*. New York: Columbia University Press.

Hanson, M. (2002). Practice with organizations. In M. Mattaini, C. Lowery, & C. Meyer (Eds.), *The foundations of social work practice: A graduate text* (3rd ed., pp. 263–290). Washington, DC: NASW Press.

Harris, G. (2009, September 2). Document details plan to promote costly drug. *The New York Times*, p. B1.

Hartmann, T. (2009). *Threshold: Crisis of western civilization*. New York: Viking Press.

Hasenfeld, Y. (2010). The attributes of human service organizations. In Y. Hasenfeld (Ed.), *Human services as complex organizations* (2nd ed., pp. 9–32). Los Angeles: Sage.

Hays, C. C. (2003, July 27). The Wal-Mart way becomes topic A in business schools. *The New York Times*, p. BU10.

Hegel, G. W. F. (1991). *The encyclopedia logic: Part 1 of the encyclopedia of philosophical sciences* (T. F. Geraets, W. A. Suchting, & H. S. Harris, Trans.). Indianapolis, IN: Hackett. (Original work published 1817).

Heinrich, S. & Kohlbacher, F. (2009, June 11). Labor market—Sayonara salaryman? Change and continuity in Japan's permanent employment system. *Japan-Inc., 86.* Retrieved March 18, 2010, from http://www.japaninc.com/mgz86/sayonara-salaryman

Henry, S. (2009, August 20). Market-driven health care doesn't work. *Des Moines Register*, p.13A.

Hersey, P., & Blanchard, K. (1988). *Management of organizational behavior: Utilizing human resources* (5th ed.). Englewood Cliffs, NJ: Prentice-Hall.

Horowitz, C. (2010, January 6). Fannie Mae/Freddie Mac bailed out again; CEO pay set for huge boost. *Legal and Policy Center*. Retrieved from http://www.nlpc.org/stories/2010/01/06/fannie-maefreddie-mac-bailout-ceo-pay-set-huge-boost

Hutchison, E. (2008). *Dimensions of human behavior: Person and environment* (3rd ed.). Thousand Oaks, CA: Sage.

Iannello, K. (1992). *Decisions without hierarchy: Feminist interventions in organization theory and practice*. New York: Routledge.

Johnson, C. (2004). *The sorrows of empire: Militarism, secrecy, and the end of the Republic*. New York: Metropolitan Books.

Kane, J., Patapan, H., & Hart, P. (Eds.). (2009). *Dispersed democratic leadership: Origins, dynamics, and implications*. New York: Oxford University Press.

Keefe, T. (1984). Alienation and social work practice. *Social Casework, 29,* 145–153.

Kirst-Ashman, K. (2008). *Human behavior, communities, organizations, and groups and the macro social environment: An empowerment approach* (2nd ed.). Belmont, CA: Brooks/Cole.

Kluger, J. (2009, July 27). Big tobacco's new targets. *Time,* pp. 50–51.

Kondrat, M. E. (2002). Actor-centered social work: Re-visioning "person-in-environment" through a critical theory lens. *Social Work, 47,* 435–448.

Korten, D. C. (2009). *Agenda for a new economy: From phantom wealth to real wealth.* San Francisco: Berrett-Koehler Publishers.

Krugman, P. (2003, February 18). Behind the great divide. *The New York Times,* A27(N), A23(L).

Lazzari, M., Colarossi, L., & Collins, K. (2009). Feminists in social work: Where have all the leaders gone? *Affilia, 24*(4), 348–359.

Lee, J. A. (2001). *The empowerment approach to social work practice: Building the beloved community* (2nd ed.). New York: Columbia University Press.

Lenhardt, D. (2010, March 23). In health bill, Obama attacks wealth inequality. *New York Times,* p. 1A.

Lewin, K., Lippitt, R., & White, R. K. (1938). Patterns of aggressive behavior in experimentally created social climate. *Journal of Social Psychology, 10,* 271–299.

Lobbying bill tops $1.1 billion for the first half of 2004. (2004, December 29). *The Los Angeles Times.* Retrieved from the Center for Media and Democracy Web site: http://www.prwatch.org/node/3148

Long, D., Tice, C., & Morrison, J. (2006). *Macro social work in practice: A strengths perspective.* Belmont, CA: Thomson.

Macionis, J. (2004). *Society: The basics.* Upper Saddle River, NJ: Pearson Education-Prentice Hall.

Marx, K. (1967). *Capital: Vol. 1. A critique of political economy.* New York: International. (Original work published 1867).

Massey, D. (2009). Globalization and inequality: Explaining American exceptionalism. *European Sociological Review, 25*(1), 9–23.

McGregor, D. (1960). *The human side of enterprise.* New York: McGraw-Hill.

Mills, C. W. (1959). *The sociological imagination.* London: Oxford University Press.

Minkoff, D. (2010). The emergence of hybrid organizational forms: Combining identity-based provision and political action. In Y. Hasenfeld (Ed.), *Human services as complex organizations* (2nd ed., pp. 117–138). Los Angeles: Sage.

Moxley, R. (2000). *Leadership and spirit.* San Francisco: Jossey-Bass.

Moyers, B. (2004, May 14). An eye on power. Address presented at the National Conference on Media Reform, St. Louis, Missouri. Retrieved from http://www.newsguild.org/gr/gr_display.php?story

Mullaly, B. (2007). *The new structural social work: Ideology, theory, practice.* New York: Oxford University Press.

Myran, G., Myran, S., & Galand, R. (2004). The spiritual dimension of leadership. *Community College Journal, 74*(4), 10–13.

Netting, H., & O'Connor, M. (2003). *Organizational practice: A social worker's guide to understanding human services.* New York: Allyn and Bacon.

Noon, C. (2005, April 8). Wagoner: GM pulls ads from 'L.A. Times' after critical column. *Forbes.* Retrieved from http://www.forbes.com/2005/04/08/0408autofacescan04.html

Ouchi, W. (1981). *Theory Z.* New York: Avon Books.

Palmer, P. (2000). *Let your life speak.* San Francisco: Jossey-Bass.

Palmer, P. (2004). *A hidden wholeness: the journey toward an undivided self.* San Francisco: Jossey-Bass.

Page, S. (2008, October 29). Campaign spending scrutinized. *USA Today.* Retrieved from http://www.usatoday.com/news/politics/election2008/2008-10-29-poll-campaign_N.htm

Parenti, M. (2002). *Democracy for the few* (7th ed.). Belmont, CA: Wadsworth.

Prigoff, A. (2000). *Economics for social workers.* Belmont, CA: Wadsworth.

Rank, M., & Hutchison, W. (2000). An analysis of leadership within the social work profession. *Journal of Social Work Education, 36,* 487–502.

Reich, R. (2000). *The future of success: Working and living in the new economy.* New York: Vintage Books.

Rendon, L. (2006). Realizing a transformed pedagogical dreamfield: Recasting agreements for teaching and learning. *Spirituality in Higher Education, 2*(1), 1–13.

Rifkin, J. (1996). *The end of work: The decline of the global labor force and the dawn of the post-market era.* Los Angeles: Tarcher.

Rifkin, J. (2002). *The hydrogen economy*. New York: Tarcher/Penguin.

Ritzer, G. (2004). *The McDonaldization of society* (4th ed.). Thousand Oaks, CA: Pine Forge Press.

Rosenbloom, S. (2009, December 20). My initiation at store 5476. *New York Times*, p. BU1.

Rusaw, C. (2009). Professionalism under the "performance-based pay" reform: A critical assessment and alternative development model. *Public Personnel Management, 38*(4), 35–55.

Schmid, H. (2010). Leadership styles and leadership change in human and community service organizations. In Y. Hasenfeld (Ed.), *Human services as complex organizations* (2nd ed., pp. 193–206). Los Angeles: Sage.

Schriver, J. (2010). *Human behavior and the social environment: Shifting paradigms in essential knowledge for social work practice* (5th ed.). Boston: Allyn & Bacon.

Seeman, M. (1959). On the meaning of alienation. *American Sociological Review, 24*, 783–791.

Shafritz, J., & Ott, J. (1987). *Classics of organization theory* (2nd ed.). Chicago: Dorsey Press.

Silverman, D. (2000). *The neurogenic roots of organizational behavior*. Landham, MD: University Press of America.

Slavin, P. (2004, May). Managing the human services business. *NASW News, 49*(5), p.4.

Somers, M., & Block, F. (2005). From poverty to perversity: Ideas, markets, and institutions over 200 years of welfare debate. *American Sociological Review, 70*, 260–278.

Stein, H. D. (2003). The concept of the human service organization: A critique. In H. D. Stein (Ed.), *Challenge and change in social work education: Toward a world view*. Alexandria, VA: Council on Social Work Education.

Stiglitz, J. (2003). *Globalization and its discontents*. New York: Norton.

Stoesz, D. (1997). The end of social work. In M. Reisch & E. Gambrill (Eds.), Social work in the 21st century (pp. 368–375). Thousand Oaks, CA: Pine Forge Press.

Stolberg S., & Pear, R. (2010, March 24). The stroke of a pen, make that 20, and it's official. *New York Times*, p. A19.

Takahashi, S., Kijima, K., & Sato, R. (Eds.). (2004). *Applied general systems research on organizations*. Tokyo: Springer.

Taylor, F. (1967). *Principles of scientific management*. New York: Norton.

Terhume, C., & Epstein, K. (2009, August 17). Why health insurers are winning. *Business Week*, pp. 35–40.

Tisdell, E. (2003). *Exploring spirituality and culture in adult higher education*. San Francisco: Jossey-Bass.

van Wormer, K. (2004). *Confronting oppression and restoring justice: From policy analysis to social action*. Alexandria, VA: CSWE.

Vaughan, F. (1995). *Shadows of the sacred: Seeing through spiritual illusions*. Wheaton, IL: Quest Books.

Weber, M. (1947). *The theory of social and economic organization* (A. M. Henderson & T. Parsons, Trans.). Oxford, UK: Oxford University Press. (Original work published 1924).

Whoriskey, P. (2009, November 29). Monsanto's dominance draws antitrust inquiry. *Washington Post*. Retrieved from http://www.washingtonpost.com/wp-dyn/content/article/2009/11/28/AR2009112802471.html

Wiseman, P., Stone,A., & Zoroya, G. (2009, May 12). Accused killer's father: The army "broke him." *USA Today*. Retrieved from http://www.usatoday.com/news/world/iraq/2009-05-12-iraq-shooting_N.htm

Zeleny, J. (2010, January 28). At Florida stop, Obama announces rail investment. *New York Times*, A12.

Human Behavior and the Natural Environment

The Community of the Earth

When the animals come to us,
asking for our help,
will we know what they are saying?
When the plants speak to us
in their delicate, beautiful language,
will we be able to answer them?
When the planet herself
sings to us in our dreams,
will we be able to wake ourselves, and act?

—GARY LAWLESS

(1994)

There can be little denying that we are living in a period of transformation on the earth generally and in all the institutions and popular cultural icons of Western society, specifically. From the recent actions of former President Bush that seemed bent on severing the United States from its responsibility to the global community, the catastrophic events of the Indian Ocean tsunami and Hurricanes Katrina and Rita, and President Obama's new initiatives to reduce global warming and spur a green economy, we are beginning a slow awakening to the possibility of impending environmental disaster. Social work itself is also experiencing deep changes in its awareness in what it believes and values and in how it goes about its business of service and care. Never before have we had so much wealth, so much affluence, so much knowledge and information about ourselves and about the conditions of the our world around us. And yet, as we are ushered into the first decade of this new millennium, most of what we know both professionally and personally is scaring us. What we know is deeply unsettling, while at the same time the modifications that need to occur to change our collective psyche and to bring our relationships to the earth and to each other back into balance seem monumental and, at times, overwhelming.

We read each day about the earth's rapid deterioration: the widening hole in the ozone layer; the destruction of the last remaining rainforests; global warming; and the toxic chemical invasions that have infiltrated our oceans, our bodies, and our genetic inheritance. Social work practitioners and students, along with most citizens from every other oil-based economy in the world, also face the growing problem of oil-fuel dependency and the difficulty associated with trying to maintain professional and personal commitments in an economy with escalating fuel prices. We have created massive problems that it seems no amount of technological tinkering or scientific management will correct in the foreseeable future.

Yet the global crises of consumer culture and impending environmental collapse also hold within them tremendous opportunity to redirect our physical, political, and spiritual energies and resources to heal our greed, to heal our planet, and to heal our relationships with each other and the earth community (Akerlof & Shiller, 2009). Essentially, we as social workers, as professional helpers, and as constituents of modern Western society are being challenged at the core of our being, at the center of our professional values, at the convergence of traditional institutions to redefine what it means to be human and what it means to be a citizen of the earth.

The challenges we face are daunting. How do we balance the needs of billions of the earth's people with the needs of the rest of the biological world? How can we replace the ethic of endless economic growth and consumption with a commitment to meet basic human needs? How do we build a social work profession of helping that recognizes the intrinsic value of all beings and how humans fit within that larger cosmic scheme? How do we balance the rhetoric of our profession's environment models, with their historic preoccupation with internal psychic problems and close social circumstances, with a deeper environmental awareness of a whole earth community? How do we build a global community based on cooperation and tolerance instead of militarism, economic colonialism, and environmental imperialism? Where does our commitment to collective justice meet our dedication to personal change?

This chapter describes the scope of the current environmental crisis, offers a history of social work's environmental conceptualizations, and proposes an expanded ecological model for social work that is built on principles of sustainability, deep ecology, and ecofeminism. The two worlds of social work and the physical environment are interconnected in that human physical problems often emanate from environmental abuses; among them are birth defects, cancer, respiratory problems, and lead and radiation poisoning. It is imperative that social welfare professionals be guided by sustainable social development concepts and sound environmental practices and that they contribute to critical policy decisions in this time of unprecedented global challenge. We ask the reader to keep in mind that, although we believe that deep ecology and ecofeminism make

important philosophical and practical contributions to assessing the congruency of social work's values and current person-in-environment conceptualizations, we are not suggesting they are the only models that might be helpful. We ask that you judge them on their own merits and continue your own journey of discovery. Indeed, our challenge is always to begin where the client is and make every effort not to impose our own belief systems onto the stories of their lives. We trust that what you find here will be helpful in affirming that core practice principle even as you broaden your own understanding of the serious ecological problems facing our world.

Note that this chapter is concerned with the *biological* component of the bio-psycho-social-spiritual study of human behavior. *HBSE, Micro Level* (van Wormer, 2011) considered this component at the individual level with respect to human physiology, addiction, and personality traits. The parallel concern here is with the external realm of the world around us. Consistent with the macro focus of this book, the emphasis is on the sustainable environment—clean air and water and uncontaminated and abundant plant and marine life. Figure 8.1 captures the essence of the forest ecosystem. We also consider the reverse of conservation—the threat to all life through the humanmade destruction of the air we breathe, the water we drink, and the food we eat. Sociology and biology come together, as do poverty and the environment. Although all humans are affected by environmental degradation, poor children in poor neighborhoods are at the greatest risk of developing health problems due to exposure to contaminants.

Ecological Disaster and Decline: Global Challenges

The overworked, overwhelmed, and perhaps skeptical social worker or reader might reasonably wonder whether this is yet another of the editorial diatribes that have become all too common as the world begins to recognize the depth of pressing environmental issues. Is it

Figure 8.1. The forest is an ecosystem in which all forms of life are interconnected and interdependent. Photo by Kathleen Besthorn and Margie Hayes.

just another boring catalogue of environmental problems that serves no useful purpose concerning the "real-world" problems of the people that social workers are trying hard to serve? We think not. We think it is of utmost importance that these issues now become a major part of how social work understands itself and its practice. As suggested earlier, recent catastrophic environmental disasters in the Gulf Coast region of the United States and the horrific tsunami event in the Indian Ocean that claimed thousands of lives are just two of a growing number of stark reminders that the world community is reaching a critical threshold in its relationship to the natural environment. Putting our collective heads in the sand and pretending that these issues will resolve themselves or that someone else will take care of them for us serves no one's best interests—especially not those of our clients.

The wholesale destruction of earth's ecosystems, in the sense of making the planet relatively unusable for human purposes, has grown to such an extent just within the past 50 years that human-induced and -catalyzed destructive activity now threatens much of nature and the very survival of human societies all around

the world. The list of deeply troubling ecological disturbances encompasses a long inventory of pressing environmental problems. These include such vital concerns as overpopulation, global warming, depletion of the ozone layer, wetland and coastal estuarial erosion, water pollution, air pollution, species extinction, loss of genetic diversity, overfishing, toxic waste, poisonous effects of chemical-based fertilizers and pesticides, desertification, mass population dislocations due to the collapse of strategic environmental systems, famine, global pandemics, and dozens of less well-publicized but nonetheless troubling environmental issues.

"As Climate Change Accelerates, So Too Will Hunger, Poverty, and Perhaps Even Social Unrest" is the title of an article by the United Kingdom's Prince of Wales (2009). In the editorial, Prince Charles argues for a new approach to climate change that would include sustaining economic recovery. "The economy is a wholly owned subsidiary of Nature," he writes, "and not the other way around" (p. 56). On the subject of tropical rainforests, he continues:

These incredible ecosystems harbor more than half the earth's terrestrial biodiversity, on which, whether we like it or not, human survival depends. They generate rainfall; they are home to many of the world's indigenous peoples; and they help meet the needs of hundreds of millions of other people. They also hold vast quantities of carbon. But they are being cleared and burned at a rate of about six million hectares per year. In addition to hastening a mass extinction of species ... this is causing massive greenhouse-gas emissions, accounting for about a fifth of the total. (p. 56)

According to the prestigious World Watch Institute (Flavin, French, & Gardner, 2002; Halweil & Mastny, 2004), the human species may have already reached the point of no return with regard to being able to gain some measure of control over seeming irreversible ecological decline. Indeed, recent history would suggest that the world community, and in particular the Global North, is not yet willing or able to respond to the global environmental crisis in any way that might even marginally begin the process of turning around ecological decline. This failure to respond even in the face of mounting evidence that a crisis is looming suggests some fundamental conceptual shortsightedness that social work must seriously weigh and consider, along with the rest of the world. First, the environmental crisis is not, at its most essential level, a crisis of nature or of biology. Rather, it is a crisis of community, of society, of spirit, and of an unrestrained ideological commitment to a set of values that are inherently destructive to earth systems. Second, prescriptions for solving planetary decline must consist of more than ardent calls for new international agreements, corporate responsibility, personal restraint, and the development of a handful of environmentally friendly technologies. Indeed, because the environmental crisis evolved in the context of community, society, and historical patterns of production and consumption, the solution to environmental problems involves a transformation of both individual consciousness and the major social bases of environmental degradation. As long as dominant social and economic relationships remain

unquestioned, little progress will be made toward meaningful environmental action. The impact of necessary modifications becomes apparent when we examine key changes necessary in core areas related to population control, biodiversity of crops and animals, environmental racist practices, consumerism, and global warming.

Sustainability

Sustainability, sustainable development, sustainable agriculture, and other associated words and phrases have become very familiar to most people today. However, it has only been since the early 1970s, during the first Earth Day campaign, that these concepts have entered into popular vernacular and the larger public discourse (Mitcham, 1997). Famed economist Herman Daly (1990) even suggested that the idea of sustainable development is a cruel oxymoron since, from a philosophical point of view, nothing that is continuously developing can be said to be sustained. Thus, sustainability's depth of meaning has sometimes become trivialized while it has become a kind of buzzword in recent decades (Edwards & Orr, 2005). No person or institution would likely admit to advocating for living in a manner that is unsustainable. Modern corporations have sometimes co-opted the concept in order to enhance their public image even while they continue with industrial and resource depleting practices that destroy natural systems and dislocate indigenous populations (Speth, 2009).

Implicit in the idea of sustainability is the belief that there are limits to everything—including our ability to sustain ongoing economic growth. It is the modern idea of unlimited growth and unending progress, whether in industrial production, population, food, energy consumption, or carbon emissions, that has been a core value of industrial nations and capitalist economies for the last 300 years (Edwards & Orr, 2005). Advocates of sustainability argue that nothing progresses indefinitely. It is, according to them, counterintuitive—what goes up comes down, humans grow to a certain height and then level off, there is birth and then death.

In 1983 the United Nations Secretary General established the World Commission on Environment and Development. It was chaired by former Norwegian Prime Minister Gro Brundtland. The extensive investigation and comprehensive recommendations of the commission have commonly been referred to as the Brundtland Report. The Brundtland Report, later published in book form under the title *Our Common Future* (1987), specifies that sustainable development is development that meets the social, economic, and environmental needs of the current generation without compromising the ability of future generations to meet their own needs. *Our Common Future* (World Commission on Environment and Development, 1987) suggests that there are two key conceptual ideas that form the basis of sustainability:

> The concept of "needs," in particular, the essential needs of the world's poor, to which overriding priority should be given
> The idea of "limitations" imposed by the state of technology and social organization on the environment's ability to meet present and future needs (p. 43)

As you have no doubt noted, the two operative ideas that have consistently run through the thinking on sustainability from the very inception of the idea are *(1)* needs and *(2)* limitations. Sustainability focuses on meeting fundamental human needs and not on satisfying imprudent human wants. While it is obvious that the distinction between what constitutes a need and a want is always culturally and historically proscribed, it is becoming increasing clear that the earth's resource base has a limited capacity to meet human needs if the definition of need is based on consumptive patterns characteristic of most Western, industrialized, consumer-oriented societies (Goleman, 2009; Dresner, 2009). Extremely high living standards that are grossly beyond the basic minimum are not sustainable in the long term. As we have seen in recent decades, high levels of economic growth and productive activity can and do coexist with widespread poverty. Insuring sustainable development depends not only on maintaining productive potential but on ensuring equitable distribution and equal

opportunity for all the inhabitants of the earth (Rogers, Jalal, & Boyd, 2008). Thus, if sustainability is to become a normative concept, it must include a trenchant critique of the full range of social institutions that guide the interaction within and between nations and societies. Sachs (1999) notes that the idea of sustainability must, at the very least, include the four following criteria:

> Social sustainability and its corollary, cultural sustainability
> Ecological sustainability (conservation of the capital of nature) supplemented by the environmental and territorial sustainabilities, the former relative to the resilience of the natural ecosystems used as "sinks," the latter evaluating the spatial distribution of human activities and the rural-urban configurations
> Economic sustainability taken in its broad meaning of the efficiency of economic systems (institutions, policies, and rules of functioning) to ensure continuous socially equitable, quantitative, and qualitative progress
> Last but not least, political sustainability providing a satisfying overall framework for national and international governance (p. 31)

Social work has also begun to address the issue of sustainability and how it impacts professional values, theories, and practice. Craig Mosher (2009), in a conceptually sophisticated piece of writing, defines sustainability as "building and maintaining institutions, communities, economies, and societies that can coexist in harmony with the natural world and each other far into the future" (p. 2). He challenges social work to develop a new paradigm of practice that is more holistic and committed to long-term sustainability of both ecosystems and social systems. Similarly, Shaw (2008) ties the ideas of environmental consciousness and ecological sustainability to international social development and suggests that, until recently, social work's efforts to cooperate in this undertaking have been ineffectual. Today the notion of environmental justice, however, has gained currency in the public arena and has a special resonance for social workers due to their concern for oppressed populations who suffer disproportionately from dangerous environmental conditions. The National Association of Social Workers (NASW) (2009) in the most recent handbook of policy statements urges that social work education incorporate "discussions of the natural environment, ideas of habitat destruction, chemical contamination, environmental racism, environmental justice, and sustainability" (p. 124). As universities heed the call, we can look forward to having a new generation of social work graduates who can respond effectively to issues of environmental sustainability.

Social work educator Nancy Mary (2008) offers a comprehensive review of social work's contribution to developing an ecologically friendly practice framework. She reviews the recent history of the profession and concludes that, while the rhetoric of environment and ecosystems has long been a part of social work's professional discourse, it has not made significant inroads into helping the profession create a vision of an environmentally sustainable world. Mary (2008) notes that the notion of sustainability is founded on four key values that apply to all institutions: "an increasing value of human life and the lives of all species,

fairness and equality or economic and social justice, decision making that involves participation and partnership, and respect for the ecological constraints of the environment" (p. 33). Mary applies these four ideas in developing a model of social work that is consistent with the evolution of a sustainable world. Population control and biodiversity are goals that are essential to such sustainability.

Population

In order to understand world population trends, as well as prospects for the future, it is important to look back at how current populations reached existing levels. Based on current estimates of an annual growth rate of 1.5 percent, the world adds approximately 85 to 100 million people to an already overcrowded planet each year (Peters & Larkin, 2008). Every 3 years, more people are added to the world's population than currently live in the entire United States. (Refer to Table 8.1)

For most of human history, human population growth was agonizingly slow, with an annual increase of about 0.01 percent. This meant that the population of the earth would double only about every 700 years. Estimates of

Table 8.1　Population and Selected Natural Resources

Resource	Description
Fresh water	Today 505 million people live in countries that are water-stressed or water-scarce; by 2025, that figure is expected to be between 2.4 billion and 3.4 billion people (near the equivalent of roughly half of today's world population).
Cropland	In 1960 there was an average of 0.44 hectare for each human being on the planet; today there is less than one quarter of a hectare, a little more than a half-acre suburban lot. By the most conservative of benchmarks of arable land scarcity, nations need at least 0.07 hectare to be self-sufficient in food. Today about 420 million people live with such little cropland; by 2025, that number could top 1 billion.
Forests	Today 1.8 billion people live in 40 countries with less than a tenth of a hectare of forested land for each person—roughly the size of a quarter-acre suburban lot. By 2025, this number could nearly triple, to 4.6 billion. Women and girls in developing countries will walk farther for fuel wood, and there will be less access for all to paper, which remains the currency of most of the world's information.
Biodiversity	In 19 of the world's 25 biodiversity hot spots, population is growing more rapidly than in the world as a whole. On average, population in the hot spots is growing at 1.8% each year, more than the global average.

Source: World Watch Institute. (2002). *State of the World 2002* (p. 134). New York: Norton.

world population in prehistory are at best conjectural but are based on reasonable evidence and interpolations from the archeological record. One million years ago the human species is thought to have numbered around 125,000 souls scattered across the earth's surface. Ten thousand years ago the earth's population is estimated to have been around 5.5 million—roughly the size of the state of Missouri. By A.D. 1, or the beginning of the Common Era, the earth's populations had swollen to perhaps 250–300 million people—still a very small number by modern standards. Indeed, the growth of world population was very gradual at first but became much more accelerated after 1750. When Christopher Columbus landed on the shores of the Western hemisphere, the population of both North and South America combined is estimated to have been around 100 million indigenous peoples and tribal groups. Europe, long decimated by war, famine, and mass epidemics, had a reduced population of perhaps 70 million, with the rest of the known world making up the remaining 200 million people. In other words, the earth's human population just over 500 years ago was around 400 million people. It had reached only 750 million by 1750 and did not surpass the 1 billion mark until about 1820 (Engelman, Halweil, & Nierenberg, 2002). By 1820, due to a stabilization of worldwide infant mortality rates, better sanitation, and a host of other improved social indicators, the annual rate of growth had increased 10-fold to about 0.5 percent per year from what it had been just 1,800 years earlier in human history. All of previous human history, a period of time of well over 1 million years, had been required for the human population to reach its first billion. But it was only 110 years later, in 1930, that the earth's population had swollen to 2 billion residents. And in only 45 years the population had doubled again to 4 billion, and in 12 years, by 1987, had grown another billion, and by 2000 had reached 6 billion. Compare that with today's global population of almost 7 billion, a 1 billion increase in just over 5 years, and the fact that the United States alone has now exceeded 300 million people, and one gets a sobering picture of just how exponentially population growth can overwhelm the earth's carrying capacity (Hillel

& Rosenzweig, 2008). It is estimated by the United Nations that population stabilization, in the absence of a worldwide replacement-level fertility plan (number of deaths relatively equal to the number of births), the global population could swell to 8.9 billion by 2050. Since only around 10 percent of land is arable, a rise in population density has important implications for how humanity can provide for itself. One begins to see very clearly that unregulated population growth has the potential of having real and significant impacts on environmental quality and resource depletion. Table 8.1 shows the gravity of the world shortage of resources.

As a species we have demonstrated our capacity for successful reproduction and species maintenance. But, as many are now suggesting, we either must constrain ourselves or end up destroying the very ecological sanctuary that gives life to our species. Indeed, as Diamond (2005) recently noted, we have perhaps another 20 years to begin making significant, even radical changes in how we live with the earth before every nation, First and Third World alike, begins to see significant decline in quality of life and other catastrophic systemic problems. A report from the United Nations suggests that just in the next 5 years as many as 50 million people will be environmental refugees—people on the move to escape the effects of creeping environmental deterioration such as desertification, global warming, and sea level changes or gradually intensifying weather events (Environmental News Service, 2005). As Ornstein and Ehrlich (1989, p. 45) noted over 20 years ago:

> Increasing numbers is a "goal" of all organisms. But never before has there been an "outbreak" of a single species on such a global scale. Unfortunately, it is not yet clear how enduring our unprecedented triumph will be, because it has created an unprecedented paradox: our triumphs can destroy us. As people strive to increase their dominance even further, they are now changing the earth into a planet that is inhospitable to civilization.

The interrelationship among population growth, resource depletion, and the environment has been known for literally decades. This is often referred to as the *ecology of population*, or the manner in which the number of people on the earth combines with other factors to affect the use and distribution of scarce natural resources. Take fresh water as a prime example. Human beings depend on less than one one-hundredth of 1 percent of the world's total water supply (Flavin et al., 2002). Only one-third of this small percentage is available for human use because water falls as rain in areas inaccessible to humans or as run-off to the oceans. Indeed, more than half of the usable portion of water available for human consumption is already being used. By 2025, over 3 billion people worldwide will be living in countries of water stress or scarcity. The tragic state of the world's freshwater supply and distribution is directly responsible for an estimated 4 million deaths annually, mostly of infants and young children. Entire cultures and social systems are disappearing as water shortages alter landscapes and habitats and lead to mass migration of desperate populations. Australia is reeling from 12 years of drought in one large agricultural region and in the United States, California's water supplies are severely threatening the farming in that state. China faces some of the most difficult water challenges on earth as the nation like much of Asia depends on the glaciers as a major supply of water. The glaciers are rapidly melting, however, and the loss of this resource will be catastrophic to the region. (See the biennial report, *The World's Water* by Peter Gleick, 2010).

The problem is not that we have not known about the interrelationship among impinging environmental concerns but the degree to which policymakers and citizens alike have paid attention to these concerns. Some, for example, obviously see that rampant population increase is a significant contributory factor in degradation of the environment (Jackson, 2009), whereas others see population increase as only one of a multiple number of variables, along with consumption patterns, values about the natural environment, climatic changes—all of which play a significant role in environmental degradation. Whether one sees a single or multiple factors, it is clear that population

pressures will continue to influence how social workers understand their relationship to the person-in-environment construct and how we meet our professional obligations in this new era of environmental consciousness.

It is increasingly becoming evident that global warming and problems of overpopulation are linked. This is because of the loss of arable land through floods and droughts. As the glaciers melt and the oceans rise, mass migrations of people can be anticipated. From the Andes region of Peru, where the glaciers are steadily melting, to parts of Africa and Asia, the resources that sustain human life are threatened by natural disasters that are associated with climate change. As stated in a Center for American Progress report by Werz and Manlove (2009), such natural disasters will be important drivers of climate migration in the twenty-first century. Drawing on United Nations and World Bank estimates, the report predicts that in Asia, warming will shrink freshwater resources from large river basins and could adversely affect 1 billion people. Bangladesh is particularly vulnerable from both a climate and a security standpoint as the sea level rises and migrants escape to India. Mass migrations into India will destabilize the whole area. Parts of Africa could see rain-fed agricultural yields fall by much as 50 percent from today's output, threatening food insecurity on top of water insecurity. Predictions are that as many as 200 million people could become climate refugees by 2050. Such mass migrations, wherever they occur, make conditions ripe for border wars, international unrest, and territorial disputes. See the section on environmentally displaced refugees later in this chapter. Now we turn to a form of harm to our natural resources that is more direct, a harm that occurs through unsustainable agricultural practices.

The Loss of Biodiversity Through Modern Farming

With publication of *Silent Spring*, Rachel Carson (1962) presented shocking data on the biological impact of chemical pollution that raised the consciousness of the world. Carson's work was so catalytic because it linked conservation of nature to human health (Dorsey & Thormodsgard, 2003). The title of her painstakingly documented book refers to the silencing of songbirds due to the spraying of insecticides and herbicides.

The term *biodiversity* refers to the variability among living organisms that maintains the health of each. Today such biodiversity in agriculture is being lost through the industrialization of agriculture which favors the mass production of just one or two crops. In Iowa, it is corn, corn, and corn and if the warm weather comes too late, soybeans. The industrialization of the farms entails the conversion of family sized farms into milk factories where cows never graze and the manure pollutes the water in the lakes and streams. Paradoxically, the smell of hog farms sends people from the country to city parks to enjoy nature.

Iowa and some neighboring states have had two historically severe floods which caused billions of dollars in property damage in 1993 and 2008. According to one explanation, the Midwestern form of row crop planting is a primary reason. In her chapter in the book, *A Watershed Year: Anatomy of the Iowa Floods of 2008*, Laura Jackson and Dennis Keeney (2010) describe a time before the coming of the Europeans to the Midwest in the mid-1800s when the prairie soil protected the land from flooding. The Iowa soil, filled with a dense and deep underground network of plant roots was able to absorb the raindrops. The replacement of these plants with annuals causes a major change in the ecology of the region. The authors point to several aspects of row crop farming that are a likely factor in the recent floods. The first is the absence of the perennial grasses to soak up water nine months out of the year. The second is the use of a substance called tiles placed below the plants to aid in drying; this process causes run-off of the water into rivers which ultimately overflow. The third factor in flooding is the compression of the soil by tractors which make it less spongy and absorbent, also leading to more water run-off.

In monoculture farming, moreover, the row crops are particularly vulnerable to invasive pests or to a change in weather conditions (Korten, 2009). A monoculture of species, such as found in the Kansas wheat farm in (see Figure 8.2), lacks sufficient diversity of the biocommunity to have resilience in time of crisis. As the average number of species found in

Figure 8.2. Wheat farm, Kansas. Influence on one-crop agriculture causes soil erosion and leaves plants susceptible to insects and disease problems. Photo by Kathleen Besthorn and Margie Hayes.

each square of earth's surface declines, so too will its biomass and its contribution to a stable, life-supporting ecosystem. Today, in the United States, only one percent of the original prairie remains, and most of the region's hundreds of species of plants, birds, mammals, and insects have been replaced by a few species of domesticated plants such as corn and soybeans (Naeem, 2009). (The photo in Figure 8.3 shows a small portion of a prairie land preserve in Cedar Falls, Iowa.)

The industrialization of farm crops is enhanced by genetic engineering of seeds designed to be able to handle the herbicides that can now be sprayed on them in an early stage of growth. Farmers have become almost totally reliant on the products from one corporation—Monsanto—to supply them both with the herbicides and with the genetically altered seeds that are designed to resist them. The extensive spraying that results has important implications for soil conservation and for humans who are exposed to them. (Refer to Box 8.1.) Because Monsanto has a virtual monopoly on the seeds, the prices can be raised at will. Reports are that the Justice Department is investigating possible antitrust concerns in the seed business, looking in particular at Monsanto, which dominates the business of supplying crop traits developed through genetic engineering (Pollack, 2009).

The recent trend is to develop markets overseas and especially in overpopulated nations requiring rapid growth of crops. As Korten (2009) indicates, the shipping of food and seeds around the world introduces alien plants and predators against which the regional ecosystems have no defenses. The encouragement of American forms of agriculture in these foreign lands eventually will lead to soil erosion and depletion of natural nutrients that will make the farmers ever more dependent on chemicals for the growing of crops.

A highly disturbing report in the *International Journal of Biological Sciences* is the most comprehensive study on long-term health effects of genetically engineered foods on mammals (de Verdomois, Roullier, Cellier, & Seralini, 2009). An examination of the Monsanto's raw data on the results of feeding trials of rats showed serious damage to the rats' vital organs following consumption of the modified corn. Of relevance to the environment, the scientists also attribute the massive deaths of butterflies and bees, the pollinators of the earth's plants, to the chemically altered crops, some of which are engineered to produce their own insecticides. As well as dangerous to human and nonhuman life, pesticides have the unfortunate side effect of developing resistance to the insects they are designed to target.

Figure 8.3. Iowa prairie. Very little remains today of the hill grass prairie ecosystem that once covered the major part of the American Midwest. Photo by Rupert van Wormer.

Box 8.1 Toxic Injury Due to Pesticide Poisoning: A Personal Account

Jamie Paige, MSW

In May, 2007, as a Hospice social worker, I made a visit to the home of a young farmer, dying from cancer. As I got out of my vehicle at his residence, I did not notice the crop-dusting plane which was spraying crops near his house for aphids. Suddenly, the plane shot up and flew directly over my head startling me. It shot up quickly and circled around for its next drop.

"I'd better get inside." I thought to myself. But little did I know it was too late, and within seconds, my life was changed forever.

As I looked towards the patient's door, a gentle mist swept by me upon the wind. It covered my car in a feather like foam. It smelled intensely of chemicals and I coughed almost immediately upon breathing it. I placed my sleeve up over my mouth and nose and made a run to the patient's house.

I greeted the patient who was watching the plane intently. "Smell that?" he asked. "The whole house wreaks of it."

I shook my head in agreement. Then his eyes became more somber as he shared, "It's killing me, isn't it? Hell, it's killing us all."

I listened to him share his concerns now of death and dying so young, of seeing it more and more himself amongst young neighboring farm families and recognizing that it was mainly from overuse and underregulation of pesticide usage in his farming life which had sealed his fate. We spoke of pollution and toxins in both the air and water. And how pissed he was that he was dying before he was ready to.

We were into this intense conversation, when my breathing had become labored and my coughing more uncontrollable. I don't know which one of us put it together first but our eyes met in recognition. I was having what was to become a life-changing breaking point in both my health and life. I was having an acute allergic reaction to being sprayed by that plane.

Soon I was on my way to the hospital ER gasping for air and coughing my lungs out. From that day forward I walked with Epinephrin pens so I could inject myself whenever I was on the road and had an attack. At that time I had one Epi pen. Now I carry two and use them at least once a month.

ER records show my blood pressure rising sometimes to 190/106 during these attacks. Early diagnosis included bronco-spasms? Asthma? Emphysema? Question marks everywhere. Soon I was on my way to a pulmonary specialist who would send me to another specialist at bigger and better hospitals. I would try to work, usually 3 days on and 5 days being bedridden sick. I was exhausted and had severe chest pains and breathing problems. My mental cognitive functioning was becoming impaired, and I was suffering from both long-term and short-term memory loss.

On June 27, 2008, at the Allergy Clinic in La Crosse, Wisconsin, I was diagnosed with a toxic injury due to pesticide poisoning, which has so far manifested itself as reactive airway distress syndrome (RADS) with multiple chemical sensitivity (MCS).

Then as a social worker I went into action. I phoned every local, state, and federal agency I could think of. No one knew of any agency which took complaints like mine. There was no organized procedure for doctors whose patients complained of symptoms after farm spraying to follow, or report for statistical data. I phoned three state representatives. Two laughed at me and never phoned me back. But one told me "off the record," that he would love to take me before our legislators in Des Moines, Iowa; however, they would eat me up and spit me out. This legislator continued by saying that without a doubt, our politicians know that whatever comes out of the back of a tractor (sprayed) or out of a crop-dusting plane goes directly off the fields as run-off and into our waterways. It is causing fish to die and making it into our drinking water. They also know that it is causing all kinds of cancers and problems like mine. When I asked why no one was doing anything, the legislator replied, "Because Crop Dusters 'own' this state."

Later I found out during the time when I became ill, that due to favorable weather conditions, Iowa sprayed three times more then they ever had before. First, they sprayed crops with pesticides for weed control. Then there was an outbreak of aphids, so they sprayed with insecticides. Then there was a fungus outbreak so they sprayed with fungicides. The most active ingredients I was sprayed with that day were the following: chlorpyrifos, deltamethrin, lambda-cyhalothrin, and gamma-cyhalothrin. (This was verified through the Iowa Department of Land Stewardship.)

I do know that FIFRA is the federal law that needs changing so that all Americans can be protected. Each state has its own laws, too. Sometimes changes can be simple such as making those crop-dusting planes have easily identifiable numbers or letters on the bottom of their wings so anyone feeling sick can identify the plane which flew over them and report it. (See http://www.epa.gov/oecaerth/civil/fifra/fifraenfstatreq.html)

Even though the doctor rendered me disabled a year ago, I am not necessarily going to get Social Security Disability Income. I am in my third appeal at the time of this writing. It seems even the government doesn't want to acknowledge it. Even though the government's own agency in studying the Gulf War Syndrome states:

> In the United States in 2008, the federally mandated Research Advisory Committee on Gulf War Veterans' Illnesses released a 452-page report, indicating that roughly 1 in 4 of the 697,000 veterans who served in the first Persian Gulf War are afflicted with the disorder.

The report implicated exposure to toxic chemicals as the cause of the illness. The report states that "scientific evidence leaves no question that Persian Gulf War illness is a real condition with real causes and serious consequences for affected veterans." (See http://en.wikipedia.org/wiki/Gulf_War_syndrome)

Perhaps the most exciting discovery for me in my personal fight to gain access to disability comes from the site MCS Beacon of Hope. I have included its petition, which our state governors have signed a proclamation on for over 4 years, and social workers and others can sign, too (http://www.mcsbeaconofhope.com/).

If you go to the above site, you will see that Iowa Governor Chester J. Culver proclaimed May 2009 to be: Toxic Injury Awareness and Education Month. The proclamation states in part: "... Those suffering with toxic injury deserve the same rights, acknowledgements, respect, support and help allotted to other illnesses and disabilities..."

Well, at least I can hope.

Printed with the permission of Jamie Paige.

Once having developed resistance, insects are more destructive than before and destroy crops at an increasing rate. Stronger chemicals are then used, and so the cycle continues.

Once the biodiversity of plant and animal life is lost, the soil becomes depleted of its nutrients. To force some life out of the depleted soil, farmers use an incredible amount of chemicals—many of them highly toxic—that seep into the rural waterways, drinking water, soil, and air. Soil that is depleted of its storage power or of the organic matter that anchors it washes away faster than it forms and is lost through erosion. Without healthy soil, we are without food. Ninety percent of U.S. cropland is losing soil because of the current farming practices (Land Institute, 2002). There is a major thrust today, however, to return to more natural methods of farming, a fact to which a trip to any large grocery store will attest. The demand for organic meat is high, as is the demand for organic milk and vegetables.

A sustainable agricultural program will go a long way toward replenishing the soil and reducing the risk of floods. As part of the green revolution, there is an emphasis on alternative land use, a restoration to a land ethic. The vision is of a landscape of farms that are natural habitats rather than ecological disasters. An excellent illustration of productive farming on a large scale is found at the Land Institute's prairie in Salina, Kansas. Biodiversity is achieved through the planting of a wide variety of native species. A major accomplishment of the Land Institute's organic agriculture is the demonstration of a healthy harvest of farm crops without reliance on synthetic fertilizers, pesticides, and herbicides and the avoidance of monoculture cropping. the Land Institute in Salina, Kansas, features perennial crops whose year-round roots hold the life-giving soil. Mixed varieties of crops are grown to be reminiscent of native vegetation. (To learn more of this process, see http://www.LandInstitute.org.)

As the emphasis on the production of cash crops is taking place worldwide the problems caused by industrialized agriculture are global in scope. In 2005, in response to an international call for a scientific assessment of the health of the world's ecosystems, the Millennium Ecosystem

Assessment, was conducted. This extensive report was funded by the Global Environment Facility, the United Nations Foundation, and the World Bank, among others. Over 1,000 researchers from 95 nations contributed to this effort. Unique to this report was the emphasis on human well-being with regard to the goals of poverty and hunger eradication. This report, which places biodiversity squarely at the center of all the environmental processes that affect human well-being, has become the standard reference for the state of the biosphere (Naeem, 2009).

The report's findings chronicling the loss of biodiversity remind us that biodiversity is a requirement for all life on the planet. Major findings from the assessment are that:

- Humans have radically altered ecosystems over the past 50 years.
- About 75 percent of the world's commercial marine fisheries have been fully exploited or overexploited.
- More land has been converted to cropland since 1950 than during the agricultural revolution of the nineteenth century.
- Species extinction is pronounced.
- Sixty percent of the world ecosystem benefits have been degraded.
- About 20 percent of coral reefs were lost in just 20 years.
- Nutrient pollution, as from nonorganic fertilizers, has led to the contamination of waters.
- Water availability is projected to decrease in many regions.
- Poverty and hunger will result for the world's poorest people without a reversal of unsustainable practices.

According to the ecosystems assessment report, human societies can ease the strain on nature through changes in consumption patterns, better education, new technologies, reduction in the use of fertilizers and pesticides, and higher prices placed on industry and agriculture for practices that are exploitative. In Box 8.1, we learned of the dangers to human health and human life inherent in the use of such chemicals. Toxic injury due to exposure to pesticide poisoning is a reality today in Iowa farm country.

Damage to the earth through warfare is another area of serious environmental concern. .

War and the Environment

Unlike the intent of the war on nature, the goal of which is the taming of nature for human consumption, wars against people may involve a deliberate attack on the environment as a part of a military "bring-the-enemy-to-its-knees" campaign. Throughout history, the environment has been one of the war's worst casualties: Romans spread salt on the fields of Carthage; Sherman's troops marched through and burned Georgia; the United States defoliated Vietnam's jungles; and Saddam Hussein set fire to the oilfields in Kuwait.

Long after the wars are over, major unanticipated effects may occur. An estimated 160 wars have been fought in the past 60 years, the majority of which have been regional conflicts (Chivian & Bernstein, 2008). The recent wars in the Democratic Republic of Congo, for example, have contributed to reduced wildlife populations in several protected areas.

All wars cause damage to the ecosystem through slash-and-burn agriculture and large-scale hunting of animal life as desperate refugees live off the land. Military preparation by itself is also a factor in the loss of biodiversity; military bases have a history of polluting the air, soil, and groundwater with toxic chemicals, including radioactive material (Chivian & Bernstein, 2008). International wars cause damage in the form of chemical pollution, such as occurred in the attack on Vietnam, and in the proliferation of land mines and unexploded munitions that endanger human and other animal life. Waves of refugees fleeing war zones further ravage environmental resources. This is what happened in the invasion of Panama in 1989 in conjunction with the war on drugs.

Fischer (1993) reminds us of this "Just Cause" invasion, which, along with imposed U.S. sanctions, broke the economy, causing the people to turn to the land and take the forests. Just as war leads to environmental decimation, so depleting the environment produces ethnic and territorial conflict.

During the Gulf War, the white mountain peaks of Iraq's northern mountains turned black, and the burning oil inferno in Kuwait blackened the skies, polluted waterways, and wiped out lower-level animal life for years thereafter. Six to eight million barrels of oil were spilled into the sea ("The Spoils of War," 2003). In Afghanistan, land mines continue to destroy human and other animal life, and the uncontrolled use of resources, such as the cutting of forests for firewood, by 6 million refugees from the bombings has depleted the land of forest cover ("The Spoils of War," 2003). Bulldozers and tanks wreak havoc on Palestine and prevent the people from disposing of sewage properly. Damage to the water system is the result.

According to Australian pediatrician and antinuclear activist Helen Caldicott (2004), author of *The New Nuclear Danger: George W. Bush's Military-Industrial Complex*, the United States, with its massive arsenal of weapons of mass destruction, is the most subversive threat to world peace and the environment. The use of depleted uranium in recent wars is a case in point. This product is used by the military because of its high density, which enables it to penetrate heavy armor and military vehicles. Such toxic weaponry constitutes a weapon of mass destruction in terms of the impact on human life and radioactive contamination of the environment. Such weaponry goes on killing for years after a war has ended, killing the victors, as well as the defeated. The use of depleted-uranium-tipped warheads against Iraq in 2003 affected not only the combatants and civilians but also their progeny, causing infertility, clusters of infant malformations, leukemia, and testicular and brain cancers (Nixon, 2005). The chemically toxic and radioactive depleted uranium dust has entered the water table and fauna and flora and will still be polluting our earth for endless generations (Bertell, 2006). Depleted uranium vaporizes when it hits a target; once released, the particles are easily spread by the wind. Depleted uranium, as Bertell indicates, is strongly suspected as a cause of Gulf War syndrome, the assortment of health problems that has affected many members of the military who fought in recent wars. (For more information,

visit the National Gulf War Resource Center at http://www.ngwrc.org.)

Caldicott attended the 2009 Copenhagen conference on global warming. Her purpose was to warn representatives of the dangers of nuclear energy. Her fears about the nations turning to a reliance on this form of energy relate to the biological dangers of a meltdown, the possibility of a terrorist attack, and the risks of radiation damage (Levine, 2009). At the conference and afterwards, Caldicott was strongly critical of environmental groups that failed to take a strong, public stand against climate bills that included nuclear power. "All of the money that will go into nuclear power," she says, "is being stolen from the solutions to fix the earth—solar, wind, hydro, geothermal, conservation." Moreover, "the nuclear power industry was formed by the bomb makers.... Any county that has a nuclear power plant has a bomb factory," as she stated in her speech at an outdoor rally at the Copenhagen conference.

In light of the global consequences of war for the physical and social environment, the Sierra Clubs of North America have issued statements on behalf of disarmament and reduction in dependence on oil and fossil fuels (foreign and domestic). The Sierra Clubs urge a move to a clean energy economy, greater fuel efficiency, and use of renewable sources of energy (May, 2002).

A related concern for humanity and the disregard for human life is demonstrated when dangerous chemicals are released in poor regions of the world.

Environmental Racism

Poverty and the environment are mutually reinforcing; as the world's poor stretch their environmental resources to the maximum for the sake of survival, they have used up their natural capital and are further impoverished thereby. Although all humans are affected by environmental degradation, women, people of color, children, and the poor throughout the world experience these harms disproportionately (Worldwatch Institute, 2009). By the same token, whereas all children are at risk of environmental hazards in that their bodies are far more sensitive than those of adults to chemical exposure, poor children are at the greatest risk of developing health problems due to exposure to contaminants in the less desirable neighborhoods in which they live. Research shows that families with low incomes, including many minorities, tend to live disproportionately close to industrial and commercial sources of chemical contamination (Rogge, 2008). The incinerators and toxic-waste dumps and the contaminated air, drinking water, and rivers are located disproportionately in African American neighborhoods and on Indian reservations. Epidemiological studies have found that individuals exposed to such environmental hazards have increased risks for certain cancers. Farm workers who are regularly exposed to pesticides and other toxic chemicals are also at serious risk (Rogge, 2008).

Mexican migrant workers carry agricultural pesticides home to their families in their work clothes while others who work in plants along the U.S.–Mexico border live in unsanitary, crowded, and hastily constructed *maquiladoras* (National Association of Social Workers [NASW], 2009). Enforcement of environmental laws, significantly, is far less vigorous in communities of color than in white communities. Most of the companies that spew the toxins that contaminate the communities receive massive tax incentives from state government and deny culpability for the illnesses that result from exposure to the toxins. Because American Indian lands are self-governed, many of the states' waste management laws can be ignored by commercial waste operations. Tribes are offered financial incentives to allow their land to be used as toxic dumping grounds (Warren, 2000). In his collection of essays on environmental racism, sociologist Robert Bullard (2000) documents the glaring disparities in who pays the price of the nation's extravagant use of energy. Contained in his book, *Dumping in Dixie*, is the story of Louisiana's "Cancer Alley." Here in the lower Mississippi River valley, where more than a quarter of the nation's chemicals are produced, incredibly high cancer rates are found. Activists from nongovernmental organizations (NGOs) such as Greenpeace that were organized to expose this fact have revealed to the world the severe health problems of children living near the industrial sites. In Louisiana the pollution is so life threatening that whole communities are fighting for relocation. Environmental groups are taking industries to court based on Title 6 of the Civil Rights Act that guarantees equal protection under the law. Built from the grassroots up, the environmental justice movement is an effort with long-term implications for changing national policies.

In a scientific report prepared for the San Francisco Bay Area Health Environmental Collaborative, Pastor, Sadd, and Morello-Frosch (2007) found that Latinos and African Americans were more likely than whites to live within one mile of an area high in toxic air emissions from industry and other sources of pollution. Even when controlling for income, race and ethnicity proved to be correlated with exposure to high levels of chemical pollution. In 2006, residents of a predominantly minority community on the edge of San Francisco scored a victory as a result of their protests in getting the Pacific, Gas, and Electric Company to shut down one of California's worst polluting power plants. Community organizing and high media coverage were responsible for this victory.

Another focal point of environmental concern is Anniston, Alabama, where a belated court settlement confirmed the damage done by industry-polluted waterways. Monsanto polluted the soil and water in their production of cancer-causing polychlorinated biphenyls (PCBs), which were used in insulation for electrical equipment. Human exposure to PCBs comes through eating contaminated fish. Residents of the largely black and low-income Anniston neighborhood won a settlement of $42.8 million in their class action suit against the company (Environmental Justice Resource Center, 2001). Production of PCBs was banned in the 1970s.

Environmentally Displaced Persons

Often overshadowed in the current impetus to protect natural systems is the impact of environmental crises on sociocultural institutions and human populations (Besthorn, 2008). The deterioration of the planet's natural systems is creating an ever-increasing population of human refugees. They are attempting to escape their unsafe, threatening, and dangerous natural environments. By 2010, there will be 50 million environmental refugees—a figure over five times greater than the number of political refugees predicted for the same time period (Moss & Ember, 2006). While it is difficult to calculate the exact number of ecological refugees, we know that if global environmental deterioration continues at the current pace, the number of displaced persons will grow exponentially (Gorlick, 2007; Townsend, 2002). As Myers (1997) suggested, well over a decade ago, we are experiencing an ever-increasing number of "marginalized people driven to [and from] marginal environments" (p. 168).

The plight of millions of persons, dislocated as a direct result of ecological decline, has become an issue of global justice. Although these people are found in virtually every nation, including the United States, 96 percent are from the developing world (McConahay, 2000; Unruh, Krol, & Kliot, 2005). In many cases, it is the major economic and political powers of the Global North that have helped create the worst conditions leading to large-scale decline of ecological systems. This causal relationship between the wealthy and impoverished peoples of the world represents a kind of "widespread systematic discrimination" (Segal, 2007, p. 309). The fact that millions of people are displaced due to environmental crises raises many core concerns for social workers in industrialized nations. The world community and helping professions alike have been slow in recognizing the reality of persons dislocated from their geographic locale due to serious environmental threats (Lopez, 2007).

One reason for this tepid response is the difficulty in formally defining and categorizing this population. Initially, this population was given the generic label of *environmental refugees*. This terminology was challenged, however, because the label requires fulfillment of a detailed criteria of displacement, usually based on political realities, and includes movement outside one's home country of origin (Falstrom, 2001). Further, the term *refugee* is widely overused and misunderstood. An example is when U.S. officials designated survivors of Hurricane Katrina as refugees, creating a maelstrom of public criticism ("United States: A Cooling Welcome," 2006).

Next, the terms *environmental migrant* or *emigrant* were introduced as alternatives to refugee, but the term *migrant* suggested a voluntary movement (Bates, 2002). This is not generally the case for those dispossessed by serious environmental conditions. An environmentally dispossessed person has little choice when leaving his or her home. In fact, it is usually a matter of survival that necessitates a person's movement (Myers, 1997). The United Nations High Commissioner for Refugees (UNHCR) eventually developed the terminology *environmentally displaced person* (EDP). Brian Gorlick (2007), Senior Policy Advisor to the United Nations, suggests that environmentally displaced persons are:

> people who are displaced from or who feel obliged to leave their usual place of residence, because their lives, livelihoods and welfare have been placed at serious risk as a result of adverse environmental, ecological or climatic processes and events. (p. 1)

This definition includes the key features of compulsion and threat but does not suggest persecution or movement outside one's home nation. This builds upon an earlier description offered by Falstrom (2001), who broadly defines an environmentally displaced person as "one who leaves his or her home and seeks refuge elsewhere for reasons related to the environment" (p. 1).

What is indisputable is that the number of environmentally displaced persons will continue to increase. Townsend (2002) estimates that at least 5,000 people a day are added to the ranks of environmentally displaced persons— 5,000 people whose "livelihoods and welfare have been placed at a serious risk as a result of adverse environmental, ecological, or climatic processes and events" (Gorlick, 2007, p. 1). The evidence detailing the significant social impact of devastating ecological damage is compelling. The struggle of environmentally displaced persons is dramatic, unacceptable, and alarming proof that human activities are seriously impacting the survival of persons in their environments.

One way to more fully understand environmentally displaced persons is to look at those contributory factors that have helped to create this new group of the dispossessed. Lambert (2002) describes five factors contributing to environmental displacement. These are natural disasters, gradual degradation of the environment, development projects, accidental disruptions or industrial accidents, and conflict and warfare.

The problem of environmentally displaced persons is also calling social work to consider new ways to think of community—that of participation as a global citizen in a global community (Nash, Wong, & Trlin, 2006). It is critical for the profession to better understand not only the causes of but the communal nature of human struggle and suffering. Social work's conventional modes of thinking, seeing, and being have too often evolved around the individual, the local—that which is near and dear—while large portions of the global world are easily overlooked (Besthorn, 2003; Jones, 2010; Schriver, 2010). Considering the prospect of a vastly different ecological future, social work must expand its traditional view of humanity as a collection of individuals confined within the borders of individual nation states.

Currently, most social work curricula focus on the importance of *cultural competence*. While the study of cultural competency encourages respecting and learning about various cultures it is, unfortunately, too often limited to theory and practice applicable to national and regional circumstances (Suárez, Newman, & Reed, 2008). An international and global culturally competent curriculum is crucial for effective social work helping with environmentally displaced persons. As globalization increases the connections between nations, societies and cultures will increasingly coalesce. It is predicted that social work will be the field that is "by definition, most likely to engage with people who are adversely affected by the processes of globalization" (Lyons, Manion, & Carlsen, 2006, p. 35) and, increasingly, the impact of globalized environmental displacement. Thus, within educational settings, cultural competence demands

an expanded definition and more discrete attention.

Curricula for examining a client's *total* environment will also have to be extended if "social work educators are to avoid creating cardboard people to fit particular stereotypes" (Dominelli, 2002, p. 23). A sole focus on social and cultural environments obscures the powerful influence of physical and biological environments on human populations. Anti-oppressive and anti-racist practice is a curricula emphasis that has great promise (Dominelli, 2002). In this framework, learning about a client would require a social worker to think of not only his or her social environment, but those institutional, cultural, local, national, global, physical/natural, and spiritual environments that profoundly impact human well-being (Besthorn & Canda, 2002). This creates a more in-depth and exhaustive understanding of the client's total environment, thus allowing the potential for better assistance.

The next section looks at values of modern society related to environmental destruction in the quest for profit and material possessions.

Consumerism

At this point in history, humanity has enough material resources to meet the basic needs of every person on earth. We have the capacity to enhance health care, sanitation, and meet concerns for cleaner environments in most areas. Nevertheless, a cursory look around during this period of rising international crises, growing alarms of global warming, international terrorism, and severe shortages of clean water shows just how far we are from realizing these goals. The world community is instead becoming a global village of two distinct and separated groups of people. There is the First World of wealth, opulence, and conspicuous consumption and a Third World of deprivation, poverty, and subsistence living.

The stratification of the world community is no longer constrained within national borders. It is no longer just an issue of rich northern economies versus struggling nations in the Global South. Increasingly, one can find relatively insulated pockets of wealth surrounded by ever-deepening chasms of misery in most countries around the world. Many of the world's nations are now being forced to adopt a kind of winner-take-all globalized financial system in which the goal is to get as much as one can according to his or her own greed quotient. Selfishness, self-indulgence, and rampant materialism have become cardinal values for many of the world's citizens (Matthews, 2005). The relentless psychological marathon of yearning and having increasingly drives the world social and economic systems. But its darker underbelly keeps us perpetually unhappy, chronically sick in body and soul, obese, and neurotically yearning for the *spirit of the buy*. In the West, our lives are lived increasingly in anticipation of the next purchase, which is always just out of reach but always imminently possible. But we are, by most accounts, as poor in collective, meaningful connection as the Afghanis and Iraqis are in money. We literally are buying our way into deep peril, poverty, and emotional destruction while believing that *this is what we ought to be doing*. We in the developed world are also endeavoring to paint the world with our highly individualized worldview. While we are spending ourselves into extinction, we are also enslaving the vast majority of the world's workforce and expropriating the lion's share of each country's natural resources to ensure what may be our own demise.

Today it seems as if almost everything is for sale—politics, sex, love, marriage, and gizmos and promises of every size and description. We seem never quite content, ever on the search—spiritual searches, romantic searches, experiential searches, searches for meaning, searching for the better deal. We have become the quintessence of the consumer culture that enfolds us.

Buy and Be Happy?

Most of us have been seduced by the delusion of the new world order, the American dream, or some combination of a promised future devoid of risk and flowing with unheralded happiness. We have unconsciously accepted the dictum that having more wealth and possessions is essential to happiness. And yet, data increasingly suggest that more wealth and consumer goods beyond a certain level do not lead to happy or satisfied lives. These realities raise a number of important questions for social workers. What is our response to the problem of a globalized consumptive ethos and its implications for human well-being? How is the profession's commitment to social justice influenced by the consumptive (wealth versus poverty) emphasis of traditional social justice paradigms? How might social work address the materialistic values and practices of late modern consumeristic capitalism, and how might a change in that perspective truly improve the quality of life of communities and the planet?

The consumer-driven economy of the Western world generally, and of the United States particularly, is based on a multifaceted constellation of values and ideologies about ourselves and the world we inhabit. In the main, these values minimize the relevance of intuitive, interpretive, communal, and quality-of-life aspects of experience in favor of the economic enterprise of consumption and amassing material wealth. The cost of industrialized consumption to the natural environment is externalized and not considered in the price of consumer products (see, for example, the recent bestseller *Ecological Intelligence: How Knowing the Hidden Impact of What We Buy Can Change Everything* by D. Goleman, 2009). Consumer culture assumes that nations and economies must grow incessantly or perish. The truly happy and fulfilled person is one who accrues as much material wealth and pleasure as possible.

Shoptimism, a popular new book on the science and art of consumption by Eisenberg (2009), reveals the subtle ways that marketers induce brand loyalty and entice us to spend, spend, spend on their products. Eisenberg lists the following incentives to buy consumer products: to assert our personal identity; to join a "tribe" of other customers whom we admire; for escape and to get a high from the act of buying. Consumerism is inevitable, argues Eisenberg, because our whole economy and culture are built around it.

To have, to have not, longing and desire, abundance and scarcity, stuff and no-stuff—these are the *real* and un*real*ized essences of consumerism in America and increasingly in the rest of the world. Global capitalism has become simply the economic tool that breathes life into that moment of sheer delight when we acquire something we have not had and the giddy anticipation that holds us spellbound before the glittering incantations of a *better and brighter tomorrow*—a future resplendent with more stuff. Most of the world's workforce is employed in the business of producing commodities and services. To paraphrase Mayell (2004), globalization and desire are driving forces in making goods and services previously out of reach in developing countries much more available today. Items that once were considered luxuries—televisions, cell phones, computers, air conditioning—are now viewed as necessities. Consumer products travel, bringing both themselves and the desire to have more to countries that have less and those that have nothing—so that one glorious day, even these places of desolation can, through spending and getting, experience the insane but intoxicating enigma of having while always feeling that they have not.

Modern culture is bombarded with messages to spend, spend, spend, in the process of which one can find real worth, deep satisfaction, and a genuinely meaningful life (Kasser, 2002). Multicolor ads flash across TV and computer screens and invade our lives in every imaginable way. Latter-day hucksters implore us to buy everything from sexually enhancing performance supplements to personalized names for recently discovered star systems. We have even been told that the best defense against encroaching terrorism or a crashing stock market is to go to the mall and spend our money. Although the content may be different, the message is the same: Happiness and security are found in the purchasing of things, the ownership of "stuff," and the status such things supposedly bring to us.

Although no one would argue that some basic level of material comfort is necessary for essential human needs, it is quite another thing to say that higher levels of material accumulation lead to ever-increasing levels of satisfaction and happiness. To the contrary, a wealth of scholarship (Besthorn, 2002a; Besthorn &

Canda, 2002; Brown, 2001; Cohen, 2003; Goleman, 2009; Kasser, 2002; Matthews, 2005; Mayell, 2004; Myers, 2000) is suggesting overwhelmingly that materialistic values actually detract from well-being and quality-of-life experiences, such as self-expression, intimate relationships, and sense of community.

The High Cost of Rampant Consumerism— The Death of Personal Well-Being

In recent years, investigators working in various fields have begun to assess the cost of a materialistic lifestyle. What they have found is startling. The reality is that people in the Western world and increasingly in the developing world are generally not adapting well to the consumerist culture and are exhibiting rather destructive ways of living (Akerlof & Shiller, 2009). In short, materialism is associated with relatively low levels of well-being and psychological health, as well as relatively high levels of narcissism, depression, and anxiety. Indeed, evidence suggests that aspiring to greater wealth and material possessions is associated with increased personal unhappiness. People with strong materialistic values are more anxious, more narcissistic, and more depressed, and they use more mind-altering substances and have more relationship problems. They also tend to be more sedentary and to sleep less, and they tend to be emptier of heart and soul (Sagiv & Schwartz, 2000; Srivastava, Locke, & Bortol, 2001).

Not only does consumerism lead to a kind of death of personal well-being and happiness, but it also has a profound impact on the social structures of society. In the United States, for instance, the period between 1960 and 1995 was a time of soaring economic vitality. The market was up, but the social fabric was sinking. Americans are better paid, better fed, better housed, better educated, and have more conveniences than ever, and yet in the 35–year period beginning in 1960, American society has seen profound social indices of decline (Frank, 1999; Myers, 2000). For example, since 1960:

- The teen suicide rate has tripled.
- The divorce rate has doubled.

❯ The violent crime rate has quadrupled.

❯ The prison population has quintupled.

❯ The number of children born to unmarried parents has sextupled.

❯ Depression has increased 10 times over pre-World War II levels.

❯ More Americans are overweight or obese than ever before, nearly two-thirds of the population.

❯ Parents spend 40 percent less time with their children than they did in 1960.

❯ Employees work over 5 weeks longer per year than in 1960 while spending fewer hours sleeping and fewer hours with friends.

❯ The number of children under age 6 on stimulant and antidepressant drugs has increased 580 percent.

Never has a culture experienced more physical comfort combined with such emotional and social misery. Never have we felt freer or have our prisons overflowed to the breaking point. Never have we been so beseeched to enjoy pleasure or more likely to suffer broken relationships. Never have we been more able to support positive global change or felt more vulnerable or threatened.

Not only is overconsumption a threat to the physical, emotional, and social health of humans, but it is also the single largest danger to the earth's ecosystems. As the world's human population grows and nonsustainable consumption of all kinds of materials increases, ecosystems are being degraded and their capacity to deliver their services is being compromised (Melillo & Sala, 2008). Nature is increasingly seen as fodder for the industrial fires of production and consumption. Earth systems are valued as infinite—as an inexhaustible resource base. Human beings, particularly in the Global North, are consuming resources at a rate far outpacing the earth's ability to renew itself. Water, forests, and clean air are being used or polluted at rates higher than can be sustained. Biodiversity is shrinking while the orgy of overdevelopment goes on virtually unabated. The United States consumes 25 percent of the world's energy while constituting only five percent of the world's population. Since 1940,

Americans have used more mineral resources than all previous generations put together (Brown, 2001). In total, the industrial countries, containing only one-fourth of the world's population, consume 40–86 percent of the earth's various natural resources.

The statistics and factual data are sobering. Consumerism, beyond a certain minimal level, is damaging to individuals, societies, and the natural environment (Besthorn, 2001, 2002a, 2004; Besthorn & McMillen, 2002; Besthorn & Saleebey, 2003). Many of the environmental issues we see today can be linked to global consumption in one form or another. A devastating toll on the earth's water supplies, natural resources, and ecosystems is exacted by a plethora of disposable cameras, plastic garbage bags, and other cheaply made goods with built-in product obsolescence, and cheaply made manufactured goods that lead to a "throw away" mentality, as Mayell (2004) suggests. China is a case in point. By 2000, 5 million cars moved people and goods; four years later the number had soared to 24 million, and it is still climbing.

The question is how to begin the change process. There are no simple answers. And yet, there is a new social renewal and sustainable development movement under way. This movement has grassroots origins and is trickling upward from far-flung areas of the world, where wealth and consumption may be low but where happiness and community pride are still relatively high. And just below the surface of the quiet desperation of industrial peoples is a perception that something in the modern ethos needs to change. A retrenchment of consumer spending is underway as Americans recognize that the past quarter century's consumption binge—for new cars, TV sets, holiday cruises, children's and adults' electronic toys, gourmet food—has left many people over their heads in indebtedness, whether to credit card companies or to the bank. Paralleling the national economic crisis that originated in the 2008 bank failures and stock market crash, people's personal finances and sense of security have plummeted. Now what Samuelson (2008) calls "the great American shopping spree" may be over, at least for a while (p. 49).

People across the globe are looking for a new story to define who they are and where they want to go. Instead of one narrowly focused on material progress, they want a more coherent vision that expresses a better balance between economics, social equity, and environmental sustainability—a vision in which these factors are inextricably linked. Unfortunately, too many national and international policy responses to the crisis of consumerism still reflect the current paradigm by which they are framed. Thus, reordering of the consumer world requires a radical change in the worldview of consumer societies and the individuals who inhabit them. As for social work as a profession, we are proposing that we consider alternative conceptualizations of social justice if we are to truly play a meaningful role in this transformation.

Global Warming

In a special report titled *The Death of Environmentalism: Global Warming Politics in a Post-Environmental World*, two long-time environmentalists, Michael Shellenberger and Ted Nordhaus (2005), created a storm of controversy in the environmental community by suggesting that pressing international environmental problems such as global warming cannot be separated from pressing social issues such as economics, politics, and social stratification. More recently, the Worldwatch Institute (2009) reached a similar conclusion. These ideas do not sound terribly controversial to social workers, because we have known for many decades the interconnectedness between environmental factors and pressing social issues.

What is interesting from a human behavior perspective is, first, that this controversy involves the realization that the realities of global warming are increasingly beginning to define the scope of the environmental debate and, second, that the debate within the professional environmental community is not much different from the dispute that has been going on in the larger community for some time now. The current discussion seems to have coalesced around two very different and dissenting voices that both support and challenge an emerging scientific assertion that global warming is the most significant and potentially most disastrous natural occurrence to face the human species in the last 10,000 years or more.

The problem is that most average citizens, untrained in ecology and unsophisticated in the politics of environmental policy, have little idea whom to believe. One group believes global warming to be a real, perilous, and increasingly menacing phenomenon that is and will continue to increase in intensity, having a profound impact on global climate and correspondingly on global social and economic conditions. The other group contends just the opposite (see for example, Fahrenthold & Eilperin, 2009). To these skeptics, global warming has not been proven incontrovertibly, air quality is getting better, world forestry is spreading, oil reserves are increasing, and the world's fresh water is cleaner and reaching more people than ever before (Barnett, 2004). For this optimistic band of environmental prophets, global warming may not exist at all, and, if it does exist, it is far too early to tell what the long-term impact will likely be. At the extreme end, radical members of this group tend to simply deny the existence of a problem or to at least argue that whatever climate differentials we may be experiencing are largely due to the natural fluctuations in global climatic patterns. They have for decades excoriated environmental naysayers as "chicken-little scaredy cats" and have set about to develop a strategic plan aimed at debunking any claim of environmental calamity.

However, it now seems clear, even for the casual observer, that three things have changed this debate significantly. Those three things are Hurricanes Katrina, Rita, and Wilma. These three hurricanes, perhaps the largest and most destructive ever, brought a deeper awareness to the general public, who saw for the first time and in real time that there exists a very genuine threat to their public safety and personal security. What has become even more compelling is the shift in public consciousness of many who now see these catastrophic natural events as inextricably linked to global warming. In addition, what millions saw in New Orleans in the aftermath of Hurricane Katrina was government complacency and politically shortsighted attempts to further marginalize an already oppressed and angry group of people. These sad events seemed to foreshadow a growing appreciation that environmental disasters have profound political and social consequences and that those impacts are felt by all but are often experienced most harshly by those lowest on the socioeconomic ladder. What seemed to come together in the hours following the Gulf Coast tragedy was a foreboding that unless we do something about global warming and do it quickly, there will be even more flooding, more breakdown of democratic institutions, more erosion of civil order, more loss of life, more racial, ethnic, and class-based victim blaming, more loss of human dignity and communitarian spirit, and an ever-widening chasm between the haves and have-nots.

So the questions can be reasonably asked: What has happened? and What do we know for certain? In short, what happened is carbon dioxide (CO_2). CO_2 is not a hideous thing. It is a common gas occurring everywhere on earth. It is a natural byproduct of living systems and is essential for life as we know it. CO_2 is expelled from our bodies when we breathe, it nurtures plant and animal life, and it is exchanged in an intricate photosynthetic process by the world's vast forests for the earth's oxygen reserves. It is essentially nontoxic. The only bad mark we can give to CO_2 is that it is the natural byproduct of fossil-fuel combustion processes. That is, when we burn anything that has a fossil-fuel base, such as coal or petroleum, we create massive amounts of CO_2. In and of itself this is not a bad thing, and in low quantities and doses the earth's atmosphere can absorb and dissipate the CO_2 over time. The problem is, of course, that we are creating too much CO_2 for the atmosphere to handle. (Refer to Figure 8.4, a chart that shows the acceleration of carbon dioxide emissions over the past 200 or so years.) Its molecular structure traps radiated heat in the upper regions of the atmosphere that would otherwise drift into open space. The net effect is a planet that acts much like a greenhouse; heat comes into a closed space but is not allowed to escape. Thus, the greenhouse stays warmer for longer periods of time, even during seasonal periods when it ought to be much cooler.

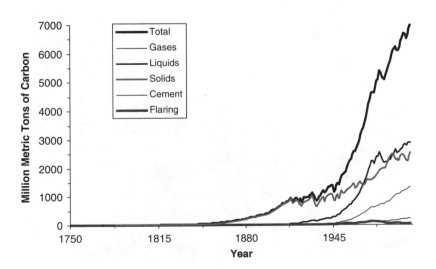

Figure 8.4. Global, regional, and national CO_2 emissions.

Did the planet betray us or did we betray the planet? This is the question asked rhetorically in Al Gore's 2006 gripping documentary film, *An Inconvenient Truth*. The film depicts the science and politics surrounding global warming. There is no quick fix looming on the horizon—indeed, none may exist at all—that will allow us to continue to burn vast quantities of CO_2-producing carbon fuels and still avoid the impact of global warming. Global warming is unlike many environmental problems in that it has only one realistic solution—to stop burning fossil fuels and totally reconfigure the ways that we have used power in our lives over the last 150 years. In other words, to reduce global warming, we are faced with the real option of having to significantly change the way we have come to exist in this world. In his most recent contribution to environmental science, *Our Choice: A Plan to Solve the Climate Crisis*, Gore (2009) gathers in one place all of the most effective solutions that are available now and that, together, will solve this crisis. Renewable energy, efficiency, green buildings, and urban sustainability are among the options addressed. He criticizes the media for disrespecting the boundary between fact and disinformation. The ethical mission of media, he says, "has been subjugated by electronic images that carelessly blend news with entertainment, advocacy with advertisements, and the public interest with self-interest" (introduction). Figure 8.5 illustrates one of the greatest solutions of all to the air pollution, carbon-emission problem in the cities—light rail. Cities such as Portland, Oregon, that have made major investments in light rail find that the environmental impact as well as commuting hassles are greatly reduced. A rail line, as Driehaus (2008) indicates, uses only one-quarter of the land needed for a six-lane freeway and greatly reduces the pollution to the air. The use of trucks to carry cargo instead of railroads is a major contributor to highway congestion, traffic fatalities, and air pollution as well. Big smoke-billowing trucks and buses are major sources of pollution—especially in urban areas. Diesel soot is a toxic air pollutant linked to human cancer. (See Figure 8.6 for a typical American highway scene.)

What, then, do we know for certain about global warming? There is an ever-increasing

Figure 8.5. Light rail, Portland, Oregon. Construction of light rail is one of the most effective ways to reduce air pollution. Photo by Rupert van Wormer.

Figure 8.6. Reliance on big diesel trucks instead of freight trains to transport food and equipment is a major cause of air pollution and highway congestion in the United States. Photo by Robert van Wormer.

amount of evidence and agreement among the world's serious scientific community that human populations and their activities have changed the climate of large areas of the world. In the last few years, it now is readily apparent that climate change is accelerating at a pace that shocks even the most conservative climatologists. Indeed, the disastrous effects of unchecked global warming have accelerated faster than scientists had predicted just a decade ago (Dunn & Flavin, 2002).

Since 1750, CO_2 concentrations have increased worldwide by over 30 percent, with half of that increase coming within just the past 50 years. The current concentration of CO_2 in the atmosphere is now at its highest levels at any time in the last 20 million years (Houghton, 2001, 2004). In response to this emerging scientific consensus, many are suggesting that humanity needs to reduce its use of carbon fuels by 70–80 percent in a very short period of time—perhaps within 5 to 10 years—in order to avoid the worst of the large-scale, irreversible effects (Gelspan, 2004). Even if greenhouse gas concentrations are stabilized at or near current levels or reduced to the levels of the early 1990s, climate change effects—many of

them quite severe—will persist for well over 200 years.

Climate changes induced by rampant and unsustainable human practices have affected food production, human health, human immigration patterns, and a plethora of climatic-related problems. For example, global temperatures are on the rise. Eleven of the last 12 years are among the 12 warmest years ever recorded in terms of global surface temperature (Pachauri, 2009). The United States has experienced 19 of its 20 hottest years just since 1980. 2005 will go down in the record books as the hottest year ever, with 1998, 2002, and 2003 ranking second, third, and fourth, respectively (National Resources Defense Council, 2005).

According to the Worldwatch Institute's (2009) latest report, *State of the World 2009: Into a Warming World*, the world will have to reduce greenhouse gas emissions more drastically than has been widely predicted, essentially ending the emission of carbon dioxide by 2050 to avoid catastrophic disruption to the world's climate. Saving the global climate will require mass public support and political will from all nations to institute new ways of living that are environmentally sustainable. As indicated by the book's 47 authors, much can be done in the way of renewable energy and efficiency improvements, agriculture, and forestry to slow climate change, but there is not much time left.

The Intergovernmental Panel on Climate Change (2005) predicts that average global temperature will increase from 2 to 10 degrees Fahrenheit over the next 100 years. The Earth's average temperature has already risen by more than 0.8 degrees Celsius (1.4 degrees Fahrenheit) since the beginning of the Industrial Revolution in the mid-eighteenth century, with much of that increase attributed to human activities (Worldwatch Institute, 2009). This rate of warming is much larger than that experienced in the past century and is without precedent within the last 10,000 years (Dunn & Flavin, 2002). Even a 1 degree rise in average global temperature can have a profound impact on ecosystems and therefore on human and plant-life systems. There is now mounting evidence, according to Pachauri (2009), Chair of the Intergovernmental Panel on Climate Change (IPCC), that grain output would be threatened by climate change, particularly if the average temperature were to reach 2.5 degrees Celsius above preindustrial levels. Some regions of the world—Africa, for example—would suffer more than others. Estimates are that 75–250 million people would experience water stress as early as 2020 as a consequence of climate change. The decline in agricultural yields would be significant. The consequences of these years of record high temperatures are greater drought, greater evaporation of freshwater reserves, and potential for increased incidents of catastrophic wildfires. In 2002 the western United States experienced its second worst wildfire season in more than 50 years.

One of the most dangerous consequences of global temperature increases is the rapid acceleration in the rise of sea levels. Sea levels have been rising twice as quickly over the past 10 years as they did during the previous century (Gelspan, 2005). At the current rate, global sea-level rises could increase by as much as 20 feet within the next 100 years, after having already risen by almost a foot in just the past 100 years. This projected rise would be enough

to swamp almost the entire state of Florida and create untold damage and hardship to island nations and low-lying estuarial areas around the world, including the entire Gulf Coast region of the United States (Environmental News Service, 2005). This rise is propelled by the steady infusion of water into the oceans from the melting icecaps and glaciers and by the thermal expansion of the oceans themselves. After existing for over a thousand years, the northern section of the Larsen B ice shelf in Antarctica—a section larger than the state of Rhode Island—disintegrated and melted into the ocean in just a 3-month period between January and March 2002. This rate of collapse astonished even the most cynical of climatologists, giving further evidence that the Antarctica ice shelf area had shrunk by over 40 percent in just 10 years. Another recent report from scientists monitoring the polar ice substantiated that another 10,000-year-old ice shelf on the Antarctic Peninsula recently melted in just 3 weeks (Environmental News Service, 2005).

All of these events are directly attributable to the rising levels of heat-trapping carbon dioxide in the atmosphere, which catches and traps heat that historically was allowed to escape into space. Atmospheric carbon levels, which were relatively steady over the past 10,000 years, have risen precipitously in just the past 150 years. This almost 50 percent increase in carbon dioxide levels in a relatively short period of time reflects an increase that could not occur by natural planetary fluctuation alone. Indeed, it is something the planet has not experienced—by naturally occurring climatic cycles—in over 500,000 years (Dunn & Flavin, 2002).

Economist Thomas Friedman (2008), author of the bestselling *Hot, Flat, and Crowded: Why We Need a Green Revolution—and How It Can Renew America*, equates solid economics with our environmental health. Just as the United States has been reckless economically, this country has also been reckless environmentally. Friedman urges that global warming be taken seriously even if there is less than absolute certainty about its cause as many skeptics suggest. He anticipates that it will be taken seriously in the form of the development of a green economy. Sustainability in the economy will be matched by environmental sustainability in what he refers to as "the Energy-Climate Era" (p. 172). In the future, Friedman predicts that the defining measure of a country's standing and environmental health will be its ability to develop clean power and energy-efficient technologies.

Let us now look at the possible role of the social work profession in attending to issues stemming from the natural environment. We begin with a historical overview of philosophical forces that helped shape the development of social work into a direction in which person and environment would ultimately be viewed as inextricably linked. This journey has not been straight forward, however; there have been many detours along the way.

Conventional Ideas of Community and Environment in Social Work

With the population increase and the environmental problems that accompanied both the rapid growth of the cities and industrialization during the late nineteenth century, a frantic search for solutions occurred (Spano, 1982). The shift in the public thinking went from blaming the individual for poverty and poor living standards to seeking out structural causes. The ideas that evolved from this national reappraisal coalesced into an identifiable political movement of conceptual clarity and social action commonly known as the progressive movement (Leiby, 1978). It was the Progressive Era that also shaped the identity and purposes of the emerging profession of social work and determined the contours of social work's early understanding of person and of how that person lived with, adapted to, and was affected by his or her environments.

The Progressive Era

What evolved during the Progressive Era was a robust belief in the environment as a powerful and dynamic force in shaping human development. Concomitant with this reform-minded thinking on environment was a growing conviction that persons had the inherent capacities to achieve positive change through deliberate modifications of their environments. This emerging focus on change through personal capacity and environmental reform, however, was limited in scope. Though it shifted attention from individual deficiency and passive adaptation toward the impact of environmental factors and the individual's capacity to change them, progressive reform tended to restrict its views of environment to very limited social and economic factors (Kemp, 1994).

This is not to say that this era's views of environment were exclusively defined in such narrow bands. The Romantic view of primitive or preindustrial modes of living as attractive alternatives to the prevailing progress-oriented, mechanistic worldview found expression in the works of early-twentieth-century writers. D. H. Lawrence, William D. Howells, and Jack London, among others, began to speak of nature as unity, as an organism that has value for its own sake, in which persons are seen as one coequal partner in the process of emergence of the whole (Janik, 1981).

In addition to the late-nineteenth and early-twentieth-century Romantic novelists' perspective, naturalistic views of environment were also prevalent in the works of the two great preservation and conservation writers of the period: John Muir (1838–1914) and Gifford Pinchot (1865–1946). It would be hard to imagine two men with like goals who were more different in specific ideology and philosophy. Much of Muir's nature consciousness was shaped by his appropriation of Transcendentalist ideas of the natural world (Nash, 1989). Nourished by his reading of Emerson and Thoreau, as well as by his years of personal wilderness experience, Muir believed in trying to merge his consciousness with nature, to seek unity in its complexity. Nature, Muir wrote in *My First Summer in the Sierra* (1911/1998), is a "window opening into heaven, a mirror reflecting the Creator" (Nash, 1982, p. 125). For Muir, it was a dangerous heresy to measure the natural world by its utility for humanity. Instead, he affirmed that there was inherent value in all organic and inorganic forms.

Muir's philosophy stands in sharp contrast to that of Gifford Pinchot. Pinchot was primarily concerned with the protection of natural resources for practical use by future generations. His ethic was driven by utilitarian ideas and infused with principles of scientific management and genetic improvement. It emerged in large part as an attempt to constrain the wholesale destructive impact of individuals and corporations who exploited nature for profit without sufficient regard for the larger social good or welfare of future generations (Sessions, 1995). Pinchot had no illusions concerning the deeper meaning of nature, so unabashedly trumpeted by Muir. To his mind there were only two relevant, guiding interests to be considered: "humans and natural resources" (Fox, 1981, p. 22). Pinchot vigorously opposed the allocation of land for parks and other noncommercial purposes. He played a major role in establishing the dominant mood concerning the management of natural resources in the Progressive Era as efficient, scientific, professionalized economic development (O'Neil, 1976).

The clash of the Romantic and modernistic ideologies represented by Muir's and Pinchot's positions was dramatized in their fight over the Hetch Hetchy Dam project near San Francisco from 1902 through 1913. Essentially, the dispute entailed whether the Tuolumne River of Yosemite Park should be dammed in order to provide power and water for the burgeoning population of San Francisco. Allied with the persuasive force of President Theodore Roosevelt's commitment to Manifest Destiny and his disdain for sentimental views of nature, Pinchot's side won, and Congress passed the Baker Act, granting the city its rights to the water and the dam (Worster, 1985).

The victory of Pinchot over Muir established the contours of American views on the natural environment during the later Progressive Era and for many decades to come. It legislated and legitimized the modern, industrial era's faith in science and technology in the service of human needs (Kasson, 1976). Hetch Hetchy became the proxy fight for a battle of competing moral visions. The lines were drawn between nature as a moral or an economic resource. The latter had ultimately won because

Americans of the late nineteenth and early twentieth centuries had become increasingly ambivalent about nature and increasingly enamored with the prospects of the modernist project (Jones, 2010). Quite willing to control nature, they at the same time sought to reform its unscientific and wholesale exploitation and to preserve a certain portion of it. Wise use, it was believed, would ensure its availability for both agendas.

This overvaluation of environmental and technological capacity, core maxims of modernist ideology, increasingly moved the natural environment into the background of the American psyche. It was believed to be in the good hands of scientific, technocratic managers. To the foreground emerged the humanistic, existential principles of environment that passed over nature in favor of the *Mitwelt* (the social world) and the *Eigenwelt* (the personal world). The natural world was oversimplified by simple linear thinking and explained in reductionist terms. Individuals and the social world became separate from and above the natural environment. It was "understood to be little more than the sum total of thwarting physical necessities" (Roszak, 1992, p. 65).

The Social Work Profession Emerges

Conventional ideas of person and environment and their relationship within social work can best be understood by viewing these concepts within the framework of social work's early history. This early history is the story of the evolution of two organizational movements that assumed the major share of responsibility for social welfare during the rapidly expanding industrial era: charity organization societies and settlement houses.

Charity organization societies (COSs) began as an effort to coordinate relief giving by operating community-wide registration bureaus in order to provide direct relief and education for both the poor and the upper class (Leiby, 1978). The work of COSs was carried out by volunteer committees that examined needy applicants and decided on a course of action. Friendly visitors had the task of investigating the circumstances that surrounded the applicants' needs and to instruct the poor in ways to better manage their lives (Lubove, 1971). The belief that the poor were morally responsible for their own circumstances is unmistakable.

By the early 1900s, COS workers became increasingly aware that the abysmal urban conditions so rampant during this time could not simply be attributed to faulty character. As one charity leader said, "I have done some psychological reading and I have still to find a single author who is willing to agree that hunger is psychical. . . ." (Frankel, 1901, p. 382). Gradually, COS leaders began to acknowledge weaknesses in the friendly visiting model. In its place arose the belief that poverty was a function of environmental circumstances (Wenocur & Reisch, 1989).

The general influence of reform environmentalism on much of early modern society is suggested in many of the early writings of COS leadership, although they do not make explicit mention of Pinchot. In 1906, Edward Devine chided the charity movement "with not having at all appreciated the importance of the environmental causes of distress, with having fixed their attention far too much upon personal weakness" (cited in Kemp, 1994, p. 79). Porter Lee (1911) argued that the foundation of social casework rested in environmental change.

The second organizational movement that assumed a major share of responsibility for social welfare in the late nineteenth and early twentieth centuries was the settlement house. The settlement house movement, like that of the COS, was a response to the urban, industrial conditions of the times. Unlike the COS, however, settlements were expressly different in structure and orientation (Chambers, 1963; Trattner, 1999). Settlement houses were established in immigrant neighborhoods by educated young men and women who themselves moved into the slums as residents. Their model was not that of friendly visiting but rather was infused with a genuine desire to bridge class differences and to develop a less patronizing form of charity (Trolander, 1987). A distinctive form of liberal Christianity and socialism were fused to form the basis of the settlements' unique outlook.

The environment, not the individual, was the locus of change for the settlers. In an address to the National Conference on Charities and Corrections, Jane Addams (1904) suggested that families experience great difficulty not because of defective character but as a result of "influences from the outside" (p. 457). Manthey (1989) writes of the settlement movement:

> The environment was both the cause and the healing agent of social problems. Social, economic and political factors had to be taken into account in understanding social problems. In contrast to the position of the charity organization societies, the settlement believed that the government had a responsibility to improve the environment. The neighborhood was viewed as a laboratory for social study. The settlements were concerned with creating a healing environment by educating the immigrant in literature, poetry, and the arts . . . recreation and leisure time activities. (pp. 106–107)

The early history of social work, especially during the Progressive Era, was pivotal to its developing conceptualizations of person and environment. The COSs and the settlements, though often involved in rancorous discord relative to the delivery of services, clearly established a philosophical link between the person and environment. The works and writings of their leaders, especially Mary Richmond and Jane Addams, established the parameters for social work's ongoing dual concern for both constructs. At the same time, the seed was planted that bore fruit in a continuous, almost exclusive neglect of the natural element of environment and the failure to develop a more expansive sense of person in relationship to it.

It would be unwise and unjustified to assume that this tendency to ignore nature and limit the person was somehow a deliberate attempt to subvert a more fully cultivated and extended view of professional development. Richmond, Addams, and their fellow social workers were creatures of their times (Kemp, 1994). They operated within the cultural framework of their day. Though marked by reformist fervor and environmental concern, the view of nature in the Progressive Era was largely framed in Pinchotian terms. Early social workers were clearly involved in limited ways with issues of the natural environment (Brandt, 1910; Kellogg & Harrison, 1910; Lovejoy, 1911) and the constructed physical environment (Addams, 1909; Deforest & Veiller, 1903; Kelly, 1895; McDowell, 1917; Sanborn, 1898), but this represented an application of the rational instrumentalist, scientific conservationism so dominant during this time (Rodman, 1983).

> Early social workers defined persons in relationship to their immediate circumstances, resulting in a view of the environment focused on social relationships and on the internal subjective environment, as experienced within these relationships. The natural environment was merely background clutter providing the medium through which social circumstance and person interacted. The period of social work history between the end of World War I and the early 1960s marked a deeper entrenchment of restrictive notions of person and environment and saw the rise of the psychodynamic paradigm as a grounding force in social work practice. (p. 83)

Separation of Person and Environment

The mood of American culture after World War I, between 1917 and 1930, was much different from that before the war. The reform spirit of the prewar days was gone, largely replaced by growing self-absorption and scientific managerialism in the arena of public interest. Business idealogues endeavored to create a new popular faith in American capitalism and in the "American way" (Akin, 1977). The total acceptance of the dominance of science, technology, and professional expertise "is symbolized by the Chicago World's Fair of 1933 glorifying a 'Century of Progress' with its slogan, 'Science Discovers—Technology Makes—Man Conforms'" (Ferkiss, 1993, p. 102). The rise of communism in Russia created a suspicious atmosphere in which reform of any sort was viewed as a threat to the traditional social order. During the period of the 1920s the American scene was characterized by a rising confidence in individual effort, private enterprise, technical rationality, and intolerance for social reform (Akin, 1977). Social work attempted to exert its influence in a society increasingly preoccupied with self-indulgence and disillusionment with the power of individual and collective action to alter historical events. Although the reform spirit was not entirely dead, its influence was largely overshadowed by social work's drive for professional status and a search for a body of knowledge, which would lead to a more refined technical expertise based on a foundation of science (Popple, 1985). The profession's shift from social action to more individual interests at this time was strongly influenced by the profession's alliance with psychiatry and its adoption of Freudian psychoanalytical theory as the scientific framework most informing to social work practice (Ehrenreich, 1985; Specht & Courtney, 1994).

The years immediately following World War I were marked by great ideological and epistemological change within social work. Driven internally by the impetus to professionalize and externally by renewed interest in the power of science, social workers took the first determined steps toward a person-centered, therapeutic model of practice (Kemp, 1994). This shift away from the situated practice of Jane Addams and the person-environment approach of Mary Richmond and others in the Progressive Era meant that social work was becoming increasingly abstract and disconnected from any environmental frame of reference. Those environmental factors that affected individual development were essentially restricted to proximal relationships: person to person, family to person, specialist to person. Larger environmental factors, economic, social, and natural, were increasingly separated from issues of personal development. Nature, particularly, became a problem to be controlled by scientific manipulation or was so familiar as to be commonplace. Attention to it was minimized, abstracted, ignored, or left in the hands of scientific managers. It was of little interest to a profession absorbed in an effort to establish its place and to develop its expert knowledge in professional, bureaucratic, and objectivist terms (Jones, 2010).

Conventional Ideas of Person and Environment

The period between the 1960s and the 1980s has been described as a multiple historic watershed. This period was marked by racial and social upheaval, gender and class polarization, wars in Vietnam and on poverty, shifts from liberal reform to quasi conservatism to neoconservatism, rising environmental consciousness, and unprecedented developments in science and technology (Marable, 1984; Siegel, 1984). Americans and others around the world were beginning to question anew the cost of unrestricted economic and technological growth. A new environmental movement was gathering pace. Its message was that humans were endangering their own lives through an arrogant, manipulative attitude toward other forms of life. A singularly important factor contributing to this feeling of national doubt was the publication of Rachael Carson's (1962) powerful book *Silent Spring*. It captured the interest of broad audiences at a time when more and more citizens seemed to be sensing that nature itself was under attack and that defending it required a more radical way of thinking. The older, far more restrained Pinchotian conservationism so characteristic of the environmental ideology and policy of the first half of the twentieth century was gradually thought to be incapable of meeting the challenges of global environmental degradation (Hays, 1987). This new environmentalism shifted the meaning of the term *environment* away from social contexts and toward nature. Worster (1994) describes this change:

> In the earlier part of this century the word "environment" referred mainly to the external social influences (as opposed to genetic endowment) working on the individual. Environmentalism referred to the belief that the "physical, biological, psychological or cultural environment" was a crucial factor shaping "the structure or behavior of animals, including man." But increasingly as the battle of heredity versus environment lost saliency after World War II, environment came to mean, particularly and especially, the *natural* influences surrounding people, including flora, fauna, climate, water, and soil; human beings, it was understood, were not passive victims of their surroundings— they were imbedded in them, they interacted with them, and they could have an effect. (p. 350)

In social work, professional self-scrutiny of the effectiveness of traditional person-centered paradigms was growing (Fischer, 1975; Hashimi, 1981). In particular, Herman Stein (1963) reexamined the conceptualization of environment in social work theory. He identified three major misconceptions associated with the concept. First, he noted the tendency to regard the environment as very narrowly related to immediate contexts, such as housing, jobs, families, and face-to-face relationships. Second, he identified the inclination to view environment as external to the individual, who "stands alone, an isolated complex of intra-psychic processes" (p. 68). Third, Stein noted the tendency to view the environment as static, unchanging, background clutter. From these perspectives, Stein argued that social work's view of environment was unnecessarily restrictive and the consideration of it merely a second-rate activity compared with the more distinguished method of psychological treatment.

A search for new ways to conceptualize the relationship between personal and environmental dimensions of practice (Brieland, 1977; Meyer, 1970, 1973; Siporin, 1972, 1980) led some theorists to explore emergent ideas in general systems theory (GST; Leighninger, 1977). GST was seen as a way to explain the complexity of human phenomena from a process orientation, without giving exclusive attention to either the person or the larger environment (de Hoyos, 1989; Petr, 1988). Early social work writing on systems theory by Germain (1968), Hearn (1979), and Hartman (1971) attempted to shift attention from a limited person-situation frame to one that was multidimensional, filled with complexity and potential.

During this same time the ecological approach of Carol Germain (1978, 1991) evolved as an attempt to bridge the gap between the abstraction of GST and the growing trend of conceiving of the world in ecological terms. The ecological approach understood human behavior as inseparably linked with the environment. In order to fully enhance human functioning, the physical and social environments of the person must be assessed concurrently. In the words of Germain (1978), "People and their environments are viewed as interdependent, complementary parts of a whole in which person and environment are constantly changing and shaping the other" (p. 539). The concept of adaptation is a cornerstone of the ecological perspective. It focuses on how an "individual's needs, capacities, and opportunities for growth and the individual's ability to adapt to changing external demands are met by, provided for, and challenged by the environment" (Saleebey, 1992, p. 113).

In an attempt to articulate this ecological perspective for practice, Germain and Alex Gitterman (1980) joined forces in order to apply the ecological metaphor to direct social work practice. For Germain and Gitterman:

> The environment is dynamic and complex. It comprises many kinds of systems, each with its characteristic structure, level of organization, and spatial and temporal properties. The *social* environment comprises human beings organized in dyadic relations, social networks, bureaucratic institutions, and other social systems including the neighborhood, community, and society itself. The *physical* environment comprises the natural world of animals, plants, and land forms, and the built world of structures and objects constructed by human beings. The social and physical environments are related to each other in complex ways. (1980, p. 137)

Ignoring the Natural Environment

System perspectives and ecological models made a significant contribution to social work by concentrating on environmental intervention as a core social work function (Kemp, 1994). The decision, however, not to attend to broader dimensions of the environment limits the environmental focus to issues in the immediate vicinity of the client (Zaph, 2009). The conceptualization of "environment", as Jones (2010) indicates, was almost exclusively limited to a person's *social* environment and relationships. In addition, the heavy reliance on adaptive processes perpetuates a decades-old social work proclivity to discuss environment while at the same time concentrating predominantly on individual agency. The essential focus of ecological and systems theory and all its variants is, according to Saleebey, "on how individuals adapt to environmental demands. While there is talk of changing environments, the message of the ecological approach in general is that, in many cases, it is the client(s) who will have to adapt . . ." (1990, pp. 10–11). The "individual determinism" (Gould, 1987) so characteristic of the ecological model's preoccupation with adaptation increases the likelihood that other important factors related to human development will be disregarded. Again, Saleebey (1990) notes that "the realities of power, conflict, oppression, and violence, so central to the survival of many groups, are given a curious and unreal patina by the adaptation perspective" (p. 11). This epistemological blind spot also inhibits conceiving the natural environment as anything more significant than data to be studied and/or resources to be procured or regulated. Social work's application of the system and ecological model's adaptive component creates a state of consciousness that suggests that one already exists on a plane of profound division between oneself and one's place in the larger environment. Person in environment becomes a kind of euphemism for what is in reality person on environment. Deeper understanding of identity with nature is then excluded and becomes an abstraction that leads to concepts and actions that cannot be reconciled with the health either of the person or of nature. Living *in* nature, on the other hand, suggests a complex relationship pieced together over time through patterns of value and restraint, through memory, familiarity, love, and respect. The result of being *in* nature is both knowledge of object and particular experience of the world and also (and this is what is missing) deep reverence for the mystery of the world and for its patterns, which lie beyond expressive understanding.

As social work moved indoors into institutional settings, what remained of an appreciation for the client's direct experience with physical and natural environmental factors was exchanged for technical bureaucratic knowledge. Though it maintained the environmental vernacular, social work's widespread acceptance of psychiatric and psychological theory moved the profession inexorably toward a central concern with changing the person through the process of relationship with the specialist and corresponding manipulation of the environment.

Alternative Perspectives on Person and Environment

Considering that the person-in-environment construct is so central to both social work's professional identity and its ability to contribute to human well-being, it is important to reenvision it in the context of contemporary circumstances and alternative perspectives. One of the purposes of this chapter is to help students begin the process of expanding person in environment in a manner more consistent with professional values and emerging global circumstances, such as recent ecological events involving Hurricane Katrina and the catastrophic Indian Ocean tsunami (Besthorn, 2008). One of the ways to do this is to look at insights from recently emerging paradigms of ecological consciousness known as deep ecology and ecological feminism. We examine how the insights from these two alternative conceptual perspectives can be incorporated into our understanding of human behavior and how this might prepare students for an ecologically responsible social work practice. These ideas may seem conceptually difficult and perhaps even a bit esoteric to the first-time reader and for those of us who look at environmental issues from a predominantly Western viewpoint. But we are confident that as you reflect on them you will discover the importance of an expanded ecological framework and that you will discover

new ways to apply this framework to your unique practice settings.

The National Association of Social Workers (NASW) Board of Directors took an important step in acknowledging ecological concerns by proposing a proactive environmental policy stance (Humphreys, 1999). The most recent environmental policy proposal suggests that social work needs an environmentally responsible conceptual framework to which professional social workers can subscribe and on which they can have influence (NASW, 2009, p. 124). This policy position asserts that social workers have a vested interest in the viability of the environment to protect the well-being and survival of all people, to counter environmental racism, to promote global equality in all nations, and to encourage human beings to exercise their capacity for intelligent and responsible stewardship of the earth. The policy states that humans are but one element of a vast, complicated, and interdependent ecosystem. Humans are not separate from, nor superior to, other elements of the biosphere. Similarly, social workers in other parts of the world, such as India, Australia, Canada, Mexico, Hong Kong, and England, to name just a few (Andharia & Sengupta, 1998; Chan, 1993; Coates, 2004; Graham, Swift, & Hart, 1996; Hoff, 1998; Jones, 2010; Lysack, 2007, 2008, 2009a, 2009b; McKinnon, 2005; Morrissette, McKenzie, & Morrissette, 1993; Ungar, 2002; Zaph, 2005a, 2005b, 2008, 2009), have clearly recognized the need to connect good social work practice to a deeper environmental awareness. Indeed, in many ways they are far ahead of U.S. social workers in this regard. Deep ecology and ecofeminism offer two conceptual frameworks to support social work's emerging emphasis on the natural environment.

Deep Ecology

Deep ecology is both a paradigm for understanding the world and a social movement for environmental responsibility (Schroll, 2007). As a paradigm, it builds on insights already familiar to most social workers, but it takes these insights to their full potential for transcending the tendency of humans to destroy the natural environment. Deep ecology emphasizes understanding of systems in a holistic way, just as social work practice commonly draws on various kinds of systems theories (Germain, 1991; Hearn, 1979; Imbrogno & Canda, 1988; Leighninger, 1977; Robbins, Chatterjee, & Canda, 2006). But it goes beyond the conventional social work view by adding two other dimensions: total ecology and transpersonal experience.

In deep ecology, the concept of environment includes all human and nonhuman beings, processes, things, and systems in the total planetary ecology and, indeed, the larger cosmic ecology. Further, as human beings are traveling and sending equipment beyond the earth's atmosphere, we are already polluting and exploiting outer space, the moon, and nearby planets. Space exploration and colonization of other planetary bodies is clearly a goal of the U.S. government and others for the next century. Social work needs to be prepared to deal with both the complex planetary impact of human beings in space and the new social arrangements and social problems that will emerge in human groups confined to vehicles of space travel, space stations, and earth orbit colonies.

Transpersonal experience refers to the human awareness of connection and unity with other people, other beings, the earth itself, and even the cosmos (Cowley, 1996; Fox, 1995; Robbins et al., 2006). For example, sometimes a breakthrough in transpersonal awareness, which Maslow (1970) termed a *peak experience*, occurs directly in relation to a powerfully moving encounter with the beauty and majesty of nature. Imagine yourself hiking to the top of a lushly forested mountain and finally coming into a clearing. Looking out, you are suddenly overwhelmed by the vast vista, feeling a sense of communion with the intricate and awesome beauty all around you. This is quite literally a peak experience, which can propel one into a new perspective on life and raise questions about how one should live life to remain consistent with this more unitive awareness (Canda & Furman, 2010). Deep ecology is called "deep" because it helps people to understand connection with the world in profound and self-transforming ways. Deep ecology leads to a

reenvisioning of both person (as total person) and environment (as total ecology). In this sense, person and environment are codetermining concepts, because person cannot exist without environment.

The term *deep ecology* was coined in 1973 by Norwegian philosopher Arne Naess (Grimes, 2008). Naess was a prolific writer, naturalist, and ardent mountaineer. He authored over 400 articles in professional publications in his almost 70-year academic career—spanning the years from 1936 to 2006. He also authored over 30 books and was a frequent speaker at international philosophical and environmental gatherings. A recently edited publication of his selected works includes 10 volumes of almost 4,000 pages (Glasser & Drengson, 2005). And this covers only a small portion of his overall contribution. Naess was widely considered the most preeminent European philosopher of the second half of the twentieth century (Drengson & Devall, 2006). His work encompasses a vast array of topics ranging from analysis of Spinozan philosophy, Buddhism, Gandhian ideas of nonviolence, and the relationship between ecology and democracy. He is most noted, however, for his work in formulating a concise and thickly descriptive ecological ethic and worldview. While Naess passed away in early 2008, at the age of 96, his work continues to have profound influences on philosophers, ethicists, and the international environmental movement around the world (Anker, 2008).

Naess sought to describe a profound experientially grounded approach to human–nature relationships. He distinguished between shallow and deep ecological movements. Shallow ecology is concerned with ecological problems only because of their impact on humans, with emphasis on privileged classes and societies. It takes an anthropocentric (human-centered) vantage on the world. In contrast, deep ecology is concerned with issues of equality and ecojustice in humanity's relationship with nature (Naess, 2005). All peoples and all beings are given equal respect and consideration in deep ecology. Thus, environmental awareness is a desirable end in itself. It is also a crucial requirement for mobilizing actions that enhance human existence in the context of supporting all beings' existence. See Box 8.2, "Insights on Deep Ecology From Norway," in which Fred Besthorn describes how deep ecology is integral to Norwegian culture.

Box 8.2 Insights on Deep Ecology From Norway

Fred H. Besthorn

The modern Scandinavian country of Norway (taking its name from *Norvegr* or northern way) is today known for its scenic beauty and a collectivist social democratic society which emphasizes solidarity, equality, and a communitarian spirit. According to the United Nations Human Development Report, Norway is ranked as the number one place in the world to live based on a number of indicators · involving health, wealth, social services, and social outlook (Williams, 2001; Zahl, 2003). The country's legacy as one of the early outposts of Viking culture is memorialized in the prominence paid to seafaring explorers, intertribal quarrels, adventure, small-scale farming, commitment to one's family and neighbors, and a very strong orientation toward a rural and earthen-based lifestyle. This legacy has shaped its image of itself and its social and economic policy (Andersson & Bexell, 2005). Norway confronts the rest of the world with seeming contradictory contrasts of outdoor adventure, grey-black hues of monotony, rugged individualism, and communal accord. Modern Norway, in ways often very distinct from its Nordic neighbors in Sweden, Denmark, Finland, and Iceland, has maintained its uniqueness as a society. It is a society rich with verdant landscape and a deep conviction to hold fast to its social-democratic tradition. It is these intense contrasts that give life in the North such great power and why this small country with just over 4 million inhabitants creates such curiosity. Without the complex mix of collective commitment and individual reserve and "without the sea and the mountains, the darkness and the sunshine," the complex character of the inhabitants would defy explanation (Ogrizek, 1952, p. 160).

Norway has remained much as it was left by the geological upheavals of eons past. Human intrusion and built artifices are rare except in populated urban areas. These natural features create a country that is very rich in story and mythology and a people who are very patient, very hard-working, and as frequently as possible turn to nature to find both physical and psychic sustenance (Lindow, 2001). Norwegians are generally known for their stout, rugged, and often acutely internalized, relish for life. They are also known for their great physical strength, their loyalty, and for their deeply metaphysical, artistic and, at times, melancholic preference to confront their destinies with a reticent stoicism that embraces rather than turns from both the light and shadow of existence. Speaking of a national spirit and soul intimately tied to the land and place, Norwegian social historian Ogrizek (1952) again observes that his fellow citizens are nearly incapable of:

> compromise and half-measures, because they are the image of . . . the imposing landscapes, where eye and mind never find rest; this all-powerful scenery that requires our total submission and complete union without which we shall never gain knowledge . . . or at best, achieve it only superficially. This land requires much of us; it insists that we give ourselves up entirely, becoming one with it; in exchange it lavishes upon us the noblest, the purest and the most lofty emotions. . . . These northern souls are fashioned of the same stuff as the glaciers, the rocks, the mountains, the island and the seas of their land; this is why they are of such great worth, and this is what makes them so full of interest, so inexplicable, and often so impenetrable, enigmatic. (p. 156, 158)

There are several spiritual/ecological constructs which are especially relevant to understanding the cultural background of modern Norwegian ecological constructs. The first, involves the spiritual investiture of common landscapes. According to Reed and Rothernberg (1992), land and landscapes are understood as having deep spiritual/existential meaning and significance. Much like indigenous groups around the world, many Norwegians share a wide-ranging belief that the land is a sacred place. Nature and divinity are one and the same. Natural environments are a spiritual sanctuary. A second concept is a belief in the free and open right of entry into both public and private lands (Andersson & Bexell, 2005). This is referred to as *allemannsrett*, or open access to nature. Many Norwegians hold to it with an almost religious fervor. The rule of allemannsrett, now codified into Norwegian law, can be traced back to the Viking period. The rule specifies that the public has broad rights to roam freely in the open countryside on foot, on skis, on bicycles, in canoes; and to stay on these lands temporarily, including in some cases private property, as long as no damage is done to the landscape. A third construct is national participation in *friluftsliv*, or the belief that all citizens ought to take part in outdoor recreation because of the restorative and healing powers of being actively involved in natural landscapes. Friluftsliv is not yet codified into law but represents a powerful set of collective norms about how to behave in nature. Unlike many of its Scandinavian neighbors, Norway maintains an expressed preference for nonmotorized and low-impact use of nature such as quiet walks, cross-country skiing, and nature-based meditative experiences. Finally, many Norwegians have a general aversion to the idea of the commercialization of nature (Seippel, 2001). They, normally, do not believe that nature should be thought of as something that can be sold and consumed. Many Norwegians have a traditional commitment to the idea that clean air, clean water, pristine forests, picturesque mountains, and pastoral valleys cannot and must not be held up for sale or exclusive private use. This has been a common refrain among Norwegian intelligentsia and rural denizens alike.

Lessons for Social Work

While the West seems in the grip of deep uncertainty and insecurity about the future, many in other parts of the world are creatively struggling to find ways to integrate new economic and social realities into ancient customs in a fashion that does not destroy the collective nurturing systems—both ecological and human—that have existed for generations. In the midst of this boiling cauldron of contending demands and competing dreams, the social work profession, especially in the United States, must again find its voice to *speak out* against a consumer-oriented, profit-driven, unregulated, and often unjust global market system that has tended to create many more losers than winners in the competitive drive for greater control of world capital. And social work must also begin to *stand with* other professionals, community associations, grassroots organizations, and global advocacy groups to facilitate collective empowerment—to assist marginalized peoples everywhere to gain access to needed change that refosters commitment to the health and well-being of human communities and ecological systems.

A growing number of social workers from around the developed and developing world are beginning to sense this essential fact and are beginning to formulate coalition-building strategies that place social work in the place of being a key ally in developing new social, political, and ecological movements to stop the pillage of natural environments and human communities. It is time for the U.S. profession, steeped as it is in the language of environment and dedicated to the principle of justice, to find ways to link with these efforts and to apply the principles of deep ecology to new forms of struggle and solidarity to protect planet and people.

References

Andersson, D., & Bexell, G. (2005). *Universalism in ethics: Scandinavian perspectives*. The Hague: Kluwer Academic Press.

Lindow, J. (2001). *Norse mythology: A guide to the gods, heroes, rituals, and beliefs*. New York: Oxford University Press.

Ogrizek, D. (1952). *Scandinavia: Denmark, Norway, Sweden, Finland, and Iceland*. New York: McGraw Hill.

Reed, P. & Rothenberg, D. (Eds.). (1992). *Wisdom in the open air: The Norwegian roots of deep ecology*. Minneapolis: University of Minnesota Press.

Seippel, O. (2001). From mobilization to institutionalization: The case of Norwegian environmentalism. *Acta Sociologica, 44*, 123–137.

Williams, C. (2001, November 11). Norway tops in health, wealth ecology: Nation isn't utopia but cares for its own, rest of world. *The Los Angeles Times*, p. B6.

Zahl, M. A. (2003). Spirituality and social work: A Norwegian reflection. *Social Thought, 22*, 77–90.

Note from Katherine van Wormer: Having lived in Norway for two years where I practiced alcoholism counseling, I can confirm Fred Besthorn's observations above. Instead of fighting nature, Norwegians live with nature. Their enjoyment of snow is just one example. Sidewalks in Hamar where I lived were not shoveled; instead, the snow was allowed to accumulate; we then glided across the icy sidewalks—young and old alike— using *sparks*, or scooters with blades. Norwegians often have a cabin in the woods where they go with families and friends during their long vacations, whether to ski in the winter or pick berries in the fall. By law, all offices and factories are required to have windows so that workers can see outside; homes have no curtains for the same reason. Finally, in my work in alcoholism counseling, the Higher Power that the clients chose was not God but Nature. Besthorn's passage comes from a longer article that beautifully places these experiences in a cultural context.

Excerpted with permission from Besthorn, F. H. (2006). Instructional techniques for social work education: Insights from deep ecology in its Norwegian cultural context. *Universitas, 2*(1). Available from http://universitas .grad.uni.edu/spring06/ fredbesthorn0306.htm

Deep ecological ideas have been critiqued, refined, and expanded by converging intellectual movements of several kinds, including holistic physical and social systems sciences (Bertalanffy, 1981; Capra, 1982; Servilla, 2006); ideologies of environmental activism (Drengson & Inoue, 1995); earth-honoring spiritual traditions such as indigenous spiritual ways and shamanism (Buhner, 1996; Glendinning, 1994; Rosenhek, 2006); Buddhism (Halifax, 1993; Macy, 1991); creation-centered Christian theology (Fox, 1979); women's alternative spirituality and ecofeminism (LaChappelle, 1988); postmodern philosophy (Smart, 1992); and transpersonal psychological theory (Roszak 1992; Schroll, 2007; Wilber, 1995). Although deep ecology is not a formally defined theory, there is a general consensus among proponents with regard to key concepts that form a paradigm for understanding the human–nature relationship (Drengson, 2005).

Naess (cited in List, 1993, pp: 22–23) referred to deep ecology as a philosophy of ecological harmony with norms, rule postulates, value priority announcements, and hypotheses concerning the state of affairs in our universe. He called it *ecosophy* (Naess, 1973).

The fundamental guiding normative principle of deep ecology is that "humans should have reverence for nature and live in harmony with it, rather than practicing domination of Nature solely for humankind" (Jung, 1990, p. 95). In the written statement titled *Restoring the Vision* (1995), the Institute for Deep

Ecology, located in Boulder, Colorado, described the moral vision of deep ecology:

Deep ecology is about transforming our way of life. This loosely-knit movement is a grassroots awakening to the root causes of our culture's degradation of nature and peoples. As it seeks to heal contemporary alienation from self, community, and the Earth, deep ecology encourages a fundamental shift in the way we experience nature and how we respond to the environmental crisis. Deep ecology arises from the basic intuition of the essential value and interdependence of all forms of being. It is committed to minimizing humanity's destructive interference with the natural world and to restoring the richness and diversity of ecosystems and human communities. (p. 2)

Naess (1995b) elaborated that the well-being and flourishing of all human and nonhuman beings is a positive value in itself, as all beings have inherent worth independent of their usefulness to humans. Social workers value cultural diversity because of the inherent worth of each person and culture and for the creativity engendered by interactions among diverse peoples. Deep ecology supports and extends this value to respecting the diversity of all life forms for each one's own inherent worth and for the contributions of each to the vitality of the total web of life. Therefore, according to Naess (1995b), humans have no right to reduce the richness of biodiversity except to satisfy vital survival needs. Because human destruction of ecosystems is excessive and deleterious to both human and nonhumans, deep ecologists are committed to creating a harmonious way of human–nature relationship. LaChappelle (1988) emphasized that human beings' dual capacity for tremendous impact on environment and self-awareness puts us in the position of needing to exercise special responsibility and care in our relations with the earth. (Consult Table 8.2 which lists some of the key concepts of deep ecology.)

These value tenets imply that humans should extend a sense of caring, compassion,

Table 8.2   Key Concepts in Deep Ecology

Axiology	Ontology
Harmony with and reverence for nature	Interdependency of all beings
Inherent worth of all beings	Ecocentrism
Human responsibility	Ecological self
Epistemology	*Social Action Methodology*
Deep questioning	Environmental sustainability
Deep empathy	Ecojustice
Holistic inquiry	Win/win solutions for human/nature

Source: Besthom, F. H., & Canda, E. R. (2002), Revisioning environment: Deep ecology for education and teaching in social work. *Journal of Teaching in Social Work, 22*(1/2), 79–102.

and justice to other beings. Nonviolence toward humans and nonhumans is necessary. Consistent with Gandhian social activism (Hiranandani, 2008), nonviolence is not only the absence of violence, it is also a proactive effort to solve problems and achieve goals in ways that are mutually beneficial to both humans and nonhumans.

From the perspective of how one understands the character of the human condition, deep ecology understands nature and the nature of humans in a holistic way. Human beings are not the prime center of importance in the universe. They are one type of being whose existence completely depends on relationship with all other beings. Naess (1973) described this understanding as ecological consciousness. The situation of our being is not well expressed in such phrases as person-in-environment or person-and-environment, because these still put humans (individual persons) in the center. They are egocentric and anthropocentric notions. Humans exist in a relational total field. Rather than experiencing humanity as separate from environment and merely existing in it, humanity must begin to cultivate the insight that they are *with* the environment (Besthorn, 1997, 2000, 2001, 2002a, 2002b, Besthorn & Canda, 2002; Besthorn & McMillen, 2002). Being with environment means realizing that humanity is part of a complex totality of interconnected relationships and that these connections among both humans and nonhumans are the very essence of existence (Halifax, 1993;

Seed, Macy, Fleming & Naess, 1988). Phrases that might better express this deep ecological perspective are human/nature or human/environment.

Human being is not realistically represented in terms of individuality or egocentrism. It is better represented by relationality and ecocentrism. From this ontological perspective, even the common Western notion of the self, as depicted in most human development theories, is transformed (Robbins et al., 2006). Devall and Sessions (1984) described the typical idea of an individualized self:

> Growth begins when one starts the long process of separating out our individual uniqueness from our socially programmed sense of self. Growth and maturity also occur when we cease to see ourselves as isolated egos and begin to identify with other humans, from our family and friends to eventually the whole of humanity. (pp. 302–303)

Conventional human development, then, according to Devall and Sessions (1984), is limited to identifying self with other humans—a social self. Deep ecology extends the concept of self to encompass a deep interconnectedness with other people and with nature—an *ecological self.*

> When a person stops defending an old ego identity—an image of oneself which does not correspond to current

experience—and misidentifies with his or her rigid social identity, growth can occur. Exploring our ecological self openly and with acceptance, no judgment is made nor is there a pursuit of anything. The self is not an entity or a thing; it is an opening to discovering what some call the Absolute or in Sanskrit, atman. (Devall & Sessions, 1985, pp. 103, 104)

Interconnectedness presupposes more than an individual sense of ego-self and more than a collective sense of social-self. The ecological self is an experience of oneself as inextricably connected with the total web of life.

Cultivating a total view of human/nature necessarily requires engagement in a process of deeply questioning all our accustomed assumptions and social norms that pivot around the privileging of humans over nonhumans and the stratification of privilege among humans (Naess, 1995a). Deep ecology's approach to environmental and social issues involves questioning "deeply and publicly, insistently and consistently" (Naess, 1995b, p. 75) the anthropocentric paradigm within which social and environmental problems reside.

Deep questioning is similar to the concept of consciousness raising in empowerment theory (Freire, 1970, 1973; Lee, 1994). But it takes critical reflection to a deeper level by questioning human-centeredness as a distortion of reality that underlies other forms of oppression directed at humans and other beings. In addition, deep questioning can catalyze a shift of consciousness for the questioner, leading to a direct experience of the ecological self beyond mere intellectualization. Practices of meditation on interdependency, rituals of honor for the earth and particular plants and animals, and retreats in beautiful places can help people learn to take the perspective of other beings and ecosystems (Seed et al., 1988).

Like social work practitioners, deep ecologists emphasize the importance of knowing others through empathy. But conventional anthropocentric empathy is limited to human beings. To coin a term, *deep empathy* allows people to sense profound connection with other beings and to extend our compassion to

them. Most people can identify with the experience of empathy in relation to loved pets. Indeed, the healing effect of connection with animals has led to the incorporation of so-called pet therapy in many of the helping professions (Barrows, 1995; Hogan, Metzger, & Peterson, 1998). Deep empathy extends a sense of rapport and communion to all beings and all things, not only those under human control such as pets or livestock.

From a deep ecological perspective, when social workers plan activities, we should gather information about the needs, goals, and potential impacts of the actions on both human and nonhuman beings. This includes deep questioning (primarily a function of sensing and thinking) and deep empathy (primarily a function of feeling and intuiting). Bringing these ways of knowing together creates holistic social work research. Client systems are viewed holistically, including their involvement with micro, meso, and macro human and nonhuman subsystems and suprasystems. Information is gathered about all these types of systems as relevant to the human–nature relationship. In addition, the process of engaging in inquiry itself is holistic, bringing to bear all the faculties of the social work practitioner or researcher for assessment and formal research studies. Deep ecological epistemology is consistent with spiritually sensitive inquiry for social work proposed by Canda and Furman (2010), because it honors the wholeness and inherent worth of the client, all beings in relationship, and the social worker. In keeping with the heuristic paradigm for social work research (Tyson, 1995), all approaches to inquiry can be brought together in forming a deep ecological understanding, including qualitative, quantitative, historical, philosophical, phenomenological, and interpretive methods. The distinguishing feature of deep ecological inquiry is that awareness of the essential human–nature connection guides the process and purposes.

Deep ecology gives the human–nature relationship central importance, both in the conception of person and environment and in the arena of activism. Many deep ecologists focus their activity on issues of natural environmental protection. This can complement and deepen

302 Human Behavior and the Social Environment, Macro Level

social justice activism. The primary purpose of the social work profession is to support well-being and social justice for everyone (i.e., all humans; National Association of Social Workers, 1996). When social workers deeply question the full implications of this purpose, it becomes clear that well-being and justice for all humans can be achieved only by working for well-being and ecojustice on behalf of all beings. Human beings cannot survive without the tiny beings within us (such as digestive microorganisms), the sustaining creatures around us (such as plants and animals), and the encompassing planetary and cosmic ecosystems.

It is reasonable for social work to make human beings the focus of change activity. However, it is not reasonable to exclude all other beings and the larger ecosystems that encompass us. Such shallow ecological activism leads to the absurd result that we inadvertently destroy the sustaining natural environment while trying to help people live better. In the short run, some people live better; in the long run, we degrade the world on which we all depend to survive. So social work practice methods need to follow a practice principle of win–win solution finding (Canda & Furman, 2010; McLaughlin & Davidson, 1994) in which our practice goals, strategies, and techniques seek the maximum mutual benefit of all humans and nonhumans who are significantly affected by the helping activity.

Many practical self-contradictions in social work practice arise from shallow social activism. For example, while traveling to conduct home studies and community outreach activities, we may be excessively polluting the air with inefficient gasoline engines. While lighting our social agency buildings, we may be using energy-inefficient bulbs. In spreading pesticides for hygiene in child and family service centers, we may be poisoning children as they play on the floor. In using computers for management of information systems, we may cause repetitive motion injuries and radiation hazards for staff members, waste of trees by using non-recycled paper, and pollution of the environment with hazardous materials such as silicon, plastics, and metals. When we ignore the impact of nature on clients in conducting assessment,

we may not realize that depression can be related to a sense of grief over the death of a pet or a larger sense of alienation from nature (Jackson, 2009; Roszak, Gomes, & Kanner, 1995). We may miss the damaging effects of environmental injustice on people who live in low-income communities and people of color.

From the standpoint of deep ecology, social work practice needs to address the problems that arise from excessive and destructive human interference with nature. We should promote social change that contributes to the sustainability and flourishing of all life. We should be active in social policy development that reshapes the basic economic, technological, and ideological structures of society (Naess, 1995b). In supporting human well-being, deep ecological social workers emphasize improvement of life quality rather than mere quantitative increases of consumption.

Ecofeminism

According to Carolyn Merchant (1990), the term *ecofeminism* was coined by French writer Francoise d'Eaubonne (1994) in 1974 to illustrate the potential of women for bringing about an ecological revolution to guarantee human survival. Since that time there have been numerous ecofeminist writers and critical theorists (Berman, 1994; Birkeland, 1991; Booth, 2000; Buckingham, 2004; Campbell, 2008; Carlassare, 2000; Cheney, 1987; Diamond & Orenstein, 1990; Diehm, 2003; Eaton & Lorentzen, 2003; Gardner & Riley, 2007; Kheel, 2007; King, 1983; Merchant, 1990; Plumwood, 1994; Ress, 2006; Ruether, 2005; Sandilands, 1991, 1994, 1999; Swer, 2008; Warren, 2000; Zimmerman, 1994) who have formulated a variety of perspectives, interpretations, and critiques of ecofeminism.

Berman (1994) argues that ecofeminism "is a theory and movement for social change that combines ecological principles with feminist theory" (p. 173). Sandilands (1991) agrees with this assessment and defines ecofeminism as "a theory and movement which bridges the gap between feminism and ecology but which transforms both to create a unified praxis to end all forms of domination" (p. 90). Ynestra King (1983, pp. 119–120) suggests that ecofeminism is based on four overarching beliefs: the concurrent oppression of women and nature, the importance of human and biological diversity, the need to change the institutional structures of society, and the fact that there is no value-based hierarchical ordering in nature.

A review of the literature suggests several major conceptual themes that run through ecofeminist philosophy. First, ecofeminism asserts that the split between humanity and nature in turn reflects a split between man and woman (Zimmerman, 1994). This split between man and woman and between humans and all other comparative spheres of existence is supported by a dualistic power hierarchy that "creates a logic of interwoven oppression" (Plumwood, 1994, p. 211). In the words of ecofeminist Susan Griffin (1989), "We divide ourselves and all that we know along an invisible borderline between that we call Nature and what we believe is superior to Nature" (p. 8).

According to this worldview, oppression and value-based hierarchical ranking are inseparable. The fact that there is a perceived value-based hierarchy of existence and that this hierarchy presupposes an oppressive ranking structure is a view whose assumptions are so widely accepted by modern culture that it is not generally questioned much less thought of as a powerful sociopolitical ideology.

The second major conceptual theme of ecofeminism is the conviction that human–nature relationships and all forms of social domination are feminist concerns (Birkeland, 1991). For ecofeminists, critiquing all oppressive power structures is the first step in forging a new standard of human–nature relationship. For Starhawk (1989), ecofeminism's power critiques are essential for societal transformation because "powerlessness and the structures that perpetuate it is the root cause of famine, of overpopulation, of the callous destruction of the natural environment" (p. 180). In a similar vein, ecofeminist writer Ynestra King (1989) argues that any movement that claims an ecological interest is simply incomplete without a critique of power. She observes that "without a feminist analysis of social domination that reveals the roots of misogyny and hatred of nature, ecology remains an abstraction: it is

incomplete" (p. 24). The sense of this is summarized by Ruether (1989):

> There can be no ecological ethic simply as a new relation of "man" and "nature." Any ecological ethic must always take into account the structures of social domination and exploitation that mediate domination of nature and prevent concern for the welfare of the whole community in favor of the immediate advantage of the dominant class, race, and sex. (p. 149)

Ecofeminism exhorts humanity to give up power as it has been traditionally conceived and move toward what Sandilands (1994) calls a "wild justice" grounded in political action. Wild justice is an exhaustive sense of justice that challenges all vestiges of power inequalities and ultimately dismantles them. This point of view is expressed by Petra Kelly:

> Our aim is radical, nonviolent change outside—and inside of us! The macrocosm and the microcosm! This has to do with transforming power! Not power over, or power to dominate, or power to terrorize—but shared power; abolishing power as we know it, replacing it with the power of nonviolence or something common to all, to be used by all and for all! (Kelly, 1989, p. x)

A third theme emerging from the literature is related to the way ecofeminist philosophy envisages the idea of *interconnectedness*. Interconnectedness for ecofeminists is a view that the parts of all energy, matter, and reality are related to the greater whole. All things are connected in complex webs of communal networks. This whole is not an abstract mentalism but has infinitely complicated characteristics somewhat analogous to the way communities of beings manage individual and collectivist realities. Ecofeminist writers suggest that humans have lost their integrated wholeness through a gradual deprogramming initiated and sustained by modern institutions, economies, and educational systems. Swimme (1990), for instance, compares the fragmentation of the modern mind with a malfunction of the brain that essentially shuts down a person's fundamental cognitive and sentient powers. Swimme suggests that this cognitive deficit began with the Western world's unquestioned faith in logical positivism as the only legitimate source for ascertaining knowledge. This knowledge system is sustained through educational and economic processes based on positivist premises. By the time formal education is complete:

> We have only a sliver of our original minds still operative. . . . It is a sliver chiseled to perfection for controlling, for distancing, for calculating and for dominating. . . . Our insistence on analysis, on computation, on categorization has blinded us to the reality of the whole. We have been seated at a table heavy with food, and instead of realizing that this is a feast we are meant to join, we occupy our minds with counting the silverware over and over as we starve to death. (Swimme, 1990, p. 16)

Similarly, Griffin (1989) suggests that modern civilization's root metaphor is division rather than connection. She concludes that:

> We no longer feel ourselves to be a part of this earth. We regard our fellow creatures as enemies. And, very young, we even learn to disown a part of our own being. We come to believe that we do not know what we know . . . dividedness is etched into our language. (p. 7)

Ecofeminism seeks to heal this cognitive dysfunction by reweaving the inherent interconnectedness in all of the universe through a revitalization of each person's direct, lived, and sensual experience with the complex whole of nature (Diamond & Orenstein, 1990). From this complex ontology of interconnectedness, ecofeminists understand human beings as not being separate from or above nature. They are one small part of a whole, rather than the pinnacle of nature. In separating nature from persons, humanity creates a nature that is made up of dead, unintelligent matter. Ecofeminists offer an alternative view of nature that suggests that "consciousness is an integral part of nature" (Griffin, 1990, p. 88) and that nature is soulful. It is this great soulfulness of nature that connects deeply, unalterably, nature with humanity.

Given this, ecofeminism rejects the reductionist tendencies of modernity by emphasizing that the organic wholeness of the universe is greater than the sum of its parts (Coates, 2004). Reductionism understands all complex phenomena as being reducible to their smallest parts. Change consists in rearrangement of the parts, which themselves do not change (Capra, 1996). When the parts of any system are manipulated, the whole is changed (i.e., the whole *is* the sum of the parts). The corresponding change is always or perhaps presumably for the better. This point is illustrated in Swimme's (1990) comparison of the tumultuous and fragmented big-bang theory of the origin of the universe with the ecofeminist vision of a Great Birth. Instead of warlike images of bombs and explosions as root metaphors for creation, ecofeminists visualize a complex and mystical birthing process swelling and growing into life. Nature was and is birthed, as we are. It is a mystery to be experienced rather than explained. And because it is a living entity, not simply a random reassembly of billions of pieces of cosmic dust and debris, there is an essential organic unity between nature and ourselves (Starhawk, 1989). This interconnected unity leads to action motivated by compassionate understanding and appreciation rather than competition; the experience of feeling with all beings now and into future generations.

Ecofeminism thus rejects the dominance, competition, materialism, and technoscientific exploitation inherent in modernist, competitive-based social systems. Ecofeminism instead assumes that healthy interactions are based on caring and compassion and the creation and nurturing of life (Christ, 1990). Compassion and caring for nature are part of ecofeminist processes because all of nature is seen as intimately connected with humans and as having inherent value. Nature has an existence and voice worth experiencing and hearing.

An Expanded Ecological Model for Social Work

The major contribution of ecofeminism and deep ecology is their focus on a new language and new understanding of person, nature, and interrelationships between the two. Ecofeminist and deep ecological thought suggests to social work an alternative framework as a basis for understanding human behavior, nature, interrelationship, and issues of empowerment, which in many ways diverge significantly from the profession's conventional ecological/life models. They offer social work an opportunity to construct an expanded ecological model more consistent with professional values and practice commitments such as social justice and efforts to end discrimination and oppression (NASW, 1996). With this in mind, we consider two questions. First, what are some of the essential premises that can be derived from deep ecology and ecofeminism to form the basis of an expanded ecological model of social work, and, second, what are some potential implications of this model for social work practice? (Consult Table 8.3 which lists the key concepts of ecological feminism.)

Several important premises may be distilled from ecofeminist and deep ecology. First, by defining nature as "other" and as essentially hostile or by hierarchically relegating it to a position of lower rank, humanity simultaneously defines itself in a way that severely constricts its ability to create individual and collective meaning.

Table 8.3   Key Concepts of Ecological Feminism

1. Western industrial civilization opposes nature and subjugates women.
2. Life is an interconnected web, not a hierarchy.
3. A healthy ecosystem supports diversity.
4. Species survival demands a new relationship to nature and society.
5. A rejection of the dichotomization of nature and culture.
6. Antimilitarism.
7. Political activism to replace patriarchal ideas and practices with feminist ones.
8. A dedicated interest is prepatriarchal societies that lacked significant domination hierarchies.

Source: Deegan, M. J., & Podeschi, C. (2001). The eco-feminist pragmatism of Charlotte Perkins Gilman. *Environmental Ethics, 23*(1), 19–36.

The reality is that there is no value-based hierarchal ordering of nature and no natural antagonism and separation between humans and nature. Nature is one with and beneficial for humanity. A second premise derived from ecofeminism and deep ecology is that, in large measure, social, political, economic, and environmental issues are interrelated and fundamentally associated with humanity's core understanding of its relationship with nature and the practices that stem from it. By constructing an integrated language of human behavior and nature, one that fully incorporates the powerful image of interconnectedness, social work enhances its ability to understand and thus act on a broader range of human issues. Adopting an alternative metaphor of the human–nature relationship—for example, that of a nurturing mother who kindly provides for the needs of her children—suggests something uniquely different and transformative in the way humans sense their place with the larger natural environment and their place in the community of being. This metaphor dramatically reconstructs a capricious and dangerous nature into a nature that provides life-giving and life-sustaining sustenance.

Important practice implications flow from an ecofeminist- and deep ecology–inspired ecological model. For example, for social work to operate out of an expanded ecological model, it must address those powerful systemic oppressions that maintain human alienation. An expanded ecological social work would fully recognize that, just as humanity and nature need to be interrelatedly understood, so too do modern social, political, and economic realities (Ungar, 2002). That is, issues of environmental degradation and concerns for a reanimated human–nature consciousness cannot be separated from those systemic forces that function to maintain all forms of injustice, whether toward nature or other human beings.

A strong social justice logic is inherent in an expanded ecological model of social work. The interconnectedness focus of the model suggests that struggles against oppressive, systemic forces that denigrate nature are intertwined with struggles against all forces that also oppress humans. The oppression that keeps realization of a dynamic, harmonious human–nature relationship out of consciousness is connected to other forms of human oppression, including economic exploitation, racism, sexism, and patriarchy. Oppressive social institutions are an expression of an alienated collective psyche, but they also structure and maintain an alienated collective psyche. Though human oppression and oppression of nature appear to exist in separate form, struggle against any one in isolation cannot be effective. Concern for any oppression necessitates concern for all oppression.

This expanded model's logic of justice portends nothing short of social work's involvement in fostering fundamental change in the social, political, and economic structures of modern industrial society. Adopting this framework changes the identity of conventional social work practice. It suggests that the profession must return to and significantly expand on its progressive, activist roots. On a larger scale of concern, deep ecology and ecofeminism alert social workers involved with political action, policy formation, and international social welfare to deeply question and deeply empathize in the process of macro service. Macro social action also can be guided by win/win solution seeking, to the benefit of both humans and nonhumans (McLaughlin & Davidson, 1994). In social development planning, deep indicators of success would replace anthropocentric and materialistic standards of increasing consumption and production with ecocentric standards of increasing quality of life, social justice, and ecojustice, such as support for the rights and dignity of all humans and nonhumans.

These same questions can be applied to the social work educational setting itself in order to create a learning environment that is congruent with the content of ideas. How can educators engage themselves in a holistic way in teaching? Can they draw on examples from their personal lifestyles and professional practice to illustrate deep ecological and ecofeminist principles? Does the social work educational program operate in an environmentally responsible manner? How are global events and issues connected with local concerns in class discussions? When educators and students investigate such

questions in their immediate learning situations, new possibilities for teaching, learning, and educational program operation can open up.

An expanded ecological social work establishes the foundation of a new sociopolitical mandate. It suggests the profession has an obligation to examine all oppressive political, social, and economic structures of modern society and the policies that extend them. It requires that social workers become professionally involved and personally committed, both within and outside the confines of office, agency, and academy, to implementing change.

One potential application of an expanded ecological social work might include the profession's active participation in critiquing modern economic theory and the way it works to sustain oppression of both humanity and nature. Western economic theory tends to appreciate only those entities and practices that have market value: material things and the flow of goods and services to satisfy consumer needs. In *Shoptimism: Why the American Consumer Will Keep on Buying No Matter What*, Eisenberg (2009) shows how marketers create needs for products even if needs for such things do not legitimately exist. They turn natural things and everyday experiences into commodities. Needs and wants become relatively indistinguishable. This practice tends to foster the collective myths that consumption and human happiness are essentially equivalent and that only those who produce have value.

As suggested earlier, this illusion of consumer happiness creates inequality as an ever-increasing number of people scramble to get their piece of the relatively scarce "good life" pie (Eisenberg). In an effort to keep pace with an ever-growing penchant for consumption, natural resources are systematically destroyed. Fewer people are able to realistically share in this vision of the good life. More and more are marginalized as they are recruited to fuel the productive fires that feed the material appetites of an ever-smaller elite.

One way social workers may think about altering this cycle would be to encourage a commitment to a core social value of material equality (Hoff, 1998). Until individuals and societies can agree to a new collective vision of the good life, the idea of material equality offers a corrective to the individual and social demand for economic progress and material consumption. If material equality becomes recognized as a high social priority, then the incessant process of trying to achieve higher and higher privilege through material possession and consumption would be diminished. Demands for economic growth and its resulting inequality and depletion of natural resources would be slowed in a society in which having more and more things was regarded as contemptible rather than as an identifier of merit or status.

Ultimately, however, an expanded ecological social work must endorse more than just an equitable redistribution of material wealth. This redistributive focus of justice does not change the underlying reliance on resource expropriation and human exploitation to satisfy human need. An expanded ecological social work must also advocate for an alternative vision of the good life—that is, a new insight into what constitutes a joyous and satisfying rather than a satiated life. It is a vision that must be compatible with a natural environment that can support the continuation of human life and well-being. In doing this we use our social work skills not only to work with others to become better stewards of the earth but also to challenge them to question deeply the underlying assumptions of our current social, political, and economic paradigms (Schriver, 2010).

This alternative vision of life must reflect a long-term commitment to identifying sources of human satisfaction that can flourish intergenerationally in harmony with nature (Moser, 2009). The focus of human satisfaction changes from quantity of possessions to quality of life. Social work must recognize this as a difficult undertaking because Western society has lost, or has yet to develop, the language and capacity to assess satisfaction apart from material consumption.

Social work can contribute to a new view of human satisfaction by helping people appraise ways of being that are rewarding, not exploitive of humans, not damaging to nature, and not based on consumptive materialism (Goleman, 2009). Things to be considered might include simple conversations, spiritual rituals, neighborhood/community gatherings, family outings, artistic pursuits, music, dance, literature, or experiencing nature. All are ways of life and being that can endure through countless generations. This is a kind of simple life vision adorned with nonmaterial sources of fulfillment. It includes the kinds of activities and associations that most people would admit are the main determinants of happiness.

For example, one might visualize an inner-city neighborhood that has been depleted, polluted, victimized, and virtually destroyed in the wake of modern economic/consumptive policies and practices. The question would then be, How might a new vision operate in this setting? An initial step would be for social workers to again take on the role of becoming community and neighborhood organizers in an effort to confront current economic, environmental, and social issues. This would mean developing mechanisms that promote participation by every member of the neighborhood and acting as advocates who apply pressure and call attention to the need for local, state, and national intervention. It also would mean that social workers would function as facilitators of skill development in order to allow residents to act on behalf of themselves and their neighborhoods.

Social workers would also need to take an active lead in helping residents construct a new conceptual vision of a revitalized and satisfying community. This would be a vision of community or neighborhood that, though not complete or perfect in any utopian sense, fosters local strength and interdependence. It is a vision of community that is not continually subject to the debilitating economic cycles and social inequities associated with the modern consumer-oriented culture. There are many models of economically viable, environmentally safe, personally satisfying, and socially flourishing communities from which social work may effectively draw (Anthony, 1995; Hoff, 1998; Mary, 2008).

Summary and Conclusion

Social work's notion of environment has been unnecessarily constricted. First, social work tends to define its activity in terms of the immediate personal and social environment of the individual. This notion of environment obscures broader elements of the environment. Second, though not totally ignoring the natural environment, social work tends to accept a shallow conceptualization of nature as something *other*, quite separate from human beings, whereas humans are viewed as the center of importance.

Alternative environmental models offer a fundamentally different view of the person-environment construct. They suggest the necessity of discussing human beings not merely in the context of relationship between individuals and the social environment but also in the context of relationship between persons and *nature*. For deep ecologists and ecofeminists, human crisis and environmental crisis are problems of a human-centered ethos. They understand that the ways people conceive of nature and portray it in social discourse have serious implications for the natural and human world. The anthropocentric (human-centered), mechanistic view of nature is very focused on technology and has been very exploitive. Nature is seen simply as a collection of resources to be used for human benefit. Destructive uses of nature then rebound back to harm humans, thus locking people into a cycle of harm and oppression for both humans and nonhumans.

We have argued in this chapter that human and nonhuman survival necessitates a fundamental shift in understanding and experience of human relationships with nature. There must be a fundamental reorientation of social work perspective from being *in environment* (mainly social) to *being with nature* (as a totality). Our perspective needs to shift from a person-and-environment dichotomy to a human–nature complementarity and unity. This chapter has presented an overview of past attempts at environmental reorientation and the current state of the environmental crisis and has provided strategies for supporting this shift through deep questioning in social work theory and practice. Human behavior in the social environment is an ideal component of the curriculum to encourage students to begin reenvisioning the human–nature relationship and to expand the scope of practice based on this new vision.

As paradigms, deep ecology and ecofeminism are works in progress. Within the environmental movement, they engender creative debate. Deep ecology and ecofeminism are not rigid ideologies or strictly formed theories. They remain open to alteration while at the same time encouraging us to reenvision the nature of social work and social work in nature. This chapter proposed a way of understanding ourselves with nature that can carry social work deeper into the next millennium with a sober sense of responsibility, a heartfelt sense of compassion, and a joyful sense of celebration for our connection with all people and all beings in this complex and amazing world. One need not adhere dogmatically to deep ecology or ecofeminist principles for this. But the profession would be served well if we applied deep questioning, deep empathy, and deep connections to all our considerations of theory and practice.

Indeed, the ideas presented in this chapter suggest the need for a fundamental change in social work understandings of environment/nature and, as an outgrowth of that, for new language and insights directed toward radical changes in our social, political, and economic structures. The challenge of this chapter constitutes a call to action for the social work profession to return to its progressive activist roots. Social work must recognize that its conceptualization of environment has had a limited focus and has emphasized in individual adaptation to environmental demands. Consequently, despite the vernacular of its existing ecological models, the profession has continued its movement toward a dominant approach directed toward changing individuals rather than systems.

Many people feel overwhelmed and immobilized by the current state of our world. They express concern for the depletion of our natural resources, the loss of connectedness that exists on many levels, and the systemic oppression that maintains human alienation. Social work can counter this sense of overwhelming isolation and alienation by adopting an expanded ecological framework such as the one suggested here. An expanded ecological social work model encompasses and addresses a broad range of environmental and social issues rather than dissecting interrelated issues into disconnected pieces. As ecofeminist and deep ecological writers have suggested, the introduction of positivist scientific strategies have often resulted in an acceptance of a fragmented view of modern life. This is a view that presupposes separateness when, in fact, all things are connected in complex webs of communal networks.

An expanded ecological social work model holds great promise for *action* that is consistent with social work's rejuvenated commitment to social justice. It emphasizes interactions and actions based on caring and compassion rather than the dominance, competition, and exploitation inherent in our current competition-based social systems. This model presents social work with the opportunity to take a philosophically grounded position that publicly and openly acknowledges an awareness of the interrelatedness of social, political, economic, and environmental issues. With this model we can form a foundation from which to work to end oppression in all its forms. We have been offered a vision and a framework. Opportunity is knocking at our door.

Thought Questions

1. "Materialistic values actually detract from the well-being and quality of life experiences." Discuss.
2. What is the evidence that global warming is real? Check out the media for recent controversies on this issue.
3. What was the change that followed the publication of *Silent Spring?* How is that change important?
4. How was ecological theory an advance over earlier formulations regarding the environment?
5. Trace the history of the social work profession's treatment of the physical environment and show how it has often been inadequate.
6. Describe deep ecology as a paradigm.
7. The peak experience in a person's reaction to the beauty of nature is consistent with a spiritual awareness.

Discuss the truth of this statement from personal experience.
8. Describe deep ecology as a social movement.
9. What is the contribution of ecofeminism? What does dualism have to do with this?
10. Discuss the various kinds of power as delineated in this chapter.
11. Discuss three advances in our thinking that an expanded ecological model offers.
12. Relate ecological theory to social justice and to social injustice.
13. Read one of the nature poems of William Wordsworth and relate the themes to this chapter.

References

Addams, J. (1904). Neighborhood improvement. In *Proceedings of the National Conference of Charities and Correction* (pp. 456–458). New York: Heer.

Addams, J. (1909). *The spirit of youth and the city streets.* New York: Macmillan.

Akerlof, G., & Shiller, J. (2009). *Animal spirits: How human psychology drives the economy, and why it matters for global capitalism.* Princeton, NJ: Princeton University Press.

Akin, W. E. (1977). *Technocracy and the American dream: The technocratic movement, 1900–1941.* Berkeley: University of California Press.

Andharia, J., & Sengupta, C. (1998). The environmental movement: Global issues and the Indian reality. In M. Desai, A. Monteiro, & L. Narayan (Eds.), *Towards people centered development* (pp. 422–449). Mumbai, India: Tata Institute of Social Sciences.

Anker, P. (2008). Deep ecology in Bucharest. *The Trumpeter: Journal of Ecosophy, 24*(1), 56–67.

Anthony, C. (1995). Ecopsychology and deconstruction of wholeness. In T. Roszak, M. Gomes, & A. Kanner (Eds.), *Ecopsychology: Restoring the earth, healing the mind* (pp. 263–278). San Francisco: Sierra Club Books.

Barnett, A. (2004, April). Bush attacks environment "scare stories": Secret e-mail gives advice on denying climate change.UK: *The Guardian.* Retrieved from http://www.guardian.co.uk/environment/2004/apr/04/usnews.theobserver

Barrows, A. (1995). The ecopsychology of child development. In T. Roszak, M. Gomes, & A. Kanner (Eds.), *Ecopsychology: Restoring the earth, healing the mind* (pp. 101–110). San Francisco: Sierra Club Books.

Bates, D. C. (2002). Environmental refugees? Classifying human migrations caused by environmental change. *Population and Environment, 23*(5), 465–477.

Berman, T. (1994). The rape of mother nature: Women in the language of environmental discourse. *Trumpeter, 11*(4), 173–178.

Bertalanffy, L. von. (1981). *A systems view of man.* Boulder, CO: Westview Press.

Bertell, R. (2006). Depleted uranium: All the questions about DU and the Gulf War syndrome are not yet answered. *International Journal of Health Services, 26*(3), 503-520.

Besthorn, F. H. (1997). *Reconceptualizing social work's person-in-environment perspective: Explorations in radical environmental thought.* Unpublished doctoral dissertation, University of Kansas, Lawrence.

Besthorn, F. H. (2000). Toward a deep-ecological social work: Its environmental, spiritual and political dimensions. *Spirituality and Social Work Forum, 7*(2), 2–7.

Besthorn, F. H. (2001). Transpersonal psychology and deep ecological philosophy: Exploring linkages and applications for social work. In E. R. Canda & E. D. Smith (Eds.), *Transpersonal perspectives on spirituality in social work* (pp. 23–44). Binghamton, NY: Haworth Press.

Besthorn, F. H. (2002a). Radical environmentalism and the ecological self: Rethinking the concept of self-identity for social work practice. *Journal of Progressive Human Services, 13*(1), 53–72.

Besthorn, F. H. (2002b). Natural environment and the practice of psychotherapy. *Annals of the American Psychotherapy Association, 5*(5), 19–22.

Besthorn, F. H. (2003). Radical ecologisms: Insights for educating social workers in ecological activism and social justice. *Critical Social Work: An Interdisciplinary Journal Dedicated to Social Justice, 3*(1), 66–106.

Besthorn, F. H. (2004). Restorative justice and environmental restoration—Twin pillars of a just global environmental policy: Hearing the voice of the victim. *Journal of Societal and Social Policy, 3*(2), 33–48.

Besthorn, F. H. (2008). Environment and social work practice (pp. 132–136). *Encyclopedia of Social Work-20th Edition (Vol. 2).* New York: Oxford University Press.

Besthorn, F. H., & Canda, E. R. (2002). Revisioning environment: Deep ecology for education and teaching in social work. *Journal of Teaching in Social Work, 22*(1/2), 79–102.

Besthorn, F. H., & McMillen, D. P. (2002). The oppression of women and nature: Ecofeminism as a framework for an expanded ecological social work. *Families in Society: The Journal of Contemporary Human Services, 83*(3), 221–232.

Besthorn, F. H., & Saleebey, D. (2003). Nature, genetics and the biophilia connection: Exploring linkages with social work values and practice. *Advances in Social Work, 4*(1), 1–18.

Birkeland, J. (1991). An ecofeminist critique of mainstream planning. *Trumpeter, 8*(2), 72–84.

Booth, A. (2000). Ways of knowing: Acceptable understandings within bioregionalism, deep ecology, ecofeminism, and Native American cultures. *The Trumpeter: Journal of Ecosophy, 16*(1), 1–14.

Brandt, L. (1910). Alcoholism and social problems. *The Survey, 25,* 17–24.

Brieland, D. (1977). Historical overview. *Social Casework, 13*(1), 341–346.

Brown, L. R. (2001). *Eco-economy: Building an economy for the earth.* New York: Norton.

Buckingham, S. (2004). Ecofeminism in the twenty-first century. *The Geographical Journal, 170*(2), 146–155.

Buhner, S. H. (1996). *Sacred plant medicine: Explorations in the practice of indigenous herbalism.* Boulder, CO: Roberts Rinehart.

Bullard, R. (1993). *Confronting environmental racism: Voices from the grassroots.* Boston: South End Press.

Bullard, R. (2000). Dumping in Dixie: Race, class, and environmental quality. Boulder, CO: Westview Press.

Caldicott, H. (2004). *The new nuclear danger: George W. Bush's military-industrial complex.* Queensland, Australia: University of Queensland Press.

Campbell, A. (2008). *New directions in ecofeminist literary criticism.* Newcastle, England: Cambridge Scholars Publishing.

Canda, E. R., & Furman, L. D. (2010). *Spiritual diversity in social work practice: The heart of helping* (2nd ed.). New York: Oxford University Press

Capra, F. (1982). *The turning point: Science, society, and the rising culture.* New York: Bantam Books.

Capra, F. (1996). *The web of life: A new scientific understanding of living systems.* New York: Anchor Books.

Carlassare, E. (2000). Socialist and cultural ecofeminism: Allies in resistance. *Ethics and the Environment, 5*(1), 89–106.

Carson, R. (1962). *Silent spring.* Boston: Houghton Mifflin.

Chambers, C. A. (1963). *Seedtime of reform: American social service and social action, 1918–1933.* Minneapolis: University of Minnesota Press.

Chan, C. (1993). Grassroots mobilization for environmental protection: Tactics and dilemmas. In C. Chan & P. Hill (Eds.), *Limited gains: Grassroots mobilization and the environment in Hong Kong* (pp. 15–28). Hong Kong: The Center of Urban Planning and Environmental Management.

Cheney, J. (1987). Eco-feminism and deep ecology. *Environmental Ethics, 9*(2), 115–145.

Christ, C. (1990). Rethinking theology and nature. In I. Diamond & G. Orenstein (Eds.), *Reweaving the world: The emergence of ecofeminism* (pp. 58–69). San Francisco: Sierra Club Books.

Chivian, E., & Bernstein, A. (2008). How is biodiversity threatened by human activity? In E. Chivan and A. Bernstein (Eds.), *Sustaining life: How human health depends on biodiversity* (pp.29–73). New York: Oxford University Press.

Coates, J. (2004). *Ecology and social work: Toward a new paradigm.* Halifax, Nova Scotia: Fernwood.

Cohen, L. (2003). *A consumers' republic: The politics of mass consumption in postwar America.* New York: Knopf.

Cowley, A. S. (1996). Transpersonal social work. In F. J. Turner (Ed.), *Social work treatment: Interlocking theoretical approaches* (4th ed., pp. 663–698). New York: Free Press.

Daly, H. (1990). Toward some operational principles of sustainable development, *Ecological Economics, 2,* 1–6.

d'Eaubonne, F. (1994). A time for ecofeminism. In C. Merchant (Ed.), *Key concepts in critical theory: Ecology* (pp. 174–197). Atlantic Highlands, NJ: Humanities Press.

de Hoyos, G. (1989). Person-in-environment: A tri-level practice model. *Social Casework: The Journal of Contemporary Social Work, 70,* 131–138.

de Vendômois J. S., Roullier F., Cellier D., & Séralini G. E. (2009). A comparison of the effects of three GM corn varieties on mammalian health. *International Journal of Biological Sciences, 5,* 706–726.

Deforest, R., & Veiller, L. (Eds.). (1903). *The tenement house problem.* New York: Macmillan.

Devall, B., & Sessions, G. (1984). The developing of natural resources and the integrity of nature. *Environmental Ethics, 6*(4), 293–322.

Devall, B., & Sessions, G. (1985). *Deep ecology.* Salt Lake City, UT: G. M. Smith Books.

Diamond, I., & Orenstein, G. (Eds.). (1990). *Reweaving the world: The emergence of ecofeminism.* San Francisco: Sierra Club Books.

Diamond, J. (2005). *Collapse: How societies choose to fail or succeed.* New York: Viking Press.

Diehm, C. (2003). The self of stars and stone: Ecofeminism, deep ecology and the ecological self. *The Trumpeter: Journal of Ecosophy, 19*(3), 31–45.

Dominelli, L. (2002). *Anti-oppressive social work theory and practice.* New York: Palgrave Macmillan.

Dorsey, E., & Thormodsgard, M. (2003, January). Rachel Carson warned us. *MS, 43*–45.

Drengson, A. R. (2005). The life and work of Arne Naess: An appreciative overview. *The Trumpeter: Journal of Ecosophy, 21*(1), 5–47.

Drengson, A. R., & Devall, B. (2006). Arne Naess, his life and work, part two: The continuing development of the long-range, deep ecology movement. *The Trumpeter: Journal of Ecosophy, 22*(2), 2–7.

Drengson, A. R., & Inoue, Y. (Eds.). (1995). *The deep ecology movement: An introductory anthology.* Berkeley, CA: North Atlantic Press.

Dresner, S. (2009). *The principles of sustainability.* London: Earthscan Publications.

Driehaus, B. (2008, August 14). Downtowns across the U.S. see streetcars in their future. *New York Times,* p. A17.

Dunn, S., & Flavin, C. (2002). Moving the climate change agenda forward. In C. Flavin, H. French, & G. Gardner (Eds.), *The Worldwatch Institute state of the world: 2002* (pp. 24–50). New York: Norton.

Eaton, H., & Lorentzen, L. (2003). *Ecofeminism and globalization: Exploring culture, context and religion.* Lanham, MD: Rowman and Littlefield Publishers.

Edwards, A., & Orr, D. (2005). *The sustainability revolution: Portrait of a paradigm shift.* Gabriola Island, British Columbia: New Society Publishers.

Ehrenreich, J. H. (1985). *The altruistic imagination: A history of social work and social policy in the U.S.* Ithaca, NY: Cornell University Press.

Eisenberg, L. (2009). *Shoptimism: Why the American consumer will keep on buying no matter what.* New York: Free Press.

Engelman, R., Halweil, B., & Nierenberg, D. (2002). Rethinking populations, improving life. In C. Flavin, H. French, & G. Gardner (Eds.), *The Worldwatch Institute state of the world: 2002* (pp. 127–148). New York: Norton.

Environmental Justice Resource Center. (2001, November 27).Chemical assault on an African American community. Retrieved March 19, 2010, from Environmental Justice Resource Center Web site: http://www.ejrc.cau.edu/cassandraroberts.html

Environmental News Service. (2005, October 18). *Global sea level rise forecast to flood low-lying coastlines.* Retrieved March 19, 2010, from http://www.ens-newswire.com/ens/oct2005/2005-10-18-02.asp

Fahrenthold, D., & Eilperin, J. (2009, December 5). In e-mails, science of global warming is hot debate. *Washington Post.* Retrieved March 19, 2010, from http://www.washingtonpost.com/wp-dyn/content/article/2009/12/04/AR2009120404511.html?wpisrc=newsletter

Falstrom, D. Z. (2001). Stemming the flow of environmental displacement: Creating a convention to protect persons and preserve the environment. *Colorado Journal of Environmental Law and Policy, 15*, 1–20.

Ferkiss, V. (1993). *Nature, technology and society: Cultural roots of the current environmental crisis.* New York: New York University Press.

Fischer, E. (1993). War and the environment. In J. Allen (Ed.), *Environment 93/94* (12th ed., pp. 73–88). Guilford, CT: Dushkin.

Fischer, J. (1975). *The effectiveness of social casework.* Springfield, IL: Thomas.

Flavin, C., French, H., & Gardner, G. (Eds.). (2002). *The Worldwatch Institute state of the world: 2002.* New York: Norton.

Fox, M. (1979). *A spirituality named compassion and the healing of the global village, Humpty Dumpty and us.* Minneapolis, MN: Winston Press.

Fox, S. (1981). *John Muir and his legacy: The American conservation movement.* Boston: Little, Brown.

Fox, W. (1995). *Toward a transpersonal ecology: Developing new foundations for environmentalism.* New York: State University of New York Press.

Frank, R. H. (1999). *Luxury fever: Money and happiness in an era of excess.* New York: Free Press.

Frankel, L. K. (1901). Response to session on needy families. In *Proceedings of the National Conference of Charities and Correction* (28th Annual Session) (pp. 381–382).Boston: Ellis.

Freire, P. (1970). *Pedagogy of the oppressed.* New York: Seabury Press.

Freire, P. (1973). *Education for critical consciousness.* New York: Continuum.

Friedman, T. (2008). *Hot, flat, and crowded: Why we need a green revolution—and how it can renew America.* New York: Farrar, Straus and Giroux.

Gardner,C. & Riley, J. (2007). Breaking boundaries: Ecofeminism in the classroom. *Radical Teacher, 78*(1), 24–34.

Gelspan, R. (2004). *Boiling point: How politicians, big oil and coal, journalists and activists are fueling the climate crisis—and what we can do to avert disaster.* New York: Basic Books

Gelspan, R. (2005). Global denial. *American Prospect, 16*(10), A3–A5.

Germain, C. B. (1968). Social study: Past and future. *Social Casework, 49*(7), 403–409.

Germain, C. B. (1978). General-systems theory and ego psychology: An ecological perspective. *Social Service Review, 52*(4), 535–550.

Germain, C. B. (1991). *Human behavior in the social environment: An ecological view.* New York: Columbia University Press.

Germain, C. B., & Gitterman, A. (1980). *The life model of social work practice.* New York: Columbia University Press.

Glasser, H., & Drengson, A. (Eds.). (2005). *The selected works of Arne Naess* (Vols. 1–10). New York: Springer Publishing

Gleick, P. (2010). *The world's water: The biennial report on freshwater resources.* Washington, DC: Island Press.

Glendinning, C. (1994). *My name is Chellis and I'm in recovery from Western civilization.* Boston: Shambhala.

Goleman, D. (2009). *Ecological intelligence: How knowing the hidden impacts of what we buy can change everything.* New York: Broadway Books.

Gordon, W. E. (1969). Basic constructs for an integrative and generative conception of social work. In G. Hearn (Ed.), *The general systems approach: Contributions towards an holistic conception of social work* (pp. 5–11). New York: Council on Social Work Education.

Gore, A. (2009). *Our choice: A plan to solve the climate crisis.* Emmaus, PA: Rodale Books.

Gorlick, B. (2007, May). Environmentally displaced persons: A UNHCR perspective. Presentation at Environmental Refugees: The Forgotten Migrants meeting, New York. Retrieved from http://www.ony.unu.edu/seminars/2007/16May2007/presentation_gorlick.ppt

Gould, K. H. (1987). Life model versus conflict model: A feminist perspective. *Social Work, 32,* 346–352.

Griffin, S. (1989). Split culture. In J. Plant (Ed.), *Healing the wounds: The promise of ecofeminism* (pp. 7–17). Santa Cruz, CA: New Society.

Griffin, S. (1990). Curves along the road. In I. Diamond & G. Orenstein (Eds.), *Reweaving the world: The emergence of ecofeminism* (pp. 87–99). San Francisco: Sierra Club Books.

Grimes, W. (2008, January 14). Arne Naess, Norwegian philosopher, dies at 96. *The New York Times,* p. A33.

Halifax, J. (1993). *The fruitful darkness: Reconnecting with the body of the earth.* San Francisco: Harper.

Halweil, B., & Mastny, L. (Eds). (2004). *The Worldwatch Institute state of the world: 2004.* New York: Norton.

Hart, M. A. (1996). Sharing circles: Utilizing traditional practice methods for teaching, helping, and supporting. In S. O'Meara & D. A. West (Eds.), *From our eyes: Learning from indigenous peoples* (pp. 59–72). Toronto, Ontario: Garamond Press.

Hartman, A. (1971). But what is social casework? *Social Casework, 52*(7), 411–419.

Hashimi, J. K. (1981). Environmental modification: Teaching social coping skills. *Social Work, 26*(4), 323–326.

Hays, S. P. (1987). *Beauty, health, and permanence: Environmental politics in the United States, 1955–1885.* New York: Cambridge University Press.

Hearn, G. (1979). General systems theory and social work. In F. J. Turner (Ed.), *Social work treatment: Interlocking theoretical approaches* (pp. 333–360). New York: Free Press.

Hillel, D., & Rosenzweig, C. (2008). Biodiversity and food production. In E. Chivan and A. Bernstein (Eds.), *Sustaining life: How human health depends on biodiversity* (pp. 325–381). New York: Oxford University Press.

Hiranandani, V. (2008). Restorative justice in international relations: A Gandhian approach in the post-colonial era. In K. van Wormer (Ed.), Restorative justice across the East and the West (pp. 163–204). Taiwan: Casa Verde Publishing. In the public domain at http:scribd.com/vanwormer

Hoff, M. D. (Ed.). (1998). *Sustainable community development: Studies in economic, environmental, and cultural revitalization.* Boston: Lewis.

Hogan, L., Metzger, D., & Peterson, B. (Eds.). (1998). *Intimate nature: The bond between women and animals.* New York: Fawcett Columbine.

Houghton, J. T. (2001). *Climate change 2001: The scientific basis—contributions of the working group of the Intergovernmental Panel on Climate Change (IPCC).* Cambridge, UK: Cambridge University Press.

Houghton, J. T. (2004). *Global warming : The complete briefing.* Cambridge, UK; Cambridge University Press.

Humphreys, N. (1999). Environmental policy. *NASW News, 44*(3), 12.

Imbrogno, S., & Canda, E. R. (1988). Social work as a holistic system of activity. *Social Thought, 14*(1), 16–29.

Intergovernmental Panel on Climate Change (IPCC). (2005). *Safeguarding the ozone layer and the global climate system.* Geneva, Switzerland: IPCC.

Jackson, L. & D. Keeney (Eds.) (2010). Perennial farming systems that resist flooding. In C. Mutel (Ed.), *A watershed year of the Iowa floods of 2008.* (pp.215–226). Iowa City: University of Iowa Press.

Jackson, W. (2009, April 20). Events heading to a 50 year farm bill. Presentation at the University of Northern Iowa, Cedar Falls.

Janik, D. I. (1981). Environmental consciousness in modern literature: Four representative examples. In R. Schultz & J. Hughes (Eds.), *Ecological consciousness* (pp. 104–112). Washington, DC: University Press of America.

Jones, P. (2010). Responding to the ecological crisis: Transformative pathways for social work education. *Journal of Social Work Education, 46* (1), 67-84.

Jung, H. Y. (1990). Shallow thinking on deep ecology. *Trumpeter, 7*(2), 95–98.

Kasser, T. (2002). *The high price of materialism.* Cambridge, MA: MIT Press.

Kasson, J. F. (1976). *Civilizing the machine: Technology and republican values in America, 1776–1900.* New York: Grossman.

Kellogg, P., & Harrison, S. (1910). The Westmorland strike. *The Survey, 25*, 605–610.

Kelly, F. (1895). The sweating system. In J. Addams (Ed.), *Hull House maps and papers* (pp. 27–45). New York: Crowell.

Kelly, P. (1989). Foreword: Linking arms, dear sister, brings hope. In J. Plant (Ed.), *Healing the wounds: The promise of ecofeminism* (pp. ix–xi). Santa Cruz, CA: New Society.

Kemp, S. P. (1994). *Social work and systems of knowledge: The concept of environment in social casework theory, 1900–1983*. Unpublished doctoral dissertation, Columbia University, New York.

Kheel, M. (2007). *Nature ethics: An ecofeminist perspective*. Lanham, MD: Rowman and Littlefield Publishers.

King, Y. (1983). Toward an ecological feminism and a feminist ecology. In J. Rothschild (Ed.), *Machina exeda: Feminist perspectives on technology* (pp. 118–128). New York: Pergamon Press.

King, Y. (1989). The ecology of feminism and feminism of ecology. In J. Plant (Ed.), *Healing the wounds: The promise of ecofeminism* (pp. 18–28). Santa Cruz, CA: New Society.

Korten, D. C.(2009). *Agenda for a new economy: From phantom wealth to real wealth*. San Francisco: Berrett-Koehler Publishers.

LaChappelle, D. (1988). *Sacred land, sacred sex, rapture of the deep: Concerning deep ecology and celebrating life*. Durango, CO: Kivaki Press.

Lambert, J. (2002). Refugees and the environment: The forgotten element of sustainability. Brussels: European Parliament.

Land Institute. (2002). Natural systems agriculture. *Land Institute Newsletter*, 1–2.

Lawless, G. (1994). "When the animals come to us." In G. Lawless (Ed.), *Poems for the wild earth*. Nobleboro, ME: Blackberry Books.

Lee, J. (1994). *The empowerment approach to social work practice*. New York: Columbia University Press.

Lee, P. R. (1911). The social function of case work. In (A. Johnson, Ed.). *Proceedings of the National Conference of Charities and Correction.*(44th Session) Fort Wayne, IN: Fort Wayne Printing Company.

Leiby, J. (1978). *A history of social welfare and social work in the U.S.* (pp. 260–266). New York: Columbia University Press.

Leighninger, R. (1977). Systems theory and social work. *Journal of Education for Social Work, 13*(3), 44–49.

Levine, A. (2009, December 22). Helen Caldicott slams environmental groups on climate bill, nuclear concessions. *Truthout*. Retrieved from http://www.truthout.org/1222096

List, P. C. (1993). *Radical environmentalism: Philosophy and tactics*. Belmont, CA: Wadsworth.

Lopez, A. (2007). The protection of environmentally-displaced persons in international law. *Environmental Law, 37*(2), 365–409.

Lovejoy, O. R. (1911). The cost of cranberry sauce. *The Survey, 25*, 605–610.

Lubove, R. (1971). *The professional altruist: The emergence of social work as a career, 1880–1930*. Cambridge, MA: Harvard University Press.

Lyons, K., Manion, K., & Carlsen, M. (2006). International perspectives on social work: Global conditions and local practice. New York: Palgrave Macmillan.

Lysack, M. (2007).Family therapy, the ecological self and global warming. *Context, 91*, 9–11.

Lysack, M. (2008). Global warming as a moral issue: Ethics and economics of reducing carbon emissions. *InterdisciplinaryEnvironmental Review, 10*(1&2), 95–109.

Lysack, M. (2009a). From environmental despair to the ecological self: Mindfulness and community action. In S. Hick (Ed.), *Mindfullness and social work* (pp. 26–42). Chicago: Lyceum Press.

Lysack, M. (2009b). Doing social work on a traumatized planet: Fostering environmental health, sustainability, and community action. *The Advocate, 34*(1), 24–25.

Macy, J. (1991). *World as lover, world as self*. Berkeley, CA: Parallax.

Manthey, B. J. (1989). *Social work, religion and the church: Policy implications*. Unpublished doctoral dissertation, University of Texas–Austin.

Marable, M. (1984). *Race, reform, and rebellion: The second reconstruction in Black America, 1945–1982*. Jackson: University Press of Mississippi.

Mary, N. (2008). *Social work in a sustainable world*. Chicago: Lyceum Books.

Matthews, F. (2005). *Reinhabiting reality: Towards a recovery of culture*. Albany, NY: SUNY Press.

Mayell, H. (2004, Jan. 12). As consumerism spreads, Earth suffers, study says. *National Geographic News*. Retrieved from http://news.nationalgeographic.com/news/2004/01/0111_040112_consumerism.html

Maslow, A. H. (1970). *Religions, values, and peak experiences*. New York: Viking.

May, E. (2002, December 11). Sierra Club in the U.S. [Press release]. Retrieved from http://www.sierraclub.ca/national/programs/atmosphere-energy/climate

McConahay, M. J. (2000). No place to call home. *Sierra, 85*(6), 66–72.

McDowell, M. E. (1917). The significance to the city of its local community life. In *Proceedings of the National Conference of Charities and Correction* (p. 459). Boston: Ellis.

McKinnon, J. (2005). Social work, sustainability, and the environment. In M. Alston, & J. McKinnon (Eds.), *Social Work: Fields of practice* (2nd ed., pp. 225–236). Melbourne, Australia: Oxford University Press.

McLaughlin, C., & Davidson, G. (1994). *Spiritual politics*. New York: Ballantine.

Melillo, J., & Sala, O. (2008). Ecosystem services. In E. Chivan and A. Bernstein (Eds.), *Sustaining life: How human health depends on biodiversity* (pp. 75–115). New York: Oxford University Press.

Merchant, C. (1990). Ecofeminism and feminist theory. In I. Diamond & G. F. Orenstein (Eds.), *Reweaving the world: The emergence of ecofeminism* (pp. 100–105). San Francisco: Sierra Club Books.

Meyer, C. H. (1970). *Social work practice: A response to the urban crisis*. New York: Free Press.

Meyer, C. H. (1973). Purposes and boundaries: Casework fifty years later. *Social Casework, 54*(5), 268–275.

Mitcham, C. (1997). The sustainability question. In R. Gottlieb (Ed.), *The ecological community: Environmental challenges for philosophy, politics, and morality* (pp. 359–379). New York: Routledge.

Morrissette, V., McKenzie, B., & Morrissette, L. (1993). Towards an Aboriginal model of social work practice: Cultural knowledge and traditional practices. *Canadian Social Work Review, 10*(1), 91–108.

Mosher, C. (2009, May). *A new paradigm for sustainability and social justice*. Paper presented at the meeting of the International Eco-Conference: Building Bridges Crossing Boundaries, Calgary, Alberta, Canada.

Moss, J. (Author) & Ember, S. (Presenter). (2006, April 23). Number of refugees in the world at lowest level in 25 years [Radio broadcast]. Washington DC: Voice of America. Retrieved from http://www.voanews.com/specialenglish/archive/2006-04/2006-04-23-voa2.cfm

Muir, J. (1998). *My first summer in the Sierra*. New York: Mariner Books. (Originally published 1911).

Myers, D. G. (2000). *The American paradox: Spiritual hunger in an age of plenty*. New Haven, CT: Yale University Press.

Myers, N. (1997). Environmental refugees. *Population and Environment: A Journal of Interdisciplinary Studies, 19*(2), 167–182.

Naeem, S. (2009, May–June). Lessons from the reverse engineering of nature. *Miller-McCune*, pp. 56–71.

Naess, A. (1973). The shallow and the deep, long range ecology movement. *Inquiry, 16*(2), 95–100.

Naess, A. (1995a). Deepness of questions and the deep ecology movement. In G. Sessions (Ed.), *Deep ecology for the 21st century: Readings on the philosophy and practice of the new environmentalism* (pp. 204–212). Boston: Shambhala.

Naess, A. (1995b). The deep ecological movement: Some philosophical aspects. In G. Sessions (Ed.), *Deep ecology for the 21st century: Readings on the philosophy and practice of the new environmentalism* (pp. 64–84). Boston: Shambhala.

Naess, A. (2005). Access to free nature. *The Trumpeter: Journal of Ecosophy, 21*(2), 48–50.

Nash, R. F. (1982). *Wilderness and the American mind*. New Haven, CT: Yale University Press.

Nash, R. F. (1989). *The rights of nature: A history of environmental ethics*. Madison, WI: University of Wisconsin Press.

Nash, M., Wong, J., & Trlin, A. (2006). Civil and social integration: A new field for social work practice with immigrants, refugees and asylum seekers. *Journal of Social Work, 6*(3), 345–363.

National Association of Social Workers (NASW). (1996). *NASW code of ethics*. Washington, DC: NASW Press.

National Association of Social Workers (2009). Environmental policy. In *NASW, Social work speaks: NASW policy statements 2009-2012* (pp. 121–125). Washington, DC: NASW Press.

National Resources Defense Council. (2005). *Consequences of global warming*. Retrieved October 19, 2005, from http://nrdc.org/globalwarming/fcons.asp

Nixon, R. (2005, February 18). Our tools of war, turned blindly against ourselves. *Chronicle of Higher Education, 51*(24), B7–11.

O'Neil, W. (1976). *The progressive years: America comes of age*. New York: Dodd, Mead.

Ornstein, R., & Ehrlich, P. (1989). *New world, new mind*. New York: Doubleday.

Pachauri, P. K. (2009). Foreword. In *Worldwatch Institute, State of the world 2009: Into a warming world*. Retrieved from http://www.worldwatch.org/node/5986

Pastor, M., Sadd, J., & Morello-Frosch, R. (2007). Still toxic after all these years. Retrieved from the Center for Justice, Tolerance, and Community at the University of California, Santa Cruz, Web site: http://cjtc.ucsc.edu/docs/bay_final.pdf

Peters, G. L., & Larkin, R. P. (2008). *Population geography: Problems concepts and prospects*. Dubuque, IA: Kendal Hunt.

Petr, C. (1988). The worker-client relationship: A general systems perspective. *Social Casework: The Journal of Contemporary Social Work, 69*, 620–626.

Plumwood, V. (1994). Ecosocial feminism as a general theory of oppression. In C. Merchant (Ed.), *Key concepts in critical theory: Ecology* (pp. 207–219). Atlantic Highlands, NJ: Humanities Press.

Pollack, A. (2009, December 17). A patent ends, a seed's use will survive. *New York Times*, p.3.

Popple, P. R. (1985). The social work profession: A reconceptualization. *Social Work, 59*(4), 560–577.

Prince of Wales (2009, December 14). As climate change accelerates, so too will hunger, poverty, and perhaps even social unrest. *Newsweek*, pp. 55–57.

Ress, M. (2006). *Ecofeminism from Latin America*. New York: Orbis Books.

Restoring the vision. (1995). Boulder, CO: Institute for Deep Ecology.

Robbins, S. P., Chatterjee, P., & Canda, E. R. (2006). *Contemporary human behavior theory: A critical perspective for social work* (2nd ed.). Boston: Allyn & Bacon.

Rodman, J. (1983). Four forms of ecological consciousness reconsidered. In D. Scherer & T. Attig (Eds.), *Ethics and the environment* (pp. 82–92). Englewood Cliffs, NJ: Prentice Hall.

Rogers, P., Jalal, K. & Boyd, J. (2008). *An introduction to sustainable development*. London: Earthscan.

Rogge, M. (2008). Environmental justice. In National Association of Social Workers (NASW), *Encyclopedia of social work* (pp. 136–139). New York: Oxford University Press.

Rosenhek, R. (2006). Earth, spirit and action: The deep ecology movement as spiritual engagement. *The Trumpeter: Journal of Ecosophy, 22*(2), 90–95.

Roszak, T. (1992). *The voice of the earth: An exploration of ecopsychology*. New York: Simon & Schuster.

Roszak, T., Gomes, M., & Kanner, A. (Eds.). (1995). *Ecopsychology: Restoring the earth, healing the mind*. San Francisco: Sierra Club Books.

Ruether, R. R. (1989). Toward an ecological-feminist theology of nature. In J. Plant (Ed.), *Healing the wounds: The promise of ecofeminism* (pp. 145–150). Santa Cruz, CA: New Society.

Ruether, R. R. (2005). Integrating ecofeminism, globalization and world religions. Lanham, MD: Rowman and Littlefield Publishers.

Sachs, I. (1999). Social sustainability and whole development: Exploring the dimensions of sustainable development. In E. Becker & T. Jahn (Eds.), *Sustainability and the social sciences: A cross-disciplinary approach to integrating environmental consideration into theoretical reorientation* (pp. 25–36). New York: Zed Books.

Sagiv, L., & Schwartz, S. H. (2000). Value priorities and subjective well-being: Direct relations and congruity effects. *European Journal of Social Psychology, 30*, 177–198.

Saleebey, D. (1990). Theory and the generation and subversion of knowledge. *Journal of Sociology and Social Welfare, 17*(4), 112–126.

Saleebey, D. (1992). Biology's challenge to social work: Embodying the person-in-environment perspective. *Social Work, 37*(2), 112–118.

Samuelson, R. J. (2008, April 28). The great shopping spree, R.I.P. *Newsweek*, p. 49.

Sanborn, A. (1898). Anatomy of a tenement street. *Forum, 18*, 554–572.

Sandilands, C. (1994). Political animals: The paradox of ecofeminist politics. *Trumpeter, 11*(4), 167–194.

Sandilands, K. (1991). Ecofeminism and its discontents: Notes toward a politics of diversity. *Trumpeter, 8*(2), 90–96.

Sandilands, K. (1999). *The good-natured feminist: Ecofeminism and the quest for democracy*. Minneapolis: University of Minnesota Press.

Schriver, J. (2010). *Human behavior and the social environment: Shifting paradigms in essential knowledge for social work practice* (5th ed.). Boston: Allyn & Bacon.

Schroll, M. (2007). Wrestling with Arne Naess: A chronicle of ecopsychology's origin. *The Trumpeter: Journal of Ecosophy, 23*(1), 28–57.

Seed, J., Macy, J., Fleming, P., & Naess, A. (1988). *Thinking like a mountain: Towards a council of all beings.* Philadelphia, PA: New Society.

Segal, E. A. (2007). *Social welfare policy and social programs: A values perspective.* Belmont, CA: Brooks/Cole.

Servilla, J. C. (2006). The intrinsic value of the whole: Cognitive and utilitarian evaluative processes as they pertain to ecocentric, deep ecological, and ecopsychological valuing. *The Trumpeter: Journal of Ecosophy, 22*(2), 26–42.

Sessions, G. (Ed.). (1995). *Deep ecology for the 21st century: Readings on the philosophy and practice of the new environmentalism.* Boston: Shambhala.

Shaw, T. (2008). An ecological contribution to social welfare theory. *Social Development Issues, 30*(3), 13–26.

Shellenberger, M., & Nordhaus, T. (2005, January 13). The death of environmentalism. *Grist Magazine.* Retrieved from http://www.grist.org/article/doe-intro/

Siegel, F. (1984). *Troubled journey: From Pearl Harbor to Ronald Reagan.* New York: Hill & Wang.

Siporin, M. (1972). Situational assessment and intervention. *Social Casework, 53*(1), 91–109.

Siporin, M. (1980). Ecological systems theory in social work. *Journal of Sociology and Social Welfare, 7*(4), 5–7, 32.

Smart, B. (1992). *Modern conditions, post-modern controversies.* London: Routledge.

Spano, R. (1982). *The rank and file movement in social work.* Washington, DC: University Press of America.

Specht, H., & Courtney, M. (1994). *Unfaithful angels: How social work has abandoned its mission.* New York: Free Press.

Speth, J. (2009). *The bridge at the edge of the world: Capitalism, the environment, and crossing from crisis to sustainability.* New Haven, CT: Yale University Press.

"The spoils of war". (2003, March 29). *Economist,* 71–72.

Srivastava, A., Locke, E. A., & Bortol, K. M. (2001). Money and subjective well-being: It's not the money, it's the motives. *Journal of Personality and Social Psychology, 80,* 559–571.

Starhawk. (1989). Feminist earth-based spirituality and ecofeminism. In J. Plant (Ed.), *Healing the wounds: The promise of ecofeminism* (pp. 174–185). Santa Cruz, CA: New Society.

Stein, H. D. (1963). The concept of social environment in social work practice.

In H. J. Parad & R. R. Miller (Eds.), *Ego-oriented casework: Problems and perspectives* (pp. 65–88). New York: Family Service Association of America.

Suarez, Z., Newman, P., & Reed, B. (2008). Critical consciousness and cross-cultural/intersectional social work practice: A case analysis. *Families in Society, 89*(3), 407–417.

Swimme, B. (1990). How to heal a lobotomy. In I. Diamond & G. Orenstein (Eds.), *Reweaving the world: The emergence of ecofeminism* (pp. 15–22). San Francisco: Sierra Club Books.

Swer, G. (2008). Gender, nature and the oblivion of being: The outlines of a Heideggerian-ecofeminist philosophy. *The Trumpeter: Journal of Ecosophy, 24*(3), 102–135.

Townsend, M. (2002). Environmental refugees. *The Ecologist, 32*(6), 22–25.

Trattner, W. I. (1999). *From poor law to welfare state: A history of social welfare in America* (6th ed.). New York: Free Press.

Trolander, J. A. (1987). *Professionalism and social change: From the settlement house movement to neighborhood centers, 1886 to the present.* New York: Columbia University Press.

Tyson, K. (1995). *New foundations for scientific social and behavioral research: The heuristic paradigm.* Boston: Allyn & Bacon.

Ungar, M. (2002). A deeper, more social ecological social work practice. *Social Service Review, 76*(3), 480–497.

"United States: A cooling welcome; Katrina evacuees in Texas". (2006, September). *The Economist, 380*(8495), 61.

Unruh, J., Krol, M. & Kliot, N. (Eds.). (2005). *Environmental change and its implication for population migration: Advances in global change research.* New York: Cambridge University Press.

van Wormer, K. (2011). *Human behavior and the social environment, micro level: Individuals and families.* New York: Oxford University Press.

Warren, K. (2000). *Ecofeminist philosophy: A western perspective on what it is and why it matters.* Oxford, England: Rowan & Littlefield.

Wenocur, S., & Reisch, M. (1989). *From charity to enterprise: The development of American social work in a market economy.* Urbana: University of Illinois Press.

Werz, M., & Manlove, K. (2009, December 8). Climate change on the move: Climate migration. Retrieved from the Center for American Progress Web site: http://www.americanprogress.org/issues/2009/12/on_the_move.html

Wilber, K. (1995). *Sex, ecology, spirituality: The spirit of evolution*. Boston: Shambhala.

World Commission on Environment and Development. (1987). *Our common future*. New York: Oxford University Press.

Worldwatch Institute (2009). *State of the World 2009: Into a Warming World*. Retrieved from http://www.worldwatch.org/node/5982

Worster, D. (1985). *Rivers of empire: Water, aridity, and the growth of the American west*. New York: Pantheon Books.

Worster, D. (1994). *Nature's economy: A history of ecological ideas*. New York: Cambridge University Press.

Zaph, M. (2005a). Profound connections between person and place: Exploring location, spirituality, and social work. *Critical Social Work*, *6*(2). Retrieved from http://www.criticalsocialwork.com/units/socialwork/critical.nsf/EditDoNotShowInTOC/

Zaph, M. (2005b). The spiritual dimension of person and environment: Perspectives from social work and traditional knowledge. *International Social Work*, *48*(5), 633–642.

Zaph, M. (2008). Transforming social work's understanding of person and environment: Spirituality and the "common ground". *Journal of Religion and Spirituality in Social Work*, *27*(1–2), 171–181.

Zaph, M. (2009). *Social work and the environment: Understanding people and place*. Toronto, Ontario: Canadian Scholars Press.

Zimmerman, M. (1994). *Contesting earth's future: Radical ecology and postmodernity*. Los Angeles: University of California Press.

Human Behavior and the Religious/Spiritual Environment

The Community of Faith

A seeker after truth must shun no science, scorn no book, nor cling fanatically to a single creed.

—ISLAMIC PROVERB

All around the Western hemisphere and all over the world generally, there appears to be a resurgence of interest in the spiritual and religious dimensions of the human experience. In the United States, the number of persons involved in religious organizations and spiritual life has been on the increase across a wide array of belief systems, denominations, and communities of faith (see Table 9.1). And this new resurgence does not even attempt to account for and attest to the millions of spiritual and religious persons represented among the early indigenous tribal groups and the early émigrés who brought with them to this country a multiplicity of both traditional and esoteric faith expressions (Mary, 2008; McGaa, 1995). Americans, suggests Mary (2008), are moving from a time of individual spiritual growth into a time of collective spiritual activism. One only need look at the many thousand best-selling books, the seemingly unending array of TV programs, spiritual retreats, religious gatherings, general interest magazines, and Internet Web sites, and the proliferation of the influences of spiritual and religious personalities to see the growing concern for things religious and spiritual in the general public. And, perhaps sadly, one sees the spirituality and resurgent forms of religious fundamentalism being mixed with virulent forms of nationalism and long-standing ethnic tensions whereby both religious traditions and spiritual sensitivities become even more tainted with a historical and incriminating record of injustice, violence, tribalism, and incipient violations of fundamental human rights. And we see the heated debates and outright hostility that seem to impregnate the political culture of this country with the ideological battles and doctrinaire apologies being bandied about between the so-called religious fundamentalists and the elitist, secular humanists (Kaplan, 2004). Battles over abortion, judicial nominations, the death penalty, prayer, faith-based welfare delivery initiatives, and the teaching of creationism and/or its newer derivative, intelligent design, in the public schools have become common in the public discourse and a linchpin to a new emerging kind of religiously driven culture war (Campolo, 2004; Carter, 1993; Kaseman & Austin, 2005). We seem to be becoming

Table 9.1   Self-Described Religious Identification of U.S. Adult Population, 1990, 2001, and 2008

Group	1990 % of Adults	2001 % of Adults	2008 % of Adults	Change in % of Total Adults 1990–2008
Adult population, total				
Adult population, responded	97.7%	94.6%	94.8%	−2.9%
Total Christian	**86.2%**	**76.7%**	**76.0%**	**−10.2%**
Catholic	26.2%	24.5%	25.1%	**−1.2%**
Non-Catholic Christian	60.0%	52.2%	50.9%	**−9.0%**
Baptist	19.4%	16.3%	15.8%	**−3.5%**
Mainline Christian	18.7%	17.2%	12.9%	**−5.8%**
Methodist	8.1%	6.8%	5.0%	**−3.1%**
Lutheran	5.2%	4.6%	3.8%	**−1.4%**
Presbyterian	2.8%	2.7%	2.1%	**−0.8%**
Episcopalian/Anglican	1.7%	1.7%	1.1%	**−0.7%**
United Church of Christ	0.2%	0.7%	0.3%	**0.1%**
Christian Generic	14.8%	10.8%	14.2%	**−0.6%**
Christian Unspecified	4.6%	6.8%	7.2%	**2.6%**
Nondenominational Christian	0.1%	1.2%	3.5%	**3.4%**
Protestant—Unspecified	9.8%	2.2%	2.3%	**−7.5%**
Evangelical/Born Again	0.3%	0.5%	0.9%	**0.6%**
Pentecostal/Charismatic	3.2%	3.8%	3.5%	**0.3%**
Pentecostal—Unspecified	1.8%	2.1%	2.4%	**0.6%**
Assemblies of God	0.4%	0.5%	0.4%	**0.0%**
Church of God	0.3%	0.5%	0.3%	**0.0%**
Other Protestant Denominations	2.6%	2.9%	3.1%	**0.5%**
Churches of Christ	1.0%	1.2%	0.8%	**−0.2%**
Jehovah's Witness	0.8%	0.6%	0.8%	**0.1%**
Seventh-Day Adventist	0.4%	0.3%	0.4%	**0.0%**
Mormon/Latter-Day Saints	1.4%	1.3%	1.4%	**0.0%**
Total non-Christian religions	**3.3%**	**3.7%**	**3.9%**	**0.5%**
Jewish	1.8%	1.4%	1.2%	**−0.6%**
Eastern Religions	0.4%	1.0%	0.9%	**0.5%**
Buddhist	0.2%	0.5%	0.5%	**0.3%**
Muslim	0.3%	0.5%	0.6%	**0.3%**
New Religious Movements & Others	0.7%	0.9%	1.2%	**0.5%**
None/ No religion, total	**8.2%**	**14.2%**	**15.0%**	**6.8%**
Agnostic+Atheist	0.7%	0.9%	1.6%	**0.9%**
Did Not Know/ Refused to reply	**2.3%**	**5.4%**	**5.2%**	**2.9%**

Source: Kosmin, B., & Keysar, A. (2008). American religious identification survey. Retrieved from http://www.americanreligionsurveyaris.org/reports/ARIS_Report_2008.pdf

Printed with permission of Institute for the Study of Secularism in Society & Culture, Trinity College, Hartford, CT.

increasingly polarized in regard to one of the only mental and behavioral characteristics that are distinctly associated with being human: our commitment to ideas, institutions, and practices that transcend self in time and space. Spiritual commitments and religious convictions, like any other deeply held moral code, can provide both the courage to resist repression and violence for some and, for others, the impulse to impose them. Strong transcendent convictions led both to the dismantling of slavery and the imposition of witch trials and inquisitorial death penalties. History is not ambivalent about those two realities. It is the best of times and worst of times for the spiritual and religious among us.

The 2008 American Religious Identification Survey is informative concerning religious beliefs and affiliations (Kosmin & Keysar, 2009). Based on over 54,000 respondents, this survey found most significantly that fewer Americans identify as Christian (now 76 percent) than formerly and, strikingly, that one out of five Americans identify as Nones or with no religious affiliation or beliefs. Other highlights of the report are as follows:

> The historic mainline churches and denominations have experienced the steepest declines, while the nondenominational Christian identity has been trending upward particularly since 2001.
> Thirty-four percent of American adults considered themselves "Born Again or Evangelical Christians" in 2008.
> Irish, Asian Americans, and Jews are substantially more likely to indicate no religious identity than other racial or ethnic groups.
> One sign of the lack of attachment of Americans to religion is that 27 percent do not expect a religious funeral at their death.
> Based on their stated beliefs rather than their religious identification in 2008, 70 percent of Americans believe in a personal God, roughly 12 percent of Americans are atheist (no God) or agnostic (unknowable or unsure), and another 12 percent are deistic (a higher power but no personal God).

> The impact of Hispanic immigration has significantly boosted the Catholic population in California and other states with high Hispanic populations.

See Table 9.1 for the breakdown of Americans by religious identity.

Definitions

In Allied Disciplines

Although, as suggested, there is increasing evidence that the study of religion and spirituality generally and its relationship to a range of human development issues has garnered increased attention in the largely public discourse, there is still little consensus about what these constructs really refer to (Roehlkepartain, Benson, King, & Wagener, 2005). Indeed, a fundamental issue that faces every social worker interested in this line of inquiry is the problem of definition. Knowing how we define such constructs as spirituality, religion, and faith development sets the boundaries for scholarly endeavor and determines whether these ideas are deemed appropriate for study at all. What is spirituality? Is it different from religiosity, and if so, how? What is spiritual development? Is there a difference between spiritual development and faith development and, if so, what is that difference?

There are numerous academic and applied disciplines that include in their field of inquiry an interest in the subject of religion, spirituality, and related conceptual constructs. Sociology (Davie, 2003; Wuthnow, 2003), psychology (Pargament, 1999; Reich, Oser, & Scarlett, 1999), biology (d'Aquili & Newberg, 1999), ecology (Besthorn, 2002), comparative religious studies (Marler & Hadaway, 2002), theological studies (Loder, 1998), human development (Wink & Dillon, 2002), public health (Miller & Thoresen, 2003), nursing (O'Brien, 2008), organizational studies (Alford & Naughton, 2001; Conger, 1994), higher education (Blacher-Wilson, 2004), political science (King, 2001; Norris & Inglehart, 2004), philosophy (Harris, 2004), and social work (Canda & Furman, 2010; Mosher, 2009; Sheridan, 2003) are just a few among a growing list, perhaps too numerous to mention, of scholarly disciplines that have historically and more recently started to vigorously pursue this line of inquiry.

The social scientific literature presents a number of helpful explorations that have tackled these definitional issues. King (2001), MacDonald (2000), Mary (2008), and others have suggested that there are several ways to think about spirituality and religion. Sometimes spirituality is defined as a particular dimension of a religious experience. Wulff (1997) notes that this focus on dimensionality was necessitated by the pioneering work of noted philosopher William James (1958/orig.1902), who recognized that religious expression contained several intertwined dimensions, such as institutional expressions of belief and ritual practices, as well as experiential and deeply spiritual aspects of faith expression. For Wulff (1997), the meaning of religion is related to the first of these two—a more or less fixed system of ideological commitments and associations with institutional or collective settings. (See Figure 9.1 of a Kentucky mosque and Figure 9.2 of a Jewish worship service.) The term *spirituality*, in some quarters, is thus used to refer to the more subjective, experiential, intuitive aspect of religious expression (Mosher, 2009; Zinnbauer, Pargament, & Scott, 1999). Indeed, some models now subsume religiousness or religious expression as one category within the larger domain of spirituality (MacDonald, 2000). The more standard delineation is summed up by Zinnbauer, Pargament, Cole, Rye, Butter, & Belavich (1997):

> Spirituality is now commonly regarded as an individual phenomenon and identified with such things as personal transcendence, supra consciousness, sensitivity and meaningfulness. . . . Religiousness, in contrast, is now often descried narrowly as formally structured and identified with religious institutions and prescribed theology and rituals. (p. 551).

Figure 9.1. When an influx of Bosnian refugees moved into Bowling Green, Kentucky, this mosque was erected on the outskirts of town. Photo by Robert van Wormer.

Figure 9.2. The lifting of the Torah, Jewish synagogue, Madison, Wisconsin. Photo by Dorith Steinberg.

This attempt to separate religion and spirituality has both supporters and detractors. For some, this represents nothing more than an artificial line of demarcation that often obscures the fact that individual spirituality and religious practice, as well as belief and experiential encounter, are dynamically interconnected. Associated with this concern is the fear that attempting to differentiate between religion and spirituality, except for important pedagogical reasons, unnecessarily fuels a dominating and hierarchical dichotomy that one is bad—often religion—and the other—often spirituality—is good.

A relatively new effort to provide definitional clarity is predicated on finding a common denominator that integrates spirituality and religion without minimizing their unique statuses. For Pargament (1997) that common denominator is the idea of the *sacred*. Examples of the sacred include such concepts as God, divinity,

transcendence, and ultimate reality. Spirituality is a search for the sacred, as well as an ongoing process whereby people both affirm and modify their sacred constructs in order to fulfill deeper needs to securely locate themselves in time and space. From this perspective, religion is one element of a larger sacred search that creates institutional links, rituals, and belief systems in order to access the sacred through collective associations.

Another definitional effort has been suggested by Beck (1992), who understands spirituality as a set of human qualities rather than a search for the sacred or transcendence. These spiritual qualities, such as insight, gratitude, an awareness of interconnectedness between persons and other living and nonliving phenomena, the experience of awe, and a practiced attitude of generosity, can be seen as developing in either religious or nonreligious persons. This way of explicating spirituality gives expression to the internal processes of being, the power and expression that comes from within as we begin to know our deepest self. Thus, it honors both the internal and external manifestations of spiritual development.

Another recent line of theory and research suggests that spirituality, rather than religion, is a core, universal dynamic of human development that shares equal importance with the more traditional venues of human developmental research: cognitive, social, emotional, and moral (Roehlkepartain et al., 2005). This core developmental dimension focuses on the human capacity to create a *narrative* or story about who one is and how one exists in both time and space. Thus, persons are active and creative participants in crafting their spirituality as they utilize materials that come from their families, their social group, their own experiences, and the natural environment. This process of creating a narrative of one's spiritual self in context is, according to Coles (1989), universal, transhistorical, and transcultural. In this vein, Benson, Roehlkepartain, and Rude (2003) summarize the active agency of humans in construction of their spiritual development:

> Spiritual development is the process of growing the intrinsic human capacity for

self-transcendence, in which the self is embedded in something greater than the self, including the sacred. It is the developmental "engine" that propels the search for connectedness, meaning, purpose and contribution. It is shaped both within and outside of religious traditions, beliefs, and practices. (pp. 205–206)

In Social Work

Religion and spirituality have long been considered important sources for shaping both personal and social life. As will be suggested a bit later, social work has its historical roots in various religious and spiritual traditions, and, though the subject of religion and spirituality in social work has often been neglected in the literature, recent scholarship has suggested a burgeoning interest in the interrelationship between these constructs and social work practice. Whereas the negative consequences of religion for various measures of the human condition, such as morality and social organization, have long been the subject of debate in the pioneering writings of social theorists and researchers; the positive contributions of religion and spirituality to ever-broader categories of human functioning have, in some ways, only recently achieved currency.

The social work profession has had its own internal debate about what counts as spiritual or religious and how the two are connected. A substantial body of literature has appeared in recent years on spirituality and religion, and an increasing number of theorists have attempted to provide definitional clarity between spirituality and religion (Besthorn, 2002; Bullis, 1996, Canda, 1998; Canda & Furman, 1999, 2010; Gilbert, 2000; Sheridan, 1999, 2003; Van Hook, Hugen, & Aguilar, 2001). To date, as with other disciplines, no consensus seems to have emerged. And one must acknowledge that that may, indeed, be preferable, given the emergent nature of these ideas. Spirituality and religiousness are not mysterious constructs. We know a great deal about them. But it may be premature and perhaps counterproductive to propose that a single definition or integration could capture the richness and complexity of these constructs.

A typology has recently been developed that provides a useful way to appreciate how social work scholars and practitioners have historically attempted to understand religion and spirituality and their efforts to integrate the two. Social work scholar Laura Praglin (2004) suggests that one may characterize social work's response in four typical ways: *(1)* resistance to or avoidance of a dialogue about these constructs; *(2)* an overly generalized syncretism or acceptance of the spiritual nature of practice; *(3)* a radical separation of the terms *spirituality* and *religion* for ideological reasons; and finally *(4)* a sincere interdisciplinary engagement of the two constructs.

The first response, according to Praglin (2004), is typical of those social work professionals who equate religion with injustice, personal pathology, and very rigid sociocultural prohibitions. The study of and utilization in practice of this kind of religious orientation would be unethical and antithetical to social work values and ethics. This seems a legitimate fear, for one cannot argue persuasively that religious systems have not been involved in the most egregious kinds of tyranny, genocide, and rank inequality. No religious system can claim exception from this stain. The second response is the opposite of the first and suggests an uncritical and simple acceptance of the spiritual dimension of human development as fully complementary to social work. This response minimizes difficulties and conflicts between spiritual and religious conceptualization by stressing the holistic nature of social work practice and the importance of addressing the whole person—including the spiritual person—rather than focusing on individual pathology, which is presumably associated with more religious aspects of human functioning. Praglin fears that this overly simplistic response runs the risks of creating social workers who are simple "avatars of spirituality" (p. 73). A profession that is too narrowly accommodating to a single and unique definitional category runs the risks of failing to incorporate broader scholarly and sociopolitical conceptualizations. In the process they compromise their own credibility and intellectual rigor.

The third typology regarding how social work has addressed the integration of religious and spiritual constructs is the almost complete epistemological separation of the two terms. This trend in social work is exemplified, according to Praglin (2004), in the ways that many social work scholars define religion very narrowly as referring to "specific worship practices, formal denomination affiliation, or explicit participation in a faith organization" (p. 74). Religion, then, is an external expression of internal beliefs. Spirituality, on the other hand, is viewed as interiorized religion—the universal quest for meaning and connectedness. Praglin (2004) notes that this kind of binomial categorization finds acceptance among social workers who are responsive to noninstitutional and nontraditional forms of faith expression.

The final option in the typology insists on a serious intradisciplinary and interdisciplinary engagement of spirituality and religion within social work theory and practice. This approach is most often associated with social work scholar Ed Canda (2002; Canda & Furman, 1999; 2010), believed by many to be the recent progenitor of social work's renewed interest in religion and spirituality. According to this strategy, the honest and ethical approach to spirituality and religion is to acknowledge conceptual and ideological differences and contending truth claims while at the same time engaging in "substantive, cross-disciplinary research and discussion" (Praglin, 2004, p. 75). Without this cross-fertilization between social work, religious studies, social psychology of religion, sociology of religion, comparative religion, and many other areas, social work will continue to remain isolated from the robust contribution of other disciplines and thus will be at risk of being intellectually constricted in outlook and practice.

The Oppression of Evangelicals in Social Work?

Praglin's analysis draws our attention to the struggle social work has encountered in its attempts to more fully understand the similarities and differences between religious and spiritual constructs. It may also help explain how this effort may have unintentionally contributed to a major backlash from some conservative, religious social workers—especially those identifying themselves as evangelical Christians. Their reaction involves the perception of a sometimes unintentional but, at times, openly oppressive discrimination against evangelicals by their secular colleagues or teachers (Hodge, 2002, 2003a, 2003b, 2006, 2007a, 2007b, 2009; Olasky, 2005; Ressler & Hodge, 2003, 2005; Thyer & Myers, 2009).

As we will see later in this chapter in our discussion of Protestant Fundamentalism, the prominent and steady rise of the Christian Right in America's social and political life has fostered a great deal of controversy. Much of the controversy tends to turn on the question of whether the Christian Right's influence on American political life has grown too extensive and whether this is a help or a hindrance to an American realpolitik—historically committed to limiting overtly sectarian influences in the nation's governance. In the current political climate of charge and countercharge, it is difficult to assess the validity of the claims that evangelical Christians experience discrimination within social work. Again, as we shall see in our later discussion, it is reasonable for social workers to inquire whether these anti-evangelical allegations accurately reflect genuinely oppressive attitudes and practices. It is also important to question whether these allegations are a part of a much larger religio-political stratagem that, relying heavily on the rhetoric of perpetual marginalization and victimization (Balmer, 2006), aims to discredit and dethrone the alleged hegemony of secular humanism in American life. Others outside of the profession have joined the sometimes rancorous debate (National Association of Scholars, 2007; Ricketts, 2008; Will, 2007). It is important to note that the current criticism does not represent a consensus opinion among social workers scholars (Bennett, 2003; Canda, 2003; Melcher, 2008; Melendez & LaSala, 2006; Spano & Koenig, 2007).

The social work scholarship suggesting a pattern of discriminatory beliefs and practices is not yet extensive or conceptually sophisticated. There have been only a small number of incidents of alleged discrimination reported in social work programs at various colleges around the United States. Much of the evidence is based on anecdotal reports and unrefined research data that undoubtedly tap into strongly perceived feelings of marginalization on the part of some evangelicals but do not establish irrefutable patterns of discrimination. While social work scholars are correct in alerting the profession to be constantly vigilant to the possibility of discriminatory practices, it is also important that social workers not overreact to allegations of discrimination in the absence of substantial, clear, and convincing data. These are highly charged and serious allegations that deserve careful scrutiny. Before rushing to judgment we are obliged to consider a number of interrelated factors. First, the definitional precision by which one can accurately assess just who is being discriminated against is, at best, underdeveloped. The scholarship thus far alludes to a voluminous, and often casually interchangeable, array of descriptors to portray individuals and groups who are purported to be the targets of discriminatory practices. One reads of evangelicals, religious conservatives, conservative Christians, evangelical Christians, practicing Christians, orthodox believers, Christian orthodoxy, devout believers, conservative protestants, fundamentalists, more traditional faith traditions, traditional theists, theologically conservative Christians, theistic believers, and people of faith. Religious scholars and survey researchers have known for years of the difficulty associated with self-identified and ill-defined designation of religious affiliation—especially among so-called evangelicals (The Barna Group, 2007; Marsden, 2006). They have called for greater specificity and cautioned that drawing broad generalizations about these very heterogeneous populations in the absence of a clear definitional framework is precarious (Harrington, 2009; Pew Trust, 2008). Unfortunately, the social work scholarship tends to amalgamate a broad assortment of socio-historical faith traditions into a kind of unitary, homogenous camp. This oversimplifies very discrete demographic, linguistic, theological, and historical differences and leads to the false impression that systematic discrimination is widespread when, in fact, this is not the case. For instance,

a sharp distinction is often drawn between liberal Christians and evangelical Christians, obscuring the fact that there is a long tradition of liberal evangelicalism in America's religious history (Balmer, 2006) and that so-called liberal Christians sometimes espouse quite conservative viewpoints on a range of theological and social issues (Campolo, 2004; Wallis, 2005). On other occasions the social work scholarship contends that evangelical Christianity is decidedly and singularly representative of more *traditional faith traditions* while presumably liberal Christianity is not. Again, this obscures the fact that so-called liberal Christianity is also a traditional faith tradition given its long historical evolution dating back to the earliest days of the American republic.

A second factor to consider is the implicit assertion that social work educators and practitioners engage in discriminatory practices against evangelical Christians because they are operating out of a kind of unconscious allegiance to an oppressive, anti-religious classism. That is, social workers are thought to discriminate against evangelicals because they are members of an elite, religiously intolerant and secularly privileged class of power brokers who dominate large segments of American society. This is, unfortunately, a simple restatement of a century-old contention on the part of ultra-conservative religionists that secularists or secular humanists have rested control of American social life. These secularists then strive to maintain their cultural hegemony through an overt oppression of religion and religious peoples (Almond, Appleby & Sivan, 2003; Lawrence, 1989). Several things should become immediately obvious. The attempt to tie social work's alleged discriminatory proclivities to the shadowy intents of a secular-humanist worldview rests on several outmoded, sometimes imprecisely explicated and loosely associated socio-cultural theories (Berger, 1986; Goulder, 1979; Hunter, 1991; McAdams, 1987; Schmalzbauer, 1993). These conceptual models, purporting to establish a theoretical basis for social work's secular privilege and the resulting power imbalances that negatively impact evangelicals, are not well established, are mostly interpretive, and lack compelling explanatory power. The arguments are, as Melendez and LaSala (2006) point out, largely tautological—based on a supposed universal, taken-for-granted, and unassailable truth claim. This tautology seriously understates the many ways that ultra-conservative evangelicals and other conservative religious groups also experience significant degrees of *faith privilege* given their disproportional influence in so many areas of America's contemporary political, social, cultural, and mass media discourse (Balmer, 2006; Domke, 2004; Sharlet, 2008).

Social workers should ask, Is there an unbridled undermining of religious values and systematic discrimination against evangelicals by people who describe themselves as secular or who, perhaps, unconsciously operate from a secularists mindset? Can we say categorically that social work teachers and practitioners commonly ascribe to a secularist worldview and, if they do, must they necessarily act in discriminatory manners because they so define themselves? We might also ask, Just what is meant by secularism, and who are these so-called secular humanists, and what is their influence? The answer to these questions and many others like them are, on closer observation, far more complex than may first appear. Historian Wilfred McClay (2003), for instance, suggests that secularism is one of the most often used but least understood words. It has multiple meanings depending upon the cultural and historical context in which the term is used and is best understood as a sociological process that evolves slowly over time—having an assortment of both humanistic and highly religious antecedents. It is not an abstract presence, somehow anthropomorphized into a malevolent force intentionally bent upon destroying religion—as seems to be implied by those who so virulently attack its influence (Berlinerblau, 2005).

Historically, secularism has been both lauded and assailed. During the late Renaissance, secular and enlightenment influences were viewed as the savior of European civilization—having been for centuries mired in the oppressive and totalizing society of Augustinian Christianity (Johnson, 1979). Holy crusades, religious wars, witch hunts, and murderous inquisitorial rampages resulting in the death of hundreds of thousands were all thought to have been brought under some degree of control as a byproduct of the rise of secular and humanist impulses. Indeed, secularism was viewed as both saving religion from religion and, interestingly, saving religion for religion. It was never seen as being absolutely intolerant of religion. It was, however, intolerant of the horrific abuses associated with European Christo-theocracy.

Today, however, Western society is caught up in the secularization versus desecularization culture war. Christian fundamentalists, especially, assail secularism as the very epitome of the anti-Christ, what eminent sociologist Jacques Berlinerblau (2005) calls the "secular tyranny myth" (p. 133). In this context, secularism has become nearly synonymous with atheism, godlessness, and immorality. It is blamed for persistently undermining Christian values and leading to untold misery and moral degeneracy while inflicting unsuspecting minds with a kind of virulent, intellectual virus. It is also contended that secular-humanist influences on college campuses and among the professorate are largely responsible for students losing their faith. This despite the fact that recent research suggests that students who attend secular universities are more likely to hold on to their faith than students who do not attend college (Uecker, Regnerus, & Vaaler, 2007). Indeed, students at secular universities do not give up their religious convictions generally and, when they do, it is because of natural maturational processes and how young people choose to spend their time while in college. It is not, contrary to conventional wisdom and the impassioned rhetoric of ultra-conservative religionists, because elite, secular-humanist professors are out to destroy students' relationship with their religion—however they may define that. Even if some faculty hold unfavorable views towards certain religious groups—especially evangelical Christians and Mormons—as a recent survey by the Tobin and Weinberg (2007) seems to suggest, this does not necessarily translate into acts of classroom discrimination. Anti-religious bias is not the same as holding some sort of latent sentiment or honestly struggling to better understand and interpret the cultural meaning of religion in the life of the university.

While it cannot be denied that isolated acts of anti-religious bigotry occur in university settings, this does not substantiate nor necessitate a discernable trend. It is more probable that the unfavorable feelings of some faculty members represent a resistance to the ultra-conservative social, scientific, and political agenda associated with certain religious groups rather than overt bias against their religious precepts and traditions. In fact, it appears that university faculty across disciplines are far more respectful of religious traditions and take religion and religious expression far more seriously than pejorative stereotypes of them might indicate. Some research, in reality, suggests that in the aggregate more than 80 percent of university faculty consider themselves spiritual (Astin & Astin, 2006) and over 56 percent hold strong theistic beliefs in God and the importance of involvement in religious activities (Gross & Simmons, 2009). An unexpectedly high proportion—almost 20 percent—of the professorate in secular institutions identify themselves as born-again Christians. This runs contrary to popular misperceptions of evangelical underrepresentation in universities and/or an anti-evangelical bias (Cooperman, 2007; Gross & Simmons, 2009). This percentage matches very closely the percentage of persons in the larger population identifying themselves as evangelical Christian—in which being born again is a fundamental dimension of their theological faith expression.

Secularism, far from being a monolithic ideology perverting the hearts and minds of the unwary, is, at best, a moderately influential and at times deeply floundering intellectual movement. It may still, on occasion, declare the prominence of its ideas and assertion that it has been the best defender of religious pluralism and surest safeguard against religious intolerance—but little more. Cultural historian McClay (2003) offers this sober assessment:

> The fact of the matter is that secularism in our day can claim no energizing vision and no revolutionary élan, not as in the past. Instead, it sits passive and inert, heavily dependent upon the missteps and excesses of the Religious Right or some similar foe to make its case, stir up its fading enthusiasm, and rally its remaining troops. Secularism sits uneasy upon its throne, a monarch that dares not speak… and dares not openly propound its agenda…These days it is rather more fashionable to be "spiritual" than to be secular. (p. 38)

Finally, social work students are encouraged to carefully reflect upon and critically evaluate the social work scholarship on this issue. They should look closely at the research protocol, how samples are drawn and from where, sample sizes, the kind of data reported, generalization made to the larger population, and interpretations and applications of the data. They should be alert to the fact that much of the admittedly small body of existing research is exploratory in nature—attempting to ascertain whether discrimination actually exists rather than identifying the extent of specific incidences and/or discrete types of religious intolerances. It is also important for students to be especially careful to distinguish between reports of discrimination based on personal perception rather than quantifiable and testable data sets of actual discriminatory behaviors. Personal perception is an especially tenuous basis for making larger, macro-level judgments and generalizations. Personal perception tends to give too much weight to single, salient experiences and to consequently discount or minimize alternative possibilities. This tendency is sometimes referred to as *confirmatory bias* or *belief perseverance* (Kahnerman, Slovic, & Tversky, 1982; Lord, Ross & Lepper, 1979). It occurs when research subjects have strongly held beliefs about a social issue or concern—in this case discrimination against evangelicals—and thus cast their responses to researchers in such a manner so as to confirm what they already firmly believe to be the case and which is vigorously supported by other members of their specific identity group. In important ways this phenomenon mirrors an often studied collective phenomenon referred to as *groupthink* (Janis, 1982).

While confirmatory bias often occurs in order to fulfill some higher, and even laudable, social calling of eliminating discrimination that respondents firmly believe already exists, it can lead to unreliable findings and questionable interpretations of the data. A recent example is the work of Thyer and Myers (2009). The researchers invited selected social work students, faculty, and graduates to submit verbal reports and written narrative of what they perceived to be examples of religious discrimination in social work academic programs. According to the authors, their collection of unsystematic, anecdotal reports came from personal e-mails, publically available reports from neo-conservative think-tanks, personal phone conversations, and editorialized descriptions found on the Internet. These self-reports may offer some useful information to consider as the profession struggles to define more clearly what it means by social justice and anti-oppressive practice. But, unfortunately, the article leaves the unmistakable impression that the issue of anti-religious and anti-evangelical discrimination is far more serious, widespread, and intransigent than, as we have argued earlier, is likely the case. These kinds of conceptual perorations, while perhaps helpful, simply are not capable of becoming the basis for establishing the claim that social work is an anti-religious/anti-evangelical profession. Clearly, there is a need for much less hyperbole and far more information before anyone can justifiably make this claim.

A Holistic Model

What, then, can we say about defining spirituality and religion for social work theory and practice? Canda and Furman's (1999, 2010) integrative and holistic model offers some very important insights. This model suggests that spirituality may be understood as comprising three essential dimensions of the human experience. First, spirituality can be seen as being one aspect of what it means to be human. That is, a human being can be said to have a biological, psychological, sociological, and spiritual aspect. The spiritual aspect motivates experience and action and orients the person toward ultimacy—giving things ultimate value or finding ultimate meaning in reality itself.

Second, spirituality may be seen as a totality—"as a wholeness of what it means to be human" (Canda & Furman, 2010, p. 243). From this perspective, spirituality is the holistic, sacred, and irreducible ultimate ground of reality. This holistic dimension is sometimes understood as the divine nature, the Atman, the Christ, the image of God, the Buddha nature, the "I am" that permeates the very essence of personhood. Indeed, this wholeness is not limited to the realm of the individual but is manifested in a myriad of relationships with other human beings, animals, inanimate objects, and the entire planetary ecosystem.

The third dimension of the holistic model describes one's spiritual nature as existing at the center of the person. Spirituality at the core of the self may be referred to as the soul, consciousness, awareness, enlightenment—that which creates connection and acts as the fulcrum point for the integration of all aspects of a person's being (Canda & Furman, 1999, p. 48). The focus of spirituality is thus to go deeply within to find the summit of unity and integration. Speaking of spirituality as both *wholeness of being* and *center of being*, Canda notes:

> Both the metaphors of the sacred center and sacred wholeness of the person seem to us to be different ways of experiencing the same thing. In theological language, this is like the dual aspects of relating to the divine: the divine as *transcendent* (wholeness) beyond; yet encompassing all particular things and the divine as *immanent* (center) within each person. (Canda & Furman, 1999, p. 48)

Figure 9.3 shows a holistic model of spirituality.

As we have seen, there is no easy way to fully understand how to define spirituality and religion and related constructs. Scholars, devotees, congregants, and searchers have been struggling with these issues for millennia. Perhaps the best we can say is that religion and spirituality are vital processes and resources in human development irrespective of the unique definitions one applies to either construct. Indeed, we know that when religion and spirituality are marginalized in our understanding

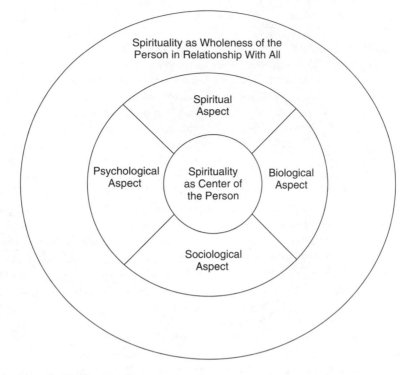

Figure 9.3. Holistic model of spirituality.

of the human condition, we do a disservice to our clients, to our profession and its ethics, and to ourselves. Without asking the hard questions, taking the risk of creating dialogue and debate, acknowledging both the light and the dark side of the religio-spiritual experience, we will ultimately end up building theory and, by extension, praxis that is based, at best, on an incomplete understanding of our humanness. A fair degree of ambiguity and uncertainty is likely to be our constant companion as we navigate the rocky shoals of understanding religion and spirituality and its impact on us. A religiously and spiritually sensitive social work is one that does not shrink from these tough issues but, at the same time, does not fall prey to the temptation to craft simple answers to very complex issues.

Sustainability and Spirituality

An exciting development today is the emphasis within the sustainability movement on spiritual

virtues and universal human values. The previous chapter discussed deep ecology, a theory that, as Mary (2009) indicates, broadens our view of systems and helps bridge the gap among biological, social, and spiritual realities. From an ecological perspective, the oppression of people is linked to oppression of the environment, of Mother Earth. Korten's (2006) paradigm of moral consciousnesss, the highest level of which is creative service to humankind as a whole, leads quite naturally, observes Mary, into the values and principles of a sustainable future. Spiritual values such as respect for human life and nature overlap with those of the sustainability movement. This approach also eliminates the false dichotomy between science and spirit and the material and spiritual realms.

In his presentation at an ecological conference in Calgary, Canada, Craig Mosher (2009) discussed several key aspects of sustainability that have a bearing on the spiritual realm. These are the concepts of the unity of all, deep ecology, and moral values.

The belief in the *unity of all* is the belief that the entire planet and universe can be considered one unified system. The unity of all is often sensed through a personal experience. Mosher cites ecologist John Muir who stated that "When we try to pick out anything by itself, we find it hitched to everything else in the universe" (1911, p.110). This sense of inter-connectedness and awe is a sense of the sacred. We saw this belief system in the boxed reading on Norway in the previous chapter on the envi-ronment and in the discussion of *deep ecology*, which focuses on the interconnectedness of human and nonhuman life. The *spiritual and moral* dimension to the new paradigm of sus-tainability that Mosher is proposing incorpo-rates spiritual beliefs common to many religions. People's search for meaning and happiness may lead to a shift in values (that are often religious): away from materialism, individual-ism, and wanting "more" for themselves, toward equalitarianism and involvement with one's family and community.

Ecological destruction and the threats of global climate change are increasingly seen as moral issues, as Mosher indicates, partly because religious groups have identified this work as caring for God's creation, and partly because people are realizing that their own society and economic system are damaging the planet so they feel a moral responsibility to solve the problems. Some see a moral impera-tive to redistribute wealth and develop a mod-erate lifestyle based on the value of sufficiency rather than material greed.

"Religious Groups Active in Climate Debate." This is the title of a *USA Today* article on the United Nations summit on climate change in Copenhagen (Winter, 2009). At a time when political leaders are struggling to get their nations to make a strong commitment to protection of the environment, numerous preachers, rabbis, ministers, and other faith-based leaders brought a spiritual presence to the conference. Repre-sentatives from the National Council on Churches, which represents over 45 million con-gregation members in the United States, Nobel Peace Prize winner Desmond Tutu from South Africa, and representatives from various evan-gelical associations attended the conference. America's religious communities have shed their long-standing suspicion of the environmental

cause, according to the article. Many have ral-lied behind the belief that we are called upon to protect God's creation, including human and all other life. Younger evangelicals are especially concerned about environmental sustainability, according to a theologian quoted in the article.

See Box 9.1, "Earth as Source of Spirit" for a social work perspective that offers a sense of oneness with nature. Also refer to Figure 9.4 for an image of nature.

Box 9.1 *Earth as Source of Spirit*

Michael J. Sheridan, MSW, PhD

Human beings have known since the beginning of time that interaction with nature can be a source of healing and renewal. Direct and mindful connection with the earth provides sustenance, comfort, wonder, challenge, peace, beauty, and nurturance in a way that cannot be found elsewhere. Social workers and many others are increasingly recognizing this ancient and ever-abiding wellspring of transformation by proposing practice approaches that directly engage the human with the nonhuman world (Besthorn, 2002; Besthorn & Tegtmeier, 1999; Coates, 2003; Cohen, 1997; Durning, 1995; Roszak, Gomes, & Kanner, 1995; Winter, 2003).

One example of an earth-centered approach to practice is Besthorn's (2003) Eco-Spiritual Helping (ESH), a multifaceted model of healing concepts and practices that is based on three overarching principles: *(1)* "healing individual alienation from the earth by enhancing openness to being nurtured by nature in a manner that is both intentional and frequent," *(2)* "enable[ing] clients to become more aware of the spiritual or transpersonal dimension of their experience with the natural world," and *(3)* "assist[ing] clients in adopting more earth-caring lifestyles and belief patterns that focus on contributing to an ecologically and socially just and sustainable society" (pp. 10–11). This third principle of ESH explicitly links "ecological, political and economic contributors to . . . personal or familial pain" (p. 11). The overall goal of this helping approach is to deepen clients' sense of their connection with nature, with themselves, and with their communities and thereby facilitate a process toward healing and wholeness.

Another example of employing earth as a healing modality is Chard's (1994) engaging book entitled *The Healing Earth: Nature's Medicine for the Troubled Soul.* He provides several descriptions of employing earth as his "co-therapist," with wonderfully transformative results. In one case, he sits with a woman in a state park listening to the sounds—the lullabies—of nature to help heal her profound feelings of homesickness and aloneness. In another instance, he sends a man out into the country during the dead of winter to answer the questions: "What is alive? What is dead? What is the difference?" In yet another story, a woman who had suffered many losses finds a way to grieve and heal through digging a garden with her bare hands. Chard offers several creative exercises and ceremonies for use with clients in their journeys toward healing that could easily be incorporated into social work practice.

In my own experience as a social work practitioner and educator, the powerful potential of nature to inspire, restore, and transform has also been evident. I share the following "snapshots" as simple examples of earth as source of spirit.

Snapshot #1

In a maximum security prison, a circle of men are discussing how they keep going within a world of concrete, locked gates, razor wire, and guard towers. This is an ongoing group for inmates with substance abuse problems who are trying to put recovery into their lives. I am facilitating a guided imaging session with them about finding a "safe place" inside, asking them to deepen their sense of this place—its visual details, its smells, its textures, how it makes them feel inside. When it is time to share what they've found during the exercise, the pervasive power of nature comes through:

"Well, my safe place is a particular spot by the river near by where I grew up. Me and my brothers would go there in the summer when it was really hot, you know. And we'd jump off that river bank into the cool water—over and over again until it was so dark we had to go home 'cause we couldn't see anymore. Man, I loved that place."

"I went in my mind to the grassy space beside the Washington Monument. There's just lots and lots of pretty green grass there. I used to lie on my back and just watch the sky and clouds for hours. No one thought to look for me there."

"Mine is this tree in a park. I could climb up there and hide out. I could watch all the craziness going on below me and still feel safe."

"I talk with the moon here every night, when I walk to the main building to polish the floors. I always pause and see if I can see her and how big or small she is and, I don't know, it just makes me feel kinda peaceful and like I can make it another day."

One by one, every man—most of whom had grown up in inner cityscapes and who had been behind bars for at least 10 years—brought forth a cherished image of earth that made them feel safe, made them feel connected, made them feel whole.

Snapshot #2

I am working with 10 adolescents in an urban summer work program. The program is designed to be a work opportunity, a lesson in ecology, and a mentoring program for "at-risk" youth. The task at hand is to clean out a creek that runs through a city park, which also houses various animals and birds. We are to start at the part of the creek that begins in the bison pen and ends at the seal pool. The creek is full of all kinds of trash and debris and, in some places, is so grown up that the water barely trickles by. All 10 kids live in various housing projects in town; homespaces of concrete, sparse grass, litter, and asphalt. All 10 show up the first day in their most fine, "look at me" clothes. I am in old jeans, t-shirt, and rubber boots, with a shovel in my hand. I point to a pile of boots and shovels and tell them they all have to get into the water and the mud—up close and personal. "Man, are you crazy, lady? I ain't messing up my clothes in that mess!" The guy from the city tells me I'll be lucky if I get them to do any work at all. I punt that day and get them to wear different clothes after that. The first couple of weeks are spent trying to get them to not automatically kill every living creature that they come across. Slowly, ever so slowly, the fear of nature is replaced with awe and curiosity about her wonders—fish, flowers, bugs, rocks, little magic pools of water. A major breakthrough comes when we spend an entire afternoon transporting fish from a shallow part of the creek to a deeper part. I'll never forget the look on each face as they lovingly carry each creature in their hands, careful not to drop them or the precious water that surrounds them. And as the reverence for the wildlife they encounter grows, the care for one another emerges. Less harsh put-downs, less fake profiling, more honest expressions of affection, more opening of painful stories. We sit one day and listen to a young girl explain why she has a scar down the whole midsection of her stomach, a mark left by a drunken stepfather with a knife. She is the only white youth among the other nine African-American kids and had struggled to belong. They listen, they witness, they do not judge. They create sacred space for her and for each other among the grass, the critters, the mud, and the water. At the end, we finish the project ahead of time and have to ask for more work to do. The sense of pride and ownership is palpable.

Snapshot #3

A specialized group is being offered for women in a residential, drug treatment center. The group is being facilitated by two graduate students who are both scared and excited about doing this "meditation nature thing" with a group of real clients as part of their research project on stress reduction. I am their research teacher—I am a little scared and excited, too. This kind of project represents "new ground" for the research sequence. The students have developed an 8-week program and have worked very hard to create what they hope will be meaningful exercises. They enter the process with fearful questions: Will the women be willing to try the exercises? Will they think it's just too "fruit-loopy"? Will it make any difference in their lives? Each week, a report comes back.

"They had a little bit of a hard time getting the meditation part, but the recording of the ocean sounds helped a lot."

"We actually got to go outside today, and they loved just being able to relax out there."

"They're really opening up a lot about their lives, especially the pain of not having their kids with them."

"They're telling us that the connection to nature is really helping with the stress of being in treatment."

At the end, the data show some statistical significance and the students are elated. But the real findings are in the stories, the reflections on the part of both the women and the students. The lines between helper and client have softened as each person has shared in the healing powers of the natural world.

Snapshot #4

I find myself to be a tired, overworked, running-on-empty academic. I feel joyless, dispirited, unconnected to anything of real meaning. A thought occurs to me one day—a frightening thought. I realize that I can get up every day, walk out of my city house onto the sidewalk, get in my car, drive to my office, step out onto sidewalk again, and into the concrete building. And reverse the process in the evening. And I become painfully aware that I have done this day after day, never putting my feet on earth. No wonder I am feeling "groundless." How did I let this happen? I make a vow to put my feet on earth every day and I discover a tiny, vibrant world of nature in my back alley—complete with an over-100–year-old elm tree that is just magnificent and gives me wise counsel when I ask. I start noticing the sky again. Feathers find me, one coming up to rest on the threshold of my front door. I bring in images of nature for opening meditations prior to beginning each class session. I bring in elements of nature for closing ceremonies in my classes, and bring my students rocks from my various travels. And with each inclusion—each recognition or remembering—of my true home, my earth home, my spirit begins to recover and I have more to give.

In these brief snapshots, the capacity of the natural world to bring power, counsel, joy, comfort, and a sense of belonging is hopefully evident. The sacred gifts of earth are truly "sources of spirit" that social work must recognize and utilize as we simultaneously address the very serious threats to existence that face us now. Some speculate that we could manage to figure out a way to continue human life on a treeless, airless, waterless, creature-less, earth-less planet through technological processes that somehow maintained physical life in some sort of bizarre, synthetic bubble-land upon a totally destroyed planetary rock. I assert that even if we could continue to exist without the natural world, much of what constitutes life would be lost. I believe that we would lose the very essence of our being, because the natural world is as much about nurturing and protecting our spiritual selves as it is about maintaining our physical selves.

As Chard so eloquently states: "there is more wisdom in the voices of wind and water than can be found in any talk show, self-help tome, or politician;

there is as much spiritual sustenance in a night sky or a misty morning as an ornate cathedral or charismatic sermon; and there is more life purpose in growing a garden than in many careers, and more education in exploring a marsh, pond, or prairie than can be gained from months in a classroom" (1994, p. 14). Earth is truly a source of spirit in all its manifestations.

References

Besthorn, F. H. (2002). Natural environment and the practice of psychotherapy. *Journal of the American Psychotherapy Association, 5*(5), 19–22.
Besthorn, F. H. (2003, February). *Eco-spiritual helping and group process: Earth-based perspectives for social work practice.* Presentation at the Annual Program Meeting of the Council on Social Work Education, Atlanta, Georgia.
Besthorn, F. H., & Tegtmeier, D. (1999) Opinions/perspectives/beliefs: Nature as professional resource—A new ecological approach to helping. *Kansas Chapter NASW News, 24*(2), 15.
Chard, P. S. (1994). *The healing earth: Nature's medicine for the troubled soul.* Minnetonka, MN: NorthWord Press.
Coates, J. (2003). *Ecology and social work: Toward a new paradigm.* Halifax, Nova Scotia, Canada: Fernwood Books.
Cohen, M. J. (1997). *Reconnecting with nature: Finding wellness through restoring your bond with the earth.* Corvallis, OR: Ecopress.

Durning, A. T. (1995). Are we happy yet? In T. Roszak, M. Gomes, & A. Kanner (Eds.), *Ecopsychology: Restoring the earth, healing the mind* (pp. 68–76). San Francisco: Sierra Club Books.
Roszak, T., Gomes, M. E., & Kanner, A. D. (1995). *Ecopsychology: Restoring the earth, healing the mind.* San Francisco: Sierra Club Books.
Winter, D. D. (2003). *Ecological psychology: Healing the split between planet and self.* Mahwah, NJ: Erlbaum.

Source: *Spirituality and Social Work Forum*, 2004, *10*(2), 14–15. Printed with permission of the Society for Spirituality and Social Work Forum and Michael J. Sheridan.

A celebration with a close connection to the bounty of the earth and the harvest is the African American Kwanzaa. Such ceremonies and rituals as are represented in the Kwanzaa holiday celebration play an important role in providing meaning and purpose in life, bringing the generations together, enhancing a collective sense of peace and harmony, as well as connections to the sacred (Canda & Furman, 2010). We can add to that pride in one's cultural and ethnic heritage. Read Box 9.2 for a detailed description of this event, which took place on December 29, 2009 in Bowling Green, Kentucky. Figures 9.5 and 9.6 relate to this reading.

Figure 9.4. Kentucky woods. Many people seek a spiritual presence in nature. Photo by Robert van Wormer.

Box 9.2 *Kwanzaa for Intergenerational Sustainability*

Katherine van Wormer

This year I attended my first Kwanzaa celebration at the First Christian Church in Bowling Green, Kentucky. I entered in time to join in the singing of "Bringing in the Sheaves," a hymn that aptly reflected the harvest theme of the celebration. As described in the program:

Why We Celebrate Kwanzaa

Kwanzaa is a Swahili word that means "first fruits." From December 26 to January 1, the African American Celebration of Kwanzaa occurs. It is a celebration based on African traditions when the ancestors gathered together to celebrate the harvesting of the first crops. After the harvest was over, the entire community engaged in singing, dancing, eating, and drinking. Everyone gathered together to give collective thanks for the collective effort that made the community prosperous. We should always remember that collective work and responsibility, living together, sharing the fruits of our labor, are traditional among African cultures. Our recovery of Kwanzaa is just one aspect of our movement towards Nationhood. By affirming the celebration of Kwanzaa, we begin to create traditions that will be passed on to yet unborn generations of African people when we become the ancestors. By coming together to give thanks and to enjoy the blessing of living and working collectively, we give concrete expression to our *Imani* (faith) in our people and righteousness and victory to our struggles.

Saundra Starks (see Figure 9.5), associate professor of social work at Western Kentucky University, was the "Mistress of Ceremonies." Standing behind a display of assorted fruit, corn, a libation cup, African sculpture, and an autobiography of Barack Obama, she explained the Kwanzaa symbols, discussed the lighting of the candles, and introduced the participants. The candles are black, red, and green; black represents the people of Africa; red, the blood of struggle of the ancestors; and green stands for growth and prosperity. Chief among the symbols was the *kinara* or display of seven candles, each representing one of the major principles of Kwanzaa.

The Seven Principles are as follows:

1 *Umoja* (Unity)—Striving for and maintaining unity within the family, community, nation, and race. Candle lit by members of the Taylor Chapel AME Church Lay Organization.
2 *Kujichagulia* (Self-Determination)—Defining ourselves, naming ourselves, creating for ourselves, and speaking for ourselves instead of being defined, named, created for, and spoken for by others. Candle lit by individuals from the New Beginnings Church.
3 *Ujima* (Collective Work and Responsibility)—Building and maintaining our community together and making our brother's and sister's problems ours to work out together. Candle lit by members of the Association of Black Social Workers.
4 *Ujamma* (Cooperative Economics)—Building and maintaining our own markets, stores, and other businesses and profiting from them together. Candle lit by guests from State Street Baptist Church.
5 *Nia* (Purpose)—Making our collective goal the building up of our community, restoring our people to greatness. Candle lit by members of Mt. Zion Baptist Church.
6 *Kuumba* (Creativity)—Leaving our community more vibrant, vital, and more beautiful than we inherited it. Candle lighting by alumnae from the Bowling Green chapter of Delta Sigma Theta Sorority.
7 *Imani* (Faith)—The Seventh night of Kwanzaa. To believe with all our hearts in the goodness of people, the strength of the community, the courage of our teachers and leaders, the righteousness and the victory of the struggle toward wholeness, health, healing, justice, and the power of the creator to sustain. The final candle was lit by members of the First Christian Church, which held the celebration.

Following the lighting of the candles, the group transitioned into the fellowship hall led by the African drummers to form a circle around the labyrinth. This symbolized community joining together and a centering before sharing the meal, which was then blessed. The celebration feast that followed is called a *karumu*. The food was provided by the host and community organizations; the menu consisted of Hoppin' John soup (black-eyed pea soup), African peanut butter soup (both regular and hot and spicy), chili, cheese, fruit, crackers, nuts, and assorted fruits. Beverages were water, tea, coffee, and juices.

In a personal interview following the celebration, Saundra Starks filled me in on some additional information. She had organized not one, but several Kwanzaa events in the community and for family members. One was at a Kentucky state juvenile institution and another at a white evangelical church. Although the latter group had been initially skeptical and concerned that there was no worship of God during the ceremony (there was a reference to the Creator), the program was well received by the church and especially by a group of sometime rowdy children whom the church was sponsoring. In the future, given the warm response to Kwanzaa by diverse community groups, this spiritual celebration of the season can be expected to grow. Next year I will be there too, as will be some of my family members.

Social Work's Early Religious/ Spiritual Heritage

Mainstream Protestantism

The rapid industrialization, urbanization, territorial expansion, and economic uncertainty that characterized the post–Civil War period marked a time of great change in American culture. But change does not come without great human and social cost. Though spurred by unblemished confidence in the notion of industrial progress, frontier-minded individualism, and the belief in self-sufficiency, these heady and time-honored ideas were gradually coming under increasing criticism as the nineteenth century progressed. They were ultimately to yield to a new and more critical consciousness of the human condition and the social contract (Axinn & Levin, 1975; Boyer, 1978).

In the pre–Civil War period, prior to heavy industrialization, "most people lived in communities with an array of institutions that afforded a high degree of self-sufficiency. Survival necessitated a degree of solidarity or interdependence

that was taken as a law of nature" (Karger & Stoesz, 1990, p. 35). Social welfare in America during this period was largely viewed as the responsibility of private institutions and individuals, often localized and coordinated by small church communities to enhance the welfare of individuals and communicants. (See Figure 9.7 of a group of Mennonites. The members of this group live on rural farms and maintain the community values of an earlier day. Hynm singing is a large part of their heritage.)

Reliance on voluntary associations to solve social problems characterized nineteenth-century relief efforts. Poverty was viewed as a limited, though inevitable, result of the social organization of communities, but with faith and effort individual opportunities existed within the system for many, if not most, to overcome its restrictive bounds (Kemp, 1994). It was "pauperism rather than poverty as such" (Spano, 1982, p. 12) that captured the attention of the Protestant church and of many concerned individuals involved in relief efforts. Pauperism was a state of mind—a moral flaw connected to a state of spiritual depravity—that contributed to a state of poverty for some. It was not synonymous with poverty, was thought to be more widespread than poverty, and existed more or less independent of the socioeconomic system. It was the result of some defect in individual character, such as drunkenness, idleness, moral laxity, or truncated work ethic, and it was best eradicated through moral rehabilitation (Kemp, 1994; Spano, 1982).

As westward expansion prior to the Civil War continued at an accelerated pace and as population increased correspondingly, the magnitude of the escalating number of social problems could no longer be easily attributed to lack of effort or individual defect. Spano (1982) summarizes the changing social climate:

> Due to this tremendous growth, cities faced nearly overwhelming problems in housing, health, sanitation, crime, unemployment, transportation and poor relief. The existing social institutions lacked both the technological capacities and the philosophical foundations to cope with these problems. The combination of

Figure 9.5. Kwanzaa. Saundra Starks welcomes the guests to the celebration feast that concludes the Kwanzaa celebration. Photo by Robert van Wormer.

sheer numbers, combined with the heterogeneity of the new arrivals in American cities, increased the complexity of the problems and the frantic search for their solutions. (p. 14)

The period of time after America's devastating Civil War was a watershed period in the history of religion and social work in American life. The ending of the war and the victory of northern unionists, although securing freedom

Figure 9.6. Kwanzaa. Children celebrate their African heritage at the annual Kwanzaa celebration in Bowling Green, Kentucky. Photo by Robert van Wormer.

Figure 9.7. Mennonites share this moment of worship during the Christmas season in the home of a former Mennonite. Photo by Robert van Wormer.

for millions of slaves, left a nation divided, economically depressed, religiously adrift, and socially stratified. The social, cultural, intellectual, and spiritual problems associated with increased immigration, urban squalor, the rise of modern science, and the dominance of an industrialized and corporate American economic landscape were not easily understood or managed by the average citizen or the religious institutions that had, for over a century, been a stabilizing influence in ensuring American social cohesiveness.

Protestantism was by far the dominant religious force in American culture from the very early years of the nation. And, prior to the Civil War, Protestantism was reasonably effective in responding to the localized, small-scale, community-centered social problems of its day. Indeed, American Protestantism was one of the main impetuses in the growth of the voluntary social service sector in pre-Civil War society. But as Manthey (1989) notes, whereas pre-Civil War Protestantism was characterized by firm theological and ideological grounding and the capacity to ward off disunity, post-Civil War Protestantism was characterized by a tendency toward disunity, inadequate theology, limited

technology, and an antiquated polity system incapable of responding to the incipient encroachment of modernism and mounting nationwide social upheaval.

At about this same time, the young profession of social work was beginning to enter the social service scene of American life. There can be little doubt that the beginnings of the social work profession in the United States had a strong sectarian heritage, which has shown a resilient and continuing historical trajectory. It has often been associated with a Christian human service ethos from its very early years (Canda & Furman, 2010). But perhaps that is too simplistic a generalization to help us understand the emerging socio-religious moorings of the young profession. In most ways, both ideologically and religiously, early social work shared many commonalities with the dominant, mainstream Protestant religious system of the day. Given the rampant anti-Catholicism of the post–Civil War period—precipitated by the influx of large numbers of Irish Catholic immigrants—the backlash against modernism, and the deep skepticism of the day, it is not hard to see how social work developed in a manner that was inherently conservative, pietistic, and focused on *interiorized revivalism*—the insistence on internal spiritual and moral change in order to energize effort toward greater outward behavioral modification. Social work's original helping creeds, particularly those of the early charity organization societies, were very often strict behavioral epigrams that emphasized individual moral failure and the need for a revival of spirit.

Charity organization societies (COSs) began as an effort to coordinate relief giving by operating community-wide registration bureaus in order to provide direct relief and education for both the poor and the upper class (Leiby, 1978). As we saw in the previous chapter, the provision of services and moralism were intertwined. Universal relief would eventually, however, also bring into question capitalism's reliance on the unquestioned sanctity of the Protestant work ethic and would be practically very difficult to control once it began. Relief was to be dispensed "only when starvation was imminent" (Axinn & Levin, 1975), for, as Alexander Johnson (1901) feared, for the poor "the first taste of alms is often like a tiger's first taste of blood" (cited in Kemp, 1994, p. 68).

Though friendly visiting was the heart and soul (Paine, 1901) of the COS, it increasingly found its intellectual grounding nested clearly in the emerging scientific paradigm. This marked a shift of emphasis away from the austere strictures of Protestant biblicism. Many social workers of the late nineteenth century saw no inherent conflict between the religious impulse and the scientific endeavor. They were not viewed as incompatible enterprises (Fitzpatrick, 1990; Kemp, 1994). Many social scientists, particularly sociologists, were committed to social reform, and many volunteered for the COSs and, later, the settlement houses.

By the early 1900s, COS workers became increasingly aware that the abysmal urban conditions so rampant during this time could not simply be attributed to faulty religious or moral character and did not lend themselves well to easy or simplistic biblical exhortations. This change toward a rational, well-organized, efficient method of relief was to eventually bring the COSs into open conflict with the mainline Protestant churches at the close of the nineteenth century.

As the twentieth century approached, tectonic shifts took place in the social fabric of American life and culture. Demographically, the country changed from predominantly rural to largely urban. By 1900 nearly half of the entire population was urbanized (Baltzell, 1964). The wealth of the nation was growing generally while at the same time the disparity between the rich and the poor was increasing. Laissez-faire economy ideology prevailed, while poverty, child labor, intermittent cycles of economic depression, tenement squalor, labor strikes, alcoholism, urban congestion, and family breakdown were on a precipitous rise. Mainstream Protestant religious institutions of the day were ill prepared to deal with these kinds of trenchant problems. Additionally, religion generally was under assault by the new scientism that was sweeping the intellectual and academic communities—most notably Darwin's evolutionary theory, Freud's new psychology of the mind, and the higher biblical criticism emanating from Europe. Higher criticism brought literary, scientific, and historical analysis to the heretofore unchallenged textual authority of the biblical manuscripts (Hofstadter, 1955).

How did Protestantism respond to the intellectual, scientific, and socioeconomic challenges of this time? In short, one could say not well at all. Mainstream Protestantism failed intellectually, organizationally, spiritually, and methodologically in its response to the social problems of newly emerging industrial America. From the close of the Civil War and through the early twentieth century, the majority of American Protestantism was conservative and evangelistic, lost in its own internal, institutional debates, largely able to shield itself from the newer thinking regarding evolution and biblical criticism while having reached, in the words of May (1977, p. 51), "the summit of complacency." Again, Manthey (1989) sums up the prevailing mood of mainstream Protestantism by saying that it:

had a great confidence in the prevailing social and economic order. It supported laissez-faire. It viewed poverty as inevitable. Any intervention was to be approached with reserve. It believed that if the poor were patient enough, the natural automatic forces would bring relief. Individual greed and an individualistic ethic would bring prosperity. . . . Protestantism did not speak out against the social injustices so rampant at this time. Those that did were very rare exceptions. . . . The churches supported the railroads against the laborers . . . accusing the unions of being despotic and revolutionary. . . . It developed an ethic of exclusiveness in relations to the new immigrants. (pp. 78–79)

The Social Gospel

Not all of Protestantism ignored the strident social, economic, labor, and cultural turmoil that seemed to be enveloping American life at the turn of the twentieth century. A new form of Protestant Christianity, sometimes referred to as a Social Gospel or a Social Christianity, was to take shape that not only recognized these new problems but also believed that a deeper, more esoteric Gospel message provided explicit guidance as to how to alleviate them. The Social Gospel movement was liberal Protestantism's response to two interconnected shortcomings perceived to exist in the social structures of the day. One was the failure of unregulated capitalism, which was running unrestrained and unfettered in newly industrialized America and as a result lavished economic benefit on a select few while marginalizing millions. The second failure was the unwillingness and lack of skill of mainstream Protestant churches to adequately address the environmental (social, economic, political, and physical) circumstances of human misery and poverty (May, 1977) and thus their failure to critique the shadowy side of the capitalist enterprise.

The Social Gospel movement had become a part of every major Protestant denomination in America during the early twentieth century. There were several major spokespersons for the early movement, including Washington Gladden, Horace Bushnell, F. G. Peabody, and Walter Rauschenbusch (May, 1977). A bit later, Harry Emerson Fosdick came to public prominence and took up the standard for social

gospelers, thus becoming the epicenter for a red-hot controversy that was beginning to emerge between modernist and fundamentalist Christians. Each of the spokespersons, in his or her own way, saw the inherent evils of unregulated capitalism and the complicity of mainline Protestantism in becoming instruments and allies of the American social and political establishment. The religious and secular establishment supported the economy's domination by robber barons, ignored extreme income disparity, and turned a blind eye to the unjust practice of sweatshops and child labor (Bawer, 1997).

Proponents of the Social Gospel also questioned the traditional Protestant doctrine of substitutionary atonement—that Jesus' death was compensation for the sins of humankind. Instead, they relied on the importance of *living as Jesus lived* rather than believing in a prescribed set of doctrines *about Jesus*. The clear focus was on the humanity of Jesus—a unique person who lived out of a distinctive and special relationship with the Divine but who himself was not divine. The Social Gospelers were open to and often allied with political science, economics, social work, sociology, and the labor movement. Many were especially intrigued by the new science of evolution, which gave credence to their emerging ideas that God's activity was immanent on earth; that is, that God was involved and present in the activities and movement of life forces on earth and not simply at hand as some ethereal apparition from on high. For them, evolution represented a compelling way in which God could be thought of as having eternal being and active participation in the activities of earth.

The Christianity of the Social Gospelers was an activist, social Christianity that identified with Jesus as master, mentor, and social reformer rather than savior and lord. The Social Gospelers' faith was in realizing the Kingdom of God now, in this place, at this time. They were instrumental in creating associations and alliances with labor unions fighting for worker rights. They formed the contours of the Christian ecumenical movement and played a pioneering role in development of the advanced techniques of social survey, investigation, and reasoned social analysis (Manthey, 1989). In the words of Bawer (1997), the social gospel:

> came to be about: spreading the kingdom. . . . the gospel was central to Christianity, and central to the gospel, in turn, was the concept of the kingdom of God . . . spreading the kingdom did not mean hell-fire evangelism; it meant seeking to lead a Christlike life. Jesus had come . . . not to die in an act of substitutionary atonement but rather to substitute love for selfishness as the basis of human society." Yet Christians had forgotten that purpose. They had forgotten . . . that Christianity is in its nature revolutionary. (p. 93)

It was, in particular, Walter Rauschenbusch who gave the Social Gospel movement one of its earliest, most fervent, and most well-reasoned theological voices. Rauschenbusch, a northern Baptist minister educated at Rochester Theological Seminary and unwavering in his advocacy for a Christianity deeply connected to the social injustices of culture, was perhaps the first Protestant minister and theologian of his day to suggest that society, as well as individuals, was sinful. That is, social institutions, social practices, social contracts, and social arrangements could be as deeply imbedded with the original stain of separation from God as any individual and that this social sin had far more severe and profound implications for the masses than did personal sin. For many, this represented the height of heresy and a rank abandonment of traditional Christian principles. But for Rauschenbusch, recognizing societal sin was returning Christianity to its social roots and away from its more recent traditions, which had become far too narrowly focused on the individual. To this end Rauschenbusch wrote:

> Because the individualistic conception of personal salvation has pushed out of sight the collective idea of a Kingdom of God on earth, Christian men seek for the salvation of individuals and are comparatively indifferent to the spread of the spirit of Christ in the political, industrial, social, scientific and artistic life of humanity, and have left these as the

undisturbed possessions of the spirit of the world. (as quoted in Bawer, 1997, p. 94)

The Social Gospel came to the forefront during the height of the Progressive Era and found natural allies with the young social work profession. It was into this world of possibility and promise that a fully recognizable and increasingly well-established profession of social work was beginning to find roots. The Progressive Era encompassed a conflicting mixture of fear, dissatisfaction, reform, and rising confidence. The Social Gospelers and social workers found common cause in the reformist fervor and political transformation efforts that characterized this era. What evolved during the Progressive Era was a cautious allegiance between the sacred and secular impulses to improve the life of marginalized masses in modern society. Progressive Christianity and social work shared a robust belief in the environment as a powerful and dynamic force shaping human development. Concomitant with the reform-minded thinking on environment was a growing conviction that persons had the inherent capacities to achieve positive change through a deliberate modification of their environment (Goldman, 1977). This emerging focus on change through personal capacity and environmental reform marked a unique integration of the personal, the sacred, and the political. It shifted attention from individual deficiency and passive adaptation toward the impact of environmental factors and the individual's capacity to change them.

The movement that assumed a major share of responsibility for social welfare in the late nineteenth and early twentieth centuries and that shared a significant affinity with the Social Gospel was the settlement house movement. Social work settlements relied on the model of so-called *institutional churches* or *religious settlements*, which were largely created in the spirit of the Social Gospel movement (Manthey, 1989). Institutional churches or social settlements were large, high-status old churches in downtown urban areas that had been largely abandoned by the retreat of the upper and middle classes from the inner city. Institutional churches often had paid staff members and large numbers of volunteers who served the religious, educational, artistic, and recreational needs of the poor and new immigrant masses. It was this distinctive form of progressive Christianity that was fused to form the basis of the secular settlements' unique outlook (May, 1977; Szasz, 1982).

Methodologically, the religious and secular settlement movements were oriented toward group change rather than individual adjustment. The focus of change rested in the collective as the source of community development (Boyer, 1978). Mutuality and shared responsibility and the desire to harness the social initiative of the poor were a driving force behind both movements (Leiby, 1978). Although they did not reject individual services to the poor, the settlements were essentially reform oriented.

The ascendancy of Jane Addams to the presidency of the National Conference on Charities and Corrections in 1910 marked a culmination of a decade-long turn toward the larger social environment as the center of change activity, as well as confirmation of the increasing commonality and shared ideological vision between the Social Gospel movement, the religious settlements, and the social work settlement house movement (Kemp, 1994; Manthey, 1989). Assuredly, there were chasms and difficulties between social work and the Social Gospel. Some feared that the secular settlements were becoming far too irreligious, and the religious settlements feared that they were losing their influence to their secular brethren.

Despite differences, for Jane Addams and others like her, the efforts of the institutional church won admiration and recognition from the early social work settlement house movement (Baltzell, 1964). Jane Addams was deeply religious and had come to social work only after rejecting a missionary career. The Social Gospel leaders of her day were very powerful influences in her personal life and on her conceptualizations of social work (Baltzell, 1964). Addams often writes respectfully about the thought of Social Gospel pioneers. She served as an associate editor of *The Kingdom*, a prominent Social Gospel periodical of its day, and was in attendance at many conferences and gatherings organized by Social Gospelers and settlement workers to address the chaotic social conditions of the day.

The significance of the movement as a contributor to social work generally and the settlement movement particularly cannot be underestimated. This contribution is evidenced by the 1903 National Conference on Charities and Corrections, which was devoted almost exclusively to the role of the church and social work in meeting the challenges of the newly stratified and increasingly poor social order. Further cross-fertilization is seen in the 1907 issue of the *Annals of the American Academy of Religion and Social Sciences*, which dedicated the entire issue to social work, religious and secular settlements, and the church's social responsibility. The Sagamore Sociological Conferences, organized by Social Gospel leaders, are another illustration of the cross-fertilization efforts among social work and the Social Gospel leadership. Addams remarked of the powerful conjunction between individual and social reform that was at the heart of both the social gospel and the settlement movement: "It is as if the Charitable had been brought, through the care of the individual, to a contemplation of social causes, and as if the Radical had been forced to test his social doctrine by a sympathetic observation of actual people" (Addams, 1910, p. 1).

Protestant Fundamentalism

Protestant fundamentalism had its beginnings as a response to mainline Protestantism's seeming accommodation to modernity, the so-called heretical influence of the Social Gospel, the new natural sciences—especially evolution—and higher biblical criticism, which questioned the historicity of Jesus and the veracity of the scriptures (Marty & Appleby, 1994). Prior to the Civil War, evangelicalism—the commitment to and effort toward bringing peoples into a personal relationship with Jesus Christ and the Christian religion through a spiritual rebirth, or a *born-again* experience of faith—was a core element of mainline Protestant identity and practice. Most Protestant churches defined themselves as evangelical. Periodic and, at times, large-scale revivals and so-called mass *awakenings* to Jesus were not uncommon. After the Civil War, as suggested earlier, significant changes were taking place in the social, economic, and cultural structure of American society. A crisis of confidence arose in established institutions, as well as a growing sentiment that traditional religious mooring could not supply the kind of stability and answers to difficult social circumstances that they had once so easily provided. America's Puritan ethic was under suspicion for being too rigid and not responsive to the fast-changing social upheavals of modern industrialism. A huge influx of Catholic immigrants had also shaken the core beliefs and dominance of mainline Protestantism. The new sciences and biblical criticism seemed to pose great dangers to the cherished belief structures of most Protestant evangelicals.

Although most of America's Protestant majorities were evangelical in spirit and practice prior to the Civil War, fundamentalism had not yet found full expression in the parlance of American religious discourse. After the Civil War, however, two distinct camps began to emerge in evangelical Protestantism. They are sometimes referred to as moderate evangelical Protestantism and radical evangelical Protestant (Clabaugh, 1974). It is the radical evangelical fringe that was later to flower into what is commonly referred to as the Protestant fundamentalist movement. Strictly speaking, *evangelical* and *fundamental* are not synonymous terms, though they are frequently used interchangeably. As suggested, most of Protestantism was evangelical prior to the Civil War. Fundamentalism slowly grew out of the more conservative and orthodox sectors of Protestant evangelical churches, such as the Baptists, Presbyterians, Methodists, and Congregationalists. The conservative wings of these major denominations had become radicalized in their beliefs that modern American society had lost its moral ground and was now adrift in the anti-Christian principles of elite, amoral, secular humanists. What gradually emerged was a politically conservative and radically doctrinaire evangelicalism that replaced the Gospel message of love with a peculiar mix of high-minded moralism and apocalyptic fear. The radical evangelicals rejected Darwin's theory of evolution, fearing that it would undermine faith in God, while at the same time accepting social Darwinism

because it tended to support laissez-faire economic policy and American exceptionalism and held people individually responsible for their own poverty (Ahlstrom, 1972; Greeley, 1972, Marsden, 1980).

The early stages of Protestant fundamentalism began with the 1878 Niagara, New York, conference of evangelicals, where the core fundamentalist principles were developed and slowly canonized into a 12-volume anthology that set out the *fundamentals* of the faith. These works, called *The Fundamentals: A Testimony of the Truth* (1913), stress individualist faith expression and the singular and utter importance of personal salvation. They opposed the new natural sciences to the degree that they tended to undermine traditional belief in God. They also opposed higher biblical criticism and any heretical faiths or ideologies that were not consistent with core fundamental Christian doctrines. These core, or fundamental, Christian doctrines were eventually reduced to a five-point declaration of fundamentalist beliefs that became a kind of primer for thousands of individual fundamentalists and for membership in the World Christian Fundamentals Association, which was organized in 1919. These five fundamental points are the verbal, plenary inerrancy or inspiration of Scripture, the virgin birth, the substitutionary atonement of Christ, the bodily resurrection of Jesus, and the authenticity of miracles (Marsden, 1980). The Protestant fundamentalist movement was to grow slowly but was finally to appear on the public stage by the 1920s as an austere, highly rhetorical, and openly conflictual movement that took issue with many dimensions of modern secular and religious life in America. Fundamentalism was adamantly opposed to many aspects of modern science, secular intellectualism, and the liberalizing—often referred to as neo-orthodox—trends of mainline Protestantism. Bawer (1997) describes the way in which fundamentalist fervor also pandered to the most desperate and isolated in the early years of its growth. The fundamentalists:

> with their dramatic rhetoric about the
> threat of hellfire and promise of heaven,
> played expertly on the miseries, anxieties

and resentments of the provincial poor, on their fears of the unknown in this world and the next, on their desperate desire for a paternal, authoritarian figure to give their lives a sense of order and direction, and on their eagerness to believe in the promise of a postmortem existence more worry-free than this one. They have always appealed to the isolated and desperate, to people living on the edge— and such people are generally not inclined to be subject to penetrating critical analysis of the rules, doctrines and faith statements that are presented to them as the key to the Kingdom. So it was with the tent meeting crowds, who early and unreflectingly affirmed the things they were told to affirm. (p. 78)

It is not surprising to note that Protestant fundamentalism was also in open conflict with the young profession of social work. There is little evidence to suggest that any segment of the early social work profession was ever greatly influenced by fundamentalist ideology. Indeed, fundamentalism had a visceral mistrust of collective social action in dealing with the problem of poverty and the socials ills related to it. The strict individualistic tenets of fundamentalist doctrine suggested that industrious behavior, individual effort, individual sobriety, and, most of all, individual salvation and obedience to the Scriptures would lead to the alleviation of poverty and social progress in the context of an individualistic-focused capitalist economy. The welfare state and government charge over the provision of relief was understood in the most pejorative of terms. Some of the more moderate wings of Protestant evangelicalism were indeed responsible for the provisions of significant levels of welfare relief and social reform. Such institutions as the YMCA, private philanthropic agencies, denominational hospitals, city missions, the temperance movement, and the Salvation Army are just a few examples (Ahlstrom, 1972; Hankins, 2009). Radical evangelicalism, however, remained mired in an unrelenting preoccupation with individual salvation as the only significant remedy for both individual and social problems. Truth was

not to be found in rational thought or dedicated study but rather in the strict and literal interpretation of the Bible and in doctrinal absolutism. For the radical, fundamentalist fringe of evangelical Protestantism, conversion and living a sanctified life were the primary mechanisms for solving social ills. In most cases, they understood the sources of poverty and social unrest to be sin, moral defect, alcoholism, foreign provocateurs, and, most tragically, Catholics and Jews (Ahlstrom, 1972; Manthey, 1989).

Modern Fundamentalism: A Religio-Political Neo-Theocracy

Radical evangelicalism, what we have come to call fundamentalism, went through a period of public decline in the aftermath of the so-called Scopes Monkey Trials in the summer of 1925. The public trail in Dayton, Tennessee, had a carnival-like atmosphere and pitted anti-evolutionary forces led by famed populist leader and former presidential candidate, William Jennings Bryant, against a modern, pro-science contingent headed by American Civil Liberties Union lawyer Clarence Darrow (Almond, Appleby, & Sivan, 2003). The trial led to the eventual conviction of John Scopes for teaching evolution in the local high school but had far more portentous ramifications for the fundamentalist victors. The establishment press lampooned and satirized fundamentalist hubris and their anti-modernist, anti-rationalist rhetoric. The public sentiment shifted away from tacit support for fundamentalist causes and commitments. Many, both in rural America and in large cities, began to believe that fundamentalist ardor and their quasi-militarism in defense of the old-time gospel was a genuine threat to American democracy.

While fundamentalism faded into the background of American religious life, this did not mean that it had become extinct. Indeed, the period between the 1920s and the 1960s was for fundamentalism not only a time of retrenchment and separatism but also a period of transition and consolidation of power (Carpenter, 1999). This new phase of fundamentalist evolution was characterized by a focus on expanding the reach and breadth of radical-evangelical Protestantism. The fundamentalist impulse, especially its anti-modernist critique and lament over the secularization and moral decay of American society, began to unite a plethora of like-minded persons and religious groups (Lawrence, 1990). Fundamentalism was slowly becoming an amalgam of disaffected mainline Protestants and Catholics, conservative Mormon, Pentecostal, Holiness, and Revivalist groups (Armstrong, 2001). New denominations emerged or split with their historic forbearers to form a distinctive fundamentalist denominationalism. Gone were the days when fundamentalist adherents attempted to influence religious life within the confines and restraints of mainline churches. Fundamentalist institutions such as Bible colleges, summer Bible conferences, youth summits, ultra-conservative theological seminaries, and mission organizations proliferated during this period.

While these groups were united in their stand against modernism, secular humanism, and their defense of the one, true, Bible-based faith, there were significant doctrinal differences and controversy. Pre-millennial, dispensational fundamentalists tended to distrust and even ridicule Pentecostal focus on the gifts of the spirit— especially *speaking-in-tongues*—and had similar concerns with some aspects of the Holiness movement. There were also misgivings and open disdain for Mormonism in its emerging claim to be a legitimate, though relatively new, member of Protestant Christianity. Many fundamentalists believed that the Restorationist history and extra-biblical claims of The Church of Jesus Christ of Latter-Day Saints were at best cultish deceptions and at worse heretical aberrations of historic Christianity (Kaplan, 2004). Nonetheless, these many new conservative traditions and orientations began to merge and become part of a discernable, ultra-orthodox subculture (Marsden, 2006). The impetus gradually changed from separation from society to joining with and ultimately changing culture along Biblical lines.

Fundamentalism was becoming ever more modern in language, education, socialization, and in its sophisticated utilization of contemporary music, entertainment models, and popular media to spread its message (Smith, 2002). There was an increasing willingness to embrace the secular world in order to attempt changing it.

Fundamentalists were taking on the cultural trappings of modernism even while they maintained a somewhat disingenuous critique of the decline of moral values and rampant secularism associated with modern culture. This period also saw a marked shift away from individual believers and institutions self-referencing as *fundamentalist* to the more acceptable terminology of *evangelical*. Indeed, it had become fashionable for fundamentalist groups to eschew distinctively religious terminology all together and simply to refer to themselves as *people of faith*. This led to the perception that Christian fundamentalists were just one undemanding member of a larger community of believers while at the same time obscuring the exclusivist claims that set them apart from and antagonistic to other religious traditions (Bawer, 1997; Hedges, 2008). In this vein, George Marsden (2006), arguably the most highly regarded religious historian of American fundamentalism notes:

> The loosely organized fundamentalist-evangelical movement was perhaps not the largest in American Protestantism; it now had, however, a solid base of growing institutions which paralleled the older denominational establishments... Their basic attitude toward culture is suggested by their successful appropriation of the more culturally respectable term "evangelical." Yet, although this new evangelical sub-culture repudiated "fundamentalist" as too exclusivist in implication, "fundamentalistic" remains a useful adjective to describe many of its most conspicuous and controversial traits. (p. 195)

American fundamentalism from the 1970s to present has seen its fortunes advance precipitously. Fundamentalism had become an influential and growing social and political phenomenon that was again pushing its way back into the mainstream of American culture. This period marked the ascendency of fundamentalism to the apogee of American political life. Again, Marsden (2006) notes, "the most striking feature of fundamentalism since the 1970s that distinguishes it from its forebears is its deep involvement in mainstream national politics" (p. 232). The rise of the fundamentalist phenomenon is a complex matrix of both complementary and competing trends. As with any historical evolution, no single calculus can be given to explain precisely how American fundamentalism went from the periphery of American public life into the hallowed halls of local, state, and national government and international geo-political power politics (Harris, 2008). Some date this burgeoning political resurgence to the early 1980s and the so-called conservative revolution, which resulted in the election of Ronald Regan (Kaplan, 2004; Kimball, 2002). Others conclude that significant fundamentalist influence did not fully manifest itself until the election of born-again, Bible-believing Christian George W. Bush in 2000 to the office of the Presidency (Domke, 2004). Whatever its beginning, the catapulting of what has come to be called the *New Christian-Right*—a loose alliance of fundamentalist theology and neo-conservative political ideology—into the very heart of American political life was bolstered by the rise of several religio-political activist groups (Hedges, 2008; Kaplan, 2004). *The Moral Majority*, headed by fundamentalist preacher and mega-church architect the Reverend Jerry Falwell; *The Christian Coalition*, founded by tele-evangelist and erstwhile presidential candidate, the Reverend Pat Robertson; the family-values focused media empire of Dr. James Dobson's *Focus on the Family*; and neo-conservative, quasi-religious think tanks such as the *Heritage Foundation* were several of the most prominent of a growing array of conservative religio-political organizations making up the New Christian Right (White, 2006).

While the specific focal points and tactics of these disparate groups varied, their interests tended to converge on a variety of theological, social, and political issues. They maintained their historic focus on the verbal, plenary inspiration and inerrancy of scripture; the substitutionary atonement of Jesus Christ; the divinity, virgin birth, and resurrection of Jesus; and the necessity of individual conversion or a born-again experience. There was also coalescing agreement on an ultra-conservative social agenda which tended to be defined in terms of the Christian Right's opposition to a number of social and cultural tendencies they saw as ultimately leading to the breakdown of traditional American values and morals. Contemporary fundamentalists take a strong stand against, among others, homosexuality, same-sex marriage, abortion, stem-cell research, the teaching of evolution, the United Nations, gun control, government support of social services, public education, mainstream environmentalism, cultural pluralism, the socialist indoctrination of higher education, and the deleterious influence of *secular humanism* (Domke, 2004, Kaplan, 2004). To be sure secular humanism, wherever it might be hiding, had become for fundamentalist a code word for the corrosive influence of rational thought, scientific inquiry, reasoned debate, and, indeed, for all that was wrong with American society.

Christian fundamentalists had taken on a strident, militant oppositionalism to godless cultural tendencies while maintaining a kind of quiescent stance of innocent victimization—a deeply felt sense of collective persecution with regard to critiques of their own authoritative and exclusivist claims. Distinguished Duke University religious historian Bruce Lawrence (1990) observes:

> Fundamentalists are oppositional. They do not merely disagree with their enemies, they confront them. While the evil other is an abstract sense of *anomie* or uprootedness, it is located in particular groups who perpetuate the prevailing "secular" ethos. Fundamentalists confront those secular people who exercise political or judicial power. Often they also confront "wayward" religious professionals. (p. 100)

A common ideological strategy of the Christian Right is to deny or significantly minimize their powerful, and in some sectors nearly ubiquitous, influence on America's political, social, and media landscape (Phillips, 2006). Still, at the same time, they claim a marginalized status—seeing themselves as under siege, a persecuted minority standing alone in a sea of worldliness and maltreated by a pernicious form of secular privilege, imposed upon them by a shadowy but dominant new class of secular elites (Newfield, 2008). In this environment, fundamentalist Christians are vocal in their demand that their absolutist claims and exclusivist rhetoric not only be heard but honored (Hedges, 2008; Jacoby, 2008). Challenging, disputing, or criticizing fundamentalist beliefs or their corresponding social agenda is seen as intolerant and tantamount to an openly discriminatory and anti-Christian bias. Again, Lawrence (1989) suggests that one of the defining characterizes of fundamentalism is "the affirmation of religious authority as holistic and absolute, admitting of neither criticism nor reduction; it is expressed through the collective demand that specific creedal and ethical dictates derived from scripture be publicly recognized and legally enforced" (p. 27).

This sense of collective victimization by the dominant, secular culture is perhaps most clearly seen in fundamentalist attitudes toward America's colleges and public universities. Fundamentalist Christian students and campus organizations routinely excoriate professors and administrative personnel for their liberal, left-leaning tendencies, supposed anti-Christian biases, and the professorate's apparently organized efforts to censor students' free expression of their religious beliefs (Adrian, 2007; Limbaugh, 2004). There has been a spate of editorial opinion, embellished punditry, and several highly publicized legal battles which purport to prove that American higher education is not only adversely coercing the consciousness of religious students but is actively involved in a campaign to suppress the expressed beliefs of evangelical/fundamentalist students (Beruhe, 2006; Jaschik, 2005; Ricketts, 2008; Schmalz-bauer, 2002; Steigerwald, 2005). A recent incident and ensuing litigation at Missouri State University is illustrative. This case involved a social work undergraduate who claimed she was discriminated against and disciplined for her evangelical/conservative beliefs, which she had openly acknowledged in a classroom assignment (Ricketts, 2008). While there is still a great deal of controversy in the aftermath of this incident and the resulting litigation, it is clear that there is a small but growing number of similar cases that continue to draw national attention. Social work has been especially singled out as advocating a particularly virulent

form of anti-Christian bias and secular elitism (Melendez & Lasala, 2006; National Association of Scholars, 2007; Will, 2007). *Students for Academic Freedom, the Alliance Defense Fund's Center for Academic Freedom*, the *National Association of Scholars*, the *American Center for Law and Justice*, the *National Alliance Against Christian Discrimination*, and *SpeakUpMovement.org* are several of the most vocal religio-political coalitions actively involved in promoting a neo-conservative, Christian-Right agenda for American higher education.

As discussed earlier, fundamentalism has become actively involved in the political life of the United States. The primary difference between the political aspirations of the new Christian Right and its historic fundamentalist forbearers is the theo-political prominence accorded to a pre-millennial, dispensational worldview and its extensive application to U.S. foreign policy and international affairs. *Pre-millennial dispensationalism* is a complex apocalyptic, pseudo-theology postulating a cataclysmic end-of–time scenario marked by the rise of Anti-Christ, the Rapture of the church of true-believers, a 7-year period of calamitous Tribulation culminating in the Battle of Armageddon, and the return of Jesus to earth to usher in a 1000-year reign of peace and justice. Pre-millennial dispensationalism is a very recent interpretive strand to traditional Christian eschatological studies. It had been, at best, a minority position among many conservative Protestant groups since its development in early nineteenth century Scotland by evangelist and ex-Anglican John Nelson Darby and it's popularization in early twentieth century America by Cyrus I. Schofield (Rossing, 2004). That changed in the late twentieth century, with the printing of two widely popular prophetic publications: Hal Lindsey's *Late Great Planet Earth* (1970) and the 12-volume, multiyear *Left Behind* (1996) series by Tim LaHaye and Jerry Jenkins. Together, both publications sold nearly 90 million copies and both were vigorously predisposed to a pre-millennial, dispensationalism worldview.

The influence of millions of Americans' preoccupation with the Rapture and the Anti-Christ in both private and public discourse is seen in the way that end-time eschatology came to be incorporated into the Christian Right's political agenda and its eventual translation into the foreign policy of the Republican Party generally and the former Bush administration specifically (Hedges, 2008; Phillips, 2006; Sharlett, 2009). This movement of apocalyptic theology into mainstream political life was given legitimacy with the popularization of what has been called Christian Reconstructionism or Dominion Theology (Diamond, 1995, Hedges, 2008). Reconstructionists and Dominionists challenge America's civil religion and the historic separation of church and state. They seek to bring all of American political and cultural life under God's rule. A common strategy is to propound a revisionist history of colonial America, especially a reinterpretation of the writings of the Washington, Jefferson, Franklin, Adams, and Madison. Thus, Dominionists claim that America was founded by Christian patriots, based upon Christian principles and was intended from the very beginning to be a thoroughly Christian nation—an American Theocracy (Meacham, 2007; Phillips, 2006; Rodda, 2006; Waldman, 2009). Marsden (2006) also notes that Christian Reconstructionism is closely aligned with hypercapitalism and corporate domination, and "advocates ultra conservative economic theory and calls for a theocracy" (p. 248).

Dominionist ideology is predicated upon challenging the belief that America works best and is most secure in the context of a pluralistic society where all religions are equally free to practice their unique faith expressions. The political language of Dominionists is peppered with the rhetoric of patriotism, war, holy crusades against the forces of evil, American nationalism and military supremacy, and ardent support for the state of Israel. The Dominionists support for Israeli hegemony in Middle East geopolitics is closely associated with the important role that the Jewish State plays in pre-millennial, end-time scenarios. Indeed, in recent years, the United States has made the ardent protection of Israel a cornerstone to its foreign policy and diplomatic initiatives. For highly politicized, fundamentalist Reconstructionists there is, in Ammerman's (1991) words:

> ...no neutral ground, no sphere of activity outside God's rule. One is either following God in all aspects of life or not following God at all. One is either engaged in godly politics or is participating in the anti-God structures that now threaten the home, the school, and the church.... (pp. 51, 53)

We have reviewed social work's early religious/spiritual development, including ways in which mainstream Protestantism, the Social Gospel, and radical evangelicalism/fundamentalism have influenced the profession and, indeed, all of American cultural life. We shall now turn our attention to the profession's more recent religious/spiritual evolution.

Social Work's Contemporary Religious/Spiritual Heritage

Social work's twentieth century religious and spiritual legacy from the 1920s through much of the 1970s was marked by a 50-year hiatus when focus shifted from the profession's earlier religious orientation to a commitment to professionalization and a secularization of social work helping. This period saw a general shift from the social action orientation of the social gospelers and settlement workers to a sustained interest on individual function and internalized problems of the psyche. This shift was strongly influenced by the profession's alliance with psychiatry and its adoption of Freudian psychoanalytical theory as a more scientific and thus, more professional, framework upon which social work practice might be grounded (Specht & Courtney, 1995).

Psychoanalytical theory provided social workers with an easily accessible and coherently secular body of knowledge that supported their professional ambitions. Even though social workers could not do psychoanalysis, the theory drew their attention away from social and environmental factors associated with pressing social problems to the primacy of individual adjustment and individual treatment through therapy. This doesn't mean there was a total absence of interest in the importance of religion to the practice of social work during this period. It was simply scant and, in the end, did not turn out to be terribly influential. One notable exception was the work of famed American protestant theologian Reinhold Niebuhr, who published *The Contribution of Religion to Social Work* in 1932. Niebuhr wrote eloquently concerning the connection between theology and social action and was scathing in his criticism of a profession that had almost completely abandoned its earlier religious orientation. Written during the dark and dreary early days of the Great Depression, Niebuhr's work made the point that both religion and social work had gone too far in their preoccupation with individual salvation and individual responsibility for pressing social problems (Rice, 2009). He detailed the importance of understanding the human condition in both scientific/rational and religious/spiritual terms and argued that collective human misery and suffering were paradoxically associated with both the oppressive inclination and emancipating impulse of religion.

During the later stages of social work's professionalization history several social work scholars (Biestek, 1956; Imre, 1971; Johnson, 1956; Keith-Lucas, 1960; King, 1965; Spencer, 1956, 1961; Towle, 1965) attempted to revitalize an interest in the profession's earlier religious moorings and to find ways to integrate religion back into the practice of social work. One of these writers, Spencer (1961), developed a six-point statement of core propositions that she felt were central to encouraging social workers involvement in the religious/spiritual lives of their clients. These may be summarized as *(1)* the recognition that almost all humans have spiritual needs and aspirations, *(2)* social workers need to understand and appreciate these needs, *(3)* religious beliefs and practices also play a significant role in individual and community life, *(4)* social workers should be able to enter into the religious/spiritual lives of their clients with the same professional skill as they utilize in other areas of professional practice, *(5)* social workers should encourage clients to call upon religious/spiritual resources in their lives when that is appropriate, and *(6)* social workers need specific professional preparation to work with client's religious and spiritual needs. In many ways, these nearly 50-year-old

central statements still form much of the foundation of the profession's efforts to revitalize and integrate religion and spirituality into social work theory and practice.

The decades from the late 1970s through the mid 1990s saw a marked resurgence of interest in religion and spirituality in social work. This was a time of uncertainty, change, and rediscovery (Marty, 1980). Many social workers were again finding religion and spirituality to be important components of both personal growth and professional practice (Canda & Furman, 2010). This era found social workers calling for a return to the profession's historic foundation of religion and spirituality (Lowenberg, 1988). A diverse range of religious and spiritual perspectives were being discussed, including the integration of ritualistic, meditative, Christian, and Eastern religious orientations into social work education, research, and practice frames (Brandon, 1979, Chu & Carew, 1990; Dudley & Helfgott, 1990; Faver, 1986; Keefe, 1975, 1996; Keith-Lucas, 1985; Laird, 1984; Marshall, 1991; Ressler, 1992; Waltz, Sharma, & Birnbaum, 1990); the importance of including spirituality in social work's *person-in-environment* perspective and the relationship between social work values/ethics and religiosity (Constable, 1983; Leiby, 1985; Salomon, 1976; Siporin, 1982); the association of church, parish, and synagogue with effective social work practice (Berl, 1979, Joseph, 1975, 1987; Linzer, 1979); the applications of shamanism, spiritism, and existentialism to both clinical and community practice (Canda & Furman, 2010; Delgado, 1977; Frey & Edinburg, 1978; Krill, 1996); the problems associated with the rise of global fundamentalism and social work practice (Midgely, 1990; Midgely & Sanzenbach, 1989); and the first efforts to address the importance of nondominant cultural and indigenous spiritual commitments to the practice of social work (Chenault, 1990; Ramirez, 1985). Many of the names in the previous citations are synonymous with the formative years of social work's reemerging interest in religion and spiritual: Canda, Constable, Joseph, Keith-Lucas, Keefe, Krill, and Leiby. This period also saw the founding of a reorganized *North American Association of Christians in Social Work* in 1984 by Dr. Allen Keith-Lucas and *The Society for*

Spirituality and Social Work in 1990 by Dr. Edward Canda. Both organizations have become leading international associations whose aim it is to bring students, scholars, and practitioners together from both Christian and other diverse religious and spiritual perspectives in order to enhance communication and encourage dialogue.

The years between the mid 1990s and the early twenty-first century have been marked by a kind of renaissance of ideas related to religion and spirituality. This reemergence of the transpersonal into social work has significantly broadened the religious and spiritual undercurrents that have existed in social work from its very beginning years. Unlike its earlier sectarian period, the focus of this new developmental phase has tended to be on enlarging definitions of religion and spirituality, while transcending professional and practice boundaries so as to help the profession be more inclusive and honoring of diverse religious and nonreligious spiritual traditions (Canda, 2010; Derezotes, 2006; Russel, 1998). As Canda (2005) has noted, the distinctive feature of this period has been "to transcend boundaries between spiritual perspectives, academic disciplines, nations, governmental and religious institutions, and between humans and nature" (p. 99). For a full chronicle of the historical phases of social work's advances regarding recognition of the importance of spirituality and religion, refer to Table 9.2 developed by Canda and Furman (2010). The timeline shown on the table records an awakening by social work educators to the need to prepare students to address issues regarding the spiritual dimension in human behavior. Note the final development: "whole earth perspectives on spirituality introduced," which echoes a major theme of this human behavior textbook.

This period also saw the return of attention to religion and spirituality within the curriculum guidelines of The Council on Social Work Education—Social Work's professional accrediting body—and marked increase in the number of spiritually orientated elective courses being offered in American MSW programs (Russel, 2006). The focus on religion and spirituality is on the increase in the international arena as well. The *Canadian Society for Spirituality and*

Social Work was founded in 2002 by Dr. John Coates and the *Staffordshire University Centre for Spirituality and Health* was established in England in 2005. Social work in Australian and New Zealand has also begun to address the imperative of integrating religion and spirituality into its professional discourse (Furlong, 2006; Gray, 2008; Rice & McAuiffe, 2009; Stirling, Furman, Benson, Canda, & Grimwood, 2009). The professional collective was also rediscovering a substantial and sustained interest in continuing to identify linkages between spirituality and religion, and feminist, postmodern and eco-philosophical worldviews (Besthorn, 2007; Cnaan, 1999; Coholic, 2003; Pardeck, Murphy, & Meinert, 1998) and is expanding more fully into a variety of social work educational and practice settings. This newfound strength of the spirit is being given expression in numerous popular books, articles, textbooks, monographs, presentations, and informal networking of both a sectarian and nonsectarian nature (Bullis, 1996; Canda & Furman, 2010; Derezotes, 2006; Ressler, 1992, 1998; Van Hook, Hugen, & Aguilar, 2001).

Theoretical Perspectives

There have been numerous and diverse attempts to develop theoretical perspectives that can help inform our understanding of spirituality, religion, and their interrelationship. Theoretical models of spiritual and religious development are useful to social workers because they provide a general framework of how people understand and incorporate these constructs into their lives. As with any theoretical orientation, it is important to keep in mind that no model captures the complete essence of any given phenomenon. They are, at best, snapshots that give us an incomplete and all-too-linear perspective that runs the risks of being too simplistic and of communicating the idea that development follows a successive hierarchical ordering. It must also be acknowledged that these models represent a modern, Western, highly individualistic worldview and may not be useful in describing spiritual/religious development from a non-Western perspective.

Table 9.2   Historical Phases in Connection between Spirituality and American Social Work

Phase	Characteristics
One: Indigenous precolonial times	Hundreds of indigenous cultures with spiritually based social welfare systems
	Discrimination, oppression, and mass destructive impacts from European colonial contact and expansion
Two: Sectarian origins (colonial period to early 20th century)	Primarily Christian and Jewish sectarian professional services
	Sectarian ideologies in governmental services
	Beginnings of nonsectarian humanistic spiritual ideologies for social services
Three: Professionalization and Secularization (1920s–1970s)	Professionalization and secularization of social work ideologies and institutions
	Increased professional skepticism of religiously based social work
	Separation of church and state more strictly enforced in social service delivery
	Tacit religious ideologies continue in governmental social services
	Social work education detaches from religion and spirituality
	Sectarian private social service agencies and educational institutions continue
	Beginnings of existential, humanistic, and new nonsectarian approaches to social work
Four: Resurgence of interest in spirituality (1980–1995)	Continuation of private sectarian social work
	Calls for inclusive approach to spirituality
	Increasing diversity of religious and nonreligious spiritual perspectives in social work
	Rapid increase of related research, publication, and networking
	Beginnings of systematic international collaborations
	Return of attention to religion and spirituality in social work education
Five: Transcending boundaries (1995 to present)	Escalation of previous trends
	General and context-specific definitions and research on spirituality refined
	Curriculum guidelines, courses, textbooks widely established
	Postmodern perspectives increased
	Faith-based social services policies formalized
	Interdisciplinary and international networking and collaborations increased
	Empirical studies increased
	Whole earth perspectives on spirituality introduced

Gordon Allport

Gordon Allport was the first contemporary theorist to present a theory of religious development, which he referred to as a model of religious sentiments (Allport, 1950). Religious sentiments are strong and fairly well-defined religious beliefs that are animated by strong emotional energy and that lead to discrete religious and secular behaviors. Religious sentiments were not just idle and/or passing religious inquisitiveness or ritualistic acquiescences to collective social conventions. Rather, they are seminal propositions that have ultimate importance to one's own life. Allport's (1950) model was based on the classic psychological assertion that there is a strong association between belief, emotions, and behavior. According to Allport (1950), the development of religious sentiment or a strong religious orientation to life occurs along three stages. As with many stage-based models, Allport's model held that a person's adult religiosity was very different from that which was experienced in childhood. Allport held that childhood self-consciousness and cognitive ability were not sufficiently developed for the young person to experience the highly complex organization of religious sentiments found most often in adulthood. Allport acknowledged that children may engage in religious activity, such as praying or worship, but that these were more social in character than truly religious (Frame, 2003). Allport (1950) also developed his highly influential distinction between intrinsic and extrinsic religious orientations. The first refers to those who find their religious orientation to be important unto itself—it is a religious expression that is lived. An extrinsic religious orientation is one that is held because it serves other important purposes. Extrinsic religiosity is always instrumental and very utilitarian—it is a religious expression that is used.

Allport (1950) divided religious development into three stages. The first stage is referred as *raw credulity*. In this stage, during young childhood and into middle childhood, children assimilate everything they hear about religion, which comes from parents and other authority figures. This is a time of blind acceptance of dogma, religious doctrine, or spiritual orientation. This first stage of development toward deeper religious sentiment is characterized by an unwavering commitment to and unquestioning attitude toward one's particular belief system. Children have a great need to bond and feel a sense of belonging and, because of this, strict religious belief systems often provide a sense of belongingness and steadfastness for children. As with many models of this type, Allport's (1950) model posits that adults could get stuck at this earlier stage of development and exhibit child-like beliefs well into adulthood that would be characterized as juvenile or illogical.

The second stage of religious development is referred to as *satisfying rationalism*. This stage begins in adolescence, when teens start to question beliefs held during childhood. This questioning may lead to a rejection of the religion of their parents and of their own childhood experience. In place of traditional religious orientations, adolescents may ascribe to a satisfying rationalism that provides a logical, reasoned safe place to stand while the adolescent more fully explores his or her unique and personal spiritual and religious evolution. In the final stage, which begins sometime after adolescence, the adult is able to find a place of comfort with spiritual and religious issues that allows him or her to move between the polarities of uncertainty and deeper commitment. This final stage — referred to as *religious maturity*—recognizes that adult religious development is characterized by an ability to stay attached to a religious tradition while at the same time critically reflecting on and questioning its core tenets and doctrines. Allport (1950) recognized that not all adults reach this level of religious maturity. Some will retain the faith of their childhood, characterized by egocentrism and wish fulfillment, whereas others will move on to a kind of comfortable agnosticism that allows for both doubt and faith. (See Table 9.3.)

James Fowler

James Fowler (1981) created the most used and arguably most comprehensive theory of religious/spiritual development. Fowler's work was heavily influenced by Erikson, Piaget, and Kohlberg and relied on intensive interviews with subjects ranging in age from 3 to 84. His model is made up of six or seven stages, depending on whether one counts the first stage, *primal faith*, as an actual developmental stage. Either way, the stages correspond to certain ages, and people pass through them sequentially from younger to older. Fowler points out that it is not possible to skip stages, nor is it inevitable that people will make transitions from one stage to the next (Frame, 2003). He also felt that there were universal dimensions to faith development that transcended time and cultures and that were not content specific to any particular religious or spiritual tradition. Thus, he chose to refer to his model as a model of faith development rather than religious or spiritual development.

For Fowler (1981), faith is understood to be far broader than traditional conceptualizations,

Table 9.3   Allport's Theory of Religious Sentiments

Stage 1: Raw Credulity	Children (and some adolescents and adults) believe everything they hear about religion and spirituality that comes from parents, clergy, and authority figures
Stage 2: Satisfy Rationalism	Adolescents begin to question their childhood beliefs and may reject their parents' and authority figures' religious and spiritual beliefs in an uncritical and haphazard way.
Stage 3: Religious Maturity	Persons move between uncertainty and faith. They are able to stay connected to a religious or spiritual tradition but can approach it with reflection and a critical eye. Religion and spirituality tend to become liberating rather than exclusivist and oppressive.

Source: Adapted from Frame, M. (2003). *Integrating religion and spirituality into counseling: A comprehensive approach.* Belmont, CA; Brooks/Cole.

which tend to associate it with religious creeds, rituals, or doctrinal belief systems. Instead, faith is a universal aspect of the human experience that centers a person's life and that *underlies* the formations of content-specific beliefs, values, and practices. Faith, then,

> gives coherence and direction to person's lives; links them in shared trusts and loyalties with others; grounds their personal stances and communal loyalties in a sense of relatedness to a larger frame of reference; and enables them to face and deal with the challenges of human life and death, relying on that which has the quality of ultimacy in their lives. (Fowler & Dell, 2005, p. 36)

Sheridan (2003) also notes that Fowler attached great importance to the idea of *ultimate environment*. She notes that ultimate environment is:

> the highest level of reality. Faith is not only your internal image of the ultimate environment, but also your relationship with that image; it is relational, not merely cognitive. Your view of the ultimate environment—as personal or impersonal, trustworthy or not dependable, capable of dialogue or silent, purposeful or based on chance—and your relationship with it is an evolving, dynamic process that is strongly influenced by your experiences throughout the life course. (pp. 231–232)

Fowler's (1981) prestage period, known as *primal faith*, occurs during infancy and is related to the infant's ability to trust his or her caregiver. If positive levels of trust are achieved, then the foundation is laid for the child and later the adult to develop meaningful relationships of both temporal and transcendent quality:

> If nurturance by caregivers is consistent, the infant develops a sense of trust and safety about the universal and the divine—or feels at home in his or her life space. Conversely, negative experience can produce images of the ultimate as untrustworthy, punitive or arbitrary. (Sheridan, 2003, p. 232)

During the first stage, *intuitive-projective faith*, children make meaning of their world through story, symbol, dream, and imagination. Their images of God largely reflect those of their parents, and they tend to create metaphors of their world that represent both evil and protective aspects of life. Faith during this stage is fantasy filled and very imaginative. During the *mythic-literal faith* stage, children begin to separate fantasy from reality through the emergence of their own rational thinking capacities. Cognition plays a strong role in this sorting-out process. It allows the child to take on the beliefs and symbols of his or her own traditions while at the same time recognizing different religious perspectives and experiences of the world. God is often understood in human terms—as a kind of fatherly ruler who rewards goodness and punishes evil in a manner that is both fair and, at times, ruthless. The third stage, *synthetic-conventional faith*, begins as the adolescent develops the capacity for formal operational or abstract thinking. With this ability to think in the abstract comes the capacity to be self-reflective, to see oneself through the eyes of others, and to think about thinking. Images of God are often populated with personal qualities of love, acceptance, and understanding, whereas religious experiences are constructed through conformity to a set of values with a fairly clear deference to authority. "Fowler maintains that this stage was characteristic of adolescents and normative for adults. A clue that persons are beginning to move beyond this stage is when they begin to question authority and established beliefs and values" (Frame, 2003, p. 41).

Stages 4–6 of Fowler's (1981) model represent a somewhat more advanced level of faith development. Although Fowler is quick to say that these later stages should not be interpreted as providing a ranking system whereby one may judge the strength of a particular level of development, he does, nonetheless, suggest that it is not unusual for many not to reach the later stages, thus suggesting a kind of hierarchical ranking (Fowler & Dell, 2005). Stage 4, *individuative-reflective faith*, marks the transition to late adolescence and an increased responsibility for one's own beliefs and lifestyle. The adolescent is no longer defined by others' goals and values. She or he must be willing to take on the difficult task of critical reflection on the stories, symbols, and rituals of one's tradition and translating those more literal representations into figuratively meaningful systems:

> For example in previous stages, persons might have ascribed to one of the creation stories that described how the world comes to be. Critical reflection or "demythologizing" involves asking oneself what the significant of the creation story is. Instead of dwelling on the details of the length of creation or how people came to exist. . . ." (Frame, 2003, p. 42)

Stage 5 of Fowler's model, *conjunctive faith*, begins at midlife and is characterized by the ability to embrace the polarities of the religious experience in one's life. That is, one is able to recognize that the divine is both personal and abstract, both transcendent and immanent, both mysterious and knowable, both hidden and revealed. There is a new reevaluation and reclaiming of one's past and an opening to a sense of deeper self. "Either/or debates become both/and resolutions" (Sheridan, 2003, p. 235). Fowler (1981) suggests that most adults do not reach this stage of faith development. Indeed, only one in six over the age of 31 meets the criteria for this stage (Lownsdale, 1997).

The final stage of Fowler's model, *universalizing faith*, is the pinnacle of faith development in which the polarities and divisions that characterize stage 5 melt away into a deep recognition of the oneness of all experiences and phenomena. Only 3 people out of every 1,000 reach this stage; it is limited to a very few rare individuals. It has been suggested that only unique political and religious personalities such as Mahatma Gandhi, Martin Luther King, Jr., and Mother Teresa meet the criteria for this stage of development (Gatham & Nessan, 1997). (See Table 9.4.)

Ken Wilber

Ken Wilber (1980) first proposed a psychospiritual developmental model that is loosely based on psychoanalytic theory and transpersonal psychology. Like other transpersonal theorists, Wilber believes that psychological and spiritual development are not two separate phenomena but are, rather, two different aspects of the same dynamic power or force urging the human species toward full "beingness." Wilber's work, referred to as a *full-spectrum model of consciousness*, is a complex system that focuses on both individual and collective psychospiritual development.

For Wilber (1995), the epitome of psychospiritual development is not the attainment of a kind of unity with the whole of the universe or with other humans. Rather, psychospiritual development is movement to a kind of full enlightenment that views the separateness of things as an illusion and not a reality with which one should seek merger in order to

Table 9.4 Fowler's Stages of Faith Development

Prestage: Primal Faith	Trust in caregivers is developed in infancy.
Stage 1: Intuitive-Projective Faith	This stage characterizes early childhood.
	Images of God and faith are reflections of children's relationships with parents and other significant adults.
Stage 2: Mythic-Literal Faith	This stage begins in middle childhood and may extend beyond it. In this stage, people appropriate for themselves the stories, beliefs, and symbols of their tradition. God's characteristics are often seen as anthropomorphic. Persons in this stage might believe God rewards goodness and punishes evil.
Stage 3: Synthetic-Conventional Faith	This stage begins when people are able to think cognitively. During this stage, faith is constricted in terms of conformity to a set of values and beliefs with deference to authority. This stage is characteristic of adolescents and normative for adults.
Stage 4: Individuative Reflective Faith	In this stage, persons critically examine their faith and take responsibility for an authoritative worldview they have chosen. People commit themselves to faith through conscious choice rather than through unexamined acceptance.
Stage 5: Conjunctive Faith	This faith stage typically emerges in midlife and beyond. People acknowledge the multiple perspectives of faith and begin to integrate the polarities in their lives. Persons in this stage develop an openness toward differences in belief while staying grounded in their own.
Stage 6: Universalizing Faith	This stage is limited to a few people. In this stage, persons are committed to universal values such as peace and justice and are "grounded in a oneness with the power of being or God" (Fowler, 1991, p. 41).

Source: Canda, E., & Furman, I. (1999). *Spiritual Diversity in Social Work: The Heart of Helping.* New York: Free Press.

find meaning. According to Wilber (1995), such new insight can occur by virtue of an evolutionary ascent to a higher stage of consciousness that integrates all previous stages and represents a *transpersonal* level of awareness. For Wilber (1995), some spiritual developmental models implicitly encourage a kind of regressive identification with older and more atavistic forms of consciousness that are somehow perceived to be more meaningful, holistic, and spiritual. But for Wilber (1995), these models "are committing the 'pre-trans-fallacy,' which encourages people to regress to an earlier level of consciousness" (Zimmerman, 1994, p. 202). In other words, they confuse movement toward transpersonal levels of consciousness by inadvertently suggesting movement toward prepersonal levels.

Wilber's theoretical framework conceives of an ascent through a series of evolutionary stages toward full spiritual enlightenment. The current personal, sociocultural, and socioeconomic levels of individual and social consciousness are not to be criticized or retreated from. In fact, despite external appearances to the contrary, the secular West exemplifies a higher stage of consciousness development than do all earlier cultures and most non-Western societies. The attainment of the final, transegoic, stage of psychospiritual development must first proceed through a transitional period, what Wilber (1995) calls the *vision-logic* stage. This stage of consciousness is a more deeply realized, existential, and probative rationality—what he calls the *integral-aperspectival mind.*

Wilber (1995) writes that "it is the integrative power of vision-logic, I believe . . . that is now desperately needed on a global scale. For it is vision-logic with its centauric/planetary worldview that, in my opinion, holds the only hope for the integration of the biosphere and noosphere" (p. 187). Wilber contends that the persistent evidence of degradation of nature and social inequality visited on humankind by the many manifestations of Western rationality are simply temporary stresses and wrong turns of modern cultural civilization that must be addressed. But he insists that an emerging world culture "is being built by international markets of material-economic exchange, and by the increasingly free exchange of rationality structures, particularly empiric-analytic science and computer-transmitted information" (p. 197).

Of particular importance to Wilber is the view that any attempts to create nonhierarchical democratic frameworks of spiritual development represent an ill-conceived understanding of human evolutionary development. He observes that many critics of traditional developmental models advocate for an egalitarian transformation. Critics of these older models suggest that they inherently separate mind and body, subject and object, human and nonhuman into a mechanistic and hierarchical dualism. In its place these critics advocate a "worldview that is more holistic, more relational, more integrative, more Earth-honoring, and less arrogantly human-centered" (Wilber, 1995, p. 4). But the problem for Wilber (1995) with this conceptualization is that it ignores a critical element of both natural and social systemic development: the notion of holons.

The linchpin of Wilber's critique of nonhierarchicalists is his belief that they have misunderstood the importance of hierarchies in system functioning. He says of them: "All sorts of theorists, from deep ecologists to social critics, from ecofeminists to postmodern poststructuralists, have found the notion of hierarchy not only undesirable but a bona fide cause of much social domination, oppression, and injustice" (1995, p. 15). Wilber (1995) contends that the opponents of hierarchy, particularly social hierarchy, are concerned with the ranking and domination associated with the rule of an elite few and prefer instead to replace hierarchy with heterarchy—rule or governance "established by a pluralistic and egalitarian interplay of all parties" (p. 16). At issue, then, is whether one's emphasis is on the parts of the whole, or

hierarchy, or on the whole *as* a whole, or heterarchy. Wilber (1995) maintains that this is a too simplistic either/or dualism. He insists that the emphasis on the whole is really not holistic at all. If one were to ask these "wholeists" what is included in their wholeness, "you find out immediately that there are an enormous number of things that they do not include in their version of 'the Whole'" (p. 37).

Wilber (1995) suggests the adoption of the concept of holon as a more appropriate conceptualization of system functioning. A holon is:

> that which, being a whole in one context, is simultaneously a part in another. . . . The whole, in other words, is more than the sum of its parts, and that whole can influence and determine, in many cases, the function of its parts (and that whole itself is, of course, simultaneously a part of some other whole . . . reality is not composed of things or processes; it is not composed of atoms or quarks; it is not composed of wholes nor does it have any parts. Rather, it is composed of whole/parts, or holons. (pp. 18, 33)

Wilber concedes, in fact, that much of his developmental work is "about holons—about wholes that are parts of other wholes, indefinitely" (p. viii). For Wilber, perpetually emerging holons, or what he calls a "holarchy" (1995, p. 21), is the best qualitative descriptor of systemic function, both naturally and socially. Holarchies represent organizations of increasing complexity and complex levels of consciousness.

Wilber (1995) posits 10 basic *stages* of psychospiritual development, which are pedagogically depicted as distinct parts of three general *phases* of development. Stages 0–3 represent the *prepersonal* or *preegoic phase*. Stages 4–6 represent the *personal* or *egoic phase*, and stages 7–9 represent the *transpersonal* or *transegoic phase*. The preegoic and egoic phases correspond closely to the first five stages of Fowler's (1981) faith development model. The preegoic phase essentially views the emerging person as progressing through a series of developmental milestones that suggest an orientation to the physical world—the body and sensuality, the establishment of a healthy and bounded self-concept, and the coming to fruition of a cognitive or mental self (Sheridan, 2003).

The egoic phase consists of three stages and is sometimes referred to as the phase most focused on the development of the mental ego. It corresponds well to Piaget's periods of concrete and formal operational thinking. The major focus of the first two stages of this phase is learning how to perform social roles and to fit within one's primary group. This takes place while one evolves to the point of making critical judgments about previous rules and roles and thus comes to an appreciation of different personal and cultural perspectives. The third stage brings a deepening of one's worldcentric view (Sheridan, 2003). That is, one begins to develop the capacity to think holistically and dialectically. This allows for an integration of previously separated constructs such as mind/body, emotion/intellect, human/nonhuman. This egoic development phase leads to an autonomous self that is not isolated but is rather integrated into networks of service and responsibility.

By the end of the egoic phase, most people have developed a truly worldcentric perspective that transcends personal ego and cultural constraints. The end of the egoic phase marks, for many, the pinnacle of human psychospiritual development, but for Wilber, it is only a doorway to a yet higher level of transegoic development. The transegoic phase is only rarely experienced or attained. Although some may be awakened to a higher consciousness, most are not able to get past the mental ego phase, which still tries to capture and impede this higher spiritual evolution. The transegoic phase is characterized by a marked reorganization of psychic processes. The ego self gives way to an *aware self* that is able to observe life as a witness rather than an exclusive participant. The evolving self becomes a *world soul* that experiences a deepening sense of kinship and community with all things—human, natural, and supernatural. During the final stage of this phase of psychospiritual development— *nondual reality*—all distinctions between subject and object disappear, and one begins to experience self as pure consciousness in a timeless and spaceless mysticism. Ultimately, there evolves a disidentification with the self

entirely. The self is no longer ego and is no longer witness and awareness but is rather dissolved into the One. This involves more than a recognition of emptiness—the awareness of pure consciousness without form. In nonduality, emptiness is not a state of awareness but, indeed, becomes pure consciousness. There is no awareness. There is just nonduality. Sheridan (2003) summarizes Wilber's model very succinctly:

> Prepersonal and personal phase of consciousness should sound familiar to students of conventional approaches to human development. In contrast, the stages of the transpersonal phase (and the language used to describe them) are most likely unfamiliar to those who are not well versed in contemplative Eastern ideas about human development. However, it is this synthesis of both conventional and contemplative approaches and the inclusion of "higher order" levels of development that is Wilber's primary contribution to our attempts to understand human behavior. (p. 242)

With this model, Wilber (1995) is proposing that the personal level of development, with its achievement of strong ego development and self-actualization, is not the highest potential of human existence. Rather, the ultimate goal of human development is the "spirit" level—beyond ego or self to self-transcendence and unity with the ultimate reality. The capacity for attaining the highest levels of consciousness is innate with each human being, although Wilber (1995) acknowledges that very few people reach the higher transpersonal levels. He describes these individuals as a "rather small pool of daring men and women—both yesterday and today— who have bucked the system, fought the average and the normal, and struck out toward the new and higher spheres of awareness" (Wilber as quoted in Sheridan, 2003, p. 245). (See Table 9.5.)

Limitations

There are no perfect theoretical models of religious and/or spiritual development. No model

Table 9.5   Wilber's Full-Spectrum Model of Consciousness

Phase of Development	Stage	Basic Structures Consciousness	Corresponding Fulcrums	Characteristic Pathologies	Treatment Modalities
Transpersonal or transegoic				Nondual	
	9	Casual	F-9	Casual pathology	Formless mysticism
	8	Subtle	F-8	Subtle pathology	Deity mysticism
	7	Psychic	F-7	Psychotic disorders	Nature mysticism
Personal, or Egoic	6	Centauric or Vision-Logic	F-6	Existential pathology	Existential therapy
	5	Formal-Reflexive Mind (formal operations)	F-5	Identity neuroses	Introspection
	4	Rule/Role Mind (concrete operations)	F-4	Script pathology (problems with roles or rules)	Script analysis
Prepersonal, or Preegoic	3	Representational-Mind	F-3	Psychoneurosis	Uncovering techniques
	2	Phantasmic-Emotional	F-2	Narcissistic-borderline	Structuring/building techniques
	1	Senscriphysical	F-1	Psychoses	Physiological pacification techniques
	0	Primary matrix therapies	F-0	Perinatal pathology	Intense regressive
				Nondual	

Source: Sheridan, M. J. (2003). The spiritual person. In E. Hutchison (Ed), *Dimensions of human behavior: Person and environment* (pp. 220–267). Thousand Oaks, CA: Sage, p. 243.

could ever be comprehensive and detailed enough to address the religious and spiritual experiences of all people in any given historical or cultural context. A persistent critique of most stage-based models such as those discussed here is that they tend to imply a kind of ranking that suggests that those at the higher or more advanced end of the continuum are more developed and/or esteemed. Most of the theorists we have addressed have tried, at one time or another, to temper this critique by explicitly stating that no such ranking is necessarily intended. However, it is difficult in highly linear and hierarchical models to completely repudiate the idea that a higher valuing is somehow not intended by a higher place on the ladder of spiritual development.

A second concern for any model of this type is that they are inherently biased in the sense that they often rely on very select and narrow theoretical underpinnings—mostly modern Western philosophical, psychological, and/or political orientations. Another concern is that those models created by empirical validation rely too heavily on a single racial and ethic cluster that usually represents the dominant cultural group, thus marginalizing a whole range of alternative voices. And finally we could reasonably argue that these models of religio-spiritual development, especially that of Wilber (1995), are too confusing and abstract to be of any real use to social workers doing the hard work of practice. Many social workers might find themselves seriously challenged in conceptualizing how they would recognize whether a client is in the formal-reflexive mind or vision logic stage of psychospiritual development. Irrespective of the critiques leveled at the models, these theories have made a significant contribution to social work's understanding of religious and spiritual development. They offer social workers a schema to organize their thinking about client's complex bio-psycho-social-spiritual development processes. They also sensitize the practitioner to the reality that clients are involved in an intricate process of transformation that often includes spiritual and religious dimensions. Our role is to better understand so that we can better assist our clients in this process.

Summary and Conclusion

The current state of discussions of spirituality and religion in social work, much as in the popular culture around it, is vibrant and appears to be growing in interest and strength. It is also fraught with controversies, and there is little consensus in the social work community about the nature and scope of this dimension of life and what if any influence it ought to be having in the day-to-day practice of social work. Although social work went through a 50-year hiatus in which focus shifted to secularization and professionalization, over the past several decades this has begun to change. Many individual social workers are finding religion and spirituality to be important components of both personal growth and professional practice (See Figures 9.8–9.10).

The professional collective is also rediscovering a substantial and sustained interest in continuing to identify linkages between spirituality, religion, and social work theory and practice. This renaissance of the transpersonal has expanded on the interreligious and spiritual undercurrents that have existed in social work from its very beginning years. Unlike its earlier sectarian period, the focus of this new developmental phase has tended generally to be on broadening the definition of the religious/spiritual construct so as to make it more inclusive and honoring of diverse religious and nonreligious spiritual traditions (Canda, 1998; Russel, 1998). The current status of spirituality and religion in social work is robust and appears to be growing into the international arena, as well as expanding more fully into a variety of social work educational and practice settings. This newfound strength of the spirit is being given

Figure 9.8. Happy Hanukah. Photo by Kathleen Besthorn and Margie Hayes.

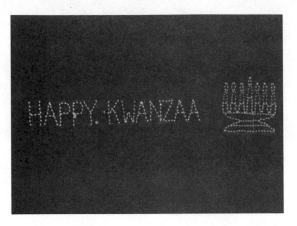

Figure 9.9. Happy Kwanzaa. Photo by Kathleen Besthorn and Margie Hayes.

expression in numerous popular books, articles, textbooks, monographs, presentations, informal networking, and formal organizational structures of both a sectarian and nonsectarian nature.

This chapter has attempted to give the reader an overview of the religious and spiritual aspects of human behavior and how these important new conceptualizations have impinged on and are currently affecting the profession. We have spent a fair amount of time looking at the ways that social work evolved as a profession and the influences of larger religious contexts on this historic evolution. We have also attempted to provide some insight into the difficulty of defining the religious and spiritual construct and how both social work theorists and those in allied fields have attempted to provide clarity in this difficult enterprise. We explored several theories of religious and spiritual development and suggested both the strengths and limitations of these kinds of approaches.

Figure 9.10. Merry Christmas. Photo by Kathleen Besthorn and Margie Hayes.

A Final Word: Ends and Beginnings

With this presentation on the spiritual dimension of human and nonhuman life, we have come full circle in our study of human behavior at the macro level. We have progressed from the psychology of groups to the sociology of the family, culture, and the organization to the biology of the natural world to the philosophy of spirituality. One of the major themes can be summarized in a nutshell: The systemic forces that denigrate nature are intertwined with struggles against all forces that oppress human beings in the space. And the reverse is also true.

To transcend the various dimensions that were considered in this book—groups, families, culture, and so forth—we chose the image of the holon. We have drawn on this odd-looking structure in both volumes of this *HBSE* set, in fact, to serve as a metaphor for human interconnectedness and to represent our theoretical contribution of an expanded ecosystems framework. The holon relates to empowerment, as well, in the sense of wholeness. As we learned in the first and last chapters of this book, the holon is about the joining of opposites and about reality as paradox. For example, each part of the holon is both a whole and a part of another whole. The first is last, and the last is first. And each end marks a new beginning.

Thought Questions

1. "It is the best of times and the worst of times for the spiritual and religious among us." Discuss.
2. How can spirituality be differentiated from religion? Relate to what the theorists say.
3. Discuss Praglin's four categories of treatment of spiritual and religious issues in social work.
4. Claims have been made that social work faculty discriminate against evangelical Christians (especially those who believe homosexuality is a sin). Discuss both sides of this issue.

5. Consider the importance of sustainability to the various religious denominations.
6. How can prisoners get in touch with their feelings for the earth? How is this meaningful to them?
7. Relate the seven principles of Kwanzaa to the values of social work (check out the NASW code of ethics for the list of values).
8. Describe the sectarian heritage of social work.
9. What was unique about the Social Gospel movement?
10. Recount how religious forces played into the settlement house movement.
11. Differentiate between moderate evangelical and radical evangelical Protestantism.
12. What is the fundamentalist attitude toward poverty?
13. Consider your own religious development in terms of Allport's theoretical scheme.
14. W hat was Fowler's contribution? Pay special attention to stage 6.
15. Describe Wilber's conceptualization of the holon.
16. Compare Wilber's ego self to his *aware self*.
17. What are the basic criticisms of these models of spiritual development?

References

Addams, J. (1910). Charity and social justice. In *Proceedings of the National Conference of Charities and Correction* (pp. 1–18). Fort Wayne, IN: Archer Printing.

Adrian, W. (2007). Is bible translation "Imperialist"? Challenging another anti-Christian bias in the academy. *Christian Higher Education*, 6(4), 289–297.

Ahlstrom, S. (1972). *A religious history of the American people*. New Haven, CT: Yale University Press.

Alford, H., & Naughton, M. (2001). *Managing as if faith mattered: Christian social principles in the modern organization*. South Bend, IN: University of Notre Dame Press.

Allport, G. (1950). *The individual and his religion*. New York: Macmillan.

Almond, G., Appleby, R., & Sivan, E. (2003). *Strong religion: The rise of fundamentalisms around the world*. Chicago: University of Chicago Press.

Ammerman, N. (1991). North American Protestant fundamentalism. In M. Marty & R. Appleby (Eds.), *Fundamentalisms observed* (pp. 1–65). Chicago: University of Chicago Press.

Armstrong, K. (2001). *The battle for God: A history of fundamentalism*. New York: Ballantine.

Astin, A., & Astin, H. (2006). *Spirituality and the professoriate: A national study of faculty beliefs, attitudes, and behaviors*. Los Angeles: UCLA Higher Education Research Institute.

Axinn, J., & Levin, H. (1975). *Social welfare: A history of the American response to need*. New York: Dodd, Mead.

Baltzell, E. D. (1964). *The Protestant establishment: Aristocracy and caste in America*. New York: Random House.

Balmer, R. (2006). *Thy kingdom come-An evangelical's lament: How the religious right distorts the faith and threatens America*. New York: Basic Books.

The Barna Group. (2007, January 18). *Survey explores who qualifies as an evangelical*. Retrieved from http://www.barna.org/barna-update/article/13-culture/111-survey-explores-who-qualifies-as-an-evangelical

Bawer, B. (1997). *Stealing Jesus: How fundamentalism betrays Christianity*. New York: Three Rivers Press.

Beck, U. (1992). *Risk society: Towards a new modernity*. Thousand Oaks, CA: Sage.

Bennett, R. (2003). Does social work oppress Christians? [Letter to the editor]. *Social Work, 48*, 273–274.

Benson, P., Roehlkepartain, E., & Rude, S. (2003). Spiritual development in childhood and adolescence: Toward a field of inquiry. *Applied Developmental Science, 7*, 204–212.

Berger, P. L. (1986). *The capitalist revolution*. New York: Basic Books.

Berl, F. (1979). Clinical practice in a Jewish context. *Journal of Jewish Communal Service, 55*(4), 366–368.

Berlinerblau, J. (2005). *The secular bible: Why nonbelievers must take religion seriously*. New York: Cambridge University Press.

Beruhe, M. (2006). *What's liberal about the liberal arts: Classroom politics and "Bias" in higher education*. New York: W. W. Norton.

Besthorn, F. H. (2002). Expanding spiritual diversity in social work: Perspectives on the greening of spirituality. *Currents: New Scholarship in the Human Services, 1*(1). Retrieved from http://www.ucalgary.ca/currents/files/currents/v1n1_besthorn.pdf

Besthorn, F. H. (2007). En-voicing the world: Constructionism and essentialism in natural discourse—How social work fits in. In S. Witkin & S. Saleebey (Eds.), *Social work dialogues: Transforming the canon in inquiry, practice and education* (pp. 167–202). Alexandria, VA: Council on Social Work Education Press.

Biestek, F. P. (1956). Religion and social casework. In L. DeSantis (Ed.), *The social welfare forum* (pp. 86–95). New York: Columbia University Press.

Blacher-Wilson, F. (2004). Spirituality and school leaders: The value of spirituality in the lives of aspiring school leaders. *Religion and Education, 31*(1), 80–90.

Boyer, P. (1978). *Urban masses and moral order in America: 1820–1920*. Cambridge, MA: Harvard University Press.

Brandon, D. (1979). Zen practice in social work. In D. Brandon & B. Jordon (Eds.), *Creative Social Work* (pp. 30–35). Oxford, England: Basil Blackwell.

Bullis, R. K. (1996). *Spirituality in social work practice*. Washington, DC: Taylor & Francis.

Campolo, T. (2004). *Speaking my mind: A radical evangelical prophet tackles the tough issues Christians are afraid to face*. Nashville, TN: W Publishing Group.

Canda, E. R. (Ed.). (1998). *Spirituality and social work: New directions*. Binghamton, NY: Haworth Pastoral Press.

Canda, E. R. (2002). A world wide view on spirituality and social work: Reflections from the USA experience and suggestions for internationalization. *Currents: New Scholarship in the Human services, 1*(1). Retrieved from http://www.ucalgary.ca/currents/files/currents/v1n1_canda1.pdf

Canda, E. R. (2003). Social work and evangelical Christians [Letter to the editor]. *Social Work, 48*, 278–282.

Canda, E. R. (2005). The future of spirituality in social work: The further reaches of human nurture. *Advances in Social Work, 6*(1), 97–108.

Canda, E. R., & Furman, L. D. (1999). *Spiritual diversity in social work practice: The heart of helping*. New York: Free Press.

Canda, E. R., & Furman, L. D. (2010). *Spiritual diversity in social work practice: The heart of helping* (2nd ed.). New York: Oxford University Press.

Carpenter, J. (1999). *Revive us again: The reawakening of American fundamentalism*. New York: Oxford University Press.

Carter, S. L. (1993). *Culture of disbelief: How American law and politics trivialize religious devotion*. New York: Anchor Books.

Chenault, V. (1990). A Native American practice framework. *Spirituality and Social Work Communicator, 1*(2), 5–7.

Chu, K., & Carew, R. (1990). Confucianism: Its relevance to social work with Chinese people. *Australian Social Work, 43*(3), 3–9.

Clabaugh, G. K. (1974). *Thunder on the right: The Protestant fundamentalists*. Chicago: Nelson-Hall.

Cnaan, R. (1999). *The newer deal: Social work and religion in partnership*. New York: Columbia University Press.

Coholic, D. (2003). Incorporating spirituality in feminist social work perspectives. *Affilia, 18*(1), 49–67.

Coles, R. (1989). The call of stories: Teaching and the moral imagination. *Journal of Narrative and Life History, 5*(2), 87–123.

Conger, J. (1994). *Spirit at work: Discovering the spirituality in leadership*. San Francisco: Jossey-Bass.

Constable, R. (1983). Values, religion, and social work practice. *Social Thought, 9*(4), 29–41.

Cooperman, A. (2007, May 5). Is there disdain for evangelicals in the classroom? *Washington Post*. Retrieved from http://www.washingtonpost.com/wp-dyn/content/article/2007/05/04/AR2007050401990.html

d'Aquili, D., & Newberg, A. (1999), *The mystical mind: Probing the biology of religious experience*. Minneapolis, MN: Fortress Press.

Davie, G. (2003). The evolution of the sociology of religion: Theme and variations. In M. Dillion (Ed.), *Handbook of the sociology of religion* (pp. 61–75). Cambridge, England: Cambridge University Press.

Delgado, M. (1977). Puerto Rican spiritism and the social work profession, *Social Casework, 58*(8), 451–458.

Derezotes, D. (2006). *Spiritually oriented social work practice*. Boston: Pearson Education.

Diamond, S. (1995). *Roads to dominion: Right-wing movements and political power in the United States*. New York: Guildford Press.

Domke, D. (2004). *God willing: Political fundamentalism in the white house, the "war on terror", and the echoing press*. London: Pluto Press.

Dudley, J. R., & Helfgott, C. (1990). Exploring a place for spirituality in the social work curriculum. *Journal of Social Work Education, 26*(3), 287–294.

Faver, C. A. (1986). Religion, research, and social work. *Social Thought, 12*(3), 20–29.

Fitzpatrick, E. (1990). *Endless crusade: Women social scientists and progressive reform*. New York: Oxford University Press.

Fowler, J. (1981). *Stages of faith*. New York: Harper & Row.

Fowler, J., & Dell, M. (2005). Stages of faith from infancy through adolescence: Reflections on three decades of faith development theory. In E. Roehlkeparetain, P. King, L. Wagener, & P. Benson (Eds.), *The handbook of spiritual development in childhood and adolescence* (pp. 34–59). Thousand Oaks, CA: Sage.

Frame, M. (2003). *Integrating religion and spirituality into counseling: A comprehensive approach*. Belmont, CA: Brooks/Cole.

Frey, L. A., & Edinburg, G. (1978). Helping, manipulation, and magic. *Social Work, 23*(2), 89–93.

Furlong, M. (2006). Observing different faiths, leaning about ourselves: Practice with inter-married Muslims and Christians. *Australian Social Work, 59*(3), 250–264.

Gatham, A., & Nessan, C. (1997). Fowler's stages of faith development in an honors science and religion seminar. *Zygon, 32*, 407–414.

Gilbert, M. (2000). Spirituality in social work groups: Practitioners speak out. *Social Work with Groups, 22*, 67–84.

Goldman, E. F. (1977). *Rendezvous with destiny: A history of modern American reform*. New York: Vintage Books.

Gouldner, A. (1979). *The future of intellectuals and the rise of the new class*. New York: Seabury Press.

Gray, M. (2008). Viewing spirituality in social work through the lens of contemporary social theory. *British Journal of Social Work, 38*, 175–196.

Greeley, A. (1972). *Crisis in the church: A study of religion in America*. Chicago: Thomas Moore Press.

Gross, N., & Simmons, S. (2009). The religiosity of American college and university professors. *Sociology of Religion, 70*(1), 101–129.

Hankins, B. (2009). *American evangelicals. A contemporary history of a mainstream religious movement.* New York: Rowman and Littlefield Publishers.

Harrington, J. (2009). Evangelicalism, environmental activism, and climate change in the United States. *Journal of Religion and Society, 11,* 1–22.

Harris, H. (2008). *Fundamentalism and evangelicals (Oxford Theological Monographs)* New York: Oxford University Press.

Harris, S. (2004). *The end of faith: Religion, terror, and the future of reason.* New York: Norton.

Hedges, C. (2008). *American fascists: The Christian right and the war on America.* New York: Free Press.

Hodge, D. (2002). Does social work oppress evangelical Christians? A new class analysis of society and social work. *Social Work, 47,* 401–414.

Hodge, D. (2003a). Developing cultural competency with evangelical Christians. *Families in Society: The Journal of Contemporary Social Services, 85,* 251–259.

Hodge, D. (2003b). Differences in worldviews between social workers and people of faith. *Families in Society: The Journal of Contemporary Social Services, 84,* 285–295.

Hodge, D. (2006). Moving toward a more inclusive educational environment? A multi-sample exploration of religious discrimination as seen through the eyes of students from various faith traditions. *Journal of Social Work Education, 42,* 249–267.

Hodge, D. (2007a). Does social work discriminate against evangelical Christians? Yes. In H. Karger, J. Midgley, P. Kindle, & C. Brown (Eds.), *Controversial issues in social policy* (140–147). Boston: Allyn & Bacon.

Hodge, D. (2007b). Religious discrimination and ethical compliance: Exploring perceptions among a professionally affiliated sample of graduate students. *Journal of Religion and Spirituality in Social Work, 26,* 91–113.

Hodge, D. (2009). Secular privilege: Deconstructing the invisible rose-tinted sunglasses. *Journal of Religion and Spirituality in Social Work, 28,* 8–34.

Hofstadter, R. (1955). *The age of reform.* New York: Vintage Books.

Hunter, J. (1991). *Culture wars.* New York: Basic Books.

Imre, R. (1971). A theological view of social casework. *Social Casework, 52*(9), 578–585.

Jacoby, S. (2008). *The age of American unreason.* New York: Vintage Books.

James, W. (1958/orig. 1902). *Varieties of religious experience.* New York: Longman.

Janis, I. (1982). *Groupthink* (2nd ed.). Boston: Houghton-Mifflin.

Jaschik, S. (2005, March 30). Leaning to the left. *Inside Higher Education.* Retrieved from http://www.insidehighered.com/layout/set/print/news/2005/03/30politics

Joseph, M. V. (1975). The parish as a social service and social action center: An ecological systems approach. *Social Thought, 1*(2), 43–49.

Joseph, M. V. (1987). The religious and spiritual aspects of social work practice: A neglected dimension of social work. *Social Thought, 13*(1), 12–23.

Johnson, F. E. (Ed.). (1956). *Religion and social work.* New York: Institute for Religious and Social Studies, Harper and Brothers.

Johnson, P. (1979). *A history of Christianity.* New York: Touchstone Books.

Kahnerman, D., Slovic, P., & Tversky, A. (1982). *Judgment under uncertainty: Heuristics and biases.* London: Cambridge University Press.

Kaplan, E. (2004). *With God on their side: How Christian fundamentalists trampled science, policy, and democracy in George W. Bush's White House.* New York: New Press.

Karger, H. J., & Stoesz, D. (1990). *American social welfare policy.* New York: Longman.

Kaseman, M., & Austin, M. (2005). Building a faith-based human service agency: A view from the inside. *Social Thought: The Journal of Religion and Spirituality in Social Work, 24*(3), 69–92.

Keefe, T. (1975). A Zen perspective on social casework. *Social Casework, 56*(3), 140–144.

Keefe, T. (1996). Meditation and social work treatment. In F. Turner (Ed.), *Social work treatment: Interlocking theoretical approaches* (4th ed.) (pp. 434–460). New York: Free Press.

Keith-Lucas, A. (1960). Some notes on theology and social work. *Social Casework, 41*(2), 87–91.

Keith-Lucas, A. (1985). *So you want to be a social worker: A primer for the Christian student.* St. Davids, PA: North American Association of Christians in Social Work.

Kemp, S. P. (1994). *Social work and systems of knowledge: The concept of environment in social casework theory, 1900–1983.* Unpublished doctoral dissertation, Columbia University, New York.

Kimball, C. (2002). *When religion becomes evil.* New York: Harper Collins.

King, N. (1965). Some perspectives on theology and social work. In P. McCabe & F. Turner (Eds.), *Catholic social work: A contemporary overview* (pp. 6–27). Ottawa: Catholic Charities Council of Canada.

King, U. (2001). Spirituality, society, and the millennium: Wasteland, wilderness, or new vision? In U. King (Ed.), *Spirituality and society in the new millennium* (pp. 1–13). Brighton, England: Sussex Academic Press.

Korten, D. C. (2006). *The great turning: From empire to earth community.* San Francisco: Berrett-Koehler Publishers, Inc.

Kosmin, B., & Keysar, A. (2008). American religious identification survey 2008. Retrieved from http://www.americanreligionsurvey-aris.org/reports/ARIS_Report_2008.pdf

Krill, D. F. (1996). Existential social work. In F. Turner (Ed.), *Social work treatment: Interlocking theoretical approaches* (4th ed.) (pp. 250–281). New York: Free Press.

Laird, J. (1984). Sorcerers, shamans, and social workers: The use of ritual in social work practice. *Social Work, 29*(2), 123–128.

LaHaye, T., & Jenkins, J. (1996). *Left behind: A novel of earth's last day.* Wheaton, IL: Tyndale House Publishers.

Lawrence, B. (1990). *Defenders of God: The fundamentalist revolt against the modern age.* New York: I. B. Tauris.

Leiby, J. (1978). *A history of social welfare and social work in the U.S.* New York: Columbia University Press.

Leiby, J. (1985). Moral foundations of social welfare and social work: A historical view. *Social Work, 30*(4), 323–330.

Limbaugh, D. (2004). *Persecution: How liberals are waging war against Christianity.* Washington, DC: Regency Publishing.

Lindsey, H. (1970). *The late great planet earth.* Grand Rapids, MI: Zondervan Publishing.

Linzer, N. (1979). A Jewish philosophy of social work practice. *Journal of Jewish Communal Service, 55*(4), 309–317.

Loder, J. (1998). *The logic of the spirit: Human development in theological perspective.* San Francisco: Jossey-Bass.

Loewenberg, F. (1988). *Religion and social work practice in contemporary American society.* New York: Columbia University Press.

Lord, C., Ross, L., & Lepper, M. (1979). Biased assimilation and attitude polarization: The effects of prior theories and subsequently considered evidence. *Journal of Personality and Social Psychology, 37,* 2098–2109.

Lownsdale, S. (1997). Faith development across the life span: Fowler's integrative work. *Journal of Psychology and Theology, 25,* 49–63.

MacDonald, D. (2000). Spirituality: Description, measurement, and relation to the five-factor model of personality. *Journal of Personality, 68,* 157–197.

Manthey, B. J. (1989). *Social work, religion and the church: Policy implications.* Unpublished doctoral dissertation, University of Texas–Austin.

Marler, P., & Hadaway, C. (2002). "Being religious" or "being spiritual" in America: A zero-sum proposition. *Journal for the Scientific Study of Religion, 41*(3), 288–300.

Marsden, G. (1980). *Fundamentalism and American culture.* New York: Oxford University Press.

Marsden, G. (2006). *Fundamentalism and American culture* (Rev. ed.). New York: Oxford University Press.

Marshall, J. (1991). The spiritual dimension in social work education. *Spirituality and Social Work Communicator, 2*(1), 12–15.

Marty, M. (1980). Social service: Godly and godless. *Social Service Review, 54*(4), 4463–4481.

Marty, M., & Appleby, R. S. (1994). *Fundamentalisms observed.* Chicago: University of Chicago Press.

Mary, N. (2008). Social work in a sustainable world. Chicago: Lyceum.

May, H. F. (1977). *Protestant churches and industrial America.* New York: Octagon Books.

McAdams, J. (1987). Testing the theory of the new class. *The Sociological Quarterly, 28*(1), 23–49.

McClay, W. (2003). Two concepts of secularism. In H. Heclo & W. McClay (Eds.), *Religion returns to the public square* (pp. 31–61). Baltimore: John Hopkins University Press.

McGaa, E. (1995). *Native wisdom: Perceptions of the natural way.* Minneapolis, MN: Four Directions.

Meacham, J. (2006). *The American gospel: God, the founding fathers, and the making of a nation.* New York: Random House.

Melcher, J. (2008). Orthodox vs. progressive: An invitation to transform professional consciousness. *Journal of Religion and Spirituality in Social Work, 27*(1/2), 183–200.

Melendez, M., & LaSala, M. (2006). Who's oppressing whom? Homosexuality, Christianity, and social work. *Social Work, 51*(4), 371–385.

Midgely, J. (1990). The new Christian right, social policy, and the welfare state. *Journal of Sociology and Social Welfare, 17*(2), 89–106.

Midgely, J., & Sanzenbach, P. (1989). Social work, religion, and the global challenge of Fundamentalism. *International Social Work, 32*(4), 273–287.

Miller, W., & Thoresen, C. (2003). Spirituality, religion, and health: An emerging research field. *American Psychologist, 58*, 24–35.

Mosher, C. R. (2009, May 9).A new paradigm for sustainability and social justice. Paper presented at the International Conference on Ecological and Professional Helping. Calgary, Alberta.

Muir, J. (1911). *My first summer in the Sierra.* Boston: Houghton Mifflin.

National Association of Scholars. (2007, September 11). *The scandal of social work education.* Retrieved from http://www.nas.org/polimage. cfm?doc_Id=26&size_code=Doc

Newfield, C. (2008). *Unmaking the public university: The forty-year assault on the middle class.* Cambridge, MA: Harvard University Press.

Niebuhr, R. (1932). *The contribution of religion to social work.* New York: Columbia University Press.

Norris, P., & Inglehart, R. (2004). *Sacred and secular: Religion and politics worldwide.* Cambridge, UK: Cambridge University Press.

O'Brien, M. E. (2008). *Spirituality in nursing: Standing on holy ground* (3rd ed.). Boston: Jones and Bartlett Publishers.

Olasky, M. (2005, June 4). Confronting diaphobia: Interview with David R. Hodge on spirituality and social work. *World Magazine.* Retrieved from http://www.worldmag.com/articles/10698

Paine, R. T. (1901). Personal service. In *Proceedings of the National Conference of Charities and Correction, 28* (pp. 330–334). Boston: Ellis.

Pardeck, J., Murphy, J., & Meinert, R. (1998). *Postmodernism, religion and the future of social work.* New York: Routledge.

Pargament, K. I. (1997). *The psychology of religion and coping: Theory, research, practice.* New York: Guilford Press.

Pargament, K. I. (1999). The psychology of religion and spirituality? Yes and no. *International Journal for the Psychology of Religion, 9*(1), 3–16.

Pew Trust. (2008, November 20). *U.S. religious landscape survey: Religious beliefs and practices, diverse and politically relevant.* Retrieved from http://religions.pewforum.org/pdf/report2-religious-landscape-study-full.pdf

Phillips, K. (2006). *American theocracy: The peril and politics of radical religion, oil, and borrowed money in the 21st century.* New York: Viking Adult.

Praglin, L. (2004). Spirituality, religion, and social work: An effort towards interdisciplinary conversation. *Social Thought: Journal of Religion and Spirituality in Social Work, 23,* 67–84.

Ramirez, R. (1985). Hispanic spirituality. *Social Thought, 11*(3), 6–13.

Reich, K., Oser, F., & Scarlett, W (Eds.). (1999). *Psychological studies on spiritual and religious development: Vol. 2. Being human: The case of religion.* Lengerich, Germany: Pabst Science.

Ressler, L. (1992). Theologically enriched social work: Alan Keith-Lucas' approach to social work and religion. *Spirituality and Social Work Journal, 3*(2), 14–20.

Ressler, L. (1998). The relationship between church and state: Issues in social work and the law. In E. R. Canda (Ed.), *Spirituality and social work: New directions* (pp. 15–24). Hazelton, PA: Haworth Press.

Ressler, L., & Hodge, D. (2003). Silenced voices: Social work and the oppression of conservative narratives. *Social Thought: Journal of Religion and Spirituality in Social Work, 22,* 125–142.

Ressler, L. & Hodge, D. (2005). Religious discrimination in social work: Preliminary evidence. *Journal of Religion and Spirituality in Social Work, 24*(4), 55–74.

Rice, D. (Ed.). (2009). *Reinhold Niebuhr revisited: Engagements with an American original.* Grand Rapids, MI: Wm. B. Eerdmans Publishing.

Rice, S., & McAuliffe, D. (2009). Ethics of the spirit. Comparing ethical views and usages of spiritually influenced interventions. *Australian Social Work, 62*(3), 403–420.

Ricketts, G. (2008, July 6). Coercing the conscience: New examples of the reign of intolerance in schools of social work. Retrieved from The National Association of Scholars Web site: http://www.nas.org/polArticles.cfm?doc_id=201&Keyword_Desc=The%20Scandal%20of%20Social%20Work%20Education

Roehlkepartain, E., Benson, P., King, P., & Wagener, L. (2005). Spiritual development in childhood and adolescence: Moving to the scientific mainstream. In E. Roehlkepartain, P. King, L. Wagener, & P. Benson (Eds.), *The handbook of spiritual development in childhood and adolescence* (pp. 1–15). Thousand Oaks, CA: Sage.

Rodda, C. (2006). *Liars for Jesus: The religious right's alternative version of American history.* New York: Booksurge Publishing.

Rossing, B. (2004). *The rapture exposed: The message of hope in the book of revelation.* New York: Basic Books.

Russel, R. (1998). Spirituality and religion in graduate social work education. *Social Thought, 18*(2), 15–29.

Russel, R. (2006). Spirituality and social work: Current trends and future directions. *Arete, 30*(1), 42–52.

Salomon, E. L. (1976). Humanistic values and social casework. *Social Casework, 48*(1), 26–31.

Schmalzbauer, J. (1993). Evangelicals in the new class: Class versus subcultural predictors of ideology. *Journal for the Scientific Study of Religion, 32*(4), 330–342.

Schmalzbauer, J. (2002). *Religious conviction in American journalism and higher education.* Ithaca, NY: Cornell University Press.

Sharlett, J. (2009). *The family: The secret fundamentalism at the heart of American power.* New York: Harper Perennial.

Sheridan, M. J. (1999). The spiritual person. In E. Hutchison (Ed.), *Dimensions of human behavior: Person and environment* (pp. 157–191). Thousand Oaks, CA: Pine Forge Press.

Sheridan, M. J. (2003). The spiritual person. In E. Hutchison (Ed.), *Dimensions of human behavior: Person and environment* (2nd ed., pp. 219–267). Thousand Oaks, CA: Sage.

Siporin, M. (1982). Moral philosophy in social work today. *Social Service Review, 56*(4), 516–538.

Smith, C. (2002). *Christian America: What evangelicals really want.* Berkeley: University of California Press.

Spano, R. (1982). *The rank and file movement in social work.* Lanham, MD: University Press of America.

Spano, R., & Koenig, T. (2007). What is sacred when personal and professional values collide? *Journal of Social Work Values and Ethics, 4*(3), 5–23. Retrieved March 19, 2010, from http://www.socialworker.com/jswve/content/view/69/54

Specht, H. & Courtney, M. (1995). *Unfaithful angels: How social work has abandoned its mission.* New York: Free Press.

Spencer, S. (1956). Religion and social work. *Social Work, 1*(3), 19–26.

Spencer, S. (1961). What place has religion in social work education? *Social Service Review, 35*, 161–170.

Steigerwald, D. (2005, February 11). The new repression of the postmodern right. *Inside Higher Education.* Retrieved from http://www.insidehighered.com/layout/set/print/views/2005/02/11/steigerwald1

Stirling, B., Furman, L., Benson, P., Canda, E., & Grimwood, C. (2009). A comparative survey of Aotearoa New Zealand and UK social workers on the role of religion and spirituality in practice. *British Journal of Social Work* Advance Access published on February 13, 2009, DOI.10.1093/bjsw/bcp008,http://bjsw.oxfordjournals.org/cgi/reprint

Szasz, M. (1982). *The divided mind of Protestant America, 1880–1930.* Tuscaloosa, AL: University of Alabama Press.

Thyer, B., & Myers, L. (2009). Religious discrimination in social work academic programs: Whither social justice? *Journal of Religion and Spirituality in Social Work, 28*, 144–160.

Tobin, G., & Weinberg, A. (2007). *Profiles of the American university volume II: Religious beliefs and behavior of college faculty.* San Francisco: The Institute for Jewish and Community Research.

Towle, C. (1965). *Common human needs* (Rev. ed.). Washington, DC: National Association of Social Workers Press.

Uecker, J., Regnerus, M., & Vaaler, M. (2007). Losing my religion: The social sources of religious decline in early adulthood. *Social Forces, 85*(4), 1667–1692.

Van Hook, M., Hugen, B., & Aguilar, M. (2001). *Spirituality within religious traditions in social work practice.* Belmont, CA: Brooks/Cole.

Waldman, S. (2009). *How our founding fathers forged a radical new approach to religious liberty.* New York: Random House.

Wallis, J. (2005). *God's politics: Why the right gets it wrong and the left doesn't get it.* San Francisco: Harper's.

Walz, T., Sharma, S., & Birnbaum, C. (1990). Gandhian thought as theory base for social work. *University of Illinois School of Social Work Occasional Paper Series I.* Urbana-Champaign: University of Illinois.

White, M. (2006). *Religion gone bad: The hidden dangers of the Christian right.* New York: Jeremy Tarcher.

Wilber, K. (1995). *Sex, ecology, spirituality: The spirit of evolution*. Boston: Shambhala.

Will, G. (2007, October 12). Code of coercion. *Washington Post*. Retrieved, from http://www.washingtonpost.com/wp-dyn/content/article/2007/10/12/AR2007101202151.html

Wink, P., & Dillon, M. (2002). Spiritual development across the adult life course: Findings from a longitudinal study. *Journal of Adult Development, 9*(1), 79–94.

Winter, B. (2009, December 6). Religious groups active in climate debate. USA Today. Retrieved from http://www.usatoday.com/news/religion/2009-12-06-climate_N.htm

Wulff, D. M. (1997). *Psychology of religion: Classic and contemporary*. New York: Wiley.

Wuthnow, R. (2003). Studying religion, making it sociological. In M. Dillon (Ed.), *Handbook of the sociology of religion* (pp. 17–30). Cambridge, England: Cambridge University Press.

Zimmerman, M. (1994). *Contesting earth's future: Radical ecology and postmodernity*. Berkeley: University of California Press.

Zinnbauer, B., Pargament, K., Cole, B., Rye, M., Butter, E., & Belavich, T. (1997). Religion and spirituality: Unfuzzying the fuzzy. *Journal for the Scientific Study of Religion, 36*, 549–564.

Zinnbauer, B., Pargament, K., & Scott, A. (1999). The emerging meanings of religiousness and spirituality: Problems and prospects. *Journal of Personality, 67*, 889–919.

Appendix

Relevant Internet Sites

Government Resources

Canadian Government Main Site: http://canada.gc.ca

Centers for Disease Control and Prevention: www.cdc.gov

National Institute of Drug Abuse: www.nida.nih.gov

National Institutes of Health: www.nih.gov

National Institute of Mental Health: www.nimh.nih.gov

Office of Violence Against Women, U.S. Department of Justice: www.doj.gov/ovw

U.S. Bureau of Justice Statistics: www.ojp, www.usdoj.gov/bjs

U.S. Census Bureau: www.census.gov

U.S. Department of Health and Human Services: www.os.dhhs.gov

Group and Family Work

Ability, Disabilities Advocacy: www.ability.org.uk

Addiction Treatment Forum: www.atforum.com

Administration for Children and Families: www.acf.hhc.gov

American Self-Help Clearinghouse: www.selfhelpgroup.org

Association for the Advancement of Social Work with Groups: www.aaswg.org

Forum on Child and Family Statistics: www.childstats.gov

Parents, Families and Friends for Lesbians and Gays: www.pflag.org

International Resources

Information for Practice from Around the World: http://blogs.nyu.edu/socialwork/ip/

International Forum on Globalization: www.ifg.orgUnited Nations Children's Fund: www.unicef.org

United Nations Development Programme: www.undp.org

Professional Links

Council on Social Work Education: www.
  cswe.org
Help Starts Here (by NASW): www.helpstartshere.
  org
International Association of Schools of Social
  Work: www.iassw.aiets.org
International Federation of Social Workers: www.
  ifsw.org
National Association of Social Workers: www.
  naswdc.org; www.socialworkers.org
Social Care Online: http://www.scie-
  socialcareonline.org.uk/
World Wide Web Resources for Social Workers:
  www.nyu.edu/socialwork/www.rsw

Social Policy

American Association of Retired Persons: www.
  aarp.org
Center for Restorative Justice Peacemaking: www.
  ched.uma.edu/ssw/rjp
Child Welfare League: www.cwla.org
Disabled People's Association: www.dpa.org
Family Violence Prevention Fund: http://endabuse.
  org
Influencing State Policy: www.statepolicy.org
Institute for Women's Policy Research: http://www.
  iwpr.org/index.cfm
Moratorium Campaign Against the Death Penalty:
  www.MoratoriumCampaign.org
National Coalition Against Domestic Violence:
  www.ncadv.org
Population Reference Bureau: www.
  ameristat.org
The Rape, Abuse and Incest National Network:
  www.rainn.org
Restorative Justice Resources (articles): www.
  restorativejustice.org
Restorative Justice Consortium: www.
  restorativejustice.org/uk
Social Welfare Action Alliance: www.
  socialwelfareactionalliance.org
Social Welfare Action Alliance Links: http://www.
  socialwelfareactionalliance.org/links.
  html#research
Violence Policy Center: www.vpc.org
War Resisters League: www.warresisters.org
World Health Organization: www.who.org

Special Interests, Human Rights

Amnesty International (type in specific country's
  name): www.amnesty.org
Campaign for Equity-Restorative Justice: www.
  cerj.org
Children's Defense Fund: www.childrensdefense.org
The Data Lounge: Lesbian/Gay: www.datalounge.com
Disability Information: www.disabilityinfor.gov
Disabled People's International: www.dpi.org
Drug Policy Alliance Action Center: www.
  drugpolicy.org
Earth Policy Institute: www.earth-policy.org
Gay, Lesbian and Straight Education Network:
  www.glsen.org
Human Rights Watch: www.hrw.org
Minority Rights Group International: www.
  minorityrights.org
National Alliance for the Mentally Ill: www.nami.org
National Coalition Against Domestic Violence:
  www.ncadv.org
National Gay and Lesbian Internet Task Force:
  www.ngltf.org
National Organization for Women: http://now.org
Office of Violence Against Women, Department of
  Justice: www.ovw.usdoj.gov
Religious Tolerance: www.religioustolerance.org
Signs of Homelessness: www.signsofhomelessness.
  org
United Nations System of Organization: www.
  unsystem.org
Women's Human Rights: www.whrnet.org

The Environment

Ecofeminism: www.ecofem.org
Ecological Social Work: www.ecosocialwork.org
Environmental Justice: www.epa.gov
Global Alliance for a Deep Ecology: www.
  ecosocialwork.org/index.html
Greenpeace: www.greenpeace.org
Midwest High Speed Rail Association: www.
  midwesthsr.org
Sierra Club: www.sierraclub.org/
United Nations Environmental Programme: www.
  unep.org
Worldwatch Institute: Vision for a Sustainable
  World: http://www.worldwatch.org/
World Wildlife Fund: www.worldwildlife.org/

Index